Slow Boat
to China

THE PERSONAL DIARIES AND LETTERS
OF PEGGE PARKER, 1942–1951

Slow Boat
to China

THE PERSONAL DIARIES AND LETTERS
OF PEGGE PARKER, 1942–1951

PEGGE PARKER
EDITED BY JOHN HLAVACEK

Hlucky Books

Omaha, Nebraska

ISBN-13: 978-0-9819034-8-4
ISBN-10: 0-9819034-8-7
Library of Congress Control Number: 2009940642
Cataloging in Publication Data on file with publisher.

Hlucky Books
13518 L St.
Omaha, Nebraska 68137
www.HluckyBooks.com

Editing: Janet B. Tilden
Book Design: Gary James Withrow
Production and Marketing: Concierge Marketing Inc.
        www.ConciergeMarketing.com

Printed in the United States of America
10 9 8 7 6 5 4 3 2 1

This book is dedicated to Mary and Mike
[Pegge's Posey and Butternut]

Contents

Acknowledgments

First, I'd like to thank Pegge for recounting the moments of her adventures in exquisite and vital detail in her poetic, vibrant style... and for preserving her personal letters, diaries, clippings and photographs for me to discover and explore while creating this tribute to her.

The undertaking of creating a book of such a vast collection of Pegge's diary entries and personal letters would not have been possible without the help and guidance of many talented and caring people:

Lisa Pelto and the Concierge Marketing crew, Gary Withrow, Erin Pankowski, and Ellie Pelto—thank you for pulling the artifacts of Pegge's life together and designing and editing a wonderful book that many people will be sure to treasure for years to come.

Janet Tilden—thank you for spending countless hours sanding down the rough edges of the original manuscript and even more time putting all of the original documents into chronological order.

Sandy Wendel—your advice and counsel in the world of words are priceless.

For anyone else I am forgetting—I truly appreciate everyone who has encouraged me to get this book into print, in a form that is accessible for anyone who is interested in reading about a life such as Pegge's.

Foreword

December 1951. I first met Mrs. Douglas Mackiernan, the Vice Consul of the United States Information Service (USIS), in Lahore, Pakistan. She and I were the only two Americans attending a meeting of the Pakistan Newspaper Association. She was one of only two women attending; the other woman was clad in a black burka and worked for a Pakistan Urdu language newspaper. I was at the meeting in my role as the Bureau Chief of the United Press for India and Pakistan, as many of the newspapers were clients of my United Press news service.

She invited me to lunch. For her, a business lunch, because she wanted to learn what I knew about Pakistan reporters and editors. At the lunch, I learned she was a widow with twins who were living with grandparents while she was on her first tour in the diplomatic service. It was not a pleasant meeting. I wanted to know why she was in Pakistan and her two year old twins were in Boston.

A few months later she was transferred to the American Embassy at Karachi. As Karachi was part of my United Press territory, we met again briefly. Then in the spring of 1952, with a consular friend, she took a vacation traveling to Goa, then a Portuguese territory on the west coast of India. Her route took her through Bombay, my headquarters. I saw her off on the train and met her when she returned. We had a few days to begin to know each other before she flew back to Karachi.

After a stormy courtship she agreed to marry me, and we were married on October 20, 1952. After a honeymoon in Europe, she returned home to get the twins, Mike and Mary, and we began our married life in Bombay. We soon added two boys and a girl. We were married for 56 years, traveling and working in India, New York, Jamaica, Miami and Omaha for United Press, *Time/Life, NBC News* (radio and television) and the *New York Daily News* and newspapers in Canada and France.

Although we worked and traveled the world together, Pegge never said much about the stories she had covered in her earlier life. It was only when, in her late 70s, she showed evidence of dementia and possibly Alzheimer's, did I learn of her personal diaries, letters and clippings. I found them in the basement of our home when we moved into an assisted living retirement center. In reading them I decided to publish them because of their beautiful writing and the story of her self-educated determination to become a brilliant and adventurous foreign correspondent. It is a beautiful history which I wanted to leave for her children and grandchildren.

Introduction

Margaret Witwer "Peggy" Lyons lived two lives. The younger daughter of a middle class Catholic family in Harrisburg, PA, she attended public schools. After graduating from John Harris High School, she went to New York to become a "famous" actress. Her mother had been a child actress and her grandparents were actors on Broadway. Her uncle, H.C. Witwer, was a World War I war correspondent and later wrote sports novels in the style of Damon Runyon. He also wrote scripts for movies in Hollywood and had acting parts in several movies.

In her own words at the time—"I had hoped to be the next Sarah Bernhardt but it was not to be."

After a brief stint as a Powers model, and writing radio scripts for the *Woman's Home Companion,* she returned to Harrisburg. After writing a series on furniture for an advertising section, she persuaded the publisher of the *Harrisburg Telegraph* to let her write, in 1940, an advice column for teenagers, 'Teen Topics. She also took a pen name, Pegge with an "e" and Parker, "because everyone had a Parker pen." Her daily column became so successful that she became a celebrity, interviewing with the likes of General Jimmy Doolittle, the Duchess of Windsor, and Rita Hayworth.

After writing over 700 columns, she took her clippings to Washington in 1942 and was hired as a reporter on the *Washington Times Herald*. Within six months she had been promoted to Women's Page editor and soon became a "star" reporter. It was wartime, and Pegge wrote stories about training with the paratroopers, riding with the tank troops, and even slogging with the infantrymen. She also continued writing about women's issues, posed for fashion photos, and became a "celebrity" culminating in being a Camel Cigarette poster girl, though she never smoked.

Slow Boat to China takes you on her journey from Washington to Alaska to China and beyond. *Slow Boat to Pakistan* continues her journey across the world.

SLOW BOAT TO CHINA

Washington, D.C.
1942–1944

1942

JULY 7, 1942—HARRISBURG, PA—"Miss Pegge Parker? One moment please. Washington calling."

A whirl of "city desk... *Washington Times-Herald*... like your work... would you be interested... come immediately... straight reporting..." And there I was—assigned to the staff of a newspaper in the most dramatic city in the world—Washington, D.C.—the vital center of political, military and international news. A dream come true for a budding reporter, especially right now while the nation is at war!

There was no sleep in the Parker household last night. I had that excited feeling of "I-must-be-dreaming" until this morning, when I rolled paper into my typewriter and tapped *"Teen Topics"* across the top. The words seem to look at me as I tapped out my final columns for the *Harrisburg Telegraph*.

JULY 10, 1942—I made my last trip to the paper to say goodbye. I also bought a war bond for $18.75 to keep a promise I had made to "help" a Washington publicity promoter, Meredith Howard, who got me a room in a guest house in D.C.

JULY 12, 1942—WASHINGTON, D.C.—Arrived by train and took a cab to the guest house at 1805 19th Street SW. Very disappointed—not at all what I'd been built up to expect.

JULY 13, 1942—Met my baptism of fire on the night staff of the *Washington Times-Herald* under noted city editor Wayne Randall. I was given re-writes, obits, and copy from the desk with instructions to "clean up a coupla paragraphs." At the end of the first day, Randall stopped by my desk to talk with me. He was so reassuring and friendly that I found the courage to ask if he was pleased with my work.

His face went into deep creases. The hard, sharp eyes behind the horn-rimmed glasses shone.

"I was very pleased with your first story because it confirmed a hunch that you can write. I didn't have to change a line. That is very unusual."

[Editor's Note: Reflecting on her time in the nation's capital in later years, Pegge believed that Randall had hired her because she wasn't a daughter of one of publisher Cissy Patterson's society pals or the many friends-of-friends with whom the staff abounded. "Crackshot hotshots not worth a damn" was Randall's comment. Kathleen Kennedy, the daughter of the American Ambassador to London, Joseph Kennedy, was one. Kathleen began as a research assistant to Frank Waldrop, the executive editor of the paper. Kathleen also assisted with reporter Inga Arvad's column, "Did You Happen to See," which profiled government officials. Kathleen was then promoted to reviewing plays and movies in her own bylined column and took over Ms. Arvad's column when she left the newspaper. Pegge, by contrast, was a kid from the sticks of Harrisburg who walked into the newspaper with a clipping book under her arm. The clippings were two and a half years of her "Teen Topics" advice columns for teenagers. (A collection of the columns can be found in her book 'Teen Topics, published by Concierge Publishing 2008.)

The Times-Herald *was losing male staffers to the draft, and Pegge was a safely draft-proof female who seemed to want to work and learn a lot. She was very serious, timid, easily hurt and frightened, but very determined and pathetically humble. She had a number of beaus in the military who occupied much of her time with letters, phone calls and occasional dates.*

Pegge made several visits home and always enjoyed reconnecting with Lois Fegan, her reporter colleague on the Harrisburg paper.

On Thursday, August 13, 1942, a month after Pegge had started working for the Times-Herald, *she had a byline story in the* Five Star Final *on the FRONT PAGE: a story about "coincidental twins" (babies born to different families on the same day).*

She was thrilled with the byline, for she was just 23 years old and had only two years of newspaper experience, with no education beyond high school. Thinking a brush-up on grammar would pay off, Pegge enrolled in a freshman English class at George Washington University, Because she worked the night shift at the newspaper, she was free in the daytime to attend class. Her first paper for the freshman English teacher was graded "Excellent."

Pegge was sent to cover a rally but was too shy to talk with Edna Ferber, who attended the rally with Eleanor Roosevelt. Pegge described Mrs. Roosevelt as "very tall, dressed in white lace, her hair quite gray."

On August 20, 1942, Pegge was tried out on the beat of the U.S. Senate. It was just a gamble, a trial run—could she be trained into the job until the regulars got back after the war? The regular reporter for the Senate beat, Frank Smith, thought "a pretty girl up here would get to know the boys and they would give a pretty girl tips and leads they wouldn't give another male reporter." That would be Pegge's special plus for the paper. She wrote later, "It was a fantastic opportunity, quite, quite lost on me. I had no training, schooling or grasp of legal affairs or the role of Congress in wartime."

A week later Pegge was still covering the Senate, and by August 31 she was on her own, without Smith.]

AUGUST 31, 1942—WASHINGTON, D.C.—Still in the Senate. Took over single-handed for the first time yesterday, but nothing much happens on Saturdays. Lunched with Frank Smith's nice wife and she tells me I'm the SWOON of the capital… the darling of all the guards, guides, elevator boys and cops! I never trolley on the rotunda that my vision is not bug-eyed, amazing. But if this is so why can't I capitalize on it to the extent of getting good slants of news? I feel myself gathering confidence and acquiring an insight into the ways of legislation. Glad I worked because my looked-forward-to weekend with Darwin in Richmond phooied into cancellation and I had nothing to do all day.

At 9 p.m. I turned U.S.O. hostess. Tall and girlish I was, in a powder-blue hat and pink princess coat.

"Good evening," I greeted the elderly directors like a nice girl. What a role I was playing being "Peggie Lyons."

I was told to write my name on a slip of paper and pin it on my dress—complete with "where from" identification. I was a little bewildered with tickets and slips and "where-can-I-check my coat" when all at once a sailor stepped up and took me in tow with unquestioning authority. He just managed the situation and me. He was all "gob" too—white ducks, flowing tie, and an eagle and chevron on his sleeve. I was disappointed that the Navy had me and not the Army or Marine Corps. Still, he's not bad-looking, I thought. When we got to the cloakroom his nice manners impressed me. The more we talked, the more interesting he became. Then I learned he studied pre-med at some western university. Loved classical music and had a curiously alert, enquiring mind. We danced carelessly and badly all evening but I found myself having fun. He excused himself once and was gone a long time. I had a sinking feeling that he had disappeared for good and was probably busy with other faces in other places. But finally he returned and said he had a 4 a.m. watch and would have to return to base. I went with him and his little rolling tough-faced sidekick "Stunky" and rode halfway downtown before we separated,

I with a grin that I'd added the Navy to my "armed services" and he with my address and telephone number. His name: TOM Sawyer. Not fiction but truth.

SEPTEMBER 4, 1942—Accomplishments since last I took up the pen: One romance and one byline. Career before love, so: I've been taken off the Senate and put back in the office. Things too slow up there to occupy three reporters. Yesterday, September 3rd, a women's conference was called in Mrs. Patterson's office and there, hiding behind a food editor, I studied the famous Cissy Patterson and what's she but a GRAND GUY. She was relaxed, responsive, receptive. We were addressed by first nicknames. Katherine Smith, women's page editor, was "Kathie"; others were "my dear." We were all "children": "Thank you, children, you may go."

"Mrs. Pat" as Mr. Randall calls her, is a perfumed, plainly but expensively dressed middle-aged woman with one of those "voices." She flips rose-tinted goggles on and off a nice round nose. Her eyes are wide and deep brown, dark glow in pale-pink puddles of wrinkles. Her hands were square and her fingers blunt, nails well manicured with a rose polish. Tension was high among the hired girls. Elaborate poise was politely perfect. Each offering of words had had a quick composition and editing before spoken for Patterson's ears. I got as far as composition and editing and hoped "she" wouldn't see me. She didn't.

But I fell heir to one of her suggestions: a series of articles on women in war jobs. All day I telephoned—everyone, everywhere. Women driving trolleys, piloting planes? Instructing in colleges? Finally landed a girl in the long-distance travel office of Bell Telephone. Much hectic last-minute confusion but got the story. Came back with NO IDEA what to write, what angle to write up, or anything. Oye! Randall was on the desk too. Your BETTER BEST Parker struggled and gradually a pretty good story thumped its typewritten trail across two sheets of copy paper. When I'd re-read it, I gained enough confidence to show it to Randall. He read the lead and second paragraph. "'s good, I like it." He put it on the desk and took pencil in hand. "By Pegge Parker" he signed it. Bless him. Oh dear God, bless this darling man who is the sky sun shines on. P.S. He even insisted I sign up for overtime and get paid extra. His praise was more than money—so I'm outrageously overpaid for today's work.

Now to my love affair. Bob Jenkins, the first soldier beau I ever had, called and came to dinner one night last week. He was to be a second lieutenant on the morrow at Ft. Belvoir. Would I celebrate with him and two friends? And would I get dates for said friends?

Finally arranged, and we met Jenkins and friends. He was one of the friends; name's George Fullmore. We went to the Shoreham, and George sat across the table from me. I thought him very engaging and nice-looking, but Jenkins was my date. As the evening wore on George and I found ourselves more and more conversant and held in a kin bond for books. It was fountain overflowing—stand-up depth going flood. Jenkins danced with George's date and the SWITCH was on. George and I danced later—and suddenly my heart had wings. I was dancing, laughing, YOUNG again—after weeks of wear, worry and emptiness. George—brains and near beauty—brought me home and the goodnight was a kiss we couldn't help, with many more to follow with whispered "oh honeys" and even "darling" which...

[Editor's Note: The next page of the diary is missing—Pegge might have deleted it at some time so we won't know how the evening ended. The diary was suspended in September after her diary entry of her date with George Fullmore. Pegge must have re-read her entries and decided they were not to be saved for posterity.

The stories Pegge wrote for the Times-Herald *must have caught the eye of the publisher. Among other stories, Pegge began a series on table manners for which she posed. Her photographer was the* Post's *Dimitri Wolkonsky. His name appears in her diaries because he was teaching her Russian words. The next entry is probably from December 1942 or January 1943.]*

My adored Mr. Randall was fired by Mrs. Patterson, and I am heartbroken for him. He came into the office the other day and I jumped up and ran over to him. He looked at me embarrassedly, the high-humbled before the worshipper, he was achingly unpretentious, a man out of a job. I wept for him. So happy to think I'm considered his friend.

Two of Pegge's featured articles.

Friday night I was getting ready to go home when Mr. Dewitt's secretary (he's a little god, archangel to Mrs. Patterson) called me into his office—would I take a long-distance call from New York? Mrs. Patterson wanted to have me do a story on Clare Boothe Luce, new Congresswoman. Flora had written a story on her, too. But orders were orders, and I was to do the piece. Flora was so upset she resigned. Not accepted—anyway, I was in a high nervous state all Friday night and Saturday. I started my chase—didn't get to Lady Luce but wheedled enough from the secretary to cut a story out of whole cloth. Flora liked it, against her better judgment, and Mr. DeWitt said it was very good. (Relief and ten years shaken from these shapely shoulders.) I stand by for reaction tomorrow.

Next day: Reaction swell. Flora quit and I've been taking over. Working my typewriter with a hand pump. Yesterday I posed for some fashion pictures and with retouching they came out very well.

No new men in my life—none that mean anything—and the only thing I look forward to romantically is visiting Lovey in Atlanta when he's graduated from Benning (March 9, 1943).

[Editor's Note: "Lovey" is the nickname of Pegge's first boyfriend. He was a regular at the Lyons family's Saturday night dinners for the servicemen.

After Pegge made her mark with her story on Clare Boothe Luce, she reported widely. She covered a sensational murder case in Annapolis, and she soon had her own daily column. She was sent on assignments to New York and Philadelphia.]

More photos from Pegge's fashion entries.

Pegge's article featuring Clare Boothe Luce.

1943

JANUARY 13, 1943—I have just come home from the Stage Door Canteen where I met a very odd boy indeed. It wasn't one of my Look—Wow nights and I walked out rather diffidently. Competition is keen if ultra-sophisticated. I stood in the back of the theater— converted music hall—for a moment, looking over the field. A tall George Fullmore-ish, clean-cut looking chap named Ray McKay sidled my way. "I've given my ankles to my country—up thar"— nodding toward the very crowded dance floor. I was delighted that such a catch came my way—tall, good teeth, nice eyes and just back from Alaska! We danced and after making with the "ankles" he turned to a lone sort of homely, shoulder-length soldier who stood with his back to a spotlight that threw an odd gold and red glow over his head and outlined his face in a blaze of radiance. His manner was in sharp contrast. He was oddly, tremendously appealing. He began by joyously insulting this brother in arms, but when Ray let go of my hand and the music began, he grabbed me and we danced. His name was Bill Spragg or Sprigg. His face was open, young-kid rough and tough, eyes wide, devilish and very brown. His mouth was large, crude, and his lips were oddly moist and shining like a girl's. His teeth were very white and straight. He was from Chicago and before the war had been, unbelievably, a stenographer. Now he was an M.P. just a month out of Alaska. The thing about him that I thought noble: Here's a real soldier who needs the Canteen and all a hostess can give for relaxation and enjoyment. He was grim, tense, fidgety, morose, bitter. "Look at these sons of b's sitting on their fat fannies—call themselves soldiers—look at the trinkets they wear (medals)."

[Editor's Note: Several pages are missing here.]

Withstood stimulating heat. I wish I were kinda madly in love with someone. I can't get to see Lovey (Bob Weborg) until March 9 at Ft. Benning—or go to West Point to work on Jerry (Capha) till even later, if at all. My favorite pastime, I find, is being in love.

Got word long in advance of President Roosevelt meeting Churchill in Casablanca for a secret conference. News breaks tonight—that the big heads were put together in AFRICA which somehow I doubt very, very strongly. Getting to know Cissy Patterson better and better. Oddly, have complete confidence in her presence. Could be because I've merited no criticism or messed-jobs in her eyes to date. Unfortunately little Flora is not missed.

FEBRUARY 19, 1943—Guess I was wrong about the Casablanca conference, which has been confirmed with pictures and newsreels. Made a special trip to the House to hear Clare Boothe Luce make her first speech. She's a slim, too pale, bony-faced madame, exquisitely smart German blonde, very confident and compelling as an orator. Spoke with harlequin goggles on her nose, reading a very marked copy of her speech on freedom of the air as dangerous to peace and international relations.

Shoe rationing met with surprised dismay. Men don't mind it, but women wear shoes as an accessory. I was fair to middlin' supplied.

Horse meat has been introduced with amusement. I'm afraid of meat a la stew or hamburger ever since.

Last night met my first Marine from the battlefront at the Stage Door Canteen. He was a tall, solid, blemish-complexioned sort of Marine, with a few dull sharp-shooter medals and one yellow, red, white and blue ribbon on his coat. The ribbon took my eye. "You've been overseas," I observed, giving him rapt awe and two free Philip Morris cigarettes. He joked back but admitted he'd seen four months of the Solomons. I got his story later walking home. He was an Italian who shied at revealing his last name with the "I" on the end. Had been in the bakery business in Philadelphia before enlisting. Went overseas as a private and came back the same but with a bullet wound in his hip and the claim of a Purple Heart medal for being wounded in action. He was common but had a kindly, chummy, well-meaning manner which, plus his marvelous STORY, made him an interesting date. His wrists were deeply scarred from bayonets. He said the Japanese are more human in combat than what we're led to believe in what we read. They're subject to fright and flight and only an officer commits hari-kari, if he can, before being captured. The soldiers, some of them radicals, blow themselves to bits with grenades. The way they try tricks of getting through our lines by speaking perfect English and wearing Marine uniforms don't always work. They've got the English but not our slang. Marines treat their buddies' wounds as they advance or fall back by each one doing part of first aid and moving on. These are the scraps I remember.

Something more intimate happened in the way of servicemen last week in New York. I was sent over for a week on assignment. While I was there, I decided to explore the Merchant Marine, Dangerous Barnacle Bill, little-known branch of the service. I made arrangements to be a hostess at a Valentine Party at the Marine Club on 30th Street (February 15, 1943). It was a small, jammed, smoky, perspiration-smelling little stuff box of a canteen, and the Marines in civilian clothes were an assortment. Some had BEARDS, scars, heads bandaged, and all appeared in a mad assortment of civilian clothes. I was introduced to a fascinating character called Charles Ripetoe (Rip a toe—got that). His nickname was "Rip," and he was an unwritten short story. Rather attractive, French black eyes, good teeth, good skin and high color, thinning black hair. He held me when we danced as though he had me alone and we were lovers long affairing. His eyes embraced me. "I want to kiss you. You got a nice mouth, and gee, honey, I'd like to go to work on it." He was story stuff, so I suffered his offensiveness. He had just come back from ORAN—Africa, troop ship. I asked him, interview-wise, what was the first thing he did when the boat landed. He looked at me with great amusement. "Really wanna know?" he asked, pulling out his wallet and fishing out a little white engraved card that looked like this:

Telephone 4-588

Madam Rosette
12 Rue de la Bleu
ORAN

It was a real HOUSE card. I was delighted and shocked and intrigued. "Oh, it's government inspected and exclusive for the Merchant Marine!" Rip put in, reading my outward disgust. The girls, he said, were French. "They show you a good time and you sleep with them. What's wrong about that?"

After Rip, a little U.S. uniformed sailor blew up, "Wanna dann'ss?" We dann'ss'd and I spied Wayne, Wayne Baxter. And here I go again. He's tall, blond, clean-scrubbed, and has STUFF, was formerly a cop in Detroit. Has three citations for single-handed captures, etc., even confessed to killing three men in a point-blank see-the-whites-of-their-eyes gun battle. He was to have come down this weekend. Feel terribly let down; I thought I was in love again—after so long.

Jerry Capha invited me to the 100th Night Show at West Point for the weekend of March 6th (1943)—two days before I go to Atlanta to see Lovey (Bob). The first time I went to West Point and met Maxie was at a 100th Night Show. I'd love to snare Jerry if he's available. *[Editor's Note: Pegge, when writing her "Teen Topics" column, had interviewed Jerry Capha when he was a cadet at the academy.]*

Wistful and terribly upset over Wayne at this writing. Waiting for him to call, I washed everything in sight to get my longing out of my system. Maybe word tomorrow.

MARCH 15, 1943—This is like writing the last chapter of a book, looking back with a sigh that so much has gone before to be written up to date. Well, briefly: Wayne came to Washington and we had a very un-enjoyable time except when he held me in his arms and gave me his picture autographed like this: "To My Darling." The following weekend I went to West Point. It was a triumph and delight. I've never been so thrilled and happy. Jerry was boyish, completely endearing and wonderful. In my flats I wasn't taller than he, I had the clothes to look the part of West Point, and at the dance met another cadet very much my style: one Jim Giles. It was one of my nights. I belonged. I was "right." Sunday Jerry took communion for me and I for him. It so happened we came to the altar rail at the same time and knelt beside each other. One of the most perfect and soulful communions I've ever received. Bless Jerry. After chapel we took pictures and went on Flirtation Walk, which was dazzling with new-fallen snow. I have never been so COLD in my life, but I smiled and tried to look beautiful. We passed kissing rock three times, and the third time I wrote "'til we meet again" on the rock. May it remain to be rediscovered someday. I missed three trains because I didn't want to leave Jerry. Wayne was waiting for me in New York. We had nowhere to go to be alone so sat in the Waldorf lobby. Sitting there he seemed so dear to me I told him I loved him. He grabbed my hand and held it crushingly. "Are you sure?" he asked with such honorable intentions in his eyes. We moved to the Roosevelt lobby for more privacy and there on a love divan on the balcony we held each other—and there he told me he loved me too. I felt oddly heartbroken when he said it—feeling, I guess, why is it all the men who love me are so ineligible, so one-of-the-ordinary masses—so un-marryable. We ended up at the Webster where I was staying—in the lobby, too—and he finally left about 2:30. I was quite starry-eyed and in awe of my triumph. Didn't think I could get him to love me.

Monday tore around the office getting things cleared up for Atlanta. Had no word from Lovey about his passing the tests but was determined to go anyway. Left Monday night on the Streamliner. The trip was seemingly short and enjoyable. Thought of Wayne all the way down. In Atlanta went to the Biltmore, unpacked, and headed for the first newspaper office. Was made welcome by everyone. Met Margaret Mitchell, who wrote *Gone with the Wind*. She adored the hat I was wearing (one I made for $2), and we became quite friendly to my keen delight. She even invited me to a press club cocktail party. I was the guest of honor, if you please, and am so under the spell of her Southern charm I'm going to make her a hat. Imagine me making a hat for Margaret Mitchell!

[Editor's Note: Pegge describes making the hat for Margaret Mitchell in her book Alias Pegge Parker.*]*

Tuesday morning at 6 a.m. I was awakened by mistake. A call from the desk. All this time no word from Lovey—got busy on telephone and half-hour later had Bob—No, he didn't make it. Flopped the second time. I was to come to camp. Flew around like mad packing and talking aloud to myself in anger and disappointment. Hopped the first train to Columbus, got a room with a local family, changed clothes quickly and grabbed a taxi for a $4.50 fare to Fort Benning. Little did I dream what a hand fate was dealing me. That the hectic confusion was all part of an inevitable scheme. Met Bob at the Service Club. He looked yellow, pink, blue and beautiful. We talked and loved.

Thursday I came to camp to say goodbye—had a reservation on the Southern for that night and decided not to go—changed all my plans at the last minute. Stayed on the post at the hostess's house. We sat up late that night. Fate hovered around as we made plans for Bob's last day before being sent back to his old regiment, the 28th in Florida. He was to meet me for breakfast. I dressed accordingly on the destined day of March 12. Bob didn't come.

I decided to busy myself with a story on the paratroopers I was seeing everywhere in the round-toed, high-buttoned shoes. Looking lacy, flowered and feminine, I strolled over to the Public Relations office. A young lieutenant with an eye to woman's kind was eager to do all he could for little Parker. One idea led to another. It ended with my being the first woman writer to be granted permission to fly with paratroopers when they were jumping. The War Department in Washington had to be called for clearance, and by miracle the officer in charge was a pal of Lt. Tukey's (the Public Relations man). Then a certain Captain (Sanford) Frank, chief of the jumping section, was consulted. He said first, "Is she pretty?" The good lieutenant avowed in kind (breakfast with Bob... trimmings)?

We piled in a jeep, and over to Lawson field we went. Walked through the hangar where the paratroopers fold and pack their precious chutes. All eyes upon me. I felt so "only womanish." The officers in charge were both young. Both tall, tanned and good-looking.

[Editor's Note: The diary is interrupted here. Pegge must at some time have re-read the diary and eliminated certain pages.

Her authorization to fly with the paratroopers resulted in two full-page stories, with pictures, in the Washington Times-Herald. The first story appeared on April 3, 1943, and the second just a week later, April 11. Pegge was featured in both stories. A photo shows her wearing a *flowered hat, interviewing Brigadier General George P. Howell, the commandant of the paratroopers. Two other pictures show Pegge standing in the plane talking to the "jumpers," with a close-up of her dressed in helmet and jump uniform. She wrote in her story that she had to promise the army brass that she would not try to jump: "No jumps for me unless ordered because of plane failure. But I did like to think about it. Did I have the nerve or not. I'll never know, I guess."*

The first of Pegge's full-page articles featuring the paratroopers.

Additional photos from Pegge's paratrooper and fashion articles.

Additional photos from Pegge's paratrooper articles.

Additional photos from Pegge's paratrooper articles.

A third full-page story described Pegge's visit to the Tenth Armored Division in May of 1943. The Sunday feature titled "Tiger Men and Iron Tanks" showed Pegge emerging from an M-5 light tank. She told her story of spending a day with the tank men, slogging through the mud and firing a carbine.

Pegge's exploits made excellent reading and led to her spending a day with the glider soldiers in Kentucky at Bowman Field. The resulting story, "Soldiers with Silver Wings," appeared in the Sunday, July 25, 1943, issue of the Times-Herald. In the story she told of spending a day in the field with the men to "really see and feel what they go through." An excerpt: " 'O.K., sister, you asked for it,' was their attitude and they spared me nothing. At the uncivilized hour of 5:45 the next morning, in coveralls, leggings, helmet and pack, Parker hit the gravel. Word went down the ranks, 'We've got a gal commando up front. Let's see if she can take it.'" The story featured four pictures of Pegge: (1) riding in the glider with the men; (2) demonstrating bayonet drill; (3) emerging sodden from the pond, and (4) shouting when sitting in a 'booby trapped" chair. The caption says: "OOPS.. A CHAIRFUL OF TNT— No one told Pegge Parker this comfy chair concealed a highly explosive booby trap of 'live' dynamite set by glider pilot shock (!) troops, and so when it went off with a boom, Pegge broke the Bowman Field shriek record."

The fourth full-page story featured Pegge falling in the control tower chute. The caption reads: "Two hundred and fifty feet down sails "Rookie" Parker, strapped into a control tower chute. Her descending screams all but brought the Marines on the run! The beginner seat harness, which is to accustom paratroopers to weight, also brought feminine yells from the American girl reporter, to the amusement of rigging instructor Sgt. Bill Duncan."

Pegge's reporting exploits paved the way for several visits to Ft. Benning and led to reporting on other branches of the service. It also led to a torrid romance with a paratrooper which was shattered when Pegge found out he was married.

Pegge went to New York in September and reported on the Merchant Marine. She was pictured on deck with crewmen, and another photo shows her pulling levers in the engine room of a merchant ship.

In October she made a trip to Camp Davis, North Carolina, for a story on the WASPs: the Women's Airforce Service Pilots. The lady pilots were civilians who wore officers' uniforms without insignia. Pegge reported they were paid $285 a month, which corresponded to the pay of a First Lieutenant. The lady pilots flew planes pulling targets for training anti-aircraft batteries.

Pegge's columns related the varied circumstances in wartime Washington. Many of her columns commented on the complications of wartime romances. One whole column was written from her experience of living in one of the two wartime Washington hotels for women.

When the diary resumes, we learn that she had a passionate romance with Captain Frank, who showed up in Washington in December of 1943. The diary reveals her heartbreak. Meanwhile, we can only

assume that her Harrisburg boyfriend, "Lovey," who had flunked out of
school for the second time, was no longer her swain.]

LATE DECEMBER 1943—Pounded out an article on the Public
Health officers. I told you how Papa Denby took up the sword against
it? Well, worse. I revised it and sent it to Mr. Randall, my original city
editor who is now working for the *Washington Post*. He returned
it with a painstaking criticism: "This is an example of the potential
writer who gets a piece of swell material by the tail and hasn't the
capacity to handle it in an acceptable manner. When you tackle a
big thing like the exploits of the Health Service in this tremendous
war you haven't the technique to put it over." It was a slingshot letter,
hitting with a zing and stinging mightily. But try harder and harder
I must. I see this writing career is going to find me gray-haired after
all… and I wanted so much to be YOUNG and be-you-ti-ful when I
began selling stories or articles. I'm so inwardly ill at ease over how
cock-surely I can sell Cissy on Alaska after the flop of my Public
Health.

And now on the drama side!

I was wringing out a lead on my Sunday story, one about Irinia
Skariatina, a Russian countess and foreign correspondent, when the
phone rang. "Who is this?" a bass voice enquired charmingly. All
unaware of impending shock, I answered, "This is Miss Parker. May
I help you?"

"Why," the voice hesitated, "I wonder if it would be possible to
obtain a copy of the paratroop article." Delighted and intrigued with
the deeply intoned modulation of his cultured voice, I bubbled, "Yes,
of course! Who is this?"

Silence fell—with silent stealth like snow on a hillside. I felt the
delicacy and wondered—the voice answered then: "Why—this is
Captain Frank."

After a gasp of anguish and disbelief and wonder: "Captain Sanford Frank?"

"Yes."

"Sandy."

"Yes."

"Oh. Oh, Sandy."

My heart broke open anew—pathetic fluttering wings beat inside me—hope—my love come back—Sandy—SANDY.

He was calling from Ft. Meade. He expected to go overseas that morning but had been left behind for some inexplicable reason. The exquisite sound of his voice in my ear and the memory it revived made me feel old and wise as God. I listened to all he said with doubt and disbelief and to my own appalled sadness I realized that the little girl Pegge is forever gone. In her place is a sophisticated woman who knows too much of the clay feet of MEN to ever believe and love and trust heart and soul again.

Sandy and I talked for an hour. Emotion ebbed and surged like a tide between us. We spoke as two about to be torn asunder, as two who bid each other a last farewell through barbed wire. I lashed out at him once in accusing him of a heartbreak and disillusionment I had not the experience and sophistication to defend myself against. Sandy protested that he loved me too—with his "whole soul."

He called me back that afternoon, and we talked again exhaustingly. I told him all the little things I remembered. The things that had hurt me so. He denied being married and said Carol had lied to me. He spoke of my adored Captain York as a bitter rival (and I was glad).

I had my friend Helen Baker check up on his record and check the veracity of his unwed declaration. Helen reported a "Mrs. Gertrude Margaret Frank and daughter" listed as dependents. My heart accepted the illegitimacy of Sandy's ardor until he called again the next day and in answer to my protests that he was NOT as eager as I for a reunion he began the Old Benning theme. He had a job to do, etc. etc., and if he ever saw me again and held me close in his arms (I wept inside my heart at that), he would never be able to leave me—and he would ask me something…

"What would you ask me, Sandy?" I put in sharply, expecting a "beautiful proposition." What with Gertrude Margaret Frank at this ironic moment, my swain newspaper man, Karl Hess strolled up to my desk. He heard my distinctly and so earnestly repeated question: "What would you ask me, Sandy?" Karl mocked an answer in fun—embracing me, telephone and all, he cried, "Will you marry me?" I shoved him away in annoyance and at that double MOCKING moment Sandy pronounced these words, "I'd ask you to marry me, Pegge." I listened, interested as a spectator in a wonderful story happening to me. Sandy, my only love, had expressed a longing to marry me.

After THAT phone call I went out to finish my Christmas shopping. Jostled around in the crowds trying dazedly to recall sizes and desired colors, etc. The desperate bittersweet agony of Sandy confronted me. Life tosses no sugar plums into your lap, I thought, Bitterly. Bitterly— BITTERLY. And why had Sandy loomed up uncalled for, out of a long-quieted well of heartbreak, to enrage my hopeless longing, to make me suffer all over again—at Christmas, too. And when I was so innocently going my way.

I spent a dull and time-dragging holiday at home. Daddy drank too much champagne at an office party and came home rocking on his heels. I recruited poor Paul from his hospital for Christmas Day. But at the last minute he couldn't come.

Always Sandy, Sandy was in the back of my mind. And the empty-shell despair that here I am 24 with no Mike McCoy in sight—and as nowhere else, in Harrisburg I am screamingly unwed, unengaged, unsought… and to offset this nothingness what have I on the career side? An equal balance of NOTHING. Nothing and a reminder of my inexperience and doubt of any real ability. I never felt so OLD. Old in my life and so frightened of my outcome. I want desperately to RUN, but I don't know where or to what.

Feeling this giddy off balance of emotion and career. I grabbed my phone and called Butch, my deepest, dearest, friend despite everything. He had received my gift and seemed pleased with it. Tonight when I came home a big package from Lord & Taylor ("our" store) awaited me. I know it's from Butch, but I haven't the delight to open it tonight.

Sandy.

Oh, my darling—why did this have to be?

1944

JANUARY 4, 1944—Midnight music, cakes and ale, exquisite setting for a story. And I have a real one to tell. My heart lamented Sandy's return and rebelled in anguish that it should be broken again. For no reason, seemingly. But yes, there was an answer, or consequence.

It was New Year's Eve. I was dressing laggingly to go to a last-minute formal press party when the telephone rang. It was Mrs. Patterson's secretary. Would I care to attend a New Year's party at her home the next day, and would I bring a BEAU. I twittered my delight and hung up, wondering where and how I would pull a "beau" out of the air worthy of the occasion (or just a beau, period). I remembered that last week a Captain Theobald had called from Ft. Meade for Sandy, requesting my envelope of clippings be forwarded to him. Ever quick on the "business business," I got as much out of Captain Theobald as possible.

Now at this ZERO hour I recalled him. A paratrooper—but still in camp? Available? Old—young? Glasses, bowlegged, big nose, pimples—married? At any rate, I called him. Trumped up the party and made it for servicemen and I was to bring a paratrooper, etc.

He'd love to go—would meet me at the hotel. I dressed nervously that night. I was overwrought at seeing Mrs. Patterson and had last-minute misgivings about this man I presumed to parade before Mrs. P and assembled guests. What a risk-all gamble I was taking. In my jittery state of plot counterplot I went overboard on my apparel for the Grand occasion. I wore the Ft. Benning pink wool suit—sewed my pink earrings to the jacket and made a hat of frosty white-pink flowers. Sensing this anonymous Captain Theobald would be a RUNT, I wore flat sandals. When he called from the lobby I went down to say hello. Oh, Heaven is Kind. He was DARLING. Had the nice face of a puppy and the manner of a sweet, shy Mr. Chips. We walked up to Mrs. P's while I warned him what to expect.

The whole office was a fascinating ordeal. The Du Pont Circle "estate" was jammed. All the women were in BLACK and diamonds. I burst into their midst like a bon bon or bridesmaid: all PINK & FROTH. Realizing my mistake, my diffidence mounted. I clutched George's hand. He stuck by me reassuringly. Mrs. Patterson stood at the top of her marble staircase looking tall, old, wrinkled, handsome in her mahogany-colored hair. She spoke in the throaty tones of an actress. She wore a full black skirt and a Chinese jacket of red, black and bright gold lamé plaid. I had hardly greeted her when she turned and introduced me to Mrs. Byron Foy as "our fashion editor." My little mama's girl pink burned into my consciousness. Mrs. Foy was dressed in black, black as widow's weeds. Near her was Justice Murphy, his bushy brows cocked over a stiff glass of ginger ale. No one paid the slightest attention to my Captain, so I began introducing him as "my paratrooper." Still no one drew him into conversation or gushed that it must take a hell of a nerve to jump out of a plane. My apologetic inferiority complex cloaked poor Captain Theobald in my eyes. It was awful.

I met the Finnish Minister, who kissed Mrs. P's hand but only shook mine. And Mrs. Lionel Atwell, the legendary Mrs. Douglas MacArthur I—she was bosomy but better-looking than I had thought.

Music drifted into the library—a deserted ballroom with a small orchestra. Two bars flowed freely. In another room sparkling with crystal chandeliers and candles, guests ate piecemeal and devouringly of a buffet spread in lavish array. I dreaded my contacts with Mrs. Patterson (with Alaska up my sleeve, she terrifies me), and taking our leave was an ordeal. I grabbed Captain George Theobald's hand for moral support. Just then our city editor came over. He is a tall, bony, T.B.-looking blond Swede. "Looks like you two are engaged or something," he said brightly with the boldness of ambrosia. George patted my hand and beamed at me in the fond manner of one who'd known me a year, not just an hour. We left, finally, and outside I was 20 years younger and possessed of a relief and gratitude for George. I wanted to hug him and say, "Thank you, darling, darling."

We went to dinner and I proceeded to work on him. The only encouragement I got was an occasional remark about my eyes. To the movies later, then home. It was a momentous evening—George and Mrs. Patterson. He was dear but strained and fiendishly polite. It was his birthday come midnight, so in saying goodnight I first gave him Sandy's envelope of clippings and then leaned forward slightly and kissed him softly for his birthday. We (at my prompting) made a date for Monday to go to the theatre if he would get out of port-of-embarkation camp. Sunday I went to an eggnog party with Helen Baker. The offering was given by Westinghouse for its Russian constituents. I went only because Helen asked me. At the first round of drinks Helen slid up to me and whispered, "The man in the grey suit has his eye on you." She brought him over then and introduced Bud WALLACE. He turned out to be the best informed, most interesting man I've met in all Washington. He brought me home by way of dinner and ended up asking if he could kiss my eyes.

Monday, January 3, 1944, was a Day of Destiny and pouring rain. (Continued in the Pullman car of the 4 p.m. express to New York Sunday Jan 7, 1944. What a week and what occurrences—on second thought this jerky writing won't do. Will have to wait till we get back in New York.)

Before I expound on the drama (Acts I, II & III) of my Monday, January 3, 1944, I must quickly record two inside stories. One is on Clare Boothe Luce, whose only daughter, Ann Brokaw, 19, was instantly killed two weeks ago in a tragic automobile accident. I had written several stories about her Annie which pleased Mrs. Luce very much. I have also become a good friend of her secretary, Al Morano (36 years old), a stocky, mild-looking, blond man with a broad, kind face, shrewd but not hard-boiled. Al gave me the inside details on the tragedy.

It seems one Virginia Blood, tall, spinsterish, rawboned, but smartly chic, secretary to somebody in the Luce outfit, told Clare outright, bluntly, terribly that Ann had been killed in an accident. Clare yelled at her, "You're crazy! You don't know what you're talking about!" But it finally penetrated in all its irrevocable awfulness. She was in San Francisco at the time. Grabbing her hat and coat, she ran out of the apartment, around the corner to a little Catholic Church where she knelt in convulsive agony and prayed her heart out.

When she came on to Washington before going to South Carolina (where the Luce country home is located), Al saw her at the Wardman Park. He was extremely emotional, nervous and apprehensive for his and Clare's future. (He was afraid she was quitting and getting out of politics.) Clare greeted him with poise. She wore black clothing, little make-up, had dark circles under her eyes and murmured something about just having had her hair set. Her husband was with her, shoulders broad and protective in his wife's tragic crisis.

Al said Clare spoke vaguely of "the office," but her mind wandered and after a while she began babbling incoherently of little things she and Annie had done and said. She wept, and her husband held her in his arms, kissing her ashen cheeks. Later, alone with Al, he said movingly, "I have really discovered my wife almost for the first time since this happened and I admire her as I never have before. She is truly a great woman. Really and truly." Al dropped a hint—discussing the fateful WHY did it have to happen to a sweet, innocent young girl—that this sorrow had brought Henry and Clare closer together than they'd been in a long time. He also told me that when Ann's body had been recovered Clare removed a ring from the slim, dead hand. It was an old, worn antique circulet she had passed on to Ann as a special sentimental keepsake. Now it was hers a second time after Ann's death. Clare resolved to part with it forever. She phoned a very special beau of Ann's and asked him to come to the apartment. He came—tall, homely, gulping his embarrassment and fear of a scene. And Clare gave him Ann's ring. "Keep this and wear it in her memory," Clare implored, "until you fall in love again and marry. Then give this ring to your bride but never tell her where you got it or whose it was."

Al is apprehensive for Clare's political future. He maintains she cares little for it now that she has been tested and proved her mettle. A list of telegrams received was prepared for her perusal. It was interesting to note or hear that the President (whom Clare has so viciously ridiculed and attacked) had sent her a personal note, as did Mrs. Roosevelt. Everyone but the President and Mrs. Chiang Kai-shek (the Chinese "issimo's" wife) were to receive printed cards acknowledging wires and letters of sympathy. Neither did her brother.

Now for the second dispatch—most extraordinary things have happened since I met M.F. [*Frank Murphy—discreet initials for a man you'll hear a lot about later*]. The first day I returned from a week of fashion shows in New York, his secretary called and invited me to tea with M.F., whom she called, as he calls himself incognito, "Mr. Williams" (at the C.S. building, no less). C.S. for Supreme Court—I had bought a fur coat in New York ($358.50 as a price comparison—knee-length skunk—very smart) and wanted to wait to wear it, so I said later in the week. Next day I changed my mind and called his secretary. M.F. picked up the phone and spoke to me himself. Down

I went, working up squared-shoulder poise from remembering the "man" I knew or thought I did from the first meeting at this hotel when he was ill. I was nervous and tongue-tied by the time a Negro servant had showed me into his sumptuous office. His secretary greeted me with strained cordiality as though to insignificant Me she should be saying "He can't be seen" when ACTUALLY she was saying "Please go right in." "In" was a huge vast office—an imposing mannish fireplace—a marvelous collection of portraits on all four walls. Three flags stood in the far corner. His desk was a plateau of leather and marble. A servant spread cookies and tea before me. M.F. was a different man in his office than in his "home." He was skirtingly garrulous on rambling subjects—especially on "ME—I— the President—the Philippines—when I was Mayor of—Governor of." I listened. I said "Yes," "No," and "Really" at the right times. I died. I made the most of my eyes. I was smitten with complexes all degrading (especially as he rambled on about all the wealthy, beautiful and charming women he knew). Worst of all, the man who wanted a "son" (somehow or other) was gone—and with him my only hold on him. The whole affair dragged on, and I was relieved when he called a taxi for me. An overpowering sense of LOSS possessed me.

But the very next day he called and asked me to LUNCH at his office. He said he'd tried terribly hard to call me after the tea. He'd dined with Jimmy Cromwell and his daughter—both feeling pretty grim after the notorious publicity on his divorce from Doris Duke. He wanted to see me very much and was quite crushed to find me out (had I only known, and to think I was only at the Stage Door Canteen trying to "forget"). This time I sailed into his office as a woman halfway sure of her charm and attraction. He shook my hand—his hand, by the way, is repulsively soft, fine-boned and fleshy). We lunched (I could have gobbled up boiled arsenic without knowing the difference). He told me he was going "away" for a week, but oh how he wanted to be held in my arms (see, grandchildren, what for granny you had?). I went around to his side of the double desks. "I'd rather deny myself EVERYTHING and have you think me a gentleman," he said, hesitatingly—vacantly—almost as though he didn't see me or know who I was. He frightened me in a way, but Clare Boothe Luce flashed through my mind and all Cissy Patterson had told me about her having used influential men to attain her ends. I tried to be clever and—if you will—alluring.

"Williams" touched my shoulder—then my throat—then he crept close to me. "Put your arms around me," he rasped unromantically. I swallowed and complied (woman of the WORLD), and then he did an odd thing he's done several times since. He felt my pulse—and in great disappointment moved away laughing. "Oh, Pegge Parker— your pulse is too steady—I can't get you excited."

Nonetheless he went so far as to give me his private phone number and to say he wouldn't go away if I could find some way or place where we could be alone and "I could hold you for hours and hours." Driving back to the office, I was astounded. Life has certainly tossed an odd experience my way. I called back at 5:00 (as planned) and Williams answered the phone himself. Then he told me his going away was just to Georgetown Hospital where he wanted to rest prior to an army physical exam for resuming this extracurricular Lt. Colonelcy in the tank forces—overseas in the big invasion of Europe. He doesn't think the President will really let him go, but he is getting ready anyway.

Well, that night—over to the hospital I go, asking for "Mr. W. in Room 7." It was after visiting hours and they wouldn't let me in. I phoned his room and he came out into the lobby in army bathrobe and P.J.s after me. We talked like two kids playing a clever prank on a lot of grownups. I laughed and kidded him and he right back. I felt I KNEW him then. I was "in" (what exactly I mean to him is something else again).

I let the next day go by without calling or hearing anything of him. Then this morning, Friday, I called. He sounded glad to hear from me and begged me to come to see him—out I went. He received me more impersonally than ever before, said my hat (self-made, all banked in flowers) was pretty, and talked politics. He trusts me, that's one thing I'm sure of. He left me with the parting speech that he has made too many demands on me and won't in the future. (I stared in big-eyed alarm at that.) He also said he might go to the theatre Sunday. I held my breath—would he dare ask me to go with him? (Instinctively knew he won't, that I am his Back Street dark lady.) However, the trip was not in vain. I got some marvelous inside stuff just by asking him what's so and so really like. I think the President must be very likeable among his associates. Williams said Churchill drank terribly, and I gather there's little love lost between FDR and Winston. In Africa when the Big Three (Stalin) met, Williams said Churchill demanded an Anglo leader and control because England had been in the war two years before us. FDR said in a grand finale comeback, "Only on the strength of USA's lend lease." Another thing—Williams said the President has gone a little too Anglo in his recent dealings and is probably acting under the influence of Anglo confidants. He amazed me by half admitting that the stories about the President and MARTHA of Norway are true. He looked me right in the eye and said, "I hope those stories are true—the President has never really had a wife and he deserves some happiness." Then he told me how the President's mother always hated Eleanor but worshipped her son. She used to call him "darling." Once, before she died, she phoned him from Hyde Park and the butler said he was out. The poor lady gasped and protested, "He couldn't be—why, he never leaves the White House! Where is he? The very idea—get him for me at once." The confused butler finally connected her with a private number. Her son answered and said in perfect happiness and dreaminess. "It's June ... moonlight and music and I'm having a wonderful time at MARTHA'S." Williams also told me the President was once in love with Mrs. Murphy. It blew over, though. He told me Harry Hopkins was the unofficial "court jester"—the joke maker, the card player, the slaphappy Joe the President needed. On official occasions when he was too busy to be charming, he owned that the President has deliberately surrounded himself with weak-brained inferiors that he may dominate and control with greater comparative power. Most breathtaking of all, Williams intimated that if the President does win a fourth term he will be made Secretary of War. (How dare I presume to have any holding charm for such a man?)

I had a sad letter from Don Ilyt this week, telling me he'd married a nice, sweet girl because he couldn't have me. Poor chap. I am his Sandy as I am also Paul's. He phoned me from Montreal when I was in New York. Alaska and my whole little world is at a drifting directionless place.

Now to flash back and quickly review events.

That Monday Butch called very unexpectedly and took me to lunch at the Carlton. Hardly was I back and busy at my desk when I looked up and saw two raincoated, big-booted paratroopers bearing down on me. One was George—the other Sandy.

Sandy—I sprang to my feet. My love! My darling! My God. I snatched my goggles off my nose, squared my shoulders and looked at my Sandy with blazing eyes and flaring nostrils. Abruptly I ignored him and showered poor George with unwarranted attention, which was a lucky move. He got rid of George later and called me back.

I had hurt his pride. He drove me home in a dreamy, maroon Chrysler. It was pouring rain and I thought how like a story in *Cosmopolitan* is this! We drove to the hotel and parked, talked. My heart was numbed with longing and sorrow that my hero should be a heel of the lowest and flattest order. But Oh—handsome. Even in the gloom his eyes were brilliant blue and his hair was so black and damp and wavy. He eventually took me in his arms, and at first he avoided kissing my lips. I nearly died. Turned on the allure like mad—and then he DID. And, oh, passionate ecstasy and unforgettable pain and sweetness. Never was such a kiss kissed in all the world! Sandy put his head on my shoulder and said the only honest and only humble thing he's ever uttered in my ear. "I never meant to hurt you, Pegge—

forgive me—please, please forgive me" and I did, really. I left him laughing, good-pals-ily, good boyishly, and ran to meet George, who BORED me so. I never heard from either of them again.

Ahmee told me an amazing thing. Aunt Marie has been married three times. What an amazing and enviable accomplishment.

JANUARY 24, 1944—My Mr. Williams and I have had the test put to us. Saturday morning I stopped in the office and he called. It seems the secret got out that he was in Georgetown Hospital under an assumed name. Only one paper in town knew: MINE! Only two persons knew: his secretary and I, a reporter on the *Times-Herald*. I nearly DIED. I gasped my protests. "Pegge, I'd trust my very life in your hands," he said. "I KNOW you are my friend and didn't tell." Later at a contact party for Mr. Wayne Randall, my hero city editor, I picked up the "leak" from the gossip of reporters. What a relief. Sunday I went over to the hospital to see him. Burst into the lobby, and there he stood waiting for me, looking very smiling and well groomed in a dark brown suit. Out we went for a walk, and it was wonderful, or rather he was. He asked me to take his arm and once he took my hand in his and tucked it in his overcoat pocket. How he talked and how we laughed—wandering around Georgetown University, stopping in the chapel—looking at little houses—every now and then I thought to myself: IMAGINE having this wonderful, world-renowned man all to myself—all alone—and just wandering around together arm-in-arm...

He did not ask me to the theater. He went alone—with his secretary and roommate (a man). He phoned me this morning and we had a gay little talk. Tonight I wrote him a cute note on bright pink stationery. Impulse. I wonder what he'll think when his secretary hands it to him?

JANUARY 30, 1944—Listening to my beloved (Dave Rose) "Holiday for Strings." HE seemed only casually amused with my little note. I have a tremorous little fear that I am losing my hold on him. To top everything else off, I had an idea for a new column—a woman seven-league booter—a gal gallivants all over creation—a femme Bob Davis, Bruno Lessing. I wrote Mrs. Patterson a note asking to see her. Wednesday in the office a little frowsy-hair copygirl handed me a stiff white envelope which I instantly recognized as Mrs. P's personal bond—the letter was a sharp, NASTY slap. It refused to see me, hear my idea. Then the tone changed. "Please, darling" it ran in chorus girl "listen, dearie" tempo: "How would it be to think a little less of Pegge and a little more of the job?" I was stung, embarrassed and then seething with hurt, humiliated ANGER—little George Keibel, who was so kind to me in the struggling days of New York, came through on furlough and I had to see him—otherwise I would have flown to Mr. Williams. I called him the next day and saw him that evening at 5:00. We walked over by the Washington Monument and sat on a bench completely oblivious of the home-going flock of government workers milling past us, I'm sure quite unaware that the troubled-faced girl in the pink (fatal paratrooper) hat was with one of the most important men in the country. He looked very well—so perfectly groomed and even natty in a fitted dark royal blue overcoat, bright blue shirt and tie, and brown hat and gloves. His distinguishing eyebrows were tangled red and gray fuzz over energetic, thoughtful deep blue, blue eyes. He was on the rampage because the big Bataan story was held up for two years before we heard anything about it and WHY? He blamed Anglo-influenced politics. The English wanted everything all set before they declared the Jap atrocities. Mr. Williams laughed delightedly: "They don't know that the Philippines are FREE beyond their meddling and INDIA will be too; you'll see." Then he lashed into the presidential campaign. "No one has a chance against MacArthur," he said. "No one but a soldier will have the right to represent them in the final victory." He went on to say how he disliked MacArthur—as does everyone in high places. His personal ambition betrays the man in his headlong drive up and up. He intimated the President is none too fond of him, either. He got off into his own affairs then, as he always does, and told me for the first time with a great catch and faraway sweet sadness in his voice about this ANN PARKER referred to in the file clippings as his constant riding companion. He told me how madly they tore over the palace grounds—"and at sunset, riding along beside her—why, her hair was the color of the sky—blazing bronze titian—waist like this"—he made a circle of his thumbs and forefingers. (I instinctively drew in my tummy and made my own waist wee tiny.) "She's 32 now—" he finished, staring at the Smithsonian across the way from us.

On the subject of women (they always come up, and they're always beauties, to my diffident discomfort)—most amazing tale of all, though. He told me about Liz Whitney. You know she always has been in love with Jock no matter what he did, and these torch bearers when their husbands remarry strike out frantically to grab somebody far over and above their past husband, just to show him up. Ah, Liz, I thought, so that's what you tried on my bachelor and brilliant Mr. Williams. "She's so rugged and earthy, somehow you like to touch her hands," he went on. "But the woman was utterly ruthless. She'd call me up at all hours of the night—make a spectacle of me in public—especially at the Madison Square Garden Horse Shows. She'd tell people she had dinner dates with me—once she called me up and said, 'Murf, if you were ever my friend, please have dinner with me tonight.' I told her I couldn't; I was dining with Doris Duke and Jimmy to see if I could reconcile them. I made the mistake of telling her where I was going. She followed and sat in the bar, sending me idiotic notes every five minutes. When I refused to see her and left by a side exit, she called me at 2:30 in the morning. My secretary said she was in tears and carrying on like crazy." I listened, feeling for Liz, pitying and understanding her headlong rush into trying to tackle "Murf" and seeing very clearly her mistake.

Abruptly he broke in with "What did Cissy Patterson say to hurt you?" I was treading on ice because he values her friendship (press), I'm sure. I implied but bent over forward and backward to apologize for Mrs. P. and say how much I really admired her. "Don't let her temperament bother you. Why, your reputation is that you're her favorite. She's very fond of you." (She was until a jealous Managing Editor Frank Waldrop put a dagger in my back.) "I've asked people about you, and everyone spoke very highly of you." (I widened my eyes in fright, surprise and relief.) "George Dixon said you were her pet and incidentally a darned good writer." (I gasped—I know Dixon only from afar.) We walked off toward his hotel facing a blazing sunset, laughing and talking about the rascally Popes of old. He left me at his hotel saying he'd call me and we'd have dinner. Oh, wonderful delight. I have the oddest emotions toward him. I want to keep perfect faith with him—to use no wiles or sophistry in my closeness to him. I want to be honorably and honestly devoted to him I know that I could love him with all my heart and soul if he could or would love me in return. He is a whole understanding in himself, though—and I am so removed from his world—the Philippines and the Supreme Court (egad).

My mind is irrevocably made up on my next move—ALASKA—some force, imaginary or real, draws me with a compelling magnet to that wild, rugged country. I spent all day Saturday at the office writing job letters to every newspaper in Alaska. To the U.S. Employment Service in Seattle, to the General Manager of the Alaska Railroad—mind you—mind you. I wrote almost flippant letters trying to make them zing and hit like a fist on a desk. I also sent my best pictures (taken by Dimitri recently for Mrs. P). I wrote to the Governor, too, and beseeched him to help get me hired. I'm afraid I'll have to pay my own expenses to Seattle. Maybe my own expenses all the way. And after laying out almost $400 for my new fur coat—whee—as a last resort I may ask "Murf" to help me—certainly Al Morano in Clare Luce's office who has become my very close friend. Funny thing, I got a cable reading "Dearest you are more than ever in my thoughts at this time writing All my love – MILTON KLEIN." I know no such person and am curious as the devil to know who wired me. And I feel sorry for poor Milton Klein's girl who will never know about his thoughts at this time. I'm just living for my jaunt to Alaska, and golly how GLAD I'll be to leave the *Times-Herald*—I almost hope they fire me.

JANUARY 31, 1944—I am a little frightened, terribly excited and very thrilled. M.F. called me twice today and once tonight—we talked for some time—and then he asked to see me "for a little supper" early tomorrow night. I hung up wildly excited—dinner with HIM—I immediately dropped everything and made a new hat of all white violets with a cloud of green veiling. Now I must "read up" on everything I think he'll be interested in—especially the (Paul just called from Montreal to beg me to come up and visit him—I promised I would but I don't know whether I want to be under such obligation to a sailor—and to make such a long trip—poor duck, he's so in love with me). As I was saying, I'll have to "read up" on M.F.'s case in defense of a conscientious objector—and a Jehovah's Witness at that. I also have to garnish the vocabulary and LOOK very lovely, plus—these men are a challenge to everything a woman's got. If he very casually calls and says he can't make it (after all my preparation), I'll swoon away kerplop! Must get busy.

I worried myself sick all day about my first "dinner date" with Frank Murphy. He didn't call all afternoon—then at 6 he did. I was to meet him in an hour at the Shoreham. I was in a nervous fidget until I got there. I never feel right—$1,000,000—looking my best when I see him. I wore the new hat, self-consciously, and not a word out of him— which increased my diffidence. I stood at the top of the steps looking for him. He rose to meet me as though preoccupied. I gasped my apologies for being late. "Oh, that's all right," he said absentmindedly. "It gave me time to say my prayers." He led me to the Blue Room. The waiters scurried. "Oh, good evening, Mr. M.—right this way to YOUR table." I was led to a table way back in the corner—a scared little busboy put down water—staring at both Frank and me. The orchestra struck up "You and I." M.F. nodded and waved to the bandmaster. "That's a salute to us," he said, then tactlessly added how many times he'd dined there with somebody else who liked that song. He ordered decisively for me: "Chicken—you'll like it." "Oh, yes—perfect," I agreed eagerly. He could have said filet of mule meat and I'd never have known the difference. He ordered soup, scrambled eggs and a glass of milk. More people came in that he knew. They eyed me curiously, "Who's SHE?" in their faces. I hoped I looked a credit to him. I had my doubts and felt MISERABLE. I thought how paratrooper George must have felt with ME. I kept trying to recall all the things I'd read up to tell him. He ate his soup NOISILY and spooned hungrily toward himself. To add to the general malaise I had fruit cup for dessert (on a rigid diet) and swallowed a full ball of melon—melon as round as a golf ball and hard as a rock. I gagged and spluttered and nearly DIED of strangling mortification. Frank very worried lest I yelp and create a commotion or something—"Just relax," he urged, patting my arm—"and here, drink some water—" I nearly swooned but swallowed quietly with all my might and struggled to get out the words "Go on, then what happened when you saw the rattlesnake at your foot?" Others danced. We sat—at the next table was a young paratroop captain eagerly adoring a frumpy homely girl. I turned my eyes away and listened to stories of beautiful and fabulously wealthy women who have been his friends. We left when we'd finished, every eye in the room on me, to my anguish. In the taxi he suddenly went "Come here and hold me" on me. I suggested a movie—but without considering if I wanted to go, he said "Oh, no" and we went to his hotel. His roommate was home. I didn't meet him. We played the records he had and every now and then he reached over to embrace me. Then he'd say, "I don't want you to go. I want you to stay and just hold me. I'll be a gentleman—but I just want to hold you." I knelt on the floor in front of his chair hugging him to me. He felt my pulse and pushed me laughingly and gently aside—"same old steady beat—I've lost my power."

A man called then, and he told him to come over. I jumped up to go, but F. insisted I stay. The man was curious and constrained when he saw me. He was heavy-set, gray-haired, somber—obviously something on his mind he wanted to discuss privately. Conversation was difficult for all three of us. I turned to playing the records—then F. said he'd drive me home. In the taxi he pressed his arm against me and gripped my hand. Surprisingly he walked me to the door of Scotts (Hotel) and KISSED me, fatherly, on the cheek. He looked a little pathetic standing there as though he WANTED me and didn't want to go back to the ugly man in the taxi. I told him I wanted to go to Alaska. He didn't take it very seriously, but I saw to my delight he didn't want me to go so far away. To my despair, I gathered "No connections, no help from him on my schemes of tackling the great NORTH."

Letter from Mother taking a very cold-eyed, use-your-head view of M.F. She said first (and she's right) that he wouldn't marry me and if he did ask me I'd be a fool to marry a grandfather. "Think of the physical side," she wrote, with cruel candor. "And no politician is honest. He won't be amused by you very long." Oh, frightening. There for a moment last week I thought I had lost him. But no, he finds me comfortable and pretty (I hope) as a relief from the glamour women. He told me a good story about Liz Whitney appearing late and unwelcome at a dinner party where he was. M.F. happened at the moment to be staring at an exquisite little statue of Christ. "HUMPH," laughed Liz. "Get Murphy looking at himself." He roared when he told me that. I observed something else tonight. He's trying to be gay and devastating for me. He'll ask me offhand every now and then, "Do I amuse you, Pegge? Am I better or worse than you thought I'd be?" Mother's cold view of him has upset me. She so icily poof poofed my awe of his importance.

FEBRUARY 3, 1944—A storybook thing happened tonight. I had dinner with Al Morano, told him about Cissy's letter and my ambition to go to Alaska. "How much would you need, really need, to go?" he asked seriously, calculating. "Oh, 300 to get up —300 back—expenses, hotels—oh, I'd say—"

"A thousand would do it, wouldn't it?' he put in quickly.

"Yes, I guess so."

"I'll give it to you—I'll back you on it and I think you'll make good. I know you've got stuff and can make a success of your book."

I gasped and cooed my "Al, darling—no, no" protests, but lordy, like a girl in a story—a thousand bucks—the only hitch is that he's expecting a commission on a South American deal. If he gets it, he said he'd have the man sign the whole thing over to me. I must refuse, of course, but gee-e-e-e! The other alternative is this: Tony Diamond is expected to return to Alaska as a judge—and why couldn't I go along as a member of his staff? I am simply obsessed with the whole adventure.

Cute story I heard last night: British Lieutenant in a bar turns to two Yanks and says, "Awfully jolly of you chaps to come over to help us out—but don't forget we're certainly going to let you in on the kill." The one Yank eyes him for a minute and then turns to his buddy and says, "For a Russian he speaks pretty good English, doesn't he?"

FEBRUARY 7, 1944—Had my first interview for a job in Alaska today with the Civil Aeronautics. Noticed a too-smart attitude on my part of being too much the newspaper woman condescending to take a job (in a way). I knew more about Alaska than the little government girl hiring me. Must sit on myself next time. I filled out two applications already. At lunchtime today I got a strange and curious V-mail letter from a First Lieutenant John Pennoch, postmarked Seattle. It read, "A Valentine wish to a very lovely miss." The message was the very first indication that any of my letters (with pictures enclosed) have been received and appraised up there. I may be all wrong. I wrote and asked him to write immediately.

I had dinner at the Statler with "Jonesy" and enjoyed being "the girl in the red velvet hat" everyone stared at, wondering who I was. I am completely relaxed in his company now. We went to the movies afterward, and before we left the Statler he asked me to call the theatre and have the manager reserve two seats. My lord, the little manager was running around all excited. He reserved a BOX for us where we sat and held hands and Jonesy drove me crazy for talking during the movie. We had hot chocolate afterward and I came home alone in a taxi. No international secrets tonight. Forgot to tell you he again boasted of the wit and conquests of women in his life. For instance, a pretty blonde out-of-town reporter sat at the court press table and all the judges, especially M.F., took note. After recess the blonde, who OF COURSE kept eyeing M. all the time, had changed her seat. One of the bench "supreme" leaned over and commented on the new seating "M—isn't he clever?" Wrote a little rhyme which he repeated three times that I might more fully appreciate its iambic brilliance. I tried to remember the exact wording for a future quote, but all I recall is this:

Of the two, the better view

Is mine

Of the blonde reporter

So divine.

Seems he had some abstruse word in there which I left out. The latest effort is: He's going to New York for three to four days next week. When I told him I was being sent to Philadelphia to cover the opening of Arabella's new play, he said, "Why don't you hop a train for New York when it's over. I'll meet you at the station—arrange for you to stay overnight with the Byron Foys, and I can even get you a plane out of New York Tuesday morning to get you back to Washington earlier than you're usually in the office." Storybook stuff again—no further details yet.

Definitely ended everything with Merchant Marine Paul. Must try a short story on the situation. How cruelly kind to bring men like him into contact—social and romantic—with girls who are only fascinated for the time and not in any way attainable for wifedom.

Writing poorly at the office. Upset when two severe and careless chops to fit my story into limited space left the context distorted and jumbled. "Oh, well," said Papa Denby, "it wasn't a very good story anyway." My Sunday story, even to ME, was worse than Class C.

I'm just barely hanging on there until Alaska opens up, and the opening up is maddeningly SLOW. Very squelched when I got a cold form letter X'd off with all my disqualifications—stressing my occupation in an essential industry and advising my staying put. DAMN—and I sent that man my picture and a long, carefully written, personal letter.

Here is a story about Clare Boothe Luce Al told me. Following her outrageous, vicious, almost fishwife attack in the press on the administration and the President, personally, the usual reception tea for new members of Congress was held at the White House. Mrs. Luce attended, on her guard. The President was lavishly, deliberately, obsequiously attentive to Mrs. Luce's rival, Winifred Stanley. When he finally acknowledged Mrs. Luce, he was cold, restrained and brief. The glamorous lady of the law moved away quickly and kept her distance. The President gloated in his superiority. He turned to a friend standing nearby. "Well," he remarked with a self-satisfied smile, "I guess I put her in her place."

"Yes, you did," coolly replied his friend, "the highest place in the room." The President has never forgiven him.

Idea for Alaska. Have a wild idea. I'd like to sing in a nightclub up there. Of course I can't sing but I can write and I can act and I can make myself look glamorous. My idea is to sing my songs as though they were letters to a soldier named Johnnie. My billing would be, say, "Sally Lee singing 'Letters to Johnnie.'" Each song would tell the part of a story and the script would be acted to theme song music. Wild idea but an IDEA.

FEBRUARY 13, 1944—If I have ever been angrier, wildly more outraged I can't imagine WHEN. I have just had a snack with Frank Murphy—there, I've named him outright. And oh, someday what I shall write about him! Tonight he phoned from the home of that fatuous imbecile, Mrs. Evelyn Walsh McLean (spelling, I know, isn't right), and said they were having a cozy dinner with Connie Bennett. Could I meet him at 11:00 in the lobby of the Statler? I dressed in a fury—I put my hair up—I sang—I sprayed myself with George's perfume. I glanced apologetically at my desk and the gaping typewriter which tonight was to have hummed with the beginnings of my story on Paul and me—Oh, well—write stories any day, sip sweetness with a Supreme Court Justice—no, not every day.

I met him. It was Sunday, and every place was closed up. We walked blocks trying to find a place. Meanwhile I listened to the most tactless country schoolboy naive account of witch woman Connie Bennett, her clothes, her figure, her jewels, her money, her swimming pool, her beauty. I shivered into my little honest working-girl skunk coat and smiled all eager and sweet. We finally went into a "Donald's" where at first the head waiter didn't recognize Frank and tried to shove us off to a little, crowded table. Then someone must have heard him whisper the name and immediately he was obsequious and helpful. All eyes were on us.

I had dressed with such care and thought I looked so well—until he began comparing me with Connie Bennett. "Yes, she wears her hair something like yours, only the way I like it—turned under in the back." I smiled patiently and with interest as he illustrated the preferred coif using two hands on his own balding wiry red hair.

That wasn't enough. The dress—it had this kind of neckline—and he reached over my simple dress and refolded the neckline like Connie Bennett's—that damned slut—that foul cat of divorced bastards! After all this he went into elaborate detail about how "really smart" women dress—How I must get one of those hats for the back of my head and do my hair so—and wear a BROWN suit. I cursed him and raged at him under my smiles. It amused me bitterly to see, as he recounted the lavish hospitality of the movie queen's, WHY he was lunched and race-tracked and swimming-pooled. Why, because he was Attorney General.

To add to my mounting, white-HOT disgust and ABHORRENCE he told me how he worked a wholesale deal with a little Jew manufacturer to get his sister a $100 wool suit for only $30 and how he has a little tailor in Detroit copy the expensive cut and fit of his FEW $150 suits—for about $35. "You remember that brown suit I wore on Sunday? I paid $25 for it in New York." I hoped my face didn't betray my scorn. Supreme Court Justice—penny pincher. Then he FASCINATED me beyond words (which he never gave me a chance to get in edgewise) by explaining how his daily diet—how he went to bed early—got up early—exercised—drank milk four times a day—no pastries—and only scrambled eggs at night and a glass of milk—made a man healthy, wealthy (count every dollar) and wise(?).

We finally got around to New York. My only reason for seeing him—well—theatre with Mrs. Foy—this one, that one. "NERTZ, brother," I thought harshly, furiously, in disappointment. So I said "NO." He kissed me in front of the hotel and kiddingly said, "I'll see you at the Ambassador tomorrow night." "You'll only see me again because you are Justice Murphy and useful," I thought viciously, in flaming outrage! I never want to see him again, but I will, of course. I feel ruthless about conniving with him now. He is an insufferable old hen—damn him to hell.

And so to bed—sweet dreams.

SATURDAY, FEBRUARY 19, 1944—Just remembered there might be a story sometime in an incident Murphy told me—about a man who was a selfish, unscrupulous old so-and-so all his life. Then, quite unexpectedly, comes the war. He was a German, so when the famous hero flier of the Nazis escaped his Canadian concentration camp and got to this pro-Hitler grocery (or restaurant) man he was sheltered and sped on his way—the one kind, unselfish, courageous act he had ever performed in all his life. For this single act, this isolated heroism, he was arrested and condemned to death. Might be a story sometime in a woman who is a witch all her life—then she does one good deed and all her evil comes home to roost in reward. Another thing: Murphy told me he was always a generous and lenient judge not because he was soft-hearted and piously forgiving but because he knew of so much more high crime committed in high places by those beyond all reach of recompense. All condemnation, all guilt, all justice, their shield—money. By comparison, few crimes of poor devils who never had anything out of life anyway seemed very dastardly and deserving of harsh sentences. Interesting and human, I thought.

FEBRUARY 20, 1944—I have had an incredible weekend. Murphy called me as I was dressing to go out. He was very glib on his trip to New York. I cut him short with cold charm. I want one thing from him: a letter of recommendation. Al and I had dinner (black market steak) with Vada Ward, about whom I am about to go on record. She's a sort of French poodle, pedigreed, snippy, sophisticated, small, handsome, choosy. Oddly enough, our only bond is MEN. As long as I've known her we've been most intimately articulate about our love affairs, mostly hers. I always thought there might be a story in some of her amours or in Vada herself—small dark, voluptuous ("I put on all my weight here—bosom—they're my hips as it were." Shrieks of tingling ice-cube laughter. Slim, leggy, Vada with her gracious, svelte femininity and her charming selfish cruelty, her French-perfume heartlessness, her I. Magnin dresses slit, lay bare heaving curves of dusky Madame du Barry breasts (in the office, around newspaper men).

Vada's man this evening was a big, beefy, gusty, loud Shepherd dog (who had provided the steaks). Of all incredible things, he told Vada the cause of most divorce is a woman's fear of pregnancy which makes her resort to artifice in intercourse. As a business and human proposition this man has consummated a smack of medical education with his knowledge of the world. And he has devised a little plastic wheel chart which determines within six days the only possible fertility in a woman. It will sell, after the war, on a national scale for about $3. Vada showed me one he'd given her—it was called the Wheel of Life.

Vada and I went swimming today. In the pool I told her about Alaska. She turned friend and offered to help through the men she knows. As the day progressed the told me about all the loves of her life. One, in particular, Ed Polling, whom I believe is Secretary of the Democratic National Committee or something. He's a Butch with self-made importance and wealth. His wife—his third—is exquisitely beautiful, and Vada met her twice, once at the Shoreham. She met her in the powder room, stared at her in the mirror as she powered her nose. Then, from an irrepressible curiosity to hear her voice, Vada asked her casually if the blackout was over. Back at her table later, where she was with two sappy lieutenants, she watched Ed dance with his wife—perfectly—as though he liked it.

Something else before I forget it. Al told an incredible story about going to Havana on a leisurely cruise boat. One day he got into conversation with a mild, quiet, liquid-eyed Spaniard—noticed he was handcuffed. He inquired of an official later what such a "meek little guy" had done. "Humph," grunted the law, "that meek little guy smuggled Chinamen into the U.S.A. for $500 a head, no questions asked. So, happens one night in the Gulf of Mexico, a Coast Guard cutter bore down on his little immigrant barge and that dirty-livered little devil bagged his Chinamen in burlap bags weighed with rocks and threw them over board! The Coast Guard had no material evidence, but they got him just the same."

Cute joke by Clare Boothe Luce. Discussing the possibility of girl pages in the House, whose ratio might be set by the number of Congresswomen, the fraction was not sufficient to make a whole. Quipped La Luce: "Well, if not a whole page—at least a paragraph." No, I think I botched that slightly. My newsgal friend, Vada Ward, was interviewing CBL for a story on page girls, and Mrs. L said the page–paragraph for the benefit of the assignment.

[Editor's Note: Pegge's diary entries in Washington, D.C., stop at the end of February. From later entries we learn that in March she received a letter from the Fairbanks (Alaska) News Miner *newspaper offering her a job as a reporter and sending a check for $1,000 to cover her travel expenses to Alaska. Pegge's last stories for the* Washington Times-Herald *were printed on March 31, 1944. Before leaving Washington, D.C., Pegge had received a "windfall" and considerable attention as the "back cover girl" in a magazine ad for Camel cigarettes. (Pegge was asked to pose for the ad even though she had never smoked.) Pegge wrote in* Alias Pegge Parker *that the ad gave her "not only unexpected mad money, but a terribly restless urge to buy a ticket to somewhere— somewhere far from the too-muchness of Washington. I was very impatient to be on my way to where the real world was, where really important things were going on." Next stop: Alaska!*

Pegge's full-page ad from Camels Cigarettes.

SLOW BOAT TO CHINA

Alaska
1944–1946

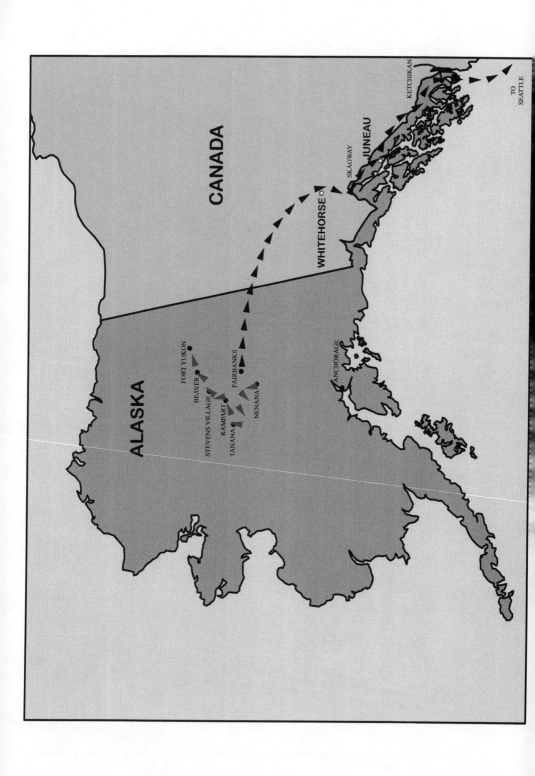

1944

APRIL 16, 1944—Left Washington at 5:30 p.m. (on train)
  Dinner en route: $1.75
  Ticket fare: $115.18
  Hotel bill: $6.60 Blackstone Hotel

APRIL 17, 1944—Met Edward Everett Horton in dining room. Very dapper, very blue eyed, very flushed-faced. Explained his comedy as a growing hallucination: "You start out in one picture sipping a cup of tea in some peculiar way that makes people laugh. Well, the next picture you make the director will make you burn your tongue on a cup of tea. Next picture, you'll spill the tea all down the front of your coat—and so it goes. You wake up someday and find you're a comedian." Horton said he loved Gene Kelly's dancing, better than Fred Astaire's because Kelly looked athletic, "like a MAN dancing." Horton's niece interested in newspapers.

APRIL 18, 1944—Breakfast $1.15. Horton wearing bright blue checked shirt with purple tie, gold monogrammed cufflinks, bright yellow PJs hung on a hook—had box of candy and ate piece after piece, picking out all the chocolate-covered cherries dipped in rum.

Riding through desert, observed the mountains were freckled with small pine trees.

[Editor's Note: Pegge stayed with Mrs. H.C. Witwer, the widow of her uncle, H.C. Witwer, who had been a famous World War I war correspondent and later wrote novels and scripts for movies as well as had acting parts. She used his entree, as well as her own celebrity, to call on the various studio press personnel. Her diaries have several references to Mr. Sadie Witwer.]

DIARY ENTRY - SUNDAY. Trip to E. Horton's -write him thank you note. Met Lucille Lemert of *L.A. Times.* Went to Irene Rich's ranch, met her beau called Pappy and a wondrous witty woman named Mrs. Jones. Dinner with them, stayed overnight with Lucille (Lemert).

Next Monday, Hedda, Brown Derby Lunch.

APRIL 21, 1944 —Toured MGM in Culver City, California. Saw sets for Dorian Gray, one stairway of simulated black marble, gilt and white marble—off in one corner Dorian (Hatfield) in Victorian evening clothes learning a Burmese dance in his stocking feet. A tiny brown weirdly fascinating Burmese dancing girl teaching Dorian. On the set a throne scene of vividly pagan-looking Japanese men and women. Yells of "Quiet—quiet, please." Then "Oh, let 'er roll." Small whirring sound; everyone in room freezes in his tracks—the nervous tenseness of the actors felt by everyone. Only 2 to 3 seconds of a scene. Then a frog call, cut from the bottom of the director's throat.

Took in a gambling scene from "Maizie Goes to Reno"—Maizie (Ann Southern), looking very Tootsie-baby in a roly poly evening gown with flowers in her hair, saying to mannish Armenian peasant-looking William Hodiak (of Life Boat), "Take a card and look at it this time." Noticed Hodiak seemed very nervous. Met him afterward, learned he was from Detroit and radio. He struck me as a serious-souled person who still feels himself unknown. Learned Ann Southern has to have "mood music" played before and after her scenes—everything from Tschaikovsky to Harry James.

Over to "30 Seconds Over Tokyo." Met cigar-smoking, friendly-eyed visitor, welcoming Melvin LeRoy. They were shooting the leg amputation scene of Larson (Van Johnson). LeRoy explained the way it's done. Larson's mind blurs during the ordeal in the hospital and flashes back to a time he crashed in the mountains and couldn't get home for Christmas. The scene showed Van Johnson talking to his wife on the phone. He's seated in a mountain cabin; behind him through the open window, lumberjacks are sawing down a tree. As the brief call with his wife ends, Larson hears the tree crack. The men run, and as Larson watches, the tree falls. In parallel, his own limb is severed. Talked to Van Johnson later. Found him a big pink and yellow rambunctious kid. He felt very close to "Larson" though he's never met him because sometime earlier in his film career he'd been in a critical automobile accident that all but cut off the top of his head. Left his face deeply gashed and scarred. The worst thing that could happen to a photogenic actor. Some kind caller at his bedside brought him a copy of "Thirty Seconds" which he read with intense kin spirit and kin anguish, never dreaming he'd play the part. Then for the hospital scene the makeup men painted in all his original head scars. "So you see I'm really playing this part from the heart," blurted out Johnson with sort of puppyish emotion.

Later we rode to the far end of the lot to the magnificent set for "Mrs. Parkington" starring Greer Garson and Walter Pigeon. An imposing regal manor house laid out on a simulated English countryside with towering hedges spread before the camera. English gentlemen in glove-fitting hunting coats and high silk hats lolled around the veranda. Poised and serene amid the hubbub of cameramen, script girls, prop men and extras stood Miss Garson. In this particular scene, "Mrs. Parkington" has come to England to lay a possessive hand on the wayward arm of her lord errant Walter Pigeon, who has been cavorting with a handsome English lady. Miss Garson's costume was chic and graceful, but she wore a matted and stiff-looking grey wig crudely glued around her face, so that delicate wisps of bright red hair showed through the gray. Her gown was a Victorian suit with a jumper bodice and hourglass-waisted skirt. The suit was made of black wool shepherd's plaid. She wore a white starched blouse with a bright green silk necktie. An arched little green silk parasol matched the necktie effectively. On her graceful head was a large white quilted beret. A tiny, old-fashioned coin purse with jet fringe jangled at her waist. And the Garson touch: Two full-blown roses, one pink and the other burgundy red, were fastened low on the bosom of the jumper. Her face was heavily painted. Her clear English eyes were deeply shadowed with bright blue makeup. Her dainty mouth was surprisingly exaggerated with bright orange-red lipstick.

Talking with her after she completed the scene, I found Miss Garson shrewd, clipped, genteel, sophisticated in a sly witty way of making remarks more witty than worldly. When the publicity woman told her I was going to Alaska, she was eagerly interested because "Richard" (her husband Lt. Ray) had been there and it was such an exciting place. Then she said, "But when you get there after traveling all the way from Washington, you'd better sit down quietly and like the pilgrims traveling to Mecca, give your soul time to catch up with you."

Hollywood remark: A friend of Zadda's is a doctor in a fancy bon bon rich-bitch sort of hospital done up like a musical comedy sawbones institute. At a party one very bright young lady asked this well-bred, well-dressed doctor if he ran "that nipple-pink place downtown where you could have a baby and shampoo and set all at the same time."

[Editor's note: Pegge made an appointment with Charles L. Pincus, known at the time as the "Dentist to the Stars." He was the pioneer in the art of cosmetic dentistry, and among his patients were Clark Gable and Bob Hope. The first reference in her diary was on Friday, April 21, reading "Dentist - 9629 Brighton Way."]

Mon. - Dentist 10 A.M.

Tue. - Dentist $300

Wed. – Dentist 9:30 Crestview 7144

Fri. – Dentist

Sat. – Dentist at 9 A.M.

Mon. – Dentist completed caps. Another $350.

[Now follows Pegge's summary of her interview with a representative of the Max Factor Company, A. B. Shore.]

- Eyebrows begin directly above corner of eye
  [Here, Pegge diagrams an eye with the eyebrow.]

- Never change body of eyebrow; trim above or below but never main body.

- For skin take slow hot baths instead of showers.

- Keep rouge high up to lower eyelashes. Use cream rouge on young skin and dry on problem skin.

- Wipe entire face and throat with tissue after covering with sponge. Women with prominent noses, no rouge. Puffy eyelids on bony structure kills highlight. At night, more rouge, eyelash makeup very moist "goo." Orchid eyeshadow with brown eyes— only at night—put a little more eyeshadow; it can show. Match eyeshadow to jewels—sapphire.

- Kids using makeup: wash face, keep skin cream, pancake on blemish healing. Doesn't harm because it's dry. Tidy-looking face—cleanliness. Most important to complexion: lots of soap and water, if water hard, dries skin. Slight film of cream. Older women put rouge near puffy eyes and use darker pancake. Wrinkles, use darker. No cracks in pancake if you wipe off with Kleenex.

[At Romanoff's, Pegge evidently met Michael Romanoff (owner?). She describes him thus: deeply brown, lined face, grey kinky hair cropped close to his head. Pegge jotted down the following remarks by Romanoff, who was one of the best known restaurateurs of the time.]

No one means anything—just a few friends and his "women a la carte."

"Rather compete with a hundred husbands than one career." Likes them—emphatically plural. "I graduated from the stage door years ago."

"Inside stories very dull. Rather be an actor in them than an onlooker."

"Restaurant not my business—my folly."

"No elevators here—everything on the level."

Likes Clare Luce's looks but not her politics. Despises Cissie Patterson's politics too.

Disclaims reading; says he has an English bulldog that does all his reading for him.

Roosevelt has blood and race, blood and race hold form. Greatest force in world today is money. Everyone criticized him for income. "Only critics fail to realize that other people rising up would have taken away their income."

Lincoln was reviled in his day, but no great man has honor in his day.

"The war is here to stay. It is a war of annihilation."

People are afraid of dying OF something instead of FOR something. We can take a lesson from Russia and prepare our fighters, not the people back here. Russia is fighting to make history.

Postwar: Victory will be exhausting and then we'll swing to right. Veterans' Assoc. will be most powerful depending on their leader.

More governmental control; Congress will destroy old legislature to make room for new.

People will be the same: greedy and grasping when they don't live up to what's expected of them.

[Editor's Notes: Hopper, at the time was the best known Hollywood gossip columnist and radio personality. To be mentioned in her column was the goal of every aspiring actor.

On Monday, Pegge had lunch at the Brown Derby with Hedda Hopper.

Pegge also noted that Hedda Hopper prefaced all of her remarks with "My dear..." and that Hopper commented, "The only time I talk is to avoid saying anything."]

Pegge's mentioning in the article
of Hollywood reporter Hedda Hopper.

EN ROUTE—Miss Pegge Parker,
former women's page editor of
the Washington Times Herald
is shown in Seattle, en route to
Alaska to become news editor
of the Fairbanks News-Miner.

Capital Woman
To Take Post on
Alaska Paper

En route from the congestion of
Washington, D. C., to the last fron-
tier, interior Alaska, Miss Pegge
Parker, former woman's page editor of the Washington Times-Herald, passed through Seattle yesterday.

She is on her way North to take
over as news editor of the Fairbanks News-Miner, published by
the kidely known Alaskan finan-
cier, Capt. A. E. Lathrop, and to
become the Fairbanks correspondent for International News Service.

Subchaser to French

WASHINGTON States subchaser

MAY 7, 1944—MAIDEN VOYAGE—Steerage deluxe, *S.S. Baranoff,* Seattle to Alaska. Company boat. Just before boarding, Captain relates that among the passengers are an English Lord or baron and wife, who have rare old scotch and have offered to host a cocktail party for all on board. When passing TAKU glacier (oldest and largest of all known and named glaciers) the Captain, as is the custom for sightseeing, blew whistles. Vibrations, broke ton-weight pieces and formed new glaciers. One of the stewards went out in a rowboat and at the barons' suggestions chipped off ice for their drinks. Englishman cabled London sitting on deck with scotch and soda, tinkling ice cubes that were 50,000 years old.

Mrs. Barbara MAPES, with a nutmeg drink, looking over the deck for defenses. Nobody spotted a gun. Man picked up a slingshot and asked, "What's this?"

Barbara replied, "Oh, haven't you heard? That's the new anti-aircraft."

Comments from Barbara: "My mouth dropped open to my knees." "My God, you'll see strawberries big as tea cups in Alaska." "God, I felt like the wart on the end of somebody's nose."

Fisherman with filed teeth, no teeth to teeth like the Morse Code. Canned fish with orchids in her hair, body rubbed with Scaparelli body oil.

Sky the color of angel's eyes. The sea had insomnia; all night long it tossed and turned trying to sleep.

KETCHIKAN, Tuesday morning—Wooden houses, Dutch clean, piled high on a hill. Hills green with snow on top. Nice chap in newspaper office. Eyed me with measuring rod, was I a smoothie? Stopped in gaudy little Catholic Church. Noticed beauty shop larger than the grocery store.

Governor's mansion—WPA paintings and ballroom furniture. Water colors—at head of stairs was painting of Peter the Great—

sparsely done and hand-done rooms. Century print cutout from Washington made by Mrs. G.

Baranof Hotel—a sort of Sears Roebuck furnished effect—chrome and stuffed furniture and glorious paintings over the door entrance. A dulled portrait of the legendary Russian painted by a local artist from an old print (ballroom of governor's mansion furnished with butter-yellow leather and white furniture). Walked out woodland path to log cabin of former mayor—wife in cotton house dress, no makeup, very sweet).

Talked with a Mr. and Mrs. John BLASÉ of Seward. Mrs. B is a typical housewife who enjoys folksy conversation.

Passenger: Harry MacIntosh, bartender from Seattle. Little, pink and brown faced, squinty eyed, rimless glasses, expensively dressed. Kept telling me about a blind pianist who played in Fairbanks nightclubs. Harry ate little—smoked cigarettes—made everyone uncomfortable at the table. Grinned, stuttered slightly. One night he didn't appear at the table. Remarks were made. "Nothing trifling, we hope." Didn't appear again. Then word raced around the ship that he was a doper and was caught trying to jump overboard. The captain roped him to his bunk and posted a guard by his cabin. They found a glass tube of yellow capsules among his effects. The Captain said he was "just a crazy man." Someone heard him remark that he had a son in the C.B's in the South Pacific. In Juneau he got off the ship and was grabbed by a detective. He was dressed in a natty blue and smart felt hat. He was still grinning but barely able to walk.

Captain C. "Squinty" Anderson—a Norwegian skipper on the line for many years. As Barbara said, he was like a little bowl of cheese. All his "J's" were "U's": "Uneau" for Juneau. Closed one eye as he talked.

Spied whale, huge black mound spouting water out of his back. Porpoises heaved and romped through the water.

On bridge—Glascock told of early days being burned one night when campfire caught tent. Missionary's wife prospectin' like ev'body else. Took some perfumed oil she had and covered his face. Took care of him. Her boat came before he recovered and he never saw her, just remembered her voice. Years later on a ship he heard her voice. Went below and saw a little old lady who didn't remember him.

Saw glimpse of a glacier called Mt. BRADY, named after some Irishman.

Ice berg—white frosty and transparent green—centuries old, looming out of the water.

Saw sudden, five-minute brilliant sunset by God or Salvador Dali. Modernistic wedges of mountain with white meringue snow peaks against a commotion of color which quickly dissolved into gray and gold. From the bridge—huge mountains.

Dead ahead on the port side, a sharp turn between two mountains and below the clean sky a mashed potato fog, whipped and fluffy and solid. Everyone on deck scurried for cover. In 20 minutes the ship sailed into white blindness. At 10:00 the captain announced over a loudspeaker that the ship would be blacked out in half an hour, which seemed really as though the only other thing needed was to blindfold the passengers. Sea very rough, the air lashing and salty.

THURSDAY AT YAKUTAT— Alaska fishery—wooden shacks. Little papoose-faced Indian infants running around the dock. Lonely looking, tall young military police. Indian or Mexican-looking Indian girls in cotton dresses, bright sweaters and worn-down old shoes eyeing the men and staring with admiration and fascination at white women on the ship. Fishermen on our ship embarked and were greeted by toothless, yellow-faced, oil-black-haired native fishermen they'd worked with the year before. Into jeep and out to air base with Butch and Mac (Lt. IRVIN L. TRESSLER, APO 943, U.S. Army Outer Alaska). The post was a covey of black bungalows, a gravel path with worn wooden plank walks. A burned hangar, a vast landing field, an Italian pottery blue sky, a vested choir of saintly white mountains, and for the few men left, lackadaisical duties, a sense of humor and loneliness. Butch, Barbara, Mac and I went down the Gulf Shore and there in my heart was a VISION of lonely glamour. The Gulf was like an ocean exquisitely marcelled in vanilla soda foam rolling up on a black sand strewn with violet and gold Japanese fishing balls *[used to hold up the nets in the water]*, tree roots, long and curled like Simon LeGree whips, and violet-stained sand, which finely sifted contained tiny bright grains of gold.

So there—imagine it—blue ocean—black sand, with fine-sifted gold. And a frosty breath of fog blowing in from the sea.

Story idea from Butch: When he's censoring his boys' mail he always locks himself up so they won't hear him howling with laughter. One day, though, he came across a poem that moved him to awe and admiration. Laid it aside to make a copy.

FRIDAY A.M.— at Cordova, where Captain Lathrop got his start and now operates the Embassy theatre and combined men's clothing and hardware store, immaculately clean—neat, busy, horsey, masculine. The day was depressing, the sky tattletale gray. The main street was like a Zane Grey locale. The buildings shacky, the streets unpaved, the sidewalks deserted except for a few shuffling old duffers in rubber boots and red lumberjack shirts. The drugstore had the feeling of an old-fashioned parlor opened for the occasion of a big family funeral. It was the most forlorn outpost of civilization I have ever seen.

Called at *Cordova Times* office and expected Horace Greeley to swing 'round on the editor's chair. Two men ran the office— or walked it. One was the all-around operating manager, a Mr. Pettijohn, formerly of Seattle. A bland, quiet-pulsed, balding man. He suggested I visit the air base buried 13 miles back by the mountains. Phoned a Capt. Ben E. CUDDY, U.S. Troops, Post Commander, for permission to visit the base. Went out to the field on the ricketiest little GI Toonerville, a bright orange boxcar that rattled down two rusty tracks on rotting logs. We passed aquamarine lakes, nosed our way round the chin of rockbound, snow-thatched mountains. At the end of the line, a jeep named the BROADWAY LIMITED waited. Beside it stood a graceful, cultured and charming man with bookish green eyes that at first studied me formally then from the sheer novelty of a newspaper girl (in the green Helen Garnell hat) his reserve broke down and he was completely friendly. The base, apparently unmanned, was as much of a ghost camp as the town, for the army had pulled out its surplus manpower. Officers' quarters were hidden under trees. They were constructed of the same black material as the ones at YAKUTAT. At the officers' mess talked to two attractive pilots and one quiet, unattractive slightly boorish Captain from Camp Hill who knew Paul Walker. His name: Captain Christian SIEBERT, Commanding Engineer Corps. Met and joshed with some cute sergeants and saying goodbye, shook hands with one who held onto my mitt. "Oh—holding hands with a white woman. I can't let go," he howled.

General impression of men stationed there for a long while. Alaska is a man's sporting paradise. They get only 12 days of sun a year, and when the sun is out, they knock off and go out in it. Their morale is fortified with a good Yankee sense of humor, and they enjoy the country. They all want to get the hell out of here, though, the minute the war is over. As a business enterprise they don't want to be bothered struggling with transportation and other pioneer obstacles. They see little thriving or population possibilities for Alaska. Some of them were looking forward to a yearly event in Cordova—The Purple Bubble Dance—where all the gals of the town turn out.

Friday night stopped at VALDEZ. Walked up by bridge to interview pilot called Captain Harry McCarthy with whom I'd ridden to the ship in a shared taxi in Seattle. He was tall, aloof, quiet-spoken, darkly attractive, slightly pudgy from lack of exercise on the ship. We sat in the ship's social hall for a few minutes comparing notes on the gossip we had created from a brief verbal clash. He was amused by what I reported. "But it's so silly," he mused, "When everyone knows I'm married." I winced slightly in regret. Looked up at him to say something and was amazed to see his eyes suddenly filled with tears. "Or at least I think I am," he added with a shrug of mock contempt and anguish. I listened feelingly. "Funny part of it is," he continued, unable to resist an audience and sympathy, "I've only been married since January." He paused. The rain beat against the ship and I shivered. Later we went into town, arm in arm, enjoying a mad impulsive gaiety in having found each other on the last night of our trip. And spending it walking down a dirt road in a driving rain looking for a coffee haven. The windows of all the local dives were blurred with steam and grime. We caught echoes of juke boxes and celebrations as we passed. Quite perfectly we then discovered neither of us drank and a quiet little coffee bistro was all we wanted. Then a barmy-looking lunchroom invited us with its name, Shamrock Café, and a huge hand-painted blob of a green shamrock on the front window. We sat on stools and laughed at nothing, toasted our cups to the luck of the Irish.

I learned that for all his distinctive reserved manner, he had a very common background. Mother born in London, father in Ireland. Mother's father had been a commander in the Royal Navy. Obviously the marriage didn't last. He never knew his father. Remarked vaguely he never sees his mother, was raised by an 80-year-old grandmother. All his life he's wanted a home—a real come-home-to home. So one day when he'd come in from a 'round the world trip and had been paid off handsomely, he went out and bought a house. His first home. He was a King with a Castle! Now all he needed was a wife. He went looking. Quite by chance he met a mite of an Irish girl who also had no home or background. Her name: Ellen. Her past: Presumed intimate with an older married man whom she's supposed to have known seven years. Harry proposed a toast over their first cocktail. "Well," said Ellen. "Here's to my nine kids." "I'd like to be a party to that plan," Harry said, eyeing her and selling himself an idea that here was the girl. "Okay," chirped Ellen quickly, "Let's start right now." Harry confided she really shocked him into stunned embarrassment. When I eyed him point blank, he hastened to add, "Of course she was only kidding." "Of course," I echoed, still eyeing him unblinkingly. "Well," Harry went on, gulping his coffee absently, "I moved in fast. I mean really fast. I never left her alone and suddenly we were married. But there was no little home. The place was rented and we lived at the Washington Hotel. Then I felt I'd moved in too fast—things haven't worked out as I expected" etc. So I sat listening, reluctantly. Then when I saw how really hurt and in love and befuddled he was, I plunged into a real Dorothy Dix. First I defended Ellen, to his eager relief. He wanted to believe he'd been wrong and it would all work out.

A sort of outside-looking-in, maiden aunt loneliness crept over me as I watched the devoted bridegroom in his emotional fog. We analyzed, we rearranged, we straightened things out to a T. We idealized too. But every now and then I let fly a jag at Ellen who sounded to me like a cheap little pickup not worthy of a nickel's worth of fidelity. Nobility was exhausting and suddenly I could stand the strain no longer. I swallowed up my last drop of coffee, stood up to go. Walked back to the ship in the rain in angry silence, writhing in self-pity that married men are my apples of temptation, and the only ones on the tree at that. Back on the ship we didn't feel like turning in so sat in the darkened, deserted social room, clutching each other's hands, talking about Ellen and life, generally. At length he was sleepy and with morale lifted, yawning tired. We parted casually to see each other the next morning, but missed. I resorted to every pretext to linger on the bridge until Harry would appear to say goodbye, but even though he was called and, I believe, told I was waiting, he didn't come.

SATURDAY, SEWARD—A dismal, cold, rain soaked, muddy day. We sat on a "toonerville" train, waiting from 1 to 5 p.m. for it to depart, then endured a ride of nearly six hours to Anchorage. No food on the train. Arrived about 11 p.m. at a small freshly painted newish station. Soldiers and frantically scrambling civilians milled around the concourse. No porters. No taxis. I had no room, either, since I had believed the train would go right on through to Fairbanks. Neither had 17 other standees, some with yelling babies and suitcases that weighed like blocks of cement. My shipmates, both with rooms reserved, had disappeared. Following woman's way, I approached a clean, scrubbed-looking soldier. Helpless as a southern belle I told him my plight. Gallant and willing, he carried the bags off the train, phoned the hotels, then called a taxi. His name was (Corporal T.) Hank Miller of Washington, D.C. By luck I learned of an agent here for Captain Lathrop. Phoned him and I was aided and abetted toward getting a room at the Westward Hotel, brand newish and immaculately clean.

SUNDAY, ANCHORAGE—Tried pricing meals here in the hotel grill. For $1 I had half a grapefruit, toast, two cups of coffee, scrambled egg and three long strips of very good bacon. Walked to Mass over a wide, cracked sidewalk bordering a mud-caked wide paved main street, the only one in Anchorage. Passed stores that made me contemptuous and eager to replace them by the most drastic measures—throwing the trash merchandise out on the street by hand, tearing down the whole shack building and putting in a smart shop. I walked all the way down to the end of the highway and suddenly, the violin strings of my heart twinkled in ecstasy! There, before me, was an elegant, beautiful white colonial frame house. I rushed eagerly toward it. Oh, Anchorage had class and style and sophistication, after all! Then, as I reached the front sidewalk I stopped. The lawn was weedy and neglected. The driveway a track of mud sprinkled with cinders. The grand façade with its almost prim colonial charm was an indifferent picture of ramshackle neglect. The fine green shutters were washed bare of paint. But, oh wretched slut who let the one fine home, the one graceful monument of the twentieth century in this unsightly, shabby town—a small, disheveled-looking annex had been tacked onto the side of the home and boldly from the front windows hung PINK GINGHAM CURTAINS. I stood there stunned with disappointment and wild with rage at the woman who was such a clod of stupidity and blindness she could hang pink curtains in front of such a home! (Later learned that a dentist owned the house and the despicable woman who presided over it was a local girl-wife—beautiful but an imbecile.)

Spurned to impatience and impassioned loathing for the people who permitted such obstructions as their so-called houses to exist in the face of royal, magnificent Alaska, I raced down the narrow sidewalk past 2 x 4's I called mere thumbs of houses, short, stumpy and above all, ramshackle. Blatant stupidity and gross ignorance of good taste rose on all sides, especially one ridiculous and pathetic Spanish bungalow—with comic scrolls outlined in bright, rain-soaked BLUE paint against a red tile roof. The pièce de resistance was a screaming chartreuse window box. Walking back to Mass, fists clenched, fear and blazing outrage burning inside me, I resolved to take Alaska in my two bare hands and remake it worth of her natural heritage. No scum of the earth robbing her of fishery profits to run back to the States and spend Alaskan wealth, no criminals, nitwits, Mrs. Plotzes, lazy rocking chair pioneers, and no scrawny, hawkfaced women would inhabit the Alaska of my impatient dream. I felt an Aladdin's Lamp passion to pave every road in Anchorage. Then to build model houses with chintz and charming women to glorify them. "I won't have this, or that, or these people in Alaska" I raged to myself. All during Mass I was a Chamber of Commerce, promoting, advertising, Billy Rose'ing Alaska.

My heart went out to Captain Lathrop. I cried out to him to be the White Father of a cosmopolitan Alaska worthy of the country. Later, back at the hotel, met Barbara and together we took in the main street. Our mutually enterprising, ambition-taking wildly racing speed. We wished we could transport some brilliant unscrupulous businessmen who would—we were laughing at ourselves by this time—sell the town insurance. Then set fire to all the shacks, or pass legislation condemning them as breeders of vermin. Anything to get them torn down or burned down so new, sparkling, smart little homes could be built in their place. We picked the site for Barbara's store over the bleeding body of one poor department store on the corner by the streaked yellow cement post office. We built a country club, we burned the pants off the satisfied codgers who thought everything good enough as it was. We even visually transported beautiful showgirls to steal all the men away from their dowdy, horse-faced wives (who would then, naturally, be forced to Barbara's store to give them clothes-for-clothes, chic-for-chic competition). We crowned the whole Utopia by making Barbara the mayor of the town, since, after all, she must make the town before she can make her store GO in this blinking little town. As we wandered back to the hotel, down a mud-and-rock road, we pictured ourselves 20 years from now, dining by candlelight, silver-haired, jeweled heroines of the STATE OF ALASKA!

(RECORDED DATE: MAY 14, 1944)

MONDAY—Father Dermot of Flanagan, pastor from Ireland direct. Holy Family Church. Tall, wiry, human priest with faint trace of brogue, found him in denims working one morning. Of Alaska, he said there were not so many marriages. Since December, he'd had only four and only one was Army. Alaskans have a different feeling about their town than an outsider's. Theirs is the one big brotherhood feeling. Let's all be comfortable, take our time, let's all share and share alike, and let's see that all have enough. He evinced only tolerant amusement at my protests over the homes.

Captain J. S. Clark, Asst. Administrative Officer, Gov. Girls Engineering Constructing Division (Colonel L. B. DE LONG commanding)—Women workers come to Alaska from all over the U.S., mostly from the West Coast. Hired in Seattle on one-year contract, not civil service. Gals come up for a lark and most go back after being here a year. They're given 15 days leave with salary, flown to Seattle and back free. Not obligated to renew their contract. Traveling on salary when they sign up in Seattle: $1620 plus 25% for Alaskan duty for a 40-hour week with eight hours or more overtime. Expenses paid and salary paid en route and back. Raised to $1800 quickly. Live in barracks. Rent $15 per month, 25 cents a meal—very good chow—half the boys take them to dinner, to Lido Club. Drinks 75 cents for weak ones. $5 full course meals, very good. Dance to jukebox. Restricted to Officers and civilians. U.S.O. gets the girls to dances. Girls very average—they come for adventure and men. Few marriages. Army can't marry girls. They are immediately evacuated. Few loopholes like being native Alaskan, having been here a long time, job, etc. Strictly office work. Women don't get on the chain. Some girls at Nome, try to promote them to get the girls up. Rooms small, hand furnished. Wear slacks and mukluks in the office from 8:15 to 5. Dates every night. After being here a year, marry and stay if work. Many save money. Boys allowed in room up to 11:00 and in social hall until midnight. Housekeeper in charge but girls take care of their rooms. Putting on chow with army boys. Air corps orchestra can be hired at fund cost for the band. Evening gowns very attractive—girls keep up appearances. Girls just having a good time. Go back and can't take the indifference. 20-30 age limit. Don't dress up in expensive clothes. In winter girls ski, go bicycling, picnics in hills and mountains. Go swimming at Lake SPANARD—cars or taxi transportation. Nightclub out there with log cabin type atmosphere, dance, get good tan. Marvelous weather in July-August. Flowers, no kissing on doorstep in summer nights. Bright daylight. Girls are FOR it, like it.

Thank a red-headed Captain Clark for his time.

FROM ANCHORAGE TO FAIRBANKS via Alaskan Railroad.

Rode halfway with Fred Hougham, city slicker turned Alaskan miner. He wore a plaid wool lumberjack shirt, hightop boots, a little felt hat—and the youngest, brightest look in his eyes I'd ever seen. His story was simple: He was second largest man in an insurance company in Chicago. Wife, dog, no children, apartment on Lake Shore Drive. He felt he was getting on in life, was comfortably successful, but had nothing to show for his time. One summer he decided to combine a fishing trip with a little prospectin' in Alaska. He bought some land, found it profitable mining acreage, and now every year he comes up from May to September, lives the Life of Riley and is superintendent of his mines. When Fred got off at the little whistle stop, TALKEETNA, he was heartily greeted by his gang—strapping, whiskered woodsmen with leathery, hearty faces.

The train, all coach, was a conglomeration of characters. Right behind me was an Indian and Squaw—the ugliest and most shriveled, most skull-bone-faced humans I've ever seen. She spoke in a swoosh, swoosh of saliva and tongue. Their language is like that—no distinct sounds. Just hissing gurgles.

There was also a woman, about 33-ish, with a sweet voice, urbane manners, good clothes shabbily worn. Her vulgar, uncouth mouth housed a sweet voice, and a fine powder of dandruff from her unwashed, straggly hair clouded the collar of her smart black suit. She spoke of "trains as bad as those in Russia." Seems she was evacuated from Burma/China through Russia. She revealed only that she was "on furlough" in the country and we couldn't figure out who and what she was. She confided girlishly that on Russian sleepers no distinction was made between a man and a woman, "But for some reason I was put in a compartment with an old lady from Belgium." She'd had her eye earlier set on a royal-looking Russian captain who apparently spoke no English.

MAY 22, 1944—FAIRBANKS

Darling, darling Mommie—

Where did I stop telling ALL? At Anchorage, yes? Well, I will give you flashes. The train ride from Anchorage to Fairbanks—almost 500 miles—was cinders, construction gangs, Indians looking like shriveled acorns, and SIT-ITUS. Took almost nine hours straight sitting. There was on the train one guy with flaming orange hair, a red-checked blazer jacket and hip boots who took favor with Parker. He taught me how to do magic tricks with rubber bands (yelled down the car "squeeze—I'm no fool. Get 'ta hold her hand this way!") But someone gave me moral support again. A very chic older gal selling (Vicki Baum stuff) greeting cards in the Yukon, representing a very nice Los Angeles firm. I tell you the copy up here is just walking around on four legs. She was as "quick" as Barbara but much more genteel. The train (much more choo-choo Baby) pulls into the little Alaskan hotel for the night, midway. It is staffed by the Army. Two little corporals came running for my four pieces of luggage—and can they show me the town, ma'am, as they're closing the door of my vast double room. I was too much cinder-ah-ella to want anything but a bath and bed. Dinner first, though. And what a dinner. Roast beef as big and thick as an hour hand, muffins made with maple syrup, four huge chunks of butter, asparagus tip salad, etc. I struggled through it somehow. On my left reposed a sober-faced, middle-aged man in a field jacket. "Uh," I began, since no one at our table had made any more noise than chewing carrot sticks. "Uh, some trip."

Nodded head.

"Wonderful beef."

"Umm. Mouth full."

"I-uh-hear Fairbanks is nice."

"Yes, 'tis."

I, while icing my third muffin with butter: "What brings YOU up here?" I beamed with all bright interest.

"Game commissioner."

"Oh really! Any minks running around I can catch with a little net or something?"

"HAR, HAW'R, HAW'R. Lady if you ketcha mink with a net I shore won't pinch ya for that! Haw'r, Haw'r. Haw'r, that's GOOD."

Anyway, he proved wonderfully interesting and had me with half a mind to tell you and Paw to come up here and start a mink farm. You know, the land is still FREE up here. All you want, if you'll just build a home on it and live on it. And the stone martins running around loose, brother!

Well, anyway—the next day, about 4:00 p.m. the train steams 'round a bend in the track and rolls into the most adorable little folksy town by a winding river tinted baby-girl pink and sky blue. With trees along the bank, slim, young and all shy green. Over yonder towered a serenely graceful Catholic Church. In the other direction, toward town, I saw modernistic office buildings, paved highways, a radio beacon—CIVILIZATION!

The sun was hot and bright. My red-headed rubber band boy piled all my luggage up against the station door, then, at my insistence, left me.

No Miriam—though I'd wired when I was arriving. Very shaky-kneed now (this is it, I'm here and snowed in financially until I write my way out). Finally, a pleasant, Irene-Dunne-type young woman rushed up, both hands clasping mine— Miriam! She is, and I say this in extreme relief, a lovely person. A darling. Just a trifle bit aloof from me, filled with the poise of her responsibility ($6 million old Cap is worth and making more every day). She took me to my apartment in front of an immaculate-looking, white cement newspaper office (would put my cubby corner of the *Times-Herald* to shame).

My roommate came in just then, up to her big brown eyes in celery tops and groceries. She is a government girl but exceedingly superior, sweet, cute, considerate, snappy in a very nice-girl way and a cook out of this world. What a dinner she sat me down to that first night, with graham cracker chocolate peppermint pie for dessert and gallons of delicious coffee. Her name is MARJORIE HAIGHT (pronounced "hate").

I didn't do anything but unpack, press and look around the first day. Miriam came in and we talked. She gave me an idea of the paper, job, etc. I liked her exceedingly and I do believe she likes me, but I had been warned by that former city ed and now Yank correspondent I met in Anchorage (remember) never to outshine her, so I play Parker straight. My newspaper boss, a man 76 years old and former Hearst man who was against their hiring a woman in the first place, has been an extremely nice, old-school-gentleman-type man, for all his prejudice—very, very nice. Not critical of my work, or even one to offer suggestions. He's too busy whipping out a paper with a staff of three (I thought the first day I walked in, it should be Lois Fegan, not me here. This is all her Mechanicsburg experience IN DEMAND, and her reporting beat, for I cover the Federal Building and the courts. And know nothing about it. By golly, here I am thinking: What would Lois do… how can I be like Lois? Honestly, my job as it is now is strictly Lois' type. I'll work into a Parker touch yet, but as is—Fegan.)

Well, my old boss introduced me to the rest of the staff, and is luck with me—he's GRAND, very much like Al, divorced, a sort of homespun city slicker and I've made up my mind, he's going to fall in love with me HARD.

He's got to; otherwise he'll leave and go off panning gold up river. I can't afford to have him go until I'm set anyway. So right away when I heard this talk I fluttered a lash. I am constantly at his heels. His name is ART BREMER, former United Press man.

First day on the job—I dunno. Not so terrific. I didn't feel right, look right, say the right things. Art was my champion, though, and stood right by me. Even so, by 6:00 I was looking for the train schedules and wondering how much it would really cost to get going.

Next day, dogging Art's heels, somewhat better. Then Miriam invited me to dinner. What an apartment she's got and didn't I sit down to Georg Jensen silver right from Fifth Ave in a room surrounded with original oil paintings, etc., and more etc. I forgot she was my boss and told her about people and places. We had a marvelous time and then went over to the little Catholic Church to a rosary service. She wanted to show me the church and introduce me to the priest. Almost everyone working for Cap, by coincidence, is a Catholic.

Art Bremer, formerly of United Press.

Right here, darling, I must tell you that the letters you wrote were waiting for me upon arrival, were the most exquisitely sweet and moving pieces of writing I have ever read. When you wrote about finding my dolly in the attic, I actually got all tearful and everything. I think I loved my Mommie at that moment so much inside it was like suffocating because I had to keep it swallowed down.

To get on—I work Saturday. All day. But—We get word in the office that the vice-president, Henry Wallace, is passing through. Hush, hush, no story. Sh-h-h, the censorship is very strict. Well to get me somewhere on the scene in case I could see him from afar, Miriam wrangled me an invitation to the officer's club dance that night at Ladd Field. I didn't feel like going because my hair wasn't done, no evening gown, etc., but of course I accepted the must-do with the best possible grace and went—with a black satin-ribboned Lily Dache net on my hair, a chignon braid over the top, and a huge red rose on the nape of my neck. I really did look bewitching—it was one of my nights. I felt full of intrigue, for I had that afternoon passed (hope the censor lets this go through) two Russian officers on the street and was SET to talk to them, dance with them that night. More interested in them than old Wallace (humph).

I accomplished my mission, well, but what a time I had. In the first place, the Lieutenant sent in to fetch me out takes one look and thinks, Oh BOY—and proceeds to hide me upstairs in the officers' quarters until almost midnight. Breathe easy, the whole apartment was filled with officers, their wives, girls, more officers. Two card games and three radios were going, etc. We were never alone. This bud wasn't bad, tall, Texan, but not too young and I'm sure married and pretending not to be. He irritated me. Finally, I insisted we go to the dance. Once around the floor when I saw them. A whole stag line of disconsolate, language lonely (good phrase to remember), erect.

"Oh," I dripped in sparkling burgundy tones, "oh—aren't they the Russians I've seen?"

The Lieutenant grabbed me and all but rushed me bodily away— all very vague.

"Please introduce me," I beg. He protested that he couldn't speak Russian, etc., but I will NOT be denied. I linked his arm through mine and dragged him over.

Eyes blazing my wonder and excitement, I opened my red lips, flashed my $650 teeth, and poured out my Dimitri-taught Russian.

"Tovarich!"

Immediately from all sides: "Ah, she speaks in RRRRoo'shun."

And they shouted in it. The poor Lieutenant was trampled and I didn't see him again for two hours. I danced with a tall, hearty, very young Lieutenant who spoke halting English. I met three of his friends. They were Russians who found their own. I kept repeating the same few phrases, over and over, to make myself speak more and more Russian. They were excited, they kissed my hand, they laughed with sudden discovery. (I had planned to say "My mother vus RRRusssian, born in Mos-kow." But somehow your hysterics echoed in my ears and I couldn't quite get it out.) I couldn't drag myself away. And I can't remember when I was more wildly enraptured. I knew from Dimitri how gay the Russians are—and they had not one single drop to drink. How they showed the American officers up too. Because the boys were getting very perspiring, rocking and noisy by this time. My Russians autographed three rubles for me, clicked their heels and the tall one I danced with led me back to my violent but smiling and sober Lieutenant. He forgave me because he had to—girls are scarce. If he showed his anger some other (hundred) officers would have a chance at something he saw first. It was a bitter and pathetic moment. I understood his predicament so completely. (Remember Lovey: "Say, Peg—do you know I've been waiting four hours and the Sgts. been here two." This at Benning as I stood talking to Sandy.)

I couldn't stand him, really, after the Russians. By this time it was raining. I was totally EXHAUSTED. Sunday, when Wallace was expected, there was a tea dance. Four or five couples danced, about six or seven showed up, but the food was marvelous. I wore my new Marshall Field pink dress (a new one I had bought en route, a darling, four bows over the bosom, four rows of tiny ruffles edged in lace around the neck, full skirt and bright, rose pinky pink. I wore white orange blossoms in my hair. (No Russians in sight—damn.) I was very bored and annoyed with no Wallace and no story and only the Lieutenant.

What's more, I was wasting time when I wanted to write to you—and was facing a dinner I couldn't get out of. Art, the first night in showing me the sights, had taken me 'round to his boarding house sort of hotel on an unpaved street, etc. The landlord, a little beady, bright-eyed Greek they call "Bill," had insisted I come for Sunday dinner. I'd said, "Sure," thinking I'd get out of it somehow. But when I realized that Art had to be saved at all cost, I got there, all smiles on the surface and Dear Gods underneath. Art greeted me lazily. "Humph, Army escort and everything," he drawled—I hope, enviously. Mr. Lieutenant had seen me to the "boarding house." Bill was all a-beam. We ate in his back room, sitting on a bed because he had no chairs, eating practically right off the stove because the room was so small. You know sanitary Sal. I was in charming agony. Then I saw steaks Bill had gotten "especially for the young lady." They were whole sides of COW—by the beard of Abraham you have never seen such meat. First came wine, and what wine, then the steaks (I have no powers to come anywhere near telling you how tears-in-my-eyes good they were). Then fresh asparagus, baked potatoes smiling with butter, fresh canned peaches and superb coffee. Not even at the Chilean Embassy did I sit down to a more royal feast, not a more GLORIOUS, unforgettable, unbelievable dinner. Just Art and Bill and me, with Bill doing all the talking in broken Greek, calling me always "young lady." A king in a shack (well, not really, but very tumble down. Except that his food was the very, very best, the labels on everything the finest that money—and he has it—can buy). I came away speechless and hardly able to walk with STEAK. Art explained, "When I first hit this town I was sent 'round to Bill—and, well, you see what he's like. I can't and won't ever leave him." Bill is just an illiterate, brilliant sort of jewel. He is rollicking funny, and ages-old WISE. He got how I feel about Art. I know he did, but the understanding passed just between us. I felt closer to Bill than to anyone else in Fairbanks.

Art and I strolled home, viewing the fire-ball sunset (at 10 p.m.) and we decided to walk off our dinner. I changed to my slacks and we walked about 20 miles straight into heaven. About 11:00 the sky was all Hattie Carnegie pink. Art was wonderful too, but strictly impersonal. I'll never know how he feels until he lets down all the way. That type. Still the walk solidly convinced me that Alaska is it. There is no defense against this country.

Monday, today, was grand. I went on my beats alone and did, I hope, fairly well. Enclosing the front page of the paper. My stories are marked. There's a typo error in the Harding Lake piece. We write our own headlines. Where it says "cooks" should be "cools." Miriam gave me the story and of course I wrote it with an eye to her reading it.

Art took me to a city council meeting tonight. I wore a turquoise velvet bow by Dache, and the whole place stared. I left early for two reasons. Wanted to write you and wanted Art to miss me, sitting there alone. Oh, yes, one more thing. See the story about the photographer? When I met him he insisted I hold up a wolf skin and he took a color movie film of me wiggling its ear, etc. Don't know where or when it will be shown.

Marjorie's in bed now so will have to close—typewriter making noise.

[Editor's Note: Pegge added the following sentences in handwriting.]

Lots more to tell next time. Having trouble finding SHOES up here. Bought polay shoes today. Feeling MARVELOUS and eating, ye gods. Who said they had whale blubber up here? My love and all of it, Baby (Address me c/o *News Miner* as per envelope.)

JUNE 3, 1944—FAIRBANKS—Just returned from my first dog sled ride. Yesterday I flew up to Point Barrow in a Navy ski plane with a group of geologists. The trip was one of many surveys for wartime emergency oil supplies that could be pipelined thousands of miles to accessible areas further south. When we landed, a young, handsome Eskimo had come on his dogsled to meet the plane out of casual curiosity. He wore a light fur parka, head tossed back, and his handsome face was so Asian. When I asked him if he spoke English, he said, smiling, "Of course, what else? Would you like a ride on the sled over to the Will Rogers-Wiley Post memorial, just over there?" So I got my ride behind seven white fluffy sled dogs to the scene of the 1935 crash of the two famous personalities.

One of Pegge's photos of an Alaskan dog sled.

JUNE 13, 1944—Met tall, tanned, deep-throated Colonel "Bill" Lawrence Costner, West Point but a soldier's soldier with a hair-trigger mind. Originally infantry, then assigned to intelligence. Hated it at first then was a natural. Arrived on November 19, 1941, a few weeks before Pearl Harbor at the Headquarters of what was then the Alaska Defense Command. Colonel Costner's Alaska Scouts were organized, called "Costner's Cutthroats" written up by George Meyers in the February 18, 1944 issue of *YANK*.

As intelligence officer for the whole of Alaska, the Colonel uncovered a saboteur—presumably German. Here, he needed a certain man in Seattle to do the job. It also happened the FBI needed him too. Costner was told he couldn't have him. He wired the crook anyway to go to Anchorage and meet him in the dark alley section. The crook, glad to duck, was ordered to change his name and leave all entanglements of travel permits, etc., to the intelligence authority at Anchorage. The crook came, met Bill, was given a "civilian worker's job." Again intelligence countered intelligence. No picture was taken—a past case history was fictionalized—and Bill hopped out into the wilderness, found good old innocent Eskimos about to die. Fingerprinted them (took six for future reference) used one set for the crook. Then trained his crook to work for him, all the time the FBI in Alaska is hot on his trail. He succeeded in his saboteur nabbing, and his sworn testimony was turned over to the FBI. But bluffing reasons why such testimony be not given IN PERSON. Crook, who was a fine fellow and the elite of his "profession," went back to the States. Went to work for the Government and is now a director of civilian personnel. When Costner was ill with a heart condition after Attu *[Editor's Note: In May 1943 Attu was a battleground in the Aleutian Islands campaign between Japan and the U.S.]*, the crook walked in to see him, decked out in the best, with "Hull'o cun'll" as a greeting to an old friend.

When Japs were getting a head start in the Aleutians, Costner asked General SIMON B. BUCKNER if he could have a free hand to supply info when needed. Buckner said okay. As Costner said, "He knew I'd have to beg, borrow and steal to get the dope I kept supplying him with." His first experiment was a radio reception or de-ception. He learned that radios are sensitive to characteristic hand movements as well as the sound of the radio itself. For months and months he tested Jap messages, and then luck gave him a break.

He found an old civilian merchant marine radio operator with a good sending hand. He was Italian and the Colonel set him to work relentlessly practicing to imitate the heavy clump, clump message sending of the Japs. He had the wavelengths measured so his radio sender would sound Japanese. His War Department backers refused to send expenses for the set so unbeknown to anyone, Bill had his Scouts build the station. Finally, he tested the first message after months of the most strained and exacting LISTENING to Jap-coded messages. As the news came in from TOKYO, Bill blurred the end of the program with a little tester message. Sent by his Italian with the Jap hand went a squib, to wit: "Admiral so and so is reported to have lost favor in high naval circles because he has been trifling with the affections of ladies of the Imperial household and has been found wanting." He slipped in a "pls acknowledge" on the end—then he waited. Finally, back came: "message received." So far so good. Then came the time when we had limited aircraft and were losing them more and more because "ambushed" Zeros kept picking them off. Bill had pre-arranged message with air bases: "quick the flit" meant rush planes. It worked.

Then: receiving message of sub in Bristol Bay, Navy checked weather and hunch. If, as Navy said, troops landing BB, very serious, all planes out. No way to confirm before taking drastic measures. Every five minutes another message from Navy. Decided to test veracity of radio set—sent message: Report heavy hostile air reconnaissance. Hold position: acknowledge. This message to tempt Japs to break radio silence and check location of sending. Waited—then suddenly clump, clump, climp. Japs wired holding positions. Bill said map showed fog.

"Quick the Flit" story: Because it was against regulations to use old gag of jamming the wires, Bill took 203 month-old regular news broadcasts from Tokyo and flooded the wires with blah, blah, blah.

End of story: Washington demanded radio operations be discontinued, cutting out frequency in AUSTRALIA AND HAWAII—Stopped sending.

Aid intelligence mission in Siberian Coast: Got a fellow for felony and blackmailed him into taking the boat to the little dot island off Cape Prince of Wales. Waited for fog, job during Russian Government alliance—out of fog, Russian destroyer—in OUR territory—tried to ram fishing boat when Bill was outraged against their daring to stop him in U.S. waters. During monsoon must have P.O.W. as Greek Orthodox missionary though he speaks (he says) no languages. Reported to State Dept on every stick and stone of Siberian Coast, even to pictures on the walls. Washington FILED his report—sent him $25 for expenses (dressed as civilian) and told him to cooperate with Russia.

(Local jargon: calling accordions "stomach Steinways")

Visit to Mr. Ernie SHERMER'S reveals time of Alaskan earthquake everyone thought he had heart attack and was imagining things. Creeks swished like water in a swinging bucket —trees tilted over— streets cracked, etc., but no one killed. Rushing out by the "line," (prostitutes section), all the good neighbors looked at the girls in their green/red kimonos, hair up in curlers—had hysterics—most frightened of all townsmen.

Fanny Quigley—funny, tarty, cussin' old character. Living alone in cabin near McKinley, tells housewives in Fairbanks the girls at Dawson and Nome had nothing on. What the soldiers are getting at McKinley, the gov girls whip down there and really go to town.

Soldiers here—the older men who find the U.S.O. too "young" for them are in a spot. They choke up under the strain of loneliness and waste existence at a post run by nitwits and moral degenerates among the officers.

One soldier was confined to quarters for refusing to study Russian. Checking, he learned that the Armed Forces Institute offers Russian as an elective correspondence course.

City slicker Jim Ryan, who professed himself Gov. Gruening's private pilot, said Mrs. G. was really a nice woman but damned naïve. Example: Called him aside one day to show off raft of new puppies. "You can tell which are the males and females by their noses," she said, girlishly. "The males all have pink noses!"

SPY SCARE—One day in St. Joseph's Hospital someone found in the waiting room a sheet of paper with scribbled instructions to "add one, drop two, add 3" etc. Police, FBI and military authorities studied the case for weeks. Finally, they found it was merely knitting instruction.

JUNE 16, 1944—Joe Louis, on a U.S.O. tour to visit Ladd Field, stopped in to be interviewed by KFAR, the radio station in our building. He asked me if he might see "how you folks live up here in the cold." I brought him to our apartment and he looked around with surprise, saying "It's real stateside!" He pointed to, and identified, a Karsh photograph of Clare Boothe Luce. Then he saw my collection of Eskimo handicrafts. When I asked about his fighting, he said, "I don't want to talk about fighting. I only wish I could do something else. I hate fightin.'" Then he asked me to tell him about Eskimos: "How do they live? Do they get jobs in town?" He was very curious.

SEPTEMBER 27, 1944—Back last night from a scheduled one-day trip to Nome. We took off in a Wien Airways new Boeing plane in sunshine with Wien pilots Rex Pilling and Herb Hager. We saw Mount McKinley in all its glory and made our first stop at the village of Galent. I stepped out for a stroll while they gassed up for the next leg to Unalakleet. No sooner had we landed when Herb Hager told us the news: "Well, folks, it looks like we stay awhile. Hop out 'n' make yourselves at home." Fog—and for five days we were stranded at this little village with a school and a trading post. I interviewed the village school teacher, the village nurse, the village trader and the village preacher—and anyone else I could find. Finally early yesterday morning, the fog lifted and we flew to Nome. Talked with the locals for the news: a new N.C. Store had opened. Then en route home to Fairbanks our plane answered an emergency call at Nenana for a little boy suffering severe leg burns. By then night had fallen, so we landed by moonlight and taxied to the Wien hangar.

An interior photo of the N.C. Store.

OCTOBER 25, 1944—What a week! I was sent to interview George Wallace. The memo had come from the Lathrop Company's front office. George Wallace, V.P., General Motors, European Division, lives in Geneva. His wife is an Italian countess. He's important, knowledgeable, may be difficult to interview because he dislikes press. Born in Yukon Territory, self-educated, remarkable success story.

George Wallace, when I found him, was reading the air edition of the *London Times* and wished not to be disturbed. "I never give interviews," he announced, dismissing me with half a glance and returning to his paper. "Oh," I murmured coolly, turning away, "I've met people like you in Washington."

"Washington?" he looked up. "You came up here from Washington. Why? What do you write in the paper?" he asked. "I will look especially for your column tonight."

Among the bits and pieces of local news. I had written a little feature about a young Yugoslav woman who was raffling a handmade tablecloth to aid Royal refugees from Tito's Communist state. It was this little story that caught his eye. He telephoned the paper and asked that the young lady reporter come to the Nordale Hotel lobby. He wished to discuss something in the evening paper.

When I arrived he was waiting with the paper folded back to the Yugoslav story. "Tell me, where did you get the information on Yugoslavia? I see, the woman came in and told you her sad tale. Did she bring the tablecloth? You say here it is quite beautiful and all hand embroidered. Did you examine the cloth personally before you wrote that? Do you know more about lace tablecloths than you do about Yugoslavia royalists or Tito, or what happened in Europe?" By the time he had finished on Yugoslavia, I could almost have written a thesis on the country. And the next morning, I found a slip of paper rolled into my typewriter with the names of books I must send away for, at once, to read.

DECEMBER 15, 1944—Another celebrity has been here for a few days. Lillian Hellman, the author of *Little Foxes* and *The Children's Hour*, came to Fairbanks on her way to the Soviet Union to do stories for the *New Yorker*. Bad weather grounded her for days. A Ladd Field Quonset hut would not do, and the Nordale Hotel was full. Someone had mentioned that if she had any trouble in Fairbanks, she should see Cap Lathrop's right hand girl, Miriam Dickey. Miriam put her up in an attractive suite in the Lathrop Building. It turned out for us to be a bonus. Lillian Hellman can cook! And for the next few days she delighted us with her cooking. We were sorry to lose her to the Russians.

Pegge posing in Alaska.

"Flashie note" —**DECEMBER 19, 1944,** Eva McGown gets an Xmas card from someone in California. The postmistress there recognizes the name and writes a note in pencil on the envelope and sends it on its way.

1945

A photo of one of the numerous plane trips Pegge made
while in Alaska.

MARCH 1945, KOTZEBUE, ALASKA—Flew over with ARCHIE
FERGUSON. Pilot, Harry SWANTON (who a month before was
stranded eight days on the ice near the Kelly Mountains).

Swanton was ferrying a new three-seater from Texas. Barren
country—brush on tundra showed through a sprinkling of white

granulated sugar. Over Easter, saw dredges that looked like robot ducks on a pond of sugary snow. Plane cold—glanced at pilot—frost exhaling from his nose and mouth, eyes watering. "Endure, Parker—endure" told myself through my teeth. Made non-stop flight—took 3½ hours. As we neared the coast, flew over flat STEPPES bound by great clumps of snow hills (mountains). No sign of life—no dog teams—went over a small village (Siliwick) half buried in snow—no life—finally Kotzebue—long, thin row of houses and blinking tower which flashed a pale spot in our eyes. A long expanse of field marked by wooden poles. Little red flags on the poles blew RIGID and trembling in the fierce wind. An Eskimo boy, with a face the color of California persimmons and a thick-lipped mouthful of teeth the color of Ivory soap, greeted us. We landed gently and stopped. The wind balked at us, tugging the ship. Harry opened the door, and the Eskimo boy grinned. "Hello," he said, in the hesitating abruptness of their speech.

Then the commissioner put his head in the door: "We're waiting for the army doctor from Nome, got this dogsled standing by—emergency case. Woman from Deering, Mrs. Ray MENDENHALL"—native woman, very sick, hesitating to say what was wrong. Harry waited. Two figures bent in the wind, heads barely visible under huge round ruffs of furs. One of the figures moved with fox terrier energy. Harry bawled out of the plane: "Hello, reception committee." The little figure, which was ARCHIE, answered abruptly. "Uh-oh," Harry muttered, "Boss's got a MAD on, G_d'd him." "How's she look?" I bubbled to Archie to cover the irate welcome. "Oh, she's a darlin,'" the little man bellowed in the wind, but he scowled and stared at the new bright yellow plane which had come all the way from Texas. He frowned at the name "BONNIE BEE" lettered on the side in honor of Harry's wife. We crawled out; the wind clawed and tore at us. I was caught without anti-freeze in the motors and stood in agony, swallowed in Harry's enveloping parka. A figure rushed up to us. "Hello you so-and-so." I was introduced to a beaming man who shipped off a burly wolf glove to clasp mine, barehanded in the teeth of the gale. "Head for the CAA houses and get thawed out, cup of coffee," he shouted. Harry and I rushed ahead, reaching a white-painted bungalow half-buried in the snow. I was too petrified and numb to turn the knob. Harry behind me struggled with the knob, finally turned it. We burst into a room that looked as though it had been furnished from a Sears Roebuck catalogue. I ran to the kitchen, which was none too warm. There was no coffee on the stove. Harry pulled off his glove, his hands were white across the knuckles. "Oh-uh-cold. Huh?"

We turned. The head of the CAA maintenance, George HENKE, a timorous man with watery, blinking eyes behind goggles, looked at us. Harry told him about our 3 hr, 45 minute flight in a cold plane. I eyed a little on the stove. Dear God, let him offer us a cup of tea, or even the plain water. He made no move. Harry and I eyed each other longingly.

We left then and piled into a dogsled—local cab system—the dogs delayed. The little fellow, AARON HENSLEY (native boy) yelled at them—drove them determinedly. Harry and I were bathed in the breath of the Arctic in the open sled which jerked along at a snail's pace. We headed for Archie's store, found it, struggled in. The room was barn-like, shadowy, with neat rows of canned food in the far end of the room. Harry's wife greeted him with restrained casualness, barking at him about some telegrams she'd sent. A beautiful Eskimo girl with a tumble of silken black hair smiled charmingly—Archie's woman. She wore a cotton dress, a dainty mukluk: "Oh Harry, it is SO good to have you home," she exclaimed in a soft, delightful voice which contrasted glaringly with the shrill rasp of the wife. Then the Eskimo girl, "BEULAH," offered us coffee and served it at a kitchen table, with the smiling grace of any well-bred hostess. Harry and I fell on it, devouringly, telling of the IN-hospitable reception at the CAA house. "Oh God," someone said, "any Eskimo would give you anything he had—but don't ask the CAA for a thing." I remembered the CAA at UNALAKLEET—Archie was distressed—he was "madder 'n' hell," Harry learned, for this and that reason. Beulah looked uneasy. He would take his wrath out on her.

The ghost of Baranoff crossed my consciousness. He was a man possessed of his spirit, bullying, brow beating, dog lashing a town into some semblance of progress. He has made Kotzebue what it is. He has the only hot water shower, electric sewing machine, washing machine, etc., in town. Angry that Harry had brought no supplies but a deadhead passenger (me), suitcases, and such, he had seized our suitcases and thrown them into the snow. When an Eskimo boy brought them in later, the snow had sifted through the crevices. My clothes were frozen like Birds Eye vegetables—my perfume ice water—pancake makeup a piece of ice.

Harry Swanton, bush pilot, tells his wife Bonnie and Pegge (right) about 8 days of defying death in the Arctic.

We left the store and came over to Harry's home—a narrow, low-ceilinged house Bonnie had painted and adorned with beautiful rose-covered draperies. An enormous dog, black malamute called

PUNCH, went through KITTENISH capers— an amazing feat for such a huge creature. He "talked" and "laid down," etc.

Harry and his wife swapped news—they relished guessing who the father of the Eskimos' latest illegitimate child might be. They shouted with laughter over who was fighting, changing women, getting drunk. Archie's latest quirks. Eventually I became aware of how glad Bonnie was to have Harry home and how much she loved him. We huddled round their stove.

For dinner we had fried frozen chicken which was delicious, "riced" potatoes, green peas, pineapple and mayonnaise, coffee and straight whiskey for WARMTH. "How will I be able to sit casually all evening when it's all I can do to keep from grabbing the nearest blanket and burrowing down in under it?" I thought.

There was a soft knock at the door. The handsomest Eskimo child I have ever seen stood there—raven-black eyes shone like polished jet—black under the white fur ruff of his parka. "Hello," he said after a minute. "Got buttons—ivory." He showed them. They were the size of quarters, crudely etched with Eskimo figures.

"How much?" Bonnie asked. "Two dollars," he answered. Bonnie counted them: "One, two, three, four—50 cents apiece. I'll take them." She handed him the money. He stood there a minute, seeming disappointed that I, the stranger, had not taken them. Then he went out into the howling wind.

The first evening was spent in the small living room with Harry's mechanic, a healthy, chubby bulk of a young man with laryngitis. He sounded like Andy Devine. He abounded in humor, he swallowed vast quantities of whiskey with Canadian beer chasers. No one showed any effects.

NEWS: School burned recently. Bottom of the stove burned. Two signal corps boys in gas masks dashed in with PYRENE guns and saved the school. (School teacher: FLOSSIE GEORGE of Barrow. Boy Scout—an Eagle Scout: CHARLES MACCLELLAN, son of Arctic unit Reindeer Manager, HERBERT "MAC" MACCLELLAN (white;

mother teaches school with Flossie). Hospital: Mrs. Clara GADDIE, Government Nurse (good egg, tends white people when sick even though not supposed to). Principal of school: Mr. and Mrs. C. L. CRUTCHER (both teach); about 30 or so students.

Mr. and Mrs. MacClellan—two children: the Eagle Scout and "TWINK" a little boy.

Father Paul O'CONNOR, Catholic priest—educated in France.

Rev. and Mrs. HENLEY of the Quaker Church—some white people go to the Friends' church.

Mrs. Marguerite ECKARDT—Husband HUGO—scared little fellow—she is an enormous woman.

George FRANCIS—postmaster, clerk or selective service man, married to Rosa, an "Eskee-mo" girl as they pronounce it.

W. R. BLANKENSHIP, who runs Bess Cross' store, married to Eskee-mo—old, old-timer—runs store way he wants to. When Bess is here he leaves town. Lives in her store when here.

PETE LEE—has an Eskeemo wife—runs restaurant, illiterate Italian (?) has nice "kids"—old-timer.

FRED FORSLUND—old, old-time whaler—born in Sweden—jumped boat at Wainright—Stephenson stayed with him when they were there. Fred didn't like Sir Hubert—"just gaw'damn panty waist"—runs dog team for Army. Has Eskimo wife.

ART FLATT—born in New Jersey—mechanic—has dainty Eskimo wife—"two kids— that he claims."

HARRY SWANTON, pilot.

JACK CONNERY, PFC, USA Signal Corps

Sgt. RICHARD COLLARD—officer in charge of SCS—studying to be doctor, about 23 or 24 years old—native girls like the soldiers— Dick here about a year—his family in Seattle.

BERT NEILY—Deputy U.S. Marshal. Neily over 60, old-timer— undertaker in Nome. Has a ne'er-do-well son.

Storekeeper Louis VROTMAN—Jew—runs store here. Oldtimer, doesn't mix much, tends to business.

Frank KNAPP—formerly had fox farm.

Gus NELSON—Catches shea fish—the town hermit—sells his fish for 7 cents a pound—catches them with net or hook.

Then the CAA and Weather BUREAU—six houses, all alike—some get along, some bicker.

Mr. "Red" TODHUNTER—former postmaster, now an invalid.

Red MULLALY—been here for years, associated with Jim Robbins.

Friday, to 7:30 Mass at St. Joseph's Catholic Chapel. Opened my eyes. Saw stars in a robin's-egg blue sky—and drifts of pink snow—faint echoes of dogs howling —the air was clear— newborn fresh as though unbreathed by any mortal—the dawning sun gleamed on a small silver bell atop the trim, prim white and green church, half buried in the snow.

Entered the church through the side door, stepped into a room of innocence and wisdom—Eskimo children in halo ruffed parkas—Father Joseph O'Connor saying Mass in a quietly intoned Latin. I knelt on a fur rug—in front of me knelt Father's pet students: one, a tall girl with hair the color of polished mahogany and Irish face, slight nose, beautiful teeth. She wore a long, flared, white pony parka—rang a little brass bell. Their responses were flawless, a perfect chant of voices and clear, distinct Latin. I raised my eyes—on one side was a wall of books—well thumbed, heavily used, read, beloved books ranging from French textbook on Napoleon to a few recent best-sellers. After Mass, the girls put the chairs away, spoke softly to Father as he changed his vestments, and left. Father threw off his Jesuit yoke. He was a cosmopolitan host in short sleeves, suspenders stretching over his shoulders—tall, grey-haired—handsome in every score—black eyes snapping—witty—utterly relaxed, sparkling and charming. We bubbled over with conversation, one interrupting the other—digressing, shrieking, laughing.

Standing over his little table, he quickly raised his hand and said grace. We had sliced oranges, oatmeal with canned milk and coffee strong as six Bombay nights. And superb conversation. Topics: Roosevelt's foreign policy. Russia dominating the place in every move so far. Father's young days in Paris where once before he was ordained he met a beautiful prima donna at a salon gathering. Naïve, he didn't catch her name when introduced. They chatted. "Rosemarie," the French adaptation of the Broadway hit, was the rage of Paris. They talked of music, Father telling her all about his own six-week course in voice. She listened with interest. "Say, let's sing," he suddenly suggested. "Oui—certainly," she smiled. Did she know anything from "Rosemarie"? A little. They began—everyone astounded at the American's daring to sing with M'lle. At first she hummed along, then with a nod to her accompanist she spread the wings of her superb voice and filled the room with joyous, amused, triumphant music. The priest was astounded, then abashed. They became fast friends.

Pegge posing with Alaskan children.

Of his whole experience he told me that the white men of his territory were "hopeless." He'd given them up long ago. His Eskimo children were the love of his life. He said in all his years as a priest he had once suffered an acute blow because his closest friend, a fellow priest, came to visit him once in a hospital. "We fell to discussing God as one we both loved—humanly, not as an omnipotent power commanding us. After listening to my friend for a while, it came to me that he loved God more than I—that his love was the most all-embracing, perfect human emotion I had ever seen. I was stunned with a sense of my own lack, my own nothingness—you cannot imagine how depressed I was."

Another earmark: He missed children to live after him. He betrayed his longing here by devoting himself more to the native children than any others. His prize possession is a collection of snapshots of children which surpasses anything else I have seen. He has also a notebook of all the Christmas cards and birthday greetings they have painted for him.

He spends his days studying the Eskimo language—making a dictionary of it—writing prosaic articles for Jesuit magazines.

Father was said to have alienated the town's sole mechanic from his congregation by stating at one sermon "there isn't a virgin in Kotzebue." ("Their temptations are enormous, poor things, and you should hear how penitent they are.")

Spent the afternoon at the village hospital taking A BATH, untold luxury—and if the well water smelled as though 50 million species of bacteria crawled in it, one ignored the odor—poured in quantities of gardenia bath crystals and wallowed in it.

My first game of poker—played with WALTER BLANKENSHIP (whose wife "Nellie" was drunk from drinking vanilla). "Blank" was a great hulk of a man, with a deep-seamed, red, kind face—the face of a surgeon who bends over a terrorized child and says, "We'll have you playing football again, Johnny. This may hurt a little."

Blank is the store manager for Bess Cross—and his kindness has been a red mark in her books and in her cheeks when she upbraids him for not tending to business. We sat in his kitchen and played at a table covered with a blanket. Blank won quietly—making only about 8 cents because we weren't putting up very high stakes. I lost $10. We played STUD and DRAW poker—drank cold apple juice from the store. We joked and laughed—we walked home over the drifted snow with the North Star glowing like Diamond Jim's tie pin. We all carried flashlights which made pools of bright shadow on the deep snow.

SATURDAY—Mass at 7:30—in that little library study converted into a chapel with the blond bear rug—the lantern hanging over the window. Father Paul O'Connor intoned the Latin with a French accent. His history (as a "jibbie," as they nickname the Jesuits)—he came from the Northwest, was educated by the Jesuits and really went into it before realizing QUITE what it meant. He said, as noted before, the hardest part of being a priest was the denial of children. "It was only years after my ordination that I saw a girl I knew I could have loved. But she was the only one." He felt the greatest reward of being a priest was the satisfying VIEWPOINT it gave one, the feeling of progress toward the only thing in life that mattered: Being a Saint.

VISIT TO THE SCHOOL—The minute I opened the door of the building burrowed down in the sparkling snowdrift, I was almost overcome with the ODOR of unwashed bodies—of furs and hides— two rascally little boys scurried out of a room on the ground floor, pausing in amazement when they saw me. The foyer was lined with little girls, parkas covered with bright pink and blue calico (Reason: the parkas are made with the fur on the INSIDE and the calico covers the bare skins; on the trail the wind blows the snow into the fur where it freezes, but on the calico it blows off). Upstairs I found Mr. and Mrs. C. L. CRUTCHER, the "dean" and his wife who was also one of the school's teachers. Mr. Crutcher looked like a city doctor on a fishing trip somewhere in Maine. He wore a sweater, dark plaid shirt and wild print tie, jodhpurs and mukluks. In his office were three little girls about 10 years old struggling to use typewriters. Long, greasy black hair fell down their slender shoulders. They wore red cotton dresses and round-toed, worn-looking mukluks. They smiled shyly when I came in, devouring every detail of my clothes. Three little boys painting ducks with paint boxes eyed me from another corner. Mr. Crutcher greeted me gladly, laughing with me at the antics of the youngsters. Mrs. Crutcher came in—a buxom, handsome middle-aged woman with twinkling eyes. She took me into the children's room where little dolls with dirty faces and running noses and shapeless ragged dresses recited some little verse prompted by Mrs. Crutcher. Then she had the children tell me their names: Grace, Evelyn, Annie, Beatrice, George, Henry, Clark. "Now, Henry"—with mild sternness—"you know we never stand on top of the desks," etc.

Downstairs met an Eskimo teacher, FLOSSIE GEORGE (formally polite). Her face prematurely old, resigned, defeated; her eyes behind slanting glasses, were diffident. The other teacher, Mrs. Herbert MacClellan, a rotund woman in high fur boots, a plaid jacket and black skirt, was herding the children around the room as they played a romping, jubilant game. Mrs. Crutcher stood at my elbow. "See the little girl in the pink dress—she is part Jap, and how the Eskimos hate the Japs. That's the worst insult they can sink to in a fit of anger— to call anyone a Jap. The little fellow tearing around in that corner, the one with the green suit on, is part Portugese. We've got almost everything here—mostly sons of sailors—the Eskimo girls take them in stride and rear them without a thought of their illegitimacy. The Eskimo girls are crazy to get white men, and will only marry an Eskimo when they can't get anyone else. How do they take the white men running off with their women? I dunno, Okay, I guess."

They showed me some Eskimo dolls they make for sale—few of the youngsters have dolls—little girls play with their tiny brothers and sisters. The dolls sell for $15, the best carved ones for $20, which are made by Ethel Washington. Ethel doesn't like to bother making them, so Mrs. Crutcher suggested I go and coax her myself.

I nearly suffocated from the smell—a thousand children crawled and tumbled over me. In one far corner on the floor sat a tiny grinning Eskimo woman about 30 years old. She wore two pair of glasses and was stoop shouldered, full busted and wore a green cotton house dress and mukluks. I tried to tell her that I came from the city she was named for—Washington—city of the President. She smiled blankly. I finally ordered the dolls and fled.

Walking home over the snowdrifts, watching my footing, feeling so helpless and citified, conscious of the natives laughing at my fumbling and sliding, avoiding the dogs who howled and snapped as I went by. Only trick I learned: Standing a moment on the doorstep when one first goes out will chill the soles of the mukluks and prevent slipping.

Arriving home, I thawed some shea fish and ate it. Bonnie and I ate dinner, chatting girlishly, enjoying each other for the first time. We were just finishing when the door opened. In came the S's huge malamute, PUNCH, and Harry—JOYFUL—he must have drunk two full bottles but he was still controlled, garrulous, ready for a big time: "God," he burst out, "I never had such a good time with my pants on in my life. I found out where the old oaken bucket is REALLY brimming over." We tried to get him to eat. "What? Ruin a hundred dollars' worth of good liquor? Hell, no."

He insisted on taking us back to the store. I was reluctant but felt I'd have to go, the obliging guest. It was bitter cold, the wind cut across the ice. At the store bottles appeared. They drank scotch with beer chasers. Harry got to dropping veiled hints about the way Pegge's been treated, etc. Malaise and tension set in. I perked up my ears without seeming to listen. Mr. and Mrs. S. really tore into each other, savagely, all "fronts" cast aside. Then Mrs. S. said, "Pegge, you might as well know that you walked into a lion's den when you came over here with Harry. He wired you were coming and we all thought what th' hell, we don't want any damn reporters around here. When we got a look at you, talk went WILD that Harry'd brought a girlfriend over here. Everyone was laying for you. That is why Archie (Ferguson) avoided you and you got cool receptions. Everyone was sticking up for ME. I had to go around telling everyone it was okay, that I liked you. (She strained that a bit and I gathered she and Harry'd probably had "words" over me. I'd been aware of "her" but thought it was just her manner.) So it went on. We returned home, Harry twice as drunk as before. Words tore at the air dangerously, and I busied myself in my room. Then I heard the dog howl in pain—a shout from Mrs. S.—more words. Harry struck his wife in the face, catching her in one eye. Mortified with embarrassment. I eased Harry out of the house and turned to Mrs. S., who was now in rage and tears and prideful anguish, now she had no defense against me. In a torrent of words the whole thing unloaded: all the little tension and hurts. Archie's miseries, misdeeds, jealousies over his pretty half-breed mistress, over passengers preferring to fly with Harry rather than with him, etc. I washed the dishes, wished myself back in Fairbanks, and offered limp Dorothy Dix advice. Hours later, Harry returned, asking for a peanut butter sandwich. Bonnie, like the woman in the poem who kissed the lover's foot that stepped on her, greeted him as though he had just rescued her from a burning building. I hopped into bed.

SUNDAY, MARCH 11—Off to 9:30 Mass. Father O'Connor said a raft of prayers and the Ten Commandments before Mass. Then he put on his vestments, lit the candles himself and said High Mass. The Eskimo women sang a miraculous Latin chant, distinct and earnest as nuns. Blubbery children crawled in and under the pews, and to my great distraction one woman dropped a baby from UNDER her flowing parka. I watched, in the middle of the CONSECRATION, between the elevation of the host and wine. I saw the half-breed mother unzip her parka and NURSE HER BABY IN CHURCH. Almost fell over in trying to double-check what I thought I was seeing.

The sermon was equally amazing. The text was about baptism, how being baptized made us children of God. The parable was about the son of the free woman and the son of the bond woman. By comparison, the gospel could have been directed at the ever-prevalent illegitimacy of Kotzebue, but he dwelled on baptism. After each three to four sentences he would pause and a woman would translate. It made listening very tedious but none of the adults stirred; only the children whined and dropped things and made faces at each other.

Someone else caught my eye: Just as Mass began a young man, full-blood Eskimo, entered with the cocky gait and graceful muscular roll of a sailor. He genuflected briefly and took the last seat in the last pew. His parka was FITTED to the curve of his broad back and feminine slight waist. Slim hips—his trousers were pulled tight over straight, solid thighs—his legs and feet were shod in tall reindeer-fur boots. The fur ruff of his parka hung about his blue-black head. A band around the waist was embroidered in brown and beige hearts—a most unusual design for a man. He went to communion, returned with a solemn, graceful tread, and knelt in submissive subjection, even remaining after Mass to pray, while the clumsy older men crawled over the top of the seats to get past him on the end of the row.

I realized as I went down the aisle in my own borrowed parka and mukluks that I was the only WHITE woman in church. I almost felt the Eskimo's shyness, as I received the gold communion plate from the Eskimo woman beside me a strange feeling crept over me—the oddity of it—my being north of the Arctic Circle, going to Communion. I looked up—the French black eyes of the priest held mine for a second. The eyes of the Pope could not have looked more deeply into my most intimate soul than his did for that second. I crept back to my seat with lowered eyes and folded hands, feeling like a little girl completing her first holy communion.

SATURDAY/SUNDAY, AUGUST 25/26, 1945—FAIRBANKS— Weather cool, early evening twilight and dark nights. Letter from Lois (Fegan) telling of book—interview with William Schoel of NC Ti Tiklas. Discussed his four years in Colombia, South America. Said they lead in culture, language, courtesy—The British influence most dominant—American and British interests have caused most of the revolutions. Americans abroad are an embarrassment—bad manners, braggarts, etc.

Jade article in the offing. Got permanent for $16. Reading *Personal History* by Vincent Sheehan.

MONDAY, AUGUST 27— FAIRBANKS—Mrs. Henry Dale at Club. Weather cool (late September-ish) Talked with Ann Schieh who gave cooking tips. Sauerkraut: quarter big apple, drop in pan with kraut. Cook slowly ½ hour.

Hot dogs: put in pan of cold water, bring to boil, don't overcook.

Liverwurst: put in pan medium-hot as is. Brown on both sides. Prepare sliced apples and onions in butter, heap on top of liverwurst.

Use finest top of lemon rind in gravy or as seasoning—a little bit.

Browning potatoes: par boil until not quite cooked. Put in pan with drippings from roast (melted and hot). Don't cover with lid; sear on all sides. Remove from grease, place in casserole, cover with absorbent paper and lid (paper drains off moisture).

Throw handful of big prunes soaked overnight into pork roast.

Brown pineapple slices in roast drippings or chicken fat. Serve with roast meat.

THURSDAY, AUGUST 30, 1945—FAIRBANKS—Moose, caribou, ducks, geese, mountain sheep—hunting season on, heavy rains.

Weather mild. Plane lost and three aboard believed dead. Both of the city doctors were hunting sheep in alternate leaves. (Note: later found to be okay—typical of this country—planes go down for days and pilots and passengers survive.)

Pegge against the Alaskan horizon.

FRIDAY, AUGUST 31—FAIRBANKS— Heard about woman in Alaska who had to help her husband deliver their baby. She read from a book while her husband followed directions. All survived.

Another story: Trapper and his wife had a terrible battle about when she should go to the hospital. When baby began arriving, long-distance call. Doctor rushed out. Husband stayed outside pacing up and down in the snow. Wife was so angry she wouldn't let him in the house—insisted his blushing bachelor, timorous partner help her. He held the light for the doctor while looking the other way. Doctor cried out, "Anything I can see you can see. For God's sake, hold that light over here!"

SEPTEMBER 6, 1945—FAIRBANKS— Leaves turning gold—pouring rain—chilly. Got assignment from BERTHA KLAUSNER to do Fairbanks article for new magazine, *HOLIDAY.* Wrote her asking incidentally if she handled lecturers. Have just returned from LABOR DAY flight to MCGRATH—ANIAK—BETHEL. Story typed in rough for book which still beats a nerve-straining toll inside, like the edgy roll of a drum as an acrobat leaps WITHOUT a net.

Went to Ladd Field on bus (fare 20 cents one way) to arrange trip to Aleutians. Hope to go next week.

Talked with a woman today who had been doing U.S.O. work in Brazil. She said the Brazilians resented the free and easy Americans with their salaries outranking Brazilian officers (American private made more than Brazilian major). "Of course, don't put this in the paper," she said. But they said American soldiers were "overpaid, oversexed and over here."

Weather: colder, heat on in apartment. Local housewives picking cranberries and blueberries. Moose and caribou hunting poor.

OCTOBER 15, 1945—FAIRBANKS— First heavy snows, flaky, the kind you could imagine looking like snowflakes under a microscope. Ice cakes floating in the Chena River. Women wearing head scarves and stadium boots. I put my savings, heretofore banked, in a prized and cherished letter from Clare Boothe Luce—$530 (representing savings of nearly two years, which is quite remarkable considering the cost of living here.)

Heard marvelous Eskimo story from D.A. *[Dorothy Ann Simpson, Pegge's close friend]* the other day. It seems Mildred Keaton, government lady dentist who's been years in the country, once was called to a mud igloo where a woman was to have a baby. Arrived and found her in bed with three other tots and a newborn babe, still attached by cord. Keaton shook mother, who was asleep.

"When was the baby born?" she gasps.

"Oh—I don't know," mother says sleepily. "Maybe half hour ago. He wake me up crying."

Jim Robbins of Candle, Arctic Circle Exploration Company.

First installment of the Aleutian series on way to clearance. Sweat blood over it. MUST be good. Also mailed jade article—pix not too complete on these—may not be good for *NY News.* To finish up on the jade series, when I heard Jim Robbins of Candle, Arctic Circle Exploration Company, was in town, I called him to arrange for a picture. "Dinner?" he suggested. "No, sorry," I began. Then I remembered a conversation with D.A. about what men-less ruts we've gotten ourselves into. Finally said "yes." Jim arrived, big and blond and perfectly groomed in a dark brown suit. Had GI photographer who works for me (Rex Wood) take two closeups of him in the apartment. Then we went to dinner. He kept remarking about my hair being "all cut off" (to wit, I discarded a chignon switch for a permanent—hair worn shoulder length—he noticed). Lively conversation on stones, rocks, etc., I brought back from Aleutians. Then to café where by soft juke box in a deserted room, with a single candle, our eyes met. We sipped chilled sherry and I said outrageous things about having liked him FROM WHEN. Amused, flattered and surprised (who, me?), Jim took it all in. Magic began and lingered like a heavenly scent we both knew would pass but tried to hold onto for the sweet, sweet moment. Our eyes met as we longed to be in each other's arms.

In an awkward sort of way, Jim attempted to react conversationally. "Pegge—you're—I don't know—so enthused—so sparkling, y'know —you're refreshing, like—a head of fresh lettuce or a fresh peach without fuzz." I got what he meant but almost split with laughter at being compared to a head of lettuce. He reached for my hand in the taxi, and before leaving at my door, sorta touched my cheek—very self-controlled and "I'll be back"-ish.

OCTOBER 23, 1945—D.A. asked me up to dinner. Captain Lathrop and I were her only guests. The conversation was memory making. Early this morning "Capt" had come into the office all in a steam because there'd been nothing in the paper about Canadian Pacific running their first passenger trips out of Fairbanks, right now with the airline—to-the-Orient—through Fairbanks. Conversation at dinner swung around to the airlines. Captain is convinced the Aleutians are un-flyable—that all planes should come overland this way. (Street experts believe the State Department will settle the air routes and that RUSSIA will fly its half of the route, using Fairbanks as a depot connecting point. Could be.) Cap was as energetically wrought up over what the air mark of FBK will mean here as if he had 80 more years to go instead of 80 past.

A school teacher was mentioned. She happened to be a blooming "Tugboat Annie" who once took a shotgun to a prowling Romeo. "Hell," grunts Cap, "if she came out of her cabin a fella'd run his legs off. She was the absolute SAFEST woman in Alaska." He chewed his green pea salad for a moment. "Y'know, she had a face red as a spanked beet." He reflected, "Money isn't everything. No sir, it doesn't mean one damn thing except for the kick y' get outta makin' it—and what you achieve with it."

Discussing his newest hog business:"God, we're havin' so many new ones born. Slogan: a squealer a minute—don' know how we're going to feed them all."

Discussing his gold mining: "Tempted once at Cleary Hill. Sank 20,000 into the venture. Then got smart and decided to let the other fellas mine and sweat." He'd take their gold away from them coming and going with his passenger ship running back and forth from Seattle through the inland passage to Kodiak, Haines. He grinned like a fox with a chicken, telling how he got the stampeders' money both ways.

Cap said the secret of his eternal youth was to keep going. Any man who retired in his mind was 100 years old and done for. Anyone with no interest in business and progress and what the other fella's doing was good as dead.

Cap said when he met Harold Ickes, he had just been put in charge of the Department of Interior that morning.

For all that Cap was perfectly marvelous in his shrewd alertness, his mental vigor, his drawlin' hominess and bland humor, one accent was on BUSINESS—his business—the Lathrop interests.

Note: Snow on ground for the winter. The nights are too beautiful to bear looking at without love. The days are like October in New York, except for the snow. A lot of Eskimos are in town, wandering awkwardly and stiffly about in their parkas and mukluks and gay gingham covers. Ladies' aids are giving bazaars and fairs. Dinners, lunches and teas are the rage.

Carol (Pomeroy) is taking flying lessons (costs $100 to solo). The mornings are not as light and clear as they have been. Ice still running in the river.

When D.A. mentioned all the different businesses Cap was in, he said, "Well, I'll tell ya. Was you ever in a gamblin' hall, Dorothy? Ever see the roulette wheel and watch the little pea go bouncing around 'til it hit the right number? If you've got all your money on one number you win or lose everything. If you spread small bets around, your chances of winning are greater even if y' don't make as much. Little bit here and there (Cordova-Anchorage-Fairbanks) and you get quite a bit. If one doesn't do well, something else takes up the slack and you know you can't lose unless the whole system collapses."

NOVEMBER 1, 1945—FAIRBANKS—Looks like an early winter. Went out this eve to mail letters and the temperature was (officially) 20 below. Great clouds of fog blurred the street. The red neon over the bars looked like fuzzy blobs of pink circus candy. Figures hurried by: girls wearing stadium boots and slacks, heavy coats; men in galoshes and heavy overcoats, fur hats.

Scurried to Mass this morn. Hurrying over bridge ahead of D.A., I had to stop talking. Air made the face taut. The Chena River was not yet frozen over, but great clouds of woolly fog rose from the water into the freezing air. Behind this white fog, the sun rose—a bowl of white-hot bronze filtering through the river fog, it had the effect of sparkling champagne foam.

As the train was pulling out this morning, a crowd of Eskimos gathered—hurried, self-conscious, but silent. Even the little tots, going to the states for a three-year dancing tour. Tough character, AL MONETTE, with five o'clock shadow and a hard shifty eye, was in charge. The women had their hair in pomp coifs—slacks—stadium boots—a smooth job of makeup (and all from Point Barrow). The kids were like dolls, their parkas covered with bright red-flowered cotton toppers.

Heard that one of my bride-shortage (*NY News*) bachelors has left Pan American Airlines to work more profitably in a furniture store. Said he, "I'm going to stand beside every bed I sell."

Rising sun of my existence: a promise from NORTHWEST AIRLINES to have a seat on the first press flight to the Orient should the Civil Air Board approve their control of the route. *NY News* by wire refused article I sent reporting on flying the Aleutians. Will try elsewhere.

NOVEMBER 4, 1945—FAIRBANKS—Just arrived home from Mass. Weather 20 below, river frozen solid and blanketed in sugary snow. Reading LAUTERBACH'S *These Are the Russians;* surprised to find it such thick copy, weighty with exact facts. Having just finished *My Chinese Wife* by KARL ESKELUND, which was such purely enjoyable reading, the book on the Russians required "concentration"—but Lauterbach keeps using Russian words which send me scurrying to check my thumb-worn Russian grammar.

Yesterday in the Piggly Wiggly grocery store, a bouncy, round-cheeked little girl clerk in slacks and apron stopped to say with almost affectionate wistfulness, "We miss the Russians around here." Not just in business, she hastened to add, a touch of unrealism in a dull monotonous routine of flour sacks and cans of tomatoes and heads of cabbage. In the midst of a Saturday afternoon rush she stopped to tell me about them.

"They were so NICE. They appreciated the way you didn't laugh at them for calling the stuff they wanted by funny names. They sorta taught me their words for things rather than their learning the English words. They said it was wonderful for them to take back to Russia so much food. They bought mostly butter, sugar and flour."

She paused, tapping her pencil absently on her bill pad while impatient housewives clamored for her to take their orders. "They gave me so many little presents at Christmas—perfume, a pretty pin, not from Russia though, local—but real nice of them, wasn't it? I haven't even used the perfume!"

This Russian interlude in an otherwise pitifully banal existence had set a pinnacle for her. This sideline share in an international scheme of American aid to a Russian ally to defeat a distant and hated enemy—it was tangible to her in a memory of romantic, red-cheeked air heroes in black boots and student prince uniforms. Smiling at her among rows of Campbell's soup, Windex and Jello—and in their absence she cherished, with her bottle of perfume and jeweled pin, a humbly ardent feeling that Americans and Russians should be friends.

NOVEMBER 5, 1945—FAIRBANKS—Dinner with Cap Lathrop, D.A. and Carol. As we sat down at an attractive table with candles and flowers, etc., Cap heaved a sigh, "By God, nobody's got anything on but Brigham Young." Later, discussing the airways, "We were really asleep at the switch up here. First I heard about the trans-Asiatic airways was in Anchorage when the editor of the paper, Bob Howard, told me he'd just come back from Seattle and they were going all out to get the route. I ran right down the street to the Alaska airlines, got a seat on the plane to Fairbanks. Next morning in my office held a meeting. We'll have to get someone to go to Washington and represent us." Cap told them, "My man is Norman Stines." (Note: Cap's cozying up to Stines for some reason. Has him billeted in the Lathrop apartments. Very friendly setup for hints of a big deal Stines has on the fire.) Cap feels strongly that Seattle does not deserve control of the air after holding Alaska in its clutches all these years.

Cap talked about the Guggenheims—"best bunch of Jews I ever ran into—fine people, best in the world." He knew them well years ago in Cordova.

Cap was leaving the next day for Seattle. Going out the door, Carol (Pomeroy) said, "Don't get into any mischief." He laughed and hugged Carol, saying, "At my age when people warn you about getting into mischief, that's a real tribute." Out he went, overcoat over arm, galoshes in one hand and a golf cap in the other.

NOVEMBER 11, 1945—FAIRBANKS—Armistice Day for World War I observed here. Last night coming home from a movie about 11 p.m., the sky ablaze with Northern Lights, I went up on the roof. Overhead was a bridal train of pale gold tulle—swirls of it—fading here, lightening there—shaft blooming out of shaft of silver glow rimmed in a gilt edge of scarlet. Through all this fairyland swirl of light, the stars shone like bright new silver dimes in the sky. Gazing down over little snow-banked Fairbanks, the wonderland phenomenon was heightened by frosty super clouds streaming out of chimney tops and doorways, hiding the town in a blur of silvery fluff.

(NOTE on Cap: One of his employees observed that as he grew older he became more active, impatient to do everything before his number is up.)

INCIDENT: LEE CARSON, well-known woman war correspondent (INS) came to town. Called her at the field and offered all civilized comforts, knowing the Army accommodations are mere bed, bath and board. When I told her who I was, she cried, "My God, What the hell are YOU doing here?" Promised to call when she finished her story on Point Barrow from which she had just returned. I kept within earshot of the telephone until midnight. She never phoned.

NOVEMBER 15, 1945—FAIRBANKS—Went to a ladies' tea at the Episcopalian Rectory this afternoon (2 to 5 p.m., the invitation said). Carol and I arrived in a cab at about 4:30, gabbing and peering thru the windows at a winter wonderland bathed in BRILLIANT moonlight and stars a-twinklin'! We were gussied up and scented as the honeysuckle rose—on our feet, though, were sheepskin-lined boots. The minister's wife, a Southern, wren-like little woman, issued us into a bandbox bedroom with a chintzy wall paper ("Did it all myself," she admitted. "Ordered the paper from Montgomery Ward.") The stout master bed groaned under hundreds of dollars' worth of fur coats, and littered over dainty scatter rugs was a collection of boots like the porch of a ski slope. The weather shivered down to 31-35 below.

What a day this has been. I made arrangements to collect war fund donations tomorrow on the line (can't wait to see the inside of my first BROTHEL). Then I fell heir to two white fox hides—a chap who works for government and buys furs on the side offered me one skin at about $15. When I hesitated, he said, "Well—tell yuh what—you just keep it. It's a bum skin anyway and I'll bring y' another one I got at home." So, as of this day I rake in my first Alaskan furs: white fox.

Finished an excellent book on Russia, *These Are the Russians*. Once you've read it through, you can't help liking the Soviets and getting the savvy on how they operate. I felt much more tolerant and less apprehensive of a Soviet-dominated Europe, and more assured that Russia vitally wants peace. Am now reading *The Idiot* by DOSTOYEVSKY.

NOVEMBER 16, 1945—What a town—went to a Ladies Aid tea this afternoon wearing a Helen Garnell Robin Hood hat—BRIGHT RED. "For the first time in my life I talked to a Prostie" [prostitute], said MARY BURGLIN (*GOOD CATHOLIC*). I set out at 4 p.m. The moon shone brilliantly over the oldest log cabins in town. Mary and I shivered—it was about 20 below—the entrances on Fourth Avenue are the kitchens—the working rooms are in the front. First stop: woman in her early 30's, hair cropped in a soft coed style, slacks and sweater without bra underneath. Attractive and refined looking except for the beady hardness in the eyes— each dark underneath as though no sleep. She listened to our blab about the National War Fund, then hesitated. "Well," she shrugged, "How much ja-want?" Put $2 in our hand. The kitchen table was covered with worn oilcloth, there was a wood stove, calendar on the wall—disheveled sort of housekeeping.

Another girl, chunky figure, merry of eye, as she dug in her purse for some money said, "Why don't you see Hattie? She lives on the corner, been here since the boom, got lotsa money. Panama Hattie they call her." Asked about the other girls, she said, "Well most of 'em aren't up yet—keep late hours." She winked with an expression that had the effect of a nudge in the ribs.

Noted: Despite all the rundown-looking kitchens, beyond could be glimpsed the most glamorous bedrooms—pale green walls— soft, springy double beds with feminine chenille covers—boudoir pillows.

Most of the girls asked us in out of the cold. One gal, pert and brunette, popped a head out the door and listened to our National War Fund spiel. "Wait a minute," she called reluctantly. Through the glass we saw she was entertaining a gent in a red plaid hunting cap and lumber jacket. Mam'selle was wearing a pink ruffled bra and pantie set "Here"—a pink-and-white arm was thrust into the moonlit night, and $5 fell into my hand.

A Negro wench had just fallen out of bed—hair like Topsy. "Come back later," she said thickly.

Conclusions: Girls much YOUNGER than I had expected. One girl, especially, was tall and wholesome looking and might have been a showgirl. Wore a black band on her hair, which was the color of a martini cocktail, and becomingly enough her eyes were the color of the olive.

Another girl came to the door in pink satin tunic pajamas, holding an ivory cigarette holder. She was frail and had the look of a woman aware of her position and on the defensive against her own loathing. She said she had a child, business was bad, but she didn't want to be the only one not contributing. Mary, wishing to turn away amiably, said cheerfully, "That's perfectly all right. We're just calling on everyone and your house was on the end of the block."

Mary grabbed my arm and we hurried off tittering like school girls. "We made $20!" Over a cup of coffee later, Mary told me she occasionally did some typing for them, and once one of the gals came in with two fruitcakes. "Say, honey," she asked, "would you do me a favor and tie these up? One goes to Papa—m' husband—he's working on the railroad. Don' matter how you fix it. Then send this one to my sweetie. He's a miner out in the sticks. Tie his up nice so it arrives in good condition." Two weeks later she came back, eyes a-twinkle. "Lookit"—she said, taking a $100 bill from her purse. "See, m'sweetie liked the fruitcake!"

THANKSGIVING DAY, NOVEMBER 22, 1945—FAIRBANKS—

Not so cold today—around zero. I covered the train departure today as the moon went down in a cloud of baby pink and sunrise turned a rosy cheek to an unheeding world. Few people were stirring at 8 a.m. when the weekly train departed.

Later to Mass with Sergei Skorik, my little Russian friend who has taught me the following sentences:

Glass of wine? Boo-desh peet veeno?

Glass of wine? (very politely) Vee–ho-tee cha staken-vena?

Sit down, please. Sah dee chess po jal-ooie-sta.

Repeat. Pov to reet cha.

Last night in the mail I got a letter from INS *[International News Service]* in San Francisco, giving me something to really be THANKFUL for—the go ahead for INS on the Orient flight.

Note: Soldiers are slowly filtering up here for jobs. The employment office reports most of the GI's asking for jobs are ones who served right here in Alaska. The other week they had a full list of jobs at $1.75 an hour (sheet metal workers, carpenters, waitresses, plumbers), but most of the jobless didn't want them. They were eventually forced to take them, however. U.S. employment official reports soldiers who are coming in from the States are high-class types upon whose shoulders a finer Alaska will grow.

Grew impatient with DOSTOYEVSKY and skipped tons of his pointless ramblings. He has not the mastery of TOLSTOY whose *War and Peace* I loved. Now reading *Insanity Fair* by Douglas Reed— recommended by George Wallace, my "hero" from last summer (ex-European manager for General Motors).

Restless to do more writing now that I've finished Aleutian series for American Weekly from whom I hear absolutely nothing as regards payment or publication. Would like to get back to the BOOK but uncertainty of angle and ABILITY (God help me) keeps me from it.

Digression to the skillets: Recipe past duplication for deliciousness. LEMON ICE CREAM: Bottle of AVOSET whipping cream—beat— add one egg yolk, juice and rind of lemon—scant cup sugar—beat— add and beat in one cup milk—dash salt—stir in stiffly beaten egg whites and pop into refrigerator tray with dusting of nutmeg—de LISH!!

SATURDAY, NOVEMBER 24, 1945—FAIRBANKS—Sergei went to Juneau this morning, but last night the Russian lesson included: Beautiful music (this Russian word used because the music is not seen) *PREV VOS HOD NI YA MOOSIKA.*

Wonderful, excellent book. *ZA MEH CHUT NI YA.*

GOLD MINER: TONY BANY—Interviewed at Pioneer Hotel. Medium height, wearing light felt hat which he did not remove, a light college-boy plaid jacket, gabardine trousers. It was apparent some smart clothier had outfitted him with a glib sales talk as though preparing him for California wear. The bone structure of his Slavic face reminded me of a native chief I had interviewed in the Aleutians. Tony's eyes were his one beauty—his teeth flashed with gold casings. When he realized I was going to put his name in the paper he flapped his hands awkwardly as though they were seal fins and I noticed they were small hands, wizened and ugly. Born in Yugoslavia, he apparently left home with no thought of parents or family. "No word from dem since I leave," he said heavily, adding he'd heard nothing of the two brothers he has in Chile in "over five years." Coming to Alaska in 1920, he worked his way inland on the railroad. Later took to mining at LIVENGOOD near here. His proudest pocket piece is a gold nugget as flat and large as a saucer, and he is never without it. When asked if he was married, he replied with no concern or regret or triumph—merely "Naw, not maddied." On his right hand, third finger, he wore a ring band of gold encrusted with a garland of diamonds. Tony is on his way to Chile and Argentina to "look over things dere"; not sure if he's coming back here—flying all the way. Had letter of introduction to minerals attaché, U.S. Embassy, Chile—from attaché's mother living here.

Pegge with Sergei Skorik.

DECEMBER 7, 1945—FAIRBANKS—Oddly enough here it is the date of World War II, and nowhere around town or in the office did I hear anyone mention Pearl Harbor. Forgotten so soon.

Interviewed a discharged GI just back from Japan. He raved about the Jap gals—"they were swell"—and was quite amazed at my irrepressible edge of resentment. They are still the enemy, etc. "Oh no," he came back, "the Japs were driven into the war. Told they had to fight" etc. Hook, line and sinker. U.S. GI, soft hearts, soft head. However, another GI—working on the paper, ex-Captain who lost a foot in combat in Italy, gave me a radio talk about a militaristic peace being absolutely necessary. "It is sad but true," he said, "that peace lies in force, not aesthetic international brotherhood. Actually all we have won from the past conflict is not peace but the absence of war."

Received check for $60 from *NY NEWS*—gave $10 to photographer for pix. Result of lengthy job on Alaskan jade. My powers are slipping. I have yet to snag a piece of jade.

Beginning to approach the NEXT MOVE, globally speaking, through industrial channels a possible job with a heavy machinery company in Russia during the reconversion. Meanwhile waiting for CAB *[Civil Air Board]* decision on the flight to the Orient. Understand the insufferable pedantic Georg Nelson Myers is coming back to FBK *[Fairbanks]* in January to do a book on Cap's life. The news urges me more than ever to get going.

Note: Weather about 20 below. Cars at curbs all kept running, making great clouds of vapory smoke on both sides of the street. Daylight breaks about 9 to 9:30 a.m. and when I come to lunch at about 1 p.m. I must turn the lights on to see a road. A boat strike which tied up operations for over a month just let up and STACKS of mail have poured into the post office.

Mother and Daddy now in Dallas, Texas, en route by car to California to live.

DECEMBER 10, 1945—FAIRBANKS—Was invited to a Russian dinner given by Jewish Russian instructor at the University of Alaska. Sumptuous food with wads of sour cream—and novel experiences. While out there I talked with a geology student—middle-aged, scrawny-haired, blonde, pudgy figure, Scandinavian. Anyway she had been at Grenfell Hospital Labrador and later in Syria. I consulted her on ways of making contacts for leaving the country. She suggested writing the Singer Sewing Machine Company (they are EVERYWHERE IN THE WORLD)—or as a teacher of English. Or, she said, write the Russian Consul. He may know someone looking for a person with your qualifications. She strongly urged knowing the language.

TUESDAY, DECEMBER 11, 1945—FAIRBANKS—Alaska is an amazing place. I had interviewed a pink-cheeked lad named Mike BISIG who was in town to arrange a passport to Switzerland. He was a baker and I became curious about Swiss baking secrets. He loaned me a pie-making book, then the day he was to leave for Switzerland, he stopped in the office. I couldn't resist asking him to give me a demonstration. He made pies until two in the morning.

Highlights of his tips were:

Don't mix dough too much.

Don't put pie shells in oven when first put into pan—let stand about ½ hour (crust won't shrink, if so).

Mix salt and sugar with cold water before putting into pastry mix.

He was a dear. For a man to spend his last night in Alaska baking pies! Of course we wished him bon voyage with coffee royals and candles on the table, all of which he appreciated. To me, there was a story in Mike; must file him away for a fiction day.

DECEMBER 23, 1945—FAIRBANKS—Christmas atmosphere background. Weather averaging 10 to 30 below. No snow. (Note: Few blizzards here. It snows quietly, efficiently at the beginning of the season and once whitening the ground there are few follow-ups.) The moon is up until about 8 or 8:30 a.m. I go out at 8 a.m. to cover the departure of the weekly train and the moon is a new platinum penny in a clear blue sky. Cars parked at curbs keep their motors running (to prevent freeze up), and the exhaust creates a foggy cloud. All the stores and houses are ablaze with lights. There is a gigantic tree in front of the post office. The tree was laboriously brought to town by volunteers who cussed every step of the way because the trees were frozen solid and when they hacked them down, the branches snapped off like icicles.

Christmas carols blast out from the top of the 5 & 10, amplified. On the circuit is a mournful record of *None But the Lonely Heart*, which is heard continuously with *Silent Night*. An ice skating rink was cleared on the Chena River but it was too cold for skaters. The cleared rink is deserted. The first 1946 Ford V-8 car is to be raffled off at $1 a chance to support a Teen Town (local teenage recreation center project) on the shortest day of the year.

DECEMBER 24, 1945—FAIRBANKS—The sun came up about 10 a.m. and by 11:30 when I was on my morning beat, it was a blaze of thunder (outranking the road to Mandalay); it blared in the sky, low hung and like molten bronze. The direct glare from the sun struck a row of cringing cabins pulling a blanket of snowbank up to the eyes to protect them. The cabins were ignited with a glow of inferno orange that was like the sun on a mirror, only this sun was getting an even more blinding red-orange glare from striking wood. I gasped as I gazed.

Have just come from a big Christmas party (dinner and drinks) that was quite a story. Cap was there, flushed-faced and kissing all the women. Holding them on his lap. He had chosen for his Christmas card this year a Santa with a bag of labeled items hastening to Fairbanks for 1946. A voice streaming out of a drawing of the Lathrop Building queried, "I wonder what's in store for 1946." Among the labeled gifts in Santa's pouch were one reading "worries" which puzzled all of us no little until one reporter popped up with "Oh, I get it—we're to guess who's to worry about getting the sack in 1946!' I repeated this to Cap who was a bit in his cups and didn't get the connection. He had only a vague recollection of what his stereotyped card was like. His answer to the quoted quip was flatly, "Oh, Miriam (DICKEY) (or "MARION" as he calls her) picked it out—was kinda nice and didn't cost much." Asked politely after that if he would be with us in FAIRBANKS for Christmas, he answered roaring, "No by God—I'll be down at the mine where I've to be all the times." I murmured regrets. He explained. "Y' don't make any money in Fairbanks foolin' around with picture shows and newspapers and a radio station. You make yer money, by God, in the coal mine lookin' after it. Now that's the truth!"

I mentioned the airline to the Orient (shaking off a drunken RCAF flier who kept stroking Cap's shoulder and murmuring, "Jus' an ol' sourdough, ain't you, sir?") Cap held forth: "Looks good, looks like we'll get it yet. We really make those boys in Washington think hard about what we've got up here." I wondered if it were a stroke of fate that my series of articles on the Aleutians was not published by the *American Weekly* syndicate, for while they were mostly devoted to the lascivious stories of the Russian "promyshleneki" (sp), I did mention the fly-ability of the Aleutians in direct rivalry with Fairbanks as the only possible route to Asia. (I have a feeling there will be two routes laid out, one via the Aleutians and headed for Japan, and the other northern, possibly through Fairbanks and cross country to Moscow. Some deal may be worked out whereby the Russians have an Alaska depot and fly over their own country.)

Noticed that the host, a lumber company owner, had hired a Negro to serve and "butler" during the drunken span of the evening. I saw the Negro calmly hob-knobbing with the nearest guest, pour himself a drink of straight scotch. He also heaped a plate with food from the buffet table and disappeared to eat it. Later a true Southern lady was kindly talking with him in the patronizing but nostalgic manner of Southerners and darkies. Even her influence did not quell the Negro to his true station. He addressed her as an equal. It may have been the scotch. I sat on the steps later getting the Southerner's life history. Her romance: the man's courting was charming, he used to say to her "hold out your hand—got something for you." Into her palm he would press three violets, which he solemnly told her meant "I love you." Once he gave her five, saying "that means 'I love you very much.'" Used to distract her in church by holding three fingers in front of his hymn book. The three fingers meant "I love you." Then 1-2-3 became their sign language. He used to note it on his letters, etc. Eventually 1-2-3 was engraved in her engagement ring, wedding ring and other jewels he gave her. Terrific romance from her report. "When miah babies were born, he was riahght there" she went on. "'It's all right, Mother girl,' he said to me, "you just hold on to my hand and press as hard as you can," and when the baby came he bent over me and said, "It's a beautiful little girl—our little baby, Mother darling. God bless you, darlin.'"

DECEMBER 26, 1945—FAIRBANKS—Here I am leaning against the top of our refrigerator with a cup of coffee and a jigger of cistercienne (beer) beside me. Christmas, my last in Alaska—is past. I got so many gifts my heart could scarcely hold the gratitude and memory-maker sentiments—want to jot down flash lines of facts for future reference. Before leaving the office, I got a check for a $150 bonus from Cap. The money, in these frugal days, will certainly come in handy. The weather was about 30 below and I froze the tip of my nose, which leaves a cherry tip scar lasting several days. (Note: I go on my beat wearing a wool bandana, wool mitts, fur coat, wool knit stockings pulled over my wartime rayons, rubber boots.) Midnight Mass, altar decked with paper poinsettias and fresh red roses. In the crowd were hundreds of glum-faced GI's with faraway looks in their eyes. Parka after parka went down the aisle to communion. Slacks, mukluks, ski suits—some chic hats and fur jackets.

The town was gay on Christmas Day. The eggnog flowed but no one seemed too gay. The atmosphere was idyllic—people stayed home and were delighted to see all comers. We lapped up many strange and potent "punches" as we (Art Bremer and I) made the rounds. The gifts given away were sumptuous. Most popular were fat bonuses, liquor, fruitcakes spongy with rum. The freight train rushed in a last shipment of mail on Christmas Eve, but the lady postmaster refused to ask the PO staff to work overtime so no gifts (parcel post) were distributed.

Perishables also were late arriving and were expensive. No one noticed. Tragic note: A man was burned to death in a Wannigan floating cabin when a faulty oil stove exploded Christmas morning. No one noticed. One woman was sulking when none of her friends came calling. Wife of a travel book author (one little-known book, on India). An attractive, bloody British wife (Betsy Fox) has paraded one man after the other before the town and set tongues wagging like dogs' tails. She is temporarily between men and at a nice party she drank too much and went around telling husbands their wives were bitches and chippies! The move was ill made just before Christmas and with her ever-loving husband returning from the war soon. He had been a professor at the University of Alaska. Interesting picture here of wives' flaunted unfaithfulness to hubbies in the army. Another great gossip concerns the adored Maisie, scarlet woman of the town. She had sent away for some record player exercises and she prepared to do them one night in her nightie on the floor. She was alone in her house. The voice boomed out—bend, stretch—deep breath—one-two, one-two, kick. The nightie groaned at the seams and Maisie stripped it off—did a bicycle exercise flat on the floor. "One-two-higher HIGHER" roared the record. At that moment someone knocked at the door, threatening to come in. Maisie shrieked, grabbed for her robe. In walked two women friends who eyed each other. Exercises in the nude at midnight, with the door unlocked. The story was all over town the next day.

As a joke, Eva McGown got a suit of long underwear (to dub as tights) for Maisie to do her exercises in! Christmas season in Alaska—moon is still a wedding night delight until 8 in the morning.

DECEMBER 27, 1945—Mark this day: a milestone—for I have had a letter from the *American Weekly* stating a check for $600 is being made out "in my favor" at the rate of $150 per article on the Aleutians! They cannot publish the series just now (I should go down on my knees at such LUCK because of the conflict with the Lathrop interests) but they liked the material I sweated such blood to get. Joy to the world. $600 is the most money, lump sum, I have yet made for writing, coming right now when I'm saving every cent for the grand Russian venture, and the work I hope to write in California. I walked on 600 clouds since getting the letter. I went around begging Art to tell me what I would buy for $600—what boat trips, what WHATS—fur coats, jewels. I relished the figures—six zero zero. The beauty of it is that now, for the first time in my life, my little pinch-penny bank account will have four figures in it: three O's and a comma!

1946

JANUARY 4, 1946—FAIRBANKS—I am disgustingly RICH. My check for $600 arrived today. A burning money bug. I want to write pieces for MONEY like crazy. Lay awake last night turning love stories over in my mind. Finished my two most valuable books, *Disgrace Abounding* by Douglas Reed (and *Insanity Fair*) and remaining impression: The Jews are an irreconcilable menace wherever in the world they alight. The Czechs were the martyr of Europe. Germany thrived during its 1918–19 period while the English masses lived in scurvish poverty—the oppression in general of the Balkan countries held under the aristocratic control. (Note: I recently hope the Socialists or Communists seize control of the Balkan countries and the masses get a chance at enlightenment.) George Preston brought me some copies of the *LONDON TIMES,* to which he has subscribed for years.

Got life story of local socialite, Mrs. Jim (Ruthie) Barrack, from Mrs. Bleeker in the flower shop. Ruthie came up in the early days, was a swimming star or something. Once dove off the bridge into the Chena River in an exhibition plunge. Looked the town over for a man with a future. Jim was a close-fisted, penny-wise Scotchman, partner of a man in the hardware business. Jim's partner died and his widow, a mild mouse but perfect lady, had eyes on bachelor Jim. So did Ruthie. Although a handsomer, more ardent suitor offered to do right by her, she grabbed Jim—eventually got a hand in the business, helped boost profits and got Jim to spend money for the first time in his life. Eventually browbeat him into building an enormous barnlike house decked with baby grand, paintings, fine rugs, etc. Had three daughters, all scattered in fancy schools. Ruthie has her way or her fishwife origin asserts itself. Once or twice has turned Jim out of his grand house with black eyes. Then last winter he developed heart trouble and Ruthie boasted that Poor Jim was going to die (of course he doesn't know it). Poor Jim did not die and reminded Ruthie his people lived to be 90 and 100. Ruthie had meanwhile gone on a diet, shed pounds, bought new clothes. Her one-time lover never amounted to much, and though she may have regretted the amour with him, she considers herself socially launched here, so the score is even.

Note on service men: All with "plans for future uncertain," many going back to school. Wearing out their service shirts, coats, etc. (a sailor's pea jacket covers work jeans, an officer's shirt under a tweed coat).

Weather mild—days getting light about 8:30 a.m.—stars divine. Northern lights.

JANUARY 17, 1946—FAIRBANKS— Just for the record, paid my 1945 income tax today and it came to $41.50 on a yearly income of $3,236.52 total, not counting tax withheld nor money made on outside articles. I still cherish the thought of the six hundred.

Since last entry the town had its worst fire in 40 years. To my chagrin I was late getting out the story to INS and Art beat me to pictures (check for $4—imagine—from INS today. I send them little, because it doesn't pay). Anyway, the memorable thing was seeing Cap Lathrop almost enjoy the holocaust because his one modern fireproof theatre building blocked the blaze and saved the entire block. For details, see clipping. The fire was a dilly; the entire town was out a-witnessin'. Dogs, babes in arms and pretzel-legged, tottery old-timers. Other funny sidelights were the wholesale "saving" of merchandise. One furniture store, NERLAND'S, had just received a shipment of very expensive mirrors—one almost a wall-sized piece. It was carted out of the store, across slippery streets in the 20-below cold, carried back again a day later—survived without a scratch. Almost no merchandise heaped on the steps was lost or stolen, except ice cream out of LAVERY'S freezer. Another highlight after fire: a Bulova watch was found—straps burned away—face frozen in the ice—the watch still running and okay.

Big moment of the episode for me was seeing DYNAMITE RED, the notorious scarlet one of Nome, close up for the first time—medium height, young, smartly but not too warmly dressed. Head swathed in enormous padded turban of yellow wool. She has no hair, and this is her camouflage. Looked very oriental and very striking, clean somehow. Was with a soldier, both very tight.

NEXT ITEM: à la Pegge Parker. I've got a maybe assignment from the *Reader's Digest* on the Nenana Ice Pool. But leery of such lofty spheres and before I can even start, I am triple checking my FACTS. Oh, the coin such a landing would represent!

Meanwhile: no assignment. Two short stories launched. No answer. Norman STINES, erudite rep. of Fairbanks at Washington CAB hearings on oriental route, returned and told me he's sure the Aleutians will not be used in the route mapping. (I strongly disagree, but am saying nothing.) He quailed my heart also by saying it may take a year or so before the route is established. I'm holding on, expecting it to come at any time. Eva McGown just called—news at 11 p.m., wee bits of "howlers" and news. Yesterday, when I checked at her desk, she suggested I just run down to the post office with her. It was an adventure leading all the way to the ROOF of the Federal Building where embedded in one of the marble steps is a wee shamrock brought from (Ireland). One step led to another until we got out on top of the roof, at 15 below zero we gazed down on a 5 p.m. little town—little snow-snuggled world of its own. We gazed down at Fairbanks with the intense and tender scrutiny with which one gazes at the portrait of a loved one seen every day but in different perspective seems newly fascinating. Stopping at the post office below, Eva fished out of the mail a dagger from someone who'd been here!

En route to her desk we stopped in at a Russian jewelry store. Eva wanted a pin made from an old Pioneer Lodge button belonging to the beloved Arthur McGown. Avalhoff looked at it. "Look, you let me give you $2.50 for this and go buy some handkerchiefs you'll use a lot more." Drawing herself up grandly, Eva snatched it from him and in a voice playing to the rafters of the top gallery said, "I'll thank you not to make suggestions; where Arthur McGown is now he doesn't need handkerchiefs." This is the highlight report. We met half a dozen people en route.

MOONSTONES from the Aleutians returned, have faint amber fire in them—really very lovely. Just read the old book *Oil for the Lamps of China* for its background on the Orient. Interesting—wish I knew where I go from here.

JANUARY 22, 1946—FAIRBANKS—Priceless remark was made at a dinner I gave here last night. I was entertaining one MARJORIE BOGARD who works for the world's craziest pilot, ARCHIE FERGUSON of Kotzebue. In that strange Arctic Shanghai lives a fabulous Eskimo, Sister Scarlet. Now a blubbery, swarthy, repulsive native weighing 300 pounds or more, at one time she was quite la belle du boudoir, slim, willing, passionate and temptingly pretty and witty. All the men in the Arctic knew Molly and visited her frequently. She is believed to have had several husbands. At one point in her career she suddenly "got religion," fiercely, humbly, remorsefully. So moved by the inner light was Molly that she sat down and crudely scribbled messages to all the men friends she had. "I have sinned," she wrote. "I got religion. Here is $10 you give me." The spell didn't last long, but the conversion and unique refunds tickled raw Alaskan humor—and for a long time it was a popular bridegroom trick to send a newly married man a letter from Molly, containing the "$10 you give me." Nothing, of course, would ever convince the sensitive bride that the whole setup was a joke.

The American Weekly becomes a household word henceforth. I just got another check from them—an expense account makes the total for the Aleutian assignment about $656.50. Oh yes, got a wire yesterday saying the sheep ranching article is accepted—another $60, I guess, for the fast-growing "kitty." Especially eager to hear knowing first fiction was received. Reading, at George Wallace's suggestion, Upton Sinclair's *World's End*. Excellent schooling in European background.

FEBRUARY 4, 1946—FAIRBANKS—Oh, someday when I'm on that Alpine peak known as the TOP, I'm going to write a good damnation article about "the struggling days" most writers hold in an ah-yes-tender-quilled sentiment. I say its damnation—the uncertainty of the PATH leading somewhere instead of just stretching out ahead. The constant reminder that OTHERS are writing for the *Post* and telling about it in idiotically bright biographies in the front of the magazine: "aged 32, one said"—and I gasp in anguish thinking how much spade work, yes, steam shovel work I've got to do to reach that first niche in the uphill climb. The book—Oh, moral and psychological challenge or torment and fear of my wee titan's talents—a desire to watch the CASH come in on quick sale pulpers (fact or fiction). The restless impatience to be off to foreign shores—yet knowing not whether. Will report anon, when chin is on a higher level.

Atmosphere: sun broke into my room this morn at 9 a.m. Gets dark about 4 p.m. Weather between zero and 10 below. Light snow. No northern lights. Beautiful moon and stars.

FEBRUARY 9, 1946—FAIRBANKS—Cold, light snow, no wind, everyone "bundled." Fur buyers busy around Nordale (hotel), frozen debris of fire on Second Avenue remains. An Alaskan steamship, *SS YUKON*, sank after being grounded below Seward; nearly all the passengers were rescued after about three days of struggle and extreme anxiety. A local Ice Carnival is being coaxed into INTEREST by a paid publicity man—HERB HILSCHER, whom I intensely dislike and who, I believe, is writing a book. A dinner was given here last night by the town's leading, socially accepted scarlet woman (British as all bully get out and man crazy—mother of three children who are gifts of the gods in looks and brains—wife of writer and traveler ERNEST FOX.) She was also the open house hostess and "friend" of the Russians here. Her quests were all complex stories of one hue or another. But it made gossip for the next day. I got a piece of Aleutian jade for my *NY NEWS* editor, Robert Sullivan—cost me $10 in a split deal. The boy (Bureau of Mines assayist) gave me the piece with the understanding that I would buy one for myself at $10 later on.

Had dinner with Mrs. CARRIE WILLIS. It was a "royalty" dinner on a children's history book she had written. We talked shop and she gave me some amazing stories. Most startling of all was Eva McGown's. Briefly, Eva, of good family in impecunious circumstances, taught music in Ireland. Among her students was an Irish-born Jewess with whom she became friendly. Jewess comes to America, meets one ROBERT BLOOM who sets out for Alaska. Once here, he gets into business deals with one Alfred McGown, businessman somewhat above average riff raff here in early days. Before leaving Ireland, Jewess has asked Eva for pix. One night dining at her home, Alfred sees Eva's pix—asks who she is, etc. Offers to pay her fare to Alaska.

Eva writes sweet note saying of course (she's a lady at this point) she can't come. Arthur, admiring her even more for refusing, writes her a letter. Eva answers in the florid imaginative way of the Irish—more letters—big meeting of minds—"Okay, we'll make it a loan." Funds to come. Eva consults poor little Auntie, a devout poor soul. "Of course you'll go—I've got some pounds saved up to buy your trousseau." Eva embarks in STYLE, lands up here. Blooms have her to dinner, and she meets Alfred. He is huge, very pleased and impressed with Miss Montgomery—suggests they leave early and walks her home. Takes her to a wee cabin where he lives. They talk. She agrees to marry him. He shows her license he'd already secured—calls for a minister and they are wed that very night. And Robert Bloom has not spoken to her to this day. In the excitement they forgot to ask the Blooms to the late evening ceremony!

Very happy, Eva later goes home for a visit in finest of clothes. Arthur ill, becomes worse and for seven years is an invalid of the worst temper, humor and tongue. Eva nurses him night and day, really TAKING it. But Arthur breaks her heart by casting up the loan of her passage to Alaska she had never returned. Frantic, pride outraged, Eva finds a friend in the witch of Denali—FANNY QUIGLEY, who hears her story, promotes a mining or prospecting deal for her and mines the money with her two gnarled, childish hands (she was only a mite, about five feet tall).

Arthur finally dies, and to hear Eva to this day, you would think he was the ORIGINAL Prince Charming, father of the well-known prince.

Oh, yes—the wife of one of Alaska's first telegraph operators called me "dynamite" because I put something in the paper about her being very sick (as he had told me, blubbering all over the telephone). She, it seems, is the leading light of the local Christian Scientists.

FEBRUARY 10, 1946—FAIRBANKS—For future reference on description of local "sassiety": Mrs. Nordale gave a tea in honor of the Ladd Field Colonel's wife who has just arrived from New Yawk and South Carolina. Madame was very chic—bony, smart like mannequin in a Lord and Taylor window—wore a hat crowned in a circlet of pink ostrich feathers. Looked as though she were set for cocktails at 21 rather than a lady's tea. The usual people were there, all women, all hatted fit to kill in flowers and veiling galore (it was about 20 to 30 below outside). The ladies came in suede sandals, nylons and taxis. I spoke to the lady and found her a little too approving, too "lovely" this and "lovely" that to be sincerely interested in Alaska (cat-cat). Anyway, the thing that AMAZED me afterward was that half the dear ladies who'd had tea and pinwheel sandwiches and chocolate cakes no bigger than the end of your finger, removed themselves to the local saloons for "post mortems." Remarks I shall never forget: "Well, we know where she got that hat; it was $29.95 at the apparel shop. I tried it on last week." "So did I, but I looked like a clown in those feathers." "Darling, I also tried on Mrs. Nordale's dress, and I almost bought that black suit Grace Smoots had on."

The town is so small, having only three dress shops, that when new clothes come in all the women make a dive for them, sort them over, try them on, then watch who buys them. (Clothes—haven't bought a thing up here—hoarding that bank account for China or wherever.)

To continue with the cocktails as per above, D.A., Carol (both gussied and looking sumptuous) and I went in for a quickie before going home. We were just having a quiet chat when two local matrons, also hatted to the hilt and at loose ends, descended on us. One of them plunked down beside me—is a story all right. Will give highlights. (Oh, before I forget it—the local tea gave me one other note. The Colonel's lady mentioned that the Russians who had lived here left their American paid-for and maintained quarters like a pig pen. They tore light fixtures out of the wall, removed everything removable and took everything back to Russia.)

Now the other story. The first time I heard of Mrs. Larry ORSINI (she is not Italian) was when she took three children into her home after the mother, stricken in an automobile accident, was taken to the hospital. A charmingly sweet voice said to me over the phone, "Yes, I've taken in the children—they're playmates of my own three and I have nothing else to do but look after children, so I love having all of them." I visualized a comfortable-looking woman with a rosy face and maternally preoccupied personality. Imagine my shock to have her turn up beside me at this cocktail bar looking shrewd and sophisticated and fashionable in an unfeminine, sharp manner. She wore an expensive black velvet hat trimmed with a band of sequins. She was a New Yorker born and bred and when she sipped her cocktail I noticed a nurse's ring (with gold caduceus) on her hand. Somehow or other she launched into tales of her nursing days in New York when she served in a hospital on the waterfront. With a nurse's forthright disregard for effete expression she told about a Turkish woman having her ovaries removed: "So I had to give her a douche. Well, such howls out of her when I tried to get near her. She didn't speak English, but it was plain enough what I was going to do. Well, for God's sake, what do you think we found? Jewels swathed in cotton crammed into her body—rubies, pearls, diamonds she'd brought from the old country for her children's education in America. She was panic-stricken at the thought of having them removed." From this weird tale she got sidetracked into how she had once worked with the New York City Police Force in tracking down dope divers, most of them on Upper Park Avenue. For this job, getting $150 an evening, she donned an evening gown and accompanied a detective—and would actually smoke some of the cigarettes while they were there. Of course she had been trained how to use them.

Amazement led to amazement until she reported her experiences as a private nurse on a pneumonia case on Long Island. The patient was a beautiful girl in her teens, in a gilt estate brothel run by a white slave ring—one of those $100 to $200 an hour places. "I stayed three weeks in this girl's room. She was terribly sick. When a doctor came in, I was asked to leave the room so that we would never know each other outside those scarlet walls. Of course the place itself was out of this world. The clothes and furnishings were divine. The girl recovered and I left with a fat check plus an extra $500 to keep my mouth shut. What an experience. The madam was a scream—you'd have loved her—what a sense of humor. And oh, the men who came there. Politicians mostly."

When this amazing paradox of a woman ducked to the little girls' room, Carol supplied the climax. Unhappily married, she has pitched in at the hospital and worked her head off. Began to notice her eyes acting up. Couldn't see out of the corners. Wouldn't focus— terrible headache, refused to believe anything was wrong, said nothing. then collapsed and went back to New York when it became too terribly apparent she was going blind from some delicate brain disorder. Underwent very dangerous operations on her eyes and recovered. Permanent effects? Back at the table later she was as gay and blithe as ever. Meanwhile, I was putting her together in my mind for a story.

FEBRUARY 19, 1946—FAIRBANKS—Signs of the times: Sun as pinkish-gold as a Swedish baby fills the apartment windows at quarter of nine in the morning. Weather about 10 above and below.

Have another assignment for the lucrative *American Weekly* if I get it: Alaska as a tropical paradise years ago. My light romances bounced from *NY News* syndicate which had asked for Alaskan backgrounds. Reason given: too artificial. Trying a new agent— PAUL REYNOLDS—got my check for the sheep ranching article in the *Sunday News*: $75. To celebrate, took Eva McGown and Mrs. Carrie Willis to the movies and dinner. We ordered chicken, and that reminded Eva of a christening party she gave here shortly after her arrival. She sent out invitations and the crème of the town came. One woman even brought a sterling silver mug. All guests bursting with curiosity. Was young Mrs. McGown pregnant? Adopting a baby or what? Eva had all the trappings laid out in style. Then at the propitious moment she drew back a curtain and revealed the "christenees"—six hens and a rooster, all with literary names: Pride and Prejudice, Jane Eyre, etc. Husband had decided they'd need chickens for fresh eggs (such a rare delicacy in the north), and Eva thought it would be fun to present them socially. The women howled.

Speaking of the women: Miriam Dickey suggested I do a piece on the 30th anniversary of the town's oldest women's club: the Pioneer Women. Members have to be residents before 1908! I called the president of the dear Ladies' Club, the red-haired, Nordic, ancient wife of an old and prosperous furniture store owner: Mrs. ANDREW NERLAND. She thought, yes, if Clara and the others wouldn't mind, okay. To the historian's house for the record book. The story really was priceless, but even more so were the touchy hides and claws and tongues and vanities surrounding the source of all their history. I carted off the history to study at the office (six phone calls to okay this daring, perilous move). Three calls before I wrote a word: "Don't put in—" "Please put in—" "Let us okay the copy first," etc., etc. Meanwhile, here was a yarn of dimensions. How adventurous, gold-minded belles du esprit set sturdy shoulders to the wheel and came NAWTH on cattle boats—walked over the Chilkoot Pass—ventured forth from there in dog sleds, horse-drawn sleds, on foot or in boats. The first president of the club was a newspaperman's wife, musically talented, the record says, and producer and prima donna of the first opera ever heard in the North. Harrowing tales told of stabbings on the boats, suicides, men lost in blizzards, terrible fires with only feeble bucket brigades to guard priceless stores brought thousands of miles into the North at such great price. All the women were "Mrs.," so for many their reward was paid off right there. The upshot of this tender yarn (none of the real gusto and sock 'em would be permitted by these grayed gals at this point of local peerdom) was that ART (Bremer) slapped a byline on the story—to my BLUSHING and

ANGRY predicament. I had dished up drool, and he made me pay for it. Of course the phone was literally jumping off my desk under pressure of quibbling: "Why was Mrs. So and So's and Mrs. Thus and Thus put in?" etc., etc.

NEXT item: for what it's worth prophetically. Had Georg Nelsen MYERS in to dinner, just the two of us—wasn't much good—he stayed in the kitchen and watched every move. Told me about the book he is doing on Cap—loaned me the carbon of a story he wrote—noted the labored preciseness of a straightaway style. The step-by-step sequence of plot evolution. Hmm-m, I thought. My own writing is at a critical stage.

A copy of the sheep ranching article in the *Aleutian* (captioned "Wool and Williwaws") came from the owner, wealthy ROY BISHOP in Portland—all praise. I read the article as they published it. All rewritten—well done, I thought ruefully—because they didn't— humbly—think my own copy up to snuff. Or what? Loaned it to D.A. She read it without a single comment. Even loaned my present incompatible roommate, HARRIET HOPKINS, the precious copy and she eyed it, also without a word. "What the hell? Is it that bad?" I worried—on top of the Pioneer Ladies byline?

News item from front page of the *P. I. [Seattle Post-Intelligencer]*: "Clare Luce becomes Catholic." Wrote Al MORANO at once and enclosed a note for Mrs. Luce saying I was happy she had joined our faith. I wonder about her husband, HENRY L. LUCE.

D.A. and I had dinner tonight and talked ourselves limp on the man she is/is not to marry. Hope it's soon, a wedding day for her, I mean. For myself, I know Jim will be home soon. There's always China in the offing. Have written a freighter line in Seattle to let me do a story on a complimentary trip to the Orient. We shall see.

Have written another entry but it must wait a bit. STORY OF THE NENANA ICE POOL CLOCK—the original one was given to me on Valentine's Day, February 14, 1946, by an amazing old-timer, Charlie Wilson. Next day, here we go on the story of the clock. It is a square box affair, greatly battered but showing its fine origin. On the left side of the box is a tiny hole through which wire was strung to pull the hands and stop the clock on the FATEFUL hour. For some reason there was a ruling that the clock should be hurled in the Tanana River when a new one was purchased.

The Nenana Ice Pool Clock

Wilson's frugal nature forbade the wasteful discard, so he tossed a cigar box into the muddy waters of the Tanana instead. He hid the clock in his cabin, then worried that it would be found and he would be shamed for an infringement of his duties. He all but begged me to take the clock and not tell where I got it. About Wilson himself: born in San Francisco, came to Alaska in 1914, prospecting. Later worked for the railroad as a construction man laying ties for tracks. Later was with Nenana Power Plant for 24 years. Idea: easy job, reap pension, lead a leisurely life. Joined army in 1917 in Tacoma when lit up with patriotic whiskey. In artillery. Early youth: at 12 ran away on a merchant ship—went everywhere from Sydney to Rio. Would catch any ship going to some exciting place. In early days Rio was a glamour center—big hotels, etc. Charlie was in merchant marine 14 years. Has been around the Horn in a sailing ship many times. Said it was very beautiful country. Rough sailing. Wilson, who has lively blue eyes and a protruding jaw with tobacco-stained teeth, has never married. He speaks well and has a forthright manner. Asked me to have some ice cream with him in the office shop while we talked of his ports of call in the early days.

FEBRUARY 16, 1946—FAIRBANKS—Weather mild—sun up about 8:30 a.m., bright sunshine during the day. Went out to Ladd Field this p.m. to see a P-80 jet propulsion plane close up. Called the FRIGID BRIGID, its pilot is 25-year-old curly-haired Captain HOWARD MARKEY of Chicago. While he showed me the small silver ship without a propeller I missed the technical details as I thought: Here's tomorrow's jet Wiz-z-z. His speed exceeds 500 mph. To demonstrate his take-off, Markey fired the ship and as I stood shivery and open-mouthed on the runway, a gust of fire burst from the tail. He assured me, however, not all take-offs backfire. He pointed out that "jet" means, of course, increased speed for all types of planes and decreased cost. He flies at about 30 to 35,000 feet altitude. With Irish flowery vision he said flying that high is like being in a cathedral of blue sky and clouds. When in trouble he flies low and follows Alcan Highway. Will be glad when he's out of the P-80. "Yah, lotta pilots feel they otter get a DFC for just sittin' in the cockpit." Markey himself minds the P-80's one engine chance. Personally checks anything that could go wrong. "Of course I wear a parachute. But one miss and at our high speed—Well, school's out. That's all." He added that the Russians were all eyes last year. The general himself, armed with interpreters, climbed all over the plane, got in the cockpit, asked minutely what every gadget was for. Harmless info, Markey said. He didn't ask a FLIER'S questions.

AMUSING INCIDENT TODAY. I had rewritten a yarn about Jim BINKLEY of Eagle (near Canadian border) being flown here for medical attention. Bad case of pneumonia. D.A. had written the original yarn and I redid it making Jim out to be an INFANT. Gad, he's a discharged master sergeant of the U.S. Army. Well, when my story was picked up and re-broadcast, there were all kinds of funny repercussions. The "baby" laughed himself almost out of bed. His mother, still edgy from the nervous strain of her son's illness, had hysterics. Nuns at the hospital tittered around the corridors and one even said to me, "Go up to Room 328 and see your baby! He's a fine lad—6'2"—a nice Catholic boy, too, so maybe—" Up I went and found said lad all grins and stammers. The nuns had told him I was a fine Catholic girl. His mother, whose name is Peggy, all but fell in my arms. "You've cured my son and me," she exclaimed laughing, "with your screamingly funny story"

Reading *THE NATIVE'S RETURN* by LOUIS ADAMIC. The book was brought to me by a teary-eyed Croat woman who lives here in town. Feels her family has fallen victims of TITO. To convince me of his vileness she supplied me with this book by LOUIS ADAMIC and another of his: *MY NATIVE LAND.* Thought of George Wallace, now that I "see" the picture of Europe.

TINY BUNTIN, my INS chief, sent me a gorgeous kimono from Tokyo—coffee cream brown lined with brilliant scarlet chiffon. After having it photographed I'm thinking of having a dress made of it. The silk material is beautiful.

MARCH 1, 1946—FAIRBANKS—Had dinner with my favorite sourdough, SID(NEY) BARRINGTON, who literally is right out of fiction (Barrett Willoughby's *Gentleman Unafraid* and *Riverhouse*). Sid is tall and slim and gallant and old-fashioned. He calls the O'Hara

Bus in which he made his entrance here last week, "The Stage." He has a touching, old-fashioned way with women. Calls me "little miss sunshine." A riverboat man, gambler, professional HUNCH player in anything from dog races to Senatorial bandwagons. Sid is now up here on a mining deal. We dined at a local tavern. Restaurant of my choosing which, unheard of on a Saturday, was nearly empty and worse, the steaks were tough as boards. I wanted wine. They were "out." "Bring us your best champagne," Sid said impatiently. NONE in the house. The young kid waiter added, "We don't get many calls for it." Sid's idea was a throwback to dance hall girls, maybe, who drank champagne—a lady's scotch, as it were.

Snatches of conversation I recall. "Once came by a man's mink coat—sweeping the floor on a six-footer—gorgeous mink with silken brown sea-otter collar and cuffs. I got it for $20. Fella had it didn't want it. Took it home to Hazel and she cut it up into capes and muff and things—AUSTRALIAN."

Sid's mother had come from the west coast. Father was a BARRINGTON with all the force of the name—a sailing man—a trader at SITKA when the Russians were there. He recalled once that another Sea Captain was beheaded by the natives at METLAKATLA and the head was bought back at a ransom fee three years later—had been smoked and preserved.

Sid told me about some kind of a solution he'd discovered (or paid for control of—in cahoots with the inventor) to wash gold out of sand. Costs only about 50 cents a quart to make and does the job for tons of sand, even solidifies the gold grains in the final process. Norman Stines once tried to borrow some of the solution and analyze it. Sid: NO Sale. It's our patent.

Next yarn takes place during the flood at Galena last spring when the ice broke up. Well, to tell the yarn in order: The Catholic missionary there, one Fr. McElwell, lived in a little cabin several feet in front of his little church. He toyed with the idea of somehow moving the cabin alongside the church but hadn't funds to cater to a whim of comfort. Meanwhile his rival religious, a Protestant missionary, seemed to thrive in his little circle.

Came the flood—the good father rushed to aid women and children, When the waters receded, damned if Father's little house hadn't moved alongside his church exactly where wanted—and saints be praised, not a thing was disturbed, not a cup had fallen from a shelf, not a bottle had broken. But the Protestant reverend lost his church and home, smashed to ruins. (Sid tells his story nicely.)

A crap game table was opened in a back room of this tavern and a few couples gathered. The very act of a game drew Sid like a magnet. "C'mon," he said, and at the table put a $20 bill in my hand. I had no lunch—managed to salvage $12 or so. Sid won the price of our dinner including the tip. It was an amazing evening. Yet I had a feeling that my own ardor was a bit one-sided. Sid thought me perhaps a nice young Miss Sunshine, period. To me Sid was an Alaskan sterling sourdough hero. And basically a man any gal would adore for a dad. A real salty-young thinking, clear conniving wits-matching old veteran of a great guy.

MARCH 5, 1946—Behold me, I'm in LOVE. Terrifyingly so because I am almost overcome with the emotional impact of sudden discovery, awareness and longing. "He"—my darling—is Jade JIM [Editor's Note: Jim Robbins—see October 15, 1945]. Amazing thing. He came into the office and my face grew warm, as though I were blushing under my skin. I looked at him standing by my desk, with all the ancient heritage of woman looking at man… Dinner? And so the magic began again. We got involved, however, and had to dine at the home of his pilot. I was so greatly aware of JIM, the way he sat in a chair, half-slouched, comfortable, all man. The easy way he made conversation. We got away finally and ended up at 11:30 looking for a place to say goodnight. He had kissed me for the first time when he came in the door, lightly calling me a "cute little monkey." But of all things we ended up in the KFAR music library, holding our breath when at about 1 a.m. we heard someone enter the next office. (Found out next day it was D.A. and Norm who ended up sitting on the steps outside the library where Jim and I were laughing but feeling giddy and embarrassed if we should be caught, like kids on the porch swing.)

We talked, we laughed, we loved and he was mine. I remember especially how he said he was haunted by a feeling of something unfinished, something uncompleted he must do—but he wasn't sure what. He is troubled with the problem of being a father—trying to launch his three (by a suicide wife) into the world. He has a wonderful mind and we talked of politics and places we must see together—San Francisco, especially. I was madly happy and enjoying the amazing, strange new emotion of being in LOVE. I must remember in a story sometime to have my girl NOT wear earrings with her beloved and to have her chin scratched and sore the next day from a wee hair growth of beard on her darling's chin. I was unable to sleep a wink and was in a perpetual state of butterflies in the stomach all day. I feel pretty sure that Jim (as he said) is in love with me, and will become more so. I had a half intuition feeling that Jim and I will end up together somehow, somewhere. But I am a bit wary until I've had proof that my Jim is completely trustworthy. But this is love and I have it terribly.

MARCH 10, 1946—FAIRBANKS—Oh, what a week. The inner trembling anguish of loving Jim. And a shocking thing that has happened to someone very dear to me. Anyway, on top of everything else a gala Winter Carnival is going on here and I want a few background notes on it.

Yesterday afternoon at 4:00, hordes of people lined the snow-packed sidewalks and street along the river in front of the Northern Commercial Company to watch the finish of the dog races. It was bitterly cold, breath came in frosty clouds, people sniffed, eyes watered and tears ran down cheeks as red as noses. Tiny tots bundled up like woolly little blanket rolls with scarves tied over their faces across the nose and chin, Jesse James style. A few natives with smiling but vacuous faces, their cheeks oddly sallow pale despite the cold. For all that dog racing is their own sport, they hung shyly among the outer fringe of the crowd and only caught a glimpse of what was happening over the heads of the crowds.

A loudspeaker blared that the first team was in sight. Great excitement—finally down the street came a string of dogs, lean, thin-bodied dogs with sharp wolf faces, snow on their breasts and noses where they had broken trail for some stretches of the 26-mile run. Behind on a rickety-looking little sled, no bigger than a child's, was a slim-legged, small-footed native in ski pants and jacket and black motorcycle goggles. He jumped on the drag brake and stopped the dogs who had been racing for two hours and some odd minutes. The dogs' tails shook like plumes. One or two black-and-silver-coated dogs flopped down, panting. Another team came in. The dogs snow-covered, but also thin-looking and friendly, begging for caresses and praise. Again the driver was a graceful-legged, trim, slim native with a strange unpronounceable name—then came an old man who fancies himself quite a dog musher. A droll little cricket of a man named LEONARD SEPPALA—who tore down the street in a white canvas-covered parka and racer's goggles, behind a team of white, fluffy-furred huskies. But the dogs became confused and headed for the bank, and would have plunged over had not nimble little Seppala run around to the lead dog and dragged him back.

Last came a Slavic boy named STEVE AGBABA whose father watched anxiously and with disappointment the outcome of his offspring's fledgling race. Steve, the high school son of a handsome Yugoslav dog man whose liquid eyes were bloodshot and whose heavy accent filtered through the sickening sweet breath of alcohol, finished last. The son had apparently lacked sufficient training to manage the dogs in the triumphant tradition of the Old Man who nonetheless rushed up to the boy and seized the sled, helping to stop the tired dogs. The man embraced his son with Slavic emotion, kissing him roughly. The shivering crowd watched without a word. It surprised me how they looked on without any uproar. Other Carnival highlights: a mutt parade, the likes of which for sheer hysterics you have never seen (100 hounds and pups and a few haughty un-submissive pedigrees dragged along by determined tots). The Carnival parade was "something" too. Floats, corny local stuff—gags—a papier maché Alaskan Capital with a Statehood Question Mark—a float of Carnival "Queens" in white bunny parkas, local advertising floats of mining equipment.

Adding to the festivities are sport star visitors—men and women CURLERS from DAWSON and BOWLERS from Anchorage. Altogether, things have been pretty hectic and exciting the past three days.

MARCH 28, 1946—Weather sun-drenched, streets snow-less, northern lights at night.

Two items: L'amour. Was coming out of the post office when a tall man in high laced boots, whipcords and very dapper felt hat ran up to me. "Hi," he said. I stopped breathing. "Oh, Jim, what brings you to town so soon?" He was off to Chicago and New York, he said—his manner very hail-fellow-well-met. Oh yes, he'd see me later this evening if I were free. Hmmm—I thought of the words to ONE FINE DAY I'd read in a little libretto of Madame Butterfly: "and when my love comes back I will hold myself apart so he won't know how I feel." By later, I thought he meant 10 p.m. or so. I was panic-stricken when the doorbell rang at 7, the apartment smelling to heaven of boiled cauliflower! Harriet faded and we spent the evening head-on-my shoulder. To my amazement he took the angle "But I'd make a terrible husband." Never did I imagine short of a portion of passion powder, he'd come forth with such committed words except he very rarely kept saying he's too old for me. I can't really be in love with him. Love isn't seeing someone now and then, etc. He is right, I guess, but adding up in my favor is an admission that he, the businessman, relaxes with me, is amused, flattered and distracted by m' charms, 'deed yes! Further, he has been "alone" and realizes it. "I haven't felt this way about anyone for a long, long time," he said, but in the next breath, "You mustn't say you love me—you be sweet and cute and I don't want to hurt you. I'm not in love with you. I couldn't be unless I knew you... oh, for at least two or three years."

The next afternoon, before he left town, he stopped in the apartment and my heart and arms and I held him close and kissed him goodbye with shiny eyes. Unless I'm just wishin'-will-make-it-so, there is a wistful quality about him that draws him to me. I gave him a little goodbye note. Yes, a half-love letter with a St. Chris medal and poem "if you ride down the wind, if you haste with the star, etc., my love shall reach you wherever you are." Meanwhile I think of him CONSTANTLY—It could be the real thing. The thought is in his mind (or am I the easily trustin' country maid—he said it and she believed it?)

Always with love comes Wednesday, mid-week. Clear vision. April one I received a letter from Jim which for crudity and triteness knew no equal. He even dotted his i's with circles. Began "Dear Pegg-o" and said how I was his charming little "mackerel snapper" (Oh, love's holy light—this will make such funny reading someday.) He said it was sweet of me to pass on the little "medallion" but nicest of all that "phony Irish talon" I will forget so soon. But someday "an old coot (Oh gad, aye, coot!) like myself will call your bluff" etc. It was a FIASCO from a man of his position and mentality. And to me it was a stunning revelation. I regretted having seen him in the acid solution which dissolved his physical attraction and my own vision of his "charm." We shall see how 't comes out. I could LEAVE him more freely though, I think, having glimpsed the clay, not of his feet, but of his sensibilities.

Meanwhile, an insatiable crying need to be OFF to see the whole wide world urges me to make plans for China. I have written three big shipping companies (freighters) about extending "press privileges" for a trip to China. I am turning my thoughts to Shanghai as a next roosting spot.

Stopped on the street corner today to talk with DONALD MACDONALD, father of the Alaska Highway. Controversy has arisen over Canada's end. The government has refused to pay the $4,000,000-odd expenditure for annual maintenance. Anyway, MacDonald contended the whole deal was a political shame. It was built without consulting engineers who knew the country. It was built to prove it never should have been built—to protect the interests of a politician with a financial interest in the rival Canadian Pacific railway. Thus he ranted while I studied him, a Scot with the passion of a LIBERTINE, shaggy brows, a rebel's eye, a full ugly humorous mouth that cursed and laughed and gave no damn for any man! His standing joke is how "carelessness" produced him a family of two boys and three daughters. He helped build the first Alaska Railroad—told off the boss, a crook and an eely snake—quit his job—put his wife and kids in a tent somewhere near McKinley and went to work as an engineer. The highway came later. As a kid he was a fast scavenging un-clown-able heller. At 17 a newspaper man who lived on crumbs paid for news writing on the *Philadelphia Inquirer*—happened to be in Buffalo when McKinley was assassinated, made nearly $400 from handling the story. Went back to Philadelphia to tell his crotchety old boss to go to holy hell—closed his newspaper career—married, went to the west coast and eventually Alaska.

Another FABULOUS tale I ran into today. The story of NELLY KELLY—(Note: For April—snowfall but brilliant sun so blinding one can scarcely recognize people on the street. Everyone wearing sunglasses—sky blue as April in Switzerland. Last night I mailed half my life, my heart's best output. A story for *Reader's Digest* on the Nenana Ice Pool. When I typed the final draft, I was exulting. It was good—ran along at a good clip. Could see Ahmee reading it and being proud of the pithy, sharp, clean description, punchy, mannish dialogue. But when I read it the next morning for type errors, my heart clung to my ribs in fright and sickening misgivings. It was raw-dusty—clipped like fingernails too short, too trim for comfort. I mailed it anyway with a personal sort of note to the editor. It is the first article I have striven desperately hard to do well for its own sake. I want terribly to place it for Ahmee to see before she passes on, and to prove to myself that I can write professionally. Everything I have sold to date has been rewritten.

APRIL 4, 1946—FAIRBANKS—This may seem a pointless theme for reading, but I have just stormed and raged inwardly through Jack London's *Martin Eden*: "Nor did he (Martin) dream that persons who were given to probing the depths and to thinking ultimate thoughts were not to be found in the drawing rooms of society.... Such persons were as lonely eagles sailing solitary in the ozone sky far above the earth and its swarming freight of gregarious life."

I recall George Wallace saying similar things, warning me. The abortive struggle and fame of Martin Eden stung me into sharp realization of the padded rut I have settled into in this too-comfortable spot. I must gird for battle, up and away. My mainstay is youth, I am still in the fleeting twenties and aware that thirties are for adulthood. I hope I can sail the world over and see everything before I must harness myself for the hell throes of solid writing. My little article to *Reader's Digest* haunts the back of my mind. After reading how Martin Eden (really London) struggled and suffered to write, my efforts are mere shop-girl prattling.

I have a story to tell you about NELLY KELLY, but it will have to come later.

APRIL 7, 1946—On this day is ascended the Olympus of newsdom. On this day I went to the post office, drew forth a letter from the *Reader's Digest*. And with agony and dread and Oh My Gods, groaned in excruciating fear of failure. Opened the letter right there to read: "I think the Ice Pool Story is highly entertaining and I have great hopes it will eventually land in the *Digest*." (That is not SOLD but "going, going, to" from the *Digest*—that's good enough). He goes on to tell me to send a wire when the ice breaks this year describing the event—and the letter went on—small talk about knowing Howard Denby, etc. Of course the letter isn't as definite as a check but considering the magazine, it's plenty good. Words fail me in describing the FEELING of having spanned the chasm of making it because I WROTE my way across. Ahmee will see it. Mother, TINY—all others on the outside "rim."

With the seasonal angle, I'm not sure when it would be published. We shall see.

In the same mail with this MOMENTOUS contribution comes a long letter from my highly esteemed GEORGE WALLACE—a letter which, like the presence and conversation of the sender, has the sanguine power of lifting me above my station, my routine existence. This letter, in answer to mine about Douglas Reed's new book, contained gems: a paper from one WHALEY EATON who offers a professional reader's service. "Events have become so complex through their own efforts to comprehend them. They must employ professional readers who know what to read. Who can tie a development in Shanghai to another occurrence in Chicago." This was an insight into the secret of Wallace's power. Perhaps his resplendent job with General Motors. He was the know all—before and behind the scene—Europe! Wallace's letter-—long and in his own hand (incidentally, oh most cherished, he invites me to visit his farm when I need quiet to assemble my thoughts. He goes on to say I must get a working knowledge of the world, geographically, atmospheric odors, what-nots. All compounded in natural divisions:

America, Europe, Near East, Cairo, Palestine, Istanbul, Athens, Bombay, Calcutta, China, South America, Rio and Buenos Aires. He says to skip Australia and New Zealand. I wonder if I should take the *Reader's Digest* money, tramp steamer around the world and do a book on it? My stars are bright tonight. Oh world, I love you. And rejoice that I was born into your midst.

Odd that I should catch up the same thread so continuously. I have had another letter from George Wallace asking the same thing. Tell me what you are thinking. Your mental discoveries—I hope someday George Wallace is very proud of me. He has made all of Alaska worthwhile to me.

The next gem of the day was in answer to a real "fan" letter to a writer whose article I noticed in *Reader's Digest*, one DONALD CULROOS PEATTIE, who wrote this in an article on William Penn: "That is how, one beautiful Indian summer morning in October 1686, the good ship Welcome glided like a weary swan whitely into Delaware Bay." I wrote him out of the worst throes of my ice pool article to pay homage unto thee for singing words. His answer must be remembered. "I would distinguish poetry from prose by saying that if a sentence or thought walks to its destination, it is prose. If gets there on wings, it's poetry!" Oh, superb.

There is no more news of my trip. No news of my article to *American Weekly*—no words on my passport—any word from the *Reader's Digest*. I am reading OSCAR WILDE'S plays every night in the bathroom until 1 or 2 in the morning. Roommate asleep in the other room. Easter has come and gone—and Jim did not remember— nor did Art—not even a card from him. We spent the day driving to BIG DELTA—beautiful day—passed a young buffalo along the road, he blinked an eye at us and stood rigid as a buffalo on a nickel.

APRIL 11, 1946—LETTER FROM FAIRBANKS

[Editor's Note: Pegge sent the following letter to her mother.]

Darling, I have so much to tell you I was all for telephoning, but Art said it might take a day or two to put the call through.

Here's the news. This morning comes a TELEGRAM that was like a honk of a ship weighing anchor. It was from the *NY NEWS*. It read:
WILL COOPERATE IN GETTING YOUR PASSPORT
LETTER FOLLOWS
It was signed "Ama Barker." Ama is the Sunday editor who has been buying my features all along. I wrote her a letter not more than four days ago sounding her out on covering the Orient and she answered by wire. The passport from the State Department is the ticket, the Navy takes me. Until I get the "letter follows," I won't know specifically where they want to send me. But, darling, I'm going. I'm a FOREIGN CORRESPONDENT FOR THE BIGGEST (CIRCULATION) NEWSPAPER IN THE WHOLE WORLD.

I was quaking when I got the wire. Art shot me a glance across the office: "Everybody okay?" he asked. I phoned D.A. and in a low whisper read it to her. She came running down from the radio station. I'm sitting tight until I get the letter. As soon as the ball is rolling SO WILL I. When the passport arrives I will let you know and scamper to Frisco to meet with you. IMAGINE SEEING YOU AGAIN! I won't be able to wait for Jade Jim, but that can't be helped. We will go to the Mark Hopkins, order up room service, buy me clothes, take in a show maybe, and have a time. More on this later, for I have another STUPENDOUS ITEM:

Sunday night (again) I almost telephoned you. At the Post Office came a letter from (oh lordy) *Reader's Digest*. I rocked on my heels when I finished this letter, for the *DIGEST* tops all other magazines for circulation and cash. Prestige still lies with the *POST*, and for reasons of the H. C. Witwer, *Collier's*, but to land plunk! In golden glory. Again I went tearing to D.A. and we had us a coffee on that one. Me off wine ev'n for Lent and D.A. dieting for her glamour trip outside. The article was really aimed at Ahmee. I wanted her to read a piece of good Parker prose before she floats away on her cloud one day... and this is it! I thought of her constantly as I read and re-read the script before mailing it. The WRITING was the thing, and it was good. I knew it. I wrote her immediately to tell her the whole thing.

Cheek by jowl in the same mail came a long, long letter from George Wallace. He was all for my seeing the world in freighters. He traveled that way even when he was top man for General Motors. It's the traveler's way of traveling; even D.A.'s friend, the Russian in Tacoma, wrote to say "Perfect" about my going in a freighter. As it is, your worries are o'er, I sail with Uncle Sam instead. Anyway, Wallace went on to lift Parker above the everyday bracket, giving me the "adopted child" treatment of training my intellect and acumen to grasp global events, etc. I WAS ON TOP OF THE WORLD, higher up than Fairbanks, literally! Talk about triple endorsement of my own certainty that I will yet be famous. Oh, Mother, what a feeling. "Soaring," Ahmee called it. I went around in a daze today. Everything's going my way. My article for the *AMERICAN WEEKLY* is shaping up beautifully (on the pre-historic heat, yea tropics of Alaska... tho' it broke me deep into geologic history for which I had no background. A word to Father: He need never boast that I never went to college. No, I didn't. But it's been that much harder for me in many ways. With one special reward: I dig so hard for the stuff I don't know that I RETAIN it like a miser's gold penny.)

My dear Waldorf lady, Ann Schiek, was in a flutter over making your Easter present. Dear darling, she ran her legs off getting extra butter (so scarce, but she uses nothing else), nuts and dates, and then hurried all the way downtown today so I could airmail the package while the nut squares were still warm from the oven! Be sure to open the box as soon as you get it. If (horrors) they should dry out, steam them over boiling water for a minute or two. I hope you like them. Art and I snitched a few samples before he tied up the box ("have to cut down the air weight," Art kept saying) and Oh, they are heavenly. Dear Ann (I keep endearing her because I see her quite often these days and she keeps giving me rolls for Sunday breakfast (Danish pastry with candied fruit!), loaves of her wheat bread, a sample of spaghetti, and such FOOD... stars that shine in heaven! and such flavors. She is truly an artist, and as temperamental and emotional over her puddings and salads and cakes as any artisan in any field of endeavor! She cooks with her whole heart in it, and no "tips" or recipes are given out. Monastery secret. But now and again she will tell me, "dear child," how to fix a bit of this and that. Wait till you taste liver made with apples.

I must end this and get busy on my article. Oh, yes, I had to go to a tea at the college this p.m. (wore the rose felt hat I arrived in two years ago, though I feel as if I've lived ten lifetimes since). Anyway, the anthropologist who was to measure my skull and detect Chinese forebears was there. I cornered him. He laughed, took a look: "Well, now, I tell you," he began, "this face shows Mongol tendencies. I would never say you are Irish, not the LEAST BIT. The very shape of your eyes tends toward a slight Oriental origin, but I would say more Russian perhaps than Chinese!" (He is a Harvard man and an international figure in this field.) So who's the China-Russo in the family closet?

Stell Wann, the social friend who is a witty gossip and little round queen and cute as a bug, has returned, and Harriet and I are lunching her Sat. Won't you come too? Ann Schiek is making the lunch, mentioned a salad that's tomato aspic with pears in it! Had note from Ahmee and wrote her warning her D.A. would call and expect to see her and what excuses she might make. She sent me the enclosed clip, which is amusing. I whisked her a fiver for any little thing she might want and wrote a Schrafft's cute note enclosing $5 and asking them to send her a pound cake, jam, turkey sandwich or something for Easter. Thought she'd rather have that than flowers. Also wrote Pattie about Stevie.

If anything more STARTLING happens I will have to phone. You will be given advance notice by the operator. Glad you have phone.

Any more word from Mrs. Willis? G'night, darling mother of a genius.

Baby bright eyes, or known as Mei Ling Maggi

MAY 22, 1946—Have dined and movie'd and coffee'd with Captain KID MARION—typical riverboat captain who told me yarn after yarn. I scribble them here for posterity.

As a kid drove a dog team. Parcels, mail, etc. One day met a girl stranded. She was on her way to Dawson as dance hall girl. Kid took her to town and when they arrived (his version) she said, "Let's team up." She worked in the dance halls—would come home and throw her money on the bureau. One day Kid said, "I'm going back to my dogs; I've had enough of this." Left her—a few years later meets her when she's on her way to the States with $50,000. "Aren't you sorry you left me? What am I going to do with the money? Take care of parents and get myself an education." Nearly 30 years pass. (I gathered that Kid and the girl had had quite an affair and there was some feeling of hindrance and pride.) Kid was going to walk to VALDEZ from Fairbanks over the railroad tracks to save money. Stayed at Pioneer, up for breakfast next day. When paying check realized he'd put all this money under his pillow—rushed back—room was made up, money gone. Kid went down to desk and the clerk handed him his wallet. The maid had turned it in. He, feeling he owed her a tip, sought her out. Nearly fell over when the girl walked out. They talked of many things. She had taken care of her folks all right, but then fell in love with a rotter who skimmed her coin. She headed back to Alaska and got a job as a maid. Years later, Kid was at a banquet for fraternity of women of the woods or something. The worthy matron was the former dance hall girl. They were introduced as though they had never met—blank-eyed.

Kid says "Yukon feathers" were spruce boughs. Every gambling trick was practiced. Says in town there was a "red-headed woman named Maggie Cobb"—a Negro with a red wig.

Lady known as Lou story. She ran the Royal Alexandria hotel in Dawson. Then the Floradora. Met the boys with a glad eye—had husband—they finally decided to go to States, went on a boat that sank and both were drowned. Each had made out will to the other. Several thousand dollars at stake. Her family claimed his will and vice versa. Trial in San Francisco, judge decided woman had the weaker constitution so she must have died first. HIS family won the suit.

Marion himself is quite a yarn. He tells little of himself but easily reveals himself. Will boast of his money tricks—how he trimmed someone out of his poker stake, etc. Marion better looking than Barrington but without Barrington's aristocracy. Kid has perpetual physical youth, a boy's physique, trim, muscular face, solid jaw. Lively expressive laughing, hard tough blue eyes—all his hair, boyish straight and smooth. Wears dark green blue suit. Noticed he did not tip waitresses.

MAY 29, 1946—A watercolor rainy evening of blurred grey twilight. My China trip is bogged down in Washington D.C.—had a wire from *New York News* saying the army wonders what my arrangements for transportation are before they can go ahead and make arrangements. I gasped with anguish, the days crawl by on knees and elbows and I live between two worlds—WAITING—even stooped to sending my news editor a gift, an ivory bird pin.

Meanwhile, a freelance writer, CHARLES LANIUS, is in town. Does stuff for *Collier's*. I flashed the magazine an outline of a pet story of mine: Stork Club of Alaska in Anchorage. They wrote back, interested—thanks for the tip. I learned they had telephoned Anchorage from New York to assign LANIUS—now must clear myself on the IDEA. (January 31 received note from Davenport saying check for $100 en route.)

No word from *Reader's Digest* on the ice pool yarn, but they have had my story for over two months. I feel in my bones they'll keep it.

Photographer here working with Lanius used me as a model for an article in color pix—trip to Fort Yukon—saw the proofs today, not bad.

Dorothy Ann Simpson, my dearest friend, went to New York for a vacation. On the plane she met a writer and his artist wife, who, flip the calendar pages—later hired her as their secretary to go to CHINA in November. Dear God—may I, too, get to the Orient. Just finished a ridiculous prattle-brained book on the Orient by Cecil Brown, *Suez to Singapore,* but it was good background. Now in Edgar Snow's *Red Star Over China*—Wallace incentive. Tell me what you're thinking, more and more of communism—with resultant awakening of objective analysis of the word and its formidable definition. The book Peattie had sent to me was a JEWEL—for one chapter alone about experimental communism in America. NEW HARMONY, Indiana—Says Peattie with sly amusement defending the essence of an idea of communal brotherhood: "We don't mind admitting that our fire department is community owned and that it serves every man according to his need and not according to his ability to pay. Hate to hear the paint on it called red even when it is!"

Other thought markers: I grow more tolerant in my views of religion—more practical than pious on some dogma.

Just acquired from the public library "the writings of Thomas Paine."

In a fit of huffed anger—**MAY 31, 1946**—Mrs. NINA CRUMRINE and her daughter JOSEPHINE who draws marvelous dog heads and portraits came to town. Filled with admiration for Miss Crumrine's talent, I went to interview them. Josephine was thin, with a pale, white-skinned face, shapely, wan looking by contrast with a long tumble of glossy black hair and a harsh brilliant red, expensively smart suit. She seemed passively disinterested, tolerant of my presence through a sense of publicity value. As we chatted, Nina came in and after a few minutes I sensed the mother lioness and her slave cub. All this in the external guise of a frail bony woman with a wrinkled pale face clinging to a girlish youth long gone—a grinning benignity betrayed by her quailing-voiced conversation and watery eyes.

Her pride was outraged at my inevitable attention to her daughter. Then in the course of the interview, I asked about Mr. Crumrine. Smoothing the pleat in her skirt with a prim, unpolished hand, Mrs. Crumrine said, "I've been a widow for 27 (or so) years." Naturally I took that to mean her husband is dead. Next day (the day of wrath), I called to see Josephine's paintings. Mama cool on the phone. The article all wrong, etc. Finally, "Don't you know there are many kinds of widows?" Josephine later took the telephone and said, "Everyone knows my father is living in Seattle and the article was rather embarrassing when you said Mother has been a widow since his death." My defense met with coolness, increasing to chill. I hung up with an abrupt apology.

SUNDAY, JUNE 2, 1946—We took two side trips across the Big Gerstle bridge and to the Big Delta airport, then went to visit old-timers the Lowells' know. One proved extremely interesting—an old man with stubble on his chin, a lean western face, a pair of young boy's eyes. His name is STEVE WALTERS. We battled mosquitoes to find a fishing spot—cast until mosquitoes drove us away. Walked back through thin-shanked young birch trees and evergreens. Saw a pink plant looking like crocus. Steve invited us into his cabin for coffee and right over his little table was a shelf of books—and SUCH books. Like the classics you read about. *The Evolution of Man— History of Ancient Greece* ("That one was right innerestin', by God!")

Joseph Conrad, R. L. Stevenson—Maugham, *Gone with the Wind,*
Berlin Diary, books on astronomy and Sumner Welles' *Time for*
Decision. Seeing these books launched us into quite a conversation
and I learned biography is his favorite type of book. Especially
Benjamin Franklin and Carl Sandburg's Lincoln. And books on
anthropology. Steve had no particular "story"—born in Michigan,
studied to be bookkeeper—wouldn't stand the servile-type clerkship
so away he went to the west. Eventually headed north—likes the
"independence" up here. Doesn't think Alaska's ready for statehood
until the population increases to support it.

JUNE 10, 1946—Art (Bremer) and I went for a drive to a mining
camp (F.E. Company) near town. Wild roses and bluebells were
dust coated, like the hem of a princess gown. Along the silt dust
roadways, we called on PETER MAAS, the cook at the camp, a
Dutchman (formerly of the Dutch army force in the East Indies)
and, to my purpose, a hobbying anthropologist. A superb cook at
various mining camps, Pete could always take time off to cover the
mining areas for bones of mastodons and mammoths. With him on
these trips went a stately German police dog named Pola (for the
actress Pola Negri) and a camera with a self-taker attachment. Pola
would smell out likely spots and Pete would dig up the bones—take
a picture of himself with the coil of tusks and decadent bones that
resembled boulders of lumber. He has saved some specimens—sent
many to museums—read up on the subject and collected data for
scientists from the U.S. Geological Survey. His disgust was classic in
describing the book theory experts who came to Alaska occasionally
on field trips. "Humph," Pete muttered through his pipe. "Pola's got
more anthropology in her nose than they have got in their heads."

JUNE 16, 1946—Ah: this writing—I've been all day struggling with a simple story on MYSELF for the *American Magazine*. Feel I've almost wasted my time. Article to be called "Snow Job."

The TIME OF DECISION has come. I am OFF to Shanghai. My passport goes out tomorrow and I am hoping to secure boat transportation by July 22-25. The Great Adventure begins.

JUNE 1946—I have just returned from my first drive on the Alaska Highway, and it was marvelous. We jostled off the bumpy Richardson highway at Big Delta and rolled onto a smooth, grey gravel road that V's ahead into a green-treed horizon with a brilliant turquoise sky overhead afloat with lamb's wool clouds. The road itself is the MARVEL, is as smooth as if it were concrete—every 50 feet or so wooden sticks marked the road bed. Ted Lowell (ranger, Alaska Fire Control Service, trapper, fur dealer) explained the sticks to me: In winter heavy snows cover the road, and the sticks guide snow plows. The border of the greatest highway of engineering undertaking is lush with flowers, a kind of vivid bluebell cluster and a purple blue flower like an Easter hydrangea.

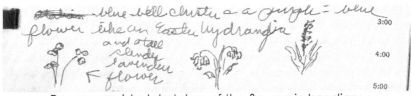

Pegge provided sketches of the flowers in her diary.

Behind all the new spring green rose the snow meringue of the Alaska range. We drove to a place beyond Big Delta called Buffalo Center, a fire guard station run by a very amiable, homespun couple, John and Linda Howard. The atmosphere of the low ceiling'd room with the wood stove in the center, sleeping cots lining the walls, stacks of magazines on a table, linoleum floor and DELICIOUS food was typical American pleasantry. One chap, an Alaskan game guide (Doc CRIPE) was just back from Honolulu where he worked for a year building an army hospital but he "didn't like to see all them Orientals and JAPS. Glad to be back in Alaska." (Learned later he had been an aviation mechanic for NOEL WIEN on a flight to Siberia when they flew out a fortune in Russian sable and fox furs from a stranded ship.)

Babe LOWELL and I bunked together, talking into the small hours about having babies (of all things). Babe says the waiting list of barren women wanting to adopt babies is pathetic.

(NOTE: June 1 Art (Bremer) got the mail from the Post Office. I was panic-stricken and faint of heart when from the *Reader's Digest* came a flat envelope—a script (the ice pool article rejected, I thought, sick with disappointment). But no. 'Twas the *Digest's* typed copy of the article for me to proofread. Still not POSITIVE acceptance. I have really in GI jargon "sweated out" this *Digest* story.)

[Editor's Note: Here begins Pegge's description of her trip on the Tanana River beginning June 26, 1946, recorded in a notebook that was separate from her diary.]

LEAVE FAIRBANKS IN A TAXI—costs $1.25 for three-minute ride to railroad station. Trip begins on June 26th on rail car from FBK through a green land of shrubs, pink fireweed clustered and tall, thin-legged trees—the sun glints on the telegraph wires and runs along ahead—a gold nerve flash against the green and blue.

On the train, which jerks and sways like an old western cowboy's nag, are a handful of passengers: a native boy in khaki—a railroader reading an Ellery Queen book—a few frumpy housewives who huddle to the neuter-sex lavatory, clutching their pocketbooks.

Arrive Nenana about two hours later—a few pot-bellied, suspender-panted old-timers, a few native kids around the station—and Bishop

John Bently, Episcopal Bishop of Alaska, who escorts me around town in the blazing hot sun. At the store, I talk ice pool and local news with the store agent and lead into a pound of butter at 80 cents a can. Then, with the Bishop, climb into a little motor boat belonging to the mission. The frail boat is run by what the Southern gentry Bishop calls faith, hope and charity—mostly hope—a young native boy is at the controls. We push off into the grey swirling, swift current-ed Tanana River—and ride a land mile upstream. The air is a-fluff with flying snowflakes—tufts of "Alaskan cotton" from native shrubs. The Bishop's residence was rustic, deep-shadowed indoors, polished logs, a stone fireplace—scatter rugs—fresh flowers in a low dish and on the end table the latest issue of *GLAMOUR*. Milady Bentley is bathing and sends her embarrassed regrets. The Bishop takes me through his church—tells me native children did some of the wood carving, etc. I ride back to my Steamer Yukon in another motorboat. I go aboard and meet Captain Ralph NEWCOMB, famed riverboat skipper. He wears a bright blue shirt, suspenders, and comfortable jeans around his paunchy middle, but his face under a heavy captain's cap is fine-featured, well molded, his eyes bluer than his shirt and the store-clerk-type glasses seem out of place in front of those eyes. He is unobtrusive, quiet spoken, studies a person slowly as though taking mental soundings if interest is stirred. I told him about George Wallace and, speaking on the mutual acquaintance-ship, he begins a dissertation on all he knows about him. We are interrupted—he murmurs some stock phrases in response to passenger banalities: "Nice day, ain't it?" Later I corner him again—he tells me he was born in Wisconsin of early English-Irish stock. Father came to St. Michael in Alaska long before the FBK stampede—Newcomb followed—has been riverboatin' ever since. In the early days the boats sailed the Tanana to trade grub for furs with the natives.

Also aboard are two genial representatives of the Law. One is Jack Buckley, old, old-timer of the Marshal's Office, who recalled President Harding's visit to Alaska. Said he was a gay dog and a great fellow in telling about an old sourdough who once served as U.S. Marshal in FBK (Harding appointee)—"Why, hell," says Buckley, "he didn't know nothin' about runnin' a marshal's office. All he done before was use the hind end of a donkey for a compass." Another yarn: Serving a SUBPOENA to a native by air (Pilot Sam White). Native needed to testify in FBK trial for drunken shooting of another native. (Cost government over $200 to bring this native trapper to town to grunt a few bits of eyewitness evidence.) Anyway—Buckley said the only way they would drop the message was to wrap the SUBPOENA in the center of a roll of toilet paper from the plane. It unraveled and the native mushed it into town.

The other Law Abide Keeper is an FBI administrator from Washington D.C. whose fellow passenger amities run to yarns about Westbrook Pegler's classic visit to the Bureau (after which he wrote a howling criticism instead of the expected eulogy) and of meeting Tallulah Bankhead at the Bureau and how she cussed on every other word.

JUNE 26 1946—LETTER FROM FAIRBANKS

Darling,

This is a quickie to tell you I am leaving Monday for Tihwa and don't know how long I will be gone. The hills of Tibet are calling me. I will be the guest of the American Consul and his wife out there and should get a terrific story. I was never so excited, next to the Siam jaunt. You should see the Chinese letters and credentials I have. My friend Fern, at the Consulate here, has given me a wonderful letter to the Tihwa consul. Will give you all details when I get back

Have a reservation on a French liner for Marseilles, Oct. 4. I will probably be able to work an earlier transport, but this is my first try. The French ship makes the most interesting stops, although the Danish and Scandinavian boats probably have better food. For once, the stops take first choice.

[Editors note: Pegge had planned to sail for Europe and Switzerland when she returned from Sinkiang.]

Have received all your clips and have put them to widespread use. Walter Logan of the UP came over to chow the other Sunday and I passed on his precious byline story that you sent.

Please send me whatever SINKIANG clips you see. Sinkiang is where the Soviets are supposed to have launched an invasion. (Sinkiang is in the far, far west, north of the Gobi Desert along the Soviet border.)

Oh yes, met the traveling publishers, especially Marshall Field. Ladeee-da cocktail party given. I went with my commanding officer. I saw Field standing deserted, tired and a bit forlorn. I went over and just quietly talked to him, liked him enormously. I also met Gannett (fuddy duddy grand-daddy) and saw Mrs. Hobby. She wore the LONGEST skirt I've seen on a street dress. It was almost 1918 length, sheer gray crepe enhanced with a jade pin of price. My Seymour Topping was down for the event. (INS is now covering from Nanking)

Write when I return. I'm going around madly getting ready. May be away a month. Bye, darling.

(Signed) Pegge

TODAY, JUNE 27—I am perched on the top deck of a gorgeous, chug and splash riverboat—a grey and white slow-knot-going stern wheeler with a trim pilot house outlined against the blue and cloud-fleeced sky with a dainty carged filigree boarder. Two barges forward (one looks like a small dock in itself, about 50 feet long) and the other holds four huge silvery, grime-smudged oil drums. The oil is beneath the barge deck and is tricky business for the weight shifts and can throw the barge off balance. But the glory of all is the spanking, splashing, brilliant orange paddle wheel on our aft stern. On the port and starb'd corners of each barge native (Indian) boys dip sounding poles painted red, green for various depths. The meals are wonderful, the scenery is mild, almost cultivated-looking for the trees are young stunted growths and the swamps are covered with new green grass a gardener would show with pride. Beyond are blue buff hills of gentle restful grandeur. One moment, I sniff the river breeze, swat a mosquito, sigh at this LUXURY. Another moment I think "if Shanghai" and fret about this or that, but the river is like a solidly plump Aunt Matilda folding her arms and saying, "Ain't nothin' t' get in a stew about. 10 years from now Shanghai'll still be there."

Riverboat *Fort Yukon*

Other flash impressions: The sun-gold sheaf on the silver-milky river along about 10 to 10:30 p.m., dazzling—gorgeous, liquid pastorale.

Wood-burning engine on the boat now, soon to convert to oil. Heavenly fragrant spruce and tamarack logs used in huge boilers— native boys in checked shirts and khaki pants shuffle about below decks. Signals given to crew by clear, crisp clangs of bells.

Progress is slow even though we're with the current—the silt is shifting so constantly two natives gee pole from port and starb'd ends of the barge—and a motor launch is sent out for about two hours to give advance soundings.

Pass Minto—first native village—smells and noises greet us—a fish wheel—few natives debark, the girls in bright sweaters, their blue-black hair hanging just to their shoulder blades—ragged filthy and cheerful urchins tumble about—dogs howl.

Was amazed that at 10:30 a veritable banquet table was spread. I thought of starving Europe as I gazed on butter—bread—cold meat—olives—jellies—pie—fruit—cake—cheese, etc., that was merely nibbled and left.

The second night we tied up at a stopping place along the Tanana. Two native boys scrambled ashore and tied up the boat, looping a wire cable around a spruce tree.

Friday we chugged into the Yukon River which was broad and full-bodied and blue-crusted, catching the color of the sky.

First stop was an Indian village, TANANA. Went ashore. Met Jesuit priest called FATHER MAC (short for MacMichael). He spoke of the natives' curse—liquor. Someone else mentioned an instance when a native trapped a beaver and came 65 miles to town in a little boat to trade the skin for a pint of whiskey.

Arranged to see the remnant of an old hotel, the TOWER HOUSE, along the bank. At one time TANANA had been an army post and General Short of Pearl Harbor fame had served here as a Lieutenant.

Father Mac also told of a Chinaman on one of the boats who turned land lubber years ago—married an Eskimo woman and brought her to Tanana (their name is pronounced GEE). The combination worked well and the children are very intelligent, especially one girl, Patricia. She is a bookkeeper in a local store—very oriental looking but trimly attired; I found her in city clothes. She must be extremely lonely, for her intelligence has cast her on a social reef, surrounded by others but alone for the white men are old and uncouth and the village bucks are beneath her. The dogs (wonderful) and children (small, moon-faced with urchin garments and runny noses) were adorable.

Father Mac also told of his early days in the priesthood when he was chaplain at Blackwell Island—there sat this twinkly-eyed pink-cheeked little Jesuit eating a piece of pie in a neighbor's house, telling about toughs and bullies in the underworld—and "hoppies," etc. Later came to Alaska—story told about him—as young missionary here Father Mac was out with his first dog team—not doing well—heard noise behind him—turned and heard a blue SMOKE of cussin' above the yelps and howls of the dogs—but the team kept moving right along. Driver warned as he sped by—the little priest looked at his dogs, took a deep breath, and let go. Later is said to have written his bishop for special dispensation for driving dogs.

Father Mac, in telling of the French and Belgian Jesuits, said Father Deschout of Nunivak Isle was once roused from his cabin by man in parka—Deschout was so used to talking Eskimo that he murmured in native tongue—"Sorry, Father—I can't understand," the chap said. "What!" exclaimed the little Jesuit. "You are a white man! Oh, wonderful saints, bless you," and he flung his arms around the man.

Chatter from various ones: LIQUOR is the number one curse on the town – beer and coke same price; the natives buy beer and get savagely drunk. Our steamer *YUKON* was docked in Tanana about five hours unloading on two wheelbarrows case after case of Schlitz beer. Captain Newcomb watched and remarked "hundreds of cases of beer and not a can of milk or cocoa for the children." Contrary to the obvious conclusion that the natives are poor, some of them have made thousands on the fur trap lines, and most of it goes for liquor.

Town character, Harry the Jap, returned last winter from an American concentration camp. The young marshal roused my interest telling me about Harry, so I had to see him. We covered the town and finally discovered him building a fish wheel. He was small and wiry, a graceful little person who looked misplaced in bulky shoe pucks and white wool socks with green borders. On his head was a

Panama hat bound in a red sash. He wore pale tinted horn-rimmed glasses over warm, friendly brown eyes which had only the slightest Oriental slant.

Harry apparently came to Alaska as a servant of a judge and his wife, remained and drifted into trapping, settled at TANANA where his cabin became a workshop for some ingenious talent. He invented gadgets—one was a flour sifter with a long handle. The housewife squeezes the handle and the wires turn around sifting the flour automatically. Harry got no benefits or royalties from this device through some mismanagement.

Then Harry invented a trap, inspired by his pity for crippled animals helplessly snared in the usual trapper's trap—his trap mercifully kills the animal the minute it is snared. Nothing has come of this so far, commercially. (Note: Harry's last name is NAKAGAWA.) Harry is also artistic—does wood carving—makes cups and saucers out of orange peel—sticks for powder puffs, bowls, etc.

His great love, though, is flowers. His garden is planted with very beautiful varieties of cultivated flowers and the whole back of his cabin is a greenhouse for flowers. Each set of plants or species is raised for someone in the village and all the blooms are taken as a gift to the person's cabin. The hospital especially gets a lot of Harry's flowers.

So far as is known, Harry has no family or has had no romances, though everyone likes him. He neither drinks nor smokes. The University of Alaska is said to have given him some award for his inventions. He is also something of a photographer and has ingeniously devised his own darkroom, using gas lights somehow or other. I did not see his pictures.

SATURDAY—At breakfast a steward suddenly remarked, "We are going thru the Rampart Rapids," and forks and spoons went down, coffee was gulped, stacks of sourdough hot cakes swimming in butter and syrup were left half eaten.

Outside on deck we beheld an overcast scene of sylvan mountain slopes rising above a brown churn of water vigorously resisting the broad charge of our boat against the current. The range stern wheeler back aft sent a splashing, determined swish thru the deserted quiet—the oil burner engine breathed an audible pulse of breath—Captain Newcomb was quiet and all alert in the pilot house.

We went through and curved out onto the usual grey-brown flow of the Yukon, ploughing gently in midstream.

Then we came upon the camp of an old Danish trapper—John LARSON—who deserted his shambling habitat to paddle out to our steamer in a small rowboat. His dogs jumped up and howled and his Point Barrow Eskimo wife, dressed in a man's blue jeans, watched from the door of the cabin, a trim log building looking about like the maple syrup cans, perched on the hill. Against the drab makeshift-heigh-ho sort of dwelling scene, a stab of color drew the eye—fresh Yukon salmon hung up to dry.

Old John, a lively cricket of a man, rowed out to the end of the barge, got his mail in a hubbub of laughter and greetings and what's news. "Mosquitoes are fierce, by God," etc. He waved to the passengers taking his picture like mad—and paddled away.

On the top deck I came across the star character on the boat—a traveling dentist, Dr. BART LA RUE, who studied on the West Coast near Portland. He's been traveling over Alaska since 1927 because the idea of having an office was too much like a jail. He has his own plane but prefers to go by boat or dog team, etc., hitting all the wayside stops, is a true Alaskan. Says there's no fun going outside for a vacation when he can travel around the Yukon calling on all his favorite characters (more on them later). He knows whole families in the country.

At TANANA this summer he bought an old horse sleigh and in June gave the N.C. agent's kids (two girls, one boy, Reedy) a sleigh ride in June on the Yukon River when they went with Mrs. La Rue to Ruby on a barge (but they rode in the sleigh). La Rue makes his home at Ruby, travels constantly.

La Rue was paid in furs and gold nuggets in the past, but now in cash. He is said to be very reasonable. In winter he carries his silver fillings and other perishable medicines inside his parka next to his skin to keep them from freezing.

Prize teeth—miners love to put the gold they've mined in their teeth. But at Beaver, a Captain Harry Healy once asked La Rue to put a diamond in the center of his China clippers. La Rue experimented with a bright piece of glass but it didn't show up to suit either the Captain's or the dentist's flair for the spectacular. Then La Rue got a brilliant idea sure to please the old salt. At the village store he found some cheap rings, one with a green stone, one with a red, and he inserted port and starb'd teeth in the upper plate. Captain was so THRILLED he ran all over town pulling them out of his mouth to show people. He still has them.

A bit of a wag, La Rue is credited with a Hallowe'en prank at RUBY where he made all the false teeth plates in town. On the pretext of checking on them and armed with one extra pair, he would insert another plate and borrow the actual one. He went all over town mixing up teeth, men's and women's, then sat back and watched the scramble when the villagers realized they had their neighbor's molars. He is nonetheless reported to be about the best dentist in the North. Eskimos are his best chair patients—kids and oldsters sit there eyes wide as their mouths but not a peep or a move out of them. The Eskimos on the Arctic and Bering Sea coast have the best teeth, almost perfect despite their age, and never saw a toothbrush.

LaRue uses a foot pedal chair, is immaculate and particular about his instruments, uses a small sterno if no other boiling water is available, uses Novocain to pull teeth.

LaRue, a Frenchman of course, served overseas in the last war. He has a true outdoorsman's life. If he hits a section of the country where the hunting is good, away he goes. If he's offered apricot brandy he downs it with the boys. He sits around at night and enjoys the best yarns of the old-timers. He hears their discussion of books, religion, or just stove-side musings.

Sketches of his best friends: a little tough 'ombre in FBK, now paralyzed in his arm, was an old whaler, later associated with the Blueberry Kid (a sort of Jesse James of the trail) at Tanana—for some years dodging the course of justice, would roam the interior to live off the land. Eventually married an Eskimo gal, had a string of kids and is now about to end his days in FBK.

Another was Kangaroo Harry, an ex-Australian prizefighter who loved a very beautiful girl. She married someone else. La Rue asked him, "Kill your rival?" Kangaroo Harry evaded, "Well, I got back at him." He came to Alaska and learned that his loved one had a daughter and years later the mother died. Meanwhile Harry, who lived like a miner and hermit, eventually died and left about $56,000 to the daughter of the woman he loved.

Another character was a French Canadian trader with a ferocious face—gruff manner, heavy black eyebrows—who wandered into Fort Yukon. He sold liquor to the natives as did all the other traders, but was not well liked because not really understood. Once he was taking a fur buyer down the river in a rowboat. He fixed his eyes under the fierce brows of the buyer, just the two in the boat in the wilderness. The buyer became increasingly nervous, thinking the Frenchman was going to kill him, rob his furs and money. Finally he removed his money belt and thrust it at the Frenchman. "Here, for God's sake—take my money but don't kill me—just take me back."

Doc La Rue fixed this fellow's teeth, reported him to be generous—ready to help anyone in trouble, etc. When he died and his will and personal papers were found in an old cigar box, it was learned he was a deserter from the American Army, a bank robber, was wanted for all kinds of crimes south of the border, and had once made a career of train robbery.

LaRue's favorite character was FRANK YASUDA, a Jap at Beaver. He was aboard the first coast guard cutter to go to Point Barrow, liked the country, stayed at Barrow a while. Then decided to penetrate the country, came down with other Eskimos, lived off the country, eventually settled at Beaver. His family was a small banking clique in Japan. A brother or uncle was a general in the Jap army. Yasuda never went back but sent large sums of money to Japan. Once in Seattle, his Eskimo wife walked behind Yasuda and the dentist when the three were going out to dinner.

According to Captain NEWCOMB, Yasuda came to Barrow on Revenue Cutter. Whalers had so much sailing trouble, boats crushed in the ice, etc. Government established a station at Barrow and Yasuda remained as one in charge. Later went prospecting, arrived at Beaver, founded the village. Eskimos of Barrow followed, coming over land. Took about two years.

As the threat of war increased, and Yasuda heard the news in letters from relatives, he decided to go back to Japan and get his money. Offered to take Doc La Rue along, but instead he went off to an American concentration camp. Yasuda is very generous with his grub and such, once insisted on treating Doc to a supply of Jap vegetables and canned delicacies. He refused to take any money, so Doc refused to take the grub. Later, when he shoved off in his boat, he found Yasuda had stowed all the food away in the back of the boat.

P.S. to La Rue story: trick on boat. At Fort Yukon, La Rue wasn't among the passengers disembarking. Learned why later. He was in my cabin turning up the mattress, tying sheets in knots, throwing towels around. On the door was this cardboard sign:

QUARANTINE—CAUTION!
WHOOPING COUGH, MUMPS, PREVARICATOR'S FEVER,
ROCKY MT. FEVER, MALARIA, RABIES, AND WHAT NOT!
DO NOT ENTER OR UNLOCK DOOR!

RAMPART, once a thriving town, now just a shambles. As we came ashore an old-timer in droopy drawers hitched up by suspenders said, "Rex Beach's cabin that-a-way" which tourist advertisement was uncalled for in the presence of JACK BUCKLEY, seasoned veteran of the country. Jack (deputy marshal) told about the squaw Rex Beach has during his brief stay in Rampart. Beach called her "Short and Dirty" and she probably called herself Mrs. Rex Beach. When tourists came around she was apt to strut herself. One tourist lady asked her if she kept house.

"Yes," replied Short and Dirty.

"And do you make bread?"

"Yes," said S and D. "Just as good as any sonofabitch."

Jack stopped along the roadway to chat with an old-timer who said, "Things are kinda dead here, Charlie." Charlie sniffed, hitched up his drawers, and replied with thick scanihovian accent, "Well, ya' shoulda' been here two weeks ago. There was more damn cats and drag lines tearin' up our streets, just like San Francisco." The street, of course, no self-respecting cow would travel to pasture on.

Noted: in boiling hot sun, native tots in saggy cotton stockings, sweaters, old rubber galoshes or sneakers.

Most noteworthy sight: IRA WEISNER, trader of Rampart—a chicken-necked, teethy, smiling, obliging fellow in a checked shirt and hobnail boots, has made a business of flying salmon in to FBK. The fish, lush beauties with white, grey and blue tinged scales, about 25 to 35 inches long, are caught in fish wheels by the natives. Then Weisner stores them in an ingenious cold storage cellar he built himself along with another old-timer called Dutch Kid Martin (an old, fiery-tempered Dutchman). The two first thawed a large section of ground behind Weisner's store. Then in the spring they dug a tunnel 55 feet long, lined it with ice blocks from the Yukon River, and plastered the blocks with "slush" ice, inserted ventilation pipes, installed a thermometer and now store the fish as is—on a shelf with chunks of ice all over it. The fish will keep about 10 days at a temperature of 20 above. His capacity is one ton of fish.

The boat tourists were shown through the cellar carrying candles and stooping as the tunnel is only about five feet high. The walls of ice encrusted in crystallizing slush, sparkling in the candlelight, threw a clandestine aura over the channel. Except for the smell of fish, the tunnel was a marvel of ingenuity.

La Rue rounds up his customers by hailing 'em: "Come 'ere, you old SOB, and get your teeth fixed." He also makes trips with old-timers. Once he traveled with HUGO ECKART of Kotzebue, who was lugging a gunny sack with a chunk of jade. Hugo went on to Vienna where he acquired Mrs. Eckart and had the jade carved into a necklace.

Once in a plane crash La Rue had his hand injured, he was so cold his fingers were numb, and he thought he'd reached the end of his career and would lose his fingers. Instead, just the tip of his fourth finger is slightly nipped where a piece of bone was removed. No detriment to his practice.

He has "siwashed" it in the arctic—heard his tales over home brew orgies—has made dentures and dropped them from his plane when he couldn't land. He flies his own plane and travels in his own boat down the Yukon.

STEVEN'S VILLAGE—We arrived Sunday morning. No Schlitz (beer) to be unloaded here, so the stop was brief. The town looked like something at the headwaters of the Amazon. No white folk visible. The riverbank was lined with beautiful but hot and disheveled-looking dogs, all tied to short posts.

Cabins mystified us for one had a man's breeches hanging outside as though he'd just taken them off. Another had shoe packs hanging from one outside log and pants from the other. Nearby in the yard was a small wood stove. Understand in summer the dogs get too hot inside a cabin so are kept outside.

Sunday at 11:00 p.m. I am sitting on the "Texas" deck, writing by the glow of a pink-and-copper sun go-down (it couldn't be sunset at this hour when all good suns are set and gone). The water, though, far from catching the watercolor wash of ORANGE–pink, is like mauve taffeta, barely rippled by the slow path of the riverboat. The low trees are deepest green margins of bank and shrub between the sky and the Yukon, resplendent and languorous in glamorous evening dress of mauve and pink. Marvelous to ponder that beneath these waters the king salmon are fighting their way north to die.

Had a long talk at last with Captain Newcomb, who told me about the YANERT BROTHERS and Ernie Pyle being aboard the boat. He (Ernie) was quiet and unobtrusive, got a big kick out of the YANERTS and a woman trapper at Fort Yukon who taught her daughter to trap also.

Technical details of STEAMER *YUKON*: on our trip we were sailing UP stream, bucking a five-mile current, the boat straining along at 4 or 5 miles an hour.

Oil instead of WOOD in the engine and no one pleased. They had to carry a round-trip supply which added weight to the ship, whereas with wood, it was light and they could gather it as they went along. The river is so shallow, current so swift and unpredictable, so CURVED and narrow, and our boat and barge are as flat-bottomed as a table. Clever maneuvering is essential to keep us afloat. The boat slips sideways going around curves, and rounding the bends is a matter of keen, unnerving judgment. Four and a half feet or five is the shallowest water we can cross. Although the Yukon is a broad, full river, the steamer must zigzag and hug the shore or else roll cautiously along midstream, avoiding shallow stretches.

HYDRAULIC GEAR in the pilot house attached to regular steering wheel which can be used in case the gear goes out of commission. The wheel has had its day, sometimes stormy. In a swift current or tricky crossing it has taken the brawn and weight of two men to turn the wheel; sometimes the skippers stood on the spokes of the wheel to steer.

The *YUKON* steamer was built in 1913. It is 170 feet long, has native deck-men and youngish engineers and mates, freight clerk, and a skipper, who is the last surviving old-timer captain.

The young pilot, who worked alternate six-hour shifts with Newcomb, said he spent eight years learning the river, hundreds of miles of it, from memory. The compass in the wheel house was closed up tight and never used. The river pilots are philosophical about their river, which is constantly changing. It keeps them as alert as green horns watching the current for the first time. "Yep," said the pilot, "when a man thinks he knows more than the river, he's headed for trouble." He referred to some pilots who feel they know the river so well they can take the upper hand in rough riding its current.

Toward the end of summer, the boats sail in complete darkness. A powerful spotlight is used at times, but when fog settles down the light is diffused and blurs the outlook. Skippers either tie up or sail on their hunch, instinct and the trace of whoever's patron saint of the river.

Tanana (river) is the toughest to sail because the soil, ground to a fine powderlike substance by glacier action, washes away on the current like cake flour under a running spigot. Constant soundings must be taken. One advantage, however: should the boat run aground, the river's silt bottom is so soft it wouldn't tear the boat's bottom. In the YUKON River the bottom is gravel and once your ship runs into that you stay put until you are able to pull the boat out by use of cables strung to "deadman" planks ashore. The steamer *YUKON* has six rudders and has had a colorful career. Once an old-timer tried to make off with gold on the boat but was apprehended.

Newcomb's story on YANERT: Came to America from Poland, was about 16 years old, served in Spanish-American War, developed great dislike for Indians, and when he decided to settle down in

Alaska, he deliberately picked the site of Purgatory because he heard the Indians were superstitious about the place and wouldn't go near it.

When he eventually carved his famous devil, he made himself an Indian (was about nine feet high, had movable arm which waved a welcome from river bank – someone would stand behind the devil and pull the arm. Also on the bank was a wood carved devil's imp who jumped out with a Yanert sound effect roar as the customer came by.)

The cabins, viewed with binoculars, were like log cabin boxes; one had a coat of arms on the door. Nearby was a weathered totem pole that mocked with ingenious ridicule the staring tourists who clicked cameras furiously.

BILL YANERT came to Alaska in 1896 or '97—settled in Purgatory in 1903. Meanwhile he undertook a special mission as a soldier, sent from Juneau or Skagway alone to inspect route for present railroad. Had letters to Canadian Mounties as a courtesy.

He and brother, HERMAN, trapped at Purgatory. Did fairly well in their youth. Bill began to carve, became a legend on the river. When the boat stopped with his mail and supplies, tourists blinked at his devil, etc., swarmed off the boat, flustered and confused the two hermits. Finally Newcomb induced Yanert to permit his place to be a tourist stop in exchange for free passage on any of the boats. Yanert finally agreed but hated the idea of being a free traveler. He would come aboard with pockets lined with cigars, bestowing them on the crew and passengers. The ladies adored Bill, who looked like Buffalo Bill in his heyday and showed his Polish gallantry and European courtesies toward womanhood, scary bachelor though he was.

Once on the riverboat, a husky, handsome nurse took his fancy with her wonderful laugh and mannish good nature. When the boat stopped at Purgatory, Bill was so engrossed with his nurse he didn't look up until Newcomb startled him out of his daze. The nurse jumped up: "You're getting off here—Oh, this looks like a wonderful place.

I think I'll get off here too." (There was but one cabin at Purgatory.) Yanert's face flushed beet red; he was panic stricken. Without a word he picked up his suitcase and supplies and RAN as though his own devil were after him. He never looked back. That was as far as he ever ventured on the jeopardous field of romance.

In addition to his brother Herman, he had another who had changed his name to JANERT (owns a sausage factory, no less). Janert had a son and daughter (or perhaps more children, for all Newcomb knew). Anyway, one time when the boat stopped Yanert was all upset. He'd had a letter from his niece saying she was coming to visit him for a few weeks. The thought of a lone young woman living there was a dreaded horror to the two brothers.

"For God's sake," Yanert said to Newcomb, "What'll I do? Will you ship me in some sheets, bedding, pillowcases and some kind of food for women?" Newcomb came sympathetically and morally to the rescue, agreed to stand by and help out during the ordeal. He delivered the female hospitality goods but after Yanert had gone through his mail, he burst into smiles and whoops of glee. The niece had gotten as far as Skagway and could take no more roughing it. She wasn't coming! Some years later her brother did brave the wilderness and come to Purgatory. The visit was agony for the brothers who felt so abashed at their humble rough abode which had no streamlining for a city slicker. Yanert told Newcomb later he was ten years younger when the nephew left. "All he did was talk about exploits with women. Hell, in my day we treated women with reverence." Called him a regular lily—didn't know a goddamned thing about livin' out. Fussy about his food just like a woman.

Bill very handy in old age. In winter used to walk on snowshoes 45-odd miles to get mail. "Not bad for a man past 70," Newcomb observed.

Bill once had a toothache and went into Beaver where YUSADA pulled it with pliers. Yanert kept the letter he'd been given for Mounties on his historic trek. He showed it to Canadian authorities.

The Mountie sergeant gasped at the signature and offered Yanert the town. Yanert took out citizenship. Volney Richmond, Sr., signed as one of the witnesses.

When he died in a hospital outside he begged doctors to send his heart back to Alaska to be buried as per his poem long ago. Instead his body was cremated and the ashes brought back.

Ernie Pyle once visited Purgatory and had a big time with Bill.

Herman was in the background doing the heavy chores, cooking, etc. But he carved a very fine totem pole for Yasuda's daughter. He lived at Beaver for a time and was to be sent to the Pioneer's Home where a whaler's relief station was maintained.

A migratory itch kept Yasuda on the move. He came to travel all over the Arctic coast before going down to Beaver. He has tried his hand at mining, opened his store about 1912 and did well, but was generous to a fault.

As the leading citizen of Beaver, Yasuda found himself forced into a doctor's role, taking care of the sick, bringing babies into the world, burying the dead and even conducting burial services. When I expressed surprise and admiration of his accomplishments, he said, practically, "But someone had to do it; there was no one else—no planes, only dog teams. After we had been talking a bit he mentioned the concentration camp. He said the hardest part was not doing anything. He had always been so active.

Yasuda (at Beaver) got on the boat to have a tooth fixed by La Rue. He was a charming, well mannered little man with a crewcut. He stepped up on deck in a trim business suit and black high-button shoes. His speech was chatty, witty and lucid with little trace of accent in pronunciation or manner. The aristocracy of his birth was obvious in the set of his bony, white-cropped head and slight shoulders. He walked a bit stiffly from arthritis of the knees.

When questioned, he told of his youth at Barrow and even why he left home. The Yasuda family had been doctors for years. When his father died it was naturally assumed Frank would follow the family tradition. Instead he ran away to sea (at 18) and came to San Francisco. In the late 1800's he joined the U.S. Navy and served on a U.S. Revenue Cutter sent to Barrow.

YASUDA CONTINUED: Has never been back to Japan since leaving. He is not a citizen of the U.S. because he didn't take out the proper papers. He said he couldn't go back to Japan with his native wife.

Note: Origin of the town of BEAVER—some mining ground developed and the Alaska Road Commission was to build a road.

(Add to legend about Dr. La Rue.) He wears a large diamond ring in a heavy gold setting. Once at Ft. Yukon he offered a reward of $100 for the ring, which he said he had dropped down the "Chic Sale" (outhouse). His cronies tore their "Johnny" apart and searched diligently before La Rue, with mock surprise, yelled, "Hold 'er, boys, I see my ring was in my pocket."

He was grounded for flying while drunk and taking passengers. Had a former wife before the present one. (Is reported to have flown to Ruby once with passengers, so drunk he couldn't even remember having made the trip. Still, he landed perfectly!)

FORT YUKON—Old Hudson Bay trading post. We arrived at midnight, riding a churning current along a high cliff-like bank dotted with tiny holes where swallows made their nests. We passed scattered log cabins that looked as though you could pour maple syrup out the chimney. The sun streamed a scorching, rose-coral ray across the serene clear brow of the heavens. Little native boys (Indian) in jeans and overalls raced shouting along the bank. Their elders hung in groups, staring. The women wore bunny-furred slippers with bright beading over the instep, cotton house dresses and old sweaters. Where we tied up closer to town, the white folks were out and Dr. LULA DISOSWAY, missionary doctor, bush pilot and wife, fur traders, natives. I took a quick trot through town, stopped for coffee with bush pilot and wife and others. Heard the local gossip. They talked avidly of the radio programs they listen to. News holds the strongest appeal. Looked in at the local dance hall; to a squeaky phonograph bushy-haired native chicks danced fox trots with local natives and half-breed lads and later the young teen-age stewards from the boat.

Then to N.C. Company to visit wife of agent whom I knew from FBK. She rose from a sound sleep (it was about 2 a.m.), to chat and visit. Their quarters are almost elegant in a rustic style. On the wall a white bearskin was stretched. Her China cabinet closeted imported china.

We left Fort Yukon after the freight was unloaded at about 5 a.m. and entered the river boatman's "headache channel": the Yukon flats where the water spreads out like a lake but is not much deeper than a pond. The boat anchored halfway upstream by one of the myriad islands. The sounding sticks went into play, a small boat was launched and jutting through the water with its outboard motor, explored all the broad expanse of channels ahead. The Captain's report on his return was a hands-on hips-retort: "I don't know where the hell we're going to get through." After a long pow-wow, the boat put out again for a distant island, strung a wire rope (cable) to a deadman (tree) and slowly unwound the cable until a buoy was set afloat. Again the pilot and crewmen in the sounding launch returned to pow-wow with the Captain. More tow line was needed. The water depth was only four feet (4½ is our absolute minimum).

Blind trapper: DAVID ADAM, 45, born and from Steven's Village, to Fort Yukon to have eyes checked. Blind in 1932, intelligent and quite sociable and chatty native. Ate with fingers to find food on plate. Goes hunting with sons after mink, beaver, rats. Can butcher caribou and moose by feeling as he cuts. Walks with cane. Once poked cane into bears' den, called wife, she shot the bear. Once heard Archie Ferguson's voice on the radio, never saw him. One day plane landed on the bar (in the river). David heard him talking, told everyone Archie Ferguson had landed on the riverboats. Sight: wants to be able to work for himself, do things, dreads sitting idle in blind darkness. He does while away the winter.

Another trapper from old time—fierce eyebrows, pale bright eyes, brown skin, tall—NEIL McDONALD. Father an archdeacon who married a native at Fort McPherson, likes to read, enjoyed *Gone With The Wind*, has never been to U.S., only Canada. Was out on the trapline when war ended, didn't know the news for two weeks. Trapline 50 miles long. Has 5 or 6 dogs, malamutes and mixed-breed huskies. Weather 30 to 40 below.

[Editor's Note: That ends her trip. Pegge doesn't record how she got back to Fairbanks. On another page in her notebook, Pegge records things to check:

- *Family in Fairbanks that bought Yanert cabins.*
- *Get Yanert book from BUCKLEY.*
- *Check University of Alaska on his honors, etc.*
- *Check Harry the Jap's story—University.*
- *Check sign about kids dog mushing at Ft. Yukon Carter's store.*
- *Check address of Cliff Hansen in Seattle.*

On another page in the notebook, Pegge records the letters she sent to family and friends in Fairbanks and Washington, D.C. She notes that the ship Marine Lynx *will sail August 28 and the fare would be $373.75 from San Francisco to Shanghai.]*

I am definitely leaving this Alaska that I love on July 22. The writing still clutches at my stomach like a stillborn child. I know it's there but don't know how to bring it into the world—a beautiful creation.

Before I go off on a tangent, though, I must record my first trip over the Alaska highway made over this past weekend, June 22–23, to the Canadian border. Leaving FBK, we drove through dust and sun to the junction of the Richardson and Alaska Highway. I went with Ranger Ted Lowell and his wife. Luckily for me, they are good

Alaskans who have roughed it in the wilds when Ted ran 2 or 3 trading posts (grub for furs) in the Tanana River Area. They told tales about their Indians and being stuck on the trail, etc. (She is a nurse and in her mid-40's, yet has a wonderful young, sturdy figure, small but vigorous hands. She, too, has "mushed" for miles in all kinds of weather.)

From Buffalo Center Saturday morning, we rolled along at about 50 miles per hour where there were deep curves and downhill, uphill grades in the road. The panorama of glacier streams (thick, bubbling, grey streams) lakes, hills inter-peaked in every shade and dye of blue, green tundra standing upright and FRESH like parsley or celery tops prime for a salad.

As we rolled along my eye was riveted to the shoulder of the road. When upturned sod furnished the spade loosening necessary for an apparently dormant growth of flowers—and what flowers—not a wild riot up-shooting of hardy field blooms, but delicate, dainty-leafed, scented and colored flowers. Wild roses with petals of pink porcelain. MERTENSIA (a blue, bell-shaped cluster), fire weed (looks like garden stock of phlox in pink mauve), butter-gold daisies, wild honeysuckle on long, slender stems, small, pink globe-shaped flowers with gold feelers in the center, wild sweet peas, a pale lilac-colored daisy, tiny white star blossoms, Indian paintbrushes (a low plant like a small dandelion bush, but with odd flowers that look like clusters of strawberries—the natives crush the flowers and dab the red juice on their faces for potlatch celebrations).

We stopped at the TUK JUNCTION RANGER (Alaska Fire Control Service) station where a young ex-GI is in charge with his young, toothy, smiling, fuzzy-permanent-wave-haired wife. He was a prisoner of the Japs—talked to me of his treatment at a copper mine in Japan. This boy lost all his teeth from mistreatment and diet deficiencies.

On to NORTHWAY, a scraggle of houses and wannigans— outdoor plumbing—slouching natives—but oh, to sleep with real wind banging against log cabin walls and blowing the mirror off the windowsill. To rise and scrub your teeth over a back fence gazing at dawn at pink snow-peaked mountains and "spit" into foliage graced with wild roses!

We drove back in one day, detouring as fancy struck us over old dog mushing trails. Once we stopped to watch a willow grouse and her young scrawny-necked chicks. The air in these byways was heady with blossoming raspberry bushes.

JULY 15, 1946—(Seasonal note—hot as NYC in July, only our sun doesn't go down at 4:00; it shines all night too. Art and I picked blueberries in fields not far from town. Dust and mosquitoes take the joy out of berry picking.)

WARD MOREHOUSE of the *NEW YORK SUN* was here the other day, a perspiring, radish-faced little fellow who amazed me by huffing and puffing his impressions of Alaska ("God, what a place—What mountains—Never have I seen such mountains—Nome was the most interesting spot in Alaska because it is close to Siberia and so remote a community"). Then, stepping out of quotes to just chat with a fellow scribe: "What the hell do people do here? How did YOU ever come here?" etc. For a world traveler he was an amazement. He completely missed the whole story of Alaska, which is the PEOPLE.

Next item: I understand there is a great deal of vigilance for Russia afoot among the military at Nome. The talk ran nervously to stories of Soviet submarines nosing about the DIOMEDES.

[Editor's Note: Now begin Pegge's notebook entries on leaving Fairbanks.]

JULY 22, 1946—On the White Pass train to Skagway. Flight to WH (White Horse) from FBK. Sat beside bush pilot from CANDLE, GENE JACK, who told tales of Mrs. J. Robbins' suicide by hanging— Robbins' political views, etc.—about a flier's common-law wife who once tried to shoot him in the air—a wild wench, she once tried to feed Archie Ferguson cream puffs filled with glass.

Flight very rough, felt so sickened with Fairbanksia, my goodbye to Eva (McGown) and Art (Bremer). Eva's giving me a wee baby shoe "to return in."

WHITE HORSE—Enter the city coming down a driveway, houses look like checkerboard of immaculate cottages. White House Inn so old—big lobby—bearskin on wall—rangy fireplace, little thin-faced lad as bellhop. I was on top floor—no bath, nothing on the floor, not even PAINT. Charge: $1.75 overnight. Main street wide, dirt and gravel. My Alaskan eye was swift to recognize the fireweed (though not as long-stemmed as in FBK), the types of houses, oil drums, wood piles. After dinner in the White House Inn (really not as glamorous as it sounds) where everyone was amused at a dinner offering of Goat Chops ($1.50), took walk around town, saw the riverboats, noticed how brilliant turquoise-green the water was (said to be the Lewis River), gulls.

Strolled by church—barnlike white wood building with bright red piping, husky and malamute dogs curled up on the sidewalks. One shaggy brute with watery, friendly eyes was curled up against the church door. It was a Catholic Church (a church of the Sacred Heart). Priest had French accent, and the altar was adorable: tiny saint's statues in blue neckties. Chatted with tall French Canadian priest afterward. Before the war, French clergy staffed the mission.

Later took in a Yukon lecture illustrated with slides at the Anglican Church. Enjoyed the clipped Canadian style of the typical vicar. He told of the Inevitable RBT Service. Crowd of tourists drank in the cold-weather sagas with round-eyed amazement; most of them seemed to be from Chicago.

Back at the hotel asked for editor of the local paper. "You mean THE Mr. Moore, our HORACE MOORE?" the hotel desk clerk asked. Mr. Moore turned up, a twinkly, spry, and clean-scrubbed Englishman who came to Canada years ago. No accent, however, or mannerisms, but quite fluttery with compliments. Talks constantly, once asked me for a story on myself but then went on talking a big stream of psychological quotes and such. He will probably mention in the paper that I passed through town.

Departed Monday morning, a gorgeous blue-sky day, with fresh-churned clouds billowing. The mountains were close as a collar, the fireweed shot up bright and pink. But O! the tourists, thick-ankled maiden ladies with CAMERAS and Robert Service poetry books. I could not associate with them, my heart ACHED inside that I was leaving Alaska. No child ever was so torn with shrinking from the unfamiliar, the strange. There was NO ALASKAN anywhere. I sat alone and watched the mountains go by. At one place the train stopped to point out the TRAIL OF '98, a mere gravel foot path, and a stumpy Canadian Customs official beside me shook his head, "God, it took GUTS to come over THAT." Another place we paused on a wooden lockout to view the DEAD HORSE GULCH and plaque erected to the memory of something like 3,000 horses driven and forced through the pass with no thought of sparing the animal—not one came out alive. The trip to Skagway would have been wonderful if I were not so damnedly unhappy.

Canadian steamer the *Princess Louise*

SKAGWAY—Walked up and down the streets with my Alaskan eye recognizing the old landmarks that remain. The City Hall should have been under glass. It was a marvel of antiquity, all painted black and a-shine. Admittedly, I didn't do Skagway justice. I was tired and dead inside and after once boarding the Canadian *Princess Louise,* I didn't go back uptown. The feeling of STRANGENESS was so overwhelming I could only withdraw inside at the de-luxe touches to which I had become so unused. The dining room was all softly paneled: stiff ironed linen on the table, flowers in a silver vase, rows of silver astride the flourish of dishes. My heart felt a pang for the dear old steamer *YUKON* where I had hollered and LAUGHED the slow pokey miles away—with ALASKANS. Oh, dear God, there are no such people on EARTH as ALASKANS.

The departure from Skagway was to me like a night on Bald Mountain. I hid in the shadows of the bow away from the yapping crowd. The night was cold, the mountains loomed up fierce and frowning, eye-pupil-black, over Skagway a grey burst of light in the sky cast long-legged shadows. The light under the pilot house was so blinding bright one had to keep looking away from it. Pinpoints of lights in Skagway winked impishly. A deck hand, surprised to find me alone, said, "Hullo! What'd you think of Skagway?" "It's the last glimpse of the Alaskan mainland, bless it!" I murmured and suddenly felt my eyes burning and blurred with tears. The words to the song "Alaska's Flag" came to mind and I sang them inwardly.

The tourists, of course, were hilarious—one had an accordion and he played loudly. Some people from Skagway were on the dock. The hubbub was maddening, bottles were passed around, one blonde(?), uncertain of her equilibrium, stood on the edge of the pier and leaned over the water to kiss a man, equally gay, on the deck. A fat woman ran up the gangway with a bunch of garden flowers for one of the tourists. At 11 p.m. with a clatter of the winch, the thin groan of the straining cables, and an uproar from the passengers, we shoved off.

JUNEAU—Sun dazzling bright at 8 a.m. By odd coincidence, the two times I have been at the fog- and rain-drenched capital, the sun has grinned with fiendish glee. We had only an hour's stop, went into the Baranoff (hotel) to look at the Lawrence paintings and who showed up walking down the steps but NORMAN HALEY, Territorial Veterans Commissioner and D.A.'s close friend. I was never so glad to see anyone. "What the hell's the matter?" Norm grunted, "Y' look like a long lost dog." We strolled around town talking, swapping news. All of a sudden Norm handed me a jade ring. "Here, keep this for a farewell token," he said. It was Alaska jade (Jim Robbins Jade) large as a robin's egg—in a gold setting, fit perfectly. I was THRILLED to death to have it and recalled how Robbins, himself, first handed me a piece of jade along the frozen coast of the Arctic Ocean, just as casually. Bid Norm a tight hand clasp g' bye and went into BEHRENDS, to meet the lyric, clothes-issimo of Juneau, JOHN BISHOP. He turned out to be a thin, grey-haired man with enormous thick-lashed Irish eyes. He whisked me off upstairs to his salon where a pink tweedy Hattie Carnegie gave me itchy temptings. We talked as he flourished suit after suit before me. Then, sinking a hand in his hair, he cried, "Oh, I know what—do you need a coat? I got two exactly alike by mistake and must get the second one out of town. I'll reduce it from $195 to $112, if you'll take it."

I almost missed my boat trying on the coat and gazing at myself, had to run all the way to the dock. We are now further underway down the inside passage which greatly resembles pictures I saw not long ago in FBK of the Strait of Magellan, purplish mountains sprigged with snow in snakey crags on top. The water is of the almost splash-less consistency of green wave set lotion as we chug calmly along, a John Charley Thomas record playing over the loudspeaker for the eternal, everlasting TOURISTS.

WRANGELL—Utterly fascinating town perched on the side of a hill. Totems leapt up the minute we stepped off the dock, staring with wild frog eyes at the gaping tourists. It was 9 p.m. and little activity could be seen. I strolled through the residential section, marveled at the modern cottage-ish homes with terraced gardens and dainty flowers. Never have I seen such daisies, big as hollyhocks, and some sort of plant with brilliant violets, although the leaf is not like violets back home. Evidence of money and smartness was shown in these homes perched high on the hill. Down in town I stopped in the town's only hotel to talk to BILL GRANT. He told me of the fishing industry and the canneries that work up to February and an interesting bit of news: that "the Asiatic Lumber Company" will soon be shipping lumber from Wrangell to the Orient. It is so much cheaper this way because the ships travel the northern route and pass by Wrangell.

I should love to come back to Wrangell and sail up the Stikine River with the people who live in those hill-perched homes. I would like Wrangell, the strong smell of the salt air, and sailing the Stikine.

KETCHIKAN—Pouring rain. Seemed odd to go back in the fishing town where so ecstatically, 2½ years before, I had first set tingling foot on Alaskan soil. Perambulatory under an umbrella, I toured the town. Loved the fishy salt air, the boats lobbing at the wharf, the houses with the lush, dripping shrubs and jumbo ferns. Noticed how in the older sections of town the houses were almost built on top of each other and the passageway would almost permit jumping from roof to roof. Grotesque totems popped up everywhere. They remind me so much of tourists I cannot feel anything historically savage in them.

AUGUST 7, 1946—SEATTLE—What a day—and change of pace. At 9 a.m. I went to the George Wachtin Travel Agency (218 Vance Bldg.) and paid $370 on account of my sailing Aug 28th for Shanghai on the President Line *Marine Lynx* out of San Francisco. Then I went to the snootiest store in town, I. MAGNIN'S, to begin a new job as "sales assistant." Too exhausted to record any more.

AUGUST 16, 1946—My precious PASSPORT arrived after two months of truly anguished waiting. And what a thrilling moment to see the cover, even IF the inside flap did contain a hideous picture of me, officially stamped and in big type letters—the TRUTHFUL year of my birth—copied too carefully from my birth certificate—wires, telegrams, and hand wringing that preceded its arrival! Have not got my visa yet but expect it soon. Have had four series of arm shots, one of which made me mildly ill. The sailing date has been postponed until Sept.11th and I shall spend the extra time in Frisco. Art Bremer is due Sunday to accompany me to the glorious town I had saved for so long to see in the amazing ecstasy of the FIRST visit with someone I loved. Art is a dear, but not "the" man.

Now for notes on Magnin's and Seattle for background material. First I hated the job and the whole setup. Each day was one day LESS I'd be there. I cringed, unreasonably under the overbearing authority of veteran assistants-to-the-department-head. I was one step above a stock girl but did the chores of one quite cheerfully because they were cute bunnies and happy hearted to shift Hattie Carnegie's around with. The sales slips horrified me first from out and out arithmetic (20% tax on furs, 3% sale tax) then a fright that I'd take a bad check or something. It was hard for me to gabble about the color flattering madam's sagging cheeks and chins and telling her, her humped old lady shoulders "fit beautifully" into the $198 numbers the old frump ruined and WASTED anyway. I didn't mind Carnegie soaking the old dears (pullenty) for little two-piece numbers. Two models paraded exquisitely in clothes they could never afford and made gay "my-my-dear–lookit the real stuff I'm loaded with" remarks. I was annoyed at their utter lack of ENVY or regret or even craving for possession of the gilt and gussie they wheeled their soft slim selves around in all day. Harder for me to "take" than the twitting around all day, bragging for trimmed coats, MANGONE'S and NETTIE ROSENSTEINS, was the mental attitude of "clerking."

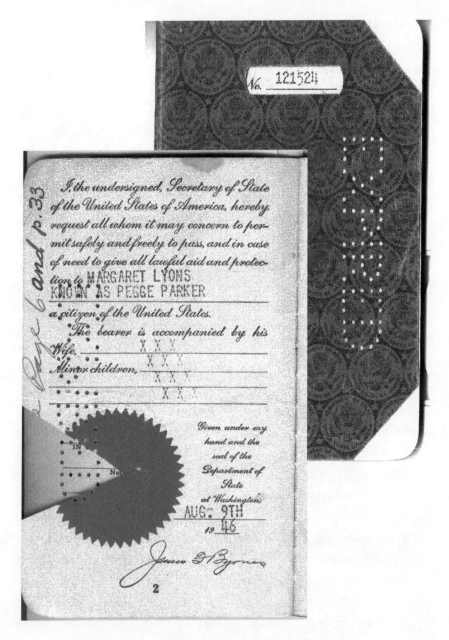

Pegge's passport, listing her pen name, Pegge Parker.

I MINDED more than total exhaustion the "new-girl-gets—
everything-so-mixed-up" or "Miss Parker" in that go-come-please,
dear don't ever—you're late this morning—here write this rep for
me—tone. I was ordered into black as the cloak of my "Tilly the
Toiler" status. First, I got a $20 long-sleeved blouse, then a crepe
dress—hideous—and paid $4.50 to have it altered. Naturally my dress
went on the last rung in the alteration room. Each time I mentioned
needing it, please, I got "Oh don't BOTHER me" shooings. One too
many—on top of my sleepless Shanghai-fretting nerves—ended in
girlish, hurt pride TEARS which created a great buzz about the new
girl, etc. A story must come out of it and the Seattle setting. How
the store hours were 10 to 5:30 Monday to Saturday but all the girls
had to be there at quarter to 10 for a fashion conference with the
buyer, a honey-haired woman of dignity and presence of about 50
who knew clothes from the seams out. Once I was called on to model
a fur-trimmed coat and nearly died of embarrassment as the others
critically appraised the "new girl."

Most interesting customer I had came in to have a dress fitted.
She had bought the gown over a month ago and casually explained
she couldn't get in earlier because she was one of the jurors at the
Sedin trial. He was a Russian Naval attaché snagged by the FBI on
charges of SPYING. Though he was freed and sent back to Russia,
overwhelming public opinion ruled him guilty.

Several husbands came in—one, a doctor who had had an argument
with his wife over the new dress she'd brought home. It was black and
he hated the deadening effect. To ease the situation he promised her
one of his selection as a gift. I enjoyed helping him decide on a lovely
deep rose gown for $65 (later the dress came back). Another man, an
attorney, came for his wife because he was afraid to trust her in an
expensive selection of a suit. I would have been intrigued but she was
size 20 and though I showed a MANGONE and talked fabric and
long wear and economy in buying the best, I thought "What a pity."

Another of my jobs was to sit at the appointment desk. I watched Mrs. America and her daughters and girlfriends by the hour. Amazing how you can spot a looker, an inexpensive, popular-pricer (our lowest was $39.95) or a woman in for one good coat, suit or dress to last for the next ten years or longer. Our prettiest model was also our sweetest, most likeable person—the divorced mother of two children she idolized. She was shortly to marry a major and leave Magnin's after 11 years.

My best friend on short acquaintance was a young Frenchwoman who had studied medicine in Paris until she fell in love. Now she's helping her doctor husband get in his last few years. They have a son and she is very content to surround herself with beautiful clothes in an exclusive shop six days a week. She intrigued me immediately when she told me about a long trip she and her husband made AROUND THE HORN before he went into the army. Her name, for future reference, is MARTINE MESSERT—daughter of a French surgeon and indefatigable traveler. She once traveled by rail with her father through the wilds of French Indo-China. I confided in her only that I was "outward bound."

The clerks got 15-minute "reliefs" in the p.m. and went to the basement for cokes, cigs and free coffee made by Joe, the one male darling of the place. Joe could show his grinning lobster perspiring face, blue shirt and suspenders in the French room's champagne beige splendor and everyone from the models down beamed on him. Then a young boy came to work in the stockroom and my cute stock girls were in a dither over Alfred, who was shy, trim and very gentlemanly, every little 5-foot-2-inches of him.

NOTES IN STOCKROOM: French pronunciation of our designers' names. I got a 20% discount on things I bought and I shopped overmuch.

SATURDAY, AUGUST 16, 1946—Last day. and guess what—my check was for a week and three days shop-girling: $10.27. Truly, it was a wealth of experience only. Just before leaving, however, some sale items on the back racks in the stockroom drew my eye. The buyer, MRS. HANNAH, came over and said I was to pick out anything I could use. I spied a Hattie Carnegie jacket in true petunia pink—coachman style with fit and flare over hips—from $175 to $24. MINE—label and all—should look divine. Everyone was so cordial, regretful and sweet over my leaving. I'll always have a warm spot for MAGNIN'S. If I ever write a yarn about the place I'll have to send them an order for an outfit or something.

Oh—added note of color—one of the saleswomen in shop talk with another burst out with this gem of a description: "So there I was with a face as red as a spanked baby's bottom."

Footnote: I am getting mild warnings on all sides about Shanghai. It's "no place" to be going, everyone implies with consoling smiles and tut-tut head shakes. I feel almost like an innocent Pauline going to a man's apartment because he promised her southern fried chicken for dinner.

SEPTEMBER 16, 1946—San Francisco still—China is still a direction, a strained look into the silver haze beyond the Pacific horizon viewed from the top of this mad city's hills. I feel now like a yawning SALMON hitting the rocks and currents and swimming UPSTREAM on a grimly determined course. Strikes have delayed my ship's sailing indefinitely and every five days I have had to jump from hotel to hotel, each time registering as two people to get in— and paying double to stay. *[Editor's Note: Hotel policy required double occupancy for a period of no more than five days.]*

Meanwhile Art Bremer arrived from Alaska. We strolled happily around Seattle, dining at the American Oyster House where Henri holds forth. We left on a train and came to San Fran, where I was so disappointed in the gay, glorious city I shall never like it. The Market Street is a NEON row of unprosperous joints: papers blowing underfoot, waffle shops, cheap jewelry, blazing movie marquees, schools of beauty culture, Negroes, Fosters cafeterias. I thought of Canal Street, Fifth Avenue, The Loop. Market Street is a poor alley in the vibrant bewilderment of thoroughfares into which streets are literally choked with people.

Art and I saw Cornelia Otis Skinner in "Lady Windermere's Fan"—lavish sets and for me, a sequence of remembrance of theater in New York. Dinner afterward at Solari's was spoiled by an expensive a la carte curb on things that read beautifully in one line of tenderness and tantalization punctuated at the end by an exclamation point of PRICE. Afterward to the Top of the Mark, but Art was the wrong man. While he pointed out hills and buildings I blacked him out and filled in the vision of another man who would lean across the tiny black-topped table, cover my hand and say, "Darling, darling." As Art droned on, "There's the Telephone Building and the Ferry Building and Telegraph Hill," I was swept with a sudden desire to get up and leave and not come back to the twinkling music-mooded places until I was with The MAN. Jim Robbins crossed my mind and I hummed under my breath thinking of him and wondering if we will meet in Shanghai. Art got into his romantic innings. "Cutie," he'd say now and then. Oh well, every woman's convenience and servitude needs a "John," and Art is that. Before he went back, Art met Mother and we dined at the EXPOSITION GROTTO at Fisherman's Wharf. Later I kissed him goodbye in front of the St. Francis Hotel as he got into an airline pick-up car to fly back to Seattle and Alaska.

Meanwhile, this town being so expensive, I went into Magnin's and got a job. Oddly enough I was hired for the identical selling spot I'd had in Seattle and was interviewed by the buyer. So I'm back to the Hattie Carnegies and Mangones and Traina Norells. It goes better because I'm more confident of my "Madame-you-look-beautiful" approach. There MUST be material in the whole experience.

I duck into the stockroom and call the President Steamship office every other day. The man said, "Lady, your guess is as good 's mine when the *Marine Lynx* will sail." I could have wept right on the spot. As I came out of the stockroom I was called into the French Room to two women—"Dresses—all the latest—EXCLUSIVES." The squat, doll-faced woman wore a camel's hair coat, felt hat, suede flat shoes. Her accent I did not immediately recognize as Russian. She was size 12, she said, but I brought her 16's. She grabbed at them or pushed them away with pudgy hands before I had a chance to "show" them with a smooth flow of "beautiful cut fabric—shoulders—buttons— etc." "Madame," I checked her firmly, "Please let me show them to you." She paused, regarding me for a moment, then decided on three dresses to try—not "Exclusives"—she had summoned but $39.95ers. In the dressing room she asked me "Are you an American?"

"Yes."

"You are lucky."

Then she said, "I just flew in from Shanghai!" I gasped. I forgot dresses and sizes and everything, scarcely able to contain myself.

"What was Shanghai like? Oh, tell me all about it. I have a friend going there."

My day was "solved" by the episode. To top it off, one of the other salesgirls—the big earring, ankle strap, French-heeled-shoetype, said, "Well, I know of a Residence Club. Split a cab with me and I'll show you."

So here I am at this place, which seems to have STORY possibilities: a residence chain of old but grand manor houses owned by a babbling Frenchman called "Papa" by everyone, and his wife, a stalking TERROR no one ever sees but whose face is felt in house rules, collecting bills, etc. Young men and gals stay in these houses, about four to a room, about $15 a week for two meals and room. My objective in taking it was: If the strike holds until Christmas I'll at least have a place to stay with no five-day bunny hop to a new place.

Well, now to my letters. I have a long list.

SEPTEMBER 18, 1946—Instead of sailing for Shanghai today, I bought a winter coat at Magnin's—green, double-breasted, $89.95 less 20% shopgirl's privilege. To add another day to my "copy" for the Magnin story: Recalling the Russian woman from Shanghai, I was surprised to see her and her husband in the store today. Madame was returning a hat she had bought to go with her dress. While she flitted upstairs to do the changing, I was all "My, my" admiration of Madame while her husband basked, talked on like Charles Boyer with a Russian accent. He lit a cigarette and went on telling me about Shanghai. Finally he drew out his wallet and handed me his card— engraved. He was JEAN GEORGE LIPSMAN, Gen. Mgr. CATHAY HOTELS LTD, SHANGHAI. In this country to buy hotel supplies, goblets, linens, etc. He and three other families had chartered a private plane (with an American pilot) to make the trip. They were returning after he had done his buying in New York. When he handed me his card, my smile was a vision to behold. "Ah, if the Broadway Mansions cannot house me," I thought, "Cathay Ltd will find room in its three inns, now that I am a friend." I was curious at the discrepancy in the two stories. The wife saying, "Citizenship, staying here, etc." Story telling. How will it be to meet her in China? Ha!

Another woman who looked very Jewish and as tho' she were wearing "good" clothes ten-years-back mode, asked me hesitatingly how much a suit we had in the window was. "My husband—we haf just come back from a long trip in Europe and Asia—saw it and said I was to come in and find out how much it is."

"Oh," I purred, "you mean the one with the white mink collar. It is about $356 plus tax. So lovely on."

She cringed at the price. Then we got into conversation about her trip. Of all places she loved Paris most, even if Paris had cost her $75 for a corset she could buy here for $15.

Another customer, with a figure like a hot dog bun but with the most twinkling eyes and rosy-glow cheeks, said, "What have you got that doesn't make me look like the dream girl I was 17 years ago?"

She laughed, then added wistfully, "You see, child, I've always bought my clothes here, only now I haven't as much money. Something with long sleeves and a high neck to cover me up. When I really had something to show, the styles were all high dog collars and high-button shoes, and now I have to cover up to hide veins and wrinkles. Oh, but I wasn't all muslin and serge. I made my blouses as peek-a-boo as possible."

I showed her a few dresses, and she ran on: "This is a special dress. You see, I have to triumph over a mistake I made 17 years ago. I'm having dinner with my ex-boss and his lovely young bride at the St. Francis Hotel tonight and I want to look marvelous but in a sly way so he'll never guess I had to run out and buy a new dress to accept his invitation. Oh yes, he is grand, not any younger 'n I am now, and I introduced him to his present wife when she used to come into his jewelry shop in Texas, years ago. Yes, that was one of the changing points of my life—to take a high-paying job traveling. It didn't last, but you know, you never go back once you leave a place. You'll think I'm crazy telling you all this. Well, I hadn't seen George in years when I ran into him at the Roosevelt Hotel in New Orleans. He told me then he was on his honeymoon. I didn't blame him. He wanted someone young and pretty around. She has everything, of course. Sweet girl. Really she is."

Another woman—I typed her as a regular army colonel's wife who came up with her warrior from warrant officer—a nut—she wanted a MANGONE—no, wouldn't look at anything else. "He's the master of them all, darling," she stated. "Never saw anyone else who could make ladies out of frumps simply by putting a suit or a coat on them." She fingered critically the suits I brought out for her selection. "No—no—my God, no—they're nice little suits but not something to wear for the next ten years. I always say when a gal's clothing budget is limited, she should spend twice as much money on everything she buys." She was terrific. She CONVINCED me to the point where I went back in the stockroom and fingered the MANGONES, weighing in my mind whether I needed one or not.

SEPTEMBER 22, 1946—SAN FRANCISCO—Just for the record, I have just returned from a marvelous weekend at the BLINNS. First, Eddie's sister, Genevieve Blinn (my step-grand aunt) intrigued me for story material. She gave me two pictures of herself —story starters. And in hasty conversation she gave me some beauty hints of the golden era: To keep from getting lines in the face give your skin a HONEY facial. Bee's honey, especially under the eyes, prevents wrinkles. For her golden-red hair she used a champagne rinse—the bubbles in the latter were believed to leave sparkle in the HAIR—and occasionally castor oil worn in an overnight dose. Shampooed the next day. What did she do for split ends? Cut them off. Oh, yes—and always stand or sit under the light.

Jennie was the toast of San Francisco. She married a lumber king, but her rigid purity and his love of wine, women and song led their marriage to divorce after one son had been born. The son was a solid citizen, strongly dominated by his mother but a forthright, intelligent, good fellow and simple underneath.

While preparing dinner and later between interruptions when Lou or Jennie walked into the room, Maizie told me the most amazing story. Through a friend she heard of a brilliant fortuneteller who does a rushing business. Maizie got an appointment and went to see her. The woman greeted her with "I'm afraid what I have to tell you will be a great shock. I see death and cupid hand in hand, coming within seven months, to completely change your life."

Maizie was gasping. The woman went on to say that a man was to come to her house on the occasion of the death, and he would be the one. His mother was to give Maizie a piece of heirloom jewelry after their meeting and that was to be the signal of her approval. The marriage would be Maizie's only wedding of the heart. The seven months will be up next month, and Maizie has been under a considerable nervous strain. Unconsciously convinced of what is coming, she is building up her strength, trying to put on weight, buying new clothes with (despite qualms of conscious) a trousseau in mind. I shall be inordinately curious to know how this turns out. Maizie gave me two evening gowns: a black crepe studded with nine stones and a red chiffon dinner dress. Genevieve, not to be outdone, gave me a green silk satin gown. All need alterations but are lovely. Believe my ship may sail very soon.

VERY LATE—SEPTEMBER 24, 1946—Someday I must write a story about a poor writer who, fearing his landlord will cause trouble over the rent, decided to flatter him by telling him he will write a long story about him and make him famous. The landlord is a Frenchman, hard with the franc, lavish with the français! Tell the story of his life to a young writer—a young artist—give some delight to the world thru the printed word. But of course, he is honored. The writer settles down. Never has the landlord treated him with such flare, such hospitality. Then the landlord proceeds to tell the most charming, human tale. The writer is moved to self-abasement that under sordid pretense he came to hear such a tale over wine and toast and wonderful cheese cut in moist strips like the milkmaid's fingers. The writer resolves to really write the story and of course, he sells it.

Something like that happened to me tonight. I knew that when I would leave my guest house without two weeks' notice after paying in advance, there would be a fuss and no refund. To soften the blow, I decided to write a story about PAPA PIERRE who runs the guest house chain where I am staying. CHATEAU BLEU, he calls it. (Why blue? "Well, blue, it is charming, soothing, cozy after the madhouse of downtown—15 minutes from the city, like 15 miles in atmosphere.") I was dead tired, mind miles away on the hurry-scurry of my sailing or not sailing in a few days. But I thought I'd better talk to him, maybe get material for a fiction piece to write en route. Papa was delighted, charmed, at my service. I called later and found him seated in a great room—old elegance—books—screens about—a desk—little coffee table. Papa, in a dark blue dressing gown, was sitting in reverence listening to the opera on the radio. Madame BERTHE BARET (his wife) was playing a violin in the orchestra at the San Francisco Opera House. Then the story poured out in self-conscious largess of words, philosophy, wit, shoulder shrugs, whimsy. I sat entranced, taking the following notes for story purposes.

One of Papa's houses was purchased for very little when the small man's irresistible, ingratiating charm had given him the family heirloom—a gold key to the front door with the family's initials engraved on the clasp that held it. Asking about the men and women who stayed at the Chateau, Papa told of a sweet blonde young girl he had noticed coming and going her quiet way. "What nationality are you?" he asked one evening by way of making conversation. "I'm a lassie," she smiled. "Oh, you shall be my little lassie from now on." Meanwhile, Papa began to look around for the right man for his lassie—a student dentist going to Stanford who loved music and played on Papa's old piano. "I have found just the girl for you," Papa announced one night as the young man was playing. "Oh, no—no," the boy protested, "I am a student—have a long way ahead—I am shy," etc. Papa went to his lassie and said, "Here, child, you sit tonight in this big chair and curl your little legs under you and listen to his music." They were married six months later.

Another—a young girl born in Tahiti of Scotch and native origin—came here and made hats, working in the millinery wholesale building on Market Street. Papa was ailing at the time and his doctor became his good friend; the doctor was a shy, inhibited man. The girl, with her exotic background, also was inhibited. Papa had them meet at dinner, at the Chateau and asked the doctor to see her home. Invited them both again, and the same thing happened. Then he worked on each individually. Told the doctor other young men at the Chateau had asked to be introduced ("God forgive me how I lied"); urged him to speak up and help the girl understand she was a woman to be loved and admired and she would not be so timid. Papa's instinct for matchmaking was a throwback of his race, from generations of fathers marrying off daughters. Anyway, the two got together, were married, have a child and are forever grateful to Papa for bringing them together.

We had gotten that far with the storytelling when the door burst open and the clatter of French heels, a whiff of perfume, a flurry of noises issued as the truly jolie et charmant Madame entered the room. She, the violinist, wore a chic coat of pale champagne wool, deep fur cuffs of silver fox—black evening skirt and soft white silk blouse—no hat. She whirled in, all full of the opera, gowns, etc. How so-and-so sang tonight, would we hear her violin, etc. Wouldn't we like coffee? Whirled around, put out her loveliest dishes—English teacups—made toast, burning every slice for the zest of her conversation—cheese and toast. Then we sat down to laugh and talk—and laugh—viva the French! Madame told of her recent flight home to Paris—of the roses Papa had ordered to be delivered on her arrival in Paree, etc. At 1 a.m. I went home through the fog as through moonlight. Papa had outdone me. They had both outcharmed me.

Note: Papa tells me the house originally belonged to a niece of the Rothschilds who married a lumber king years ago. The marriage had ended in divorce and the house lived a long legal history before coming to Pierre.

SLOW BOAT TO CHINA

*China—Shanghai
1946–1947*

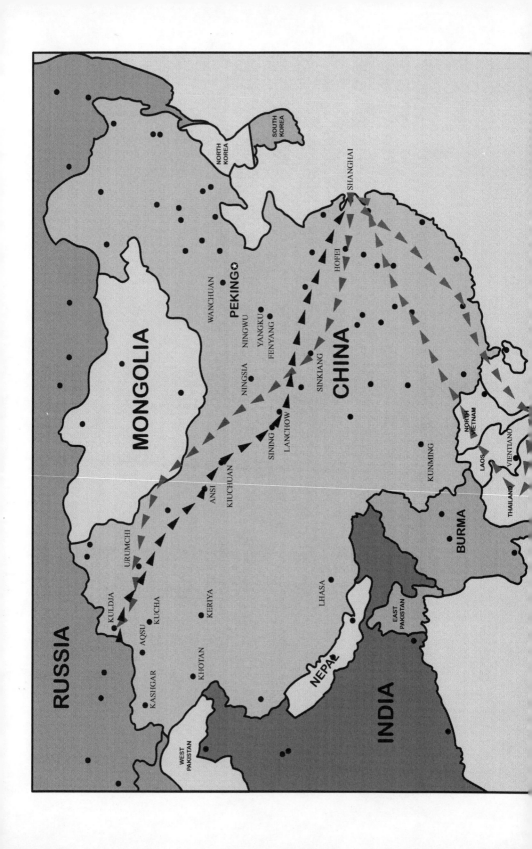

1946

The *Marine Lynx*, former Navy transport

SEPTEMBER 29, 1946—MAIDEN VOYAGE—The ship glides through the starlit night down a dark and glistening aisle of blue-white sparkling foam—the President Lines' *MARINE LYNX* en route to Shanghai. A thousand souls aboard, 408 of them missionaries who sang hymns on the dock before we left. Maizie and Genevieve BLINN saw me off. Hot day—taxis—cars—men in shirt sleeves. Cabin Class was deluxe by comparison, but the stateroom was like the galley crew's quarters—for 6! And what a 6 we are. A very beautiful and ultra chic young woman, MARIAN GRAY, and her two children: one button-nosed boy and a little girl about 10 who showed me a toe she'd recently had an operation on. Sleeping on the bunk below the little boy is a slim, shy creature—a Chinese NUN. In the midst of our utter confusion of luggage and cluttering she had two tiny suitcases. She lies sleeping as I crouch here writing. A small, sweet young face sunken in a sheaf of long soft hair. Beside her bed a pair of black silken Chinese slippers, the heels crunched down from habitual stepping into them as though they were toe slippers. The little boy was utterly bewitched by her habit—especially her hat, which was a sort of small bowler with a long sheer scarf down the back. She also carries a fat red-edged bible.

The woman was a source of curiosity to the passenger over me, wife of a President Line official—Jewish—with lavish hat boxes, a wilted orchid, Whitman sampler, a movie magazine. "My mother was down to see me off—y' know—When she saw the NUN she sez 'Well, this trip'll be an eye opener—always did wanna know what went on under those skirts and hoods.'"

The dining room is a mess hall strictly—food, very poor—howling babies—Chinese—Filipinos—but when the ship finally sailed at 6 p.m., I rushed out on deck and watched the Frisco skyline turn a pink misty fog—under a glistening moon in a gray-blue sky. Oh, that was really something. For myself I have no feeling of actually being on a ship going to CHINA. I think the trip will be INTERESTING, though.

Still outward bound a week later. I should be a master of WORD POWER now. So much of LIFE is here on this ship. I feel my inability to TELL it—To TRANSPOSE it to others. To hold the richness of the EXPERIENCE for more than my own personal RECEPTION. Ah, would that I were a great craftsman since great material has been offered me.

The first impression of a week's travel is that the discomfort and seeming steerage accommodations seem quite OK, and the PEOPLE absorb me to the point of exhaustion. People are VOLUBLE before an audience to tell their life's story. Some of them I want to recount here for my "material" record: The little nun I mentioned has impressed me most. Just a few minutes ago I sat on the edge of a suitcase in our room and talked to her. RESPONSIVE instantly and ardently. Her name: Sister Candida, after one of the first Chinese converts and undeclared saints. This lovely, sweet person sat crouched on the edge of her neat bunk with fawn's eyes and small hands graceful as a ballerina's. Observation note: The Chinese are extremely EXPRESSIVE and emotional, not dead-panned and immobile as I had imagined. Sister was the second daughter of a Buddhist tea merchant. The family was prosperous and she was sent to a Catholic convent to be educated, not for the religious aspect but because even with the Chinese, a convent's reputation for endowing its students with social culture and fastidious womanhood drew their confidence in sending their daughters. Another sister went with her but she had no interest in becoming a convert. When moved by her inner conviction, the little sister went to her father for permission to become a Catholic. He refused. Without a word she withdrew and obeyed, but her exterior unhappiness finally touched his heart. "Second sister," as he called her, "you are not happy. Do as you wish, only do not become a nun." The sister readily agreed, for she had no intention of taking the religious vows. She later became a social service nun to work out in the world with young people and others. Her father? Her sweet eyes filled quickly with tears. "He is in heaven," she gasped. "I am sorry not to have seen him again to explain and tell him why this must be my life's duty." Duty is the key word of her conversation, but not in the reluctant sense of something that MUST be done. America was a difficult experience for her because for the first time she was aware of being not only a FOREIGNER, but a Chinese among Americans. Her resentment she told me about with flashes of temper equal to a

Parisian. When she learned I was going to China to write, she begged me not to judge China from what I see in Shanghai or by the officials and others I meet. "Go to Peiping," *[Editor's Note: now Beijing]* she begged. "It still retains the culture and grace that is the real China."

Another story: RUTH KUNKLE—about 40, very chic, wears exquisite Chinese jewelry, slim legs—a cosmopolite in every sense. Why was she going back to Peiping after all the war destruction, prices, etc.? Frankly, to make some money—after all, when you get a few gray hairs jobs aren't easy to find in the States. All they want is YOUTH, so she felt secure in going back to what she knew and where she was known. Her background: daughter of a doctor, she is a medical technician of some sort and was attached to the Rockefeller Foundation. Ruth explained, "I loved PEIPING because only there could I, a working girl, afford a home with a flower court—servants—and only there could I assume a social status I would never have had in the States." She said she had given a talk to a women's club somewhere in the East and when she completed her description of life in a Jap internment camp, the hostess said the speaker would be glad to answer any questions. She did, but there was one woman in a silly little hat who waited until afterward to ask her question.

"I didn't want to ask you before the others," she gushed, "but my dear, I was dying to ask: were you RAPED?"

Mrs. K was equal to her. "No, I wasn't. But if I had been, I'd have remembered what Confucius said: 'When rape is inevitable, relax and enjoy it.'" The woman's mouth fell open and she hurried off.

Then there was a little gentleman about, like a character out of a play starring Robert Donat. The little man was obviously a missionary, but his black homburg hat, his urban mannerisms and liveliness belied the usual primness of his colleagues. He turned out to be the REV. DR. DUNCAN MACLEOD, a 75-year-old Scottish-born Presbyterian sent to Formosa in 1907 by the United Church of Canada. He had been on the island under the Jap regime until just before Pearl Harbor. He took his Canadian bride with him, and she bore five children in Formosa, which in its way was a paradise to live in, abundant with fruits, flowers, every living convenience. Greatest interest—the 150,000 aborigines who live in the mountains and are headhunters. The Japs tried to control them by herding the savages into carefully policed villages. First difficulty—the attempts to convert them to Buddhism. The priests could not resist the women, and the men would avenge their maidens by beheading all the Japs they would lay their hands on.

The headhunters are not cannibalistic but are simple people living in their beautiful mountains, Dr. MacLeod maintains. He feels a fatherly affection for them and wishes to help them. A spinster daughter is to join him later and help re-establish the mission. "Let me tell you," the earnest little Scotsman peered over his spray-dimmed glasses at me, "my head hunters are far more moral than a lot of whites." He did admit, however, that they permitted the old and helpless to die, and the women practiced some crude form of birth control. "How, I don't know," he remarked, his eyes intent on the heaving Pacific. "Of course, I never asked them."

Products of Formosa—under the Japs: opium, camphor (75% of the world's supply), salt, tobacco, timber (mahogany), liquor, manufactured goods, sake, tea and rice. Mandarin language spoken. Under the Chinese now in control of Formosa. MacLeod is not sure of his beloved island's future. "Corrupt politicians," he muttered.

A few days out, I learned we had a stowaway aboard. The first officer gave me permission to interview him. Down to the clean, freshly painted brig I went to meet a pale Romanian peasant: GEORGE DAMEAN, a sailor who wanted desperately to join the U.S. Navy. His eyes were pale blue, his features cloddish, but his manner quite appealing and civil. He was immaculately clean, had the run of the deck, but shied away from people because he was so immersed in his own misery. George was born in 1912 in a small village. At an early age he went to sea and worked on freighters on the Black Sea. Later, returning home, he served a year in the Romanian Army. In 1936 he left, fearing a great uprising ahead. From then on he worked on German and Swedish ships going to Egypt, Java and China. Finally beached in Shanghai—struggled for existence during the occupation, always hoping to become an American citizen. He will be turned over to immigration officials in Shanghai. I pitied him, recalling Paul Jorgensen's efforts during the war.

Next day—the plot grows. Last night in the dining room I met a young Spanish girl with skin the color of sherry wine and hair a raven cascade about her sweet and passionate face. She is ANGELA LOBATO of Long Beach, en route to Shanghai to marry a flier in the CNAC airline, one GERALD R. SHRAWDER of Fargo, North Dakota. We sat on the lee side of the deck and in the half light I watched her face as she told me her brief love story. "He is absolutely perfect," she said, "all I've ever wanted in a man—he just hasn't any faults—I've looked for them. We have everything in common, even eat the same food!" She was a nurse and said after the first date with Gerry, he sent her American Beauty roses with a card— "To a beautiful FRIENDSHIP"—and she was taken aback at the "FRIENDSHIP" note. I will see the follow-up of her romance and hope to do a magazine article on it.

My stowaway takes on a plot, too. He walks the deck like a caged animal, looking at no one except eyeing me occasionally. When he caught me alone he stepped up eagerly to talk. He hopes to get to Canada and somehow work his way into the U.S. I warned him against pulling any sneaky tricks. My surface pity moved him to boldness: "Perhaps I can see you in Shanghai?" I was tactful. Today he told me he went to the ship's entertainment last night and though he spoke to no one, he enjoyed it. (He is particularly ashamed that any of the young ladies aboard should know him to be an outcast—a prisoner.)

I dread our arrival in Shanghai. The feeling of orphan-ism both as to job and a place in the newspaper world makes me diffident of others. So sure, so "set," so prepared for someone to meet them.

To add to my consternation, two lovely women in an effort to be of assistance said they would introduce me to the wife of a Chicago newspaper correspondent in Shanghai—a Mrs. DOWLING. In delighted anticipation I put on a clean blouse, my Carnegie jacket and went to meet her. I was taken aback—a cow-eyed slut greeted my introduction without enthusiasm. I had noticed her before and thought her a "lady known as Lou." Egad, what AM I getting into?

It has been my luck whenever there's a moon to step to the railing and be accosted by some man of God who props beside me on hairy arms and lets loose Ideals: Love of Fellow Men—the great clean life. To top it off, all of them are CONSCIENTIOUS OBJECTORS going to China for a year with UNRRA to teach the Chinese to operate tractors. This is part of their non-military service since they refused to be doughboys. One struck me as a MAN, though I am skeptical of all this pious pacifism. He is DARWIN SOLOMON, 27, of SUNDANCE, WYOMING. Methodist, lean, clean-cut face. If he were a woman he would be a prim-lipped frump, but male sex, he looks the part of the young idealist, Scout leader, but withal a masculinity and air of strength that is appealing. He intends to devote his life to China, according to *TIME* magazine report. The boys had to fill out questionnaires set to discourage them. Such questions as these: "Are you annoyed by flies, bedbugs, human pests? Do you worship the flush toilet? If you can't stand smells you will be wearing a clothespin on your nose from the day you land in China. It stinks, but so do you to the Chinese!"

OCTOBER 11, 1946—I grow increasingly uneasy as fellow passengers say "Three more days." This morning I had to confer and confide with myself. Why was I so internally frightened (as I really am) over the arrival in Shanghai—that I know no one—that I have no job—that I know not where I will be staying—blank! Someday I will look back and recall this in self-condolence, I suppose. I have more to record, so will become more journalist than self-confessor.

Last night was October 10, a special anniversary of the Republic for the Chinese. At 10 a.m. a cannon was fired. Then the flag was raised to an ovation of CAMERAS in the hands of Chinese on board. A Chinese professor made a speech about a brave new future, fraught with many difficulties. Then the Captain stepped up to speak, his lobster-red face wreathed in the conventional smiles. Suddenly a jovial, chubby-jawed Chinese rushed up, pushed the Captain good-naturedly to one side and excused himself to the grinning assembly. He was to introduce the Captain first. When he finished, there was great applause and the Captain again stepped forward, said a few words and the heavens opened up, rushed themselves of a torrent of rain, sending babies, Chinese, missionaries, and sundry tumbling over one another.

That night in a jammed below-decks dining room a Chinese program was presented and the Chinese anthem was sung, as well as a screeching, quaking Chinese opera. I enjoyed watching the Chinese, their faces brown-gold, teeth large and very white, eyes black half-moons behind their rimless glasses. Their shoulders narrow, their arms somehow awkwardly short and always clasped in front of them. China's sons, I thought, facing what? For all this ardent devotion to studies for the modernization of China, how much heartbreak, patience and disillusionment lies ahead.

Just talking to a woman en route to Shanghai to join her husband, an ex-Naval GI, who bid his wife and son to China on this basis: "War isn't too far off, and when it comes the government will send you two home and I'll re-enter the Navy here." War—War—War— when we've just finished one.

To return to my journal: I met a most beautiful European woman, so typical of Milady the Countess one reads about in short stories by authors with unpronounceable names. Her name is Mrs. G. L. VICTORIA MOWATT (address Rue Cardinal Mercier, 229, Apt. E,

Third Floor, Grosvenor Garden), wife of a General Electric agent. She has eyes of her family of origin, Romanian, and the French features and accents—shoulder shrugging of her French mother. When she was very young she was sent to school in Paris. Here she met Mr. George MOWATT, who was young too, sent abroad by General Electric. Shortly after their first courtship he was sent to Poland—letters, flowers, telegrams—finally they were married in Romania, she wearing pink—honeymoon in Budapest. Then began her life. Glamorous and idle and lonely. Travel where her husband's business took them. He would be off in the daytime and she would be left with her hotel life. All over, meeting "first-class people" or "high-class people" as she referred to them, but never for more than a passing acquaintance. Finally home to America and to Boston to meet the husband's American family. They greeted the foreign wife cordially but the mother implied it was to be regretted her son had not married an American. Then to Rio for six years—and to China. A short stay of two months before the year when her husband was interned but she, a Romanian subject, was free. Her struggles and perils in the Cathay Mansions hotel (the very best), and finally back to America. To the family, and later Chicago where she got her own house and was so happy to settle down at last. But not for long. The Company sends her husband back to Shanghai, but she was the setting for a story—the lonely hotel wife, the husband seems devoted to her but more in the way of one who humors a child or an elderly mother. She seldom stirred from her stateroom (shared with five others) and the husband had to visit her there in the morning. She would occasionally interrupt him as he explained some phase of Shanghai. He would turn in annoyance and cut her short and she would murmur submissively, "All right, darling." I noticed on the address she wrote for me she misspelled telephone (telefon) and once she remarked her husband wanted her to speak proper English.

The other story of NATASHA—blonde, very emotional, beautiful in a voluptuous way, she became ill, underwent operations which were blunderously performed and she ended up BLIND—was flown to Philadelphia from Shanghai in six days. Doctors there refused to operate, offering treatment, half-reassuring promises. I sympathized with her. Learned she had been a model in Shanghai and later had her own shop. The rest of the story is vague. But what struck me keenly was not so much her misery at being blind as the loss one of her great beauties: her EYES. "My eyes were so beautiful," she moaned, "brown by day and so black and shining at night—but now—?" Sorrowful shrugs.

[*Editor's Note: Pegge wrote the following letter to her parents while she was on her way to China.*]

OCTOBER 1, 1946—OUTWARD BOUND

Dearest Mother and Dad,

Have just received your GRAND wire after getting Harriet's this morning. Boy, it was wonderful to be out in the middle of the Pacific and have "Mummie and Daddy" pop up in writing. Don't know where to begin telling of the bon voyage.

Sunday morning, Gen, Lou and my aide de camp, Maizie, drove us to the house and loaded me and the suitcases and typewriter aboard. It was a clear, blue-sky, hot day. I wore a new black sheer crepe dress I got at Magnins and the Hattie Carnegie jacket. Down to the ship, cars and taxis, crates labeled Shanghai... and see-offers in DROVES. Lou drove the car down to the end of the ramp. Cabin class, I learned, was FIRST CLASS. We had our own gangway. While Maizie and Gen watched my bags, I went aboard to find my cabin. I walked into a little 2 by 4 with 3 bunks in two tiers, all starchy clean and fresh, walls painted white, two portholes. And a very attractive young girl came in (Linda Darnell type) with two children. She is the wife of a Shanghai importer and was returning to live there since the war. The kids were yammie at first but the little boy is so cute no one minds him. He is up top over the sweetest and prettiest Chinese nun you ever saw. "You wear a funny hat," the wee one pops out, etc. Over me is the wife of one of the Pres. Line officials in Shanghai, young and very nice. She had a load of magazines, among them *LOOK*, and I saw the picture. Too much mouth and of course I didn't write the quote, but it was okay.

Well, after hanging up my coat and looking around, I went back to the dock to join Maizie and Gen, blazing hot. Lou had to go uptown on business and was to pick the ladies up after the ship sailed. We decided to stroll and see if we could find a place for a spot of tea. Ended up at the Southern Pacific depot having lunch. I kept saying to Gen and Maizie, "I still have no feeling that China's the next stop. Have no SENSATION of getting aboard the liner and tally-ho." Back to the ship about 3:30. Decks lined with the missionaries, grimy hats, no makeup, gardenia corsages, cameras. Below on the wharf, all Harrisburg-type housewives and Rev.'s Press boys and photographers. As the last stragglers went up the gangway, Gen, like Eddie, began to get nervous. "You'd better go, child," etc. She was all prayers and "Remember the holy water if you are in danger," etc. Maizie gave me a tight hug and a really SWELL few last words. What a gal she is! Up the gangway. Lost in the jostle and shove of Chinese students and missionaries. Up to the rail. Gen and Maizie, melting in the sun, stood there for an hour. Ship still loading. Finally, they blew a last kiss and went as it was nearly 5 p.m. and there was no certainty when we would get away.

Boy, after they left and there was no one down there to wave to, I began to think: On your own, Parker. I was TERRIBLY, AWFULLY SORRY you both weren't there. We might have arranged to have you come aboard and you could have met some of the people. There are many Jesuits and nuns here too. In fact, this morning the Shanghai wife came back from breakfast shaking her head: "Well, I've seen everything. Two of the Jesuits at my table were sitting there humming that song, "Doin' What Comes Natcherly." They say mass every morning at 6, I believe on the top deck.

They announced dinner about 5:30 so I went inside. Was just finishing up when the people still at the railing got all excited. We were pulling out. I could see streamers of paper ribbon in the sun. Ran out. Sunset. The sky was aglow with rosy-silver fog, but the skyline as we went out was BREATHTAKING. The missionaries burst into hymns. Onward Christian soll-l-jers. Sinners in the crowd exchanged dry glances. The Chinese students said nothing but gazed hard at the steeples and spires and shapes of Frisco standing out in navy-blue relief against the pink-and-gold wash of the sky. Lights came on. The arch of the bridge twinkled through the gathering fog. The ship's whistles blared and growled and honked deafeningly. We sailed past other ships riding at anchor. We knifed thru the gray-blue water out to sea, past the lighthouse, past the blinking shore lights. The fog muffled us in and the whistles became explosive. About an hour out from shore the ship stopped and the pilot crawled over the side, boarded a small inflated rescue craft and rowed through a dim spotlight to a blurred fog-shrouded launch which was to take him back to the harbor.

Then, Chin-ho… outward we went into the night blindness of fog. The decks began to heave. I ran to my room to change into slacks. Strolled the decks until the wind drove me below. Passengers began eyeing one another, the main number being classified as either missionaries or teachers. Standing in line for dining room seatings, I met a bunch of young wise guys, tractor experts no less. Very collegiate, red-checked shirts, etc. They heard of this UNRRA deal which would give them a year's free jaunt in China so they all signed up, took a three-week course in running tractors and were hired. Another girl had a tiny spaniel puppy aboard. She was to work in the Embassy in Shanghai. Another young couple were going out to join the girls' parents. Everyone intrigued over the "correspondent." After arranging my seating I went up on deck before turning in. Ahh. The fog had lifted. The night was balmy and the stars were low and bright. One of the tractor boys followed me but he was a little on the chubby side and quite a nitwit to boot. I couldn't shake him so went below and to bed.

The first morning was clear and blue-blue, the sky and the sea. Breakfast wasn't bad, though the meals on the ship are like, oh, Foster's cafeterias. They had to buy food for the trip so quickly they had to take what was available and quick. There are OVER A THOUSAND of us jammed on this ship and it's hard to prepare and serve any delicacies for such a mob. We've had meat, though, and it's been good quality.

I saw my name on the mail and package list and went to claim a gorgeous basket from Maizie and Gen, all done up like the Hicks baskets—grapes, peaches, oranges, etc. and underneath, a box of soap, jar of nuts, cookies, etc. and a darling note. The mail was from them too, courage, never fear, new experience, etc. Maizie even included a recipe for making cold cream should I run out over there. I tell you, if I were Maizie's daughter she couldn't have thought of more things to do and give me. The fruit was marvelous, though we get oranges and apples at the dinner table.

At breakfast there was a note that my seating was to be changed to the purser's table. I also got a carbon copy of a letter that I was to be looked after, etc. I turned the traveler's checks and my jewelry over to the purser in a sealed envelope. Most of the time in between I have walked the deck, talked to the passengers. Oh yes, before I sailed, Maizie got the address and cost of a cable to the INS man in Shanghai, so I hope he'll be there to meet me. I never could catch the INS man in San Francisco in person and he seemed cordial enough over the phone, said to use INS whenever I needed it. The purser said I could use this desk and typewriter so I think I'll do that article on myself for the *American* magazine. (Boy, are we ever rolling now; haven't been ill, though, or even uneasy.) I'll write more later.

Oh yes, everyone at Magnins was very nice and the girl who found me the place to live gave me a box of Blum's candy.

As for the Fr. Landlor: The "adventure" got him—did I tell you on the phone—champagne which I brought with me (no way to chill and pop on the wharf) flashlight, tuna fish, powdered coffee.

October 11th—Want to close this note and mail it on the ship. The meals have improved to the delicious stage, so that's a feature. The moon and sun have lent travelogue enchantment. I have an UNRRA beau (who doesn't drink or smoke and who is a staunch Methodist). I have met SUCH people—brilliant, world traveled, prisoners of war, a white Russian glamour gal, Natasha, the wife of a *Chicago Sun* correspondent going to join her hubby at the Broadway Mansions. She knew Howard Denby very well, is a young glamour gal type. The life stories I have heard will keep me in material for the rest of my days. Several former residents of Shanghai have offered their assistance in landing, etc., so the strangeness is alleviated. Actually, the trip has been worth everything, just for the sea and the people. Met the wife of the General Electric manager for China and she seems to like me. Has invited me to tea, etc. The husband reminds me of Mr. Wallace, only younger—good contact. The Chinese nun comes from a very aristocratic family and she has offered her assistance in getting to know the Chinese. The Chinese students on board (mostly Yale, Harvard and Columbia men) are wonderful. We even have a political refugee stowaway on board—a Romanian. I interviewed him, of course. The Chinese Republic's "Day" was ceremoniously observed, speeches, the flag raised, dinner, and a Chinese Opera—tea and cakes.

Weather's been very warm. Deck chairs are aplenty too, despite what the instruction sheet said.

Went to mass this morn and saw the sun rise. The ocean is so BLUE out here. Wonder where you are by this time. Hope you're not worrying about me. (All the passengers raving about my COMPLEXION so I guess I'm holding up okay.) Have discovered a little kitchen below decks and make myself tea at odd hours. Lots of fresh fruit on dinner table. Have the article on my Alaska ventures almost finished. Everyone on board had read my *Reader's Digest* article. Well, bon voyage for now, my two loved ones. Must "dress" for dinner.

Saturday, October 12th—Am really getting excited now. Two more days and China. Will write soon as possible. All my love across the ocean. Pegge Mei-ling.

SUNDAY, OCTOBER 13, 1946—What a day of days. I was sitting on the sun deck this a.m., reading *Reader's Digest*, while a dreamy-eyed Russian Jew from Shanghai sat nearby. A deck steward passed by and handed him the ship's newspaper. He read the first item about the Catholic Archbishop in Yugoslavia being condemned to death for betraying his country (TITO Government charge). The Jew read it, nodded his head and said "Good," then glanced at me, whom he knew to be a Catholic. "Oh, pardon me." He got up and left and I sat thinking of all the religions on the ship. Suddenly I had an idea. Religion on the high seas. God takes to the bounding main. I went the rounds of the deck all day interviewing missionaries and sinners, all hand-picked.

The revelations I heard were amazing. The sinners especially interested me because they gave such deferential replies to those who had so carefully derided them in witty social groups. I was so absorbed in their replies to my questions that the green ramparts of JAPAN rising out of the blue Pacific didn't distract me. But a personal experience has distracted me even more. A vicarious romance—casting a very tall, blond, charming and intelligent hero and a young college professor in the leading roles. They met on deck the first night out, talking in the half-light of fog and blurred moonlight, so that the hero couldn't see the girl's face but was enchanted at her voice. They discoursed on subjects they had both taught—English, Greek, Latin—the girl was amazed at the coincidence. They talked on. Both going to China for the first time, etc. Both had a feeling of "Gosh—I'm glad YOU'LL be on board for this long trip." First friendship made. Then, with belated necessity, the hero said he was a Jesuit priest. The girl was stunned into embarrassed silence for a moment. Then she ended the charming moment abruptly and went to her emergency hatch where she is quartered with 50 million others. The Jesuit, oversensitive and sensing the strangeness of the experience on a now full-moon-drenched deck, felt perhaps an irresistible PANG of his young male and so human nature. His curiosity was greatly roused to see his young lady and talk to her again. One day he recognized the VOICE, turned to see only the back of a head, a curly dark head and a tall sturdy figure. Someone called her Audrey and he learned her name later. Saw her on deck alone. Walked up and down, then approached. She was very cool—hurt. He took his leave. One night at dinner the head dining room steward invited the priest to his room to hear a steward boy play a guitar. Scotch was served with the music; the priest was shocked to see his lovely Audrey seated in the stateroom, lounging, very much at home. (The chief steward is an unctuous Portuguese.) On the last day of the trip, the priest confided his intense desire to talk to her one last time. The night was stormy, windy but moonlit. I observed the priest wearing a blue collegiate sweater, shirt open at the throat. He was facing the windward deck because "the good nuns" were wrapped in their chairs on the opposite deck. Truant moment—irresistible— the man dominating. He asked me if I would help locate Audrey. Half uneasy at doing the devil's work but absorbed in the byplay of psychology, I went after Audrey—couldn't find her. But this same priest had agreed to read the BOOK to a lovely Spanish bride-elect on board who has been carrying on mild flirtations with susceptible men on board. I wondered at putting the bug in his ear.

Also, the stowaway reveals more character: he asked me to appeal to the first mate to let him go in Shanghai and not turn him over. Acting partly from fear of future annoyance in Shanghai, I cut him off coldly, with qualms of being a Good Samaritan, which I took to the Jesuit hero. "Oh no, Pegge, you have no conscience to examine. He has broken the law of the sea as a stowaway. He is no innocent victim" etc.

A day or so later, I talked to a young man, a very earnest, Southern-accent-rolling Methodist youth leader. I pointed out the stowaway, and he accosted the poor devil on deck, had a talk with him, felt sorry, and offered him $2 as an acid test. The stowaway refused to take it. The missionary persisted, "I'm only loaning it. You don't owe it to me but to the next guy who comes along and is worse off than you. And he's to repay you by loaning money to the next unfortunate." The stowaway hesitated, then took the $2. "I'm going to take up a collection among my bunk mates," the young Southerner went on, "to ask that he at least has a decent pair of shoes and a little money to start out on." I cautioned him, "The fellow's working a racket. The purser told me droves of them work the stowaway deal. Free meals and sympathy purses raised," etc.

"Who doesn't have a racket?" the missionary went on. "I know all about them. I've investigated all the secrets of panhandling by doing it myself in old clothes. I've slept in flop houses—even went into a jail one night and asked for a bed. I've talked to tramps, taken drinks in the street. Jesus Christ said everyone is our brother, not just the nice people or my classmates at Yale" etc. I leaned back in my steamer chair pondering with stirred emotion the difference between the Jesuit (on two counts) and this drawlin' Methodist.

To continue the plot: Father Ryan waited until midnight for his "mysterious lady" as he had christened her in his diary before learning Audrey's name. She was with the second officer who was sporting khaki shorts (in the mild heat) and long, straight white legs fuzzed with curly hair. At breakfast I was the diplomat in this unique illicit love. Audrey said she was out until three somewhere but was vague on details. We were in the middle of our soft-boiled eggs when a voice intruded between our two heads: "Audrey, may I see you after breakfast?" Fr. Ryan, his face very red and sunburned, his sport shirt immaculately white. Both Audrey and I were embarrassed and jittery. I feared she would be on the defensive and shut out any attempt at understanding. She put on fresh lipstick before going on deck.

Later that morning I saw Fr. Ryan chatting properly with a group of pale-faced, shivering nuns—prim, remote ladies with black hairs above the corners of their beige-colored lips. The Jesuit came early to chat privately with his emissary: Me. "How was the rendezvous with Audrey?" I asked. "Oh, she was quite understanding but in a reserved sort of way." We chatted on—more and more he revealed himself. We practically agreed openly that he had fallen in love! "You must have some lonely moments," I observed feelingly. He looked out over the sea. "Brother!" he exclaimed with colloquial vehemence. "You have no idea—sometimes it takes days and weeks to become reconciled." He paused then, as though appreciating the opportunity to confide in someone. "I find the weakness in myself of liking people and enjoying women's company. In fact, I volunteered for this China project to get away from entanglements in the States, I thought, devoting myself to the Chinese. Oh, you can't imagine what young college girls are like—they call you up—get you alone—come to confession, and the things they say." We discussed his admitted infatuation for Audrey. He wanted to give her his chair at the Captain's table and he would have gone to eat in the hold. How the mental torture he has been through he has offered up for her benefit. "Oh, well—I may meet her someday in heaven." We even discussed his renouncing his vows under a similar situation. "Oh, I'd regret it, I know. If I were really tormented to extreme I'd join the Trappist Order rather than lose my priesthood." Then he told me of experiences where priests had renounced their vows. Once a priest's palms have been blessed, they are not anointed on his deathbed—rather, the BACKS of the hands are blessed. "Once a brother Jesuit told of going to an old man's home for absolution. He found the man unable to speak so he went ahead with the ritual. The old man's hands were clasped together and when the priest began to pry them apart to bless the palms, the man made a supreme effort and turned them over. He had been a priest!

We are about to arrive in CHINA. I can hardly believe it. Tomorrow I set foot in Asia. We entered the China Sea today. The water was soft jade green. The ship's speed was slowed down to make our arrival hour more convenient in Shanghai, so the China Sea rolled languidly past. A few small birds whirled overhead and lit on the ship. The pace was brisk around the decks. The room steward was suddenly very attentive and helpful. Service at the table was never better. The autograph hunters went into action. Overwhelming greetings were exchanged and invitations to visit Manila—Hong Kong—various places in Shanghai. The ship's barber did a rushing business in haircuts and beautifying. Cocktail parties were flourishing. The Captain put DO NOT DISTURB signs on his room to keep out missionaries trailing up with pamphlets. Petty squabbling broke out under nervous excitement. Bathrooms were plagued with hair washers. For myself, I am terrified to land and cannot imagine what it will be like—the Customs and Broadway Mansions housing leaves me quaking.

OCTOBER 15, 1946—BROADWAY MANSIONS—SHANGHAI, CHINA—The Scene: me wrapped in a blanket from the bed, writing at a rickety table but pausing irresistibly from time to time to look out the window at SHANGHAI by moonlight. The city from the window at night, a-winking with lights—street lights and shadows of people. I am exhausted from the trip's grand finale. The excitement began when at 6 a.m. we entered the Yangtze *[Editor's Note: now known as Chang Jiang]*, everyone on deck in bedclothes under coats. The terrible dread of ARRIVAL began in my diaphragm and stuck there with miserable persistence. Everyone was a-babble at breakfast and ravenous—ate two helpings, etc. Later in the day we began the really wonderfully picturesque approach to Shanghai via the Whang-po—

brown churning water, blue sky and river traffic of great hustle and bustle—dilapidated, rusting, wood-fraying old crates touched with the vibrant scarlet of the Chinese flag aloft.

The arrival was one of beauty and horror—the skyline rose into the gold and old-rose aura of the sunset. Below on the wharf was a screaming torrent of babbling excited humanity, including Chinese. I was impressed at the imposing façades of the European buildings untouched by destruction. Then, as people all around me began recognizing friends and families—SOMEONE down there in that wall of TEEMING FOREIGNERS—an almost indescribable feeling of self-pitying ALONENESS. I never felt so forlornly, achingly unwelcome, unwanted, un-greeted, unseen even in the midst of those who BELONGED TO SOMEONE on the wharf and TO SOMETHING: a JOB.

The wife of a correspondent from the *Chicago Sun* was on board, bound for the same hotel. When I suggested we "stick together," she wriggled away—had other plans. Later, when Mrs. Mowatt suggested I, alone and with only three pieces of luggage, come in their group, Mrs. Jack Dowling said, "Let her look out for herself— newspaper women know how to get around." Such a white fierce tigress anger at her welled up in me. So that was the "press" and its affiliates, was it? I knew then the INS man from Shanghai wouldn't help me, or meet me, or have reserved a room for me. These things I felt in eternal flames of fear and dread as everyone on the ship went wild with greetings and reunions. Mrs. Mowatt stood by, bless her, and suddenly a girl from the State Department (seemingly the most sophisticated, uncaring soul aboard) took me aside. She was a guardian angel with witty blaspheme and courage on her tongue: "Stay in my hotel if you're desperate. I know what you're up against, kid. I've stepped off boats with $5 in my pocket." The Customs men checked my luggage off OK—another TERROR fixed in my mind— cleared the dock OK—and two incidents stamped themselves on my mind: While watching luggage on the wharf, a Chinese, well dressed, was jostled by my witty angel. He turned on her in seething racial offense. "I'm a passenger from the ship," he bit out sharply, implying "NOT A COOLIE." She apologized tactfully, adding, "I've lived in your country six years and love your people." He turned his head away and said something deprecatory about Americans to another Chinese. The fiancé of a girl on the ship met us with a jeep—drove up to the hotel, to my relief the China Manager of INS, FRANK ROBERTSON, met me. Young, Australian, even unattached. He got me a room at the Broadway Mansions, spacious, square, overhead a dull-eyed gold light, but down below Shanghai.

This morning I had breakfast with Robertson but a strange nervousness came over me. Later I met the dear old AP (Associated Press) correspondent, SPENCER MOOSA, and walked with him to the National City Bank of New York—got $40 for some traveler's checks. The AP correspondent said I was lucky he gave me clean bills—there is a discount for soiled, crumpled ones. The smell of corroded airlessness on the streets made an impression, and the way people STARE at one on the streets—like the eyes of Bluebeard looking for a victim.

OCTOBER 17, 1946—SHANGHAI FIRST LETTER

Well, my darling, I am here—exclamation point. Luck or all the family prayers have been with me ALL DOWN THE LINE. The letter I wrote you on the ship may arrive after this one, so I will explain. The trip at first was a disappointment in stateroom and food. After the first few days, though, everyone settled down, the food went from very poor and COLD to marvelous, really.

There were more than missionaries on board and we banded together—had a WONDERFUL time. Maizie's contacts made good, and the officers really snapped to when I was around. I wasn't seasick a minute, but the weather was beautiful, the nights divine and I had an UNRRA lad at my elbow (Art's type).

Now for the landing—we came upriver on a day like a watercolor painting. Thrilled to death to see the junks, the little fishing hovels along the Whang-po. We arrived in Shanghai about 4 p.m., October 15. Took hours to clear everyone through Customs, so I really saw this city of my destiny for the first time from shipside at sunset, and Chinese sunsets are filtered coral and gold. The Customs men were all young Chinese officers, which was marvelous LUCK. I opened my blue suitcase. He took a quick look, wrote a Chinese letter in chalk on the lid and also on the other suitcase without my even opening it. He looked at the typewriter. "Is new?" "Heavens no." He wrote the chalk mark and I was cleared in two seconds (after all we heard). Haven't cleared the things in the hold as yet, as the ship hasn't been unloaded.

Came ashore with young nurse who is to be married to young American pilot for Chinese airline (partially owned by PAA). He met us with a jeep, carried all our bags, etc. So about 9 p.m. Angela, Jerry and I piled in the jeep, shrieking like mad—"SO THIS IS SHANGHAI"—and they drove me to the B'way Mansions.

It is like the Roosevelt Hotel: attractive lobby, mirrors, leather divans. All army and press living here. Luck was with me again. Cal Hirsh was nowhere in sight. Apparently never got my wires as he is not living at the B'way Mansions. BUT, the China Bureau chief, INS, met me in the lobby (me in Carnegie coat, etc.). One Frank Edward Robertson, who looks like Hodiak of the movies only more homey type, young, unmarried even. He got me a room, welcomed me in, invited me to breakfast next morn! The room was a gigantic thing, bathroom enormous, closet like a separate room, furnishings old, bed soft. Two Chinese boys jumping around fixing for missy. Then I was alone. Went to window and from my perch on 13th floor looked down for the first time on Shanghai by full MOONLIGHT. Lights twinkling around the Bund and throughout the city, which has many skyscrapers like New York. The dining room is a vision on the roof, a solarium with Chinese boys, American food, butter, jam, milk, eggs, everything! Frank and I discussed a job for me. Introduced to AP man, very suave with Russian wife. He was en route to the bank, would I care to stroll along. I got some American money and was introduced to a man to help in banking money (can't give all details). Coming out, met people from the ship who were in town with an American Lieutenant. Transportation officer, with jeep. We chatted. He offered to show me the city in his jeep (free transportation, which is a miracle here). So, bringing along a friend he lives with, we went driving. Stopped for lunch in Russian restaurant—marvelous food and army approved for safety. Then through the French Concession, American to Shanghai University campus, to the airport, saw General Marshall's plane. Back and all around. Getting dark, so we stopped at the best Italian restaurant for dinner. Chefs are refugees from scuttled Italian ship during war, divine. Music, dancing, inside dope on how to get around in the city, etc. The Lieutenant is married and expecting his wife on the next ship. He is also good pal, strictly, from an old army family (luck again). He offered the army address so that I could use the APO service for my first hurry-up dispatch.

This morning, Angela, a girl I had met on the ship, called. Wedding Friday in Jesuit church, would I stand up for her. (She is a knockout and very sweet.) She's coming here to lunch with me today. Next, Frank calls—come upstairs (he's three flights up); he has news for me. Up I go. "Think I have a good job lined up with UNRRA, which means American privileges to save you from Chinese prices, etc. Gal in charge recalls you from Washington."

Went over to see her, recalled her vaguely, but she is young, ex of *NY Herald Tribune*. Name: Ann Cottrell (might watch for her byline on UNRRA dispatches). I had my *Reader's Digest* magazine right in my hand, which made an impression. (That article has given me unlimited prestige, on ship, everywhere I go.) Ann's to call me back this p.m. about job—writing publicity for UNRRA, and features too, right down my alley. Won't mail letter until I can let you know the final word. Frank says local papers pay nothing.

Now for Shanghai. It's really HORRIBLE on first glance and I just died when I first saw it, but riding in the jeep (we drove everywhere, at least 100 miles, all day) gave me a complete once-over. Some of the homes in the French Concession are little palaces with enclosed gardens. Oh yes, the Lieutenant took me to the Army PX, said if I needed anything from food to silk nighties he would get it at army prices, sometimes LOWER than in San Francisco. Until I get permanently settled, please don't send any food boxes or anything. I have the feeling that the less I have cluttering around, the better. My General Electric lady called to invite me to lunch Saturday. I can't begin to tell you about this place as my mind and eyes are JUMBLED from all I've seen from the jeep. There are rickshaws and the Chinese who run them are young and BAREFOOT. The men on the street, Chinese, wear long gowns. The heart of the downtown district is like San Francisco's Chinatown, multiplied a thousand times and dirtier. American faces on the street are positively EXQUISITE, one is so glad to see them. I'm not on to the money setup yet but it only costs $35 a week to live here, though if I go with UNRRA they will house me. Will continue later.

Had letter on arrival from Al Morano wishing me well. And today a long letter from Father Ehardt. Today is Friday and I have just come from the wedding of my friend and her flier. I stood up for her, and the Vice Consul of the Argentine Embassy was best man. We had a luscious wedding breakfast at the Cathay Hotel afterward, wedding cake and champagne, etc. And from our window, the bund and all the ships.

I am off to two parties tonight, one for the correspondents by the National City Bank, then to a birthday party for a British (woman) correspondent given by her brother, *London Times* correspondent, who just arrived two weeks ago via the TRANS-SIBERIAN RAILROAD. He and I have breakfast together every morning as we're first ones up. The UNRRA job isn't set yet, but Ann says at least

I could be a secretary pro tem. She's to phone in an hour or so, but I want to get this letter off.

Ignore the address on this letter and write me c/o PRO Shanghai Det. Nanking Hq. Command, APO 917, c/o Postmaster San Francisco. My Lieutenant said he can get a trunk for me at much less than Frisco prices, at the PX, so I can move my stuff around. Met the woman whose pic was in the Los Angeles paper, remember. She despises the place and wants to go back on the first boat. I get more used to it every day, though, and the correspondents and wives have been wholehearted here. Cup of coffee, drink, tips on this and that. Anything I want for just tapping on their door.

The church where my friends were married was beautiful. The Jesuits married them. I keep thinking it must be about time for Patty's *[Editor's Note: Patty was Pegge's sister.]* wee one to arrive and I wonder what it is and if Mother is there or what is happening.

From the sublime to the ridiculous, I had to buy johnny paper as they supply none at the Hotel. Paid one thousand dollars, Chinese, for it. As I gaze out the window I see the Russian Embassy and across the parkway the British. Haven't been to our Embassy yet. Still the luggage isn't all checked off the ship. They made a terrible bungle of it. My newlyweds and I were down twice to locate our things. Impossible. The *Lynx* sails tomorrow for Hong Kong.

Want to mail this today for sure—all my love—I'm making out with blessed LUCK, so don't worry. Takes a while to get settled. Love to all, Baby Mei Ling.

OCTOBER 18, 1946—SHANGHAI—What a day. Honestly, everything about Shanghai should be written in italics. Today, Angela married her CNAC flier and I was a witness. Because I haven't received my luggage from the ship, I had to wear a red dress. To my amusement all the Chinese mistook ME for the bride because that's their color for weddings. At the wedding breakfast at the CATHAY

HOTEL they poured my champagne first, served me first, etc. Angela, of course was in white. The church, Christ the King—old, charred brick exterior, mild aesthetic ivory inside—candles, etc. To add to the plot, Father Ryan—my hero of the Jesuit romance—was on hand. He got me aside and confided he was being sent to Peiping where Audrey will be teaching. By oddity of fate they are again brought together, and having to prepare himself to save the Chinese. He's coming around to see me before he leaves. After the wedding I made the job rounds—to UNRRA for a secretary ship, was undermined when told I must pass a dictation test. But I go back tomorrow. Off to a cocktail party for some unknown somebody of the Chase National Bank. I devoured hors d'oeuvres because I'd eaten nothing but wedding breakfast. Coming home with the other correspondents, the AP man, Spencer Moosa, was very affectionate and suddenly grabbed me—kissed me—I cringed but remembered he was the housing chief at the Broadway Mansions. The thing unnerved me, though, and when the INS man called and asked me to come up and talk a bit, I went up to see him. He told me he was a Communist out and out and that he is working on a story which proves the Generalissimo was selling supplies to the Japanese all during the war.

But during dinner came the real story of the day. The wife of a correspondent, who had had several martinis and exhausted her vocabulary on how much she hates Shanghai, took up a new angle: how much she loathes her fate as a newspaper man's wife—admitting that although she is the mother of her scribe's three sons, although she is still young and extremely blonde and attractive, she still comes second in importance. The basics of a short story came out. Wife struggles along—husband walks out to cover stories as babies are being born in his own family. He is away months sometimes on assignment. When he gave up a local paper to get "somewhere" as a foreign correspondent they sold their home and haven't had one since. Hard on wife and kids—but the family ties are tight and loyal, the sons gallant and adoring to their mother. Husband losing out. All he'll have eventually will be a few congratulatory wires from forgotten editors saying "great scoop, etc." and maybe a few tearsheets of page one—his stuff in his heyday (for short story material). The wife gets to 35, thinking it's not worth it—from sweet, forgiving, lonely wife she, as husband is recognized and has means, has her revenge in extravagance in clothes, etc. She finds the more perverse and ill-tempered and demanding she is, the more attention she gets from the husband who tries too late to win wife and sons.

AFTER ONE WEEK IN SHANGHAI—OCTOBER 21, 1946—I still cringe at the convulsion of humanity on the streets—the city affects me physically. I have been ill from an international stomach (too much foreign food) and have cut the inside of my lower lip from nervousness. I battled my way through Customs to clear my crated luggage, with the aid of an army sergeant I got a little British limey Customs official with a nose like Cyrano's and the piping accents of Fleet Street. "What's in 'ere?" he asked, eyeing my two nailed and wired crates. "Don't answer that," he cut back before I would reply. He scribbled something on the boxes and my Customs paper—the Sergeant hoisted the boxes on his head and away we went. The U.S. Army can't be beat. Yesterday drove out to the palatial, verdant estate of one RALPH OLMSTED, who has taken over a little radio station. Spent all day talking business with him and BOB COOK of UNRRA. I was to manage the station, etc. But the money angle was very vague and somehow Olmsted didn't hit me—a self-made, opportunist and shrewd apple (with a worm in it) business—later got in with T.V. SOONG and now is knee deep in business deals. I disliked him cordially and still am angling for a job with UNRRA. Tonight I had dinner with ANN COTTRELL and came home in a taxi. She said I was to pay only $4,000 CN—arriving at the B'way Mansion, I handed the driver the money and hustled inside.

"MISSIE. MISSIE—$6,000—$6,000." The driver, an ugly, twisted devil, stood behind me, smiling, bowing and holding out his hand. I banged for the elevator and escaped, pitying the taxi man for all that I very haughtily said, "No—enough—go away." I still am overcome with remorseful pity for the yowling little, thin-shouldered, spindly-legged coolies who carry great weights through the streets on bamboo poles. Today, at noon, the Sergeant and I drove the jeep through two street fights—WOMEN—I saw two victims, one a young, clumsy-looking girl, her face filthy and covered with blood. The other, being driven away in a rickshaw, was pounded and battered and spouting hot, crimson blood on the rickshaw and spectators, mostly grinning, toothy men. I felt queasy ill at the sight of such violence and raw living right on the street. While getting my luggage ran into a blond young BAPTIST missionary who said, perched on the top of a barrel of dishes and cooking utensils, he will devote his life in China to getting one point across—FORGIVENESS—and doing away with the hypocrisy of gifts and face and civic or social ostentation.

OCTOBER 23, 1946—Today I endured my first Chinese lunch in a very cheap Chinese restaurant. We had chicken's feet SOUP that made me ill to think of where the chicken's feet had been in life. But most startling, when I sat down at the table, a boy thrust a steaming washcloth on metal tongs at me. Chinese napkins! You wipe your hands and give it back. The girl I was with tried to teach me to use chopsticks, but it was too much. After the ordeal of lunch I met my bride and groom friends who drove me out to the famed Shanghai orphanage Zikawei. A young American Jesuit, Father BOB DAILEY, met us and showed us through a place that made an impression which cut through one's sense of observation to the raw nerve—babies in tiny cradles, covered with vermilion quilted covers—all that showed were writhing, tiny faces covered with ghastly red marks, syphilitic ravages on gasping, air-sucking babies. The priest clenched his hands together—hurried us through—"Even after six years here, this place still gets to me." He apologized. We three visitors were speechless. Next came children's classrooms and large liquid eyes fastened on our foreign faces—then the chapel like something out of Marco Polo—all black-lacquered and gilt-trimmed. Then the deaf and dumb children's classroom. Live-wire tykes, making babbling sounds. (Note: Just interrupted by firecrackers going off—I rushed to the window for a moment thinking riot—guns. Ran next door to photographer's room—was properly laughed at, so retreated.)

We had to cut our visit short, but I want to go back. Have just come in from a dinner party at the KING'S LION restaurant. I was the only foreign woman present, accompanied by HARRY CLARK of Montreal (met on ship). I was so carried away by the food and the hot washcloths served, I almost missed the conversations under current of one J.S. TSOO on my left—a runty, moon-faced smiling little man. He wanted to know all my connections. Then, as we talked with derogatory agreement of old CHINA HANDS, he began to carry the anti-foreign feeling to smiling, chatty extremes. I asked him where most in the world he would like to travel, what to see— Paris, not America? "No—America not so much, I like Europeans much better—not so—rough—not so much business-business as Americans. Europeans are more intellectual, more gay," etc. This went on to an extended length, I thought. "What about the Europeans here in Shanghai?" In a flash he answered "Jews? You mean the Jews?"

I gasped inwardly. I wondered at the blend of pre-war Jap and Nazi in his attitudes and the tenor of his remarks. If it had not been for the hot Chinese rice wine in silvery goblets and the carnation flower tea in a tall glass, Mr. TSOO would have spoiled my evening. To top it all off, when I told him I'd been to ZIEKOWEI University today, he dismissed the orphanage and school and asked with good old Chinese practicality if I'd seen the Conservatory. I remarked that the whole University had continued unharmed during the Jap occupation. "Yes," he said, smiling brashly, "the Jesuits were controlled by Rome, and Italy was in the Axis. They were not harmed by the Japs." As he picked at the Chinese serving dishes, he stormed out his resentment of U.S. troops' occupation of China.

OCTOBER 24, 1946—Just for the record, I'm overjoyed I'm in Shanghai—this has been my first wonderful day. First, I've a good lead on an UNRRA job in Canton. Next, I've a chance to go to Manchuria for about three weeks on an "assignment," and I had my first round with the money changers. After approaching all the little Shylock cages along the street in my best casually shrewd manner, (quaking inwardly), I came to one run by three young Chinese. They took my $10, and while waiting for my wad they looked me over, grinning, and nodding their heads. Somewhat undermined in my HARD BARGAIN front, I asked what they were saying. The cashier looked at me twinklingly: "They said you are very pretty." I beamed and took the money, thinking OK if you've cheated me—no U.S. banker ever cashed my check with 10% compliments.

OCTOBER 27, 1946—LETTER FROM SHANGHAI

Sunday, sunny—I sit here gazing down on the treetops of French Town—Darlings, the luck of the angels continues, for I have a JOB—a really marvelous one—and I wish you could see me in my new home in the heart of swanky French town—Cathay Mansions— and my No. 1 boy has just brought missy a pot of coffee. The saints have really, REALLY been at my heels that I fell heir to an Army Public Relations officer job in the Shanghai Headquarters. I am to write a guidebook for new personnel in Our Town, which gives me a chance to dig up all the old history of the most famous places, etc. My own photographer and jeep, plus a chance to travel around. Oh, I have so much to tell you that I hardly know where to begin.

Pegge in the military AGRS jeep.

I had written the NEWS a frantic letter saying it is too expensive to stay out here freelancing as their correspondent without a regular weekly income (the local papers pay less than a living wage, I had heard). My friend Annie at UNRRA trotted me in to the chief economist there and had me all lined up for a job in Canton when this job came along. Annie's beau, a former *Times Herald* and *Time Magazine* correspondent, broke his leg (think I mentioned him before) and landed in the army hospital. He had been PRO here. When he heard of my plight he grabbed the phone, called his Colonel, and said he had a Find, Grade A—come right to his bedside. I was not so keen on it, thinking I'd be stuck in Shanghai and see nothing else of China but I was quickly informed that this job makes me almost my own boss and to get material for the press here I have to go scouting at various times. Well, the Colonel turns out to be rather young, perfectly GRAND, very impressed at my *Reader's Digest* in... so at Gerry's bedside, I get hired at $75 U.S. a week, with all army privileges: medical, hospital, PX, grocery, meals at 25 cents each and my room at the Cathay Mansions. Practically every cent is clear. I have jeep transportation (a luxury here), and am all taken care of. My room at the Cathay Mansions is about like the Chancellor, only larger and more grand: enormous bathroom, whole row of French windows overlooking French town. Afternoon sun exposure. And I am right around the corner from the Jesuit church and my two very good friends from the *Marine Lynx,* the General Electric man and his beautiful wife. Stopped in to see them after Mass. Their apartment is like the magazine article pix. I invited them to dinner over here (costs practically nothing) because they had so royally lunched me at the American Club. Honestly, I can't tell you what a difference it made to move over here, to have the army protection and be in this elite neighborhood. All the small, exclusive shops are over here, just across the street. Our dining room is like the roof of the St. Francis— such linen and silver and strings, and of course, American food. I went over to my new office yesterday morning and met my fellow officers. The Captains and Majors were very delighted to have a gal in their midst. The major in charge quickly whisked me off to dinner at the town's snooty French Club which is right across the street from us. Saw the white Russian glamour gals (very European-looking, heavy eye make-up) with the brass hats. Dinner ran through about six courses and ended with fresh fruit, all with skin so it is safe to eat, (Note: Regardless of how safe, I didn't eat any.) The sun is just going down and my desk overlooks the skyline... nothing is so gorgeous as a Chinese sunset... has such a filtered quality, and almost always looks exactly like the one before. A round, hot sun in a gauze of coral and gold. For the first time since arriving here, I am actually all a-bubble with excitement at being here. (Oh, that sky.)

To top off everything, I got a radiogram from the *NEWS* saying they had forwarded MY RETURN PASSAGE c/o National City Bank as they felt responsible for me and couldn't use enough Shanghai copy to support a regular correspondent. I have just sent Ama Barker a note thanking her and saying I'm okay now, and can still go on writing for her.

Now to the unpacking. I found the Pacific Crating Company really knew its business on boxing things up, but oh, how they crushed things down to make one small tidy box. My hats almost made me weep; they were crushed to smithereens, but I filled the bathroom with steam and just steamed out the creases. Nothing was broken or spilled. I believe I did tell you how I cleared the boxes through Customs without even having to open them…such LUCK is unheard of, but I got by. Since my stay here is indefinite, I think I'll just have Art (Bremer) forward my things to you and maybe Mommie Patty can use some of the things. I'll have you ship the really needed items; the rest aren't worth long-range postage. What I want to do is save my $75 a week and maybe next August go to Switzerland. I hear it is the one place on earth where American money will still stretch out and you can live charmingly. If not Switzerland then Stockholm, as I have a recent report on that from a correspondent who just arrived. He said the prices are very, very reasonable, food abundant, etc. So that's what I'm aiming at. I think China will pay off financially for I intend to write like mad for the *NEWS* and *Digest*. This big desk and my comfortable and sheltered room just makes me feel like FALLING TO……

Gosh, but I'd like some news from home though. If I don't hear soon about the Bostdorfs I'll be very worried. The letters from Al *[Morano]* and Fr. Ehardt *[Pegge's priest]* are all I've had.

Went over to the American Consulate to register my passport and the State Department girl I met on the boat (the one with the cocker puppy) invited me to lunch tomorrow at the American Club. Oh, but she was a grand morale booster when we first landed at the Shanghai waterfront, up to the time when I met my nice Frank Robertson (haven't seen him since as all the spot news correspondents are going to Nanking for the big political doings).

I also don't want to forget to tell you that if you don't hear from me for several weeks, think nothing of it. I can't gauge the length of mail delivery, etc., yet. And I have a possible trip up my sleeve with Ann (Cottrell). She has to go to Manchuria for UNRRA on an UNRRA ship, and correspondents are permitted to go too. We are to arrange all final details early next week. If it's set and I do go I'll try to drop you a note, though I shall be scurrying around like mad. I will be gone for an indefinite period as we see the trip right now. The Jesuit fathers I came over from Frisco with are to embark on the same ship, so we're looking forward to continuing our cruise up the China Sea. The one priest who was my favorite took me to lunch at the local Schraft's, a place called the Chocolate Shop—very pre-war in its décor AND food. Oh, Baby has been getting around. The other night I dined with two Chinese newspaper editors and a chap I met on the ship. He took us to a marvelous Chinese restaurant, and the two editors did the ordering. I hope they have Chinese chefs in heaven. Mandarin fish, for instance, is prepared with a sauce of honey, brown sugar, and tomatoes. Baby shrimp no bigger than the end of your little finger sautéed. And Chinese rice wine served in silver goblets PIPING HOT. …oooh, brother! When I think of Chinatown in San Francisco it is with disdain, after this fare of the gods.

Pegge riding in a pedicab.

I have at last ridden in the modern version of the rickshaw—a thing called a pedicab. The coolie rides a bicycle and you jog along in the cart... really FUN. I also met a girl who does PRO work for the British Embassy. She invited me to her billet for dinner—very,

very good, too. She had formerly been in India and showed me the saris she bought: Carnegie colors, pure silk. (She is, by the way, much in love with my broken-leg job provider and rather a rival of Ann's. I have to be nice to both, like them both very much.) I have seen some satin brocades here that almost defy description; they are just entrancingly exquisite... at $4.50 a yard. Golds and greens and blossom pinks, purples. But I haven't bought a thing yet. When I see some at a good price (friend tells friend where to buy and what little man to ask for, you know), I will get some.

Must sign off now and dress for dinner and my guests, the General Electrifiers!

[Editor's Note: The letter was typed, but the next paragraph was added in handwriting at the bottom of the last page.]

Next day: had nice eve last night and saw free movie, "Leave her to Heaven." Today went well. Got to commissary... food at less than state prices... not that I need it now but for future starvation yet! (Box tea 5 cents.) Just getting onto my new job. Going to like it very much. Nice girl from ALASKA is the Colonel's secretary. She's been showing me around. You can breathe a sigh of relief, Baby's in the army NOW! Love from Baby Mei-ling

NOVEMBER 3, 1946—Aboard the UNRRA transport *WAM KANG,* sailing up the YELLOW SEA. It is a sea of unexpected loveliness. The nights are starred and moody. The days are surfaced in a porcelain blue as the sun moves low on the landless horizon. Aboard our slovenly tramp freighter are over 1,000 Chinese refugees returning to Manchuria—some are smiling, toothy students going to Peiping. Smiling when you say something nice about their country, smiling when you offer discreet criticism of their government.

The high point of the trip was the birth of a baby boy the second night out in the teeth of a raging sea. When word of this reached us through casual conversation with a moon-faced, excitable Chinese lady high school principal, we scurried around like mad trying to remember what one does after a baby is born. The mother was a bewildered peasant girl who permitted the UNRRA worker in our group to recoup up her bundle of sodden, wriggling life. The poor thing had been brought forth like a puppy! We found him wrapped in an old scrap of navy blue silk, tied up with a piece of rope. It is a premature baby, but will survive to struggle for its life as it gasped and twitched and squirmed in its human muck at the moment of birth.

We are bound for Manchuria, and as I sat wrapped in a blanket on the stern, a windless spot reeking of galley smells from the stoves just below, I am thrilled that THIS trip, this adventure came out of the misery and fright of Shanghai. We have seen little except the sea, but the weather has been so beautiful even for this late in the year. This has been wonderful—I have had little contact with the Chinese aboard and my instinctive withdrawing from them has concerned me somewhat. Shanghai fright—though these poor people, huddled on the open deck under a canvas cover, are not the coolie class of the streets.

Various crew members aboard the *Wam Kang*.

A copy of the menu on the ship enroute to Mukden.

NOVEMBER 4, 1946—HULUDAO—At last glimpsed through the morning fog, the port looks like the end of the earth. Bold mountains frowned down on us and held up defenses against our approach. A primly white lighthouse crouched watchful on the far ridge—houses, tracks in good condition, and on the gravel roads, mule carts and a few coolies running along with water cans splashing over—lovely, ladylike trees graced the green hillsides, like soft-leaved weeping willows. Nationalist soldiers were everywhere— smiling, apple-cheeked, white-toothed youths. They stared at the four white women. Our refugees—about 1140 strong (on a boat equipped for 300)—began a babbling, helter-skelter disembarkation, were herded onto open train cars for an hour's ride to their destination. I walked along the trains, observing babies being held over the side of the car for bowel movements. Women with straggling jet-black hair, bright blue padded jackets, and their cloth-covered bundles clustered around them. Youths with skin the color of saddle leather, eyes black as midnight, perched atop their belongings—jaunty and self-possessed, black Persian lamb hats on the side of the head. The whole impression was of a housing transportation movement or a weekend outing. As the train pulled out, they waved and smiled. We waved in pity and compassion at the ordeal ahead.

Huludao itself has little development as a city—no shops, restaurants or the like. We learned that Huludao is the port of repatriation for all the Japs in Manchuria. The Chinese (Nationalists) rout them out, bring them here and the Americans load them onto LST ships manned by efficient, well-ordered, Jap merchant marine officers and crew. The American Colonel in charge said the Japs were mainly glad to go. He admitted the Chinese soldiers searched them for valuables and the "little spoils of war" went into their hands. The Colonel had a little Jap interpreter working for him—a Honolulu Jap girl with a flower face enhanced by make-up. She lamented that her husband was taken to Russia as a prisoner, but said she will be glad to return to Tokyo.

I have just seen my first Manchurian sunset—a fireball that scorched the blue sky until it merged behind the blunt hills. Then a flush of fragile blossom-pink tinged the somber sky—exquisite...

By 5:30 p.m. a cheese slice of moon turned on its thin radiance. The Yellow Sea was jade green and cold, choppy in the rising night wind.

NOVEMBER 7, 1946—MUKDEN, MANCHURIA—(Imagine where I am—always I will be thrilled to refer to the winter of '46 as my voyage and safari to Manchuria.) I am perched on a worn Japanese lounge chair in Room 249 of the SHENYANG Railway Hotel, having just returned from a buffet and movie party at the Soviet Consulate, observing a Red Revolution anniversary or something. We went into a barn of an unheated room draped with red bunting—a picture of Stalin and a Red Square painting arched a buffet table of dry meat sandwiches and cheese. In the center was a stage platform. Drinks were passed, Russian greetings exchanged. The movie was a worn film with Chinese translation. Uproarish applause greeted close-ups of USSR officials, etc. During the musical portion of the program, Chinese military police stomped noisily into the room, partook of sandwiches and drinks, and stomped out. The Russians became absorbed in the music and appeared not to notice. I met a lovely Russian girl who sang two songs nervously but charmingly. She was born here. Lived here during the Jap occupation and hated them. The style of the women was dowdy, the "party" touch being a scarf of mangy fur worn over the shoulders. Withal, the party was like a mid-week shindig of an Elks Lodge somewhere in a burg of America.

Now to flash back and describe our approach to Mukden. We drove from Huludao in an army truck, rutting and gutting our way over country roads. The autumnal Manchurian farmlands were restive brown ploughed plots, lying in barren respite after the year's desperate, hard-pressed harvest. Trees of ladylike delicacy and grace stemmed the flat scene. A black sow ran across the fields, a litter of curly-tailed squealers at her squat ankles. Once a flock of chickens got in the way of our truck and we downed a rooster. Color flared up in a late crop of Chinese cabbage whose vivid green leaves clustered in well-kept garden patches near farm villages. All along the way we passed donkey carts, some hauling farmers in earth-soiled padded jackets and trousers, others tightly packed bundles of cabbage. The donkeys watched our traffic down the road with furry ears raised and wide brown eyes curious and defiant. We adored those donkeys! And the Chinese children, straggly urchin-looking tykes. But laughing-eyed, their peach-shaped faces bursting with excitement to see the foreigners. China's greatest charm unquestioningly is its children.

We arrived in an inland railroad center called CHIN-JO too late for our train, so spent the day and night there. The Chinese lunch we had was divine. One dish in particular—taffy-covered potatoes, with pineapple slices. Highlight of the visit here was seeing a Chinese comic opera. The presentation was held in a barnlike wooden building with standing bleachers and a balcony for the audience. Soldiers and good healthy garlic-reeking yokels composed the appreciative horde of spectators, mostly men and boys; sing-song girls pranced and prattled through their parts in high-colored, glittery costumes, supported by rustic actors who performed with spontaneous gusto their roles of bandits and lovers.

Hardly had LEE MARTIN, JACK CHEN and I entered when heads and eyes turned our way. The stares were open-mouthed appraisal, notably human, not hostile as in Shanghai. We came out and the warm sweet scent of roasting chestnuts, chicken and other Chinese dishes flavored the night air. In the golden but faint illumination over the small table stands we saw red apples, peanuts, bright coral-colored chicken and other savory scented morsels in straw baskets.

Back to the local Ritz, or Chin Jo's leading hotel, where we all put in a night of horror—rats—a porcelain potty, one wash basin for four women, sleeping bags, luggage piled one on top of another—all night long, sing-song girls, poor frizzy-haired, crudely made-up youngsters in bright blue long dresses, their legs clad in uncomely long underwear and faded orange cotton stockings, plied their entertaining charms up and down the corridor. Low-ranking Nationalist troops probably found them diverting.

In the morning we boarded the train and traveled uncomfortably Second Class to MUKDEN—fare about $3 U.S. Black leather seats facing each other. The conductor's ticket taking gave us a chuckle. He had about four assistants and three rifle-bearing soldiers. All along the way we observed concrete firing blocks or squat towers with machine gun slits, barbed wire protected the tracks. At each station there were troops and vendors in neat uniforms selling those peculiar bright coral-skinned chickens, pears and apples in little wicker baskets.

Finally MUKDEN—an imposing, modern-looking railroad station facing a sweeping cobblestone approach. The station was unheated and without lights. Lining the driveway were pedicabs and droshkies—marvelous horse carts with drivers straight out of a Tolstoy novel.

OBSERVATION NOTE: All the Chinese civilians stopping at my hotel go stalking about in beaver-collared overcoats. Some wear matching beaver hats. Spent the afternoon with the Army Graves Registration Service Lieutenant viewing the burial place of an ancient emperor and his empress. The individual pagodas were red and weathered-looking; their coiled roofs with the little strings of dogs on the rim were multi-colored, and weeds sprouted out of the rims. Underneath the roofs were glazed porcelain-like designs, brilliant green and royal blue; lining the cobblestone approaches were stone animals of unique design.

This morning our guided tour took us to see the Jap-built Isolation Hospital, a two-story modern building which all Chinese dread more than death. The Superintendent was a chipper character who raved over the mortuary, actually rubbing his hands and saying he hoped to have "some practice" there soon, as post mortems were his favorite phase of medicine. The hospital had two patients—one TB, one jaundice—and no heat. The little guy in charge was Dr. T. M. TEOH, a Hong Kong University medical graduate. He told us something would be done to treat the opium cases, aftermath of Jap devilry.

According to figures Lee Martin got from the MUKDEN PRODUCTION BOARD (NATIONALIST CHINESE), the following factories are in operation in this winter of 1946: one cosmetics plant, one digestive tablet factory, one brewery, one soy sauce manufacturer, one candy factory, one vehicle license plant and two machine shops, and the factories taken over by this Board up to November 1946 included iron works, machine shops, 88 chemical industry factories, 32 manufacturing factories, 12 fabric factories, etc. While I have not gone too intensely into the mechanics of the situation here, the general opinion is that the Chinese will ruin Mukden, great industrial center though it was under the Japs.

We spent an afternoon in the thieves' market today and it was an adventure in the alleys of ancient Jerusalem—my skunk coat drew curious eyes and in the jostle of the crowd many an astute merchant got close enough to blow on the fur to examine the skin and stroke it with grimy speculative hands. In fur shops I was constantly being blown on and stroked by curious prying fingers. Jap kimonos being sold in the gutter brought $5 U.S. and obi's over $10. I got a lovely piece of pale jade yesterday for $1.25 and a length of raw silk for about 60 cents a yard. The shopping district is a street bazaar, and a teeming stream of Orientals in padded coats and fine western man-tailored hats shoved and eddied by. Chinese bargaining was brisk, donkey carts ploughed in the midst. A Chinese circus of sorts even drummed up trade with a tiny band. Food stalls made little cakes and meat pies in the open air and polluted dust of the street. ROBERT SHERROD of *Time* was in our party, incidentally. We saw little jade, some tempting teacups that looked like loot from Jap households— overcoats with fine beaver collars and fur hats ranging from dog hair to other furs of mystifying and uncertain origin. Highlight of the tour was our unexpected straying down a side street lined with gay porcelain-bricked houses of prostitution. The girls were all dolled up and ready for business, made up with orange-tinged cosmetics and horrible permanents kinked the ends of their hair. But their faces were babyish and pretty. They wore brilliant-colored jackets reaching to their ankles and cheap paper flowers in their hair. The sight of two American women was a thrilling curiosity and they romped outside to see us, but shooed the kids when Ann (Cottrell) tried to take a snapshot. Their houses were impressively clean, like a tile hotel lobby. The madam was a young man with a shaved head and hard eye for business. Immediately off the foyer were small dens or bedrooms with flaming scarlet drapes over the entrances.

NOVEMBER 18, 1946— CHANG CHUN—The day after our arrival here, we learned that the railroad bridges we traversed were blown up by the Communists. The trip up was a cold, but observant one. We passed over the richly dark, brown fertile Manchurian plain, now ploughed in deep ridges that catch the eye in waves of curved lines, like threads in brocade. Each railroad station approach was guarded by pill box entrenchments, one almost built like a small medieval castle. Everywhere were pink-cheeked troops in their powder blue padded garments. Many of them were mere kids, hardly taller than their rifles. Vendors sold those orange-skinned chickens through the train windows, the buyer taking his lunch in a sheet of Chinese newspaper. The eating method is to carve with a pocket knife and cut off the germ-exposed outside skin.

Another time our train went past the LIAO River bridges blown up by the Communists—such carefully wrought destruction by the almost scientifically hand-placed charges impressed us.

Fellow passengers were mostly plush fur collared and hatted officials, few women. We got into brief conversation with one man who had studied in Paris. (He was Chinese—the handsomest I have ever met—had banking connections.) His overcoat was long, of a fine wool fabric lined with cross fox—the collar was unclipped beaver and his hat matched. Most of the men wore identical coats, but their hats were very fine felt, western style. As on American trains, hawkers went up and down the aisle with trays of cigarettes, apples and candy. There was no heat in the cars and we were all wrapped up in blankets. Our arrival in CHANG CHUN was a cold one, about five below zero. Street lights were dim and the coolie redcaps hauled our luggage on their backs to the sidewalk. There droshky drivers and such stood around waiting for business. Their presence was advertised by lanterns—candles encased in very lovely painted oilpaper designs, like hand-painted lampshades. In the cold night the effect was decidedly travelogue and picturesque. The droshky drivers wear fur hats ranging from the helmet type to the true Manchurian-looking Cossack hat. None speak English, all Chinese. We went to the YAMATO Hotel (a second in the railroad chain from Mukden). This hotel must have really been palatial, but it is now under army management, the Executive Headquarters gang.

NOVEMBER 16, 1946—CHANG CHUN—I have just had a very revealing interview with a French-American physician attached to the U.S. Executive Headquarters (Dr. Godet of the French hospital) who told me what is meant by "this is China"—the deeply entrenched niceties of squeeze—and amour. On the squeeze. He told of taking 60,000 doses of vaccine to some Chinese port of embarkation for the Japs. The doctor was to administer the vaccine before the Japs departed. Three Chinese generals met him on arrival, invited him to a lavish dinner, arranged for him to have a special house to live in, etc. Meanwhile they tried to snatch his medicine. After much embarrassing polite but insistent conniving, the generals got 20,000 (measurement) of the vaccine and the Japs 40,000—the only way they would have gotten any. Then he told about the amours: the Japanese girls the Jap high command had in Formosa. And how, after VJ day, they turned them over to the Americans. Procedure: A lavish dinner, then upstairs bedrooms, the doctor examined them and then told the officers OK if they wanted to. He himself talked to one. She hated the Japs and through some inveiglement got a job as a maid in a hotel in Formosa. Another Chinese girl from Peiping fraternized with Americans, later came to Shanghai, was snubbed by her former bedfellows and one eve was asked to leave the French Club. She was outraged for herself and because the Russian harlots of Shanghai were accepted and permitted in the Club.

REFERENCE NOTES ON MANCHURIA—Primary farming crops: soybeans, kaoliang *[Chinese sorghum]*, millet, corn and wheat. Other crops were rice, beans, green peas, buckwheat, cane, rye and barley, cotton, tobacco, flax, hemp, cabbage and fruits. Timber: In Manchuria 350 species, most common pine, silver fir, spruce. Lumber industry was carried on in ANTUNG, KIRIN AND HARBIN districts, which supplied lumber for extensive building development and railways. Also pulp industries flourished in Eastern Manchuria. Textile industry was one of the largest import forces in Manchuria, cotton being the most needed type. Flour milling was one of the three main industries in Manchuria. It was carried on either by old-fashioned native mills or by modern machinery-propelled mills. HARBIN was the center of flour milling. There were over 90 flour mills in Manchuria, all told. (From *Manchuria: A Survey*, by ADACHI KINNOSUKE, published in 1925.)

In 1896, year of the Coronation of Tsar Nicholas II, the Russian minister in Peking was one Count CASSINI who dealt very successfully with one LI HUNG CHIANG in Peking. Shanghai newspapers exposed their dealings in what was called the "Cassini Convention." Their secret convention may or may not ever have been signed, but out of it came the concession of the right of building what is now called the Eastern Chinese Railway, extending the Trans-Siberian Railway through the heart of Manchuria to Vladivostok, with permission to station armed railway guards along the way, and for good measure the right of exploiting mineral wealth along the route was included. The final treaty was not ratified until 1896, when Cassini persuaded the Dowager Empress to the Alliance with Russia. Construction of the 500-mile shortcut between St. Petersburg and Vladivostok made the shortest international highway between Europe and the Far East. HARBIN on the SUNGARI RIVER was the junction of the Chinese Eastern main line with the South Manchurian branch to Port Arthur. At the time there was only one building there—a Chinese distillery. The city was built in a mad rush with no thought of expense. At the time of the BOXER REBELLION in 1900, Russian troops had a fateful excuse for occupying Manchuria. Came the revolution and refugees found Harbin a flourishing town which gradually became an industrial shipping center. Money was God—stories originated of how Russians lit cigars with 3-ruble notes, poured champagne on the floor, etc. Wine, women and song for Russian engineers—extravagance galore, social life centered around the Railway Club—lavish cuisine and wines served at banquets there. The Revolution shot the works. Chinese got the upper hand to repay abuse during the boom days. Harbin became an agricultural center under Chinese control. Twenty-four flour mills in operation, some built by the Russians. Other industries: bean oil, leather. Heavily wooded slopes of the KHINGAIN ranges east of Harbin are thick with fur-bearing animals—fox, sable, leopard, tiger, ermine, otter and wolf. Mongolian ponies which can survive on coarse and scanty food were the sinew of KUBLAI KHAN'S famed cavalry. From Jap-printed South Manchurian Railway Company booklet, SOEURS FRANCISAINES MISSIONAIRES de MARIE have a hospital and clinic at Harbin and Changchun.

NOVEMBER 17, 1946—To go from the reverent to risqué, I must tell thee about our night on the town of Chang Chun with four colonels from Executive HQ. We piled into droshkies and drove to a Chinese restaurant. The night was starry, bright and clear. Our restaurant was a two-story building, obviously a veteran of the wars. As I stepped over the bare-boards threshold into an uninviting-looking foyer, a complete entourage of a Chinese maitre d'hotel bowed to us. We went upstairs to a specially heated room, (bean cake used for fuel), where a flock of young Chinese boys in tattletale gray-white jackets—always too short in the sleeves and waist—shuffled about. Dinner included the ancient egg dish and my favorite: taffy-covered young potatoes. From there we went to the town's flourishing hot spot: The BEAU MONDE—up a curved chill cement stairway we filed. Crudely westernized nightclub posters lured us on to this den of dine and dance, or drink and dance. At the top of the stairway was a bare-board counter and a fat-faced young Chinese boy—hat check—no heat warmed his stall or the adjoining café, so he wore a fur hat and padded coat. We entered a room pulsing with jazz, crowded tables and huddled figures. A neon-bordered stage where a three-man orchestra produced surprisingly better music than Broadway's Danceland. The "girls" were Japanese (Ironic note: The technicians left behind when others were repatriated). They were young, rather lovely and even fairly well groomed. Some wore outmoded evening gowns of dark-colored silk and over them wool sports suit jackets for warmth. Their hair was permanented, their make-up excellent. Few spoke English but would understand the pidgin Chinese of the Americans.

Once seated at the tiny, inadequate tables, they accepted cigarettes and scotch. Eyed the two white women (Lee and me) with superficially smiling appraisal. When the colonels danced more with us than them, one girl got up and stomped off insolently. The patrons of the place were mostly male, middle-class Chinese in clumsy boots and leather jackets. A few Nationalist soldiers of middle rank. It seemed outlandish to watch a Jap gal and Chinese moon-faced lad clutching each other as they rumba'd or tango'd. The songs were all circa early 1930—some were foreign but most American. Another surprise: the joint closed at 9:30 (on a Saturday at that) to save electricity or for some other reason. The girls mayhap were invited to the Yamato for the night. One or two probably went for early the next morning (6:30 a.m.) when I went out to Mass, two Jap girls stepped out of a room and hurried down the hall, giggling.

On the bank of the Sungari.
(From Left) Pegge Parker, Jack Chen, Lee Martin and Ann Cottrell

NOVEMBER 18, 1946—HARBIN, MANCHURIA—I write this dateline with a feeling of incredulous awe. Imagine me, here after being in China only a month. Harbin—remote other-world-novel sort of place. And here I sit in the Communist Guest House, a lavish, European-type manor house, built originally for a Russian lumber king who later went bankrupt. Thinking of my first day's impressions—and more personally of D.A.—Dimit who lived here—and Pana, my first Russian teacher who lived here as a refugee. Flash impression: Russian atmosphere—and RUSSIANS. The first even semi-Russian city I have seen—Russian signs, all of them seeming to be "magazines" too. We flew here this morning from Chang Chun in an American Executive HQ plane. China's soil seen from the air is like brown coarse fiber combed by hand into neat furrowed patches, broken only by family graves. Little patches in one section of the field—irregular mounds marking the graves and willow trees surrounding the burial place. China's villages consist of pathetic-looking mud houses that for all their poverty seem to have been constructed with an eye to the crudely picturesque. They are wretched by our standards, but not ugly. The Sungari River has a green-blue serpentine artery, not as wide as the Yukon or so potent looking. Harbin spread out over a vast river-bordered area. The houses, from the air at least, looked imposing, built for the prosperous and parvenu families of Railroaders. (NOTE: Approaching Harbin, we observed that the Communists had dug deep ditches across all main roads leading to the city.) The automobiles that drove us to our guest house were a wonder to behold. They had wood-burning stoves on the rear, sending up furious clouds of smoke and the odor of charcoal. The cars were built by the Japs, we were told. Our drivers were poor Russian lads in worn clothes, but our Communist guide was a handsome young Chinese who spoke perfect Americanese. He wore a well-tailored long gray coat with a fur collar (beaver, I believe) and a gray squirrel hat, leather gloves and his olive drab uniform.

As we gathered around the small tea table, we were told to advance our watches about an hour and 20 minutes to northeast time. Lunch was served in the master dining room, and lavish it was. Three glasses were lined up at each place, one each for beer, wine and vodka. Water was served only if requested. Lunch consisted of hors d'oeuvres on a plate, cheese, cold chicken, fish, pickles, etc. Toast, butter in puffed curled balls, soup, chicken Kiev with fresh vegetables, stewed apples and coffee. After all this we went out to see the town. The day was sunny, but getting cold. Everywhere my eyes picked out Russian faces, old men with van-dyke beards, young men with Nordic coloring in Russian hats and boots, women with outdated fur-trimmed coats, boots and head scarves. When the Russians spotted us they stared, unsmiling, with a hard look. The Chinese were wearing gauze masks over their nose and mouths, fur hats and padded garments or long overcoats. Droshkies rolled by, drawn by Japanese horses, somewhat larger than the ponies in Mukden.

We stopped to take a picture of an old cathedral, and a very American-looking man drove by in pedicab. He was the first person who looked American and who smiled with his curious stare. "Americanski," I called out—imprudently but irresistibly. Ann Cottrell turned on me after that, saying didn't I know there were anti-American demonstrations and the situation was tense? I was squelched somewhat, but that man's face stamped with humor and good nature was the one I most remember.

We went to a large bazaar—the Sungari bazaar by name—dark, lit by candles and daylight, cold, jammed with Chinese. Goods were labeled and little bargaining was done. Prices were much lower than elsewhere in China. Going through the rest of the city we attracted some notice, curiosity and interest. Once our guide suggested we move on (we were taking pix) because "too many people" were gathering. Once a Russian woman in rags approached us begging—the first panhandler I've seen since Shanghai. The most beautiful chrysanthemums are in bloom—not the gigantic ones of flower shops back home, but white ones, mauve and butter-gold ones.

We cannot figure out where the Russians work here, as none of the store clerks anywhere were Russian. A theatre here shows Russian movies left behind by the Soviets. Posters of the Communist leader Mao and of course, Sun Yat Sen, appear in shop windows. Cigarettes are sold at small street vendor stands, as are nuts of every variety from peanuts to melon seeds. Also small bundles of tobacco. Soldiers were everywhere, drilling in a field, marching by in their bilious green padded uniforms and fur hats of the football helmet and ear flap variety. I passed, in the Russian section, a fur store called in English, ALASKA FUR STORE—was sorry it was closed. After returning to the guest house which is guarded by a soldier and wooden pill boxes on either side, we were taken to a local Chinese restaurant by our guide and the billeting officer who spoke no English. The meal was wholesome and delicious (not sickening and richly overdone). Conversation was manufactured at first. Jack Chen, the British correspondent, told some jokes that ridiculed Chiang and Madame. Books were discussed, and it appears Edgar Snow is still top man with them. Emily Hahn? They shook their heads, not sure who she was. Pearl Buck—one good book, the rest of little account.

Alaska Fur Store in Harbin.

NOVEMBER 19, 1946—Today we called on the Danish Consulate. The Communist escort permitted us to call there. He seemed reluctant but dropped us off anyway. The consulate was as helpful as any in Washington, D.C., and the drawing room was exquisite. The Danish Consul's wife was French and very charming, though apologizing for disarray. No make-up on, etc. She was in consultation with her dressmaker, and a pitched French dissertation was underway. We sat on a sofa looking at a Chinese screen inlaid in mother of pearl, rose quartz and jade—silver vases, Mongolian silver ashtrays, amber colored rugs—a silken but soiled white cat curled up in a chair. The Consul received gratefully the letters and packages we brought. A red wine was quickly forthcoming and conversation bubbled. Being women, we asked about furs. Madame said Kolinsky skins, tanned, but not dyed, were priced at 100 male skins for $350 U.S. The furs are trapped by Chinese and Russians. Kolinsky is the typical Manchurian fur. She said Russian Jews buy the raw furs from the trappers and tan them, holding back their prime skins for export to America. The merchants are getting quite rich. During the war they made money.

The Russian Church functions here on a usual scale—Easter and Christmas are great events.

Today we visited the largest cigarette factory in Harbin, a subsidiary of B.A.T. (British American Tobacco). We called on a MICHAEL LOPATO, factory manager, who had attended Duke and Columbia universities—a squat, small man with a small mustache and pale blue eyes. The factory was a dank, old wooden building— the cellar where the initial sorting was done smelled of malt, like a brewery. Chinese and dowdy looking Russian factory gals in high black leather boots, bulky, old sweaters, and overdone make-up or none at all. All but one: a small brown wren of a Russian girl who was a "checker." She checked against stealing. Chinese girls at the various machines were for the most part very good-looking, young, slight, their hair hanging in a thick braid down their backs. On the walls of the building in Chinese was this anti-Uncle Sam talisman: "Dumping of American commodities will destroy China's national industry." Tobacco and wine are the only two commodities in Harbin that can be taxed. Incidentally, there has been considerable talk about the good Lopato. He maintains he was under arrest during the Jap occupation, but others say he collaborated and very profitably. The air of profit is very evident. He met us today on the street and drove us to the Danish Consulate in a beautifully upholstered car running on gasoline instead of wood or charcoal.

We went shopping today, and Oh! I got the pièce de resistance, a pair of exquisite Paris opera glasses for only $7 U.S. And two yards of silk for 1200 CN or about a dollar a yard. Ann (Cottrell) got some fur hats for about $2 each.

Pegge bought these Parisian opera glasses at a Russian shop
in Harbin, Manchuria.

NOVEMBER 20, 1946—We got word that the talking truce war is over. The Communists have called off the executive headquarters teams in the field. It will be time to clear out in a day or two. We correspondents are the last to see Harbin. I myself feel too inadequately versed on China proper to interpret significantly the tide of events. The order to cease truce talking was a direct result of Nanking embroilments. Six C-47s flew into Harbin this morning and evacuated eight Danish missionaries who had been in Harbin six years. Field team members, an UNRRA sanitary engineer and the foreign correspondents—one American Executive HQ representative will remain a week while his counterpart, Communist General WU HSIU CHUAN, remains in Chang Chun, Executive HQ Advance echelon stronghold. Aside from American Airlines C-47's, all other means of communication have been cut off as a bridge across the Sungari River is blown out and rail lines cut. (NOTE: The Russian population of Harbin was estimated at 30,000, most of whom are Soviet citizens.)

NOVEMBER 24, 1946—**PEIPING**—Jack Chen and I flew down from Chang Chun, a freezing and long flight in a C-47. The day was sunny and clear, however, and I gazed long and ponderously at China's tight, combed patchwork of farmland. Some places looked like fine inlaid woodwork. We flew first to ANSHUNG, the Pittsburgh of Manchuria—factories of destruction under the Japs, now idle and rusting. The city itself is scenically laid out, bordered with rich iron-ore-veined hills in the distance. Nearing Peiping we flew over mud flats and a patch of the coffee-colored Yellow Sea, dotted with a few forlorn fishing junks. Next came mountains, barren and jagged, yet cradling humanity in their gently leveled valleys. I gazed on those ranges and wondered if bandits or Communists were sheltered there, and if Marco Polo had been forced to traverse such forbidding passes.

Peiping is too exquisite, too golden-hazed, too other-worldly for other than rhapsodic description. I am now at an old French hotel, the Wagon Lits. Spent the day at Mass at a Sacred Heart School, where an American nun from Brooklyn told me about some German Catholic nuns and priests who had been driven from Shansi province by the Communists after agonizing torture and a forced march. The 10 sisters and 22 priests, who had devoted about 20 years to educational and physical welfare work in that area, are now convalescing here.

Thence to the Peiping Hotel to lunch with Jack (Chen) and then on an army sightseeing tour to the fantastic and exotically fascinating Summer Palace of the Empress Dowager.

LATER—I have just had an extraordinary evening. Lee Martin, Ann Cottrell and I had dinner with Jack Chen and a British correspondent named Gerry Sampson. He was held in esteem by the others, although I'd never heard of him. When he joined us, I thought him quite scintillating with news of his recent stay in Yenan, telling us that the Communist stronghold was being evacuated and the cave dwellers displaced to unnamed places. Then he told us of meeting Mao Tse-tung, having a brief interview and then going in to dinner. In the dining room there was a prominent portrait of the Generalissimo (!). Sampson kept looking at me from time to time, although as usual I had next to nothing to say. After dinner we repaired to the hotel lobby to talk and I sat next to Sampson. Because I thought him interesting in a reaction of emotion as well as fact to his China experience, I began asking him about his own life. He spoke revealingly personally to me as a man enjoys a rare privilege of indulgence, even telling me of a lost love in America. The others left for one reason or another and we talked on, comparing notes. Then I asked him, as one who has done all the things I have wanted to, what is the price? Loneliness at rare unexpected moments, he said, quickly advising me to see what I want in the world and to marry before waiting too long. Then he returned to his own experience. How his travels and war coverage have kept him always on the move and he has never had time to be in love, except for the American girl he met at the beginning of his career. Now that he's reached his mark and is shooting at a seat in Parliament, he wants someone sitting in the Gallery. "In a pretty hat—waving slightly in recognition," I responded, and on that he said suddenly, feelingly, his face flushing slightly, "Will you—will you come and help me with my campaign—and sit in the Gallery when I win?" I was uncomfortably aware of his urgency, his longing, his asking… Jack Chen reappeared then, saving me, but when I rose to leave he asked me to lunch tomorrow. Now I'm thinking how frightful it would be to become Mrs. Parliament Member.

Next day, my prospective MP made a grand gesture. He took me to the Temple of Heaven and at the whispering wall he told me he loved me madly and I must marry him and fly back to London. On the center stone of the three-tiered Temple of Heaven he kissed me ardently, to the bewilderment of our little Chinese guide who quickly turned his back. Oh well, lest we forget, it was an interlude.

I love Peiping and am enthralled in a serenely indolent way at just being here. The only disappointment I've had was my first Peking duck. Sampson was host to our party. The duck is eaten rolled in a pancake with very strong fresh onion and mustard sauce.

DECEMBER 12, 1946—LETTER FROM SHANGHAI

Darlings—enclosed are two newspapers well splashed with Parker's copy for the gravediggers. I'm sending the whole paper, as I thought you would be particularly interested in seeing the ads and other news items. That my first output should be so well received naturally has pleased the colonel, and of course I feel right in stride.

The one paper that used maps to illustrate the story is British-owned. I made personal "charm" calls on all the editors and when I called on the British editor, he told me about being interned in

Shanghai during the Jap occupation and putting on Shakespeare. The cast studied their parts from script written on johnny paper.

The editor of the *China Press* turned out to be a blond young chap with the jaw-jarring name of Schneierson. He is part Russian, so I, of course, began my spluttering Russian, and with one thing or another he used my AGRS (Army Graves Registration Service) handout in its entirety, and exactly as I wrote it. The reaction was really very "ding-how" *[Editor's Note:* ding-how *means "very good" in Chinese.]* to even my amazement. The United Press called—why hadn't they received the release? Cal Hirsh of INS finally called me. He had picked up the story and filed it for the States. (This was the Manchuria yarn, Manchuria having great news importance these days. The INS correspondent in Nanking was fired and my nice boat-meeting Frank Robertson has repaired to the capital to fill in. The general reaction I got from the correspondents and my Britisher was that the piece was well written, and that relieved me, coming from them.

I really feel, at last, I've settled into my job and will get a lot out of it. At first, though, the army system and the chowderheads wearing major rank, etc., exasperated me.

As I sit here plinking away I am waiting for young Johnny Powell, son of the editor of the *China Weekly Review,* to come over for lunch and an interview. Thought I might be able to do a *Coronet* piece on his experiences as an American editor in mad Shanghai. Believe I mentioned him once before— little and goggled, but smart and very nice. This will really be my editorial day, as after doing Powell, I will scurry home to dress for dinner with friend Schneierson.

Sunday will be a highlight, too. First to mass at the Jesuit mission down the street, then to meet the Colonel's Russian secretary, Nina, and off to the Russian cathedral with her, then to high brunch at the Chocolate Shop in French town. The two Chocolate Shops in Shanghai are like Rumplemeyers. After that I have a dinner with a friend of Frank Robertson (my INS chief). This man, Sam, is older, divorced and the brother of a foreign correspondent, so even though he is in the importing business he goes 'round with the press crowd.

This has been quite a week. With Gerry here (the Britisher yapping at me to marry him before he returns to London), I've been dining out. One place was the most elegant in town, also the coldest. We ate dinner with our coats on and were about the only people in the entire room besides the shivering waiters. Another night we dined at the Palace Hotel where all the bigwig visitors stay. Again, cold and expensive and forlornly empty.

Monday morning—It's wonderful to be in the army; as long as you look busy everyone thinks you are. So here I sit dashing off a letter to you. What a wonderful, out-of-this world weekend. Romance and everything. After predicting how things were going to be, this is the story. Johnny Powell came to lunch and we talked ourselves hoarse. He is darned nice. We talked straight through until 5 p.m., then I called a jeep and delivered him back to his paper, but not until he had asked me to dinner; then home to dress for the next editor.

It was pouring rain and most of the curl was coming out of my hair but I had borrowed a Hattie Carnegie bonnet with a little nose veil (something like my brown wee bonnet I got in Seattle). We went to the New Palace Hotel rooftop, marvelously colorful in atmosphere— Chinese officers, Europeans, Russians, very good Chinese food. The Russian orchestra playing "Symphony" (and me thinking vaguely of Jade Jim) and other American smoothies. Schneierson turns out to be a wonderful dancer of the cheek-to-cheek school. We stayed on dancing and dancing as others left. Then we were the only ones there (all cafés must close at 11:30 because of electricity shortage). Then the real fun began. He waltzed over to the orchestra, all friends of his, and they played just the music we asked for, and we danced. Meanwhile, much eye work is going on, and telling each other the words to the songs. He the Russian, me the English. ('Twas a coy Parker, no tellin' the poor boy the words to "If I Loved You"... words wouldn't come in an easy way... something about being "afraid and s-h-y.")

From there we went seeking the little places that don't close at 11:30. Found one called the "Arizona," of all things. It is owned by Austrians. Very smart and small. British officers there, and the best groomed and dressed women I have seen, looking like Embassy staff. All in formal dinner clothes. Again, the best music I have heard. Most of the musicians are European, and what they can do with violins, even playing things like "White Christmas." Anyway, so home at 1:30 in the pouring rain but with the marvelous feeling of music and lowered lashes. He's young and WITHOUT WIFE in any form... bookish, and alas, a Soviet citizen. Well known among the correspondents. The next day he used another of my AGRS releases in prominent position. And today the Colonel's secretary hands me a memo: "Have noticed the fine coverage you are getting. Good work."

I rushed to my two church services yesterday morning, had an Amah in the afternoon to do some odds and ends of sewing jobs (for 50 cents she went over buttons, hemmed three swatches of silk for scarves, etc.). Then a basket of flowers arrived with a Russian card, wee blue bow on the handle. I was in raptures, of course, thinking they were from Schneierson after all the eye work. Sam arrives to take me to the concert and of course I never mentioned the flowers. As he was helping me put on my coat he said, "Could you read the Russian on the card?" I was terribly, AWFULLY disappointed (remember little George's roses) and naturally embarrassed. Sam will be my Little George, Al Morano, Art Bremer rolled into one here. The symphony was packed but no heat. We kept our coats on. The musicians were German, Austrian, Russian and some Chinese. Excellent. Then to dinner at the CUTEST Viennese restaurant where we had "itzel" just straight down from above. And Viennese coffee in a glass with two inches of whipped cream on top. Had to sip it with straws!

Oy, then to a Russian café for music and more atmosphere, and home at 11 p.m.

Funny to think of Christmas. No decorations, snow or even much talk of it around here. There are parties and such planned here at the Army, but I hope to be with my editors and correspondents. Don't think of me "minding" Christmas over here. It just won't seem like THE holiday so far from Mommy cat and Alaska. Hope I have a letter or two from you SOON. Mail has just been nil. See the *Marine Lynx* is in. Did you ever receive the letter I sent from the ship? Could use a little black veiling, by the by, the kind with either the tiny chenille dot or fine cross stitch. If you could just enclose it in an envelope, a yard would be plenty. "Shay-shay" (thank you in Chinese). Will be writing again very soon. Baby Mei Ling

DECEMBER 20, 1946—LETTER FROM SHANGHAI

Dearest pussy-pie Mommie,

Duckie, just have to rush off an answer to your wonderful letter which arrived the other day with all the clips. The one on Newsreel Wong really got me in action, quick.

I phoned the correspondent's bailiwick, namely the B'way Mansions, and in two minutes was talking to him. Went down to see him that afternoon and waved your clipping at him. "From my own dear Mother to YOU," I told him. He hadn't seen it and knew nothing definite about the Columbia Pix deal, so he was ELATED to read the clip. "Tell your darling mother many, many thanks," he said. He is Chinese, but very sophisticated, smooth, dapper, and quite good-looking. I am trying to round up a press tour to the hinterlands for after the first of the year so went to sound him out on that as well as to meet him and do a story on his life. He agreed to both and we will get together on it later. He has to cable New York "News of the Day" first.

KEEP YOUR EYES GLUED FOR ALL AMERICAN GRAVES REGISTRATION SERVICE ITEMS IN THE PAPER or LOLO LAND stuff (on those five "Americans believed held captive"). If all works out okay I will take Wong and the *New York Times* photographer on a field junket to last about a week.

Think I told you about my first press conference and how it went. The press notices the next day were super… My Russian editor (the young one who took me dancing) splashed his copy all over the feature page. Two separate stories he wrote, with good headlines smacked on the top. He is taking me to a Russian USSR movie Saturday night.

Meanwhile I got an ardent airmail from British Gerry (Sampson) in Hong Kong. He enclosed a clipping from the papers there. He made front page with an interview he gave on his impressions of China. Ye gods, they billed him in inky BOLDFACE as "British author, politician, special correspondent of the *London News Chronicle*."

Then later that evening when I came home from dinner, I was surprised with a basket of ROSEBUDS. Mommie, it was the dearest darling basket you ever saw! From my Sam, whose very cute card said, "Looking back and looking forward." They were pink and red talisman rosebuds snuggled down in ferns. With them came two Russian grammar books. He really is a wonderful person… you know, all understanding, all sympathetic… the perfect older man. We had dinner Wednesday night and saw a Russian version of "The Idiot." The play went from eight to midnight and not a smick of heat in the theatre.

I also got a box from Maizie (Blinn), and since I had sent her the money for some make-up sponges (which I FRANTICALLY need), I opened the box to fish them out. Instead I found a very lovely silk blouse from Magnin's! No sponges, though. I'm sure she'll send them later or I'd beg you to send a couple. I also got a small airmail box from Lois (Fegan)… no idea of contents.

Through my Alaska friend I met the man who does all the Shanghai purchasing for the Army's PX in Japan (some kind of a deal where all the best things go into MacArthur's zone and we get NOTHING right here where it comes from). Anyway, he is very nice and asked if I'd like to visit some Chinese "factories" with him. Had a marvelous time because things like rugs, cigarette lighters, etc., are made in the Chinese homes and compounds. He then took me to a linen merchant and I got some pure silk, all handmade slips for $3.50. Also some handkerchiefs like the enclosed for much less than they sell them around town.

Sam just called to say his brother, a foreign correspondent and author of four books, is flying in from Tokyo today. He writes for *Collier's* frequently under some pen name I can't recall.

I myself am off to the Associated Press cocktail party tonight after my Russian lesson.

The Christmas schedule will be busy enough… many army parties and things planned in the hotel where we all live. And I suppose I'll see Sam. My Soviet is too anti-religion for a holiday. There are several parties planned for New Year's too. Of course, I will MISS Christmas "associations" like you and Daddy.

Just had another telephone talk with Sam. His brother's name is MARK GAYN (ever heard of him?). He also said HE didn't send me the Russian books I was ardently thanking him for… my editor? How stupid to send a gift without a name. Jeepers—like the first time he sent flowers and I was sure they were from my editor.

As I was saying about Christmas… it is a strange feeling to be in such an exotic place for such a "homey" holiday. Having been away a month, I really have had little time to feel "close" to anyone. The contrast after Alaska is rather slim. But I will be busy and not mind too much.

I have always New Year's, anyway, but because of the drinking and with the Army it will be pretty bad. Sam doesn't drink any more than I do, so he is a blessing in many disguises. Neither does my editor…

Sudden thought: NOT A WORD from Art all this time. I hope he's good and embarrassed by Christmas because I airmailed him a carton of cigarettes I got in Harbin.

As for your box, I seem to be a true "Lyons"—we never let the exact deadline of a holiday or birthday bother us in the least. You will be getting your Christmas box one of these days. Meanwhile the little token inside this envelope is for you to get many dishes of ice cream at Rumplemeyers. I sent Ahmee the same with a hankie, and Aunt Marie some hankies…

Lottie (Kent) sent a cute card and note (which I shall answer). Also, remember the Swiss baker who taught me how to make pies on his last night in Fairbanks? He sent me all the latest info on living costs, etc., in Switzerland and said he will be waiting with open arms "in the snows of Switzerland" when I arrive. He has been going to a Swiss pastry school (can you IMAGINE the divine things he must be making now?). He's young and blond and pink and white, I think I told you, and was very much liked by Cap Lathrop because his marvelous bakery turnouts kept his coal miners REALLY HAPPY.

As for a few items I need: the black veiling I requested in my last letter (would prefer the kind with the wee chenille dot), a yard would be plenty… some nice writing paper… either pink onionskin or light blue. And earrings… gold ones, roundish… I'm in a muddle trying to figure out whether to have Art send my clothes here or to you. Until you get settled somewhere, I feel any extra shipments from Alaska would only laden you down. I'd also love a bunch of violets (the ones I had must be in the Alaska boxes), the true purple-purple kind. I guess these items will hold me for now.

Must get busy now with my gravediggers. Keep the clippings coming in, and send me the article on Cap Lathrop, please. My love to Lois. I will write her soon and send her something along.

Mistletoe out-louders

(SIGNED) Baby Mei-ling

CHRISTMAS EVE 1946—SHANGHAI—I must give you this briefly as it is very late and I am so tired, but I have just had a most unique Christmas, spent in the arms of a Soviet city editor of H. H. Kung-owned *China Press:* VICTOR SCHNEIERSON, who wants someday to enter the USSR diplomatic service. He came out to be with me right from the office. I, meanwhile, had tried to Christmas-ize the room with flowers, presents strewn about, candles, etc. I wore slacks, sweater, etc.

Victor Schneierson (left) and his interpretor.

We sat in a chair, unwrapped and basking in the sweetness of nearness, then bit by bit, conversation. He maintained the remoteness of war between Russia and America. We felt our friendship— American and Soviet—was symbolic of how we can get along once distrust and political antagonism is removed. We discussed religion in connection with Christmas. He does not believe in immortality except that the works or achievements of man live on. Then, as a paradox, he quoted part of Francis Thompson's *Hound of Heaven.* We sipped Nescafé coffee and brandy and kissed each other until midnight when we opened presents.

He gave me a lovely silver link bracelet on which he will have "mulaq" *[Editor's Note: "dear"]* engraved. I gave him an assortment of Russian books and some cigarettes. Then he went and I sat reading this diary until 3 a.m. What was I doing last year at this time? That was the thought, and then came Christmas Day and calamity. It was dreary and foggy. The air was misty liquid that filled the fibers of one's clothes and left them sodden and limp. I received my *CHINA PRESS*, checked Victor's placement of my AGRS story and went off to breakfast. At 10 a.m., Sam Ginsbourg, an ugly, but kind and wonderfully worldly and understanding older man, was to come by to plan the day. He has become my special friend and Shanghai adviser, and in many ways sympathetically close. I thought we would spend the evening quietly somewhere. He gave me no gift, to my surprise, but a ridiculous wicker horse with a cluster of rosebuds tied to its tail. (I had presented him with Harbin brandy and two cartons of cigarettes.) In the middle of conversation he mentioned very casually he had to go to a boring dinner, but would get away as soon as possible and stop by for me at "Oh, about eight. Is that all right?" The casual convenience of my having dinner alone and being picked up, you know, left me stricken. After he left I tried to dress for Mass, but suddenly a hysterical flood of bathos overwhelmed me. On Christmas Day to be crashed until 8 p.m. so casually by someone I made a special concession to be even seeing AT ALL. That was to me symbolic of Christmas Eve in Shanghai in 1946. The anguish I suffered was bitterly self-pitying. I dressed then and went down the street to Mass. Of course I had missed the last one; the church was half empty, cold and vapid, sodden damp. I sat there like a truant kid, tears just spilling down. So this was "seeing the world" and meeting such interesting people. Later that afternoon, Sam came by to take me downtown to the Pepper Martin's Christmas Party. Instead we talked until 5 p.m. and I contributed to the dampness by weeping some more as I accused him of the casual touch for Christmas and he tried to plead his cause. I never want to see him again. I almost don't want even to see Victor. (What point, reason or ultimate end?)

I ended my beautiful day by going to the army hospital to see the poor lad whose job I now have, ate my dinner—cold cuts and melted ice cream—at his bedside laughing with him and listening to a Chinese boy with a broken leg, in the next bed, singing opera arias. I came home in an AGRS jeep and in the half light noticed my driver was a young foreigner. Almost automatically I went to work on his life story. He had studied music in Warsaw, was a Polish Jew and two years ago had escaped through Russia on the Trans-Siberian Railway to Shanghai. He is to leave soon for Baltimore, Maryland, where he will live with friends of his father, a one-time light opera orchestra conductor. He responded, as have all the jeep drivers I've interviewed, to my sympathetic recognition of his being. When I wished him a "Merry Christmas" at the door of the Cathay Mansions, he held out his hand and thanked me for talking to him.

Christmas night from my window: French town is a muddle of blurred lights, echoing honks of taxis and the faint lyric tinkle of the rickshaws and pedicabs.

DECEMBER 28, 1946—I am growing impatient to leave Shanghai and go to Switzerland through Russia. My lessons are progressing with a complete vocabulary on amour—for Victor's sake. I have become somewhat aware of the implications of a Soviet romance. I wanted to invite him to an AGRS dinner dance, but thought better of it. If we are firing all the Soviet citizens we can spare, how can I invite a Soviet to join us socially? Vic and I have not yet been seen in public among Americans. Something tells me it would not be wise to have our relationship known; in political discussions where we differ I avoid argument by saying nothing. It is obvious the Soviets are indoctrinated and injected under the skin with their principles. The only special point I have tried to drive home to him is to retain his INDIVIDUAL REASONING, to think things out for himself thoroughly before he subscribes to a policy.

Meanwhile, I have had some interesting sidelight experiences. I interviewed one of our Sikh guards—a handsome fellow with a silken soft black beard and mustache, who told me the Sikhs *[Editor's Note: pronounced "seeks"]* of Shanghai are quite wealthy. For all they appear merely as fierce-eyed guards most of the time, they have private businesses in their homes, namely money lending. Their methods are fictional—they have Chinese agents who know everything about a "client" (as he called them) before the loan is made: why the money is needed, etc. The Chinese merchants are their most hard-pressed clients, and because of their unscrupulous, unpredictable cunning, the Sikhs charge them 3 and 4 times as much interest. The Russians are also bad risks, because they too will do "funny business" unless watched like a hawk. The best businessmen are the German Jew refugees. Women are sometimes clients, when they sell jewels for money to run their houses and feed children, or leave their jewels as security for a loan. The Sikhs charge only the amount of interest a bank would charge, otherwise God would punish them. I thought there might be story value in another thing he told me. At one time the client of a Sikh was a part owner of a Russian nightclub—KAVKAS. He made good his repayment, but if not he would have lost the club to the Sikh owner. I have been to the club, which is frequented by Chinese, Chinese officers, Russians and a thin sprinkling of American officers. The Chinese dance without pleasure, never varying their steps or speed to the music, never conversing while they dance, never holding their women any closer than necessary. The women as a whole look very well groomed and beautifully coiffed and made-up. But their main interest on the dance floor seems to be scrutinizing close up the clothes of the other women dancing around them. The Russian women, garishly overdone, with towering pompadours or harsh artificial hairdos, also seem to stare at foreign women around them. The music in most clubs is exceptionally good, for the musicians are of symphonic strata, being mostly European and Russian.

I had occasion recently to visit some factories around Shanghai and found them revealing. One was a camphor factory where tables and chests are made. In an inner compound we were led into a ramshackle hovel with a sagging roof and dirt floor—the warehouse where exquisitely carved chests were stored. Then we saw where they are carved, the panel inlays which are sometimes of peach wood, sometimes teak wood. In a room not much larger than a hotel closet sat about six young Chinese bending over wooden slabs; a row of wood chisels lay nearby. After a quick glance at the visitors escorted by a slick-haired westernized Chinese factory owner, the artists went on carving. They work every day and during rush orders, every night. The manager said they are paid (and this is probably exaggerated) $3 U.S. a day. The room was fragrant with the exotic fragrance of camphor shavings laying in pale gold curlicues on the floor. The carvers laughed school-boyishly at my attempts to tell them their work was good. Their hands were noticeably slender and their fingers shaped like those of poets. Their clothes were grimy, padded jackets and trousers. Below were the carpenters who get paid more for putting the trunks together than the artists for carving. Occasionally a woman put her head out of a doorway and watched with beady eyes as we examined the work. They were at once wench-like and sweet, their hair drawn back, knotted and greased smooth. Usually children in nondescript long coats hung around them.

We also inspected a cigarette lighter factory in the hovel of a Chinese family where all members of the family lived, from an old grandfather with just one evil-looking yellow tooth in his head to pale-yellow-skinned children with bobbed hair, dirty faces and bright jet eyes. The lighters were made in a stone-walled dungeon, behind an enclosed dark, dank vestibule used as a kitchen. Wheeled instruments whirled while shaved-headed youths watched attentively and did part of the operation by hand. One was reminded of the industrial revolution in America.

DECEMBER 30, 1946—My Sikh friend, Corporal of the Guard at the Race Course, invited me to a temple ceremony observing the founding of the Sikh religion. To attend, I had to walk out of the office and meet him at 2 p.m. Then began one of the most fascinating experiences of my vagabond heritage. He crossed the street with me to get a pedicab—I had no idea we'd take one together and was mortified when he climbed in beside me. I wondered how we must look going down the LEADING street in Shanghai—Nanking Loo— the Sikh and the lady in the bright green coat. He wore a gold uniform and olive drab turban. I was in misery until we went to the "HAN KEW" or foreign district where the "temple" was. We went into an inner stone court, past sundry whiskered, turbaned, wild-eyed, but paunchy and "tamed" looking Sikhs who saluted the schoolmaster and his white lady guest. Then into a house, up some dark, shabby and filthy steps to a hallway covered with men's shoes: boots, GI combat boots, stub-toed hightops, oxfords, and gaiters. My guide told me to remove my shoes, which I did, standing there in my nylons. Up more stairs and then I heard a strange shrill chant and the metallic clink of symbols. He pushed open a door and a burst of music, perfume, vivid scarves hanging from the ceiling and a solid mass of turbaned heads overwhelmed me. All eyes—black as Arabian midnight—stared at the shyly self-conscious white girl. The schoolteacher indicated a spot on the rug and I sank down among the turbans, primly covering my legs and feet with the hem of my coat. The music went on. Beside me a roly-poly pinch-nosed fellow in a bright orange turban burped and wriggled his fat bare toes—children seated in front squirmed and peeped at me, ducking when I smiled at them. In the front of the room was a little clearing where each man as he entered bowed and touched his head and dropped an offering of money. Beyond was a raised altar on which reposed their sacred book. Behind the altar was a turbaned religious with a white plumed switch—at intervals he switched the open bible. To one side of the altar my schoolteacher was explaining who I was and all heads turned curiously. Singing went on; occasionally a little girl stood by the schoolmaster and sang. Suddenly, I felt drops of water descending on me—PERFUME was being scattered in solid drops on the devout. After an hour of this there was a stir, and a well-groomed, ultra-sophisticated young man came in, his hands thrust deep in the pockets of his perfectly tailored topcoat: the Consul for India, I. J. BAHADUR SINGH. He bowed like the rest then sat on one side with his hand over his eyes. I watched him, thinking: He's not meditating, he's lost in thought of where he's just been. (I was RIGHT—he told me later he'd been to a terribly amusing luncheon party and had drunk entirely too much—actually fell asleep until it came his turn to make a speech.) The schoolmaster was his interpreter. He spoke in English with a clear, trouncing Oxford accent. He said the usual things: that in the political changes in India all Sikhs would be able someday to hold their heads up proudly and take their place among all great nations. The ceremony ended after a prayer chanted when the whole assembly rose and knelt by turn. I was handed a bag of apples, and my schoolteacher introduced me to the Consul who was immediately a smoothie and jolly what-the-heller. We went downstairs, recovered our shoes, then filed into a freezing schoolroom for Indian food, served in a large metal plate. Some kind of pudding like a sweet suet, boiled rice, then curry and "bread" served pancake style, very doughy and hot. The curry prepared without meat was one part fire and two parts double strength pepper. I swallowed hard and kept smiling. Finally asked for water—served in a metal glass which made me shudder for cleanliness. The Consul meanwhile was very quite amusing and a cosmopolite "more western than Indian." Could he give me a lift? We, the schoolteacher and I, climbed into his car and my heart winced slightly in resentment at the glib diplomat's supercilious amusement at the whole thing, although he said, "I'm not so sure but these chaps really are better off for their religion—gives them something to go by and hang on to."

1947

JANUARY 4, 1947—SHANGHAI—CATHAY MANSIONS—
Hello—it's a new year—little did I dream 1946 would bring me to
China, so whence shall I be by 1947's close? The New Year celebration
was memorable in the extreme. I spent it with Victor. We joined a
group from AGRS at the ultra swank, in a formally restrained way,
French Club. Victor, who is socially on the Soviet pedestal gazing
down on dissipated capitalists, struck an attitude of diffidence and
sardonic observance of everything around us. In the first place, after
promising me he would, he did not appear in the prescribed tux. As
he walked across the room to our table, he made a self-conscious
apology. My heart quailed for a moment and his detachment from
the vivid, whirling, waltzing, gay throng struck a pang in me. He had
not sent me flowers, and I felt a little unadorned and neglected among
the others. The food was atrocious and cold, the music rather tinny,
the room smoky and noisy and in motion for the occasion. We were
not in the sumptuous main ballroom (another pang of feeling our
not belonging), but after a few automatic movements constituting
dancing, Victor and I went upstairs. Here was a scene: All Europe, all

races united and democratized by wealth, all type, all ages, danced on a slightly mobile dance floor. Such gowns, bare shoulders, arms, bosoms. Silks, brocades, velvets, jewels, white fox capes, ermine, hair coifs extreme and as consciously chic as the wearers. The men looked puffy-eyed, regally suave and with the night shade of boredom bemused only by a searching eye constantly sorting the crowd, missing no detail of among those present. A few glossy-finished, wealthy Chinese danced in the throng—ultra-sophisticates they, the only Chinese I have ever seen dancing who looked as though they were enjoying it. I saw Mrs. Mowatt, my beautiful lady from the ship, and she looked like a portrait by Reynolds. For a New Year's Eve crowd, the gentry kept their liquor content under control. Victor, who was journalist enough to share my keen sense of the writer-observer, kept painting in the picture of the world's own wives and husbands and amours all awhirl around me. Speculators, cutthroats, pals of the Generalissimo. I became oppressed with Victor's interpretation of glamorous stagnation and scoundrel-ry, although I had to agree with him that they represented the shrewdest survivors of the back wash of Europe.

At midnight we went back downstairs "where we belong," Victor said. I regretted the condescending implication. The Chinese waiters poured champagne into our glasses (they did not cheer the New Year, but looked to their waiting duties all night long) and at midnight we clicked glasses and drank, Victor and I both thoughtful of the significance and prophecy of the New Year. "Let's go to my club now," Victor said, and I wondered what the Soviet Athletic Club would offer on such an occasion. It was astounding. The night was vibrant with gaiety and a wild exuberance that came from Russian hearts and Russian vodka. But nowhere was that restrained, self-conscious lordship. The newly built club was barnlike and rough-hewn by comparison with the splendor of the French Club, but it was dazzling and rhapsodic. From the moment we entered, shoving and wriggling through the tight-packed dancers to our table, we were caught up in the spontaneity of the mass. The whole room was united in its all-embracing goodwill—as the only American in the midst of them, I responded to their Russian spirit, the deep thump of drums in the midst of violins.

The Russian Consul entered and was led to the stage. Immediately one was conscious of the background decoration posters of Lenin and Stalin—the Soviet flags—the CAUSE. In the midst of the HOLIDAY, the eternal SOVIET had to roar out a silencing reminder of the work and struggle of the Soviet Union and the dedication of every Soviet to the tasks ahead. A few hoarse salutations to Stalin and a boisterous shout on all sides. As he departed, a Russian general followed and he yelled thunderously at the mike that Russia's battles were not yet won—we must unite to fight harder, etc., producing trumped-up applause from the men and women. Russian women of great feminine instinct in their holiday gowns looked on submissively. Victor translated every word. When the roars of response burst forth (I had the feeling that it was like Soviet etiquette to SHOUT at appropriate pauses), I turned my head away to look into the faces of the people and to hide the pang of apprehension I felt, realizing these were SOVIETS, not Russians, here. Victor was instantly solicitous—if he suspected the mere trace of doubt in my expression he was immediately defensive, patiently careful to explain every fault I might discern. I tried to hide my resentment of the heavy-handed Soviet trumpeting in the midst of such music and laughter. (The Soviet masters seem to view a festival like this with the indulgent tolerance of parents who permit their children to romp and play, then solemnly remind them their toys are SOLDIERS, their games endowed with gymnastic purpose and planned strategy. Not for one moment would they permit the children to play for mere happiness and indulgence in recreation.)

The moment the General left the stand and filed through the throng, the music resumed and the people relaxed, became mere human beings, Russians enjoying themselves. I studied them. The young men were brimful of vodka and best wishes. They kissed each other, on the mouth. The girls were glamorous and dressed in all the glitter and swishing silk of their French Club sisters.

Many of the men wore tuxes and cutaways, even a dusky carnation in their lapel. As the night wore on they began dancing in the center of the floor—the famed Russian squat, heel-kicking step and some Georgian dance.

We rode home about 4 a.m. in a pedicab. I was frozen in my sheer crepe dinner gown, but Victor held me very close to keep me warm. I was aware of the sweet dear stars overhead, instinctively looking for the North Star of my homeland: ALASKA.

Then came New Year's Day—one of the happiest in my whole life, completely making up for Christmas Day. Victor, whom I love very deeply, despite the estrangement of our two worlds, took me to a New Year's cocktail party at the swank Park Hotel. It was Mayor Wu's reception. Never have I seen such an ARMED guard around a public building, and the place was isolated by a Chinese equivalent of storm troopers holding machine guns in their hands, as casually as though they were rolled-up newspapers. The reception was going strong. We filed past the receiving line, shook hands with toothy Chinese officials and their shy and neatly groomed, fur-coated wives. There were no introductions; one merely said, "Happy New Year." Cocktails were served, an orchestra played, hors d'oeuvres were displayed lavishly. At 12 noon!

Victor's Chinese boss was there and we chatted with him, drinking a tomato juice toast. An American correspondent who wrote a sensational anti-Soviet article after a sneak trip to DARIEN stood across the room and I was dying to meet him, but Victor refused to even acknowledge his presence. We moved on and walked to SUN YA's for lunch. Anti-American posters, paper banners and streetcar stickers were all around. "Get thee home, beasts" was the general tenor of their slogans. This was the result of a raping of a Chinese girl student in Peiping by drunken Marines—whether the demonstration was set and organized by the Communists I don't know. As Victor and I walked down Nanking Loo, we saw flocks of Chinese police with guns and clubs. In a crowded street-section, a coolie jumped in front of a street copper—the policeman grabbed his arm and pelted him with his stick, not actually hurting him, but just impressing his authority. The coolie slipped away and hurried off in the crowd. Victor, in a flash of anger, threw away his cigarette. "Fascists, brutes, goddamn this government which permits its people to be clubbed on the street," he said bitterly. We went to D.D.'s *[Editor's Note: a popular Russian restaurant in Shanghai]* for dinner and to dance and came home to snuggle into our chair. For the first time Victor mentioned "our situation." "I love you—despite all the complications," he said. "I don't know how it will work out, but I don't know if I can let you go off to Switzerland—maybe you won't. I'll keep you with me." Actually I am in a quandary myself, but to Europe on the Trans-Siberian I will go. I am trying to get an assignment to take me to Moscow (expenses forthcoming if possible). Switzerland is my objective, some little place next to Alaska where I can settle down, feel "at home" and WRITE.

JANUARY 6, 1947—SHANGHAI—Victor has certainly brought world events to my door. His Soviet Club has a propaganda program called the "living newspaper," where articles are read to the audience. He asked me to write an article on the New Year's Eve celebration for the next newspaper. He will translate and read the article. I said I would write a brief article, and then as I sat struggling with it all the implications and possible dangers of the affiliation confronted me. I had to word my article carefully so that nothing would be misinterpreted or used to stamp me pro-Soviet, which I clearly and carefully AM NOT. I quote from my article: "On New Year's Eve I came to your club as an outsider, a stranger, and an American and you encircled me in your midst, made me one of you. Sharing the holiday with you gave me a great insight into your hearts. I felt very deeply that Americans and Russians are alike in their enormous capacity for making the most of an occasion." I then went on to describe the contrast in the French Club and the Soviet Club. I did not refer to the French Club by name, but said it was one of the most decorated, self-consciously elegant and snobbish gathering places in town. I danced to Russian music, which I love, in a throng of foreigners who did not even hear the music. Neither their ears nor hearts had the capacity for music. The women wore lavish gowns and jewels and a strained expression on their faces. The men were dissipated, not from the gaiety of New Year's but the decadence of their own lives. All Europe was represented and all political creeds or lack of creeds, save the unscrupulous cunning for wealth. They represented all that has been banished, cleansed from our world because as Shakespeare said, "the fault is not in their stars but in themselves." Then I referred to Victor. "My companion was a Soviet. I as an American and he, a Russian, were isolated from the crowd, united in our feelings toward those around us, we felt it was significant that our two countries stand virile, strong and democratic for the future against the moral corruption and inherited aristocracy of Europe that is past." I wound up with a platitude: "As an American, as one small representative of the United States here, I shall always remember the perfect understanding, happiness and friendship I shared with you on New Year's Eve.

I told Victor he could use my name if he wished. As a test case of Soviet endorsement, even in this obscure connection, it will be interesting to see how it comes out.

JANUARY 6, 1947—LETTER FROM SHANGHAI

Dearest Darling Mommie puss,

According to my little record of letters writ, I have not dispatched to you since Dec. 20—seems impossible I haven't written you about Christmas and New Year's in all this time. I hope I don't repeat myself. I was going to send you a CABLE on Christmas Day, and then I got your letters with the uncertain date of your departure from New York and should you be delayed it would have missed you entirely. For future reference, will you find out the *Harrisburg Telegraph's* cable address and I will use it c/o Lois Fegan. In cables you pay for every word of the address.

I was overjoyed to get your letters. Plane service was nil for a time, but now letters are getting through. Can't tell you how grateful I am for the clippings. Did I tell you before I went calling immediately on Newsreel Wong? He has invited me to dinner and get his life story this week. I hear there's a new magazine called '47 in the offing. Please send copies if you can get them. I have a copy of *COLLIER'S* with an article on Cissy Patterson in it, haven't read it yet, but it looks good. How was Aunt Marie, and dear Lot (Kent), who sent me a cute card. Daddy has sent me some very nice letters and please tell him I enjoyed them and will be delighted with the papers although magazines are my godsend, because they are also my buying market. I study them to see what kind of articles I can send them, for CASH. Now that the Trans-Siberian is open to all travelers (it has been thusly advertised) I am straining at the leash to go to Switzerland. Will wait until D.A. arrives this spring or summer and probably go in the fall with, I hope, some good fat assignments lined up. Want to stay in Moscow for a few weeks if I can wangle it. Anyway, any magazines beside *Life* and *Time*, which we do get, will be particularly WELCOME. Even old *Vogues*, if Lois can get her hands on them.

Did you read about the Northwest Airlines plane? I am standing by here to go out and interview the passengers when they come through.

I have finished my article for the *AMERICAN* (on Parker) and have lined up a picture taking with the best photographer in Shanghai: George Alexanderson of the *New York Times*. We'll have to fake in the background to look Alaskan. My adored Eva McGown unknowingly came to the rescue. She sent me a handmade Alaskan flag for Christmas, plus a handful of Alaskan newspapers, which scattered around will give atmosphere.

This week I also hope to get out a short article on young Bill Powell (father is J. B. Powell who lost his feet, remember?) as one of those "Report to the editors," *Saturday Evening Post*—half page of copy.

On the personal front—much news. I am much in loff! Think I indicated how much I liked this young blond editor of the *China Press* (largest paper in Shanghai). Victor is the first name, and the last is Latvian: Schneierson (pronounced "sneer-son") He's quite the "You Will Love Victor" boy. But his catch is a killer, a dead stop: He's a Soviet Russian! Getting international in my loves these days. His father was born in Latvia of Russian parentage (hence the blondness) and his mother is Russian. His English is pure "American" without the slightest trace of accent and his Russian is the most cultural I have heard. Sounds almost like French. I'm sure I told you about going out dinner dancing in the pouring rain. He took me to a Russian movie after that, and to a little place afterward where Russian gypsies play sobbing violins. Then we spent Christmas Eve together at home, because we wanted it quiet and cozy and because he had to edit the Christmas Day morning paper. (I'm sure I told you all this before somehow... or was it to Aunt Marie? Knowing how she loves the Love Affairs of Parker I sent her a gay version of it all.) He gave me a box of candy and a silver bracelet with our names engraved in Russian on the inside. With Victor I am terribly happy. We're in the Terribly in Love stage. And I call him baby, etc., and he calls me all the incredible baby names in Russian all ending in "itchka."

New Year's Day Victor took me to the most elegant cocktail party in town: the one given at the décor Park Hotel by Mayor Wu of Shanghai. Everyone was there and I even got my name in the society column for having been there with my darling, drinking tomato juice. The party began at 11 a.m. From there we went to the most famous Chinese restaurant for lunch: Sun-Ya's. Ate with chopsticks with one hand, held hands with the other. I was all a-twinkle and

a-bubble... The day was sunny and blue-skied. We had each other
and were young and lyrical. Little did we guess a big Anti-American
demonstration was taking place on the bund. Two newspaper "men"
cooing at each other and going to the movies, not knowing a thing
about it until the next day! We saw *Fantasia* and wallowed in the
music. Then to a Russian restaurant (fabulous story about the place)
called "D.D's" (will make a yarn for me yet). Then home to change
and off to another nice place to dance and have dinner. A day taken
out of my life. I have never been so happy. Intellect and laughter!

To go on with my daily news would be practically to say Victor
took me here, there. AGRS gave a dinner dance at the Navy Club
and I asked the man who does the PX purchasing for Japan. He takes
me to visit factories with him. One day I watched camphor chests
being carved, and he has gotten me things wholesale, so this was an
obligation. He's quite nice himself, too. The boy whose job I took is
being flown home to the States because his broken leg isn't healing
just right. I have been down to see my friend Ann Cottrell of UNRRA
and the *New York Herald Trib*. She was sick so I took her a bottle of
sherry. And just as we opened it, in walked the British correspondent
who had been to Harbin with us. He was en route to Hong Kong and
on his return goes off to London through Russia. He gave me some
valuable tips on getting assignments which will be an entrée to the
ballet, concerts, etc., in Moscow. And one of his contacts there (news)
is a Rose PARKER! It turned out to be quite an evening. Ann ordered
dinner and we dined in her room, howling our heads off, trying to
decide what we're going to do about eventually getting married to
SOMEONE. She's a few years older than I, but very pretty and about
in my spot. Never met the right one, but oops, he was already with
wife.

Nothing new on my next field trips for AGRS. When I get my
magazine stories lined up, will take off. Want some bread on the
waters while I'm out with the grave diggers. My stories continue to
get a good play locally, especially in Victor's paper, which everyone

reads. And everyone tells me what a "fine writer" I am. Really, no output of mine in the past has roused such continual comment. Coming from the top-flight correspondents themselves, that's pretty good.

You mentioned Durdin of the *Times,* whom Aunt Marie reads. For heaven's sake, send me his stuff. Would really RELISH a few copies of the *Herald Trib* and the *New York Times.* Politics have never ENGROSSED and absorbed me so much before. I am in the big league now and can't sit like a dummy in their company. Anything on China or foreign policy in Asia is vital. Vada Ward sent me a note, saying she is working for the American Weekly, my old customer. Must send them some stuff. It's hard to get around in Shanghai, and there is still no heat in my room, and over the weekend there wasn't even hot water. My PX man loaned me one of his quilted robes with enough lap to bury me inside. Had a letter from Gerry Sampson, my Britisher, from Cairo. He was still en route to London by air. He mentioned in a purely British understatement how he regretted I wasn't making the trip with him because "it would have been such fun." (It would have been our honeymoon, actually, and fancy such an experience being "such fun.")

Would still like the longies (about size 29 girdle I wear), if you can get them, also one snuggie shirt. I have written Art (Bremer) to send on my clothes. If you ever see any cute little hats, like a snazzy Magnin job, (à la Macy's), I could use small hats. Everyone loves the little brown one I got in Seattle. Haven't worn the others yet—too big and showy for riding in jeeps. Come Spring and strolling, though... or a pink short-sleeved sweater, (or a white one, or baby blue) still size 34... and bunches of violets in deep purple. Keep these things in mind for gifts, and bill me in between. Lois sent me an adorable compact with two fat cherubs on it. Arrived unbroken and perfect. A can or two of G. Washington or Nescafé welcome. Harder to get now that Army wives shop in the commissary.

Must get to work. Some correspondent, Christopher Rand, from the *Herald Trib* coming over this morning. (Chris Rand was the picture of Jade Jim!!!) All my squeeziest love. Hope you get to see your GRANDCHILD soon, and that Patty got the white silk I sent her. Your box will be along before Easter I guarantee.

Baby Mei Ling and in Russian "pegu," Pegge in Russian

JANUARY 18, 1947—SHANGHAI—I am enmeshed in international emotions—a controversy of newspaper editors: one, American, Bill Powell, *CHINA WEEKLY REVIEW,* and the other, Victor, Soviet, *CHINA PRESS.* (Perhaps, before I launch into this, I had better complete the report on my article at the Soviet Club. It poured rain the night Victor was to read it. Few attended. Victor deleted the reference to vodka, gave his own introduction, as I did not attend myself. I don't know what the audience reaction was.)

To return to the lead subject: I went down to the press building one day last week, saw Victor and went across the street to the Ritz Bar. At a little table with a spotted cloth and ketchup bottle on top, we sat semi-holding hands and Victor pulled from his pocket a 3- page story for the *China Weekly Review*'s monthly report. Subject: LABOR. He had worked very hard on it and felt diffident about turning it in. Would I give it a test reading? Although only slightly informed on the labor situation here, I read the three pages with outward panic and inward disappointment. It was poorly written, I thought, buried in his inbred, one-track policy of Sovietism, oppression and the workers, down with government tyranny, etc. Even if his stuff was 100% accurate, my eye quickly judged the writing. I thought it very badly done. I, however, was not the editor, so I let it go. Today, I went down to see Bill to finish up my story on him, and as I waited to talk to him, I heard Victor's name mentioned, and a long discussion of his article, which they contended was a lot of windy hash—prejudiced and presented with few factual statistics—deadline hovered and there was little time to redo it. I winced inwardly, got through my interview and Bill walked me to the stairway, to my embarrassment, as I waited to go upstairs to see Victor. After the discussion I'd overheard, I didn't think it diplomatic. I hurried down the steps, waited until Bill returned to his office, then went up to the *China Press.* Victor leaped up when I walked in—told me his grapevine of a fellow Soviet on the *Review* tipped him off Bill had been mad over the Labor article. Called Victor a damned Red trying to pump up Communist propaganda into his report. Victor went down to see him, took a few criticisms from Bill, and agreed to let a *Review* staff member cut and rewrite part of the story. He was quite upset over the whole thing. (I told him nothing of what I had overheard.) He suggested we have some coffee, so we went to the Ritz Bar. Seated at a table in the corner, we discussed the article and Powell. I could see Victor was upset over being called a "RED" (which he IS, of course— brilliant RED) —admitted to me he resented the stigma attached to the accusation. I sat there, as a woman all sweet sympathy, as a deeply loyal AMERICAN and impartial reporter I championed my fellow American editor—BILL POWELL was RIGHT—justified absolutely—my romantic ardor for Victor became estranged. At that moment, in walked Bill Powell. Our eyes didn't meet, but he must have seen me. I DIED of embarrassment— felt "caught" somehow in a delicate deception and being in agreement with Powell over the controversy, I resented my position with Victor.

Never have I been so strained in personal and political loyalties. We left, and Victor put me in a pedicab to come back to the Race Course. He asked if I had the change for my fare. I said yes, of course, and he didn't make any further offer to pay my 50 cents (approx.) fare back. As I joggled along, past the golden-globed open-door Chinese shops, past dens and hovels where steaming cookers boiled up coolie chow, past kids banging brass platters and old men sawing away on Chinese violins, I considered Victor—the Soviet—I think I fell almost completely out of love with him, regretting the loss of our haven of romance, confidence and his inevitable POLITICS. Chinese New Year's coming up next week. I mustn't bid him adieu yet. But oh—Soviet-ism and American-ism are inexorably incompatible. Someday, maybe in Switzerland, I will write a story about an American girl and a Soviet "believer."

It is almost with seeming malice that I now record my two bones of contention. (1) His Soviet ABSOLUTISM—blind and bull-headed intolerance of any other ideology, but Communism, almost childishly so. (2) As a woman, his—is it Soviet tendency—utter lack of thoughtfulness. I have given him many little things, cigarettes, a book, shaving cream, etc. He has retaliated with "I'll get you this—that" etc., and never does he come through. The other day I showed him a Russian dictionary I had. "Could you get me one?" he asked casually. It would have been an easy matter, (army education manual) but I deliberately didn't. All the time I was sick, he never sent me flowers, brought me a magazine, nothing. Enlarged to a Russian policy, I think there's a parallel there: American generosity—the giving from largesse—Soviet grab-ism, no tokens in return.

FEBRUARY 1, 1947—PEIPING—I was recalled up here on special lend-lease assignment to publicize the 332nd Troop Carrier. The pedicab, truck and aerial delivery wagon outfit for Executive Headquarters (UNRRA). Plane crashes in China these days seem to be occurring every five minutes. I prepared in advance for any emergency. Hardly had the plane taken off, than I hustled around with notebook and pencil getting everybody's middle initial and home town, including a Chinese colonel who spoke English, but gave me an orange stamped with the equivalent of Sunkist. The flight was cold but atmospheric. China's winter scene was a scroll of earthen colors offset by bright clear blue sky. Ponds, lakes and rivers were frozen royal blue splotches. The brown, minutely cultivated patches of land were lightly blown over with dry white snow. No friendly sign of life was visible—no smoke coiled up cozily from the Chinese farm compounds of mud brick. Peiping was cold, crisply clear, snow-spattered, the red walls and green-roofed pagodas rising vividly above the white and brown of the ground. I am staying at the same "Grand Hotel des Wagon Lits, Ltd." The talk around is all about the Marine rape case (Marine raped Chinese girl student) and the big evacuation of Executive Headquarters, dependents and personnel.

FEBRUARY 4, 1947—PEIPING—Yesterday was miserable. We flew over the Great Wall, rigid, incorruptible bastion on the ridge of deep gnarled bold mountains. As I gazed down on the most incredible engineering monument of antiquity, I kept re-echoing inwardly American GI sentiment about the "stupid Chinese." I find among Executive Headquarters personnel and other officers a great respect for the Japs and a bitter disgust and derision for the Chinese.

On the return flight over snow-swept brown patches of most frugal agricultural "gardening" (this is China) we swept over the Ming Tombs, but from the air all we could see were scarlet-walled compounds, clumps of secluding trees and green pagoda roofs. Peiping from the air on a clear winter's day is scroll-like in its artistic conception and exquisite charm. I was disappointed today not to have made a promised flight to YENAN, Communist capital. Maybe next week. Dined with my Russian friends, the FRIEDS, last night and learned they are Soviet, but careful to conceal it. One of their vodka-toasting dinner guests revealed the political creed of the family.

Have just come in from a freezing but magical, entrancing rickshaw ride in the Peiping moonlight, so coldly spell-creating, so detached and suspended—the Peking Hotel all ablaze with lights looked like New York or Washington D.C. I had been to interview the editor of the strange little paper, the *PEIPING CHRONICLE*, owned by the Nationalist Government. The paper is published in a Chinese compound. Coal is so expensive, the editorial staff is confined to one lattice-walled cubicle. During the interview the lights went out. The editor explained that electricity is so scarce that outside of the legation quarters where the Americans are, the lights are snapped off for hours at a time. The type for the paper is all set by hand, but by Chinese who do not understand a word of English. A printer's devil hustles about. He is the shaved-headed, apple-cheeked but undersized 13-year-old son of one of the typesetters. The paper sells for $300 CN (about 3 cents). More details of the paper will go into a magazine article, I hope. I miss Victor very much. I'm afraid I'm quite mentally and physically attached to him.

FEBRUARY 6, 1947—PEIPING—Peiping is a storybook town. Never have I seen such dawns break over the countryside as I ride out to the West Field Airport each morning. The stalwart hills bordering Peiping look beige-pink, lined with purple gorges. The road stretches straight ahead—on the shoulders are the Chinese, astride their docile trotting baby mules whose baby-faced, yeoman ardor is so appealing, tiny red tassels hard on their brown-haired brows between flopping furry ears. We pass Chinese houses of dried mud. Occasionally a woman in trousers and padded tunic, her hair braided down the back, stares at us as we whiz by. The fields are dry and plowed and barren. In the distance the tiered, aged, gray jade fountain rises into the aquamarine, fresh blue morning sky.

I put in a hectic day—was informed Executive Headquarters was worried about my releasing any stories on the Chinese Nationalist-Communist situations. So would I be sent back to Shanghai immediately? Some quick appeasement prolonged my stay until Monday.

Went to a unique cocktail party at the Peking Hotel yesterday, given for the Communists by the Nationalists. I arrived about 6:30. The place was so quiet I wasn't sure it was the right party. I was issued into a dimly lit, bare-looking room; lined up in a straight line were about 10 Nationalist officers. I murmured how I was Miss Parker of New York (no mention of scandal sheet *News*). They all bobbed their glistening black-haired heads and grinned toothily. I was handed a weak kind of cocktail in a small wine glass. I eventually got into conversation with a French correspondent and his wife. Met John Roderick, Reynolds Packard, Mark Gayn and Seymour Topping.

When a dinner date (interview) I had with the editor of the four-page local paper, the *Peiping Chronicle*, was rather suddenly cancelled, I took matters in hand and suggested Topping and I have a chat at dinner. He gallantly countered by inviting me to join him at the Peiping Club. We paused to observe the Communist General, seldom seen, being surrounded, or blacked out, by Nationalist Chinese reporters. They really suffocated him in a circle. The Communists and Nationalists did not blend too well. An air of stiffness and vague smiles pervaded. The Communist girls looked like students from an old-fashioned boarding school—they wore padded tunics, dull-toned or black color, and their hair was cut China-doll bobbed. Only Josephine Sun, English-speaking PRO for the Communists, seemed at home among the crowd. She remarked she would be glad to get to the liberated areas as she had never been in Communist China.

Topping and I walked down Legation Street to the Peiping Club, by cold clear immaculate moonlight, which silvered the sidewalks and aged walls and bulging-eyed lion guards by scarlet compounds. The grandeur of the Club amazed me. By custom, we entered by a side door, women not being permitted in certain rooms of the Club. Upstairs, in a discreetly carpeted and draperied cocktail lounge, we chatted before sitting down in the adjoining dining room to a superb steak dinner, concluded with a unique dessert called "Peiping Dust"—a mound of ground nuts (chestnuts) topped with a fluff of sour whipped cream. Topping and I got off onto some comparing of notes on the Chinese situation and foreign corresponding in general. To our surprise, over a gradual sharing of confidences we found we were very much alike in our reactions—had endured the same qualms and sharp swallows at times. I recalled my conversation with Gerry Sampson when I asked him if seeing and studying the world is worth the price. Topping drives himself and lives alone in a cubicle room lined with books and a typewriter. If he is lonely, though, he fiercely staves off that diagnosis for a restless longing. He begins to write or gets himself engrossed in a book of solid informative content. "Some of the things I learned about being a foreign correspondent," he declared, "were cultivating my own company. Learning to live alone." I understood what he meant. It was a wonderful evening— the first time I have shared my reactions to China with someone who completely understood, as a writer and American. Maybe Topping will prove to be an important contact in the future.

FEBRUARY 7, 1947—LETTER FROM PEIPING

Darlingest honey duck Mommie,

Here I am in the city of a thousand temples and scarlet walls and Empress Dowager's palaces. I left Shanghai about a week ago to come here "on assignment" to write some stories of the Air Force which has been flying General (George) Marshall's truce teams around, (without a single accident). The flight up was beautiful, such a clear day, and I was seeing Chinese winter for the first time.

I am staying at the genteel Wagon Lits (pronounced "wagon lee") hotel, Peiping's No. One hotel. The weather has been cold and divinely clear, moon drenched, snow brushed, sparkling crisp.

I had dinner Monday with my Russian family (what food) and have been with the local correspondents in between. Keep your eyes peeled for bylines by Seymour (no less) Topping. Also clip and send any Peiping datelined news items you see, on Manchuria.

When you know the correspondents personally, it is instructive to read their output. The other correspondent who took me dancing was this Robert Pines of INS who tells me he is on a world-roving assignment. He just left for Harbin. Watch for his stuff too. Pines once did the police beat for the *New York Times*. He's very slicker-ish, my age, but loose-jointed, á la Jimmy Stewart. I do love talking to fellow writers.

I am running around on the side trying to get material for other stories to write when I get back in Shanghai. (I am using a very old typewriter and the letters pile on top of each other.)

The other evening I went calling on the local newspaper editor who again gave me a big write-up in the Social column. This paper is called the *Peiping Chronicle*, has a Chinese staff, all but the editor. All type is hand set by Chinese who speak no English. They just read the lettering. I went from the hotel to the paper, which is in a Chinese compound with scarlet doors and various pagoda-roofed buildings, in a rickshaw, by moonlight if you please, having memorized the Chinese words for "newspaper office." "Ya, ya, missy, *Peking Newspaper*," the boy answered, as he tucked his blanket over my legs and started off. This is quite a place, haven't been shopping yet because I've had no time.

I suppose when I get back to Shanghai I'll have letters from you enclosing stories of the AGRS plane that made a forced landing near Canton. I told you I handled the release of that story. They finally salvaged the plane, flew it safely out to Canton. No one was hurt, so don't be alarmed. The reason for the plane crashes in China has been politics and stupid or callous mismanagement. Planes just now inspected, etc., parts missing and the planes still being flown. Army regulations were never more strict, and our planes have been flying regardless of the other crashes, and we have had a 99% safety record. DON'T WORRY, in other words, Darling, although I will know how you would feel.

Think I told you to watch out for the Lolo Land story about the American boys believed held captive. That will be MY STORY too. Or I'll be in the middle of it. There is some tension around Peiping, everyone wondering what's going to happen in the Chinese war when the Americans pull out. And that will be pretty soon. The other night, driving to town from the airport (a great butter-gold moon riding low on the azure horizon) we passed at least 100 Chinese Nationalist troops marching down the highway in formation, their rifles with fixed bayonets on their shoulders. There will be lots more bloodshed before this is over. I borrowed the book *Thunder Out of China*, by Teddy White, from the Communists' press receptionist here (a very pretty Chinese girl named Josephine Sun) and read it. Instructive indeed, certainly damns the Gimo. *[Editor's Note: Generalissimo Chiang Kai-Shek.]* Saw my Jesuit priest who came over on the ship with me for a quick cup-of-coffee visit.

Will finish this up when I return to Shanghai. Got the darlingest farewell gift from my Russian dispatcher in the AGRS motor pool. The young one who sends me Russian grammar books, candy, etc. This time, a wee round basket of fresh violets with a big red rose in the center, and the cutest toy doggie for a mascot. Victor's farewell—a jar of G. Washington coffee and some chocolates, and an argument over Yugoslavia. We parted almost in a wild fury.

Love and big verbal hugs until I get home, Baby

[Editor's Note: In the same envelope was the following continuation, written after Pegge had returned to Shanghai.]

Back safe and sound in Shanghai. Darling, I know you'll think I did nothing in Peiping but EAT. (Just glanced back over the notes leading up to this one.)

The flight home was freezing, no eating in the plane, Bob Pines of INS sleeping on my shoulder. Arriving back at the office, I found a real STACK of mail, including your colossal flirtin' Valentine. I propped Suzy up on my desk and all my fellow gravediggers adored it. Daddy's too, with the feathers on and the CUTE CUTE verse, was precious. Lou (my Alaskan girl friend) presented me with a big, big basket of red carnations as a welcome-home gesture. Yes, I got all your letters and the rolls of papers for which I THANK Pap a thousand times. I comb them for reports from China. It is valuable to get a stateside perspective on copy. I was surprised that my airplane accident received such a small mention. Here it was headlines for three days. Understand my New Year's message written for the Colonel to the Generalissimo was picked up and printed in a paper in Rochester New York. Oh yes, before I forget, I had a letter from *COLLIER'S* (Davenport himself, the editor, you know) saying I was certainly entitled to compensation for tipping them off about the nightclub in Anchorage, and they were complying with my request for $100. Was I thrilled. That's the first time I've sold an idea out and out. Long letter from George Wallace about Victor. I had mentioned my slight Soviet contact. "I told you to look out of all the windows of the world, not fall out of them," he reprimanded me and went on for pages on how I am to control my mental searching and physical adventures in the geographic and political world. Sound, sound advice from a fellow world traveler.

I also had a very nice letter from the *NEWS* asking for a story on the personal ads. I have meanwhile dashed off another story for them on Peiping's most famous unsolved murder. I will ask them to omit my name as it will probably tramp on toes.

Letter from George Keibel (from Alaska) saying he has two relatives in Shanghai he hears are destitute. He asked me to look them up, give them what money they may need and he will reimburse me. He was a good, good friend to me in the struggling days so I will comply at the first chance.

Would LOVE to see pictures of my wee niece. Just can't imagine her existence.

Lois (FEGAN) sent me a grand box of things, including a pair of snuggle panties, white wrapping paper and ribbon, a lipstick and writing paper. How darling of her. Will have to continue later.

SUNDAY, FEBRUARY 9, 1947—PEIPING—Ah, Peiping. What things happen to me here! Topping (whose real name is TOPOVITCH or something Russian) took me to a dinner party given by the French correspondent JULES JOLSON and his très charmant wife. Their home was a scarlet-doored compound, so truly old Peiping, a dimly lit foyer with screens and black latticework over a dim old mirror. We were led into a combined dining and drawing room where massive black carved furniture was offset by scarlet Chinese rugs. A fire crackled in one corner of the room. The guests were international, mostly French. I had a goggled goon next to me who said he was from Paris ("Oh, no!" I groaned inwardly). Topping lent his opinion of the Communists, etc. I was surprised and reassured somehow that the Peiping press anyhow is not as underdog championing of the Reds as the gang in Shanghai. I also felt, as I listened to fine-print discussions of Chinese strongholds and giveaways, that the mass public would know less and care less than I. And I am in business to sell the greatest number: the masses. Topping would occasionally share my glance and thought, and once he sat in a chair beside me, trying to touch my arm and hair in an obscure but meaningful way. We came home about midnight and sat in the lobby of the Grand Hotel des Wagon Lits talking about Topping. Somehow I lost interest as he babbled on. He needs a good ten years on him yet, I thought as I bid him goodnight.

Today I went to Mass, then to call on a photographer who has snapped everyone who ever came through here. Poor man, he was a broken-down wreck of a Russian émigré. His compound was cold and shabby and the room where he received me was covered with dust-grimed equipment and cameras. As if conscious of his fallen state, he went through a painful demonstration of grand duke courtliness and ended up playing a nocturne on a tinny piano in the next room.

I then met Topping and we went to lunch at Reynolds Packard's place—WHAT AN OCCASION THAT WAS. His Chinese house was utterly garbed in atmosphere of a disheveled American mandarin writer. We had Chinese chow and I happened to ask Pack how he became a newspaperman. For the following two hours he regaled us. Verily, he said, the way of the wandering scribe is fraught with trials and strong passions. Aside from all this (Pack calls himself a "fat Peter Pan"), he described Ernie Pyle, late beloved war correspondent of the doughboys, as a renegade. It was a thundering shock, for while I properly discounted most of it, I thought the gist was probably true. I felt a bit of Washington D.C. degradation (my shock and disgust findings out there).

Yesterday afternoon I lunched with my friends, the FRIEDS, and then Mrs. Fried and I went shopping. I acquired the joy of all my Chinese treasures: a Chinese Princess done in silk embroidery on royal blue mounted on pale gray-green. Oh! She is magnificent and cost only $15 gold. I also got a black kimono for $5 and some exquisite obis. The bargaining was hard to do. The Chinese seemed reluctant to sell and were quite indifferent to the threat of a Communist grand swoop or the Americans leaving.

No one seems to fear a siege or war event here. I've completed one bargain by getting a jacket for $5, provided the shopkeeper paid our fares home in a rickshaw, plus one stop on FLOWER STREET. We were laden with obis and bundles and it was cold. After sundown, the rickshaws took us into the most Fu Manchu looking alleyways, mud roads where Chinese bent over boiling, steaming vessels. A Chinese funeral procession passed in the jostle of the traffic. Then tiny shops appeared, marked outside by ancient medallions of various gilt designs, usually with a scarlet cloth attached. The shops were painted red, mostly. The minute customers step inside, electric lights go on, clothes are pulled aside and then you see—petit point bags, embroidered boxes. Prices were higher than we expected there: $20 for a really exquisite petit point evening bag about the size of a volume of poems.

FEBRUARY 15, 1947—SHANGHAI—Returned home—a trip back that should go in the record books for endurance. For over five hours in a freezing airplane I sat huddled next to INS "roving" correspondent BOB PINES, who upchucked and turned pale green when the going got rough out of TIENTSIN. Only by the fact that I had an Armed Forces pocket edition of *A. WOOLLCOTT* by Samuel Hopkins Adams did I survive. But before I go on, a sum-up of

Peiping. The OUTSTANDING EVENT was a grand orgy lunch given by JOSEPHINE SUN and her PRO boss of the Communist Branch, Executive Headquarters. The lunch began at 12:30 and ended at 3:30. Among those present were all the foreign correspondents and wives. Most noticeable: BEN WELLS, who looks more as though he were Leopold Stokowsky's son than Sumner Wells—pink-faced, goggles, lanky, very nice, though regarded with jade jealousy by the other correspondents because his father's name gives WELLS a "pipeline" of contacts not open to others. He has a wife who looks like a Powers model—paints her mouth on beautifully with a brush—wears a leopard coat and bright red kid boots. Communists present included two Generals: General YEH and Major General HSUEH. These two were to afford me the unique experience of my first direct conversation with Chinese who spoke no English. We chatted in Russian, which they spoke without a trace of Chinese intonation and with easy grace and command. I spluttered through my few phrases, ending by asking General HSUEH if he had seen the ballet at the Bolshoi Theatre in Moscow. The Russian word "ballet" escaped me, so I held up my hands ballet-like and moved them over my head. The two generals roared. The "lunch" was delayed an hour, while the hungry but voluble correspondents stood around munching sweet Chinese candy and nuts instead of the prerequisite cocktails. We then adjourned to a dining room across the court. The tables were charmingly spread—napkins were stiffly starched and stuffed in the top of water goblets forming flower baskets. The dishes were sulfur yellow with royal blue dragons. Soup spoons matched, as did hot rice wine decanters (teapot shape) and porcelain wine goblets—everything being "gom bay." *[Editor's Note: "Gom bay" means "bottoms up" or "dry glass" in Chinese.]* SUCH a lunch. Peking duck was a mere snack amid a rush of steaming ginger and brown-sugar-sauced concoctions. John RODERICK sat on my left, BOB PINES, right. Roderick kept making the most amazing barbed wise cracks about the Communists to General Yeh, who got the point, howled and gombayed like any regular guy. I watched Josephine SUN, the Communist PRO. I had met her as a happy bride in November when she wore a smart tailored suit ordered in the U.S.A., plus make-up and a becoming hairdo. Now she appeared in a padded China-blue long gown, no make-up and her hair combed down as straight as possible and pulled behind her ears. She had rendered up her prettiness for politics.

It was the gayest of parties. I was never so thrilled to be a "correspondent" among correspondents. Peiping was never more ENCHANTED looking. Heavy snow had whitened the background for a Chinese paint box of color and design: red walls and green swooped pagoda roofs rising into a brilliant blue sky. The Chinese themselves never looked colder or more picturesque, their sallow skin tinged rosy pink. And their predominantly blue gowns daubed the mingling street scene with vividness. Peach-cheeked babies were wrapped in red satin coverlets. The climax was a camel caravan warily footing it down the main drag (described by some florid writer as the Champs Elysée of Peking). Just beyond the main gates to town, the Chinese shops were like toy emporiums with tiny windows and boarded-up doors. Gilt Chinese lettering proclaimed their wares in wide signboards over the doorway. Often the roofs were sheer ramparts watched over by stone lions and dragons.

Politically, Peiping is anticipating a purse-touching economic pitfall with the departure of American truce teams. All the foreign clerks employed by headquarters will be jobless, not to mention the Russian gal friends of the landed colonels. The clerks at the PX and commissary were all but throwing themselves headlong at the American officers in a last desperate PREDATORY gesture. On the outskirts of town some threat of Communist menacing action was felt. As close as an outsider could prophesy, the town will be isolated, prodded and made uncomfortable, but it will not be taken.

P.S. Met another "interest," briefly: one lieutenant Phillip "Pete" Peterson, a "nice" boy, Catholic too. Our one date was for Chinese chow. We went forth in rickshaws, single-seaters, so we had to talk to each other from a distance.

MONDAY, FEB. 17—This is the last gasp. Got a hand-knit pink sweater from Eva (MacGown) in Alaska (sent airmail) and your envelope of clippings (thank you, darling!) and a letter from Art Bremer scolding me for writing more letters to Eva than to him (he has written about three since I came to the Republic of China!). Want to catch the mail boy before he leaves. Bye, darling, sweet... will send your Christmas box this week! Easter box combined, I guess.

Hugs and grunt-tight squeezes from a very twinkling-eyed Baby white jade!!

P.S. Victor just tipped me off that the Northwest plane with Hunter aboard is due today.

FEBRUARY 19, 1947—LETTER FROM SHANGHAI

Darling ones,

This is a rush-quickie to tell you the newspaper stories are inaccurate as usual; AGRS WILL REMAIN IN CHINA UNTIL NEXT YEAR. Only General Marshall's truce team will be withdrawn. After I sealed the Peiping letter and mailed it, I realized I hadn't told you.

FEB. 21: Well, things have been happening since I began this letter. For one thing Cyril Hunter of Northwest Airlines arrived. A small cocktail party was given and I was invited. This was to be an EVENT with much hanging in the balance. I borrowed from Lou (my Alaskan friend) a gorgeous muskrat coat (looked wonderful) and her Hattie Carnegie hat. Hunter, a few cocktails under his belt, greeted me cordially. We chit-chatted and were in the midst of a "conversation" when some goon who wanted to be introduced to me charged over and began one of those "I KNOW I've met you somewhere before" things. Hunter turned away. Furious, I tried to get his eye again. General Chennault was there, very weather-beaten face, otherwise looks like any businessman. As I made a move to depart, Hunter got me off in a corner. Offered me a job as their PRO in Shanghai!! How much salary—which gave him pause. Anyway, we agreed to a part-time handling, and I was to see him for an interview this morning (as a NEW YORK NEWS reporter). Arrived at his fabulous suite. General Chennault was there, waiting. Hunter nowhere in sight. Chennault and I were introduced, but as he is almost stone deaf didn't attempt small talk. Finally a talk with Hunter, now very chummily calling me Pegge, etc. Big group of men waiting to rush him to a mayor's lunch. No mention of job, but I am to see his press representative for the entire airline, later on. With all this in the offing, my mind has been in the good old Washington D.C. whirl, doping out angles, etc. I will be delighted if I get a part-time job. Army hours are so liberal I could do it very easily. After the cocktail party I had a date with the young navigator I'd met in Peiping with 332nd Troop Carrier. He, poor boy, is sitting outside in the jeep, watching it like a hawk by sitting in it! He took me to a beautiful hotel dining room afterward and though I went through the motions all I could think of was Northwest Airlines. As even a part-time staff member, how easy it would be to fly back to the USA sometime. Not to mention the other points on their run: Manila, Japan, and OF COURSE, ALASKA.

The two magazines, *Coronet* and that interesting READER'S SCOPE (very glad to see it) arrived, as did a roll of newspapers containing the *Times and Tribune*. Lou and I pounced on them... the clothes... the cheap prices (compared to Shanghai), and I got one AGRS clipping on our missing plane. Thank you both a thousandfold.

Ann Cottrell came over to lunch yesterday and I showed her the clipping on the man shortage and "Better Get Married," etc. We both howled. "The trouble with getting married is ruining your whole life just to be happy at 50," she said. Her mother is getting after her in a similar vein—and she's a few years older than I.

My Chinese tailor (found another girl) is making me a black skirt from that wrap-around job I got in Seattle. Looks very smart. And is fitting a Jap brocade jacket for me I got in Peiping for $5. The coloring is exquisite. Also, he copied the jacket to the red dress I got in Magnin's from peppermint pink silk, ruffled peplum bow tie neck, luscious color. He is very reasonable and a very cute little man who speaks the most balled-up Chinese you ever heard. Got your box packed, but am looking for something for Father. May get him a briefcase or something. Chinese leather is very fine.

Thanks for the envelope of clips you sent. One from the *Trib* about the AGRS in Europe was part of an official memo. As usual the clips you send have far-reaching effects. I passed the Spring hat clips around, too, and everyone gasped. They look the same as those they wore when I was a veiled and flower-topped model. Keep your eye open for the violets. Really need some for Spring. Won't need any face powder or pancake make-up for a while. I got some in the Peiping PX and Mary Allshouse writes she is sending me two cakes too. My British correspondent sent me a complete file of his dispatches on China—very stiff, HEAVILY FACTUAL style of writing—maybe, though, that's what the London scribes like. His name was plastered all over the place, which is unusual. British papers aren't so byline happy as American.

We have a Washington's Birthday holiday Saturday. Will be busy writing my *NEWS* features. Pete may be down from Peiping again. He's cute, red-headed and you'd like him, but as Honey Gal would say, "He don't kiss goodnight"... sweet and slow on the uptake.

SUNDAY, FEB. 24: One last powwow with Northwest Airlines. I'm to work with the *New York Times* photographer in doing travel lure stuff on Shanghai and to do other publicity chores as per direction from the home office. Should be profitable and wonderfully interesting. I told this Publicity Director about the article you sent me on Shanghai clipped from *HOLIDAY*. He suggested I try one from the tourist angle. My great secret delight over the whole thing is more the TRIP home than the extra money. Northwest operates flights all the way into NYC. Imagine Ahmee's reaction if I walked in on her one day. Working for the company would, of course, give the ol' pass privilege. You and father would of course whip up to New York to see me or I could come to Harrisburg (probably easier and so wonderful to see you BOTH, and Lois too). Would LOVE to know if Lois got her silk slip Christmas present. Was waiting to hear from her before writing about the box. Well, will write anyway. She sent me so many "thoughtful" things, bless her.

My Pete arrived in town Saturday afternoon and took me dancing Saturday night. We were dancing and arguing about Tolstoy's *War and Peace.* Planned to go to Mass together the next morning, but his plane took off for the Lolo country (that story will break one of these days, I guess) at 7 a.m. I should have known him in Fairbanks. He's the type to cook for.

Bye-bye, Mommie duckie sweets, for now. Loved the little poem you sent about a special treasure. Keep the *Tribs* and *Times* coming this way if possible. Just LOVED reading them. Also please let me see the snaps of Lynda. I'll return them. Squeezie hugs and Outlouders, too, my own dearest darlin' No. 1 Mommie.

Baby Mei Ling.

FEBRUARY 24, 1947—SHANGHAI—For the record I want to quote a few lines from a Washington's Birthday address, given here by ambassador J. LEIGHTON STUART (at very fancy best-bib-and-tucker dinner sponsored by AMERICAN UNIVERSITY CLUB) after discussing Washington's life from the angle of a man of wealth who sacrificed all for the revolutionary cause of a new republic. Stuart struck out with: "The real enemies of China are now INTERNAL... the real enemies of China are illiteracy, poverty, disease, the exploitation of public office for private gain, including that of relatives and friends, narrow and ruthless partisan bigotry. The hope of the country lies

in the awakening of a new form of national consciousness which…
puts the welfare of the vast inarticulate suffering masses above all
personal ambitions."

Also, for the record; Northwest Airlines zoomed across the North
Pacific a few days ago to lay initial foundation, politically and
operationally, for their first payload runs in May. Talked with Cyril
HUNTER, president of the airline, and hoped I laid the foundation
for a return hop to Alaska this summer.

MARCH 3, 1947—SHANGHAI—Making an earnest, searching
effort to know the human story of the Chinese, I went calling on
HELEN SUN—shy, flower-faced sister of the Communist PRO I
knew in Peiping. Helen took me to a Chinese restaurant—man-on-
the-street variety and a hubbub of Chinese chatter and clatter. Helen
in her sweet, halting intoned English was telling me about a growing
feeling of tension among the people. A Chinese newspaper here wrote
a witty satire on the words of the Chinese National Anthem under
the present regime. The next day the editor was given a full yardstick
of the Authorities' displeasure. The paper was suspended for a day,
the editor must recant the scathing levity of his satire and make a
most abject apology for insulting the Chinese people. Henceforth, a
government censor will sit in judgment of the editorial output. Helen
remarked, as she deftly chopsticked sweet sautéed fish, freedom of
the press is a mere phrase in the new constitution. She also told me
the mail is frequently opened and read by Chinese postal authorities.
She went on, charmingly at home and comfortable, where before she
had been restrained and tacit, telling me how much she is enjoying
Elliot Roosevelt's *AS HE SAW IT,* where a description of Mme. Chiang
includes her familiarity with the late President Roosevelt. Seems she
was given to resting her exquisite hand on the President's knee.

I have resumed studying Russian (Trans-Siberian Railway, here I
come) and have an excellent teacher. But she has given me a new

textbook with CHINESE to explain the Russian grammar. As I was studying my lesson in the Army dining room this morning, the Chinese waiter almost dropped my soft-boiled eggs. "You study Chinese?" When I explained it was Russian, he was not a bit convinced and on the spot began teaching me Chinese (ah, deep ORIGINAL instinct in all men to hear their own tongue spoken). I learned NEE HAO means "How are you?" and TSI CHANG "Good-bye." Tonight another waiter told me how to ask for tea or coffee in Chinese. Word must have been passed around that I was studying languages.

MARCH 7, 1947—LETTER FROM SHANGHAI

Dearest darlin'nest Mommie,

The veiling, ('zactly what I wanted and just the right amount!), arrived and five minutes later the wee box with the soap (mmm… thanks) and sponges—the PERFECT order came, too. Bless you, bunny sweets, for sending them.

Glad you got my letter about my staying here as usual. Prompted by the clips you sent and the impression you got, I issued a "memorandum to foreign correspondents"—see enclosed. (Am also enclosing the Peiping paper that gave me a write-up.) A recent issue of *TIME* mentioned the few troops remaining here and omitted us. I wrote a letter to Henry Luce for the colonel's signature explaining what we were and that we were remaining. Naturally, I hope they print the letter in the Letters to the Editor column—prestige.

A young lieutenant I met in Manchuria—with AGRS engaged in the grisly chore of locating bodies of American airmen, victims of plane crashes during the war—is in town and keeps me busy LOOKING MY BEST... putting my hair up every night, etc. You should see me doing that... with my Russian book propped up by the wave set bottle and bobby pin box.

Think I told you I had engaged a private tutor for Russian? An elderly and very earnest woman (nose specs et al.) who gives me a full solid hour of instruction (leaves me gasping with exhaustion when she leaves…not a second wasted). Price: $10 a month, two lessons a week and everyone says that's a bargain. She is really the best teacher I have had, all down the line. My textbook is written in Russian and Chinese. When I take it along to breakfast, my Chinese waiters flock around and read off the Chinese to me. I have ended up having Chinese lessons instead of minding my "itchkes"…Your famous Until Tomorrow is pronounced "t'si-chee."

Have had a very interesting and whirling week. First my red-headed navigator came back from the Lolo country and asked me to dinner. In his innocent way he always brings his pilot along on our dates. Pilot is a dreamy, baby-faced blond, really cute, aged about 21, whose wife has presented him with a little girl. We call his wife "Gin darling" because once in Peiping he used my typewriter to start a letter and left that much in the machine when I got back. Well, anyhow, we took in my favorite Russian restaurant and had a lot of fun. I was just saying bye-bye at the door to Pete (my navigator) when the phone began ringing off the wall… Victor. He has been waiting around to sail up the Yellow Sea to some port town where the last batch of medical supplies of UNRRA are to go into Communist hands. He will leave for the Yellow River country as a guest of the Communists. I envy him the trip.

A nice young girl I know with United States Information Service invited me to a Chinese "cultural relations" dinner one evening. Two other young gals from the State Department were also going. It was quite an evening. Four young Chinese girls, two begoggled and college professorish Chinese lads, and a very instructional and educational American "leader" from the YMCA. The Y here has a terrific prestige…all the best Chinese families "subscribe," and it has great educational and cultural programs, etc. I spent FAMISHED AND FAINT hours perched on a cushiony divan in a beautiful Chinese parlor being cultural to two doll-faced and very serious (hence the cuter) Chinese girls…telling them about Alaska. Finally, about 8:30 (after we American Gals had exchanged glances), dinner was served. What Chinese chow! Baby shrimp with almonds, hard-boiled eggs stuffed with meat and covered with a yolk sauce, glazed fish, mushroom soup, etc. The hostess explained that her cook happens to be a woman, and highly temperamental. "All I can do is tell her how many people and what kind of people and she does all the rest. She does not appreciate suggestions and wants no one in her kitchen."

I really got a big kick out of my "cultural relations" and the next day had lunch with a young girl news translator (Chinese). We went to a real Chinese chow house… all the businessmen, agents and clerks sitting around drinking glasses of boiling hot tea, their long gowns brushing the floor… My hostess, Helen Sun, is the sister of the young girl Communist Press Officer I knew and liked so much in Peiping. Helen is not Communist and her sister has been more or less black-sheeped from the family (an upper-middle-class bracket, daughters all Peiping-educated). Helen was telling me in great delight that she is reading Elliot Roosevelt's book, *As He Saw It.* Especially about what Roosevelt recounts of Mme. Chiang…how once she put her hand on the president's knee! Madame is certainly not loved by her people. On a regular round of Chinese society now, tomorrow I am to go to a luncheon and "cultural" (they're great on that word) gathering commemorating International Women's Day or something. My USIS friend and Helen Sun are going with me.

My Chinese tailor (a riot, my Mr. Wong: "okay, okay, okay, Missie" he keeps yelping when I tell him "you fix sleeve so-so") has made me the most EXQUISITE pink blouse you ever laid an eye on…pure sheer silk, bow neck, self-covered buttons to the waist and three tiers of ruffles form the peplum. A true Hattie Carnegie pink… the blouse was copied from my one Magnin dress (blouse cost about $8 or a little more for material and making). My Japanese obi (lamé effect with gold, royal blue, green and tangerine on pale crème background) jacket is finished will be initiated soon. Remember the wrap-around skirt I got in Seattle? Mr. Wong made it a closed skirt from a *Vogue* pattern (for $4). It is really something now.

My story sent to the *AMERICAN* came back with a nice note. "Didn't jell," the editor said, and wasn't exciting enough. I'm going to redo it anyway and try it on *Pageant* or one of the other mags you've sent.

Glad you sent the clip about the opium queen (*Journal* piece.) Will go to work on it immediately. Interviewed the UP correspondent who wrote the story and he promised to collaborate.

Am also all aglow over another idea I had for a story: I cover the Shanghai waterfront. Cornered the ship's columnist on Victor's paper, a crazy young Russian, and on one of these nice sunny days when I can take pix I will go with him on his beat. The waterfront, you know, is right smack on the Bund, under the windows of the swanky Cathay Hotel.

My friend Annie quit her job with UNRRA to give vent to "serious writing." She got into a snag when the correspondents at the B'way Mansions refused to let her live at correspondent rates in their hotel. Haven't heard a word from her since she gave up her fat-paying job.

My friend Lou (from Alaska) is to be married to the mess officer (such a NICE kind, homely, short but darling chap) a week from Saturday. I gave a wedding luncheon for her and three other attendants at the Chocolate Shop (local Schrafft's). Got little corsages for everybody for atmosphere...was a nice event...and we gave her slips, which she badly needed. Lou is very attractive and comes from an old Seattle family and has always been wonderful to me (as has her beau, taking care of my traveler's check, giving me a bottle of vitamin tablets, bringing me cheese, apples, etc.). I will be her attendant, and there will be a wedding breakfast in a very nice hotel here that has a penthouse, sort of private dining room.

So Missie will be rather busy for the next few weeks. I had your CHRISTMAS (dear Lord) box all ready to go but was abashed and smitten to think I'd tucked in nuttin' for Father... so am scurrying around trying to find something he would like, that will fit in the box. Meanwhile, exasperated to have kept you waiting all this time, I finally mailed off a little part of your box airmail. Everything in the package came from Embroidery Street Peiping. I got you one wee thing exactly like one I got.

Peiping mail is routed through Shanghai, and that's why I waited. Had to send my *Collier's* check back to New York for a money order. Otherwise would have had to take $100 worth of Chinese currency— dead loss. Banks have to pay out in CNC, (Chinese money). Did Lois get her silk slip airmailed in January? Sent her a thank-you note for her box. Oh yes, could use some Revlon BRIGHT FORECAST lipstick if any other packages are coming this way. HOW GLAD I am to have the sponges. Long lovey-dovey letter from Art Bremer surprised me the other day. Now must run.

Squeezy hugs, Baby

MARCH 14, 1947—SHANGHAI—Queer atmosphere and attitude: Beethoven on the radio (symphonic program announced in Chinese). On my desk, stuffed into an inadequate jug, a gloriously beautiful bridal bouquet of cinnamon-scented white carnations— and of all things, I just kissed a young, crew-haircut-thatched Lieutenant and he patted my shoulder and said, "There, there little girl." No heartbreaker I. No entanglements—and in the background of all this, Colonel Kearney read a telegram to us today from the War Department stating that AGRS was to shut up shop as quickly as possible. In a few months I'll be scavenging for a job or a train ticket to Russia. Very uncertain what's what from here. Meanwhile, for the moment, the story of the bridal bouquet. We have in Search and Recovery section, a young, tall interpreter—G-2—American citizen. Background briefly: studied medicine, later resigned to go to Spain. I guessed on the Loyalist side. From there his story blurs and comes into focus again in Burma where he was parachuted at night close to a Japanese-occupied town. He entered the town disguised as a coolie and made a survey, was challenged once and ducked. Later he came to AGRS. Somehow he must have expressed some pro-Communist sentiments and was sent packing as on some rigged chore in the hinterlands. He returned to headquarters somewhat wary of revealing his true feelings politically. He kept to himself and avoided the slap-happy rough housing of his fellow officers. Once he took offense at kidding remarks about having been seen "staggering" and with women in his room. He reacted as a Chinese to personal derision, however jocular. I once showed him a Chinese newspaper from Harbin and though tremendously interested, he was reluctant to translate it for me, turned it over to a small moon-faced sergeant.

Next incident—he asked me as a civilian capable of jumping army channels, if I would suggest to the Colonel that our AGRS signs should be translated into Chinese so the passersby and others wouldn't think us spies, as had been reported. I mentioned the sign translation to the Colonel, who grunted in uninterested, half-hearing approval. Later, I mentioned the sign translation to the news editor of USIS. From here, it got to the State Deparement Gestapo and Colonel K. got a calling-down on the "spy" business at AGRS. "Where did you get all this spy talk," he demanded of me. "Why, Lieutenant Chen," I burst out, not in tattletale, because it WAS his idea from the start, as I had previously told the Colonel. Result: Lieutenant Chen got a calling-down. Afterward he came to see me, intending strict censor, a breach of confidence, etc. I resented his preliminary attempt to deny everything—Hadn't he the courage of his convictions? He had learned, he countered, that only a fool brandishes his ideals from a white horse; the smart way is to retain your convictions and seek to work them out in devious ways—a little here, a little there. This was an opinion, but when he dared ask me to "cover up" to the Colonel where the spy stigma originated, I made it clear that I did not believe in MEN coming to WOMEN for protection. He had fallen flat in my estimations of his mental and moral stamina. He quailed, parried, finally resigned himself to "that really hurts, coming from you." In a small, ingratiating way after that he'd catch my eye. "We're still friends?" he'd ask. I was always warmly smiling, regretting my "sermon on the mountain."

Then I heard he was to be married and in the OFFICE. Understanding how he would shun any undue attention or commotion, I kept my distance, but when his DARLING, sweet, tall and smiling bride, a CNAC airline hostess, came shyly into our barren, unwelcoming, strange office in her serenely simple white silk Chinese dress and wearing a small cluster of white flowers in her jet-black hair, I couldn't help rushing up to receive her and make her feel less quakingly conspicuous. I helped pretty up her hair and re-powdered her nose, etc., and then led her into Colonel Kearney's office. I did not go into the room although a host of others jammed in. When the brief Army ceremony was over, the bride came straight to my desk.

"It is Chinese custom for the bride to give away her bouquet. This is for you," she said, and into my arms she passed her lovely spicy white carnations with their train of gossamer green fern. Oh, China. Outsider though I am, you have made small sweet gestures I have received into my heart and shall remember. Chen watched this gesture of his wife and when I clasped his hand and looked right into his eyes, I was forgiving and begging his pardon as from the lips I wished him every happiness.

MARCH 18, 1947—SHANGHAI—Someday I must write a story about a young news gal who gains information and a wellspring of "material" by purporting to "interview" top newsmen. Relaxing in a cozy "magazine article" mood, they will go on as confidingly as in a confessional, giving a gratis store of prize stories and background information. I will be writing about myself. Today I went to have lunch with HANK LIEBERMAN of the *NEW YORK TIMES*. When

I went in, ANNA LOUISE STRONG was cushioned solidly on his divan, clad in black satin PJ's with Chinese embroidery trim. This 60-year-old Trojan of the press leaves me torn between amazement and compassion for that gray hair worn Monday-wash-day style. She finally left and Hank and I lunched in his room.

I began the interview, more to tap his file of stories than to actually market a Lieberman yarn. His report was good (quick background): born in St. Louis, Columbia grad, got news start by covering Columbia for the *New York Times*—did NOT study journalism. During war, worked in the OWI *[Editor's Note: Office of War Information]*. Later sent to Chungking and after the Jap surrender became a correspondent for the *Times*. An excellent theme for his story was consciously proffered at the outset. "A Columbia sociology professor, who taught me more than anyone else, once said the word of truth can be designated as X and Y. X is truth, facts, incorruptible, inviolate, ACTUALITY. Y represents what we hear most—biased half-truths, modified to an end, obscenities, shams, pretense (and in China, "force"). The important thing is to get the X's. Truth will stand all tests, sustain time and tempest. In China, a shocking or cruel or evil X is baffling, alluring by diverting, hard to penetrate. I've missed some of the X's in China, but to sum up, here are the truest X's I believe on the present situation:

(1) True middle-class revolution has never been completely carried out in China. There must be a CHANGE in China. A change in HABITS OF THOUGHT. Change in INSTITUTIONS. 'Face' and its attendant sham obstructions to progress and directness can't disappear until China creates modern economy, etc. Talking democracy doesn't create democracy overnight. China must create the conditions of democracy: industry, transportation, breakdown in the tight family system.

(2) National unity is preeminent.

(3) Economic unity: key cities are affected by fluxes of regulations, etc., but the rest of country—small villages—continues unchanged

in a CELLULAR economy. For the Communists to create a tight economy, they would have to establish an iron, blanket control."

On Russia, Hank's X is "We have got to beat RUSSIA by offering people of the world a better proposition. Americans, to project their ideas to other peoples, must first view the situation from the Chinese psychological aspect. The Chinese do not think as Americans or visualize themselves as Americans. Americans have a haughty self-benedictory, all benign attitude toward themselves and all things American."

Touching on Manchuria, Hank said there is a great rivalry of U.S.–USSR interest there. Hank felt the Russians have no real love for Chinese Communists, would swap them without a qualm in a strategic maneuver with the Nationalists.

MARCH 23, 1947—SHANGHAI—Have just had dinner with the AGRS mess officer, wonderful Armenian-looking chap, Lieutenant ED TORIAN and his Memphis belle bride from Alaska—Lou. During the pleasantries and kiddings of newlyweds, we got off on the subject of the Chinese. I expressed my benevolent pity and all-forgiving compassion for their thieving ills, etc., and Ed spoke up: "Well, Pegge, you would only see them at their best. They all know who you ARE. Even the waiters know missy with green coat, long hair, put articles in paper. I tell you, it's an EDUCATION in the ways of the Orient working in the AGRS dining room. The waiters miss nothing. They tag everyone. First of all they observe table manners. They know who has face, background and the cherished education, from the way different officers use their knives and forks. Officers with slovenly table manners lose face. The worst offender on manners and treating the waiters as if they were feudal slaves is a Polish-born Captain, who is of unmistakable peasant origin and never had a servant in his life. Before a meal is served the boys (waiters) are drilled on the words for various dishes so they'll know what to bring. When they go into the kitchen, the pantomiming between waiter and cook is a scream. Chow hounds get heaping plates and the accompanying pantomime is a rubbed stomach and blown-out cheeks. The Chaplain, staunch Methodist, gets a crossed finger on the collar, stomach rub and blown cheeks. Cook teehees and lays on the chow. Colonel Kearney gets a "rank" gesture. His Colonel's eagles are the MARK of overlord-ism. Various others are hilariously indicated, and how they LAUGH at their diners. How quickly they pick up everything."

I have the habit of asking for an apple occasionally instead of drinking tomato juice, and this causes much walla walla as the apples are locked up. The waiter goes to Ed and says "Missy green coat, long hair, want apple"—amid much laughing. Overlord of this gang is a caterer, Mr. WONG—a self-made man, conniver Number One, who runs a thrifty kitchen (a pound of butter here, a few pork chops there) but on the whole, isn't so bad, although Ed has to WATCH— watch—watch or the whole gang would snatch and make for the gate. This despite their being paid sufficiently and being fed. Ed was maintaining that theft and dishonesty is inherited, inbred, part and parcel of the Oriental way.

Ed, this time on the liquor course, also told marvelous Hemingway yarns. Here, in tersest style: Two GI's, both sergeants from small towns in North Carolina, were buck privates together in England, Iceland, France. All through the war, the littler and smaller of the two was a lady killer until his buddy moved in. For three years the little guy harbored his hatred of his "best friend." Finally after the war in a drunken brawl in Belgium, he shot and killed the smoothie with a carbine, was tried and hung. Took the finale like a man, without an apology or whimper or indulgent confidence in anyone. Another man in the outfit, a stolid citizen soldier, never drank or went out. Dullard, middle-aged, huffer puffer, but faithful if uninspired soldier. One day "turns up missing," and no one could understand it. No clue—nothing. Military intelligence goes to work, finds his body miles from camp in the Seine River. The story is pieced together later. One eventful day charged with swift drama this man's prosaic existence. It was payday and mail day. The man got both, but the letter was more a payoff than the finance officer's stipend. It was a "dear John" letter: "Dear John, I want a divorce. I've fallen in love with another man." The soldier struck out, bewildered by three years of war and hell and mud and death and now this. He stumbled away from camp, went to Paris, rambled blindly about, finally a young but knowing mademoiselle got him, made him drunk, rolled him clean, then pushed him into the Seine.

MARCH 26, 1947—SHANGHAI—Got a marvelous story today about Japanese war dogs being used by Chinese police to track down opium. We drove to a compound beyond Shanghai in a seedy police car. Accompanying us was a tall hulking Russian sub-inspector in a black uniform, which made his colorless eyes and face seem Oriental. His unctuous civility reminded me vaguely of an undertaker, slightly fussed and impressed over a "big" funeral. He was a Harbin Russian, may have been a railroad conductor before coming to Shanghai in 1936. Throughout the afternoon he had an annoying way of injecting observations into my notes and mouthing rather obvious flattery of the Chinese Government, the police station and its valiants on the hunt for criminals. When I mentioned an interest in Shanghai's jail being the largest in the world, he anticipated a request to visit it. "Unfortunately," he waved a pale hand—his one physical beauty, they might have been a sculptor's or a surgeon's—"Unfortunately the jail BUILT BY FOREIGNERS is not a very pleasant showplace, and visitors are discouraged." As a character for future background, this clumsy henchman interested me. He had a palling effect on the moments of humorous outbursts during the interview. Though the inspector laughed, he was morose and sucked in his breath with a noisy, slushy sound reminiscent of the Japanese. Incongruously, he told me his great hobby was collecting the history of Shanghai and should I need any reference material I was to call on him. "After all," he observed, bluntly insensitive as the peasant stock he sprang from, "I am not always busy in the afternoon and I like to talk with someone I can learn something from, and he can get something from me." With characteristic lack of grace he directed the car first to his office, then told the chauffeur to take me where I directed. The inspector smiled a ghastly square-toothed smile and disappeared into the ultra deluxe police station near the American Consulate.

Now to the story: Once issued into the low-walled compound, we faced long rows of heavily wired kennels. Piercing brute barking announced our arrival to moon-faced, nattily uniformed officials in charge. One kennel housing two beady-eyed, tail-wagging puppies drew me, cooing and adoring, to them while the officials waited, pointedly, for me to acknowledge them first. Much bowing, smiling, and handshaking. Then into a bare, narrow room where peeling paint and tumbling plaster walls were adorned by gaudy calendars bearing the Generalissimo's likeness. Scalding glasses of green tea were served. The story of the dogs began: The dog department opened with 90, now has about 20, the others having been weeded out for being "too stupid." The breed is German sheep dogs (or PINTZER police dogs) and although some looked ranger mangy, they are undoubtedly pedigreed. A staff of 10 looked after them. The local newspaperman accompanying me hinted in a muttered aside that Jap attendants had lurked hidden, but actually did the training. Every dog has a name. No. 1 is CHARLIE, No. 2 is CHAO LIN, and No. 3 is MEI LING. As the interview progressed, I asked about the intelligence of male and female dogs. The Chinese dog master smiled at the lady reporter. "The female dogs are friendlier, but very clever and good at sleuthing." Then he admitted that Charlie, the No. 1 dog, is a female (or bitch, if you will, although in his halting English the inspector did not use that word). So also is No. 2 a female, as obviously is No. 3, Mei Ling.

Japanese war dogs: Charlie (left) and puppies.

The dogs' aptitude is studied, and those good at scenting and man hunting are specially trained. Others, just like the human police force, are better at guarding. They will stay by property on a post forever until relieved. What do they guard? "Oh, Government property." I wondered in the back of my mind if they train the dogs to look the other way when cumshaw (tips), thefts and sales of guarded goods are transacted. The four-legged detectives are fed better than any coolie or rickshaw boy, according to a wall chart and the testimony of the officials, although the dogs themselves looked darned lean around the ribs. The inspector kept telling me when we visited the kennels, "The puppies are very fat—see," but I thought I'd seen fatter ones. Anyway, their diet is supposed to include milk, meat, rice, eggs, vegetables and biscuits. The dog training has been going on for only two months, so few actual cases are chalked up on the record books. It was amusing that in true Chinese style, the dogs have been reproducing, and eleven puppies have cropped up recently. The one dog, especially trained for opium detection, is male, and his name in Chinese, I-ASZ, sounds almost like "hush." Opposite the kennels is a small obstacle course, and the best dogs were put through their paces, jumping hurdles, halting, trotting, lying down, scaling a wall. Charlie was the performer, though. She was taken out of the compound and turned loose on the trail of a young trainer who had trekked across a rice field and hidden behind a farmer's shack. Charlie also located and dug up a key ring buried in a dirt pile about 100 feet down the road. The trainers showed a mild amount of affection for the dogs, patting them briefly on the head after each demonstration. After all, had they failed to perform correctly, the trainers and a whole dog detachment would have lost face and the dog probably his life.

MARCH 29, 1947—SHANGHAI—Getting restless. Scheming up trips and pot-boiled articles for money, sweet stuff that giveth courage to LEAP into things.

Last night went to a housewarming given by BOB SHERROD of *TIME.* He had received an assignment from the home front to do a story on AGRS. A bit cowed by Sherrod's prestige and perfected skill in delivery, I rushed around getting all the material lined up. Sherrod, impeccably groomed, polished as a cavalryman's boots, patrician in every tone and gesture—Gad, to handle an approach to a story as he did. He insisted we go have a drink somewhere afterward, so we ended up at the Park Hotel. The streets were lined with the scarlet flags of the Republic, as we sat at a wall table sipping our drinks (sherry for me, of course). Uniformed policemen, by the HUNDREDS—more than an army division, Sherrod said—marched by.

Today, to the vague bewilderment and indifference of everyone, was being observed as Chinese Martyrs Day. Not even the army demonstrated such a show of strength. Had they goose-stepped we would have imagined ourselves in Italy or Berlin. Reaction from street crowds seems to be more curiosity than fear.

One of my Russian bus drivers left a note inside my textbook. I had forgotten it on the bus and for about two weeks carried the paper around without realizing it was a shy billet doux. At the close of my lesson the other eve, my teacher suddenly spied it and translated: "I have a heart. In my heart is a song. The song is a secret and the secret is YOU." This is a Russian song, I learned. The sheer romance of the incident charmed me and here is the Russian memento:

In her diary, Pegge copied a four-line song in Russian.

PALM SUNDAY, MARCH 30, 1947—SHANGHAI—Unique day indeed. Walked down Bubbling Well Road after breakfast. Ah, Spring—zephyr of dust-laden breezes swept the strollers. Toddlers in open-crotched pants, reed-thin Chinese in their vibrant blue gowns topped with western felt businessmen's hats and usually a hand-knit scarf around their necks, ice skater style, one loop over the shoulder.

Elegant Chinese missies in full-cut great coats with Russian influence, balloon sleeves. Street urchins with rouged cheeks and lips, devilish-eyed, Chinese style TOM SAWYER types, as well as useless daughters as yet too young to be married off. Flower vendors in San Francisco were never such a riot of color and wistful eye-filling delight as on a Shanghai street. Flower girls in that China-blue gown—selling scarlet cinnamon and all-spice smelling carnations, pink branchy blossoms, chaste daffodils and narcissus and hydrangeas. I bought three bunches for less than 25 cents. They scented the whole room. Oh, China!

Was visited this morn by a lonely-ish young demure secretary of the Netherlands Consulate and mentioned the Dutch East Indies. She expressed resentment of an American merchant ship and Chinese vessels trading in rubber and other natural resources with rebellious natives. Holland needs to re-establish herself after the war.

Later to the Race Course building to write up a Peiping murder mystery for the *NEW YORK NEWS*. Then home to study my Russian.

Have a feeling in my bones something is brewing. I shall be doing something LOCOMOTIVE soon.

MARCH 31, 1947—Oh, Shanghai—you are wooing a discomforting wistfulness. The city has groomed for Spring. It was a very warm, brilliant-sun-goldened day. I went downtown to see FRANK ROBERTSON of INS who, with his bride-to-be, is soon to trek across the Gobi desert.

Coming back to the office I received a cable from my beloved TINY BUNTIN. I was to scout for a job somewhere in Shanghai, but the real impact came in a long, long letter from my dearest friend, Dorothy Ann Simpson. She wrote that she is getting married. Now it is odd and self-searching that a pang of jealousy ran over me as I read her effulgent lyrical account—the romance—and John. I had to philosophize. Work on myself. It seemed incongruous to be sitting in China in the midst of political embroilments and to read about sipping Manhattans in the Wedgewood Room of the Waldorf. I could see myself marching across the universe in the wake of disasters and near wars and getting letters about babies being born, anniversary dinners, etc. Ah well, this is my life and I'm in the driver's seat. But I sat lost in contemplation, in inventory. Feeling very much in the red. No accomplishments to date. Not even the *Reader's Digest* story means a step toward the goal! To see and study the people of the globe, and to write WELL about what insight (not mere visual SIGHT) I glean. Then I think of Dorothy Ann with her John—greener if tamer pastures.

The study of Russian becomes more discouraging—maddening.

APRIL 10, 1947—SHANGHAI—I am distraught—distraughter I have never been. Today I yielded my final transit visa application papers at the USSR Consulate, and a Soviet smile threw me for such a loop. I was a 100% Dostoevsky IDIOT. The papers for weeks have been filled with headlines of USA-USSR clashes at the Moscow Conference— over reparations, Germany and China. Into this frigid international parlor, I burst on roller skates of brash impudence and went into the Consulate the other day with a friend of Victor's—a Russian Soviet newspaperman. The Consulate, bastion of Soochow Creek, is like a liberated manor house run by the former servants in a barren, frugal, stringently unadorned fashion, except for conspicuous portraits of Lenin and Stalin everywhere.

Gospodeen FEDIAEFF, whom I called on, was pasty faced, his mouth a straight line adding up a column of unhappy features. I sat on the edge of my chair throwing off radium waves of entreating smiles and anxious supplications. He gave the form to fill out *[Editor's Note: Pegge's notes read in Russian "in Russian or in English" (phonetically, ruskuu angleesky)]* I took them back today and saw

Gospodeen FEDIAEFF without my Russian aide. A blond young interpreter filled in—Gospodeen Fediaeff speaks as much English as I speak Russian.

When I walked in (my timid misgivings fortified by my Hattie Carnegie shocking pink coat) the Russian official greeted me with beguiling smiles. He smoked a cigarette in a jet holder, his pallid look was gone and he seemed pink-cheeked and buoyant. Our first remarks were an exchange of jokes—we all laughed ourselves "at ease," and as we became such good friends, I opened my mouth and volunteered the information that I'd met my first Soviet in Alaska— all interest. I bubblingly ignored any political or spy implications and gushed on to tell all about the Russians in Fairbanks. Warming to my subject, of course, I noticed, however, either a marvelously clever control of facial expression or lack of information when I identified Fairbanks as the point, where during the war, American lend-lease planes were picked up. Both looked as though they'd never heard of such a thing. Then, later, I added—half in jest—"If you don't let me go to your country I shall be very sad." Blank looks. Then they asked where I was working in Shanghai. When in doubt, always tell the truth. I told them AGRS—and explained what it was. When I came away, after nearly an hour's session, I first had a very warm feeling of friendliness toward the Consulate official. But later, I worried much over my answers. The mention of Alaska especially worries me, and I WANT TO GO (having studied Russian until I'm blue in the face) so TERRIBLY TERRIBLLY MUCH. He said I might come back in June for an answer. We shall see.

APRIL 14, 1947—SHANGHAI—I'm in the throes of events. First, I'm waiting for a survey flight to SIAM to materialize. Have many shots and visas all in order and am terribly excited over the prospects of going. Next, some 332nd Troop carrier pilots were having a wild farewell party Saturday night and got to talking to a reporter (SAM

SEBBA) about the LOLO story. Fortunately he called me and tipped me off. I got very busy trying to check any premature breaking of the story. Things got involved and commotional, so Colonel Kearney, the boss, and two aides descended on me Saturday night. The original plan was to fly correspondents and photographers to HSI CHAN when we got our hands on a survivor. This morning the Colonel called me into his office and told me the plan now is to whip a plane into Kunming and fly the survivor DIRECT TO WASHINGTON, D.C. The Colonel then added, "I think you should go along on that plane to represent the AGRS-China Zone when the story is released in Washington." I gasped and felt a wince at having to cheat the *China Press* of the story. They've maintained confidence all along. Now to have the STORY and the GUY snatched out from under their noses. But oh boy, to get a trip home.

This p.m. went to see a correspondent just in from Japan. He says MacArthur has pulled the greatest snow job in history in Japan. The whole occupation has been a complete fizzle. He tops off his news roundup by saying my Tiny Buntin was tossed out in Korea for "attempted rape." I was quite shocked and felt a little foolish after rushing off a $10 cable to him about another job.

Incidentally, as we were driving down Nanking Road this afternoon en route to see the correspondent, our car got blocked by a parade of Chinese soldiers. The tired-looking, sweating foot soldiers were as interesting to observe as the average pedestrian's reaction. Instead of watching from the curb, the people got right out in the street about two feet from the marchers to gape and stare. Their faces registered complete detachment, as though gazing on the peaks of the Himalayas. Some of the more sophisticated merchants and business clerks looked on with a superior air of amusement at some scrawny devil trudging along, sweating under the weight of his rifle. The guns looked good, but dusty and utilitarian, not polished for a parade. The men wore calfskin combat boots and faded blue padded uniforms. Their faces were complete blanks as they moved down the crowded street. They were as oblivious and far removed from the Shanghai Chinese, as they were from the pathetic-looking military.

Incidental note: Russian Easter was marked in Shanghai by church services and great socials all over town. I went to my Russian teacher's home and there met a charming Russian straight out of Tolstoy, one GOSPODIN WOLKOWSKY, distant relative of my first Russian friend, Dimitri, photographer on the *Times Herald* in Washington. The Russian lessons continue.

APRIL 17, 1947—SHANGHAI—The army march through Shanghai takes on a footnote—and that's no pun from their being Infantry. The Chinese lieutenant I described a while back, Lieutenant Ch'en, happened to be a spectator. He knew the marching men, part of the 202nd Youth Army, composed of partially educated soldiers. He had helped train them in Burma during the war. At that time he had entreated them to train well, arduously and for a common objective, and his main plea had been "You are being trained to fight the Japanese, not the Communists. You are soldiers in the Allied army, not in the civil war." One of the men in the marching ranks recognized Lieutenant Ch'en. He shouted his name. The dull apathy of the squad fired into excitement—they broke rank and rushed up to him shouting their surprise and delight to see him. Then their bitterness was voiced. "You said we were not being trained for the civil war, and here we are." They were bitter to the point of desertion and near insurgence.

APRIL 30, 1947—CANTON—The setting is unique, and if print had ears you'd HEAR the thread-thin trill of violins and sidewalk hubbub going on along the Canton waterfront beneath my window. After many maddening delays, I was able to get aboard the survey flight by CATC plane to SIAM. We left at 6:30 a.m., circled the field and returned at once to the same field—engine trouble. Hours of waiting while they fixed another plane. Meanwhile, I was having quite a chat with another correspondent who was aboard, one bespectacled nice-eyed BUD (WALTER) BRIGGS. Also met my fawn-like little college student who has a brother at the University of Pennsylvania in Philadelphia and a young girl secretary from the Siamese Embassy in Nanking. I shall love the Siamese if these two are citizen samples A & B. The flight to SWATOW on the China coast was interesting. We climbed out, mopping our faces and peeling off coats and jackets. Chatted with tall Lord-Byron-looking British chap, who was overseeing the loading of our plane (oil company man). Understand there's a small foreign colony of about 30 people. Recalling my Alaskan experiences, I mused over the Cat and Kitten relations among them. The airfield bordered seeded green rice paddies and new green-fleeced hills—and just beyond is a harbor, lazy and liquidy blending with the atmosphere. Bandits with pirate tactics at low tide are said to infest the area. Aside from that, all is peaceful, no anti-American feeling, no Communists. Then back aboard the plane and on to CANTON. The approach to this historic home of the Chinese Republic is storybook sequence. First the celery-top green green-ness everywhere. Rice paddies—the phenomenal architecture of the steeply tiered levels of irrigated fields. Chinese farmers looking the way they should, wearing COOLIE HATS and running along with their shoulder bar carryalls. Women looking exactly like the men, except for a screw-knot bun on the back of their heads. In certain sectors where the ancient soil was cut open and momentarily untilled, the earth was red—bright copper red—a gaudy appliqué on the Canton green.

I am now housed at OI KWANG hotel—"love all or love hotel"— with a cloud of mosquito net to crawl under. Two floors down is the street, waterfront and the stream of hot, restless, jabbering Chinese. A rudimentary gander at the town shows its charred and black-smoked evidence of Jap and American bombing.

MAY 1, 1947—CANTON—"This place is seething," remarked a seemingly informed American oldster with USIS *[Editor's Note: United States Information Service]* here when he invited fellow correspondent WALTER BRIGGS and me to lunch at his home on SAMEEN Island, former exclusive foreign colony (furnished like something out of a French colonial novel). Our spokesman pictured Canton in the restless throes of discontent among the people, stalemated internally, because no foreign or Chinese capital will be expended under the present regime, although an American HYDRO ELECTRIC Company was said to be risking its cash, welcomed by the Chinese for its rehabilitating new life injection, economically. He said bandits (or "communists") were pillaging outlying villages, usually raiding arsenals and distributing leaflets. In the villages they killed the magistrate and set up a tentative People's Government. No redistribution of land yet, but the subjugated villages were "promised" land. CNC (Chinese Nationalist currency) is now 14,000 (to one U.S. dollar) Prices are only slightly lower here than in Hong Kong.

I heard about an American freelance correspondent, a girl, who managed to get into Vietnamese country with a Vietnamese friend of the USIS informant. I envied her daring. In the afternoon with an AGRS Captain, went exploring the murky, foul, filthy wonders of Ivory Street. Found in dank and mildewed hovels some exquisite carvings but very expensive. Some ivory carved powder boxes tempted me but bargaining seemed to little avail. Great hoards of urchins, cooliehatted begrimed workers and street loafers gathered wherever we went. As we drove away, I noticed women pulling wagons laden with mat-covered produce, sweating and straining their delicate might like pack mules. They were barefooted and wore their hair either in thick glistening braids trailing down their taut spines or twined in a chignon at the back of their heads above their dust-streaked necks. The streets are, of course, encrusted with HISTORIC filth and deeply rutted. The people, closely watched, seem enduringly languid and preoccupied—poverty is glaring. Exceptionally few foreigners are seen on the streets.

MAY 5, 1947—EN ROUTE TO SIAM—(I am thrilled like a kid riding piggy-back on a cowboy to think where I'm going. BANGKOK—the ends of the earth are mine!)

As I sit gazing out the window, clouds like soapy, sudsy foam float over a strange patchwork of Indo-China countryside. If there's a revolutionary behind every rubber tree, so much greater the atmosphere of intrigue.

We have just had a two-day stay in overlord warring SAIGON. This morning, as Amah was drawing my "bawth," I was panic-stricken to hear an explosion of bombing or artillery fire. Amah never looked up. Driving to the airport we passed an unbroken line of French guards in white knee pants uniforms armed with rifles. I am not sure if they were "en garde" for insurgents or, as we later saw at the airport, guards of honor, protection for the high commissioner and other French bigwigs coming and going out to the airport.

The waiting room was a vivid scene. French women melting in cotton, housewifey-looking dresses, offset with smart head scarves, exquisite imported Paris shoulder bags and hideous platform-soled wedgies. Officers in wrinkled white linen "parlez vous-ed" while smoking cigarettes distractedly. RAF pink-faced boys looking beastly hot in heavy khaki, their blue caps almost afloat in perspiration on their young curly heads—American oil company representatives looking limp and unhappy, so far from God's country and plenty of scotch—and in our honor, a sprinkling of Chinese attachés. We waited in the small bar for the French planes to clear the runway. I got trigger happy and despite warnings from the others about cameras being restricted, caught a few quickies of the French planes. We saw British spitfires, American transports, and mostly German JUNKER (JU-52), British Mosquitoes, a French plane (like a cub-trainer), a privately owned observation plane—charter service supposed to be making money from it. Ex-French air force Messerschmidt flew in from France—trying to get more—no land communication on these flights. This was the French version of bush flying, like the Alaskan bush pilots. While we waited, a British Mosquito bomber took off. I nervously tried to get a picture.

Our flight from Canton took us over a high range of mountains, very cold. I got everything out of my suitcase and covered up—studied my Russian. The arrival in Saigon was like stepping into a Dutch oven set for cooking deep-dish strudel.

A busy street (left) and airport in Saigon.

We sank in asphalt. Little brown men in shorts that reached to gnarled knees came aboard and began handling the luggage. French police politely herded us into a sweltering office to register and present our passports.

Strolling around the modern-looking airport I noticed posters of Charles de Gaulle and droves of RAF chaps, tasted my first French cognac (out of this world). We were billeted at a grand hotel on the waterfront; some sort of light French cruiser was anchored across the street. The hotel lobby (tiled and high ceilinged and hot as HELL) was trafficked with French naval and army officers, a few chattering French girls. A sign was written on the bulletin board: CURFEW 1900 HOURS. The night of our arrival was to have seen some Vietnamese action. We met a young obliging Cal-Tex man who squirreled me to the leading department store to shop. Paris perfume—I went mad— and French purses. Spent only $39 and marveled at my restraint. Among the thin milling of customers were the high-class native women in the most beautiful costumes. Sheer silk straight gowns over sleek trousers, their hair worn sleek and severe, combed back from the very roots, drawn tight as possible into a low chignon. One woman comes into vivid focus: tall, sylph-slender, wearing white trousers and a brilliant orange over-gown; in her arms was her son clad in a turquoise sunsuit. I couldn't take my eyes off her. The store was like a Miami Bergdorf's, ultra swank though sparsely stocked except for Paris imports.

After shopping, we drove through the residential district, which was like something out of a stage setting for a French colonial melodrama. The shuttered windows, balconies, grillwork gates, lush green palm trees—plants—flowers—a tree drenched in scarlet flowers held up like sanguine sacrifice to the blue, blue sky God. Dear heavens, how gorgeous and inducing, linger-luring everything was. Most of the French maisons were a beige plaster over brick or cement—ideal structures in so emerald a setting.

Before dinner, we stopped at little "Champs Elysées" or Café du Paix. This place was a gay and lively sidewalk café—the Continental. The electricity had gone off so the entire scene was in semi-moonlight. Troubled skies and a black clouded night hung over the cognac-sipping Frenchmen. Women seemed scarce—most of the men were in stag groups, with rolled French newspapers sticking out of their pockets. I presumed they discussed events of brewing disaster. Indo-China is an unhappy country at best. Its political malady is an ugly scourge. American sentiment is predominately pro-independent

VIETNAM. Relations are cordial from the teeth out. Dined and danced at a smart, charmingly furnished French rendezvous just outside town: THE CHALET.

Next morning for breakfast there was fresh pineapple. I ate two dishes of it. Spent the morning at USIS. When I went in, the American girl in charge was out, so I talked to the doll lady, her Chinese assistant (she is CRUCIN-CHINESE or ANAMITE). Her face was Malay, her smile enchanting. She spoke English but asked me to write it down, saying she could understand better that way. Later I was asked not to print the pictures I took of her as it might get her in trouble with the French. A slim, young Anamite boy sat at the next desk. He was artistically gifted and made all the picture bulletins of Les Etats Unis (U.S.).

Pegge with members of the Thai Embassy

MAY 6, 1947 AND HOT—LETTER FROM SIAM

Hi darlings,

Guess where the galloping gal is now – in the land of temples and dancing girls. We flew down Sunday from Shanghai with stops in Canton and Saigon (French Indo-China) This place is like a story book and I wish you could see the local Waldorf where I am staying. It is named after a historic Siamese King and the jaw jarring name is: RATANAKOSIN HOTEL. My room is big enough for an army.

An advertisement for the Ratanakosin Hotel.

The little girls room (modern job) is built like an Egyptian stone chamber – FABULOUS!! I am to send you a cable this afternoon but you may receive this letter first. I went shopping the other day and got some gorgeous silver – went to the Tiffany of Siam (His Majesty's silversmith, no less.) Will send you something from Shanghai.

The whole junket seems so unreal now that I'm down here. Last night a wealthy Siamese boy, who was a guest passenger on the plane, entertained us at his home (furniture black teak with inlaid mother of pearl), Siamese orchestra playing a shrill version of "You Belong to My Heart". Food not so good – mostly fish dishes and rice. I'd been warned about eating it so just nibbled. The fruit for dissert tho out of fruit fairy land – the COLOR – the SCENT – the strange new flavors – dear God! Siamese dancing girls entertained us later – met some very, very charming Siamese people (like them ENORMOUSLY) three sisters especially who spoke gay and bouncing American English. One works at the Siamese foreign office and she arranged to have me visit the ROYAL URN this afternoon – that is the crypt of the late young king who was murdered (suicide? Never proven) last June. The country is still observing deep mourning (they take their kings solemnly, devoutly here) Fortunately have my black dress along and will place flowers on his golden urn. This is a great privilege.

This morning I had a long interview with His Excellency (no less) the Chinese Ambassador, and after the Royal Urn visit, I go with my letter of entré to His Excellency, the American Ambassador. This is my first tackling of political interpretation of a people and a country and though a bit uncertain, I LOVE it. You see so much more than sight seeing – although a grand, Dorothy Ann-like-girl I met at the U.S. Information Service (like O.W.I. somewhat) took me to lunch and tea at her home. Gave me a gay earful of local color and tuned her jeep and Siamese driver over to me.

The Chinese ambassador is throwing a party for us here tonight. Which timely function delays our departure another day. Must rush to TIFFEN now (money here is called TIKALS – say 50 "tickles"— like an itch tickle—for a lunch). Hope you received my cable – Love, Love Baby.

MAY 6, 1947—SIAM—I am writing this in the plane, en route to Canton, after three days in an enchanting city. The plane reeks with the sweet heady odor of tropical flower leis (several Chinese officials and the wife of the Chinese Ambassador to Siam are aboard, as well as three bamboo baskets of Siamese KITTENS!). Forgive me if I go into a travelogue, but Siam is like an ancient Oriental storybook kingdom. We flew over Bangkok at midafternoon with the sun blazing down on the stucco and gilt, sharply narrow spires and the famous temples with SNAKE roof edges, in tribute to the Snake God, sweeping curvy straight into the brilliant blue, cloud-foamed sky. Temples gleam in a compound of lush tropical greenery—immaculately white, or gold, or black with multi-colored stones a-glitter with a gaudy, gypsy ostentation that is somehow entrancing. Roofs of temples are sometimes bronze bordered in emerald to jet. Against the fever flush of sweetening sunset, the silhouette is magnificent. The bondsmen, or priests, walk around barefoot, with shaven heads swathed in a sari of brilliant, butter-yellow. I'm immediately impressed with Siam in contrast, in order and courtesy so unlike the Chinese.

The Siamese spoke English and were very nice, checked in at the local Waldorf—no elevator—a wide, hand-scrubbed stone stairway. From my balcony I gazed on the unicorn of the Imperial Palace. Mosquitoes fierce—chewed me to a fare-you-well. I look as though I have small fever blisters of the legs and ankles.

During her trip to Siam, Pegge witnessed a kickboxing match.

As our first move after a French tiffin (very fine gleaming silver on table) we all went off to a Siamese boxing match. In a medium-sized sports bowl, two fighters mounted to the ring. Before the fight both bent on their haunches, bowing heads to canvas—supposed to be praying to their instructors to remember their training and win the fight. Then Siamese music began a chant—and first one, then the other, enacted brief pantomimes of the fight to demonstrate physical fitness. The music (a shrill, very Siamese-sounding flute, drum and hand cymbals) and the people themselves kept me looking around pop-eyed. Great sports fans relished the strange wrestling sport, where contenders struck each other with hands and feet. One very young wrestler got a bloody nose right off the bat, and my girlish and shrill protests at such savagery had dark heads turning and big square-white-toothed grins observing my presence.

We dined in an elegant Chinese restaurant and came home by white silver glow moonlight in leather-cushioned, clean pedicabs called "tricycles." The main street leading to our hotel is wide enough for all the weekend traffic in New York City, and it is almost completely deserted except for a few diminutive strollers, bondsmen (priests), Austin-sized cars and pedicabs.

Monday I began hustling around to get my Siam snapshot politically, economically. The Siamese position during the war (occupation with virtually no resistance) leaves an unsettled doubt of sincerity in many people's minds, despite the underground activity and other gestures in the right direction. The Chinese infiltration into Siam is casting shadows of things to come. They hold the country in a powerful economic grip, and it is the indolent, easygoing Siamese's own fault. The Chinese émigrés were willing to work like water buffaloes to make a bare living, while the Siamese sat back and permitted them to do so. Now the Siamese are caught in their own snag. In an attempt to curb the overwhelming migration from Swatow to Siam, a new immigration act went into effect May 1, fixing the quota at 10,000. Considerable walla walla over this. The Chinese have intermarried so extensively that even high-ranking government officials have Chinese blood. Bit by bit, they would attempt to grip the power reins (backed by their economic wealth).

Communist activity has been noted among labor groups, following the great PARTY LINE, adopted undeviatingly, ALL OVER THE WORLD. The leaders have hit the "oppressed" and stirred them to unite in the omnipresent Red Brotherhood. The Siamese generally, who have a personal devotion to their King, are not enthusiastic about the Communists.

Two street scenes from Pegge's trip to Siam.

A party was given for the ship's passengers by a wealthy Siamese boy who flew down with us. The house was palatial, but I was annoyed to find his frail and charming mother standing in the reception line barefoot. A buffet of many fish dishes was spread, but I had been warned about eating fish dishes and just nibbled. No wine was served, just an orange soda pop and water. The guests, somewhat timidly withdrawn at first, were endearingly responsive after the meal. One small, deer-eyed man, who held a master's degree from MIT, told me he was forced to resign his government post because of inadequate salary and the higher cost of living. He is now with the rice commission. Rice is quite a factor, being the main wealth of Siam. Some of it is rationed for local consumption. The rest is supposed to be allocated to nations made most destitute by the scourge of war. But the smuggling inducement is irresistible. Rice brings a fortune in Malaysia and Singapore, so junks and small boats spirit the rice to more lucrative markets. The Chinese blandly accuse the Siamese of this subversive profiteering, even though the rice millers and wholesalers are all Chinese.

At this same party I met a Siamese girl who works at the Siamese foreign office. When I heard about the Golden Urn containing the body of the young somber-eyed king who was so mysteriously slain, I asked if I could visit the Royal Mausoleum. She called the next day saying 2 p.m. was the appointed hour and asking whether I had a black dress to wear. Fortunately I did, but it had long sleeves and 2 p.m. is the hottest time of the day. She took me to the Imperial Palace and presented me with flowers to place on the King's altar. We were escorted into the royal courtyard of history (*Anna and the King of Siam*, of book and movie fame). A serious and very dignified guard from the foreign office led us into the most spectacular place of interest I have ever seen. A royal red carpet matched hand-painted Buddha-figured walls that towered to domed ceilings of scarlet and gold. A gold Buddha, before which the King (now in Switzerland) worships, faced us. To the right was his late brother's fantastic crypt. Within the Golden Urn, the young man's body is buried in a sitting position, arms and legs interlaced, head down, the corpse being swathed in a white shroud.

I was slightly incredulous when I heard of this strange burial, but my Siamese hostess was so earnest and intelligently devout that her interpretation was contagious. The urn is the climactic gem, resting on top of a tiered altar of gold. Potted palms surround the altar and amid them an honor guard of soldiers stood, rifles in hand. An enlarged photograph of the swarthy handsome monarch stood on a pedestal in front of the altar. Bordering it were garish, rainbow-colored flowers (one from the 13th U.S. Army Air Force) that lined the walls. I was fascinated by the urn. In this day and age, to think that a modern, European-educated monarch should be so mysteriously assassinated in his own palace. To this day no arrests have been made and the government's attitude is to hush it all up. The Siamese themselves are still sensitive regarding the manner of their beloved young king's death. Bondsmen priests eyed us scathingly as another foreign lady (British) and I approached the urn to place our flowers on the altar. Our two Siamese friends prostrated themselves on the red carpet.

I then drove out to the American Embassy for an interview. Checked the information received that morning from the Chinese Ambassador and found some of it slightly misleading. Picked up a few Communist newspapers, one showing Uncle Sam being booted out of China. Had afternoon tea at the home of the British lady and then stopped at the shop of one of the Siamese ladies. I got some hand-loomed Siamese cloth. To my surprise, when I asked the price, I found it terribly expensive and when I asked the exchange rate into TIKALS (pronounced "tickles") they knocked off a few tikals from the open market rate. The incident was a minute insight into Siamese business dealings.

Later the Chinese ambassador hosted a party which had the redeeming feature of opening windows on psychological threads of INTER-TANGLED lives. I was sitting to one side, balancing a plate of cold and not too tasty Chinese chow, when adorable little KWAY LONG, who is with the Siamese Embassy in Nanking, sat down beside me. She whispered that her parents, particularly her mother, had forbidden her from going to Russia when diplomatic representation is exchanged. The country was the objection, and Kway herself admitted not liking the Russians. They entertain in Nanking, and the Siamese staff must go, despite disliking the unctuous manner of the Russian servants (every other embassy has Chinese servants). This did not bother her as much as gossip about her and the Siamese boy, her old playmate (OSAN). The Chinese ambassador asked if she were engaged. To a Chinese girl (never mind the Siamese citizen DISTINCTION) such jokes are not taken lightly. She began to weep, put down her plate of food and tilted back her head so no conspicuous tears would roll down her cheeks. The Chinese ambassador then insisted she sing for the guests. She was so angry over his suave inference of her being engaged to Osan that she was openly rude and obstinate—the first time I have seen such behavior from a Chinese. (KWAY LONG is from Swatow.) When we departed to go home, she barely uttered the standard pleasantries and sneaked across the lawn. Kway Long will have to buck her parents and tradition in attempting a modern career in China. Also among the guests was a diplomatic couple of interest: a thin-faced, but not unattractive French woman with a Chinese husband. They had just come down from Afghanistan. Apparently the two met when the man was a student in France. There are several such combinations in China but she (or they) were the first such couple I had met.

MAY 20, 1947—SHANGHAI—As I close this journal I have to offer for the future –my first significant step on the way to the OBJECTIVE. I have just completed TWO POLITICAL INTERPRETATION articles for the *China Weekly Review* (editor Bill Powell). The first appeared in the May 17th issue, obscurely buried near the back of the book under the title "WORD IMPRESSIONS OF SAIGON." Possibly prejudiced on short notice (I was only in Saigon two days) the lead gives the theme away. "Saigon is a city under siege of an ill-tempered political war in which the French fight with all the insidious subtleties for which they are famous." It was a sophomoric effort stirring little comment except from devoted followers; nevertheless I still felt ¾ of an inch better.

MAY 29, 1947—SHANGHAI—I have just come from the French Consulate, where I was summoned by a young, attractive Vice Consul who was "greatly interested" in my report on Saigon which appeared in the *China Weekly Review*. He summoned a translator, a doughty Frenchman of gallantries and gestures and twitches of a white brush mustache. I was a bit a-twitter myself at this intrigue-ish interview. There is so little firsthand information on the situation. "Tell us, Mamzelle, what would YOU like to see emerge from the complicated situation?" I pled aversion to opinion founded on superficial study— two days. What was my overall impression of French Indo-China? "Very sad; I thought it an unhappy land with much suffering now and in the future." This puzzled them to know for whom my heart bled. S'il voux plait. French control—puppet (pseudo independence) rule or VIETNAM control absolutely? Having had no opportunity to observe the native organization, I could draw no absolute conclusion. They injected a word about the natives being like the Chinese, once given a ruling hand, observing that their cruelty to one another is beyond bounds of mercy. I listened to this with an earnest façade. "I have pictures to show how they cut up bodies of prisoners," the interpreter added. More conversation and I gathered a subtle trend: that they wanted me to put the blame for French colonial sins on the old regime "functionaries," which they sympathetically agreed were like "old China hands" and had to yield to the new French authorities. They repeated their questions about what kind of RULE I wanted, and I repeated NO COMMUNIST DOMINATION. Blank, reserved "reaction" to this from them.

I was amused at the French maneuvers during this petite conference. The interpreter, possibly responding to a subtle hint from his superior, regaled me with a tale of the Vice Consul's heroic wartime activities. He had been with the underground, had been in prison in France and Italy. Had even grayed at his temples in his wartime rigors. Later was in Bern (which sparked my interest) and then was sent to Nanking. As I rose to bid my au revoirs, the interpreter translated a remark that I should marry a Frenchman and learn French so that I could read a book the Vice Consul had written. QUELLE EGO!!! I thought as I had my hand caressingly shaken in farewell.

JUNE 10, 1947—SHANGHAI—To continue from the previous record book, I find myself beginning with a Siamese theme. First, my article entitled "Siam's Chinese Mother-in-Law" (my title) appeared in the *China Weekly Review*—the same day the Siamese ambassador to China arrived in Shanghai to meet his wife and daughter coming in by ship from Bangkok. The ambassador was a hickory-nut-skinned, bouncing, laughing little man with eyes like polished jet. Playing up to my nationalism, he told me proudly he was called "Sam" during his wartime associations with the OSS (Office of Strategic Services). Learned more at a Chinese dinner party—behind the napkin, so to speak—that he is not of the vested autocracy, but got his post by DESERVING it for wartime activities. When his sweet-faced, shy wife arrived with her dusky-hued but delicate-featured daughter (SANGUAN TULARAK) he gave a lavish cocktail party at the Cathay Mansions. I arrived late, having been to another party earlier, and after greeting the host and hostess, I was standing in brief conversation with my friend KWAY LONG, when someone boomed behind me. It was Tovarich Fedayoff of the Soviet Consulate—MY INTERVIEWEE FOR THE VISA ON THE TRANS-SIBERIAN! In difficult but pleased English, he clasped my hand and we held a laughing conversation. I gushed charm and flattery like a French pompadour. (Note of anguish: I see by the *China Press* society page that the Soviet ambassador and Madame Sun Yat Sen were also invited to the party. God, how I want to go to Russia on that train.) Then a curious thing happened: the Ambassador insisted I stay for the dinner (a small, flatteringly select group). We chatted amiably, and I was amazed at how brashly frank he appeared to be about distrustingly disliking the Soviets (his guests). At the dinner, we discussed Sinkiang province, and he proved himself extremely well informed on every move the Russians might make to "absorb" this desert province literally floating in oil down under. I chattily confided I too was going to Tihwa on a CATC plane the first of July—that I had just this afternoon been to the airport to see MOON CHEN who rather unenthusiastically said I could go on their July 7 flight. But what is the game Siam and Russia are playing? (Head's awhirl with ways and means of working out that USSR visa... wonder if there's a Siam angle I might play?)

JUNE 12, 1947—28TH BIRTHDAY—Just to recount the passing parade, this year's age adding began when YUKANA JUST, ex-actress with hair the color of scrambled eggs, swept into the office to present me with a wee painting of Soochow Creek. Eva McGown rushed to me airmail a bottle of mosquito lotion! Mother sent a stack of birthday cards and the news that Ahmee has been in the hospital (dear God, that I may see her again before she floats away on her cloud). In the afternoon I went out to an Army radio station to send a message of good wedding love to Dassie *[Editor's Note: Dorothy Ann]* Simpson who becomes a wife on June 28th. Then to see my new discovery—one George Vine, just out from England to take over the *North China Daily News*. He has fierce blue eyes, and I have the feeling when I'm talking to him that our separate stars will cross paths, at least briefly. Anyway, we talked of Douglas Reed, our writer hero. Then I went down to the Soviet consulate to see my Tovarich Fedayoff. We laughed—spluttered each other's language—and I was wished a happy birthday. Home to dinner alone, reading witty reviews of a book by Brooks Atkinson's wife, *Over at Uncle Joe's*—giving me bright-eyed, breathless ideas about doing syndicated columns on gay-giddy-globette! Then off to interview Russian refugees from FASCINATING SINKIANG Province, where I still hope to God I'm going July 7th.

JUNE 15, 1947—Tartars aren't burly, bearded, coal-eyed rogues out of the Mongolian wilds. No, by God, I talked with one today in a Chinese hotel and found him mild, fragile and twinkly to talk to in interspersed Russian and English. I am on the trail of SINKIANG leads and went this p.m. to a white Russian charity home for refugees, who trucked and trained in from TIHWA (a mere jaunt of two months).

Staring, sallow-skinned kids followed me and my bombastic guide, red-haired Zoya (a Russian who supports herself and four cats by various and very sundry means, including making professional matches between "reech" Chinese and foreign "ger'l") into a bare-boarded, splintery school room. It was converted into a flophouse-style dorm by a crude arrangement of tablecloth and tattery sheet "screening." Russian housewife types with vacant cowish faces and man's hands watched me uneasily as I conversed with four of their men and a waspish directress of the club. (Tacked to a far wall: a dapper ink sketch of Tsar Niki!)

One woman with leathery skin, half-moons under hard brown eyes and wearing rosary beads as a necklace accessory to a hand-me-down (four times at least) green dress with pathetic lace trim, spoke her bit with Slavic overtures of "teddible"—and oh my God, "teddible" it was. Born in Russia of farm peasants, she fled to Sinkiang after the Revolution with her husband, an ex-colonel in the Tsar's army. She started a dairy farm. The Bolsheviks were everywhere in evidence. Finally, in 1940, they arrested her husband and other males of the family, closed up the dairy and drove her off to prison in KULDJA. She was imprisoned for one year, finally escaped and returned to Tihwa to trace her husband through the American Consulate. Told he'd been shot by the Russians, she stayed in Tihwa working as a cook for an American radio station. Then a few weeks ago, with hard-saved separate money, she slipped aboard a CATC plane and flew to Shanghai. With her came two leggy, mousy-looking daughters. Others escaped in refugee parties aided by Chinese, who loaded the Russian families aboard trucks headed for LANCHOW. Here, they took the train to Shanghai. Zoya as an interpreter was distractingly dramatic and in between times vouched "everybody dey kneel, everybody dey runnink away. Everybody die—fodder, modder, brodder, everybody." I was discounting 80 percent of the hysterics, but gathered this much: Russia wants to make a pro-soviet sister autonomy of SINKIANG— rich, rich Sinkiang with a heart of gold oil in her veins and uranium in her pocket. Warring Tartar tribes, provincial uprisings, all manner of disharmony and disunity, the Soviets have utilized. Their officers helped train provincial military. Scientists were also legion, making tests, maps, examinations of natural resources. The Russians were greatly annoyed at the American consulate opening in Tihwa (in 1941-42). Up to that time they had full sway.

Eighty percent of the Revolutionary refugees are said to have taken Soviet citizenship. The others took trucks for Shanghai. One man, knee boots, a schoolboy face, in a seared and aging frame, happened to mention one American correspondent's guide, Bairu Gofyrob (in Russian, BALU Gofygov) a Tartar about 40-ish stopping just now at a Chinese hotel just off Tibet road. Bale welcomed us without so much as a stern look or security check. I spread my *National Geographic* magazine on his marble-topped table and heard how he escorted one BARBAR STEVENS from Tihwa to Kuldja, his birthplace, where letters zealously acquired from an (phonetic spelling) AHC MADJUNG (rep. to National assembly last winter) was a safe conduct pass. The two flew on a Soviet airline, very cheap. Bale himself was an interesting chap (a pity he was so diminutive, so bald and gold-toothed—in fiction he would be a tough Cary Grant with whiskers to his knees). In 1923, he went to Tashkent and Moscow. He worked in a fabric factory, going to school at night to study engineering and English. His entreé a Chinese passport. Returning to Sinkiang, he worked as an engineer for the Chinese government ten years. Taught math, physics, and engineering in a Turkish school. Now his home is Lanchow, No. 40, Jung Yung Loo to be exact. He wrote his address and name in Turkish, Russian, and English for my future reference.

JUNE 20, 1947—Just for the record, I received a note from the National City Bank, East midtown branch, that $659 was deposited in my name. Today I mailed $500 additional money orders. We are having a howling typhoon today. Through the blur-blotched glass doorway overlooking the Race Course, I see the scarlet Chinese-lettered neon sign of the Wing On department store, the hotels and

the winds. I've got a terrific Russian lesson to be tackled. I'm in the throes of an article on Bill Powell, the young editor of the *China Weekly Review*. Also for the record, I spent an absorbing and exhausting evening talking with one ex-government gal turned correspondent, who ventured into Indo-China and had an interview with Ho Chi Minh. (Caroline Cooley is her name.) I was amazed that she spoke so dishearteningly of a Sovietized Vietnam. No freedom from fear there. Ho, himself, was a droll and evasive little man, straining every minute to say or avoid saying newspaper headlines. In Caroline's article appearing in the June 21st *China Weekly Review,* she said in gist—all local fledgling officials are slaves of the double police force —street clique variety and secret "suspect" sleuths. Either you are with the government or you are against it, but if you value your life, you will be for it. The dreadful fear of personal danger pursues those who think that all is not perfect. It struck me as odd that when Caroline sat on my bare and uninviting balcony overlooking the Race Course, blackness rimmed in the distant spangles of downtown Shanghai's neon, she told me of the political mechanisms, but her warmest and most enjoyed conversation was about her personal reactions, her slumping reluctant interpreter, shopping in a mountain barter market, getting "worms" and being bed-stricken in Hong Kong. The old angle of human stories dipped in picture words.

JUNE 24, 1947—I have come closer to China at last. How glad I feel somehow. I want to KNOW these people and like them, warmly, humanly. Lt. Chin took me to dinner at the home of one Anna Wong, a Swedish-German doctor who married a wealthier and politically prominent Chinese in Germany as an escape and bore him a son, an intelligent, strange-looking child with a shaved black stubble beard and sharp-featured face, speaks Chinese and some German—no English. Anna, as I gather, is an intelligent woman, a depot for travelers from significant parts of China and elsewhere.

She must be a Communist, not sure. More on her later. Anyway, after Chinese chow (worst I have ever eaten) at her home we went to a tattered cement block house building, ineptly named the Municipal Dramatic School. We climbed steps and finally came to a reception table in a blinding glare of a single overhead light, which made the eyes of the eager, milling Chinese glitter like polished jet. We were handed brushes to autograph scarves of immaculate white satin, then led into an auditorium muggy, airless and hot, so jammed with Chinese I thought they must have been drawn in with a suction pipe. A young UNRRA lad at my elbow, an agricultural specialist, was timidly accosted by a slight, brawny, and strikingly handsome Chinese boy in white cotton shirt and rough blue trousers tightly belted, seaman style, around his flat, hard waist. His teeth were very white as he smilingly, self-consciously asked Philip what to do for a kicking cow. He was a student at the most unique school in all China. In a few minutes he was to go on the stage and play superbly the poignant *ANDANTE CANTABILE* of Tschaikovsky, but his job at the school is taking care of the cows—precious and prized UNRRA henna-hided moo-cows. One of them had taken to savage kicking and he was at a loss to cope with her. Later, it was the tight muscled, charming and boyish YANG PING-SUN, who made me feel—here was SOMETHING. The story of the school came later.

The next day, Philip drove me out to the "school" (actually an unhoused "effort" on the site of a landowner's dilapidated villa outside Shanghai). He was to diagnose the kicking cow and I to interview his keeper. A young, thin-shouldered "director," wearing a sun helmet, which dwarfed his small face, escorted us. My YANG PING-SUN came running. Farm boy "Paganini" wearing the same clothes he had worn for his performance the night before. He spoke English fairly well and we laughed together as I praised his playing. (I shall NEVER sit in a gilt opera house and hear a violinist without thinking of YANG, who played with such lithe vigor. He has had no lessons for a year and a half and very little music scores.) When he had finished playing, with complete lack of self-consciousness, he pulled a handkerchief from his pocket, mopped his face and blew his nose.

We trailed out across the courtyard, down a mud aisle to the bamboo-thatched barn, where about six cows were tied. The kicking cow occupied the attention of Yang and Philip for a time, then my Chinese musician came over to where I was swatting flies, and we talked about him and the meaning of music. As a Chinese, he fascinated me. Did he feel the same emotional exhilaration we drew from western classics? He was awkward about expressing what music means to him, but his director said he lives with his violin under his chin when not tending to the cows or studying in regular classes. He is poor at math and un-artistic subjects—plays the piano very well. He said he was 18 and apologized for not being his best: "I was sick" he told me, "I had an attack of my old malaria." He is an orphan and was taken into the school's fold by the founder, the late Dr. W. T. Tao, whose idea was to import ART as well as the rudiments of literacy to orphans and war refugees. The founder apparently liked Yang's obviously quick, bright eagerness and taught him personally until his death. Yang has studied violin for only four years. His teacher was a Chinese from Peiping, who had studied under a remnant of the Imperial Russian missionaries. Yang hopes he can go to America to study music, but that possibility, in his humble position, is quite remote. Philip called him about the cow and then we started back for the jeep. Couldn't resist asking Yang to play. He got his violin, a cheap one like something salvaged from a pawn shop. We squatted on stools, and he played again the *Andante* (his favorite, although he once heard Mendelssohn's concertos and loved them). His accompanist, CHEN YI-SHIN, had listened to my interview with Yang with such hungry timidity I had to acknowledge him, too. He beamed at my secondary praise. "Chen," said the director, son of Dr. Tao, "was adopted by Edgar Snow." Chen smiled slightly but without any seeming response. Curious, I probed a bit. Snow had heard of the school, wrote Tao, and said he wanted to adopt a boy and girl student. On merit, Chen was selected. At first, letters followed. Then, and now, nothing. Chen has never seen Snow and never expects to. He loves music and just wants to be a teacher. A 20-year-old, beginning in a new and marvelously ideal form of educating the heart and creative art instinctive of Chinese, who might otherwise grow up rickshaw boys or peddlers. Dr. Tao, it seems, was the son of a wealthy wine merchant near Shanghai. Educated in the States, he returned to China, conceived the idea of reviving art among the common people, saw his greatest chance during the war in Chungking, teaming with refugee families and rich financial assistance from the United Services to China (U.S., Cambodia, Britain).

As I write this, I know badly, I am exhausted. Have completed plans, almost, for going to Sinkiang and just came from a cocktail party where I talked to Marshall Field, just in on a round-the-world flight. He was standing isolated for a moment, looking TIRED and very, very alone-ish. With Seymour Topping at my elbow, went over and talked. He said, tiredly, he'd found the trip depressing, especially India. To leave the U.S.A. and so abruptly step into this tortured part of the world was a saddening experience.

China—Sinkiang
1947

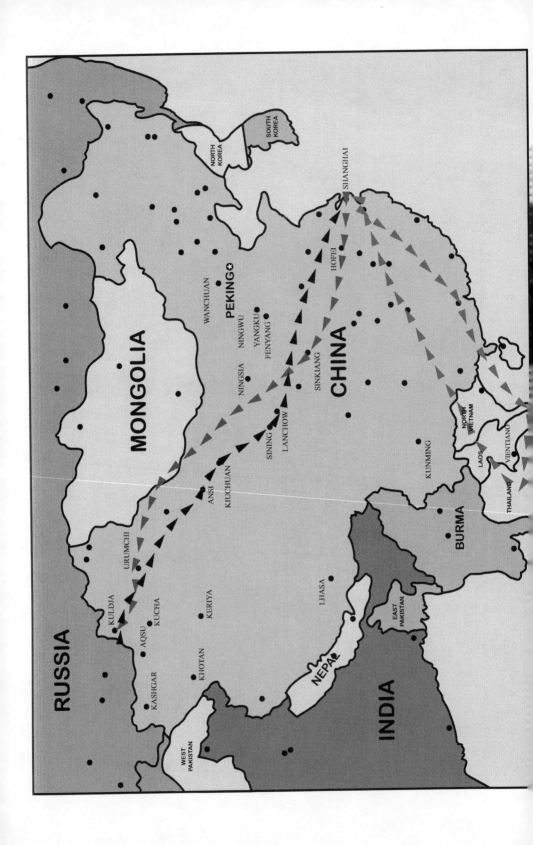

1947

JULY 3, 1947—TIHWA—SINKIANG PROVINCE—Of all my travels everywhere, this place looks most uncivilized, most historically original. A lush, green valley in the palm of a mountain monarch. Our CATC plane droned tiredly down out of a cold altitude into the sun-bathed, green-treed, neatly squared off meadowlands of this remote and now politically interesting province in all China. The tiptop peak of snow cresting the arid, unadorned mountains of mud, rock and sand stirred visions of Alaska so far, far away.

Two timid customs men, who of course never came near us, and airline officials, coolies, swarmed around the plane to receive the dangerous cargo of 250 gallons of gasoline, mail pouches, and merchandise. Three Chinese generals, sub-ranking military. A Chinese postal clerk told me in he had left his wife and five babies in Hangchow to come to Tihwa for three years. He was having his first plane ride but he seemed more impressed with sitting between a tall, rather distinguished Chinese general and his sophisticated, attractive wife (pearl earrings, makeup) to notice the airplane. I was the only white person in the party, though our pilot, slim 16-year-old looking

SHOE WING GEE (of New Orleans) was American Chinese. We stopped the first night in LANCHOW, capital of Kansu Province, which is leisurely, mystically, colorfully attractive, walled in by mud-bathed mountains.

We stayed at the No. 1 hotel, a lavishly western-minded edifice called the Northwest House (single room 61 cents a night). The manager was a tall, English-speaking sheikh-ish Chinese clad in a trim U.S. khaki uniform. He told me Frank Robertson of INS had just departed for Tihwa via truck. I set out in a rickshaw to call on the Tartar interpreter I had met in Shanghai. Rickshaws in Lanchow are uniquely awninged so that the driver is umbrella'd in the spotty rain that was blessedly keeping down the dust and cooling the evening. My Tartar was not in Lanchow, his Russian shopkeeper neighbors told me, so I pedaled around town sightseeing. Streets were muddy, skinny Chinese police stood listlessly atop mud pedestals with umbrellas overhead. Wahlies and peddlers wore enormous picture hats of rough straw (men only—no woman was considered important enough, I guess, to have a hat). Shoulder poles were different from others in Asia. These were gracefully edged like pagoda roofs, in curves.

The most Russian-looking utility vehicles were covered carts like vague remnants of old circus wagons, painted in bright colors. A whole family rides inside, taxi style. Streets were lined with Tibetan-looking Chinese mixed bloods and Russians. Many women hobbled on bound feet. Old men were whiskered and skull-capped. Many villager male folk wore Russian boots, Russian-type blouses and van dyke beards. A few shops had Tartar script on the sign boards. Fresh fruit is the greatest natural endowment of this sand-mud-sun-baked outpost. The overall color of the street, buildings, and people generally is mud brown. Suddenly a coolie passes with his curved shoulder pole. On two swinging baskets are a Sultan's salad of brilliant apricots, apples and other kinds of orange-red fruit, and especially melons.

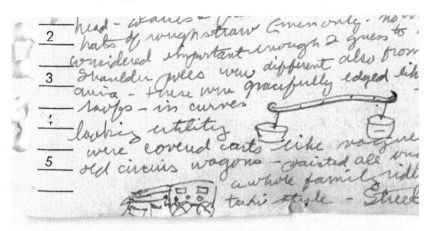

A sketch of a utility cart and shoulder poles from Pegge's diary.

The early ride to the airport the next morning was a setting for a story. A silver fume of dawn mist hung over the streets. Poochy dogs followed at the heels of early-rising Chinese. Vegetable and fruit farmers passed, shoulder poles laden. We passed an extreme military garrison of mud structure. The flight to Tihwa was interesting and rough going. I was most thrilled by my first glimpse of the Gobi Desert. It looked so rumpled and trodden somehow. Even more impressive was the mountaintop cultivation and even cliff-edge farming. Incredible the way desperation for food has driven the Chinese to hook one arm around a cloud while wielding a hoe with the other. The vegetables themselves must hang by teetering roots, and cabbages are afraid to look down for fear of turning green. I must say Tihwa itself was worth the long trek. I have a very casual agreement with Associated Press to send out whatever I find—also *Chinese Weekly Review* (Bill Powell) and my *New York News* of course. Meanwhile, I have lost my passport—frantically, madly the night before I left I tried to find it. Gone! I phoned Fern Cavender, my friend at the American consulate. She said I could get another one in Tihwa, but J. HALL PAXTON, the missionary-ish consul, says he can't issue the passport. I hope to God it turns up in Shanghai somewhere.

The consulate itself is like a farmhouse being converted with the aid of Sears Roebuck. Everything is sticky with new paint. We walk on planks. Russian cooks, handymen, work women are busy about. I am bedded down in the radio room. Last night a Chinese general gave a dinner for the American courier (tall, well-bred, outgoing lad) who was his tennis partner and another departing Chinese. The Chinese food was elegant, but Russian cognac like straight brandy was served. I got hold of the bottle and noted with interest it was from "CCCP." Two young Chinese women were present, both speaking English and acting very cosmopolitan, enduring the province as best they could, thinking fondly of Shanghai and Peiping. We drove home, all very gay and joyous, under a full, haunting low-riding moon in the cool, star-twinkling sky.

Pegge and Valentina, the cook, outside the consulate.

This morning I was the first one up. Found the number one Russian cook, a plain and lovely faced woman named Valentina. She and I made understandable conversation in Russian. Breakfast was interesting and native: prunes the size of olives but very good. Scrambled eggs, local bread like French long bread, then a kind of mushy porridge of barley kernel, I believe. The table sugar was rough, unrefined—from Russia. Mrs. Paxton, ex-nurse (who dotes romantically on her spouse and honeys him ardently and coyly), explained she has concocted a mixture of sugar and water boiled—she keeps it in a bottle on the table. This and American coffee completed the meal.

I then got some local currency (no black market, 5 to 1,000 CNC) and set out to see the town. I was gaped at in amazement, but I gaped back as I wound my way down a mud and horse dung paved road at the foothills of massive mountains, mud brown against a brilliant turquoise sky. Housewives looked very "native" in shocking pink blousy dresses, skull caps of velveteen, sometimes embroidered. Little girls' hair hung in thin snake braids, about six or seven, down their gay-clad, narrow shoulders.

Many youngsters and farmers ran past me with shoulder poles laden with fragrant fruit—green grapes, yellow apples, apricots— many sidewalk stands drew my eyes, especially those selling what undoubtedly came from CCCP. I found soap, matches, cigarettes, much vodka, canned butter. I did not find as many Russian-speaking shopkeepers as I had expected. In one bookshop as big as a postage stamp, a mixed breed, knobby-cheek-boned keeper had distinguished his whitewashed walls with posters of Dr. Sun Yat Sen and the Generalissimo. I also passed a deserted-looking place that resembled a United States information service. But this was CCCP again.

An occasional Chinese soldier or policeman appeared and eyed me keenly but did not approach. Kids timidly followed me. Open-air butcher shops appalled me. Flies and indescribable odors and gizzards hanging on iron pipes—odors of soy sauce, garlic, and fresh fruit mingled with street dirt, dust, and human filth. The streets are lined with running-water gutters. Most pristine were the rustic-style droshkies and horse-drawn wagons with flat board passenger space. The arched halter is trimmed with jingle bells and cow bells.

When they clop over the rutted streets, a tinkle of bells blends with hucksters hawking a genial, many-tongued babble. I stopped once to take a picture and two 1930 model sedans passed, bearing Soviet flags on the fenders. Before turning back I was determined to buy a hat: one of those plush skullcap jobs everyone to the lowest peasant wore. When the kids and general onlookers understood, they led me to all kinds of reeking, fly-swarming hat merchants. I finally got a pine-green one for about 30 cents. At lunch I learned from the Paxtons that no news of the so-called Sinkiang invasion has ever been announced here. Paxton himself got it from a "reliable source" and sent it on to Shanghai. I understand there are local clashes here at night and occasional street shootings.

JULY 3, 1947—The wife of the Soviet Consul general, CEBELUEB (approximately) or SAVELIEFF, has just come to tea. We are giving a 4th of July dinner tomorrow evening and Madame has just returned from a leave in Moscow. She arrived in a limousine which cast impressive magnitude amid the carpenters' shingles and shambles of the American Consulate. The chauffeur was a young girl with a frizzy "perm." Madame was a Brunhilde titian blonde with a sweet and lovely, merry-eyed face. She wore a navy-blue felt hat with veiling and a silk dress of black and white check enhanced with brilliant satin stripes. I found my Russian self-consciously halting and badly pronounced, but she was cordially responsive. The only leading question she asked me was how long I would stay in Tihwa. In the conversation (which was somewhat consciously careful and banal) Mrs. Paxton invited Madame to dinner tomorrow (purpose of the visit).

Last night I got young (Art Bremerish) DOUG MACKIERNAN to take me for a jeep ride outside the city proper. We had the Chinese provincial general's interpreter with us—a slick Chinese lad educated in Shanghai, given to whistling Hit Parade songs and rattling off slang witticisms. Down the main street we went, jostling over the ruts. Every mud hut had an electric light (at least 150 watt). Nearer the edge of town we passed the male Walla Walla circles—some lounging over small tables, others hunched in the oriental frog perch (on their haunches).

Pegge and Doug Mackiernan.

Outside of town we passed tradesmen on horseback or families on wagons. Then we cut out over a wide Alaskan-like gravel road winding along the mountain and a river bed. So odd to see green, lush land uncultivated in China. The sun was a smoldering red striking the mud mountains and turning them to brilliant bronze against the eight o'clock twilight sky. My heart went out to Alaska and in part to Tihwa too. Still haven't got my political bearings, although I learned Doug and the Pao General's interpreter made a quick trip to the scene of the "invasion" and learned the bombing did occur and in part the Chinese were justified for their protest.

JULY 4, 1947—Outside my window a temple of shrill babble. Carpenters, plasterers, Chinese Russian Uighur fixing a garage door.

We four sat down to breakfast to the tune of a victrola recording of "My Man" and the distant rat-a-tat of machine gun practice! The American Consul, in response to my comment that we had a beautiful day for the fourth, remarked, "Well, I don't know. At 11 p.m. last night I had a telephone call from commissioner Liv Tse Yung saying he and most of the leading Uighur politicos could not come to dinner tonight as they had to have an important meeting to determine the status of the central government appointee (also a guest at the party), MESUD SABRI. Paxton became very indignant and said, 'The American Embassy would be highly displeased if they did not come. We will wait dinner for you.' He finished. LIV telephoned the Central Government's number one, Gen. CHANG CHIH-CHUNG, and apparently he agreed they'd better come." It will be interesting to see what happens.

JULY 5, 1947—Oh, dear God—never have I been in such internal agony and fear. I have just come back from the most nerve-twinged nightmare interview of my entire life. The worst self-damning point is I feel I was INEXPERIENCED, INEPT in a situation created by my own stupidity. I wish I could undo the last four hours by hand, second by second. I have been to the SOVIET CONSULATE to call on one Consul GENERAL SAVELIEFF, a truck-driverish, horn-rimmed goggled character who smoked cigarettes like a French Apache. As an interpreter I had to take the slick-haired Chinese who works as a translator at the American consulate and at Gen. SUNG HSI-LIEN'S headquarters. "Kwang" (the interpreter) and I drove to the consulate, which is palatial in space, tacky, paint peeling and barn-ish in furnishings. Peasant-looking servants or tovarich staff members slinked around, eyeing me with furtive curiosity. My heart quailed. I knew I was not fully prepared to launch a difficult and suave interview, but the days were passing and I had to see SOMEONE. We were shown into a room the size of a ballroom, covered with a threadbare rug, faded wall paper and around the room pix of STALIN, LENIN, and others. Savelieff lit a cigarette, sat in profile beside me, and prepared for what would be what. I began at high pitch. What were his comments on the Peitaishan incident? (Kwang was taken aback at my question and murmured his reluctance to ask.) I insisted. Savelieff replied: many stories about incident in American magazines and newspapers. No stories in Soviet papers. If I want to know about such an incident, I must ask the proper authorities (i.e., Gen CHANG, the Central Government's No. One boy). Having gotten off to a bad start, I went on from there. What are the Soviet activities here? I added I had been to the cultural relations office which is plastered with pictures of political significance. He was rather abrupt on this question. Why didn't I ask the Chinese authorities instead of him? Then came the KILLER: out of nowhere the idea came to me to ask if the UIGHURS OR KAZAKS in areas under revolt had taken out Soviet citizenship and if they were eligible if they were so inclined. Kwang turned pale. Did I really mean to ask this question? I insisted. Nervously he translated to the Soviets' Chinese-Russian translator. Hardly had the Russian interpreter gotten half way than Savelieff turned to me angrily in English and shouted "WHY DO YOU ASK THIS QUESTION?" assuming I was not a correspondent but a spy! I flushed but coolly turned to the mortified Kwang and said, "Explain that I wanted to get my information direct." Savelieff interrupted, "If you want this information you can go to the POLICE." I winced and dreaded the implication this might be for the American Consul. Then he turned to insult and as an irate instructor to a child explained that my question was ill advised and impossible for a diplomat to answer and I was out of grace for being so unschooled in the diplomatic world to ask it. Then began a long walla walla on my qualifications as a correspondent—following my embarrassed answers with damning remarks about how young I was and what a "bright" future was in store for me. I tried to lift the conversation to a light vein though dying inside. I made an attempt to tell him in Russian that I regretted having to bring a Chinese interpreter and next time I would come alone. He did not quite understand my Russian so to make sure I spoke the translation aloud in English, to the complete loss of face to KWANG, who was by this time muttering under his breath, "Let us go." I sat on the edge of my chair, but the Soviet refused to recognize my signal to end the interview. To gain mastery he then proceeded to advise me as a correspondent: "You have used the wrong tactics entirely coming to see me first. You should see all the others and then check with me." Actually all the others were at a meeting today. I murmured this and he was instantly insulted. Oh, I came to see him because everyone else was busy! By this time I wanted to hide behind Stalin's mustache. I felt small and humbly damned to a microbe. When we returned to the consulate Kwang could hardly speak, he was so angry. I was of course aware that a full and outraged report on the conversation would be rushed to Kwang's Chinese Provincial command. I reported the full text of the interview to Paxton (American Consul) who either played the role of arch diplomat or else merely was mitigating the whole situation. He expressed the hope that next time I see the Soviets I plant some source for my question on citizenship to throw suspicion away from himself.

In a small capacity I wondered what must have passed between Marshall (Gen George) and Stalin at the recent Moscow conference. If frank words were exchanged, to flash back now on the July 4th story the American Consulate was surrounded by bodyguards and soldiers armed to the teeth to celebrate a revolution in the midst of a modern one, with a full star cast of rebels and rulers. First to arrive was the provincial military leader: moon-faced, Burma-trained, sophisticated Lt. Gen SUNG HSI-KUEB (without wife). Next came bent, white-haired MESUD Sabri (Kuomintang-backed provincial chairman), who reminds one of a gentle Virginia colonel, retired. Next came the Soviets: Consul General (my bugaboo Rooski), with his very feminine and gay-hearted wife, who sat beside me. She wore a black velvet dress with a white collar trimmed in beads. In her plump hands was a small, white, beaded bag she confided was made either by her mother or grandmother before her demise. "She giff me and say—take diss and do not forget me. Very sad." Madame fingered the glittering purse. More guests arrived and the teetotal atmosphere became a strain. The men smoked. The women carried on desultory feminine chatter. Fortunately Madame and I in Russian had a little gossip corner to ourselves. Time dragged—the Uighur rebels did not appear. Russian became the language of the room. MESUD SABRI broke out in the dread language. Finally after the provincial Chinese general confided in me that he was hungry, there was a stir and in came a slight, silken-mustached youngish man with liquid midnight eyes and a green Moslem cap embroidered in sprigs of pink flowers. He wore his western clothes with ease and also spoke in Russian. Behind him came a dusky wife with long braids down her back. She wore a dark green dress of plain housewife style and carried a patent leather purse. The Turki maid spoke not. She knew neither Chinese nor Russian nor English. We finally went to dinner at nearly 10 p.m. and confusedly tried to find our seats. Liberty Bell placecards were labeled in Chinese. I drew the Soviet Vice Consul (peasant stock and non-conversant) and the Chinese personal secretary of the Northwest Headquarters. The meal was a dragged-out ordeal with some watery punch served as wine. Russian food was the bill of fare, cold by the time we put a fork into it. At the end of the meal Mr. Paxton toasted the President of the U.S. It was translated into English by KWANG and Turki by the pro-Chinese-Government Uighur AISABEK. Then we sipped a mediocre brand of champagne. Coffee was served in an adjoining room and I got a chance to sit next to the rebel chief VICE CHAIRMAN ACHMAD-JAN. He was very attentive. To make light conversation, I asked him how to say "I love you" in Turki. He roared—and told me. His enemy AISABEK was sitting right beside him listening and laughing. Considerable twitter resulted from our conversation by all those who understood Russian.

JULY 7, 1947—I have just interviewed the rebel leader Achmad-Jan, small, close-knit man with his green velvet skull cap, black western suit, Parker pen clipped to his coat pocket. I was shown into an interview room of color and domesticity. The chairs were swathed in white dusters, a full-length French mirror stood between the windows. On the opposite wall dangled a red silk banner the size of a bedspread. In gray Turki lettering the emblem probably bespoke the Ining cause. For the interview I went without an interpreter and he had none either. I took two dictionaries with me—one Russian to English for him, one English to Russian for me. The lead questions I wrote out for him in Russian and he wrote the answers in Turki. The translation will be made in Chinese and from Chinese into English. I took three pictures of him and he took three of me sitting in the chair. I asked if I could go to Ining territory, and he blandly said, "Yes, of course." All I needed to do was make arrangements with the Chinese representative of the Minister of Foreign Affairs, LIU TSI-YUNG, whose three children are in school in Moscow. I asked Achmad-Jan if I could take his pictures, and he boyishly was pleased. We went into his courtyard and found it well promenaded with Turki soldiers of what might have been high rank from the spruce, trim uniforms they wore (very Russian looking in boots and cut). As we sipped our tea I stumbled along in Russian asking if he liked music ("OYEH!" he said. In KHUGU? DA, OYPH—then he told me he had read Upton Sinclair but had never heard of Edgar Snow or John Steinbeck.

I have just gotten out my first stories for AP and stepped out of the room for a second. In a flash the translator KWANG came into my room and read my stories (not exactly complimentary to the Chinese). A complete report will be passed soon, I'm sure.

Doug Mackiernan (Lt. Col. stationed at Consulate in various and sundry capacities) and I ferreted out the message and got a line on the story anyway. Apparently some local Turki, Moslem faith, was mugged and beaten. (The definition used in the Russian dictionary with which the note was obviously written listed "TRITE (BANAL)" at the top. The good man's finger slipped on the final type and he actually meant the word above: ZBUHAT—to beat unmercifully, to beat until losing consciousness, UZBUMTR—a beating, to beat to a mummy, to beat one into a cocked hat, to beat to massacre and slaughter! I love the lingo straight out of the dictionary.) Anyway, from all indications the Chinese hand probably being played in these beatings—a put-up job of terrorism to put the rebels in a bad light.

Doug and I went for a walk in flame-sky and twilight over the back road out of town. Donkey caravans and family groups astride horses (Turki) passed and eyed us, boring in with their eyes. Doug carried a loaded pistol as he is assuming the Chinese hand in assaulting Americans would be a fine political move against the opposition. He has warned me about taking off on my own in future. Beatings have been occurring daily and usually in broad daylight.

JULY 8, 1947—I think I am about to embark on the most exciting junket of my entire wanderings. Today the school teacher turned revolutionary who taught me how to say "I love you" in Turki gave me three letters of entree to ILI—Kuldja, near the Soviet border in Sinkiang (pronounced Sin Jang). I will travel on the Sino-Soviet airline and jeepers, what a story now, as the situation is very tense! My first bit of news came from the provincial military commander, a Chinese version of General Patton. He told me the Provincial Consultative Council (local government body) had broken off all negotiations, had been locked in adamant disagreement for a long time. The general was charming and even handsome but I would not like to be his underling or at his mercy. I spent all afternoon composing a letter in Russian to my rebel Achmad-Jan, asking for confirmation of the PCC ending its session. I used about three dictionaries and I must have made many mistakes, but when I went to deliver the note I found Achmad-Jan at home and very willing to receive me! He looked quite the picturesque young rebel in a white silk roughly smoker style blouse, rough trousers, and his green velvet Moslem cap. He read my letter as I murmured apologies for the mistakes. As I was leaving he said in rapid Russian, "One minute, I have something for you." He handed me three letters in bright blue envelopes, addressed in Turki. I nearly fell over in excitement because I believe the next Soviet plane comes through on Thursday. Must stop now—back later.

JULY 10, 1947—96 degrees in Tihwa. I have just been hat buying, wonderful Moslem skull caps in velvet—black-red-green and one in gold and scarlet thread (about 40 cents each in gold). To find the bazaar we turned our jeep off the main street and edged zig-zaggedly through food stalls—entrails of cows hanging hideously from steel spikes, sun and dust blazing down on them. At dingy hovel stands, funny, wrinkled, filthy-whiskered Turki sold the hats and adored bargaining.

A crowd gathered immediately, and eyes were riveted on the American, especially on my clothes. This done, we went to the Sino-Soviet airline office—an old compound like something from biblical times—mud and whitewashed walls. In a low-slung room with a dipping board floor I found a mongrel-faced Russian woman overflowing a small Chinese desk and a peasant-type Russian clerk in a seedy business suit. A map of the world covered the arid dungeon-like effect of the office. I had come to buy my 3 and 1/2 cent U.S. ticket (350 Sinkiang). My Russian driver, Dimitri, was translating. It seems my friend the Soviet Consul General Savelieff is going to Moscow on the same plane and maybe for that reason they said there was no room for me. I am to come back next week.

Meanwhile I went through an ordeal last night. The No. 1 Chinese general here, Gen. CHANG CHIH-CHUNG, director of field headquarters, Northwest China, gave a small family dinner for me. What an ordeal—the strain of "nice" conversation and elaborate jokes, all having to be translated. The general is about 50-ish but with his crickety manner, shaved head, and apple-pink cheeks, he could pass for 25. I got the impression very quickly that the whole thing was business. I was to interview him before the audience of Doug (of whom I was personally very conscious), the Paxtons, the General's wife and daughters. I wasn't in the mood and hadn't prepared my questions. I thought I fumbled in expressing myself and the gist of the central government's diplomat militaire was thus: In reply to my query here and in Ili zones—"Chinese proverb: all crows are black"— or Red, I added. I asked about Soviet citizenship in the rebel zones, and the General estimated 7 out of 10 persons hold Soviet passports either from fear or willingness. USSR uses the excuse that they were originally Russian citizens and are only resuming their citizenship. (Thus they would be Russians as well as Moslems.) He added that undesirable mining is going on (of tungsten) in Kuldja, oil in WUSU and ALTI. When warlord General SHIH SHIGH TSAI was in cahoots with Russia, oil was being drilled in Wusu. When he broke with them they plugged in the wells (with cement?) and removed their machinery and equipment. It is said the drilling has been resumed with primitive methods. In ALTI, as we have information also, mining and oil drilling is taking place on a grand scale.

To add to the atmosphere of intrigue par excellence, I took one of my letters of introduction from rebel chief Achmad-Jan to an odd, salaaming little man who lived in a stable-barn-mud compound with a yard full of black-eyed Moslem kids (all wearing caps), chickens and grimed, gnarled workmen. This man, whose sympathies are with the Chinese, studied English 20 years ago in Syria. I was very reluctant to have him read the letter but wanted to be safe and especially to know if Achmad-Jan had concealed anything when he sealed the letter of introduction. He hadn't. The note in Turki requested fullest cooperation. Then I had the added insight into visual interpretation of a politically potentially unsealed political regime in a whole town. I was completey briefed on COUNTING machinery—soldiers—

guns—everything possible and of course looking for the bear's paws in all things. If I only manage my story well and get it out before anyone else appears—dear God, what luck.

JULY 14, 1947—TIHWA—Mark ye well the day of July 13th in the year of our Lord 1947. I don't know whether to record this in language for posterity or merely to make note and await future developments. Maybe the latter, for how can I be sure of something as drastic as marrying this darling love of my life DOUGLAS SEYMORE MACKIERNAN, and damn, I'm not sure of the spelling of his name, though I asked him twice and have seen it written!

During my stay here I have been in mental throb (as per the hell from the Soviet Consul General) and bewilderment figuring out my angles. Always it was Doug I went to, and from the first it was into his arms. I was (underlined) bound to fall in love with him but did not think it was seriously the real thing. On July 13th, however, we connived to get a jeep for the whole day and early in the morning took off. Under lowering clouds on a spine-jarring road we whipped along, singing, laughing, occasionally clutching each other's hands— the marvelous Holy or Heavenly mountains as they are called, were melting in mists of storm clouds and were for a time gas-flame blue in the distance. The stubble of sage under our jeep was gray-green and fragrant. Doug charged across country off the main road as though the jeep were a Kazak horse. About 10 a.m. it began to rain. Our jeep had no roof, so we bailed out—tied an old chunk of canvas tentwise over a patch of ground on the lee side of the jeep and snuggled down. The sage was close and smelled sweet. The rain was a companion to our wanting each other. We ate a quick lunch under the canvas to which would have been a puppy to a pup tent and moved on. We drove about an hour and again the rain came down, this time PELTING. We pitched another lean-to in the grooved-out river bed of an ancient river. It was marvelous being with Doug—more than that—he didn't exactly say will you marry me—for just now I know he isn't entirely free—but "Don't ever leave me, darling. I won't ever let you go" led to "Are we lost in a dream—is this POSSIBLE?" "It is," he said, and I had the feeling, "Here he is"—at last to get him and not let go.

We began swapping family backgrounds and what we'd have to put up with, etc. We more or less set this Fall for WHEN—and Tihwa for our first winter—from there "Connivers Inc." as we call ourselves, operationally. I am torn between feelings of ecstatic bliss and terrifying physical attraction and mental appreciation (my darling's a smart lad—from screen doors to science) and a feeling of uncertainty. Is he REALLY the one? I take very thoughtful looks of dread and incredulity at him at times and think: Doug forever and EVER? (JEEPERS) Then there is the angle of his (underlined) divorce or whatever he's got to get. I have turned away from even hearing the story—and that I never need know it would be okay too.

By the end of August we should know more about our future, which we pray to make exclusively romantic and mobile. If Doug's eligibility, legally, were more certain, I would rant madly on. I am happy, though, even perched here in a weedy old garden. Birds a-chirp over head, bees a-buzz, getting some shrimp-colored pink suntan on my belly and legs. God, I love Doug, and just for the record and just because I do, with all my heart. We decided to remember the date of our proposal plans, made in a dry riverbed in the middle of no-man's-land, in the Republic of China on the day of July 13, Sunday, 1947.

JULY 18, 1947—The INCIDENT recorded above continues and deepens. I have never been so happy, and no man of my life has loved me with the boyish adorable desperate wanting and ardor of my DOUGLAS. I go over to see him every night at the British Consulate next door. Sometimes we sit on rickety chairs in his tangled weedy garden neglected lovingly by his Uigher caretaker. We sip coffee from GI mess kit tin cups, look at the stars, "COGITATE," as Doug says—and hold each other in wonder and clinging determination that no obstacles will separate us.

The nightly visits to the British compound have not been without drama. During the street beatings Doug would come halfway to meet me. A Chinese soldier with a rifle as big as himself stood in the road on guard. Occasionally we would stiffen, alert and listening when we heard a strange noise. Tonight Doug and I went house hunting. Really the setting for all this is fantastic. Mud walls and horses in Russian halters all a-jingle with tiny bells—Uighers gaping as we pass. We looked at one house which has vague possibilities, but as we wandered farther on we came to a clearing overlooking the heavenly mountain. We would smell the sage which will forever hold endearing memories of July 13th. I wished we could pitch a mud house plunk where we want it, facing the mountains. So much for my love, which seems pretty hard, fast, and sure to be.

At dinner tonight we had a guest—a little dark-skinned young man from Ili, the rebel zone, who may be my escort when I arrive there next Monday on this strangely political airline known as XAMUats (Russian). It runs between Hami, East of Tihwa to Alma Ata in the USSR. The ticket cost me exactly 3 and a half cents U.S. I was up and set to have one day this week but the plane was suddenly switched to go to Hami instead of Kuldja, the opposite direction. I waited nearly two hours at the ticket office before sheer exhaustion drove me to order the jeep back to the Consulate. Incidentally, the Consul tells me one of my stories about the split between the Ili rebels and the Chinese Government caused quite a stir in Nanking where officials confirmed the news. Paxton (the Consul) incidentally uses copies of my news cables in composing his own reports. The other day when a KAZAK chieftain's son came to visit my darlin' Doug, who early in June went on a special mission to a border outpost called Peitaishan to investigate greatly exploded reports of an Outer Mongolian invasion of a Chinese territory, the young (26-year-old) KAZAK who was dressed in Russianized western clothes was the most fascinating human I think I've ever seen.

On his head was a hat of glory—the likes of which would make Lilly Dashe herself shriek. Here's a quick sketch—the backdrop lined with fox leg-fur, the border of honey brown marmot—the shock of owl feathers dangling from one side. The velvet chin ribbons and the tower crown itself of dusky blue silk. VOT! What a bonnet.

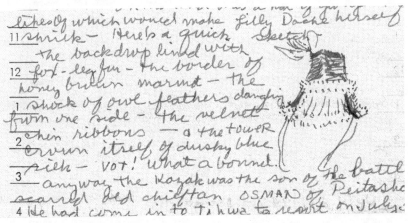

A diagram of a hat from Pegge's diary.

Anyway, the KAZAK was the son of the battle-scarred old chieftain, OSMAN of Peitashan. He had come to Tihwa to report that on July 5 Red Star marked Outer Mongolian planes had dropped 13 bombs on Peitashan, killing one Kazak and a dozen horses. On the ground 100 Kazaks repelled an attack by 200 Mongols, captured and killed the Mongol commander in chief. Light machine guns, 30,000 rounds of ammunition, 70 grenades and battle orders were captured, the latter commanding the Mongol troops to take the Peitaishan mountain range from China. Also found were Soviet medals for the war against the Japanese and pictures of Stalin. Paxton, Doug, and I late last night called on the No. 1 military chief here, Gen CHANG CHIH-

CHUNG, to confirm the story. The general hedged awkwardly at first and while he didn't deny its veracity he strove to mitigate its significance. Something's fishy about the story, but I hated to miss sending it. Today I called on the Provincial garrison troop commander, shrewd, double-dealing Gen. JUNG HIS-LIEN, who also reluctantly confirmed the story. He showed me a bundle of loot from the Mongol captives and dead, and he permitted me to take some of the Mongol photographs—hard-faced characters in ultra-Russian uniforms down to the star on the caps. I also have a picture of Stalin from the Russian army for heroics against the Japanese. I got several telegrams from FRED HAMPSON, the Shanghai bureau chief, all saying my stories are good and page one in Shanghai papers. Then plunk in the middle of the Kazak interview comes a wire saying he can't decipher my telegrams and "complicated over writing" in mailers is difficult to edit. It was a letdown, but right into my darling's arms I went for restored confidence. Hampson has guaranteed my expenses here at $3 a day plus extra for the news value of my stories. Doug and I have had a merry whoop over my $3-a-day livelihood, which was all the job I needed to keep me here until we can be (strange word, so extravagant to use somehow) MARRIED. Have written Mother a long letter telling her the first news of my fate. Won't feel "engaged" out and out until Doug feels free to tell Paxton our intentions.

JULY 21, 1947—Doug and I took a long junket yesterday into the Bog-do-lo (approximately) Mountains. I can't begin to tell you how wonderful the day was for me and how much I LOVE, LOVE, LOVE him. So much that it is a little sad and overwhelming. I have never before been in such throes of sheer ecstasy and longing. We bounced way up the mountains (honestly should have had saddles instead of seats in the jeep). The sun beat down on us. Doug singing like a Gaucho—all his boyhood Mexican songs. I took pictures of him to be sent to everyone when we announce the Great Event.

Finally we found a crest of a hill with a gushing splash of waterfall. I was cook—wonderful fun, especially with Doug kissing the back of my neck and grabbing me every time I turned around. I know that he loves me very much, so much so I see how shallow and empty the "love" of others really was. We laughed by the hour—as I did my cooking and kept telling him all the grand things I'm going to cook for him. Oh, yes—'twas said he wooed and won her true, true love with visions of soufflés and waffles and deep dish strudels—bedded into our very private and full-flowing waterfall were our thermos bottles and a can of apricots.

As we were finishing up, lo, a strange rider appeared—a Uighur. He hobbled his horse and came over for a visit. We gave him some apricots and he loaned us his horse later for me to take pictures of Doug.

When we got home (very late for dinner purposely), we lost ourselves from the others by having dinner in Valentina's kitchen. A storm blew up, and as we had no electricity Valentina brought forth a candle and bottle of divine vodka. The wind flickered the candle wick in a fascinating disturbance which threw golden flickers of light over my beloved's well defined face, turned raw red from our day in the sun.

We went next door to the British consulate and with the rain pelting and beating down, were close together in a chair—the conversation was one to bind us closer, if that is possible now. All day we had laughed and bounced around. Then in the night the uncertainty of WHEN we can be married (when his divorce would be final) plagued us. Because in the period of uncertainty we might lose each other, I decided to pray for a happy solution, to pray as I haven't in a long, long time. I wondered too if the obstacle to marrying Doug wasn't deliberate. Perhaps it was a means of bringing me back to my knees—and maybe, bringing Doug along with me. If he has been baptized (he's not positive), I don't know what I'd do. We swore to each other to cling together during the uncertainty and agonized

WAITING period and never to let the other down. At one stage of discouragement I thought if by the end of next month we still don't know when we can be married, I might go on to Switzerland and let him follow. If it's to be it will be, no matter what. I do love him with all my heart and some. He is the only, the perfect one to spend my salamander's unconventional life with. It is the very height of bliss to plan how we shall live together in Tihwa this winter if we can be married in Shanghai and have our very own mud hut. Meanwhile, as far as my professional life is concerned, I haven't heard how my Peitaishan story was received or what's the outcome.

JULY 22, 1947—KULDJA—Behind the Rebel curtain! At six o'clock this morning Valentina, wild-eyed and excited out of her head, came into my room and said, "Airplane go to Kuldja today—pilots are here for you. The plane leaves right away." I rose like a flying swordfish out of the deep and flew in all directions, including next door to the British Consulate to awaken my beloved (my darling husband to be). We cogitated, quickly kissed hand and foot. Then I finished packing and was off. Doug drove me to the airport on the edge of town, a separate one from the field used by CATC. A fairly substantial but tattered-looking office building was our check-in point. I was charged about four U.S. cents for excess baggage, then all aboard. The plane was American made, olive drab with XAMUATA emblazoned on the side. I was stared at out of the corner of all eyes and began to get that walled-off feeling which now that I'm here is deeply entrenched. A representative of Achmad-Jan, diminutive, small-footed, in a brown pin-striped suit and natty trim of a French velour western style hat, escorted me, more or less. I was armed with two dictionaries and my three months of Russian, tough going. I watched for WUSU, scene of the oil mines, but couldn't see a thing that looked like a town or mine. There was no activity on the roads. I saw no barracks or gun emplacements. Coming closer to Kuldja we flew over a high plateau—green, treed—rich looking "Yurts," their form of tent dwellings populated the remoteness of this green velour-looking lofty domain. Kuldja itself is a lush green, fertile place. I goggled out of the window to see everything.

At the airport I got my second taste of being stared at as an interesting freak. It was an odd feeling of being completely alone—no one speaking your language and your country and its politics barring you from every acceptance. I especially wanted to talk to our pilot, having met so many Soviet fliers in Alaska. I made a pointed request twice and I was vaguely put off. But when I saw our weathered and whimsical-looking pilot come striding toward us, I all but flagged him down. He came over and shook my hand, and I sensed at once his guard was up and he was being conspicuous for coming near me. To ease the awkwardness of the situation I tried to tell him about the fliers I knew in Alaska. He shook his head. No, he'd never been in Alaska, he told me. Trying to make myself more clearly understood, I went on about the planes Soviet fliers picked up in Fairbanks and flew to Russia during the war. "That's an American plane we came up on today," I finished. Everyone in the group looked increasingly uncomfortable. Was it disbelief or distrust or what? The pilot hastily took himself off. Silence fell. I sensed an isolation more complete than the language barrier.

Unloading the luggage took considerable time, and I sat plunked on my suitcase waiting and watching. I saw six planes parked to one side of the runway—mid-sized, twin engine, silver finish. Off to another side was a small model with USSR in black letters on the side. In the far distance I caught the outline of other planes. Small number, or else the others were concealed. Two long barrack-type buildings flanked the airline office and a straggling group of local soldiers in Russianized uniforms lounged about, some helping unload the luggage. A few motorcycles were parked by the entrance doors. Intermingled with the local low-ranking soldiers were Russian-looking, bony-faced officers in trim uniforms, new and well-made boots, and new-looking shoulder epaulettes. One of them, blond, hard-knit but very young, caught my eye. I watched him as he maneuvered around near me. Suddenly he turned and said quickly in Russian, "Do you understand the Russian language?" I knew from the way he sprang the words to me he had worked his way around to speak to me. I answered quickly that I had studied Russian a short time. He barely waited for me to finish before he began something else, but a goon-faced Uighur officer stepped up immediately and called him by name in a warning tone. The young chap stopped at once in extreme embarrassment and moved away, though he kept watching me. The time dragged. Finally, the goon-faced Uighur officer took me into the airline office where with another Russian chap I was to tell them my name, where born, how old. With the dictionaries going in both directions, Russian-to-English and English-to-Russian, we figured it out. "Where born" stumped him. Pennsylvania they'd never heard of, so they put down Washington, D.C., which they knew, instead. This over, I again waited on my suitcase. A local politico who identified himself as the Minister of Education attached himself to me and shared the long wait. I forgot to note that on arrival ABASOFF was greeted by a paunchy walrus-mustached looking Mongol-Kazak-Chinese—racial origin unknown, but not Russian nor Uighur—with a considerable splash of gold braid. Asked ABASOFF'S Chinese wife who he was and she replied, "The General." I was not introduced to him, but he eyed me carefully from afar. In fact I was introduced to no one and given no welcome of any sort.

To further flash back, I want to tell about the plane. Chinese customs officials were at the airport and one or two Chinese stood at the gangway as I went aboard, but they were purely functionary. The Manager of the Airline from the Tihwa office was aboard the same plane, but he and some other civilians rode up front in the cockpit and pointedly avoided even looking at me. I bobbed my head in mere civil recognition of the airline manager, and he pretended he didn't see me. All the luggage was dumped in one side of the plane, almost up to the ceiling—suitcases, trunks, and bundles upon bundles all tied in shawls, blankets, and bedspreads. As the plane bumped down the runway, the mountain of luggage teetered toward us and would have crushed us completely had it come down. No ropes secured it. No seat belts held us in our seats, either. A long metal pole had been inserted behind the usual bucket seats and we hung onto that. There was only one pilot and a tough-looking little fellow acting as crew chief. The other passengers were Russian peasants, despicably impoverished, and one little girl with a disfigured eye and an old man with his head in bandages. I saw a stack of passports at the airport office when the Chinese police official checked me out. All the passports were Soviet.

To resume my increasingly uncomfortable position at the airport—FINALLY a car arrived to take me somewhere. The car was a dilapidated, spine-shattering lizzy whose ancient seats were swathed in beautiful, violet-hued rugs. As we bounced along past fields on which country fair prize specimens of cattle grazed, the schoolmaster politico explained that here a great deal of fighting had taken place. We passed shattered, pock-marked mud walls and he said (I believe) for three weeks (months) the Chinese soldiers and Uighurs had fought here. We drove past a target practice field where Uighur enlisted troops were taking a 10-minute break. I glanced without undue interest at them. Guessed about 50 to 60 troops with fairly new looking rifles were sprawled on the ground.

Entering the city I found Kuldja more picturesque than Tihwa. The streets are mud and dust clouded, but the sidewalks are lined with towering poplars. More homes are whitewashed and some of the compounds house very modern-looking buildings. The people on the streets were about evenly distributed—Uighurs or dark-skinned and Russian, fair-skinned, bulky type.

In our drive through town, we came to one massive fortress of a compound with towering trees and solid-looking rooftops showing above the wall. This was identified as the Soviet Consulate, the only foreign government establishment in town. Finally we came to the Minister of Education's home. Unable to understand half or three-fourths of what he was saying, I was in a constant state of what-the-hell—not knowing WHAT was coming next.

In a lovely garden pavilion with grapevines climbing over a bamboo latticework and apple trees branching above, chickens clucking underfoot, we sat drinking bowls of tea that tasted like liquid mold. Apples were placed before my ravenous eyes, but no attempt was made to "serve" them. I went on struggling to communicate with my schoolmaster. Learned he had studied one year in Moscow. During all this a tall, eager-beaver young man in a brown corduroy uniform, with a pistol snapped round his lithe waist, hopped about doing chores at the schoolmaster's direction. "KTV OH?" I asked. "He is my adjutant" was the answer. "Oh, you are also in the local army," I followed up. Blank, forced reply: "No. No." But an adjutant is a military aide, I explained simply, feeling an inner cringe that again I'd said the wrong thing. We let that one pass, but the adjutant, whose name is Momyeta, was to be my escort, I gathered. He had been a delegate at the National Assembly last winter in Nanking, and that gave him great "worldliness." He indicated by his boyish masterliness that he was sufficiently sophisticated to manage the trials of escorting a young American girl about town!

Lunch was finally served. It consisted of peeled apples (at last), the usual Turki bread biscuits (on which flies were black as pepper), a syrupy jam and some hot lardish dish deathly sweet and oozing oil. This and the mold tea. I clutched at the apples and smiled. Finally, the exhausted (I'm sure) schoolmaster indicated I should rest and at 2 p.m. we would do some sightseeing. He disappeared and far from rest, I was surrounded by the ravenous women of the household who apparently were waiting for their crack at the lard dish bread and jam. I drew out a compact and they giggled when I held the mirror up to their faces. The women, wife and daughters of the schoolmaster, were dusky-skinned but dressed western style except for make-up.

The adjutant and some other gangly youth joined the group until finally in sheer exhaustion and discomfort I plopped down on an immaculate chaise longue, freshly spread in snowy sheets and pillows, and closed my eyes. Everyone shooed but the chickens, who clucked furiously. I closed my eyes and thought about Doug and how terribly alone I was without him in this garbled, strained, and very strange city. At 2 p.m. the women appeared and my luggage was carried out and stowed in the carpet-lined auto. I got in and the adjutant suggested we go to the bazaar. As we drove I eyed the people. Surprisingly few on the streets, but about an even mixture of fair Russians and native conglomerations. We stopped at a department store—went in—the shelves were piled to the heavens with Russian cotton print and bolts of woolen cloth. Several of the military uniform color, olive drab. The cottons, I gathered, were cheap, but the wool was about $10 U.S. for about a yard and a half. But the material is very wide. Vodka, cigarettes, matches and other knick knacks were in the counter holds under glass.

Two young Russian girls in dainty white embroidered frocks, western style, spoke to my adjutant who was a bit flustered for a second, having me in tow. Just then I moved, smiling deliberately, in a circle of bulging eyes. No mob of Chinese ever, ever stared more microscopically. We left and headed deep into the native quarter— many Kazaks astride fine-looking horses turned to look at me. Their hats were a joy to behold. Herewith a sketch.

A diagram of a hat from Pegge's diary.

I will of course have to go back with umpteen hats. Fruit and vegetable markets were overflowing. We stopped deep in the heart of a bazaar sector and penetrated an inner cubicle place where rugs were displayed. Nothing I liked. Meanwhile the place was MOBBED but literally FLOWING OVER BY THE HUNDREDS with people staring at me—not friendly or unfriendly, just pop-eyed with curiosity (and there I was on this majestic occasion wearing old khaki trousers, my black seamen's sweater, and a twist of scarlet silk around my head).

When we left the rug place the crowds were overwhelming, and I had to take my adjutant's arm to thread my way to the car. By this time he was assuming the role of a gallant and suggested we might find some music and dancing tonight (EGAD). Suddenly we stopped at a compound—very modern and tidy-looking. My baggage was hauled off—plunk. There I was. A young woman in western house dress with a scarf over her hair greeted me in Russian, showed me to an attractive guest room, and the adjutant left, saying he'd return at 5.

I put on a dress, brushed my hair, and asked for some hot water (dying for some coffee by this time). I heard a knock at my door and opened it—PLUNK—two young men stepped into the room. I was quite taken aback. Finally it was explained that the younger, darker and more somber of the two was the local newspaper editor. He assumed I spoke Russian and was going to interview me. I mustered a bit of far-fetched poise and sat him down with a dictionary. I had just gotten started on my name when in came a tall, slim, western-looking man who said in Russian he would be my interpreter. He worked at the local electric plant and had studied English many years in Constantinople. I could have wept with relief to have him break down into easy, fluent English—to be able to SPEAK—to say to someone "What is all this? What's what around here? Why is everyone so reluctant to let me have an English interpreter from among the local people when I KNOW there are English-speaking residents here?" I gathered even this chap was not altogether too free in acting as my interpreter.

The interview amounted to one question. "How long will I be here?" I was put into the embarrassed position of asking my host how long I might stay. Two weeks seems to be the time, although I can stay longer if I express a special request. The newspaper interview dragged out to a tea served from a Russian samovar (DELICIOUS) but poured into bowls. Preserved fruits and some kind of cakes like small waffles curled into cones were served. The young newspaper editor sat glumly eyeing me as I girlishly chatted away about wanting to buy things here—rugs—hats—etc. I turned to him and said, "I am afraid my colleague will think I am not very serious." His reply through translation was "You Americans are very rich; you do not need to be serious." I drained every drop of gaiety from my face. Resenting slightly his remark, I explained that America is very seriously concerned about the troubles and struggles of others in the world. "But we are very small remote people," he went on. I replied, "America is particularly concerned over small people who by fear or helplessness from powerful oppressors may not be free." Whether this was accurately translated I don't know. To my regret I felt he went away thinking me an outsider, not a sympathizer to his cause. My attempts to make him laugh or smile only embarrassed him. After tea I went to my room, which I almost forgot to say was adorned with a picture of STALIN and glossy prints from Soviet movies.

I rose about 7:30 for dinner served by one overhead unshaded electric light. My English-speaking host, who explained he and his family were all TARTARS, helped me to an excellent Russian meat dish, soup, and later red raspberries from his garden. My adjutant came in and said something about my having to pack up and go somewhere else. I begged to be permitted to stay where my host spoke English, and for that night was granted permission. But the adjutant was none too smiling when he left. Too worn out to care at that point, I went to bed.

Next morning I woke to a beautiful blue sky, white-fleecy-cloud day. At breakfast there was some talk of where I was to stay. As I dug into a heaping mound of fresh butter (marvelous), jam, fresh fried eggs and bread, I wondered what NEXT. A man appeared and said two carts were waiting to move me where I was to live, with a Madame CAPBU (Sarbee) and her son, an army officer, PABUL (Ravel). They were to leave soon for a resort in the mountains and I would be left alone. The cordial attitudes of all this chilled me a bit and I sought some excuse to stay with the man who speaks English, my Tartar, but he told me, "It is better you go to the other place." I packed and on a horse cart rode to a very charming home painted blue and white. A porch embracing the side of the house was lined with blooming potted plants. A Russian housekeeper showed me to a room which was properly prepared for a guest—in the European sense. A table laden with fruit (heavenly local apples, red-speckled or cream-colored skin, and the fruit itself dead white) stood to one side. A European dresser with an old-fashioned mirror—plates hand-painted in peasant scenes hung on the wall together with STALIN'S portrait and a huge poster of a Russian soldier casting a vote in a ballot box, the Hammer and Sickle flag flew behind his head—a local rug in screaming red, pink, and green designs hung over a narrow iron bed covered with a hand-loomed wool blanket.

The son of the house finally put in an appearance—tall, slim, rather attractive lad in boots and jodhpurs. I spluttered to him in Russian. He smiled, bowed, and went to his room across the hall. A few minutes later he came out, noisily locked the door and went away. I just ducked, spotting a soldier with rifle standing outside gazing in here with interest. I don't want to go on record prematurely, but something tells me I am not among friends here. The whole thing has been awkwardly and clumsily managed. No one yet has presented himself as a spokesman or guide.

I have just returned from my first stroll. Quite luckily a young Russian girl, daughter of my hostess housekeeper, said she would go walking with me. We had only gone a few steps when a little urchin approached, begging. He was the first of about ten—men, women, Russian children and ragged nondescripts—who presented themselves to us. We passed more "Veno" (BИHO) shops than anything else, and the equivalent of bars. We stopped in one clean and fairly busy looking bakery and I decided to take down prices. One and a half pounds of butter, called a "NOL," was 1,000 rubles. I was amazed to learn that the money here is called by such a Russian name. I do not know yet if it is Soviet money or not. Bread was 500 rubles. The old fellow in the shop was quite awed to have an American in his shop. We walked on, past numerous bicycle repair shops. I checked to see if I was being followed but didn't believe I was. We came to another shop where I priced samovars (thinking always of Doug and our home, even though we keep telling each other our idea of a home is a bed with four walls around it). A big spanking new samovar was about $14 to $15 U.S. Gloves of very soft brown kid lined with wool were about 75 cents to $1 U.S. A pair of Russian boots about $4 to $5 (I hope to have a pair made to order here). Russian victrolas about $15 U.S., records about 10 cents apiece, and there are many Soviet records here. I asked my Russian friend about sending a telegram. She said there is only one telegraph office and that is at the Soviet Consulate. As beggars kept approaching I asked if people were hungry and Moosa answered, "There isn't much money here." She pointed out several movie houses where Soviet movies are shown. As we neared the edge of town, we came to street hawkers with rough hand-loomed woolen cloth from Kashgar for sale. Further on was a marketplace of stalls selling spice, tea in odd lumps that looked like chewing tobacco.

We came home exhausted and on the way passed Abasoff, who told me I was to see the governor after lunch. Lunch consisted of three soft-boiled and very fresh eggs, dry bread, and tea. After that we went to see the governor, taking Moosa as interpreter, which wasn't a good idea as we barely understood each other with pigeon

Russian. The governor, HAKIM Bek Hoja, an elderly Uighur with a thin chiseled face and gray van dyke beard, greeted me on the walk of his shaded garden. We sat in a carpeted pavilion drinking tea and eating apples as Moosa struggled to be my interpreter. It was arranged that I should come back at 5 that evening with Masood, my Tartar English-speaking host. At the set hour we went to the governor's residence. I presented Mr. Paxton's gifts: a can of pineapple and a box of sugar (these, I must say, were received with very casual interest and thanks).

These are the nut kernel facts I gathered from our interview: Kuldja has a population of 2,000 including 14 different races. People are taxed on their ability to pay and in the form of barter or goods. The tax is two cows out of every 100, two horses from every 100, three sheep from every 100. Sometimes there is trouble collecting when tax collectors try to get four or five animals from the livestock owners. Farmers give two pounds of every hundred (wheat, for instance) to the government. Other taxes come from property purchases, land used for family gardens, etc. Stress was placed on how the government helps poor families with grants of seed and farmland too if they are too poor to pay taxes. I said here that the tax situation was so attractive I would like to live in Kuldja. If so, what tax would I pay? None. If I bought a house to live in, however, I would pay $6 U.S. for every $100 U.S. the house cost. I checked this money exchange quoted all through the bazaar as rubles. "No, no," I was hastily informed. "No rubles here, only Sinkiang currency." As a point of conversation, I pulled out some CNC and asked how I could have it changed. As he examined the money, which was brand new and bore the image of Sun Yat Sen, I asked what the governor thought of him. Allowing for misunderstanding in translation, the answer was "The whole world knows Sun Yat Sen, who worked for his people and country. When we were under the Chinese government we admired him also. Now we have our own leaders." As I began to write this down, repeating the words, the governor interjected a correction:

"We also admire Sun Yat Sen." Following this was a comment: "After the Revolution we presented 11 points to the central government. If they keep them we will join the Chinese government. But we sent our delegates to Tihwa and they had to return because the Chinese government did not keep its agreement." He added, "We believe big governments (American implied) will help. The more they know of the true situation, the less chance China has of disposing of us as she wants to." I concluded the interview, not wishing to tire the elderly gentleman with whom I was favorably impressed. He said I was an honored visitor from a great distance and could place the town at my disposal. I said I had one request: to learn to ride a horse. He laughed and said "Gladly." In return I offered to give English lessons or lecture on any phase of America that an interested group might want to hear. Nods and smiles.

JULY 24, 1947—This morning as I sat sunning myself and copying my notes, a slim little man in a scarlet Moslem hat appeared: my riding teacher from the governor's office. After considerable walla walla and furious use of the dictionary and drawing pictures, it was decided I must have riding boots and breeches. Sunday was set as the day for the first ride. The little man went away and two Uighur officers, trim, slim, and striking in their blue tunic uniforms and slim, soft leather boots, appeared. They would see that I got boots and breeches. Away we went to a boot maker. The shop was a busy whitewashed mud hovel, but the boot maker obviously knew his trade. He plunked me down on a stool, drew my foot on paper—measured my arches, ankles and calf. I get them in black leather as a gift of the government. Then began a round of tailors for the pants. No material available but heavy wool. We went to several shops where skull-capped Uighur tailors almost stumbled head-first in their eagerness for business with the foreign woman. Finally in all the shops I saw American sewing machines (Union & Singer models in fairly good condition) and the walls PLASTERED with pix torn from Soviet magazines. Stalin, Moscow, Lenin, army parades, the works. It was decided the only suitable material would be regular Rebel Army gabardine (a heavy twill—not wool—in a fine medium blue—oh boy, Parker joins the revolution. Incidentally, I learned one kind of rank: 3 stars and one bar is a captain. With great difficulty I learned I cannot (as I insisted) buy the material which will come from the army. I can only pay for the tailor's work! Oh, yes—flash back—as Masood (my Tartar interpreter) and I left the governor's home and I made praiseworthy remarks. Masood said, "Any questions you want to ask, bring to the governor. He will tell you the TRUTH. He is an old man and always tells the truth. Sometimes the younger men in the government"—he hesitated and framed his words with care—"have their own ideas."

Just for the record—my observations: I have seen no Soviet soldiers in Soviet uniforms, but I have seen Russians in Uighur army uniforms marked with the half moon and star. I have seen no evidence of mechanized activity militarily or industrially—no trucks, no heavy or modern equipment beyond rattletrap autos and a number of bicycles. Nowhere have I seen Chinese characters used on shops or offices and of course no Chinese flags or pictures. I have seen no pictures of local leaders or champions—only Stalin. I have been surprised that most of the army officers and the governor do not speak or apparently understand Russian. I have seen few Chinese here, and these were mostly very old women with bound feet, or old men who are miserably poor shopkeepers. Last night Moosa took me to a Soviet movie version of Cinderella. It cost us a very small sum for paper tickets and we entered an open courtyard lined with bleachers. A victrola played screeching Russian records until 9 p.m. when the movie began. I did not realize at first we were at the Russian Club, but when Moosa told me, I looked around with great interest. Directly in front of me sat a young blond soldier in a dark green tunic with navy breeches, boots, belt and pistol around his narrow waist. His hat, snap visor style, bore no insignia. Moosa and I sat

conspicuously in what would pass for "box" seats. An older officer
in a gray faded tunic, visor cap, and insignia epaulette of black and
silver came over and made a special point of talking to Moosa. His
arm was bandaged in a sling. He was careful to look me over without
acknowledging my presence. Out of civility I smiled and nodded as
he stood there, but he pretended not to see me. When he left I asked
Moosa if he were high ranking, and she nodded with some irritation
at his approach.

It is odd that I have not been given the cook's tour treatment I
expected. On the contrary, I have been left quite to my own resources.
The most amazing thing just happened. I have just had a burst of
confidence from (best I not name him), and the story was revealing.
If the border were let down to China or India or any other EXIT
but Russia, there would not be a single person left in Kuldja—even
the poorest, oldest and most wretched would somehow flee. A reign
of terror here is in full force. People have taken Soviet citizenship
from fear. Officers of the revolutionary army have been called
back to service. Achmad-Jan is the No. 1 figurehead taking orders
from the Soviets. The real leader during the actual duration of the
revolution was taken away in 1946 when Achmad-Jan went to Tihwa
to sign the peace treaty and assume the role of No. 1. The name of
the UZBEK who was the people's true leader: ALE HAN TOO RAY.
He had the role of "president," was 65 years old, and is now believed
to be in the USSR. First military leader, a local man, rather weak—
ALEXANDROFF. Before the revolution, say, in 1943, people were
free to talk—now not. Under General SHEN SHI-TSAI people are
afraid—father afraid of son—now the same. My informant broke
off now and then to gasp "I will die in prison if they find out I was
saying this," but he said it as though it would be worth the case to let
the truth OUT. I was deeply moved by his risky despondence—at
the same time I would not ask questions fast enough to get them
written down. I had the feeling it was NOW and never again. He told
me my interview with the governor yesterday was rather out of line

on security. The elderly statesman is a native stock type leader and not schooled in the political approach. He will answer a question truthfully. "It was so dangerous for me," my friend said, "to translate what he told you about small merchants going to the border to trade with Russia, giving as barter our wool, leather, horses and cattle. You are not supposed to know that, and I should not even have translated it."

JULY 25, 1947—Having just polished off a breakfast of three soft-boiled eggs, so fresh the chicken feathers were still on 'em, a salad of baby cucumbers under a blob of sour cream, Russian sausage and bread, I am ready for another bout of what's going on. Yesterday was quite a full order. After my friend departed, Moosa, my bouncy, singing young Russian companion and I, took the one in-hand carriage and jolted down to the bank. It was a dilapidated building, whitewashed and trimmed in weathered baby blue paint. Were it more spruce, it might have done for light opera background. The "bankers," though, were material for Hemingway. No. 1 and No. 2 came tussling out from their abodes in the back of the compound and gaped at me. No. 1 was a bull of a man overflowing his boots, trousers, and shirt. His head was shaved, and he looked like the world's wrestling champ, 1950! He led the way into a family dining room sort of office and sat me down at a table covered with a butterfly-sprigged tablecloth. I pulled out my CNC and indicated I wanted it changed into Sinkiang currency. I had with me some brand new 5,000 and 10,000 CNC notes. The two picked them up and gazed in rapt fascination as though I had flung down gold from King Tut's tomb. The bills labeled gold units they were too bewildered over to touch. They handed these notes back to me with a bow. Finally a young Turki girl emerged from the mysterious extremities of this place with a Chinese abacus, but for $162,000 CNC I got 32,400 Sinkiang. This arduous transaction took about 1½ hours of counting, explaining the money value in inner China, and interpreting through poor Moosa, who fell to chatting. (Gad, how conspicuous I felt—every breath I took was closely observed to see how Americans inhale and exhale.) I mentioned U.S. dollars casually, and they told me there were some circulating in the bazaar. "Really?" I said. "What is the value in exchange." "$3200 Sinkiang," they said, or only 16,000. (I base my figuring on $45 to one U.S.)

After all this, we departed and galloped around the town just sightseeing generally. Moosa pointed out the few modern trucks in the town (as though I hadn't noted them with an eagle eye myself). One passed us, a heavy canvas over its low packed cargo and turned into a compound used as offices by the Soviets. A soldier (not sure of the uniform) stood guard. We passed only one other truck that looked new and sturdy. Moosa told me it was an American-made truck owned by a Chinese. I did not see it close up.

Before coming home, Moosa took me to see the Chinese bazaar. Down a mud and stench trailed passageway we drove. Sure enough, Chinese were sprawling out of hole-in-the-wall shops with Chinese-lettered signs. The shops were mostly vegetable stalls, a few silver trinket junk shops, and a few very tiny cloth and general miscellaneous goods "shops." I would roughly estimate the Chinese population in this district at about 200.

On the way home, Moosa and I, laughing together and singing "y dugs lim spate," began talking about our darlings. I showed her a very poor snapshot I have of Doug, and she, in a burst of confidence, showed me her Misha in uniform completely Russian even to the fur hat. "He is a local boy," she said. "Now he is working in the ALTI zone as a technician, having been discharged from the rebel army." "Does he write?" I asked. "Da," she coyly replied. "Often?" "Da, several times a week." If this is so, communication must be good between Alti and Kuldja. Interesting.

When Moosa and I returned, I began taking some notes when a tall sort of celery stalk of a chap, colorless eyes, soft white fingers, came in to inform me my past interpreter (my confidant) was no longer to be my translator. "The governor said I was to assist you" (I groaned and felt some anxiety for my other friend) "and be your interpreter. But for 15 years I have not speak EEEnglish, and ees very difficult." I listened to all this with great impatience. Finally it was suggested that the only other person in town who speaks English is one Russian dame who works at the newspaper office. Backlog G-2 on her, though, rang very phony and I didn't want her. A short while after he left, however, this woman, about 45 and in her day a beauty, walked into my room. She had come entirely unbidden and because she had been an interpreter for Barbara Stephens (American correspondent of sorts), she assumed I would grab her too. I was as formal as she would permit—not very—and she plunked herself down for a bivouac in my room. Her English was very slow and weary (she was like the 10th stanza of "Owchee chornia"). I couldn't dope her out except that I disliked her with enthusiasm and didn't want her at any cost. She stayed to dinner without invitation, and when little Moosa mentioned we were going to the Russian movie at the Soviet consulate, she promptly decided she was going along. As my annoyance increased, in came the celery man again (who never removes his hat in my presence) with an illiterate sort of note indicating NICKOLAI (the celery) was ordered to escort me at night because to go out unescorted by a man placed me in danger of hoodlums or other ignorant people. So he promptly joined our party—off we went in our droshky—I noticed many little hovels with electric lights but somewhat faint. Fruit and vegetable hawkers jammed one square with torches casting a flickering bronze glow over their Asiatic faces and fruit.

At the entrance to the Soviet Consulate a jam of people shouldered each other roughly to get in. The women wore cheap pale chiffon scarves over their heads and shapeless cotton dresses. Whole families came—sleeping babes in arms. Also, at one end of the garden an elevated screen stretched out among the trees. The movie was a

Russian fairy tale, not very well done or acted. Between each reel was a long pause, and once the sound track went dead and all the kids set up a whistle and stomp just as in America. Everyone around me stared until their eyes bulged and as we made our way to the entrance I watched Nickolai. He went ahead and with the uneasy glance and alertness of a trained guard moving through a crowd he steered us through the people to our droshky. The night was filled with clear needle-pointed stars, and my heart was in Tihwa with my dearest beloved. I am now haunted with a fear of unreality and an incredulous feeling that it was all make-believe. I have almost forgotten what he looks like.

Moosa and I took a long walk this morning, and though today is the Moslem Sunday, most of the small shops, boot makers, and tailors were hard at work. As we penetrated the heart of the shopping district called "the bazaar," I drew whole mob crowds. Chinese beggars beset me and I had to give to them.

Coming home, Moosa and I talked of our wedding days. I was able to learn that her Muhq gets what is considered a high salary in Alti—80,000 Sinkiang a month. He writes, though, that there is no food up there but meat. They cannot live in Alti—no facilities, etc. Moosa and I took a walk this afternoon after I washed my hair with two wonderful fresh eggs that were just born for angel's food cake! As I put my hair up Moosa and Madame CARON came in and watched with awe. I invited them to inspect my cosmetics. Then I really flustered them by manicuring their nails with some Revlon polish I had with me.

To return to Moosa and I walking, we went after my confidant up the street. He was not home so we took a stroll—to a city park if you please. There were tree-lined walks, garden after garden of hedged-in vegetables and flowers (with signs in Russian and Uighur: "Do not pick flowers!"). In the center of the park was a star pattern, and if one's mind runs to the Russian stamp, one's mind runs to the Russian star. Near the edge of the gardens was a large circular swimming pool and young kids (all boys) about 10 to 15 years old were having the time of their lives, au naturel and not a whit disturbed by the gazing American.

After a dinner of chicken borscht, local honey (milky variety but very good), bread and coffee, Moosa, my celery man, and I got out the cart called a phaeton (fie-ton) and went for a long ride in the country. The trail leading out of the city went through a dwelling meadow of mud shapes called houses in which lived Uighurs and others, including hundreds of yelping dogs. Past this we went into true countryside of old trees spread against the sky turned to dusky velvet. Finally we came to a rich, wide, sweeping river—the Ili River, I was told. Of course, as I stood on the high cliff bank and looked down at the silvered, giddy gleam of a half moon on the water, I thought in a sweat of anguish of my beloved in Tihwa. Coming home, the horse stepped into a creek crossing—the cart lurched and my own Moosa (she is a darlin' kid) went into the water. The driver was also thrown. But we all got home okay and I am now doing an Elizabeth Arden on Moosa—facial and make-up. The Arden deal was an amazing psychological study. As I worked on Moosa, whose skin was young and firm but showed the effects of poor diet, soap, and negligence, Madame came in to watch. She is a tall, handsome (in a stoic, earthy way) Tartar with seared skin, a beak nose, and jet silken hair. I stretched her on the bed, doused her with cream, and her startled complexion drank it up like champagne. Then Mama, bouncy mother of Moosa, peeped in. Her, too, I worked on—a complete facial and make-up, even mascara very lightly on brows, explaining my technique as I went along with one hand in the cream jar and one in the dictionary. Moosa emerged a raving beauty; Madame, an aristocrat. Mama interested me most of all. There she sat, a merry soul of about 40, without the least droop in her skin. I gave her a rounded mouth with light lipstick, removed her head scarf and did a 5th Avenue uproll on her hair, covered her work dress with a soft blue chiffon scarf and added my pearls to her throat. She was absolutely transformed. She gazed into the mirror, her face ready to burst with novel amusement. Then, as I called her "Madame"—très chic, ready for the theater, etc. She slipped into her role as any woman queened thusly would. She, who has spent her life on horses, hauling loads, cooking on mud stoves, bearing children, burying her husband, living through political and military revolutions—there sat Mama in broken shoes, disreputable stockings, a frightful towel apron—and about her shoulders and throat chiffon, pearls, and Elizabeth Arden. I enjoyed myself immensely and promised to send them all face cream and powder. It also interested me to observe they had not the slightest scruples, religious tradition or otherwise, to using cosmetics—even lipstick on my Tartar hostess of at least 50!

—Photo by the author.

Moosa and her mother, friends of the author, enjoy tea at the house where Miss Parker stayed in Kuldja.

Moosa and her mother, friends of the author, enjoy tea at the house where Miss Parker stayed in Kuldja.

I have just returned from a shopping excursion with Moosa trying to get this riding garb ordered. The "captain" either forgot or couldn't get the material he offered, so Moosa and I combed the bazaar for suitable blue material. Finally had to settle for blue as a tunic, Russian style, and black for the trousers, plus black boots and belt. The material, about seven meters (or yards I suppose), came to about $5 U.S. It is Chinese heavy cotton but looked pretty good. It may be noteworthy that all the tailors were busy and we had to coax a mention of the "Goob-er-nott-er" (governor) to get the Russian tailor to promise the outfit in five days.

SUNDAY, JULY 27, 1947—Without doubt, this is the most exasperating place I've ever been in my whole life. Yesterday I went to see the dear Goobernotter to arrange an interview with the general. We found the Goobernotter holding a trial of five spindle-shanked, bearded, withered-looking millers—all in velvet caps, boots, and bulky robes though the temperature was 95 at least. (Light clothing here is a heathen idea and the locals wear the same clothes all year round.) Moosa and I sat for one hour WAITING for the trial to end. Then briefly we stated our business—yes, yes, at 5 p.m. I could see the general. At five I donned my pink dress—nylons—did myself up for fare and set out for Masood, my interpreter. Not home. Went to his office—not there. "No, we know nothing of the interview." In a panic, I had Moosa telephone the general. Not home, knew nothing about the interview. I came home in a wrath. Now this morning I was to have a riding lesson. But the boots we ordered weren't finished. I would have to pay for them and the government would reimburse me later. Meanwhile, in counting out my money I find I haven't very much with me. The material for the riding outfit took most of it, and I haven't paid the tailor yet. I'll have to sell something, I guess. The only thing that saved me yesterday was a visit from my friend who gave me more vital information on things generally. Moosa and I took a short ride in the "fieton," though we were warned about "hoodlums." Moosa said these were many here and frequent robberies. NOTE: I want to put in here a line about the attitude of the people here—no "face." No lacquered politeness, although they are extremely courteous. The average village yokel is more intelligent and calm than his Chinese counterpart.

JULY 30, 1947—TIHWA—I had to leave the never-never land of Kuldja very suddenly for many reasons. One: basically, exasperation and high blood pressure temper at the shilly shally treatment—the one interpreter who would make anything intelligible was ordered to keep away from me! I had to struggle with Vladimirova and the celery man. The other morning when I went for my shawled and bemoaning Vladimirova, she was not home and wouldn't be back for the rest of the day. This, plus M. being barred and EVERYTHING, positively EVERYTHING, down to small issues going wrong, snapped my last smudge of patience. I just ordered Moosa to the phone for a plane ticket and this morning in a wake of positive hysterics I boarded the Xactuama plane for Tihwa. The hysterics were occasioned by the three different times in the city—one airline—one daylight—one regular—and nobody knows which is which. I was up at five, regular time, and in the midst of packing in comes a heel-clicking lieutenant from the governor's office. The plane would leave in 15 minutes (it takes at least half an hour to drive to the airport). On top of this the peasanty but appealing young wife of a Russian employee of the consulate, Dimitri, came to see me with a bundle of clothes. Would I return them to her husband in Tihwa? She said something in Russian about going back on the plane with me—then when she left the compound my vested soldier barred her path with his rifle. She came tearing back hysterically frightened. Her anguish at missing the plane—I was never in such a state of near insanity as the morning I made my escape—escape to return to my love, my life, and my fate: Doug. The flight home was very cold—the necessary altitude over the mountain. We had the same pilot I'd seen the first day I landed. I deliberately ignored him while waiting to board the plane, but in mid-flight he came back to where I was sitting, asked in

Russian if I were cold—plugged up the air whatchamacallems—told me we were 20 minutes out of Tihwa, etc. I wondered at his sudden amiability. I telephoned Doug, and after an hour's struggle on the phone, and having to call the minister of foreign affairs and ask him to relay the message of my arrival, Doug finally arrived. I took one good, hard look—as though making a last, last decision—and was SURE. The week's separation was hell for Doug too, he said. I love him, I love him for all my life.

AUGUST 2, 1947—We have another date to remember for the Mackiernan history. It is AUGUST ONE. We knew we'd have to break the news to the American Consul, J. HALL PAXTON. Right after breakfast when Doug got him alone—plunk—he told him. Paxton was all smiles, congratulations, and admitted he'd been suspecting something for a long time. I saw him later myself and he said he was so happy because Doug is a splendid fellow with a very fine background. I was proud in that moment, but when I girlishly broke the news to Mrs. Paxton she made remarks about "It's good you're American—foreign women just don't make out as wives of Americans. There were so many quick war marriages out here. It's a pity so fine a boy as Doug" etc. I listened in growing alarm, for the comments did not fit the briefest outline of the former marriage Doug had told me about.

J. Hall Paxton and his wife.

As soon as I could break away I went to my dear Valentina for some cookies and a coffeepot. Then, feeling quaking and lost inside, I went next door to see Doug. We ate the cookies and met the most anguished climax of our lives. There is a past—to my great, extreme sorrow. But at least he told me, not sparing himself or the incident, though he realized it meant risking me and our future. I was deeply saddened to think this had to be before we'd even had a chance. I felt so sophomorically immature and unsullied and regretted with frightful tremors of doubt and RISK—having to hear of my adored's aberrations—the secret which we must both bear now—the THING we must hide. The dread I must fear of past association coming into our future lives—our children. But when—bent over in his chair, his head bowed in remorse and hopeless, abject penance almost to his knees—Doug gasped out the words, "So you know now—you HAD to know why our dreams are hopeless. I don't dare ask you to share the crucifixion. It would always be there, so we'd both know it. I guess it was a tragedy from the start. God, how I tried to keep from loving you." I was utterly numb with terror at the thought of losing my darling. I could not say "Never mind, I love you enough to forgive." My love for him changed in the moment of revelation. Pity and sorrow were added—his and my own.

"One thing," he added tonelessly, "one thing I can tell you: keep your religion—when that goes, there's nothing." I had been aware of God's hand at work here somewhere and felt that was it. Here was a fellow creature of His—a man with a self-loathing eating out his heart—and there was I, Pegge, a woman now with a responsibility to sustain him, help him, love him, live out my life with him. In return for this voluntary deed to which my whole soul must be dedicated and bear the trust—in return for all this I have the compensation of Doug, himself. In absolutely EVERY—EVERY other way he is the PERFECT delight of my life, dreams, and terrible longing. But I receive him at an expensive and frightening RISK which will keep me hard fast on my knees at the feet of my beloved God. And some day

Doug will kneel there beside me, although I will never ask him. He has never had any religious tie to my church. Oh, dear Heaven—this must not go wrong. The knowledge of his other marriage and a child was bad enough. Now this—I cannot pretend that I am as SURE as I was before or that I love him in quite the same way.

The fact that Tihwa is associated with the incident and the Russian language (my keen delight that we could speak it together) were also pangs of bitter futility in the hope and dream I had that here on earth was SOMETHING—SOMEONE—so humanly perfect. Even as I write, I have the feeling if I am not absolutely POSITIVE, ABSOLUTELY CONVINCED he is the only, only ONE by the time I leave on the next plane for Shanghai (next Saturday), I will never come back. I have no "out," no second chance if this doesn't work out. I, a Catholic, what a pity I had to know, but I of course bless him for telling me NOW. We concluded this dread interview by striking a bargain: I would assume responsibility for helping him and becoming his wife if he would assume the responsibility of making our marriage endure to the end of our days. And of giving our children the best manhood of which he is humanly capable. He was beyond speech. We clung to each other.

AUGUST 5, 1947—Oh, my love. It is a revealing insight into the human experience of LOVE—to realize how much more, and more, and MORE I love my dearest darling Doug. Despite everything—I knew a bad moment after his confessional, and the days that followed were tortured with dread that under all decrees of Catholicism I must never have him. The heart, too, looked askance—in accusation that the beloved, destined someday to be mine, should have gone so far from me in his past. The days passed and the nights too, which are more terribly, wonderfully binding. We walk to our hillside ditch (he just stepped in for a minute to muss my hair and peek with intrigued amusement at what I'm writing. Someday I'll read it all back to him

and we'll howl or clutch each other's hands in remembering the days),
sit and talk until it begins to get dark. Then we walk back to the
consulate, get the big coffeepot, etc., from our Valentina (who must
know how terribly in love we are), and go to the British consulate
to be together. These are our days and nights. A short time ago I
sent a cable home to his parents which will, when we get an answer,
tell us WHEN THE DIVORCE is to be final. All our plans must be
made accordingly. But one plan is irrevocably set. We will wait out
the waiting together here in Tihwa, we hope, although Paxton feels
"the strain" will be too much and we should be separated until we
know more definitely when we can be married. Had a wire the other
day from Colonel Kearny ordering me (his very words) to stop filing
for AP and return at once. The plane leaves Saturday for Shanghai,
and how I hope I won't be on it. I have never been in love before in
my life, if I must compare my feeling for Doug with anyone else.

AUGUST 11, 1947—The WAITING for my love to regain his eligible,
marryable freedom is maddening in the extreme. We have had no
news from Doug's cable to his family and so the days go by—not
knowing, not knowing. We are happy to the skies and above when
we are off alone together, like yesterday. We took the jeep and went
to our Heavenly Mountain, passing donkey and horse caravans—
Kazaks, Turki—brown-skinned lumbermen in a lone lumber camp.
Way up we went, to our special spot populated with three big pine
trees, a gushing outpouring of sloshing mountain stream, and donkey
a-grazing. Truly love in the "boondogs," as Doug calls it. Hardly had
we settled down to be at home when a long-nosed neighbor poked his
face at us—a furry-eared donkey. More followed, and how we howled
at undying love amid the jackass pastures. Valentina had prepared
a chicken for us to cook over a fire, and Doug manned the Turki
pitchfork Valentina had borrowed from some mysterious friend.
Doug, amusedly listening to me, plunked nearby reading a Tiffany

ad from an old *Sunday Herald Tribune,* burned the tail end of the poor chicken—a true black bottom. We howled and turned him over with a basting of cold water. FUN—We got home at sundown after a long wind-burning bronzed ride across the sage and dust and chalk-white boneyard desert on the outskirts of Tiwha. We returned to the British consulate for a "night cap" of Soviet cognac. On Doug's radio we picked up a symphony from New Delhi. Never have I listened to Rimsky Korsikoff's Capriccio Espagnol with more thrilled delight. I have heard no music in months, and to hear a symphony bell-clear seated in a big old chair with my beloved, sipping true fire water (Russian brandy at about $2 a small bottle is liquid inflammation), was heavenly. We rose at dawn the next day, met at the consulate for coffee, and took to the open road for a wonderful walk. Then the day settled down with nothing accomplished except outlining articles in my mind.

NO NEWS at all, and we just live from day to day to hear SOMETHING—GOOD OR BAD—Alack. Last night, driving across the desert, we dreamed up a small Catholic wedding to be performed in Paris after a civil service to be performed (we hope) here by the British Consul, or in Kashgar. To be married in Paris and go to Geneva to have our first Mackiernan—ha!

AUGUST 13, 1947—Today is the anniversary of one month's betrothal and we two, Doug and I, are celebrating in fitting manner—dinner for two at the British Consulate. Of course dear Valentina is on the whole thing, and we had the menu all planned before I carefully announced our intentions to Paxton and his very difficult wife. They were a bit befuddled over the whole thing, even though I made it very clear we had paid Valentina for the food. Oh, well. We shall have each other tonight.

Monday (Aug 11) was a bad day for us. And part of the story I must do—called "the waiting" (before a divorce can be final)—the strain began to get to me, and I wondered if I really wanted Doug after all. I left the compound after dinner and walked out beyond town to our ditch—whereupon I sat alone and held a board of directors meeting with tears of helplessness (not to know what to do and so much in the balance—marriage or going on alone). I know my AP stories have suffered from the strain of distraction, and that worries me. I almost decided to go on to Switzerland and tell Doug when he was free to come after me if he hasn't changed his mind. I went back to town and met him coming after me. He, too, had been thinking things out but had no answer except that he would have me if it took forever and every cent he has. We went to the consulate, made some coffee and finally helped sustain each other. And then the next day the answer to the cable came and it was blessedly lucky—the decree should be final this fall, which means we can stay here in Tihwa together waiting for the final word. Be married here—civil ceremony—and still go on to Paris, or so we dream. What a sleepless night I put in last night, thinking of everything, from what kind of wedding dress I want and could use up here, to knowing that the news will be announced to the waiting world. I decided I will tell no one in Alaska, not even Eva McGown, until I am actually married. Only Mother, Lois, and D.A. will know the progress of the romance.

AUGUST 16, 1947—The romance continues, but with exhausting connivings to be alone, to wangle our precious privacy. What fleeting moments of doubt I know are dispelled when I'm with Doug. One morning I wrote a long letter to Father Ryan, a Jesuit I met coming over on the *Marine Lynx*, going into detail about Doug's past, necessary for obtaining advice on how we can be married by the church. I became engulfed in profoundest sadness that my love, the love, forever and ever should be a man with a shadowed background—good story material. Fine for a novel, heroines—but not for a one-chance Catholic compromise with reality, denied a dream, even a human dream, not a star-in-the-sky dream that my love's soul would be purely untouched. This is a continual REGRET—a pathos at our lives so young, so early beginning. I leave for Shanghai next week and will return at the dictate of circumstances. If I've still got an army job I'll stay, otherwise return. I hope the waiting for Doug's freedom will not be LONG. Where we will be married is also uncertain. Doug said once he hoped it would not be Tihwa, and we both know a thorn thrust of guilt for his past involvement there. How oddly strange that we should meet and know such ecstatic HAPPY BINDING discovery here in Tihwa, which had already marked my life for penalty.

AUGUST 24, 1947—SIAN, CHINA—Death, or at least his second cousin, brushed close to me this morning. I am en route to Shanghai on a Central Air Transport Corp. (Chinese government subsidized airline) plane, and as we prepared for takeoff here in a pelting drenching rain and nosed toward a gray clouded sky, the plane gave a jerking, rolling shudder and as I glanced up with wide eyes at a young American Consulate courier traveling with me, suddenly the plane shuddered convulsively and swerved toward the ground, coming to a life-saving thud stop! We had a flat tire jammed tail rudder and were at the very brink of the runway. I was completely terrified (after writing the obit notice for Barbara Stephens, *TIME* freelance correspondent, on her flight to Lanchow). The courier's face went dead white. Bales of luggage and postal sacks tumbled in dull thumps from the roped-down aisle of the plane. Our pilot, a slight American Chinese with a brisk air of command, came down the aisle crawling over a gaping row of Chinese soldiers, mothers clutching babies limp with sleep, the rain pelted drearily against the fuselage and stung at the windows. Dear God—in a flash of panic one could grasp the stricken terror victims of a crash must know just before the shattering obliteration. I thought of Doug in that instant—a flash of telegraphic contact—knowing how alarmed he would be if he had seen our narrow escape. We had to remain overnight, and I was relieved. Even if the plane had been in perfect order, the weather was deadly.

Sian is a wide-streeted semi-westernized interior town. Markets overflow with brilliant-colored vegetables in wicker baskets. Rickshaws are awninged—shops look leisurely prosperous. A few open-walled fur shops were invitingly interesting, but the tanning is such a risk that I decided not to buy anything. We were driven to a low-structured squarish Chinese hotel with a pretty courtyard. In the center of the driveway was a round fish pond banked with potted flowers. During the afternoon a Chinese wedding was held in the dining room. What a to-do—the dining room was plastered with a gaudy bunting of screaming scarlet-blue, yellow and green. Two candles burned on the low table in the center. Finally a hullabaloo of firecrackers. A regular blitz of bang bangers announced the arrival of the well-rounded bride and her shy and trembling Chinese army officer. The two were led over a red cloth trail (after every two steps, two coolies snatched up the red cloths and rushed to lay them before the couple's wavering footsteps). As the two progressed, hordes of Chinese friends pelted them with what looked like green dyed flour (no rice in this hungry land) and bits of paper. The poor bride got her white veil and gown smeared with the colored dust flung in her face and over her head. A brass band played fit to burst the walls with crescendo! What a scene and what an ordeal for the hapless two who were to be wed.

I dread the takeoff in the morning but will continue my prayers for the plane's safety (I, who have hopped in planes all over Alaska and China and have seldom given safety a second thought). To flash back to Tihwa, I must record the horseback trek to the famed TIENSHIEN mountains (means "celestial" or "heavenly" in Chinese), so named for their entrancing beauty as well as their rising, towering altitudes (23,000 feet at their highest peak). Gen. CHANG CHIH-CHUNG invited the American Consulate staff and me to visit his mountain resort, a Buddhist temple turned into a compound rising above a grass and treed terrace which overlooks a lake of purest aquamarine—a glacial lake of brilliant green-blue water completely bowled in the foothills of surrounding pine-treed mountains. At the far end the peaks were banked in white new snow. Out of this world, indeed. But the greatest part was the arrival at the remote splendor of this spot after three hours on horseback up the mountain trails rising about 6500 feet (my second time on a horse). Doug and I were accompanied by "Irving" (our Austrian-born chauffeur, an eyes and ears man around the consulate). A long-time resident of Kuldja, he picks up lots of tips from friends and informers. Aside from all this, he's a bronzed, agile mountaineer and superb horseman. Our horses were laden with so much luggage we were riding sky high in saddles backed and padded with English herringbone wool cloth—a misplaced import reaching China markets via India. Across gushing green and white-foamed rivers we went, eating strips of DELICIOUS melons Irving kept cutting and riding down the caravan to pass out. As we neared the resort I knew one lone moment out of TIME. I was above a giddy high trail—below was the sloshing gush of glacial water crashing over rock beds. On both sides rose emerald mountains cutting sharp jut-out lines into a blazing blue China sky. My horse, veering slightly downhill to another river ford, broke into a swift gallop and my amateur fright at being bounced in the saddle at a downgrade slant vanished as I raised my eyes and looked up, up over the horse's furry ears—up to the pine-green mountains just ahead, with blinding snow on the crest caught in the afternoon sun. Alone, flying over the trail and looking UP at that was a moment to—my dear God. So this is in your world and I have seen it. Flushed and a little wobbly-kneed from three hours in the saddle, we approached our host—lobster-faced from the sun, but regal in a long blue fur-lined robe. He waved us to a table to eat as the other Chinese guests flocked around to welcome us.

Doug and I were radiant from the ride and zest of climbing the mountains. When a birdlike Chinese woman interpreter, a Mrs. Lu, in prattling Chinese fashion began the traditional courtly questions of personal inquiry—to Doug she said in her softly piped English voice: "When is your wife coming to Tihwa?" "Oh, dear God," I muttered to him under my breath. Doug paused before saying in a strained tone, "Why, I really don't know." She caught the tone, "but where is she now?" Doug's color rose in anger and embarrassment. "In Shanghai," he remarked dryly. "Oh" Mrs. Lu said, then turned to translate to the general, who smiled briefly and made no comment. The day was suddenly STABBED for us, and we became tediously surrounded with Chinese. At dinner I sat on the general's right and Doug was placed at the FOOT of the table. I lay wide-eyed on my bunk that night, shivering in Doug's sleeping bag—aware that his PAST is alive and with me always in the future. Loath to remain at the resort among the Chinese, Doug promoted a mountain trip to the snow peaks. I went along and knew sheer TERROR as our horses, following a native KAZAK guide, slithered and stumbled up and down vertical ROCK trails. Several times we had to dismount and scale the rocks ourselves on hand and knees. Doug was not very sympathetic to my fright, his only help being a shouted "Hang on... dig in your knees and hang on. You'll be all right." We rose to about 6,000 feet, sat in the middle of a mountain stream on rocks to eat lunch, and then rode back 6 or 7 hours on the horses round trip. (My third try, of course, and this junket was really rugged—twice my horse passed so close to trees my knees crashed into the trunks.) What a trip. We came home in the boat across the lake. The next morning we rode down the trail to go back to Tihwa. Doug had a spry horse and couldn't resist letting her step out so I had the tail end of the caravan to myself and was quite content—wonderful to think things out, and I was thinking out the question: to marry Doug or not—at the moment, the decision hovers between rushing to Europe and forgetting him (the past is a deadening shadow to bear into the future) and marrying him in a civil ceremony only and having a legal exit if it doesn't work. He knows my doubts and is pathetically eager and endearing in his boyish effort to distract my serious thinking. (He knows when I'm lost in "decision" clouds which bear me away from him.)

Worst of all was the day I had a final session with Paxton. I was scheduled to leave on the next CATC plane and wanted to settle things politically and personally. Politically, Paxton said he doesn't think there'll be any military outburst but politico-relations will drag out in future to some compromise. Then we spoke of Doug and The PAST. "Frankly, Pegge, I'm not satisfied with Doug's story and before I will witness any ceremony between you two I will have to have legal documentary proof that his entanglement with the Russian girl here is completely cleared up. Otherwise you'd be letting yourself in for all sorts of trouble in the future—scandal and heartbreak." I felt inner convulsive anguish—to think that my Doug should be so MARKED—to have committed so despicable a fraud as an illegal mock marriage in a Russian Orthodox Church to an innocent, very young Russian girl, when he was not divorced. To have lived with her as her husband in Tihwa (where he made such poetic plans for our little home!). It is fantastic, but I was driven to him to help me bear the threat and ugliness of the words Paxton told me parent-wise. Doug went wide and taut under his leathery suntan—the rim of his mouth was white. He clutched me in panic, then put me aside to sink into a chair in spent contrition. "Something is wrong with me—something terrible must be wrong with me," he gasped. "You can't marry me, Pegge—you can't." I listened, stunned and anguished with dread. Catching the slight Bostonian accent as Doug repeated "Can't, can't."

He gathered his determination about him then. "I'll go to Shanghai on the next plane and settle this thing once and for all," he said, as I sat deadened, numbed with pain more awful than I've ever known. I was beyond speech—my lips were dry and sealed—only my eyes had power to gaze on this young lover who so graspingly, desperately wants me to help him atone for the dreadful commitment of his life. Pity came as a release. I stroked his young gray head. He wept.

AUGUST 27, 1947—Oh, dear God. Life is a churn of crest and undercurrent. My return to Shanghai was marked with considerable bitterness and defeat. All the pictures I took in Sinkiang were lost. The most important dispatch of stories on Kuldja, that cost me dear, were lost. Only one or two unimportant stories—one on the facials and make-up of Mama, Madam Cepean, Moosa—made every paper with a byline. That, and nothing else of value, was received. When I heard this, I felt the life blood of all resistance run out. My reception at the army headquarters was cool. The Colonel told me what trouble I'd caused but said I was still in the family. There are reasons for that which for the moment save my life—Walter Logan of UP did all he could to stir up trouble that I, an Army Pro, should be off filing stories for a rival wire service. Threats of court martial were brandished about, but nothing came of it. When I phoned my AP bureau chief early this morning to say I was back, he coolly disposed of me. He was on "vacation"—call Tom Masterson who was on duty in the office. He muttered not one word of how-are-you, good-or-bad-stories. NOTHING. I called Fern. She was too busy to see me, perhaps tomorrow. How would I send a State Department wire to Tihwa to say I got back safely? She hesitated. Then vaguely—can't be done—awfully sticky around here on sending messages up there. I went to work and finally dug up a long-lost contact to say I'd at least gotten back safely. The wire had to be coldly impersonal and addressed to Paxton instead of Doug. My poor darling meanwhile was sent two wires asking for news of the trip, and both have been signed "all my love" and "much love." The wires were worth pure gold for their sustaining powers. This was the only bright ray, along with a very witty letter from the wonderful English writer, DOUGLAS

REED. I had sent him a snapshot of myself and then noted I'd had a girlish impulse of regret—seemed presumptuous. Reed writes: "I'm very glad the girlish impulse not to send the snapshot didn't come until the snap was gone. It's lovely, and I am filled with awe when I look at those excellent legs and think of their perfection-shod feet picking their way thru VIETNAMESE (god preserve us) politics." He ends up with "Benedictions on you, brave but not yet blithe-enough spirit."

I had a letter from D.A. Wilson (now) and put it away for a later reading. In my present state of "will I/will I NOT marry Doug" (or rather, "may I—legally, safely—hiding his past, dare risk marrying him"), I couldn't take on a tome, hand writ, of dear orange blossoms, tulle, and the family church in full blessing.

AUGUST 28, 1946—LETTER FROM SHANGHAI

I am sending you a cable today telling you of my SAFE arrival in Shanghai last evening. Well can I imagine how worried you must be—and this is one time I don't say "Oh, Mother!" I was praying hard, believe me, on every take-off and landing. After sending out the Barbara Stephens stories—and she went whipping out the very morning I came back from Kuldja (the rebel capital)—I can imagine how her mother feels. Jeepers. Everyone has a scare when something like that happens too close to home.

The flight was really marvelous aside from the breath-holding. We stayed at beautiful hotels. At one stop word had been cabled ahead of my arrival and some Chinese general met me with a private jeep, whisked me to dinner, escorted me to the plane the next morning. The hotel overlooked the entire village spread out at the foothill of a purple mountain. At Sian, the next stop overnight, we stayed at a hotel with a pool in the driveway and flowers everywhere. Delicious Chinese food, of course (STILL eating, although I've lost some weight, I am thrilled to report). I was traveling with a young chap from the State Department who carried diplomatic mail.

We got into Shanghai at about 7:30, checked through Customs and came right on in to town. How amazed I was to see civilization again. The pilots (all Chinese-Canadian boys) brought me in to the Race Course, carried my bags, were WONDERFUL to me. One of them was Cedric Mah, the boy I wrote an article about for the *NEWS*.

Cedric Mah, pilot of the CATC plane.

I had quite a talk with the colonel this morning, and expected to be fired on the spot. Not so. All is forgiven, I suppose because they NEED me just now. I would still have done the same thing all over again, no matter WHAT. It was THE experience of my life, Doug included. He rushed a cable down to me which was waiting on my arrival. He too was worried about the flight and praying-out each day's stop-over. Wait till you see me on the HORSE. I'm still very much in love with him, but the more I think about marrying him the more I feel my DOOM or four walls or something closing in on me and I have moments of utter dread and fright, as though I should RUN now before I'm all snared, held and chained. Marriage is such a drastic step, isn't it? Would you be DISAPPOINTED and shocked, etc., if I married him with a justice of the peace?

AUGUST 30, 1947—The black of my Shanghai homecoming yields to gray, even cream tones. My precious pictures have all been found—but considerable anguish—the most VITAL, most irreplaceable shots—pictures removed from bodies of dead Mongolian soldiers at Peitaishan are now blessedly again in my hands. For over a month they reposed under the desk counter of the Park Hotel. All during extensive renovation and swankying of the "lobby." I had another wire from Doug today, asking how my employment situation is now. He still signs them "love." I eye them fervently and continue to weigh Doug in my mind: Yes or No. I had a call from the Swiss Consulate today saying I'd been granted a six month's visa. That and the magnetic power of Douglas REED are a slight balance against Douglas Mackiernan. But when I stood in the AP office casually gazing at strips of drying negatives showing my dearest beloved! Oh Oh—my heart held out its arms.

AUGUST 30, 1947—LETTER FROM SHANGHAI

[Editor's Note: The letter was written on stationery with the following letterhead:

HEADQUARTERS
AMERICAN GRAVES REGISTRATION SERVICE
CHINA ZONE]

Darlingest Mommie,

I can imagine the state you must be in wondering what your baby duck dotter is up to. First the airplane, then the Doug Mackiernan project, etc. At last I have some pictures to present evidence. He has wired me every day since my return (no, he missed yesterday, or else the telegram wasn't delivered yet) and I have whisked up to him but one. I STILL am of two minds: either take him on with a quick, not-so-terrifying civil ceremony or run while the running's good and be off to Switzerland or London and Douglas Reed.

I just had a call from the Swiss Consulate that a six-month entry visa had arrived for me from Bern. They give you six months and if you're respectable, etc., and a good citizen they give you an extension. I can jump in either direction and will TRY to decide definitely when Doug comes down next Sunday. I can also imagine the state HE's in, poor unlucky lad, being stuck so many miles away and knowing my wavering dread of the shackles of matrimony. (Seems such a dreamy thing when you're merely holding hands and saying, "Oh, darling," but when it comes to the ACTUAL plunk-this-is-it—jeepers—DOOM!)

AP gave me in us cash $275 for my assignment in Sinkiang and I will get extra, and quite a bit I imagine, for my pictures. The whole packet Doug sealed up and sent down on the plane was lost for weeks, just turned up. Carefully processed and developed by an expert AP photo man just in from New York, they're excellent. Will be released probably before you get this letter. For heaven's sake, watch every possible paper and send the clips choppy-chop.

I understand AP gave me bylines in the States. Only hope you caught some of them. The mail has been held up and nothing has come in for three days, but perhaps your next letter will spill forth the precious contents.

NOW: Did you get my telegram? Are you in Florida or where? I sent the message to Patty expecting you to be there. How is the baby snooks and how in the saints' names does it feel to be Nana? Does the baby look like Patty or any of us or like Lynnie boy? Have some pix taken of Muvver duck, GRANDMUVVER DUCK holding the wee bundle. How cute, CUTE, it must be at this age. Just think almost a year has gone by since I came here. Patty had a baby and I came back from Harbin. (Note: That reminds me, the "odd picture" as you called it, with the head of Christ is a Russian "icon" I bought in Harbin with the assistance of the wife of the Danish Consul. They're usually terribly expensive, but I got mine for a song. And the wooden box that arrived was the special container made to ship my precious scroll with the Chinese princess on it. Better keep it boxed up for the time being. If I do take on Doug and we come home someday I'll retrieve it and hang it somewhere.

I understand the duty you people have to pay on incoming packages from China is terrific. I sent Mary Allshouse some petit point bags to be made up in Detroit and mailed out to you and Eva McGown and she send me a postcard: "Sorry, couldn't afford the duty so am returning the box to you!" Won't send another thing until I hear further. Understand the Army has extended its duty-free time or something.

There was nothing to get in Tihwa but stories, pictures and a romance. I hope the weather is cooler when Doug comes down as I've NOTHING to wear except fall clothes. Don't bother sending anything now. Wish those nail scissors had been forwarded. (Or they might be held up in this next mail.) I desperately need footie-nail choppers. I also need a list of other things but don't want to write until—dear heaven—I know whether I'm going to be wedded or not. If Doug does the trick on this next visit, and I'm not too hot and fussed and scary, and you write quick-quick and don't upbraid me for not wanting a Catholic wedding (I just can't help it. I'm too DREAD frightened to think that Doug would be the only, only chance I'd have. Ahmee always wanted a change of husbands, too. I'm just like her. She and Eddie were never married by a priest either, you know. And they stand a fair chance of being saved from hellfire.)

I wrote Doug's mother a little note. Couldn't be Emily Post "nice," so just made it a gay introductory. Doug says she's like you, which must be pretty wonderful. I dread hearing from Father Ehardt, but at least will hear the WORST before I move in any direction.

Watch for some AGRS stories. We've got some good ones coming, our field teams being shot at, etc. The Colonel has been almost too nice to me since I came back and it may be I'm keeping my job only because he wouldn't want me to write any inside stories I know. It really doesn't matter because this month will decide my fate and I'll be moving out of Shanghai, anyway. Sinkiang or Switzerland.

Received a beautiful basket of pink rosebuds from one of my local "nice lads." And the British editor, George, who looks like Rex Harrison, has dined, movied and lunched me. So I'm not neglected. Had lunch yesterday with Chris Rand, you know, of the *Herald Tribune* and he said to tell you he'd work twice as hard so you'd never yield up your good nickels or dimes for a *Trib* that "didn't even have a Rand story in"—as you wrote me once or twice. I passed on to him your past wad of clips and again he marveled at this mother o' mine. Asked if you're a writer, too. Chris wants to go to Tihwa and will probably go up on the plane that returns with my darling. Finish up later after the mails comes in.

SEPT. 3—Baby darlin'—your letter just came rolling in with all its tut-tuts and wise words. No, lovey duck, I wasn't "cross" or "fussed." You haven't told me anything I hadn't already cogitated for myself. I don't think I did Doug justice, though, in the blithe way I described him as a gay wanderer (Yes, that gave me a hoot when I read it). I was going on the old standby you gave me once: I don't care who or what he is, so long as he makes you happy. DOUG DOES. With slingshot-ZING. He's so up-and-AWAY and ready for anything, but withal is soundly practical and responsible. He'd have to be for the job he has. No mere dreamy "wanderers" or boys-of-the-broad-highway could be entrusted with the work of a Vice Consul. I don't want to DEFEND him or explain him. We're not at the altar yet, and meanwhile I have ENOUGH doubts, dreads, and mind-changings. Fear not—before the final leap is taken I will have the American Consul and his wife do you a note, Doug also, and perhaps you and his mother might exchange a few words. She's very accessible, living just outside Boston.

I'm still expecting him down on Sunday (Sept. 7th) as he wired me yesterday. Not only because of Doug, but the whole country up there lures me back to snuggle in for the winter. And my "scotch"

Doug will take care of me, he said, if I can't get a paying-supporting stringer connection. It won't cost more than about $1.50 to $1.75 A DAY to live up there, and when I'm traveling outside Tihwa, it costs nothing at all. I ride as the guest of whichever government I'm "covering." I feel as strongly wanting to go back there as I did wanting to be back in Alaska. More so with Doug, whose personal PROTECTION is one of his most endearing traits. He helped me over all the bumps and bewilderments; when his "baby girl," as he calls me, had one moment of "upset," I told you he was right at my side asking, "Darling, what's wrong?" I was worried over my AP stuff and Frank Robertson—remember the INS correspondent who met me that first night in Shanghai—well, he got in some nasty digs, always casting the inference at me that I was a mere "stringer" and not a full-fledged correspondent. He got me to the point of tears once and I ran to Doug who just tucked me into a big chair and cozied me up, etc. Naturally, all this is balm to my formerly taking-it-alone little selfie. And I go to him intellectually with all my problems. He is superbly grounded in history, literature, social science, and MATHEMATICS. (He figures out all my money deals. In fact, he's so good at figures he handles all the money business of the entire consulate.) He has nice ways of coming in when I'm working, quietly, just letting me know HE'S THERE, for spelling, a quickie kiss or a cup of coffee. He's a comfortable, unobtrusive person to have underfoot, which is what gives me the idea he'd be thoughtful, unfussy and COMFORTABLE to live with.

Suppose we put it this way: I'll go back to Sinkiang with him (possibly by train and truck, he prefers it that way, though it takes a long time) and do no marrying until Spring when we'd be ready to depart for Europe anyway.

I gave you an inaccurate steer on his finances, incidentally. He has most of his Lt. Col.'s pay salted away in war bonds, plus a bank account, plus enough property owned outright at the Consulate to clear a quick thousand right in Tihwa if necessary. He's very definitely aware of MONEY, but just doesn't want to make it for the sake of having it. He wouldn't take a desk job he hated JUST FOR THE MONEY. Neither would I. The State Dept. doesn't pay much, you know, but it PROVIDES for its help: quarters, food, PX prices, medical care, etc., so that the salary you do make is practically untouched while it's coming in. That's how I saved so much with the Army.

Have no sleepless nights, though, darling, until I write you we're about to tie knots. It's wonderful to be loved and looked after, to see a strange new country, to be among really nice people (the Consul and his wife) to learn as I go (language and history) and to feel the ALIVE energy that mountainous, rugged country gives me. And being ready to climb into the jeep and GO GO GO with Doug, campfires and chow chow by babbling brooks in a bed of posies, moss and sage. I was just happy to be alive, and all a-sparkle. When I came back to Shanghai among the cocktail sippers, the bored and sophisticated, I felt like a college junior who'd BEEN SOMEWHERE DOING SOMETHING.

Now that I've got the picture to complete the "likelihood," I await your final words. Will write what comes of his session with the Jesuits here, and what's what about my going back to Tihwa.

Was all a-goo-goo beam to read of my toothing niece. Must have been a thrill to gaze down on the third generation. Try to send a pic of you all, want to introduce Doug to the family also. Do you think it's possible you'll be living in Orlando? What about a place to live? Hope you stay on the East Coast as the Mackiernans, Douglas and Margaret, "maybe" expect to hover in that vicinity.

Note: The "farm" idea for us was more isolation than raising cows and peepers. He has a project, scientific-radio, he wants to work on in his own lab. And I want to write. WE will not be farmers. We may have a couple of horses to gallop around on but that's all. I'm crazy about them now that I'm not afraid of them and know how to "hang on."

I'm enclosing the letter I had from Douglas Reed (the British Walter Lippmann—only more "popular" to the reading public than Lippmann). I sent him my picture and the Saigon article. I LOVED the way he made no other comment than to chide me on the one silly mistake I made in my French. "Avant" must mean to "come" instead of to "go," as I used it. Professionally he was wittily kind, and I appreciate his not whacking into polite "very goods." I know it's not "very good." Someday I want to be able to click off the politics so that it reads like pearls and velvet and peach ice cream. If I go to England (being torn, she is, between two Douglases—the elder and professional, the younger and romantic), it will be to see Douglas Reed and beg him to let me work under his tutelage. I've come to the point in my writing where I KNOW I need direction. I have to work for an editor. I wrote Douglas Reed three pages of my Sinkiang experience and took him up on the "book" collaboration idea. Even if I worked as his secretary I'd learn a lot. (Return his letter, please.)

Having lunch with Bob Sherrod of *TIME* tomorrow. Want to ask him for a job as "stringer" if I go back with Doug. *TIME* and AP together would be sufficient "support." Love, Love, Baby

SEPTEMBER 1, 1947—Oh, Shanghai. With nowhere else on earth save Washington D.C. do I associate such bitter, unfeeling, uncaring, on-my-own-ness. I have just had another session with Tom Masterson over my stories. I begged him not to release the stories for the Shanghai papers as I'd certainly lose my job. He hedged. I explained that losing my job meant losing the roof over my head. He shrugged, tapping my stories in his hand with annoyance that it was so hot and he'd have such a job going through them. I shook my head. "The lot of the stringer is a note of illegitimacy," I remarked, self-commiseratingly. Masterson snapped back, "Damn lucky getting a byline play in the States and local papers. More'n UP'd ever give you. And after all, Parker, a stringer doesn't 'belong,' as it were. You're just what you're called—holding by a string." He had previously tipped me off that I really earned my $275 for the missing-plane story alone, and I wouldn't have to turn in the blood-sweat-tears stories I wrote day by day. Keep the stories and rewrite them into a magazine piece. Money conscious as I am, my PRIME interest was getting the story OUT. It had cost me dear. It was exclusive by dint of a plane crash removing the only other correspondent ever in that area—and how would I keep the facts from the world? It sickened me to have no one concerned in particular here—to have no one CARE an iota that I had come back with a great story of things to come in Turkistan. When I walked out of the AP office I felt I MUST go back to Tihwa—there, people at least knew and cared what was going on. I wired Doug today although I have heard nothing from him so far on WHEN he is coming. If I do get back and settle down to a long hard winter of much writing, I'm going to do this story of my return: "Stringer"— the correspondent who doesn't belong, warrants casual concern for his vital story and is left to himself on his arrival. I haven't even had an offer of a cup of coffee from any of the AP-ers. If I do go back and a BIG, really BIG thing happens in Tihwa, I have my doubts about caring whether Associated Press gets the first news flash. As soon as Doug comes down, if we can get his past straightened out, I will go back to Tihwa with him, though I hope we can figure some way of not FLYING.

SEPTEMBER 3, 1947—I guess I did come close to death's awful oblivion in that airplane at Sian. I learned from the State Department today that courier service to Tihwa has been temporarily or indefinitely suspended. Will be praying hard for Doug's safety on his flight here Sunday. I sent him a telegram today reading "Darling Returning Tihwa With Your Separation Impossible Love your Pegge." I've quite definitely made up my mind unless his visit here changes my love and my mind. I don't want to marry him FOREVER AND

A DAY—but if it can be done, civil ceremony, and say we have 3 to 4 years—that will be enough. If it were not for the dread secret of his past, I would feel differently about the lifelong alliance. But I cannot STAND this dead existence in Shanghai. When I think of Sinkiang I feel ALIVE, SET, READY—and always there is Doug. I sent a long letter off to Douglas SR. that is the strongest professional tie—Douglas Reed in London—hinting that should he want an assistant, I'll be right there. Long conference with FRED HAMPSEN of AP on my stories. He's doubtful if *NY* will be much interested in some of the stories and pix. "They were rather cool on the first batch of mailers," he declared. Then, "Would $300 for the batch of pix and stories be about right?" I was insulted. "$275 for stringer duties—$ 25 for about eight rolls of film and the shots from Peitashan!" We left it unsettled so far—I tried to feel him out on stringer support if I returned. "Well—hard to say, place so obscure, far, far away. Spot stories don't pay much." "But the situation is climactic," I faltered. "Well"—the fifth placating "Well, if something really did break we'd send our own man up to cover." BASTARD—the STRINGER MUST do the story of the stringer, and I'll bet I could make more money on it than on all my hard, blood-wrung news dispatches.

As I was tearing myself out of the office with leaden heart, the blonde Russian girl who "helps out" in the office handed me a clipping. "One of your stories with a byline," she said. It was from a godforsaken sheet called the *Schenectady Gazette*. And the story, as rewritten by AP, was dull, wooden going. I was ill, embittered, LOST after reading it. The only stray virtue the story had was accuracy. DULL, UNREADER-HOLDING-FACTS. Damn them. Bring on the fiction. I'm lunching with BOB SHERROD of *TIME* tomorrow and will try him for support of my intended move to Tihwa.

SEPTEMBER 17, 1947—LETTER FROM SHANGHAI

Darling Mother Duck—

By this time you are gasping with your tongue out! You must have my cable, if you're still in Florida. Your letter of stern disapproval was in the back of my mind when Doug and I decided NOTHING ON EARTH was as important as being married AT HOME, the right way, with our families, and in the Catholic Church. I have been to see the Jesuit here, as I believe I wrote you, and Doug will have to become a full-fledged Catholic for our marriage in the church. He is, of course, perfectly willing to go through that, and would rather do it in America at a little church near his home in Boston than in China among strangers.

Next reason for our coming home: Washington D.C. is the place for Doug to present himself for a transfer to Switzerland or Europe where we both want to live, rather than back in China. These string-pullings are most effective in person. So—after we are wed, down to Washington we go to continue with the State Department and execute passports, etc., for leaving the country again as soon as possible.

I've written so many letters and have been in such a hysterical rush I've forgotten who's heard what. And I HAVE HAD NO MAIL FROM ANYONE BUT MY BANK IN NEW YORK IN WEEKS. Anyway: we had a frantic time trying to get on a ship. Naturally, we are avoiding overseas planes like the plague! (I hated to have Doug leave this a.m. on the plane for Nanking, but he went with the air attaché at the American Consulate and that arch air-expert only flies when the eagles do, so I guess he's safe.

In our ramblings around for a ship, I recalled at luncheon once Mrs. Robert Sherrod said she knew the President of the American President Lines very well. In fact, she entertained him and his wife (now Ambassador to India) when they came through this summer. Ahhh, so down I rushed to the Sherrods. As the fates would have it, the whole Sherrod family had reservations for the *Pres. Polk,* but THAT VERY DAY were going to cancel as they had decided not to go. Sherrod very nicely took over the personal wangling so that his reservation could be split into two singles. Some conniving indeed. The *Polk* is the lines' round-the-world glamour ship and the only thing going out of Shanghai, next to sampans and tugs we could PRAY our way aboard. Such ins-and-outs. But finally the top man got us aboard. Unheard of, about two weeks before sailing! But we are on. We are set for Marseilles. But yesterday the office called and said that space was taken, so Doug and I would have to disembark in Italy—Genoa—which suited us even better as land travel through Europe would give us a chance to see more, and save us a few pennies. We are all set now with the *Polk*. I have cabled my bank to send on the fare to Genoa.

We went to the Cook's Travel office (which everyone out here swears by... they really know their stuff and LOOK AFTER their clients). Anyway, we're booking through from Genoa to Switzerald (Geneva and Lausanne) to Paris (by train). We will be in Paris from Nov. 22nd to Nov. 26th when we leave for London. We will be in jolly England, where Doug knows the Embassy staff and I know Douglas Reed, until we can get the first and fastest boat to New York. The agency is cabling for reservations on the *Queen Mary*, leaving London Dec. 4th. (We will come Second Class, probably, just making it on the finances.) The crossing will be quick, and we should be in New York by Dec. 9-10 at the very latest.

Now, the complications. Where can you and I "put up" in New York? Of course you will meet our ship. If you are in Florida I will die—you MUST MUST be in New York on the great, great homecoming day. I will send you the money or you can check with Lois. I sent her $150 in money orders to buy clothes. I cabled her yesterday, too, so she'd know not to send them to China. If she hasn't spent the money, you take it and use it for your travels to New York, for a hotel room, or a new hat or whatever. But I want you to have that money cozily in hand. Don't give me REASONS and "WHY, I WOULDN'T THINK OF THIS OR THAT." Doug and I aren't rolling in wealth, but he will carry the financial burden. So, Mother, I want you to take that money and SPEND IT.

We will cable from London of course and send letters en route. Damn, I wish you had an address where I could feel secure in reaching you. This business of Lois Fegan, *Harrisburg Telegraph,* and now where to go when I come in FROM AROUND THE WORLD. Oh well, we'll be home for Christmas and together somehow I hope. We can stay in New York or go up to Boston on the train and meet Doug and his family there (and D.A. and her husband), or whatever.

Naturally Doug and I want to get this wedding arranged as soon as possible. Once he gets his Catholic instruction we can make arrangements immediately. The smallest and fuss-less-est wedding possible. Just his family, you and Daddy, D.A., her husband and Lois (Fegan). Doug says there's a cozy and very attractive little Catholic church in Stoughton not far from his home. Perhaps that would be the place for the ceremony. Or a church in Boston. Not too awesome. I will wear just a suit or soft, simple dress, street length, and that will be that.

I can imagine YOU when you read all this. But remember... you can still have firm words to say when we get into New York. Meeting him will explain a lot. Seeing us together will give you the PERFECT-COMPATIBLE-MUTUAL-MATCH picture a thousand letters never could. Which won't change the "divorce," naturally. His conversion and becoming a Catholic will satisfy the church. Perhaps you, too. And you'll be right on the scene to watch and know and have anything to say you want.

Naturally, I am positive he is the "ONE." But the instinctive dread of "matrimony" lingers away in the back of my mind. So your last words will not be as to a stone wall, or be resented or argued over or anything. I especially want YOU TO BE HAPPY WITH ME when I take the fatal plunge. And I want Ahmee to meet him... for all these reasons I was determined to COME HOME TO BE MARRIED. And Doug only too willing, too.

The trip to Europe, the pix taken, etc., will pay off. I will naturally be working, possibly even "stringer-ing" for AP as I go along. Not a minute will be idle sightseeing, except at night along the railing as we swish thru the Mediterranean. Ah then, with my sweet darling—he is, Mother, he is—and oh how happy he has made me! I have never, never been in love before. I know that at long last, NOW.

I told you, I believe, about the *Collier's* assignment on Sinkiang. That must be written on the ship with Doug to help me. And seeing Douglas Reed in London, THAT is utterly vital. So I'm not off in romantic clouds. Nor was I just willy-nilly in urging this trip.

Enclosed is a schedule of our stops and mail addresses. We don't know what our hotel stops will be yet. Cook's will provide. I hope we make the *Queen Mary* out of London and get home EARLY, quick, quick. (Just simply beside myself to see YOU. Oooh, darling Mother. After all of China. To be snuggled up home with my Mommy duck. Get us a nice, nice room in New York for the first few days anyway. Like Seattle. NOT the Webster. We'll manage! Save your energy on writing what the prices are, etc. I DO know. I DO... DO... DO KNOW, but I have a different gauge on things now, at this point in my momentous fate, and I will scurry for pennies later. I'm going to have THIS and have it RIGHT if it takes every cent. It will be worth it.

From the Nanking Embassy's post office Doug is sending home the furs presented to me in Sinkiang by the Chinese general. They are astrakhans and perfectly exquisite, silken soft, jet black. I will need a fur coat made up at once, and am enclosing a picture of the cut and style I want. Please, darling, have it made up and ready to wear when I get home. December is rather chilly, as I recall, and I will be coming home with only that Magnin coat. It is a "winter" coat in name only, and I have just turned it over to a tailor to have it lined with baby lamb's fur (a light, white fur). But I will need that astrakhan immediately. All measurements and details are attached to the picture.

The way Doug will mail the furs, there should positively be no duty. He will send them to Lois. I hope, again, there will be no difficulty in getting the stuff in.

Gad, what a crucial time for the airmails to go flooey. The typhoons are keeping all planes ground bound, I guess. But time is running out on when I will be able to receive any mail. I will have all APO mail returned to Lois. I hope she doesn't mind being my mail-information depot. I'll try to send her a little gift or something before I leave.

Doug has had not a line from his family, either. Just cables. His father tried to telephone Doug Monday but the lines were out and we had to cancel the call as Doug was leaving for Nanking for 4 to 5 days. He has been absolutely wonderful to work out plans, ways, and means with. He's got a good solid head on his shoulders. Knows money exchanges, how to do things railway express, etc., all of which leaves me in a muddle. I'm having my Alaskan household effects shipped from Fairbanks to his family in Stoughton. Fortunately they have a spacious place for storing things indefinitely. I cabled Art Bremer, too, but did not mention the reason for coming home or anything about Doug, of course. No one in China except the Sherrods (who had to understand our desperate plight to go to so much trouble for us) know and they have been sworn to secrecy. I'm not even telling Fern. After we're married we'll get out some announcement cards.

Well, that's all I can think of now. Hope you got the big envelope with my front-page pictures of Sinkiang. And how I'd love to know what AP did with my stories in the States. This complete "blank" on the mail is awful. Give my love to the Bostdorfs. Hope they don't think I've COMPLETELY lost my mind. Oh, darling Mother, see you in a few months—imagine! Will keep cabling Lois so you get the news from her of which ship, etc. Write to us en route. Be terribly thrilled to pick up a letter from you in Genoa.

Love, Love, Love, Baby

SEPTEMBER 24, 1947—So much has happened since I wrote last, some of it happy, some of it, like tonight, a bewildering dread—and of course I mean Doug. He arrived the following Sunday after my departure, getting into Lungma Airport ahead of my arrival to meet him. He telephoned at once, his voice trembling with anxiety over my absence. I rushed right out to get him in an Army jeep. He looked forlornly alone, mussed, wrinkled and nondescript with insignificant luggage and a raincoat over his arm. But it was Doug—as soon as he checked into the hotel we found shaky-kneed means of telling each other we'd never be separated again, come what may. In the days that followed he was ardently mine—with me every second: for breakfast, lunch, and dinner, of course. I had the wonderful feeling that I would never be alone again—that here was Doug to shield, protect, and love me forever and aye. To my reassured delight he fit into the Shanghai scene with ease, in a quiet ex-army brusque way. It was fun looking glamorous for him—wearing high heels, hats, sniff-swooning perfumes, etc. We were terribly close and terribly happy just knowing we were in the same city together. For the first time in my life I experienced the one-ness of being "together" heart, soul, and mind with another person who was somehow part of oneself.

I got—through some wrangling with Jack Beldon (author of *Retreat with Stilwell)* an assignment from *Collier's* magazine to do a story with pix on Sinkiang. That elated us. We tried to settle our wedding plans after much discussion. His family is either very desultory about DOING things or I'm only overly impatient or something. Anyway, these awful doubts and the most insidious of all—DISTRUST— DISBELIEF, that second fiendish self that is always on the alert to imagine something fraudulent or false in something or anything Doug said. "Of course if you just say the word, honeybunch, we'll go home—get everything straightened out and be married right." That was enough: GOING HOME—dear God.

I went meanwhile to see a Jesuit Priest about Doug—divorce and "past" all explained. The Priest took it all with routine concern.

Shrugged at Doug's past in China. The divorce and its grounds would have to be investigated, and if all was OK, Doug could take instruction to become a Catholic. I put this up to him. Yes, he would go through with everything. Meanwhile a furious RUSH and operations PRONTO get underway.

And then Doug went to Nanking for a few days. Being alone again did something odd to me. I felt, no matter what happens to Doug, I'm going on that ship—the RETURN TO SOLO OPERATIONS PARKER got hold of me. Doug telephoned me every night but the last evening, and I wondered where he was—DISBELIEF and this dread but very genuine DISTRUST were at once raised in my mind, shutting out the "belonging—one-ness" we had before. I got letters back from Mother—horrified at Doug's divorce. If she really KNEW the intention to marry him with a civil ceremony, more HORROR: "Why, you wouldn't be married at all in the eyes of the church." She's now in Florida with my sister and the first grandchild.

In the push of having to get ready to go home I had to discontinue my Russian lessons. When my teacher and I were having our last session she got off onto the wrongs (very true, too) Americans have done to Russians here in China. As she went on talking she mentioned all the promises of marriage and "even untrue marriages." I was panic stricken—I was in frightful dread and disgrace for Doug. I walked home afterward in the throes of despair. Stopped in the Jesuit church: "Our Father," yes and one part: "Forgive us our trespasses as we forgive those, etc." Yes. Forgiveness. Doug offended God, himself, and an innocent Russian girl—not me. Forgiveness and forgetfulness are hard. I was so late getting home after the dread session that Doug met me at the Race Course gate FRANTIC with worry. Had a rickshaw run over me? What could have happened? I laughed and reassured him. But patting his arm and being very blithe, I pitied him with unutterable sorrow that I will never, never be able to love him freely and with FAITH.

His return from Nanking was interesting. He had all sorts of news to intrigue me as a news observer. But later when he held me, the feeling of one-togetherness was gone. He knew it. "We're not as close as we were before I went away," he puzzled out, waiting for me to reassure him—women's greatest wile. I kissed him and smiled but did not answer. We are still full of plans for the trip home, but again tonight I had a reminder of the perfidy of the MALE SPECIES. The little Russian girl who does my hair (at Madame Chiang's) told me how desperately she is trying to get to America. The Army Captain she had been living with and really loved has of course tried to outsmart her—lying about being married and the usual story. I was deeply hurt all over again—inside—the disgrace of Doug. I gave Luba all the womanly advice I could think of, but after she left, I took you out, diary of my thoughts, and instead of telephoning Doug as per schedule, I had to release this DREAD feeling. I am FAR— FAR—from the happy girl in love and have been only in snatches and moments with Doug—and naturally wonder if our whole future will be like this. Something always to remind me—if not Doug—of the SECRET of Tihwa. On top of everything else I may have some trouble getting myself cleared out of the army confines. Colonel Kearny said I possess certain secret information and until the ban on that is lifted I must be retained (the only reason I wasn't fired on the spot when I got back from Sinkiang). Fern Cavender is right at my side on all this, though, and I'm sure she will get me cleared. She assures me I cannot possibly be "held" here no matter what.

I had a long letter from LOIS FEGAN today explaining her version of marriage. When I read it this morning I felt terribly happy, close to my best friend and Doug. Now I regard her sentiments with a lonely feeling—with accusation and with sad anger that Doug should have denied me the simple human bondage of FAITH and TRUST. Such basic, root-earthy holds on love. "Pegge," Lois writes, "the relationship between a man and a woman is the most important thing in the world. Don't let the fact of a divorce keep you from taking your happiness, and once you've made up your mind don't look back and think what might have been. That's fatal." (Oh, Lois, if you only knew the real story.) "All I can say is just be sure it's what you want." I'm not, I'm not. Oh, dear God, how can I ever be? What can change this feeling? I deliberately blocked seeing him tonight. Pretext: Luba was still doing my hair. His disappointment only steeled me against him. He's going to Nanking tomorrow, to be gone two or three days, and I know he was expecting to hold me very close tonight. I never wanted him less, nor despised the race of men more. Am I emotionally unbalanced or making a horrible mistake? I will be glad with all my SOUL with all my being to get out of China.

OCTOBER 3, 1947—Gliding down the China Coast. Notes from a green-striped cushioned steamer chair beside Doug, aboard the *President Polk*. Here we are—lovers of Sinkiang—the wild and the rugged—the mountains—our jeep—our horses. AND THIS: a FLOATING WALDORF—buff and chrome—recorded music— unctuous stewards, push button when we want service—swimming pool. Dear God, half the deck is enclosed in glass lest a nervy spray or whipping breeze filter through, like an ardent adolescent into a girls' dorm. I'm sure if it were possible even the heave and roll of the ship would be evened lest it annoy the cultured stomachs and quivery livers of the pedigreed voyagers. Doug and I go around smirking—laughing with disgust at U.S.—so miscast in this watery ermine cage.

The leave taking was dire and drastic, but I see I haven't typed this to date. The ship was to sail October 3 from Shanghai. We had to expedite other gaps in our chartered way through COOK'S TRAVEL AGENCY. Fortunately we got reservations on the *Queen Mary*, which means the last lap of the fateful journey will be repulsively luxurious but QUICK—HOME. We'll be in New York December 8, and meanwhile we will take the European and near Eastern world in stride.

We have isolated ourselves as much as possible from the lolling fellow passengers, and that has led to the natural assumption that we are married. Since I am traveling under two names anyway, it is equally bewildering to be taken for Doug's wife. I keep thinking of George Wallace and his warnings of the sheep-minds of my state-side fellow Americans. At the dinner table last night I asked a solid-citizen-type businessman and his bosomy, chicly clad wife if a ship's newspaper were published. "Yeah," our solid citizen buttered a roll as though spreading cheese on a cracker—"yeah, but nothing interesting. Politics and that stuff—few baseball scores." My mental toes turned under—Doug sent me a communal glance.

Pegge's photo of Doug Mackiernan

Leaving China was a calm retrospective experience. With my arm linked through Doug's and our shoulders close, on a top nook of the deck—one year—1946-47—slid by in my mind. I never expected it to be in ANY—ANY RESPECT the year it was. But the months were well accounted for. Doug beside me—with me—our coming union—this made the difference. I looked back on China—for the experience, the political sophistication, the human initiation it was—as though looking back on another existence. Loving Doug—despite the times of anguish and remorse—makes me another person—part of him. (He is plunked here lazily intent on a Tibetan grammar someone gave him in Shanghai.)

OCTOBER 6, 1947—HONG KONG—Our ship lies off the twinkling gold-lit harbor of this intriguing spot. The approach to the harbor—a blue-green waterway spread between green hills—reminded me vaguely of the Aleutians, except that the air of habitation and civilization was prevalent. Then we came closer to the structure and water populace of a harbor: ships, skiffs, motor launches, docks, wharfs, and on the hills as night fell, houses of habitation agleam through the torrent of rain which suddenly burst from the heavens. I was standing wide-eyed on the top deck, or under the semi-shelter of the promenade deck near the plush green and pink leather cubicle bar. The rain roughed the surface of the water. All about passengers scurried. Three little Chinese children clucked excitedly about seeing Daddy soon. And then a blonde woman of the indefinable age caught my eye. She was staring out at the hills with the dull gleaming lights. In her hand was a martini. Suddenly she gulped the entire drink and hurled the glass into the water. I turned quickly to observe her more closely but she turned her back—an impersonal black dinner dress back—and was lost in the mingling crowd. It has stopped raining now, and the land lights of the foothills and those glistening from unfathomed darkness are a composition of loveliness and imagination. The habitation on the sides of the hills.

Doug and I went ashore on the ferry, walking a while along the government building'ed avenue that curved around the harbor. Flash impression: Hurray for the British and the orderly, smartly well-organized air of the "colony." And a tribute to the Chinese—I noticed the difference in them at once—Anglicized, even to their clipped

British accent. They seemed to be individuals, sure of themselves and aware of their part in an orderly modern society.

OCTOBER 7, 1947—Off the green-gray harbor of Hong Kong waiting for a typhoon. There must have been some hitch in the ship's command, for last night in the middle of unloading we suddenly pulled out into the harbor leaving half the crew and passengers ashore. One word did it: TYPHOON. This morning Doug and I watched as other freighters around us lashed down booms, deck obstructions, etc., in preparation. We ran out on extra anchors but our booms are still up like soda straws. "Not enough crewmen aboard to lower them" was one explanation. All the junks and busy cutters and chuggers and other oddment seacraft flung out all over the harbor yesterday are gone. A warning and air of watchful waiting has cleared the waters of all but sturdy freighters (how longingly Doug and I gaze at their rusting, slow-riding hulks and wish we were aboard them), all of whom are stripped down, booms lowered, riding the lulled heave of the harbor waters—waiting.

To further record our day in Hong Kong, October 6, 1947: The weather was clammy, sultry, but the sky was brilliant blue with fluffy white clouds. We took the ferry and chugged across to the city. I noticed many Chinese girls leaning against the rail, clad in simple Chinese-cut cotton dresses and flat-heeled shoes, smoking cigarettes with the purposeful air of American lady executives. Once ashore we strolled the main thoroughfares—wide streets—massive gray-stoned, weathered government buildings—shiny green, double-decker electric trams glided by, fast-moving and intent about their business. Chinese motormen conducted the 1st, 2nd, 3rd class passengers very well. (Note: sitting top side in the first class section, I was amused at the signs all around: "In case of typhoon passengers will cooperate by lowering windows immediately, keeping their seats," etc.)

At each street intersection I loved looking down the cement corridors of babble, commotion and Chinese to the rising green hills. Riven into the sides were apartment houses and imposing dwellings done in the manner of opera houses of Olde England master homes. We went to the Windsor House (or Hotel) Provisions store to send DOUGLAS REED a box of food. We stopped briefly in Whiteaway and LAIDLAW'S, the British Lord and Taylor's which had more haberdashery than women's clothing. We found all the famous bargains in English wool cloth very elusive.

At noon, casually stopping in a coffee shop, we were embarrassedly recognized and greeted by FRED HAMPSON, dear old bureau chief for AP in Shanghai, doing a lend-lease stretch for some vacationing scribe. Seeing Doug in close attendance, I'm sure he was CURIOUS. The situation of our being together has incidentally caused considerable situations (on the ship everyone assumes we are Mr. and Mrs. Mackiernan—somehow we got immersed in the assumption before we could explain). Removed from the coffee shop, we moved on to "The Grips" in the Hong Kong Hotel where a Chinese pianist masterfully rendered Gershwin, Chopin, and Irving Berlin from a crème-colored baby grand as diners lolled in the pastel luxury of one of the loveliest dining rooms in the Orient. Ah, what Hong Kong must have been in the old days. Mirrored walls, a mobile chef's table, scarlet gladiolas, gleaming silver, and a graceful terrace effect wherein diners could with a gossipy eye observe everyone coming and going. Many Chinese sat around looking very white linened, sophisticated and secure.

We had a four-course luncheon, served with flourish, for about $1.25 each. After this we wandered down to the Peak Tram, an ultra-modern, efficient and quite immaculate cable car which hoists one about 1200 feet above sea level and presents a VIEW to behold. The city, the harbor, the cliff's edge, sheer drop-down perspective on British capital in lump building form. We got off our little car (takes about ten minutes to ascend as the car goes up very slowly in certain places) and walked around the cliff. A sidewalk-wide promenade curved around the mountain amid green shrubs and late fall flowers. For us—two in love—it was a dreamy delight. We returned about 5 o'clock, had cocktails at the Gloucester Hotel (old fashioneds, very strongly stocked), and I went calling on a girl correspondent I'd met in Shanghai. Caroline is now married to a merry-eyed elder sea captain named PALMER. We talked about Barbara Stephens, and I gleaned the further insight into my unknown's past that she'd "only loved one man and he was married, so that's that." (Someday I MUST do a story on her—the wreckage of her ill-fated plane was reported found by the Chinese Air Force, Hampson told us.)

I rejoined Doug, and we proceeded to hunt down a good Chinese restaurant for one last Chinese chow blast before leaving China proper. Caroline had recommended someplace called TAI TUNG (let us remember the name WELL that none, nay, not even deadliest enemies, chase up and down Queens Road, the main street where Caroline had directed me). We stopped cops to ask for directions, and I finally went into a drugstore (called dispensary) for further directions, complete with written directions in Chinese. When we got to it—a five-story department-store-looking place—Doug saw the Chinese waiter write $10 on his tablet after my first mention of one dish—chicken and walnut. We had a quick argument in Russian, ordered rice, ate it furiously, paid and stomped out in a huff. Ended up using our last remaining Hong Kong dollars in the original Windsor House coffee shop having a chocolate soda (Doug a waffle cone), then back to the ship.

SUNDAY, OCTOBER 12, 1947—Just past Corregidor Island, heading SW to Singapore. Behind the blue-creped ruff of water: the PHILIPPINES and MANILA. We were there two days, and all the remarks to be listed here are rudimentary FLASHES—IMPRESSIONS. Damage to public monumental buildings was extreme, and misshapen manglings stand out harshly against languid vivid skies. The downtown sectors are more provincial than I expected. Streets are narrow lanes with attractive shops and stores. Conspicuous are the number of cable offices. (Every wireless firm in the world is bannered in headline signs on all sides.) Also glance-conspicuous are the number of American branch offices for every electrical device gadget—machinery and heavy equipment. A glance down over two streets marked with U.S. trade products is reminiscent of an industrial "fair." Contrary to widespread notions that the Philippines are dawdling in repairing the war damage to their capital, I found shovels and putty knives piled everywhere with intent and purpose. Pock-marked buildings were having shell holes puttied up. Wood super-structure supported trembling buildings, and little brown men in flimsy dungarees crawled along the structures, WORKING. Bailey bridges (makeshift wartime spans) arched over the rivers. Public vehicles for transportation were like beetles at a circus, streaming down the narrow thoroughfares. Jeeps, converted into small "buses" or private conveyances, were the most predominant type of vehicle. Horse carts, picturesque but out of place somehow with their exaggerated high wooden wheels—gaudy carriage for two—and a tiny pony sweating under a metal rail (can't think of the term I want) adorned harness trimmed with a little brass arch from which hung small medallions. Also picturesque were the slim, brown grand dames who wore old-fashioned Philippine gowns of organdy—long-skirted—off-the-shoulder puffed sleeves and a kerchief shawl or scarf of matching material.

After cursory looking around with Doug, I called my old UP friend, MADDOX (TED) BROWN, a gawking, horn-spectacled young Englishman with a glowing personality and wonderful sense of humor. Ted resigned from penurious servitude to UP and took on a lucrative and interesting job with an American concern out to rehabilitate industrially the shambles of the Philippines. This organization is the BEYSTER CORP., and Ted is PRO (public relations officer), writing a report of their previous programs. He told me about their plan for mining and setting up various types of manufacturing plants. Then he said in trailing-off irony, "I'm getting so I almost believe this stuff myself. On paper it sounds impressive, but the Filipinos just aren't industrialists. They just don't function as American industrial planners decide they should. Same way as China. The educated learn HOW to be engineers. Then all they want to do is save face, sit back in a big office, look important, and do nothing. The poor devils who must do the work haven't the technical training or education to go ahead with the job."

But meanwhile, as PRO, Ted has an almost unlimited expense account and can wine and dine the press unendingly. I looked at him and wondered how it was all working out for him. He mentioned, after three old-fashioneds, my one-time timid Romeo, Lt. Pete Peterson. "He was very much in love with you," Ted decided, "and wanted to marry you—really." Doug, sitting right at my elbow, took passive interest.

The next day Ted invited me to lunch at a brand-new restaurant on ESCOLTA ST. (main thoroughfare). In the party was a sometime newsman turned radio man, PAUL RAPPAPORT, who carted me off to the Manila Press Club where I met some Philippine newsmen and listened to some interesting views. In snatches, the lingo ran: The Filipinos don't resent or dislike the Americans. The visa difficulties are mutual. It is as hard for Filipinos to go to the States as vice versa. Seems a society matron applied for a temporary visa to go to Reno. When asked the purpose of her trip, she said she wanted to get a divorce. "Immoral reason" was the judgment of the Embassy, and she was refused a visa. (No divorces can be granted in the Philippines, I was told, but somehow doubt it.) American commercial ties with the Philippines are just as strong and indispensable as ever. If the Filipinos feel no particular gratitude for what American development and capitalism has done for their country, at least they admit the aggression was benevolent. Even the poorest native in the outreaches of the land speaks English, and most can read and write their own language (which incidentally is the tongue heard by passersby on the streets, not English). The president, ROXAS, in the opinion of the newsmen was put into office because MacArthur and McNutt were behind him. He is at least "trying" to do something for his country—for one thing, buying land and reselling it at moderate cost to poor farmers. In the hills, however, is a people's hero—TARUC—a leader of guerilla bands during the war and an insurgent people's reform party known as the HUCKS now. It was felt TARUC would never come into prominence because he is being sold out from among his own followers.

The American Chamber of Commerce in Manila has dictatorial power over the press—no strongly worded political commentaries, columns, etc., could be written for fear of ads being "pulled." Chinese infiltration in trade is on the alarming increase and governmental steps are being attempted to oust Chinese traders. Incidentally, American currency is useable in Manila shops but a slight deduction is made in the exchange value. After leaving the Press Club, Rappaport took me to the AP office where one SPENCER DAVIS told me one of my Kuldja stories came through—with a byline and a little explanatory note saying I was a "stringer." I was somewhat gratified that my precious stories were even used. Ted has steamed me up to cashing in on the Collier's article, but somehow I never seem to get started on it. Trivia seems to interrupt on all sides. The first day I saw Ted, he took Doug and me to the Manila Hotel for cocktails. Doug was amused at the sign in the lobby: "Guests will check their guns or firearms at the desk." He also noted many rifles, revolvers and such in stores and on American and Filipino soldiers and private citizens.

OCTOBER 19, 1947—EN ROUTE TO PENANG—The horizon over the tops of my tattered Chinese slippers looks like this (drawing of mountain over the sea) and all variance of blue-sky-sea-mountains—even the clouds are blue-sheened billows.

A sketch from Pegge's diary of the horizon as recorded below.

SINGAPORE was a surprise. All the lurid, shadowed, low-note suggestion of the name was lost in actuality. British prominence in building, parkways, cleanliness, trams, efficiency, "order" are staunchly vested in this lush, sweltering, vivid Malay city. Flash impression: police in khaki shorts and berets adorned with crimson crest silver pins and native order-keepers look snappy, decently provided for. Unlike China, this colony seems to have instilled a sense of "belonging" to the country. Whatever colonization has fostered on its subjects, contingent rule has been a godsend for the people. The natives have adopted their masters' sense of well-being—order and blessed cleanliness. I had dinner with the AP chief and his wife, Mr. and Mrs. Leif Erickson, and enjoyed hearing them discuss Singapore and the situation here in general. Sum gist: the Chinese infiltration, economy and biological majority is the most serious threat to the Malay Peninsula. This is not communistic but a belated filial tie with the Mother Country. The Malays are easy-living indolents. The Chinese, since the year one, have been voracious "industrialists"

---

from street chow-chow hawkers on up. As in Siam they have finally gained economic control of the country (excluding the British rubber interests). Now while perhaps little love or blind dependence on Chiang Kai-shek is felt among Malay Chinese capitalists, the feeling seems widespread that the day of China's dominance of all of Asia is not for away. Far-sighted, these money lords wish to have their claim in future rule. Their political thinking—and remember, they represent the majority of the population and greatest store of capital (compared with British interests—don't know)—is along the line of patience for the present queasy status of the Kuomintang. Tomorrow will bring another stronger government, "their" government. This interest and participation in Malayan government affairs is transitory and mundane. Communist endeavor was mitigated by Erickson to a *Straits Times* man also at the dinner. Prices were exorbitant, and the women present talked endlessly of bills and extravagance.

We had four days in Singapore. Doug and I took a bus (Chinese enterprise) to an historic, ancient port town about 150 miles NW of Singapore: MALACCA. I LOVED it and was very happy there, partly because I had Doug close to me. We were truants from the ship and its chilling confines and we were seeing the people's part of the country. It was wonderful—the palm and coconut trees I had never seen before—great, slender edifices with sloped trunks as though bent by the wind, and a fountain of branches hung with glistening, shiny leaves. Really, a tropical patch of palm trees is lush intrigue for the eye. Rubber trees are also slim-trunked upstarts— mild and domestic-looking, they might be garden-variety "shade" props around the old homestead in Ohio but for the bias cut slash on the trunk and little affixed cup catching the world's precious utility: RUBBER. Amid these trees were houses.

This is a vague, atmospheric vision, but the houses have dead-gray working grass roofs—are built on stilts and some have porch panels of carved wood—ooze and mud and a pond of water lie under most houses, and sometimes the family offspring swim around their front porch. The people, non-Chinese, did not exist on a degenerate, oppressed level. Their homes may have been shacks, but their visual upkeep was fairly tidy and comfortable.

A drawing of a Malaccan hut from Pegge's diary.

The people looked busy and intent on doing things. Women were shopping in the markets. We passed several open-air schools (wooden structures like picnic pavilions on stilts) and we passed modern buildings. All villages had paved streets and regulated maintenance: city buses, telephones, beauty parlors, shops without doors or windows.

Malacca is a story in itself. Forgive me for adding tourist notes, but the town is as clean as though scrubbed by Dutch housewives. In the old days, no doubt, Dutch wives of early colonists did slosh the scrub buckets around. But there, facing the blue ruffled watery plateau of the STRAITS OF MALACCA, lies this prim, white plaster-walled city. Under its British orderliness, its wide streets, scenic trees, and slow-moving daily routine, lies a lush, bloodthirsty past—like a torrid history in a family closet, or glamorous lustiness embodied in a pirate's chest or attic trunk. An Indian correspondent to the *Straits Times* was our guide. He pointed out the government administration

building known as the STADTHUYS, believed the oldest Dutch
building in the East, circa 1641 or 1660. The walls are a clay red rust
color piped in black. Inside, the corridors are agedly crème colored.
The floors dip, the stairs are uneven, but atmosphere is prime. The
library upstairs, a musky room housing ravished books, posts a
sign: 1st and 2nd class members and rules. As my escort was on the
opposite side of the color line, I didn't ask too many questions about
the qualifications for membership.

Malacca Rest House—to add another tourist note—is a dream
place and will always be dear in my personal memoir. From the Malay
boys who glided in with tea and bananas to the private verandah we
had overlooking the blue straits of Malacca.

From its antiquity in the realm of historic European buccaneering
(Portuguese), Malacca is a literal treasure chest for a historic chronicle
and fiction piece. One could live on very little while doing the actual
research and writing. Authenticity would be garnered from many
sources which remain intact, especially tombstones nearly six feet
high, in the Dutch language.

Doug and I drove down to the shoreline on the edge of town and
a small native kid shimmied up a tower of stubby trunk to knock
down a green coconut for me. My first—surprisingly, they are like
green melons. A Malay woman slashed the top with a knife and I dug
in, cupping it up in one big "slurp," as Doug put it. It was a watery
substance, non-sweet, faintly fragrant, and the fresh fruit was moist
and at first taste flavorless. You had to chew on it a while to get the
coconut flavor.

A curious, timid group of Malay children gathered shyly around,
and I have never felt my heart go out to wee strange folk so endearingly
as to them. One little fellow proudly began to count for me in English:
"one, two, one, five, one, one, one" one was obviously his best bet. A
lovely girl of about five struck my eye and must go down in my story
somewhere. She was slim and brown and her eyes were soft as fawn's.
She wore a faded sarong rolled about her flat abdomen. Her hair was

already done in an unruly chignon from which black wisps curled and blew about her delicate face. A group of mature women came down to gaze on the whites. Our guide said we had come from far away. Were we Dutch, they wanted to know. "No, Americans," the man exclaimed in Malay. "Am-errikan" rang all around the smiling curious women and children. Families of fishermen long gone out in their boats by that time of day. One woman who had stood staring at me closely, arms across her bosom, one hand and forefinger framing her broad homely face, suddenly pointed to an infant and enquired how many babies "mem" had. I had to turn to Doug for an answer, also in pantomime and giggles, to that! All the women howled, as did the Mackiernans.

Some impressions on leaving Singapore: Damn less the British colonial rule after being under its working influence and comparing it with China, ruled by the Chinese, and Manila, under the Filipinos.

OCTOBER 21, 1947—PENANG (sometimes Georgetown on certain maps of Malaya). The waterfront gutturals of Malay-Indian from the sarong'd stevedores lends a tang to the blue-hilled, gray-green harbor of Penang. Its source of wealth, RUBBER, is a strong sweet odor below on the quarter decks where the brown men in turbans and skirts are loading the crude produce of modern industry into our hatch pit.

If I raved about Malacca as a dream spot for romantics—here I go, only more so, on Penang, or rather a resort in its tropical mountains. Quite by accident Doug heard about a small place over 2000 feet above sea level where from primly immaculate cottages one views the harbor and sleeps at night under blankets. From the suffocating heat of the city and ship, Doug and I got us hence. The town seemed predominantly Indian and was decked with shops—signs all in English and Malayan (we presume). We rode past large, old-style British homes—some on stilts—painted beige, bordered in black and red burgundy. These stiff and complicated-looking edifices sat back in green harbors of trees (coconut), flowering shrubs. We passed a Chinese convent with wide-open classrooms.

The cable car was similar to Hong Kong's but goes twice as high (one-way fare about 40 cents U.S.). Riding slowly up a tropical mountain was an experience, yielding a view usually obtained from horseback in wild places. I saw tropic plants, ferned trees with great spreading leaves like a fringed canopy, lush orange (burning on fire orange, that is) flowers—red ones redder than flame (hibiscus)—at the top cool, crystal-balmed air—languid but cool—blew through the lush greens and over the Mackiernans riding down a curved paved roadway leading from the cable car to the hotel.

Malayan boys in tropical hats and khaki shorts drove small pedicabs to the hotel. There was the hallowed spot for us. Mark ye well the name that we may someday return. For we were in love—young and happy here—at the CRAG Cottage (CRAG HOTEL) establishment. For less than $15 U.S. (about $11) we had heaven with each other, and all that a poet could ask for, surrounded by ferns-flowers-trees and at night the sparkling, twinkling lights of Penang. The cottage (No. 8, remember it well) was a "house" really, having its little verandah where on a rattan table and lounge chairs we were served tea (a scarlet melon, marmalade squares, tea with all the trimmings), two spacious bedrooms with sheets as white as tablecloths and white English blankets at the foot. A sitting room and TWO private baths completed the suite. Outside we had our own private garden and the boy thoughtfully placed our chairs there, facing the harbor.

After our tea we eased into the chairs and Doug read Kipling to me until dark. My heart stood tall and wide-eyed inside—aware of the moment and not wanting to miss a bit, or let it slip away. "I've taken my fun where I've found it," read my love. The sky was 4 o'clock blue and the breezes fluttered the pages of his book. "I've rogued and I've ranged in my time. I've 'ad my pickin' o' sweethearts." He read other passages—lyric, sardonic, laugh-lined. Then Doug closed the book, rose, stretched, and held out his arms: "Come on, honeybunch, we'd better go for chow."

The cottage was special for us, and we shall never forget it.

As for the political observations of Penang, all I know is what I gleaned from the paper brought in with the tea this morning, the *STRAITS ECHO*—Chinese infiltration and grasp on the money bags—granted the Malays are indolent and like to live without making more effort than absolutely necessary to support themselves and family, and the Chinese have worked through the heat like galley slaves to amass their capital—still, as Doug says, they are doing in Malaya what foreigners did in China, carving fortunes and never putting back into the country what they take out in mass capital. And the wealth made in Malaya goes back to China in some form or another.

What a long, long trip this is—how the days idle by. If I could be working I wouldn't be so impatient, I guess. With three in my stateroom and one dear old lady of 70-odd who sleeps all day, I can't use my typewriter, although I see some story material here. While crossing the Indian Ocean we ran into the tail end of the monsoons, and things were really rough. Even my man Mackiernan admitted only after I had spoken up, that his hard-hide stomach was feeling "rocky." We steadied ourselves on the top deck and recalled the misleading lines of Kipling: "The Injen Ocean sits and smiles. So soft, so bright, so blooming blue. There aren't a wave for miles and miles." Ceylon tomorrow.

OCTOBER 25, 1947—COLOMBO, CEYLON—What can I say of this charming, brown people'd, lush and alluring spot? No vague notion of Ceylon prepares you for the British modernization. The British solidarity of sweeping highways, downtown banks, cement fortresses, hotels with rattan cocktail lounges in the lobby (Scotch is dispensed right smack upon entry—one can sip and stare and lolly-

way in the most strategic locale to see everything—getting clear of the immaculate dockside buildings and a huge GEM museum, shut up tight when we were there. We saw apartment buildings with rattan woven drop curtains shielding verandahs against the sun. Turning into an upgrade boulevard, we passed shops mostly laden with velvet frames for GEMS (on Sunday and Saturday afternoon all shops were closed). At the end of the street was a towering old red brick lighthouse—a historic landmark. Plastered on the side was a huge yellow placard exhorting the populace to "spend less money on yourself and more on your country." Slogans and banners in two languages—English and something else—marked the town, urging one to DIG HARDER—MORE LARDER—save money—do this, do that. I had been interviewed on the ship when we first arrived, so I went to the newspaper office. First we (Doug and I) called on earnest, articulate, politically informed though very young, slim and small FRANCIS ASHBORN of the *Times* of Ceylon, Colombo. He looked up back papers to give me an idea of the new-independence background. When we were leaving I asked where the post office was. Instead of pointing it out, he took us there—afoot in the heat. It cost about 40 cents U.S. to send two airmail letters (one to Mother and one to Art Bremer (Alaska). The post office was a fine counterpart of U.S. postals. Old, barn-ish—a flourish of yesteryear trim outside. From here to the *Times'* opposition, the *Ceylon Observer*, where S. G. Perera was ensconced in a sumptuous news office called the LAKE HOUSE (it might have been an Upper Central Park West apartment— black and white marble foyer—rose window border motif of inlaid handwork. (Will save the political notes until later.) After bidding the press adieu, we got on a streetcar and rode to the end of the line. Fabulous. First the little conductor in his khaki uniform was not only polite to his only white riders, he was courtly! The narrow house-shop-temple-bazaar-market-lined street was more like a cross-section of Little India than Ceylonese—or else the natives are Indians. Women in saris, workaday models of cotton topped with deep U necklined (front and back) blouses of white cotton—many so décolleté as to almost show the stomach! The brown race is not so unseemly as the poor class Chinese. No human filth or intimate acts on the sidewalk. Some women with bundles on their heads. Oxen carts with bushy-haired male drivers in pink check, blue, green or purple sarongs reaching to the ankles. Betel nut chewers sitting on door stoops or in the Oriental hunch (resting in a crouched position) lined the barely passable streets, their gums, tongues, and mouths a revolting raw vermillion. Sidewalks stained with splattered betel spittle. Women walked together, trailed by clusters of kids, or behind their husbands. The men were knit by fraternal custom, as in China. Caste marks were evident but not universal. Neither were turbans or Moslem hats. If what we saw was the slum areas, I must say that aside from the acute shortage of rice, the poor class here is far better off than in China. Returning to the ship from a jetty, we saw a group of cocky young French sailors, all with boxes of tea under their arms. Ashborn told us Lipton's isn't as good as it used to be. The port of Colombo, braced from the sea by a broad sea wall, was lined with ships, mostly British. More ships than we've seen congregating in any one port (weather had held up loading and unloading).

OCTOBER 28, 1947—COCHIN, INDIA—I've just come back from a junket ashore with the wife of a Swiss export agent (company name VOLKART—main product COIR—COCONUT ROPE). Name of people BUELER (not sure of spelling—no card). I had dinner at their home last night and this a.m. Mrs. B (a rebellious American colonist who "hates," "detests," and "loathes" this South Indian hinterland together with her one British kin-spirit friend. (For contrast, her friend "really" doesn't mind living here—is amused at the oddities and customs—considers herself lucky to be so well off—in fact, was quite blithe, gay and stoic.) Anyway, they took the visiting fireman to tour—we went to the Jewish synagogue, which was a marvel—a whitewashed building rather suggesting a Dutch manor house than a church. The doorway (one entered from a courtyard through an ancient door bolted like the King's treasure chamber) cut in scallops. The building itself was hospital white piped in royal blue. An old English map post leaned at an angle. Oh—gem curio, a Canton-tile floor of white and blue squares.

A diagram of a synagogue from Pegge's diary.

Overhead hung marvelous crystal chandeliers, somewhat chipped and unwashed, but exquisitely formed. In the center of the comparatively low ceilinged chamber was a chandelier of princely elegance. The globes cupping the tapers were embroidered in gilt flowers. The origin of the chandeliers was vaguely "Dutch" but one wondered. Across the back of the synagogue hung globes of colored crystal—rose—bottle green—pastel blue, delicately frosted with flowers. Borrowing a note from a book Mrs. B's husband loaned me, the *LAND OF LINGAM* by ARTHUR MILES: "The Jewish colony in Cochin has existed since the days of King Solomon. It is believed Solomon drew some of his treasures from the Malabar Coast and thus established the earliest trade in this area. Clashing with the Portuguese, the Jews sided with the Dutch against their blunt and bloody overtures." A clock over the synagogue was dated 1760, probably a gift of gratitude from the Dutch (consisted of a square plaque with blue figures).

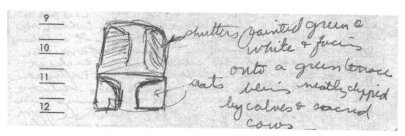

A diagram of windows from Pegge's diary.

When the original synagogue was razed and the Jews were rebuilding, tiles were needed for the floor. By chance the RAJA, who favored the Jews and granted them privileges, had ordered some tiles from Canton. The Jews cunningly and expediently contrived to inform the RAJA that the beautiful tiles were compounded of bullocks' blood—therefore an insult to his religion. The RAJA waved the entire lot out of his palace and so today they lie intact in the synagogue—blue and white Chinese scenes and flower designs. An old, sallow-skinned Jewish fellow attached to the synagogue was our guide. He was barefoot, unshaven, wore a print fabric skull cap and spoke with an odd side tilt of his head. To the British lady he was deferential. She spoke up that it was a "pity" they were having so much trouble in Palestine: "Beastly business—all the killing." "Yes, yes, such a waste of money," the Jew lamented profoundly. "Such a lot of money wasted, all WASTED." From the church we went in rickshaws through narrow dirt and sand streets, along which the black bony people passed about their business. Stopped at some ancient RAJA's palace where the walls of the rooms are marked with murals from 500 years ago—deep rust red and mellowed gold paisley confusion of Indian figures—birds, cows, women with naked breasts. I was more charmed by the Dutch windows than anything else, feeling the carving and artwork was really inferior to the Chinese. The Dutch window seats were incongruous, an historic touch.

Then to a bazaar where we looked at saris. Oh, truly the hand-wrought cloth of India is a treasure of gossamer froth, bordered with intricate, smooth and coiled designs. Color was also subtle, off greens, misty beige, blue and pink. But the price, $40 to $50 for six yards, was prohibitive. I looked, Ah'd, but bought not. Returning to the ferry jetty in a bubble of typical ladies' shopping chatter we passed a tall, slim woman clad in rough white cotton—her face was a blotch of chalk white and brown spots. "My dear," piped the American wife, "LEPER." I felt ill, the clash of her face and the black curious eyes. And the fragile cloth we'd just been idly admiring—fabric of sultan fairy tales—and the other poor devils who suffer some malady causing the legs to swell out of shape. Dear God, what a country.

Noted on one beige plaster building—a black sketch of a hammer and sickle. Recalled conversation last night of Mr. Bueler that the leftist influence is strong, despite the religious hold. He seemed to feel the Indians will suffer more under their own leaders than they did under the British, who still had human instincts.

Under some new idealist movement prohibition has taken hold. Only foreigners may drink, and then only with a permit. At the Cochin Club, where the Buelers took me before dinner, I was only permitted to drink ginger ale—and that incidentally was served in a glass as big as a bucket, the size of a flower vase. Both admitted the DRINKING of this place TRIPLES any comparison. The imbibing begins after sundown and continues almost until the next morning without too unseemly effect.

The ingrown social world is a strain on nerves and endurance and Christian instincts. Said the American wife: "The British women are hysterical when they gossip or rip another woman to shreds. Not only are they vicious cats behind your back, but downright rude and insulting to your face. They will walk right up to you, tell you you look terrible. 'Are you ill, my dear?' Or say 'That dress is really horrid on you. I must be truthful.'"

An airplane just zoomed overhead—Air India—said to be very good and quite safe (cheap also). One case of gossip suggested a possible story: There are a few bachelors here and they are in a tough spot. No white women but wives (with whom they have to be exceedingly discreet) and the brown women forbidden. Once in a while a girl whose name begins with Miss gets off a passing ship. There is a terrific rush—then she goes. Once a young New Zealand lass was delayed two weeks here. In the rush she and a young, earnest chap seemed to care for each other. The gossips went to work, making them self-conscious and isolated in the club, and then she went off and he was miserable. He wanted to marry her. "I hope she does accept him and come back," the American girl told me with vengeance.

(Note: All houses called "bungalows.") No running water, no plumbing, mosquito nets on beds, clothes must be carefully aired or kept in a closet with an electric light bulb strong enough to heat the air or the tropic musk will get into everything. The one room of their house air-conditioned was the bedroom but because so much time is spent there, entertaining guests, etc., they have it furnished as a rumpus room. Their servants have to be hired on a caste system because only certain castes do certain chores.

NOVEMBER 3, 1947—BOMBAY—Memorable spot, but for me personally a bitter lotus. I went ashore one morning alone, the launch making such quick hops back and forth I had to rush like mad to change clothes and return on time. Not seeing Doug, I couldn't tell him where I was or what was up. I'd met some young folk at the American Consulate and was making the most of it. Doug was deserted so teamed up with the radio crew and went on a bender. When I came back Sunday night he was red-eyed, surly, hurt, lonely, beastly. I learned what a job of stamina, subtlety and ardor handling a man is. I knew the things he said—verbal slaps, smarting and cutting—were said in anger and hurt. But though I meekly let them pass and held him in my arms, I was infuriated and raging to white fury. When I finally unleashed my held invectives, the ebb tide surging between us changed and he was adoring, conciliatory, blindly, passionately begging my forgiveness. When I left him after nearly three hours of this emotional wrangling, I loved and wanted him not at all. I have come so many times to the point of neither desiring nor wanting him as my husband. I begin to think of alternatives. These next two weeks before Geneva may decide the issue. The plan is—if his parents wire the divorce is final, we will have a civil ceremony at once. If I do marry him I want to go home with him in hand. Otherwise I must play my role well and pick my spot to remain somewhere in Europe. If I don't marry Doug I don't want to go home right away.

The day after our battle we were reconciled through great effort on my part and now all is apparently serene. As I feel now anyway I would marry him. Counting the days, these idle listing lasting days until we arrive in Geneva—about 12 more days.

Bombay was wonderful—most striking feature (coming out of China and the Malay Straits) was the hustle, zip and aliveness of everyone here. People, the Indians in their white cottons, from saris to the low-slung diaper jobs the men wear—look and move as though they're going somewhere. A Marine Drive of apartment houses, all cement and streamlined, faces the ancient harbor, bowl of blue before them—ship lined and a dance of ancient rigging (I am no nautical artist—ships are the CATAMARAN—meaning "out rigger"), making the waterfront more conspicuous in the imposing, domed Taj Mahal Hotel, which from the flowering court to the lobby and second floor air-conditioned dining room lives up to its name. Beyond that, I hear it's as backward and unplumbered as the rest of India.

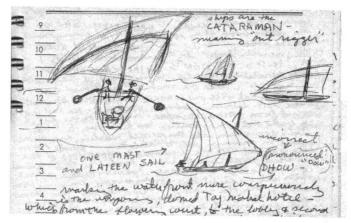

A diagram of catamarans from Pegge's diary.

The streets are wide, and traffic whips along at a twentieth-century pace. So unlike loitering, absent or blank-minded China. Policemen in navy blue, short-trousered uniforms topped with yellow berets (or beret-like hats) direct traffic and look as though they know their business. Beggars were innocuous shadows, a whine or whimper barely heard in the metropolitan noise and bustle. Saris were exquisite, a flutter of color—scarfy softness and sensuous suggestion, figure faults marvelously concealed. Leather thong sandals on straight-toed feet were a final wise accessory. For all that woman's status in India has been background, I give them credit for knowing what they are about in no uncertain terms.

The first day ashore Doug and I afoot went down the wide, tree-shaded, HORNBY ROAD to an enormous bookshop. In the musk of the back shop we found a worm-eaten tome on Turkistan which Doug immediately recognized and wanted—but had not enough rupees (about $9 U.S.) to get. (Note: Money is called Rups (to rhyme with "loops") by American residents.) I went back the next day and in my poor woman's way (for which I get no thanks or even recognition) I told the man I wanted the book but lacked the full amount of rupees and needed taxi fare to the Gateway of India (a launch pier). The man then reduced it to about $6 and got me a taxi. We also got a book of Douglas Reed's *GALANTY SHOW* in the lobby bookshop at the "TAJ" (as everyone calls the hotel) and K. P. S. Menon's *DELHI–CHUNKING* book describing his trip over the GILGIT pass which Doug and I are intent on making. Had an interesting chat with one WAYNE HARTWELL, librarian at the USIS library, about Kashmir. He had just returned from SRINAGAR just after the first riots broke out. The province has gone over to the Indian dominion, though the people, Muslim, are more bound by common ties to Pakistan. Aside from being ecstatic over the beauties and cheapness of the resort where people live on houseboats, he told me about a concern called COCKBURN'S AGENCY (British) which outfits mountain expeditions. Foreigners are immune from attack by even the most frenzied rioters. This seems true at present all over India. One MERRIT COOTES, American consul, Lahore, Pakistan, Hartwell said, might have some information on the pass (Gilgit). He is supposed to have come down that way from Russia or through Afghanistan.

I went to the Taj for dinner with a young chap from the consulate. Ultra-modern, saris worn only by Indian women. The British women looking horsey and deliberately "dressed." A few undetermined foreign women looking elegant, worldly and Far Eastern somehow. The food (costing about $5 U.S.) was scant but good, the coffee like that in New Orleans. The wine—superb, the little girls' room was a line personified from H. Allen Smith, who described the "johnnies" at Radio City Music Hall as a Taj Mahal of toilets. The Indian women, glamour girls, wore no make-up but did all the other turning, looking and primping possible before the forest of mirrors on all sides.

Crawford's market with its American rayons by the bolt and its Indian merchants sitting around indifferent to sales, gossiping and shop talking on the stall stoops of this fascinating bazaar. On raised platforms are white cotton cushioned beds, and this is their "shop." Goods expensive—noted much organdy from Switzerland. Went barefoot and reluctantly through a Muslim Temple. In the foot bath two whiskered devout were soaking their feet and passing the time of day. Across the pond another pious was scrubbing his teeth. Goldfish swam about and pigeons swooped down for a bath and drink, Allah be praised.

In a little tea shop had some Muslim cakes, baked in triangle packages—delicious, though my consulate friends thought them and me repulsive. Incidental note: The former French Consul General in Bombay is a passenger on the *Polk*. Traveling with his wife—bony, bespectacled, and disappointing somehow for her lack of aptitude for her role as Frenchwoman, diplomat's wife, and mother. With them is their retarded or moron daughter of about 14 or 15, though she could be older, poor thing. Anyway, the Consul had a casual conversation with Doug this morning and mentioned that the Hindu-Moslem strife will eventually be settled. "But then," he added, "The British are behind Pakistan."

NOVEMBER 10, 1947—I have been using a notebook to list my decisions to marry or not to marry Doug. I have several No's and once lay awake for hours deciding how I would spend my time traveling around Italy and go home sometime after Christmas. Last night I think Beethoven's *Fifth Symphony* suddenly pealing out over the loudspeaker saved us, but not until after I'd made a check mark next to "No" in my marrying book.

We are cutting our way in the face of a sharp wind sweeping down the Red Sea (Arabia on our right looking parched and hilly, Egypt a beige outline of the white-capped BLUE RED SEA). We were sailing near MECCA, past ancient landmarks of human history yet aboard this detested "modern" steamer. I feel completely frustrated; even my hunger for reading palls. Doug, loath to pass a word with fellow passengers (only diversion on board after all), leans against the railing staring glumly, oblivious, unheeding my nearness—over the water. I am torn between wistfulness for a lover—companion—a role he fits not at all—alas, such BOREDOM in the isolation nearness to him compels me to endure. What a dreary recital of vacillating emotion this record will be. If I don't marry him after all—as in coldest LOGIC and reason I SHOULD NOT—what a sad frustration at the expense of YOUTH and TIME. Meanwhile, let me recount a few marks of observation. I am trying to think out the details for STRINGER, my story, and I am turning over in my mind plots for checking with an agent in New York. How far away New York and all contact with civilization seems. The other passengers are bored, confined and irritable in the dining room. A long, unbroken trip like this is an endurance test. If I venture forth again it will be to work. We are due at SUEZ at six. Cholera will keep us from going ashore. I have had two casual conversations about India—one expressing the feeling that Pakistan and India to survive will have to unite—the other that the country will disintegrate without the British.

NOVEMBER 11, 1947—SUEZ—Entering the Mediterranean, a scene to remember: a 4:30 sunset of coppery fire as we slowly edged out of the canal and at the edge of the famous waterway—in lonely, steady grace stood a green bronzed image of the canal's hero, the French engineer Ferdinand de Lesseps. At his feet—the day being a blurred, dusky finish—a line of fishing boats rode gently on the water's motion. They, too, were deserted. The statue and the rumble of workaday ships—the cold, gray Mediterranean behind—the rolling waters of the canal's entrance a brown wash behind a cement (looking) sea wall. That scene was Suez to me. That and the leech-crawling Egyptian bum boat merchants who besieged the ship from the moment of arrival until departure. A raging cholera epidemic confined everyone to the ship as we loaded on fuel, and the boats swarmed around—raw boats with swarthy young louts aboard—out to leech whatever a bat's eye and hawk's claw could snatch. One young, kinky-haired but not unattractive chap was caught on the quarter deck by Fez-headed police. Such Egyptian cursing you never heard as he was thrown off the boat. His English being limited, the only invective he could hurl back at the ship's quarter master was "JEW—JEW!" Stung to fury, the American—probably not a Jew at all—ran for the hose. Other ships around us in the busy corridor were hosing the little men who cursed, shook both fists and rowed away, their unsold wares bobbing perilously on the gunwales. (For sale: leather satchels, rugs of the souvenir type and pocketbooks with Egyptian designs.) I thought vaguely the bum boats would make a story of some sort.

Incidentally, I am thinking of doing Europe until after the holidays—or until my money gets perilously low—and going home later on. Still very undecided about Doug. We were on the top deck this morning watching the bum boats. I called down to a voluptuous Russian girl who had traded some clothes for a hand-tooled purse. "Bargain?" I asked and went down the ladder to take a look (it was a monstrosity). Once on the lower deck I decided to stop by my stateroom for a second—brought an apple back for Doug (he's been devouring them en route). He was gone. I mingled with the other passengers until nearly noon—then when he didn't appear I sensed uneasily that something was wrong. Went to his state room, where he was scowling, petulant. "If you wanted to be alone, why didn't you say so? You were gone for over an hour without saying where or when or anything, leaving me standing there" (alone with four radio operators and cadet pursers!). I kissed him, bidding "Darling, I didn't mean to. You aren't seriously angry. Look, I brought you an apple" etc. He was unresponsive—lunch gong called—we were forced to discontinue.

When the other couple had gone and we were waiting for our dessert order, Doug resumed, "I'm not going to trail around after you any longer. If you want to be alone that's OK." Emotional me. I clenched my teeth—put my napkin on the table with a gesture of finality and tried to rise (from the table). His hand on my arm held me in my chair. He murmured something penitent and conciliatory, but to me it was more to prevent a conspicuous move on my part. His slashing remarks on my sensitive ears went through me like a current. Tears welled quickly, and I tried discreetly to hide them. Finally cleared the dining room with long strides. "Come on up on deck; I want to tell you something," he said, taking my arm. The old familiar pattern, but the charm is broken. "There is nothing to say, I'm finished," I rasped out, rushing to my stateroom, banging the door. I stretched out on my bunk, trembling, hurt, angry, too infuriated to weep. I thought of Italy—how I'd connive to fend for myself.

I received a letter from George Wallace, saying he hoped to see me on my return and have me and my husband (pardon me while I writhe briefly in bitter irony) down to visit Weems. He thought my decision to return home rather "sudden," but I must have "good reasons." Humph! The hours passed. Finally a knock at the door. Doug. Inhospitably inquired what he wanted. "You," he said, sure that all he had to do was sweep me into his arms. He tried, but only annoyed me in the sweeping by knocking off my braid. I coolly edged him out of the room. "All right," he cut back, leaving, "but remember I came to you." I felt little other than regret I'd opened the door to his knock. I often wish I'd left him and all memories (gloriously happy, exotic ones) far behind in Tihwa where he really belongs. This has been an ordeal love affair. As a marriage it will be a disaster. I may yet be persuaded, lose my head and go through with it. But I will have only my own dread of young aloneness to blame. My heart is out of it from this point on. If I can just steel myself to face the strange turmoil of Europe alone.

Europe
1947–1948

1947

NOVEMBER 12, 1947—MID-MEDITERRANEAN SEA—(which incidentally looks exactly like every other ocean we've seen—blue—awash with sudsy foam and a crest of spume). We are midway to NAPLES, going at half speed to conform with a cholera immunization. I just want to add a line in adoring, all-my-heart defense of Doug. I was so fulsomely upbraiding yesterday I must tell the reverse. He did not appear at dinner in the dining room. After I'd finished I went looking for him on deck. In the darkest, coldest, most forlorn part of the run deck, I found him. I handed him an apple, saying nothing. He took it. A ship passed just then, a strange freighter with masts barely visible in dim deck lights. I moved toward the railing to look at it, and Doug, sensitive to my moving away, put his arms around me. "Baby girl," he gasped, his faced burrowed into my hair and throat. I did not relent at first. We sat down then, backs to the heated main stack of the *Polk*, shoulders touching, strained toward and away from each other. "Come here, close to me," he said. Then he put me down tight, warm and close to him. We were reconciled and a feeling beyond mere kiss and make up engulfed us. I became, with every bit and part of me, and with all my heart and mind being HIS. I have never loved him more—not even in the beginning. Nor anyone else. This one perfect forgiveness marks out all the other marks on doubts. Damnation on the record. I love him. In the fullest, most perfect, whole, complete, radiant, and happy sense of the word, My darling, beloved, dearest Doug.

NOVEMBER 17, 1947—NAPLES—Here I sit in the Little Girls' Room of Cabin 17, *S.S. Polk,* drinking black coffee and deciding my fate. Mostly that I must not marry Doug Mackiernan—and this on the eve of a day when I should love him more than before, and think only of being his wife and mother to the wee Mackiernans. How bittersweet and oddly strange that the end should come at the beginning. After being very heavenly happy close and loving each other more than ever, ever before, we started for town—always our disaster. Doug charges into a casual sightseeing excursion grim as a soldier marches toward the front. Crossing a street he clutches my arm fiercely—in the shopping district he gallops scowling through the loitering, ambling people. If I stop to look in a window he could be a full block away before he sees me. He returns in a fury.

We stopped in a little place for coffee. I wanted some of the divine, tempting cakes I had seen in the window. The waiter, who looked vaguely like biography photos of Caruso in his prime, brought dull, huge, globby cakes. I wanted "petits fours." Doug, annoyed at my "conspicuous behavior" and never having heard of tiny cakes called petit-something, was choking on his demitasse. But we finally got them. As we were leaving the place some beggar kids picked up the scent of "Amerikanos." One little girl pulled at my sleeve. "Oh, Doug," haven't we got something?" I asked. Charging 10-miles-per block beside me, he cut over his shoulder, "No, give to one and you'll have the whole pack after you. They're just professionals anyway." I looked down at the little girl with the large eyes and pale pimply face and cringed inside.

Then I wanted to take a streetcar ride because I was so tired from walking. Very curtly, disinterestedly, he said, "We don't have any idea WHERE they're going, and we can't stand here because all those pests (the kids begging) swarm around if you stand still." I moved on beside him, angry now, no consideration for how I felt—that I was tired. "Let's call a taxi—carriage or something" WITH MY MONEY WHICH WE HAD CHANGED TO BUY HIM SOME SMOKING TOBACCO. Doug glanced sharply at me. "I wish you wouldn't go into your tantrums on the street where everyone—" He broke off and we walked BLOCKS in grim silence. In my heart I thought, "So this is love—this is what I'm to marry? After loving him with all my being only a few hours before—THIS?" Then, after dinner, No, he was tired—didn't feel well—didn't want to go ashore. "All right." I was disappointed but fussed about. Did he have a fever? etc. At nearly 10 p.m. he finally trundled off to bed. Very WIDE awake. We'd been talking to a radio operator who gave us a pep talk on champagne at a Trocodero. "Want to go?" I asked Doug. He made a face—he was tired—"But I guess if I don't take you you'll howl about it six weeks from now." I looked at him, the FINAL DECISION "No" for a second—then smiled. But enough of this. The fault, dear Brutus and dear grandchildren who are NEVER to be Mackiernan—I want to make Doug into a charming romantic and he-man lover and companion. By nature, temperament, and background he is a very STOLID, ordinary, wholly selfish, and INSENSITIVE man. I am guilty of resisting SUBORDINATION of my own professional and personal inclinations to his, and refusing to accept or recognize his limitations. Keep martyring myself and draining my emotions in sorrow and tragedy at his neglectful oversight. He is a lover only in the bedroom. Outside of physical ardor he is part boor, part boy—and all Douglas Mackiernan. The story is finished unless a quirk of fate decrees otherwise. I am sorry to write this all out in picayune detail but I am doing some searching analysis, and writing my candid reactions and surest thoughts helps. I will try to have Doug's assistance—quote quote—until I land in Geneva. If I can't get a refund on my *Queen Mary* ticket, I will go home; otherwise all Europe awaits a look.

As for Naples: I must see Europe. I never want to go back to China. I have enough money, my youth, vigor, and Irish luck. It is worth the gamble. It will be difficult hassling Doug in Genoa. I dread it but will be so relieved. So "free" when it is all over.

From July 13th to November 17th—the most formative romance of my life.

NOVEMBER 21–25, 1947—LAUSANNE, SWITZERLAND—
How marvelous to have a phone call in a strange country. When the phone rang just now I didn't answer, assuming it couldn't be for me. But it was MIKE BISIO—Cap Lathrop's ex-baker, who once taught me how to bake pie crusts and kissed me quickly before he left Alaska for his native Alpines. Oh, dear heaven—to be so intrigued with all this—so enthralled with Europe and its possibilities—and still being tied to Doug. I wrote above that it was over. I think it is old-married-couple prosaicness to a certain extent. Emotionally we are accustomed to each other, and Doug by nature and army indoctrination for five years past is no gallant or sentimentalist—no pretty speeches. I am sick of this "Do I love him-don't I love him" debate, and fate has formed no resolution. We had a cable from his family. "No definite date yet." Mother's letters about no housing on arrival and Doug's mother warning that I had better not be conspicuous until the divorce is on the dotted line, all gave me a natural exit. We cancelled my ticket on the *Queen Mary* and Doug will go on alone. Doug and I will remain in Lausanne until December 2nd. The status is—if we get a cable—divorce final, we will be all set to be wed at once. Otherwise I stay in Europe. Well, so be it. But I

have a feeling I will not marry Doug if he goes back and I remain. We loved Italy, Genoa, that is. The city was smart-trim—tidied up since the war. There was an air of brisk self-assurance about the city, and the people—vive la Italy and the Italians. They were attractive, charming, snappy and keen-eyed, soft-spoken, ultra-sophisticated and smart. I was astounded at the furs—the chic feathered hats, the metallic inflection of Italian spoken at a smooth, inhaled, exhaled pitch. There were more candy and bakery shops than honest-to-gosh FOOD stores. But there were some fresh produce markets and the coffee BARS—they drink coffee in Italy that is like a heady coffee liqueur—a tiny cup, midnight black—made fresh to order. Doug and I walked all over town drinking it and gaping at the Italians. We had one elegant night dinner at a place called CAPUERO'S —the local Waldorf rooftop overlooking the twinkly lights of the harbor. Dinner and wine out of this world. And such swish-and-bow-style service. Afterward we went to a symphony and all during Tschaikovskys' 5th, I kept thinking "It will take more than Douglas Mackiernan to get me out of Europe. I'm not going home and leave THIS."

The train ride to Switzerland was an ordeal, except that lunch on the diner—with wine, of course—was a riot. One little man scooted down the aisle with wines and mineral water—chasing hard after him was a cork popper aide de camp—pop-pop-pop all down the dining car, filled predominantly with men in pinstripes buried in newspapers and puffing cigars that smoked like campfires. Doug and I loved Switzerland and this enchanting Lausanne. We walked all over, nosed into the shop windows—the heavenly, divine pastry shops—strolled by the lake, so blessedly unpopulated, so restful in its out of season blue-gray idleness. This country and its people is heaven on earth. We took the train to Geneva yesterday and had a heavenly happy day just walking ourselves to death. Looking, looking. Stopped in an ultra-elegant place for lunch and for $2 had a king's banquet. Zurich tomorrow and the problem of handling Doug and Mike together.

DECEMBER 2, 1947—LETTER TO DOUG

My darling, darling,

On the morning of our third separation (Kuldja, Shanghai, now Switzerland), I want you to know when you are off there in the vast away-from-me-ness (call it London or mid-Atlantic—it is all the same) that I love you with all my heart. You, darling Doug, are mine, my life, my happiness, my fulfillment. Our togetherness is our own perfection of that young, instinctive, swift, discovering romance of July 13th.

We have already been through a turmoil of events—for love is a human, not a poetic experience after all—and our closest "oneness" has transcended the differences, the regretted angers and clash of temperaments. The places dotting the globe between here and Shanghai where we were happy, alone and together, were compensating gem-abodes, our very own—and darling, I was terribly, terribly happy with you. All through the ordeal of traveling, customs, currencies, etc., I marveled that I had YOU beside me when I watched the other women who were alone. But for you I would have been so frighteningly alone. So when I say thank you, my beloved, for taking care of me, I mean another way of being loved by you.

I remember the frantic day you jeeped me to the Hami-Ata airport. I would have been giddy kneed had it not been for Mackiernan at the wheel saying, "Don't take any guff, honeybunch. Send for me if you need me." The feeling of your fightin' protection nearness would have sent me into a roaring jungle prepared to take no damn guff from anything that crawled.

Here's a wee poem to bless you, darling mine:

If you ride down the wind
If you haste with the star
My heart shall o'ertake you
Wherever you are
For as swift as the wind
And as fleet as the star

Is my love that shall reach you

Wherever you are

God love you and keep you for me until you send for me to come home. I love you, darling, forever and the day after, Pegge

DECEMBER 5, 1947—LAUSANNE—What events have marked the interim since my last entry. Doug flew to London (3 hours) because the strike in France endangered rail travel. I went to Geneva to see him off—a chilly, snowy, slushy day. I felt so odd that the parting should be so casual. We sat in the Swiss Air terminal, talking as though we would see each other the next day. In my mind was the question if we'd ever meet again, but Doug was preoccupied with physical mechanics of the trip. Odd assortments of people—men with mustaches, spats and walking sticks sat vacant-eyed, smoking Women in leopard coats, some with dogs on scarlet leather leashes—family groups in a glop-glop guttural huddle in foreign languages—airline attendants very brisk, blonde marcelled shock of hair, deep cleft chins—spouting clipped French right and left. I had a little girlish goodbye note—romantic and very naïve for the knowing tenor of the writer—for Doug. And felt quite embarrassed passing it, half hidden, folded, into his hand as we crossed the sidewalk to the airport bus. "Well, take it easy" was Doug's farewell. He waved his hand slightly and stepped off the bus in the line of overcoats, fur jackets and blue gabardine airline uniforms. I felt a rush of tears which filled my eyes, not so much for Doug's departure as the uncertainty of our ever being united and my alone adventure in Europe.

I walked around the licorice-black, wet streets of Geneva for a long while—called at the American Consulate and began my chain of "contacts" which someday may place me somewhere. Called the AP bureau man for Switzerland, one ED FISHER, who casually mentioned I might follow up a story in Lausanne. King Michael of Romania and his reported "fiancée" are stopping at a palatial hotel in Lausanne. "Get a picture of them together" said Fisher. My first move was to call on the local newspaper editor. He was out, so I was steered to a second man who offered to take me to meet the King's guard—a Swiss detective named Monsieur Jacques, just as you'd expect. We went to the hotel, paced the scarlet carpets of lobbies and foyers big enough for railroad stations, and walked to a rear elevator. The detective was a 5-footer, bald, bird-like. If we would sit for a minute the royal family would pass by on their way to the elevator. I was really thrilled, put on my specs and pretended to read a newspaper. My God—the electric eyeful of the robust, strident, footballish King towering over a flock of fuddy-duddy women in black—his mother—aunt—a woman attendant—and the princess, wearing a pale, colorless, daub-in-mud brown tweed to match a bob of mud-mouse hair—flat heels. My heart went out to the King—no country to call his own, and hemmed in by a lot of spinsterish old gals who watch every move like a hawk. The detective said as far as he can see, the "match" is no great romance. No attention is paid to the princess, no flowers—they seldom, if ever, go out at night and almost never alone. I am thinking of trying to have a word with his highness.

DECEMBER 7, 1947—LAUSANNE—I have had a cable from Doug (a nice one beginning with "darling") and a letter (long one) with much detail on how to fend for myself in London. I was surprised to receive both and hadn't expected to hear from him until he reached the USA. If only he were the Doug of Sinkiang. I feel almost estranged from him already, but I do want to go home. I have a strange, empty feeling of wanting BELONGING—old friends' faces around me. And I want the Mackiernan affair finished once and for all—or to marry him—at long last.

I have given up the Romanian chase, though I may work on it after I finish the Sinkiang article—which Doug won't like because

I'm going to call the Ili area Soviet Turkistan—at least, I've got it that way on the first draft. I'm also taking Russian lessons from the University professor, a spidery little Jewish lady who speaks very wispy Russian but who gets her points of instruction across very lucidly. For Russian grammar, that is a lot.

DECEMBER 9, 1947—LAUSANNE—(Ha! Note how I "file" each squib, with a dateline.) Want to set down in flash freshness a new window on the world and certainly a story. The college story of Lausanne—First the picture is disjointed and full of unhappy contrasts in young American and young European, femme et male. The males predominate on the campus, but they are mostly ex-GI's on a bill of rights or shoestring, spending no money, using other people's generosity, hospitality or gal if possible. The American girls have all or most of the money—society backgrounds. They are eager for the exotic touch or finishing to native-ize themselves—adopting local modes, customs, phrases, food, manners, etc. They had come to Switzerland thrilled: Didn't Kings go to school here and what not? To their dashed hopes and resentful chagrin, they found the Swiss extremely reserved, and being a "schoolmate" was no entrée to having so much as a cup of tea in the native old-family multigenerational home. The boys were nice, but went to school as if being apprenticed to higher learning. They worked at it and answered to their families for their grades. They are given no mad-money or allowance, so they can't take a girl out, and the idea never seems to occur to them anyway. Saturday night is just the end of the week. The girls SIT home, and that is that.

I have an adorable "bug" in mind—the cutest gal this side of a Bonwit comb. She spoke so forlornly of being in Switzerland. She hasn't met a single Swiss outside of school. She has long, soft hair and the eyes of a fawn—and would be adored and cherished by any Yankee. "Oh, this isn't like back home," she said with hurt bewilderment. "I'm going to France as soon as the weather is warm." Her roommate—a very nice Greek girl from Athens who speaks colloquial American (her first name is Helen and her last name has an "opolis" on the end)—agreed on the men situation but put in a word defending the Swiss: "After all, they haven't any money." Barbara (fawn eyes) must not have much either—she wouldn't touch her salad at lunch until she called the head waiter and begged to know if it cost extra or went with the lunch. She is tiny and thin as a cricket, but the way she asserted herself in her classroom, French was a study. Helen corrected her accent, and then when the waiter, all bows and tolerance of youth, looked puzzled, Helen cut in with a flood of perfectly accented French and the fawn was immediately self-conscious. But she tried again. She had a dog at home and wanted bones for it—this in French. The waiter tried very hard but his sixth senses—gallantry and imagination—were not up to comprehending what she wanted, please God! Helen again cut in, and this time the fawn gave up.

Helen and I had a few words together. "What is Greece like?" I asked. "Wonderful" she said, and that faraway longing for home-home-home—dear and familiar—came into her brown eyes. "Athens is sophisticated and modern. The society people are snobs and profligates—disgusting—but the simple people, the little Greeks, are grand. Give you half of their last loaf." She forked her salad absently. "I'm afraid there will be civil war at home—the Communists are very strong—all because of the nasty Russians, of course." She sloshed lettuce around in the dressing in a jabbing gesture. "I HATE them," she said shortly.

Then, to complete the picture, there's Sandra Gyranesko, who is figure one in the story. She is European—tall, blonde hair streaked the color of buttercups in the sun, in striking contrast with her black-brown Romanian eyes. Sandra represents all that Europe was, and, as she has been raised to believe, still is and will be. In the front of her mind is an instinct—I say instinct rather than THOUGHT because she doesn't let herself think too much about it—that her escape from whatever may happen in Europe is to marry an American. In view of the situation at school she has checked off all the clunky GI's with no money and concentrated on one Bob, who has money and a car. He is short and she hates wearing flat heels for him, but he is the American! Bob had some kind of trucking business in partnership with three brothers back home, so he has money coming in all the time. He's what is generally meant when a woman calls a man she is not in love with "a darling."

Sandra's European background has matured her in the strictest worldly sense of the word—she realizes MEN run the world after all, and the more you know about them the better off a pretty woman will be. I don't know what Sandra knows about love—the real, real thing—because she lives in an atmosphere of fake and frivolous affection for this one or that, as she is momentarily amused or intrigued. She calls her father "darling" or more rarely, "Papa." He was a Romanian ambassador (minister?) to Paris. She knows the diplomatic world and rather dreads it, except for looking divine on long-dress occasions. Sandra reports on shocking inside scandals about the titled and royal of Europe (that my handsome Michael "chances an eye" and that princess Margaret Rose of England is a "sexy little b....." I gasped. "Oh, Pegge, don't you know about English women—they're either one thing or the other, in extremes: horsey and flat footed, or—" and she whistled.

Sandra has odd little ways. She makes FIRST always a study of the MEN in any situation. If anyone even glanced at her Bob, she would annihilate the girl and be purring sweet to Bob. She makes a terrific play for any man casually met—touches his coat lapels, stands very close and looks UP at him, even though she's as tall as he is. She concentrates on being amusing in a smoothly frivolous way. Let anyone inject a thoughtful word into the conversation and she will quickly turn it aside with something suave, making the serious spokesman feel vaguely as though he has made a social faux pas and

Sandra is covering it up for him. She is trying desperately to keep Bob "amused" and babied and a bit smothered, I think.

Sandra is always late and today was downright, cruelly thoughtless. Her Russian teacher, and mine, is an elderly woman in her 50's. She made a trip to the Mirabeau to give Sandra her lesson after I'd had mine. The dear soul has a bad sniffly cold and made quite an effort to come for the lesson. And she arrived exactly on time—I met her in the lobby, having walked home, taking my time. "Oh, mam'zelle," she came up to me, "have you seen Sandra. She is not in her room." I could offer no suggestions, and went, with a little apology, to my room. Ten minutes later the phone rang. Sandra said gaily, "Oh, Pegge—do come and have coffee with me." "But where are you— your Russian teacher—" "Oh, but I'm having the most marvelous manicure and the polish didn't dry in time for me to dash back to the hotel. Tell me, is she terribly angry?" Pat phrase for anyone left forgotten somewhere—are you terribly angry? So coyly put that the poor victim becomes the brute by inference.

Another thing: Sandra adores American men—in preference to European. Aside from the money and passport security, "they're so sincere, so clean, so real—so generous. They're casual, a bit crude. Their manners are frightful, but I'd rather have a 'not-bad-chum–not-bad' from them than a European on his knees spouting sonnets."

"AMERICANS ARE SO SINCERE." It struck me that all she said about European men goes for European women, herself included at the top of the list. And now Bob, studying physics—rather unsure of himself underneath—feels physics is a good deal—know that and you can tinker around with a lot of things. He had been to Italy recently with a stringbean from Texas. They hit the bars and the back road villages. "They don't like Americans over here worth a damn. We bought our way in and so long as we're paying for it, OK." What did he think of going to school here as compared with the States? "Well, y' got a helluva lotta good professors, I mean real whizzes. For the rest, I dunno. It's different all right." And Europe? "Oh, people over here have fixed habits of thinking—you can give Mike Hoolavich out in the fields all the liberation y' want but he still feels his class. There's gentry—blood for a hundred years' generations. And there's peasants—the underdog expects to be in his class. That's what he's always known. This communist stuff goes over very big with them, but nothing will change until the habit of thinking has a complete turnover." For the story, I think he's torn between being attracted to Sandra's novel ways and struggling to be serious about his work. About getting hold of himself somehow and finding what he can do and wants to do.

Fine on this for the time being. I had a card from Mother, taking the postponement with innocent good faith. She doesn't realize yet why I'm staying on in Europe. When I think about Doug—counting the days until he should be arriving and the fateful cable will arrive—it is with impatient watchfulness. But when I think of "us" together I am filled with the same dread uncertainties and a feeling that it is over for us. But we are both reluctant—or refusing to admit it. I am torn between wanting to go home and dreading it. Meanwhile, I am working on the Sinkiang article. It is tough going. I've spent two days wrestling with the rough outline and now I've re-worded the whole framework and will dig in from there. I want TERRIBLY to write a smooth piece and with the pictures to produce an important article. I may go strong on the Russian angle and Doug may object, but this is my very own field of endeavor and I've got to do my own thinking.

Back to my story of Sandra. I've just had dinner and an evening with her. In return for the lunch I took her to dinner at the hotel. She arrived in a long swishy skirt, Italian handmade slippers, spike heeled, and enveloped in a cloud of exquisite perfume. Bob was downstairs reading a paper. A terrific act went on: "Oh, darling, you MUST have coffee with us—come, come, now da'ling. I'll feed you all the leftovers—you'll love it." After much protest—rather loud in a hush-hushy lobby, Bob was dragged into the dining room. Immediately a mild explosion of French began because the salad was not Sandra's special favorite—the poor waitress smiled and apologized as though Sandra were asking her what she did for her beautiful complexion! What training the waitresses get over here.

Sandra ate ravenously in between floods of café conversation, sweeping scandals and gossip, with a goodly sprinkling of references to her beaux—at one point I said to Bob quite lightly, "How do you think Sandra would like York, Pennsylvania?" (Farm town, with Pennsylvania Dutchees galore.) Bob was seriously thoughtful—"I don't think she'd go for it." The lovely twittle bird went on twittling "Bob, da'ling" and missed the doomful obvious. We adjoined to a frigid, heavily furnished drawing room under the lamp so the light would fall on her hair and cast well-placed shadows over her figure beneath a white silk blouse. Another chap from the University had joined us: the son of the Turkish ambassador to Rio de Janeiro. He was a typical pretty boy, I thought—suede shoes, hair slightly long in back. A little pointed thing he said to me: "The Russians are very, very clever" as Bob, having a beer as we sipped coffee, held forth vacuously. He seemed to express proper respect, or at least acknowledged American defensive aid in his country. Sandra, conspicuously out of the conversation while all this was going on, would after a pause switch the chatter to herself—center stage.

DECEMBER 11, 1947—LAUSANNE—I had a cable from Doug this morning: DARLING ARRIVED TODAY etc. LOVE DOUG. I had a shivery thrill when I first opened it, not knowing if I were to be summoned home or what. I hope he will cable something definite tomorrow. Every day I am faced with two things—my Russian lessons which I enjoy, and the Sinkiang story which I dread. Odd spurt I got today, though, from an odd person—the tall, bald, suave secretary to King Michael of Romania. I went to see him today through the efforts of M. Jacques and as we sat chatting about how chances were

for an American correspondent to visit Romania—the secretary fell
to talking about reporters in London where the King had attended
the wedding of Princess Elizabeth. "How they talked—what a nice
guy the King is and the stories they wrote." That got me—somewhere
in the outside world news "guys" are writing stories, and here I am.
It's an ordeal, and I feel so suspended waiting to hear from Doug.

DECEMBER 14, 1947—LAUSANNE—What an odd day, blowy
and cold—the famous lake mist—veiled and from the top of a hilL
looking down—all a platinum blur of brightness. When I rang for
my breakfast tray I was surprised to see several letters and a cable
from Doug. "DARLING LEAVING FOR WASH. MONDAY WILL
WIRE NEWS REMEMBER TODAY LOVE" "Wash" means State
Dept and Divorce. The 13th: was our long-standing anniversary. I
had quite forgotten it until in Cook's office I had occasion to write
down the date. In a flash I thought, I must cable Doug. By coincidence
we sent each other night letters so must have received the news of
remembrance simultaneously. It was a lucky happenstance that we
BOTH remembered, although I think we're both aware we've come
a long way from the original July 13th—that happy, mad rainy
Sunday afternoon in the desert of Sinkiang, China! After the cable
I read Mother's letters and wept. She is heartbroken to think she
contributed to my decision to stay in Switzerland by overemphasis
on housing and economic problems attendant on my return. That
was partly it but not all—Doug was 75% of the reason. I don't want
to record all the things Mother wrote and I felt reading them. It was
rather awful—I think she senses my uncertainty and unhappiness
over Doug and is more worried FOR HIM because he won't see it. I
feel I will give Doug one more chance. I want to see what he's like on
home soil. As he was here, I don't want him. I finished reading the
letters, including one very unnecessary and crudely well-intended
letter from Daddy, condemning Mother for having written anything

to change my mind about coming home. I really felt terribly sad thinking of my poor, poor darling Mother. What a nasty deal life has given her. Nature did not equip her to stem the currents—she just took them as they came, defenseless. The whole situation engulfed me. I went to Mass and sat oblivious of the service. I'm drifting away, away from the church, I guess. I came back to the hotel and actually worked on my article all day, then had dinner. I took to dinner an English girl I met.

I leave Friday for London, taking the midnight sleeper straight through to Calais, then on to Belfast and Christmas (Dear God— how blessedly lucky she's there) with Eva McGown.

DECEMBER 17, 1947—BERNE—I set the date more pointedly by noting the conclusion of the Foreign Ministers Conference in London. The Secretary of State, aging George Marshall, said: "I reluctantly concluded no useful purpose would be served by further debate. Soviet claims in Austria, if accepted, would be the price of Austrian independence, agreements on Germany could be reached with Russia only under conditions which would enslave the German people and seriously retard the economic recovery of all Europe." This is contemporary.

Personal history: I had the friendliest, pleasantest day I've had since I came to Switzerland. I went to Berne and from the Bahnhoff called the press attaché, Mildred Allport, who cheerily welcomed me. She sent me to Minister John Carter Vincent to literally say hello. Period. (I had Cavender's letter of introduction but caught him at an odd moment. Tall, twitchy, stuttery, nervous.) The press attaché was more sit down, tell-all-ish. She even put a call through to Berlin for me and I talked to Howard Denby—my dear, dear Pappa Denby of *Times-Herald* days. He told me to come to Berlin in a hurry and stay with him and Linda (Frau). I spent the p.m. shopping, happily befriended by sales clerks, and got a cashmere sweater, Hungarian hand-painted

cup and saucer, plate set, and four Swedish crystal wine glasses. That
evening went to Mildred's for a cup of cheer—heard lots of news and
gossip about the news hounding world and went home on the train
later.

I re-read a letter I received this morning from Doug, written on
board the *Queen Mary*. I quote a line or two: "Honey I miss you
very very much. This has been a most boring trip." (This, despite
the fact he is laden with over $100 worth of Stein's Innermost Asia
purchased in London.) Solid page of sea-side tips, do's and don'ts:
"Naturally when you come back I will meet you in New York, so you
won't have anything to worry about (customs, luggage etc.). Write to
me soon and tell me you love me, too." THAT was the only line in the
letter my eye lit fondly on. From Mother, a Christmas card—much
comment on the status quo and "Well, we'll see what comes of it."
(Doug and I do), then penciled between the lines: "If anything, that
was unnecessary."

DEC. 20,1947—LETTER FROM TRAIN TO CALAIS—France is
speeding by... a pastorale of wheat gold fields, stark, winter trees, and
modern, solid-brick looking houses.

Darling dear Mother,

Ah, yes, I have my moments. Yesterday, for instance, Doug
telephoned me from Washington, just to say, come home darling as
soon as you can! He cabled this morning that his trip to Washington
has been deliberately postponed to keep an appointment with his
aunt-lawyer. "Expect definite news in few days, miss you, love," he
said. I was so relieved to hear this on my last day in Lausanne. Then
that night I was clearing the hotel desk and my French news editor
and his mountaineer Lt. were in attendance to see me off. (How very
nice and warmly friendly they both were. No eye work, no suggestion
of more than just being-kind-to-a-lone-American.) Anyway, the
hotel manager came running. "Oh, Mem'zelle, Berne has just called.

You must wait for a call from Washington, IN AMERICA." I nearly swooshed plop on the red Persian plush! Then I expected Doug had something definite on his mind, but he just said, "Hello there," and I knew he'd called JUST TO TALK TO ME. I was giddy, of course, but the connection was bell clear. I asked him if he'd called you and he said, "No, I wanted to talk to YOU first." I begged him to ring Harrisburg. And am sure he will. He minds Christmas coming on without me, and said the divorce should be all FINI very tout-suite! We must have talked TEN MINUTES. (France is really lovely. The countryside—I have to stop and glance up every now and then…) I emerged from the phone booth very giddy, and had to rush for the station. My two escorts however rushed me first to a very pretty café where the walls are lined with real birds all twittering. We had a bon voyage quickie then they put me on the train. My editor presented me with a beautiful book of photographs of Lausanne and the Lake Lemon (Geneva, Lausanne and other cities are all edged by this lovely pool.) I will in turn present the book to YOU as I took no pictures, being far from in the snapshot mood. It was blizzard snowing when I left and Switzerland looked really like a poster of itself. Up to that time there has been no snow whatever. The two lads got me all set on the train, waved me away and were very gay! I was all champagney inside—Doug and this send off. The train is a marvel. Here I am in a compartment all to myself—little table for the typewriter, wash stand, closet and English-speaking porter. My bed was clean and warm but I was saucer eyed all night long. Snow blew in gusts against the pane. Gold glows illuminate the night as we came into France. Bang bang on the door. Passport s'il vous plaît mam'zelle. Whoosh, the door was opened and I rose up in the nightie. Looked so bewildered they didn't even ask or inspect my luggage. I was much too excited to sleep. Then about 9:30 we arrived in PARIS! My porter came to say we could stop about an hour and if I wanted to go for a stroll I could. I flew… and walked down Rue de Lyon (by coincidence it was the nearest boulevard) to the station. I was thrilled. Had only enough

French francs to eat on the train, or I would have brought you a wee token. I'll get back to France tho before I come home. The street was wide and glistening with drizzling rain….. the people shuffled along, straggling and apathetic. I passed a shop that had MEDALS for sale, war decorations that is. Only the wine shops and perfume stores had goods that looked abundant. The cafés had a few customers, odd face lads with pointed cheek bone and gold caps on one side of the head. The railroad station is a sight. Looks like some dilapidated freight depot. The countryside from the train windows looks better. Just had lunch in the diner with a British man and his wife who have lived in Paris, going home for Christmas. So he's got a dozen eggs in her suitcase and is praying they won't break all over the clothes til she gets home – and past the customs. I'll write again from London, darling. Baby

Sunday morning—Russell Hotel—LONDONTOWN

Well, darlin', could you but see baby now! Through my open window is a park and gentlemen in darbys and walking sticks strolling round. The day is misty—sunny and almost Spring-like. The grass is green in the park. I LOVE and adore the English in their own country. Everyone, down to my luggage porter, has been laughin' and havin' a nice word—"Pretty smile there, miss. You must keep it that way," etc.!!!!

The trip across the English Channel goes down on permanent record! It was a rough, wind-whipped, and ablaze with sunset. Decks jammed with Britishers caring not a jot for the cold – gazing on Dover. No wonder England is England. The people AREN'T stiff and stand-offish at all. Maybe hard times and the holiday—everyone in same boat feeling has changed them. But they're the greatest people I've come across yet. A doctor at the immigration post was exceedingly charming and a young Lovey-type British bobby saw me to the train and into my seat. He was too cute for anything. The train trip from Dover to London takes as long as Philadelphia to NY.

Gerry (Sampson) met me and nagged this porter (old timer-seaman's cap and picket on him) and given me tips on how to get through customs without trouble. Gerry was marvelous—I just stood by and things happened. Our porter said he'd just put Noel Coward on the train for Paris. So jammed Coward and valet had to go 2nd class in UPPERS. Imagine Noel in an upper bunk! Had an awful time getting a taxi. There's a black market in the fares—either pay twice the legal fare or, sorry governor. Finally got to the Russell—looks like a British Club—room warm, bed sink-down, nice fireplace and on the bureau a huge bouquet of mums and a box of fresh fruit. Welcome to my native land. We went to dinner in a supper club all white and gilt and smart with a Christmas tree decked in gold. Women all looking very ta-ta—waiter in cutaways. Had quite a good meal—butter, meat, wine—everything. I was so exhausted by this time. I was really making a supreme effort for Gerry's sake. I never, never dreamed he'd go to such welcoming extremes. He wants me here for New Years but my only evening gown is in Harrisburg. And I would rather be with Eva, of course. (Or Doug, naturally—in my heart, I am always with him.) I just hope he telephoned you after talking to me. I'm glad I'll have time to really see London. In the taxi we passed the palace where old *Queen Mary* lives. Lights on in the upper windows. Gerry and I will go sight seeing today and I will take pictures. Must hurry off to Mass now. Just wanted you to have a word from London. Tomorrow at Cooks I will try to definitely get myself booked for a ship about the end (or middle) of January—want just enough time to make Paris and Berlin. And by that time, Doug's divorce will certainly be final. My London address had better be to Cooks for the time being. Had darling card and note from Lou Torian's husband from Carlisle barracks. And have guest room all set for me. Housing in an emergency if a little long range and they want me to be Godmother to wee "LUCIA."

Bye darlin' dear—or should say—cheerio (they do here all the time). Baby

DECEMBER 20, 1947—LONDON—England is, absolutely without doubt, my favorite country (next to beloved U.S.). The British are my favorite people. Today I walked down a blowy street, turned a corner and saw Big Ben and Parliament. Then down a bit and Westminster Abbey. A service was going on (loved the tones of the tomb-like interior, restrained and pale by comparison with florid St. Pat's in New York). Then walking back, entranced, to pass a lanky stone kinsman, Abe Lincoln—Buckingham Palace and Victoria's Monument. Standing there in the late afternoon looking at them I had conflicting impressions. Buckingham Palace looked like a fenced-in railroad station. I shuddered at the thought of living there, calling that "home." I was even more taken with the bronzed statue facing the Palace on the avenue side of Victoria's Memorial, a workman in apron and open-throated shirt, opposite his woman, with a sickle in her hand—the pair are so unlike the British and so like the dread workers' country across the way, even to the sickle in the woman's hand. I was drawn to staring long at them. Gazing at ample dumpling Victoria in stone, I thought of Kipling's *Widow of the Windsor* and again of Kipling when I saw the foreign office and a statue of Clive.

In Westminster, I was most strangely touched to see a tablet of dedication and tribute to General Howe—our Revolution enemy who died at 34 in New England. I passed the mounted guards at the Admiralty Building and was charmed with the homey sight of parents holding up bug-eyed tots to pet the horses' noses. What London gives her citizens in showmanship is worth the hide-bound datedness of her tradition. It is the people's magic, their flight of fancy—their decorative distraction from their ordinary lives. You felt and understood it when you heard the affairs of the royal family discussed as intimately by people on the streets as though they knew their majesties as well as their own families. The King and Queen are not imperial society above the people. They belong to the people, really, and are part of them. I adore the bobbies—they are so handsome and vested in righteousness somehow. You could go to one of them as to your own father for some guidance beyond a mere street direction, etc. They are lovable, chatty with a HUMAN. In fact, all this business about formality and standoffishness in the British is sheer fiction. Everyone speaks right up—they're wonderful and I love them.

I needn't flash back into too much detail on leaving Switzerland, but I must note that Doug telephoned me from Washington. I was afraid he'd placed the call to tell me about buying some scientific gadget but no. I'm not sure, but I think he just wanted to say hello. He didn't speak up much, and all the "I love you darlings" came excitedly and giddily out of me. Then I found myself saying, "Doug, do you love me as you did in Tihwa? I've got to know; it's terribly important." "Yes, I do" from Doug, but with no outpouring. I left the phone booth quite excited (Lausanne to Washington, after all) but just as uncertain about us. The divorce, coming home, etc., as I had been before. I told Doug I wanted to come home. "Well, why don't you?" he said. He said he hoped it would be before January 13th—at least he remembered that.

DECEMBER 23, 1947—BELFAST, IRELAND—Eva McGown, my beloved Alaskan second mother, has just checked off another notch in my lifetime experience. I asked her how she HAD taken all the things that life has given her (in unhappiness and bitter awful moments). She twitched a bit in her chair. "Well, darling," she said, "it's not what life gives—it's HOW YOU TAKE IT." Then she spoke sweetly about faith in God, etc. But as she meditated a bit, I found her saying the wonderful graces and blessings life gives at times are SUSTAINING AND COMPENSATION. I'VE HAD THEM TOO—many of them—so they will have to sustain me now.

Eva and I have just lost our Christmas, so specially planned. I came from London to Ireland to be with her. The boat ride is just an overnight trip, but I met the gayest Irish girl and young man. We sat up howling and shrieking—the boat was very nice, even attractively furnished. This morning we docked in a blue mist fog, but as I stepped on deck I saw a vision in green—coat, hat, everything—EVA. I greeted her swimming-eyed.

But the family—Eva's three sisters—all hard-bitten Irish—not shanty Irish but they've had a hard go of it, I guess, and the Irish way of speaking with a verbal back-of-me-hand t' you—I sat back amazed. It was hysterical. They all yapped at once, at the top of their lungs. The house is Eva's own—ancient as a museum—the mold and tomb-like chill rolling out at us—a wee coal fireplace barely giving off a flicker of heat. I heard nothing but rations and points so that I felt conscious about touching a bite. The head of the house is a stalking terror—a spinstery sergeant-major who at first amused me as a character to whom only an Abbey player could do justice—but when she and the three sisters turned on my Eva, saying they thought she must be mad the way she talks, etc., I became furiously resentful.

An alcoholic younger brother wandered in and the scene domestic was like a witches' banshee. It was a bit too much to take on top of being terribly cold and somewhat hollow for food. (The gas lights in the house—dear God! No central heating.) Tonight the tipsy but good-hearted brother had all the sisters to his apartment for a drop of cheer. Going home, a violent argument began about which bus to take. By the time we reached the house the witches were baring their fangs. Eva burst into tears. And I was distraught—super sensitive for HER sake and she mortified at this demonstration before me. "Come on, Peg," she gasped, red-eyed and trembling, "We leave and go to your place." Howls and fusses, with the elder sister having a word to me that extra food has been bought and no matter how they fight I've got to eat with them, etc. I was weeping for both Eva and myself—Christmas—and Doug. When we two walked down the foggy street together, gas lights sent up greenish-yellow glows in the mist. And the streets were wet and shiny. If only it weren't Christmas. I want to go back to London at once, but can't hurt Eva and am afraid I wouldn't get a boat, train, or anything until after Christmas Day. If I'd only stayed in Switzerland—if I'd only known—but maybe it was meant to be. My heart aches for Eva. Ireland is drab, dour and hideously ugly—at least Belfast is. I am too cold to write more tonight.

CHRISTMAS EVE, 1947—BELFAST, IRELAND

Life, life, life. This trip to Ireland has been the most jolting contribution to my kit bag of experience. Here's the picture.

Pegge's sketch of her bedroom in Belfast.

This whole junket has been so strange. I'm sure it was meant to be. Perhaps the Montgomerys, Eva's family, are a story someday. And Eva herself, very sustaining ramrod in days to come. We spent all day downtown, trailing around in the pouring rain which reminded me vaguely of Shanghai, Christmas Eve 1946. Belfast is the ugliest, squarest cut, clod-solid, old-old and damn proud of it city I've ever seen. The streets are cobblestone. Fortunately there was no Christmas trim in the stores or on the street so the gay holiday was pretty much in the background. I felt sorry for the people—points and coupons for everything and dear-to-the-skies what they had. And queuing up for everything from buses to being helped in the shops. We called on one of the newspaper editors and that was another insight—the old-oldness of everything, including the people. I talked with an editor who gave me a bit on the political side. In a fine rollin' brogue "an' you'll pardon me but it's my own opinion, that etc." All virtues to the North, which is industrial and PROTESTANT, and all hell to them in the South. "Now wot's happening," my characteristic informant edged about in his chair, "wot's doin' now is somewhat a delicate situation—an' you'll pardon me—all the fault of the Roman Catholics. They be sendin' their people up here now an' you know their religion—all have big families and in time, all the votes—Devil of a way o' getting at this good part of Ireland wot remains true to England. They've only got agriculture in the south an' we've the best manufacturing up here" etc. etc. etc.

Eva and I lunched at the town's best—the Carlton—sitting for hours talking about this human life and about Doug. Eva took a look at his picture. "Aye," she nodded. "He's a man that's got a head of his own and wants his wife to be HIS an' nothing else." But from bits and scraps of her own life going to Alaska, Eva drew the harvest of her experience to help me. (I listened rapt and touched—two bits for the story I didn't get down before. When Eva came over the trail to marry her unseen correspondent, admirer—she was met first by her Jewish-Irish friend who helped arrange the whole thing—Jessica Bloom—and another man, Jim Barrach. Eva was trembling, thinking at first he was her Arthur. Jessica, once back at the house—a horrid cabin with odors and babies' didies being washed—told Eva if she didn't want Arthur after the first look, she could have Barrach. Eva, fuming and frantic and frightened. Time passed. No Arthur. Finally at eight p.m. the doorbell rang and Arthur stepped in—immense in a black fur coat. He called her "little girl." Told her she stepped into the room like a stricken fawn, all wide, frightened eyes. Later they took a walk, and Eva learned Bloom had gone to Arthur with the news that

Barrach was starting out in a sled to meet Eva, but for a wee matter of $200 he would see that Arthur got there first or Barrach didn't go. "I'll see you in hell first," roars Arthur, and was so enraged he wasn't going to see Eva at all. Later thought her the innocent victim and got her.

That lunch and our conversation was enough compensation for coming to Belfast. I got the feeling that my fate is up to me. If I'm happy with Doug it will be because I made it so. Eva is certainly example for what she preaches. We returned home later and I had a cable from Doug which sent my love across the miles in sheer pity and sympathy. He must have called Mother and she told him I was going to Berlin, not coming stateside. "Please cable right away what change in plans." How he must have felt. I rushed an answer by direct wire: "Returning first possible ship—love you always."

Much as I have pitied myself for the way Belfast turned out, I think it must have been harder for Doug, feeling worried about my status and trying to keep up a holiday mood in front of the family. At least Belfast's grim, unadorned ugliness was no contrast in mood and holiday. Must stop—freezing by inches.

DECEMBER 27, 1947—BACK IN LONDON—I have just been through an extraordinary awakening. Coming to London on the train from Liverpool (as long and tiring a ride as the stretch from New York to Washington D.C.), I opened this journal (Doug's pen leaks, damn it) and began reading the story of Pegge Parker from June on—even the diary pages of the trip on the *Polk*. So much time has passed that the whole thing seemed impersonal. My reader reaction was quite detached from myself. And thus I summed up an abstract portrait of a P. Parker of concentrated and utter self-centered, self-intense, self-predatory girl. My sympathy for Doug mounted, I was so stricken with suddenly seeing myself as he must (or others less gallant) and I wanted TERRIBLY to telephone him—and I was

POSITIVE I wanted to go to Cook's office and book passage on the first ship to cross the Atlantic. I was so mortified with the self-portrait presented I was completely abject—staring out the window at England's rain-washed pastel country scene and thinking of my beloved Eva McGown. I do think that oddly hilarious, wretched trip was meant to be. I had a plain lesson in character just watching Eva. I saw her giving and GIVING and GIVING, even when her "cracked"—to quote them—sisters harped and shrilled at her in that frightful dressing-down, hell's kitchen Irish way. She cooked the Christmas turkey (working on it in a dark, dilapidated, tomb-cold kitchen three nights running), and Christmas morning her sisters had not the consideration to let her take off one hour for church. She grasped my hand and whispered, "Pegge, darling, you say prayers for us both. I can't go and on Christmas day." Oddly enough, there were moments when I felt providence had sent me to Eva because SHE needed me. (I went thinking it was the other way 'round.)

Calling back to Doug for a minute. He sent me flowers which arrived with a note "roses ordered but unobtainable." I loved them (pink carnations) anyway, and Eva pinned three on me to go to Mass. "Here, darling—one for Doug, one for me, and one for you." I've just cabled him: DEAREST CABLE DIVORCE NEWS IMMEDIATELY FLOWERS BEAUTIFUL BUT CHRISTMAS UNHAPPY WILL TELEPHONE MONDAY NIGHT LOVINGLY YOURS." I couldn't get to Cook's as I impulsively wished on arrival from Belfast. If I had, I'd have grabbed the VERY FIRST SHIP OUT. I want to go home to him, my darling, immediately. Will the fates decree otherwise?

To finish with Belfast—Christmas Day I ate breakfast alone, in my Irish boarding house and thumbed an old copy of the *Ladies' Home Journal* for company and marveled at myself sitting there—oddity of happenstance—Mass was more quieting to my unhappiness. Doug's flowers under my chin—the fine rolling Irish choir—the droll, Irish brogue'd priest saying a few words to one and all. When the choir softly began *Adeste Fidelis* and *Silent Night*, my heart ached for Doug beside me. My religious concept being in a distant state at the moment, my prayers were less ardent than my thoughts during Mass.

After dinner at Eva's vocal household, we two went for a walk and as we loitered along the wet streets, we half-planned to see each other in Paris if she can come over while I'm there. We two managed to whoop and howl with laughter talking about Alaska and the Belfast situation. The evening was more hilarious still—tea in the upstairs drawing room—a spinster friend of elder sister Jane came in and younger opera-singing sister Molly read her fortune in the leaves. Irish soothsaying: Gentleman expectations kept cropping up, and the lady (buxom and with a slight tendency toward lady-like intellect) told of a Piccadilly Johnny she had gone out of her way to repulse and insult as he pursued for her favor. Months later she was shocked to read in the papers that her Picadilly Johnny had married an English society girl—and that he was teddibly wealthy in his own right. My own fortune was told but unfortunately I was warned that my heart's interest will be DELAYED INDEFINITELY. Sometime earlier, Eva's younger brother alcoholic Dick (in a nice, brotherly, quiet way) and I had a long talk about love and marriage. He advised me to marry Doug and "LOVE THE HELL OUT OF HIM. Lots of LOVE. Very important to a man. Now do you follow me there, girl? Ya' know what I mean and I don't speak too plain?" He told me his love troubles too. His wife is spry, pretty and quick-witted. After their children were raised, the wife packs up and goes off to Glasgow to open her own business. Dick can't follow very well—he's not young enough to start a new job in the ministry, as they call government time served here in Belfast. Yet he doesn't want to come home every night to an empty house. As he talked, I could hear Doug reading Kipling: "For a man he must go with a woman, which women don't understand." As Eva said, briefly summing up poor Dick's status: "Poor dear—he's not old enough or young enough." He was unusually kind to me. Went to all kinds of trouble to get me a bottle of Irish whiskey which I'll take back to Daddy.

Eva and I spent my last day seeing the other side of Belfast. We got on a bus and I glimpsed almost two worlds of Ireland—lace curtain and shanty—with gas lights and cobblestones and square cloddish, dull unimaginative houses in a tight sunless row, shut-in like the Irish, prejudiced, old-old habit mentality, and a few others with lawns and gardens and gay Christmas trees trimmed with lights. I saw the Irish Parliament building, a figurehead of stone, for Ireland (I believe) is really controlled by England. Before we said good-bye, Eva opened up a wee bottle of Benedictine, poured it into my red wine goblet, and we drank sip for sip, toast for toast, to our beloved Alaska and all our loved ones until it was gone. The room was so cold we sat talking with our coats on. Eva took me to the ship (which was quite deserted) and in my cabin, we sipped Johnny Walker and she repeated the scene of my last evening in Fairbanks, Alaska. She re-read Arthur's letters to her and hers to him. His were very fine, mature and earnest. Eva's were more distant and less charming (surprisingly). The steward knocked and she had to dash. I saw her last waving from the dock, three pink carnations pinned to her fur stole. Doug's.

I'm staying at a middle-class boarding house Eva recommended, and as I unpacked the wee landlady, fluttery, mousy with a face like a faded flower, couldn't resist going over my clothes—fingering the materials lovingly, simply in awe of my Chinese silks. My heart went out to the English so long denied.

DECEMBER 30, 1947—LONDON—I love the people of this blessed isle. I went to have my glasses fixed today (frame snapped) and the man switched lenses from my sunglasses—took about 20 minutes in all. He refused a cent of payment. Wished me bon voyage when I told him I was sailing Thursday. I looked at him gratefully. "I'll have a lot to tell them back home about the people of Britain. You have all been wonderful to me." "Americans have been wonderful to us," he said warmly. Everywhere I went—alone—the little clerks, underground attendants, etc., were kind and the two who own this very middle-class boarding house have been kindness personified. I got my final confirmation on a ship home—the Cunard's *Mauretania*. I'll arrive about January 7–8.

I spent the p.m. in two art galleries—most thrilling seeing the Vincent Van Gogh originals. I stood gazing amid a jostling throng, marveling and raving inwardly. This rather uplifted me from the chill outsider-ness I felt when I went calling on two friends of Doug's (he is with the State Department). The smuggest charm in a lavish apartment—not once was a human word extended or a thought that I was entirely alone on New Year's. This stretch of being isolated in London has taught me a deepening lesson in humanity. The people who have been human to me have been the darling bobbies—clerks—shop ladies—telephone operators, sight unseen. God love the humble, anonymous British. Called Eva in Belfast—seeing her was worth all that Ireland had to offer. Terribly glad to be going home, though I don't feel festive about it. Just tired, tired, tired.

1948

JANUARY 1, 1948—ABOARD MAURETANIA—FIRST NIGHT OUT—New Year's Eve in London was an unexpectedly charming and HUMAN event. John Lloyd, bureau chief of AP, a 50-ish, blue-eyed, white-haired but youthfully robust man in well-tailored gray, gave me another insight into the professional life. I had gone to see him for advice on a Russian language AP post in Europe. My entrée of being from AP in Shanghai received the usual, brotherhood cordiality. But when I mentioned my speaking Russian, the blue editorial eyes blinked and his whole attitude changed. He advised me to check the New York office, etc. As I rose to leave, he consulted his desk calendar. "Well," he said, nicely (for he is truly a very, very nice person), "Well, I would like to take you to dinner before you leave. How about—" he glanced at the page in his book that was completely blank. "How about Wednesday night?" I knew, but he did not, that Wednesday night was New Year's Eve. And the one night I shudderingly dreaded (after my frightful Christmas). Then it came home to me that our domestic-less job excludes us from any ties with holidays that bind kinfolk stay-homes, close, dear and gay.

And so here I was in an elegantly posh London restaurant (which, they say, was a favorite of the Duke of Windsor), seated amid Lady London in bare-shouldered evening gowns and MINK and Lord London a bit paunchy in white tie and dull red carnation attire. With this important and homeless, attaché-less, and charming man. Another couple was with us but left early. John and I sat talking, admitting to each other the oddity of the situation. That we could watch the news circus of events go by and give up our own lives, in a sense, to observe and report on others. Our understanding was so mutual that comment was almost superfluous.

We spoke then of Moscow, where he had been stationed years ago, and of King Michael of Romania abdicating. Midnight came and went. Everyone around us was very gay and shrill (though not rowdy or yelping as Americans would have been), but we two talked interestedly on and on. Then in the pouring rain we ran from corner to corner for a taxi and home. He patted my arm and kissed me, more as a gesture and perfectly human for the occasion—and was gone. I came home to my English boarding house to find the dickie bird landlady and her mainstay, doughty brother in their basement kitchen doing odd chores. I sat down and had a folksy chat with them and the bird (reminds me of a wee sparrow, the landlady) brought me hot tea as I faced all the packing.

I was quite happy inside and so GRATEFUL and thoughtful about John Lloyd—he made my last day in lonely London the only gay one. He got me a ticket for a matinee too. I saw flippant Noel Coward's "Present Laughter" and was amused at the tea served at the end of the second act to the audience still in their seats—trays went across rows of laps like a church collection. The music was like a quaff of brandy. I've heard so little that gay twinkly Coward airs were tingling to my ears.

The day was marked with another memorable event, reminiscent of Tihwa. Shortly after I returned from Kuldja I sent out a scoop flash on Barbara Stephens, *TIME* stringer and gal adventurer in

China's hinterlands and blond, laughing Brian Sorenson, son of a British Labourite MP, being killed in a plane crash near Lanchow. I had sent the family a note saying I was in town, and as my last day in London was so "busy," the only place Brian's father could think of for us to meet was the AP office. The insight this exposure gave me into British family life and the human, human feeling behind the reserve was deeply touching. Brian's mother got up from a sickbed to come, and his older brother stood by her saying nothing but holding his mother's arm. Brian's plain but incredibly sweet and rosebud-fresh young sister who ADORED Brian. As we stood outside on the chill, foggy street, trying to get me a taxi, Mrs. Sorensen, whose blue eyes were tear-drenched, kept clinging her arms around me and kissed me, wished me bon voyage and stood waving until I was out of sight. Oh dear God, bless these people, these English!

When I got on the underground en route to Fleet Street, I asked a porter (or agent) the quickest way to exit. A young girl standing near said, "I'll show you. I'm going there myself." We left the subway together talking as two Americans. I told her how warmly I admire the people I've met, and she glowed when we parted at a crossing. Miss Britain clasped my hand—"Good trip home," she smiled, "and all the best for the new year."

Doing a bit of shopping earlier in a very posh shop with a large, fancy grocery department (so fancy all the clerks wear cutaways and red carnations), I had a soul-baring conversation with a tall, twinkling-eyed chap who'd been in the navy during the war. When he heard my American accent he came scampering to help me. "I was in your country during the war," he enthused, and went on to tell me about North Carolina and a young lady he met there with whom he still corresponds (she even sends him food parcels). I enjoyed all this and commented on the nonexistent reserve (to my experience anyway) of the English. "Well, no," he admitted, "We may be and usually ARE bursting to talk to people on trains. But we've got to be INTRODUCED FIRST. Yes, we're sticklers for that. I must say, of course—" he coughed a bit embarrassedly, "It's perfectly proper for me to talk like this to you in the shop and I can't tell you how terribly I've enjoyed the little chat." He, too, sent me off with best wishes, then stepped into Dunhill's.

Next day—ink in the pen—my talkative grocery clerk added, in a flow of political views, "This island just pulled through by the greatest miracle, I tell you, but believe me, we're still quivering. We're just now beginning to get over the worst." I had a similar chat with a thin-faced young chap in swank Alfred Dunhill's. He showed me pipes for about $12 U.S., and my comment on the price led to a political discussion. He, too, was an ex-serviceman. He minded the food situation, not so much for himself but because he feels the working public can't do the doubly hard job allotted them on the food they're getting. He said a word about Russia—"Obvious they don't want agreements and conferences"—but he ended with a sporting shrug of his shoulders as he carefully put the expensive briar pipes away. "We'll pull through. We'll come out all right. It'll take time, but we'll make out in the end." That personified or typified all Britain's outlook: We'll make out all right.

Glamour luxury ships will be my undoing. By mistake I went into the dining room half an hour ahead of time (no gongs on this ship, and I thought 7 p.m. late enough to appear). The proper mien'd waiters and I communed silently in the Grand Central dining room. My waiter, a tall blond chap, solicitously inquired if I wanted olives or something while I waited. One word over the olives led to another (me being me) until he was forgetting the shackle of reserve and was telling me with gusto of being with the RAF in Singapore, etc., and I was telling him about China when suddenly he flushed and stiffened. "I beg your pardon, but I'm getting frowns from the head steward for talking to you like this. I guess we were both thinking we were on one of your freighters for a moment." Then very stiffly he served me caviar from a bowl set in a silver bowl with shaved ice. (The delectable Russian dish sent a pang of nostalgia through me—

Sinkiang—Valentina—and Doug, with whom I'm feeling very much in love, longingly at this point). The other guests filtered in, and a little midwestern Dr. Wang, provincial despite his tux for dinner, sat down, dug into his caviar and proceeded to discuss Russia and the Soviets. How stupid they are—how overrated—how we should declare war on her—blow Moscow off the map. Then what'd they have left, etc. This was too much for me, especially when another American across the linen and yellow chrysanthemums commented, "Yes, the Russians think they're so superior." I don't know if my RAF waiter caught that. If he had, he might have spilled the roast beef for we had been commenting on the typical luxury liner passengers, "American, you know, forgive me, you're an American of course." He apologized. But I was so appalled by the American's ignorance. He spends twice as much time and money on education as the average Englishman but he can't discuss anything but his business. He is utterly foolish and embarrassingly ignorant about world affairs, politics, and so on. I remember when our troop ship was in New York I sent out some laundry and it came back wrapped in paper imprinted with the words "It's wonderful to be an American" all over. I was so amazed I couldn't even laugh. Really, now. "It's wonderful to be an American" wrapped around an Englishman's underpants! I whooped, then remembered the decorum of a first-class passenger, Cunard White Star Line, and reached for an olive. The sailing has been rougher than anything on the *Polk,* and to keep my mind off it I'm reading *Kim*—the Kipling classic, of course, and great favorite of Doug's. I love it for R.K.'s deeply human understanding of the Indians—not in the slightest inferior to the overlord Englishman but marvelously unique, physically and imaginative, vividly bizarre and wonderful philosophical:

Oh ye who tread the narrow way
By thrumphet-flare to Judgment day
Be gentle when the heathen pray
To Buddha at Hamakura!

United States
1948–1951

1948

FEBRUARY 9, 1948—NEW YORK CITY—How much time and tide has issued past until I come to this notation on a twice memorable day. First, Eva McGown arrived on the *Queen Elizabeth* from England and I was the only one to meet her. And what a time we had getting her a hotel room. She's at large in the city now and I'm catching a breath at my humble 3rd class domicile, Hotel Webster. Next time marker is one month to the day I have been in the USA, and what reactions and jagged impressions my native land imparts.

To flash back on scenes briefly, I arrived on a FREEZING day—missed the Statue of Liberty for last-minute packing. Standing on deck to catch a glimpse of Doug on the dock, I heard every language under the sun being spoken BUT English—perfect gales of Russian, French, Yiddish, Italian, etc. Doug met me on the dock. I was beside myself, but he barely kissed me for looking over my shoulder to see about the luggage. I kept asking him, "Aren't you glad to see me? Do you really love me—really love me?" "Yes, yes," he replied without looking at me. "Now count your luggage, and when it's all assembled, get a customs inspector, etc."

Mother was waiting behind the passengers' fences. She greeted me with "Why, you look MARVELOUS, absolutely marvelous." Quick introductions to Doug and confusion over the baggage. Doug passing out tips and me protesting, talking to Mother—worried over Doug's odd manner. Taxi ride with me between them. Mother: "Weren't you THRILLED coming in? Why DIDN'T you go to Paris?" etc. etc. Doug: "I'll have to rush. I got tickets for us to go to Boston. Train leaves in half an hour." Mother: "But I have a Grand Hotel room for us here," etc., "and I've come all the way from Florida to meet you." (Visiting Patty and baby and Lynn.) Doug adamant, staring out the window—didn't know when he'd see me—had to go to Washington soon. I stared straight ahead—the lights, the orange NEON of New York, not seen in four years, flashed by. "If you had only wired or telephoned," Mother put in, pointedly, to Doug. "Yes, it's all my fault," Doug admitted with an edge. So THIS was what I had come to. I was beside myself. I was sorry for Mother but I knew I'd have to find out our status from Doug. He had brought me home. The upshot was I went off to Boston with him, leaving Mother alone in the Grand Hotel room with the bottle of sherry and all the gifts I'd brought back—her little watch from Switzerland just left on the bureau.

Doug and I talked four hours straight on the train going up. Boston is such a long way from New York. His brothers Stewart and Malcolm met us—fat-cheeked, bouncy and grand young boys. At about 2 a.m. I arrived at Doug's home looking my worst, just numb with cold and completely worn out. Mother and Dad Mackiernan tumbled out of bed in bathrobes to greet me. I loved them both and felt at once they had accepted me as though I'd always belonged to them. I loved the room I was given—the library—so surrounded with BOOKS that I almost had to burrow my way in and out.

The next morning Doug took me for a walk in the snow. He held me in his arms and I knew he was glad I'd come home—and he knew I'd come home to him.

Next day we went into town and I telephoned my dear friend, Dorothy Ann Simpson Wilson. When she answered the telephone and I heard the sound of her voice, I could have wept. She saved me, I think, from nervous collapse. I would go in to see her and we would talk and TALK. We went over marriage from every angle. She met Doug and was utterly charming to him. Had us to dinner—memorable evening—her John quizzing Doug about Sinkiang and Doug, sure of his authority and audience, simply outdoing himself. I was proud of him and loved D.A.'s John for so genuinely and sincerely setting Doug in his element.

Doug and I observed our anniversary—the 13th—having dinner at the Parker House. As the days passed, and the nights when Doug was close to me, I began to relax and feel I'd come home, knowing my own mind and heart: to marry him. I was never more in love with him, not even in Tihwa. He was never sweeter. I had long talks with his mother about Doug's boyhood in Mexico, etc., and then talks about his first marriage and the daughter. Her picture, quite adorable, adorned the bookcase in my room. Talks with D.A. about foster daughter sustained me in quailing moments about Doug's child. D.A. was a handmaid of heaven when I needed her most.

I left Doug and the bulk of my luggage in Boston and came on to New York to see Lois Fegan and attend to business. Lois is so ultra glamorous I hardly knew her—sweeping long skirts—cartwheel hats—fur coats—chunky earrings, etc. LOIS FEGAN!! The change in her outlook and grab-as-can-grab in this world left me feeling very odd. She was a little loud with my feeling for "poor Europe"—the starving, the cold and homeless. She was covering fashion shows—and each day's hemlines, braid trim and hat styles she absorbed in dear earnest. She never ONCE asked me to tell her anything about the world I'd seen. She was concerned for Doug—that was all. I guess we live in different worlds.

Doug sent me flowers twice and I loved him. He telephoned too and stopped to see me on his way to Washington, D.C. I never loved him more. He keeps begging me to assure him I'll never leave him, that I'll not go back to Europe and leave him (as I once threatened in a burst of tears).

Then I went to Harrisburg—stayed at the Penn Harris, and everyone was simply grand to me. Had an exaggerated, immaculate but impressive write-up in the paper—picture and all. Then Doug (who has been sending me flowers two and three times a week) called and said he'd come for the weekend, which pleased Mother not at all. I went to Boston. This was HER visit with me. What could I do? Doug was very distant and self-conscious, I think, with mother and Daddy—which Mother quickly picked up. I stayed three extra days in Harrisburg to pacify Mother. We spent one very pleasant day visiting my dear Shanghai friends Lt. Ed and Lou Torian and their wee baby—both very nice to Mother, which I did appreciate.

Back in New York saw Peggy Jenkins and George Keibel, neither of whom has changed. Began a slow process of job hunting, as Doug and I won't be wed until April—or so—it now looks.

Al Morano came into town and we had lunch. He was grand. Allan Witwer *[Editor's Note: Pegge's cousin]* also appeared, very nice and very charming. Oh yes, I took Doug to see Monsignor Ehardt who turned Doug over to the legal high rankers of St. Pat's Cathedral. Very upsetting day. The Monsignor chillingly informed me Doug's first marriage was legal and binding in the eyes of the church and our only hope was Doug's conversion to Catholicism, and after that was completed a petition could be made to the Pope and "perhaps in about two years we might have a special dispensation." TWO YEARS. So Doug and I will have to have a civil ceremony. Ahmee sustained me there. She and Eddie to this day were never married by a priest. She was the only one I told about the interview with the legal authority. Doug was up for the weekend. His plans with the State Department are to set up an international weather station in Boston, with two of his brothers in charge, and to take me with him back to Afghanistan into Sinkiang where Doug will hold the rank of Vice Consul.

MARCH 7, 1948—WASHINGTON, D.C.—I have just come from Union Station where I kissed my darling goodbye for six weeks. He has gone to Las Vegas, Nevada, to get his divorce. Oddly enough the train was called the *Liberty Express*, and so I remember the beginning of another ordeal—a separation—Doug—two suitcases, one laden with a set of Russian-language records and books on Turkestan. He was very, very dear and "close" to me before he left. I think he was wary of the trip in advance—a vague awareness of loneliness in a parched, arid sort of place—"Las Vegas." A curious catch in his mind: Will there be any hitch—will a strange woman who was his wife cause any delaying counter-action? He was smoking a cigar and kept saying over and over "I wish you were coming with me, baby girl." I love him. I love Doug, my darling, now more than the lyric—giddy—sun-wind-and-mountain days of Tihwa. He was wonderful and really makes up for all the other days following my return. After weeks of seeing people, *Reader's Digest, Ladies' Home Journal* (sub-deb page offer—maybe) the hopes rising—looking my best, speaking my piece brightly, and NOTHIN—dragging home to a costly (at my bank figure) and dreary hotel room at the downtrodden Hotel Webster. Doug came up from Washington, revived my spirit—that and the boxes of flowers that arrived—roses, carnations and daily phone calls. We saw one wonderful play together: K. Cornell in Shakespeare's *Anthony and Cleopatra*.

Finally, I decided my expenses in New York didn't justify staying there. I moved to Washington and right back to my old headquarters: Scott's Hotel. Before coming down, Dassie Wilson (with Daisy Mae tucked under her waist, et al.!) came through New York on her way to Washington to see her John. I told her the incident of Doug's rejection by the church and what it will mean to us. She was unduly concerned on the religious angle—as I am myself at times. She urged me to contact Monsignor Ehardt again. I am getting more and more estranged from the church and feel too remotely apart to even pray with any conviction. One thing is certain: Doug and I will be married as soon as he gets back, decree in hand, church or no church.

MARCH 19, 1948—WASHINGTON, D.C.—How much I love, love, love my Darling Doug. Here I sat on a dreary rainy day when a dozen divine red roses arrived with a card: "All my love, Doug." I sat on my bed looking at the red vivid flowers through their garlanding wrapping. I must go out to him, I thought with resolve, I must go out to him, some way. This first stretch of the separation is a frightful strain. His letters are moving outpourings of almost ungrammatical, half-spelled little boy lover yearning. I never could have really LOVED him before if this that I feel now is the supreme emotion. I love Doug to the point of eyes-misted for sending the flowers I know he can't afford at the moment. If years from now there are no flowers, never mind. I've had it now.

Now to catch up on events. I've got a job with the State Department, but the security check takes nearly a month, I was warned, and all this to be a little secretary at about $40+ a week. Well, no matter what, I have my beloved love and the remembered triumph of my weekend at WEEMS, Virginia, with my SUPREME MENTOR, George Wallace, and his Countess, lovely, exquisite SONIA. I went down to Fredericksburg, Virginia, where they met me. With them was an old friend from Alaska, Mrs. Carrie Willis, who lives in historic, homey, American Fredericksburg. I'll tell you about her first, as my visit with her concerns my heart. I discussed the marriage difficulties and what Doug and I planned for as soon as he gets back. Mrs. Willis' brown eye glowed. She was more my mother than my own. "Darlin' child, may I offer you my own house. It's so old and historic. See the bullet scars from the War Between the States. Right here in this parlor you and Doug can stand up and take your brief vows. We'll have the room decorated with fresh flowers," etc. It sounded so perfect, and she is such a dear. I wrote Doug all about it. If all goes well and he has the final uncontested decree in six weeks, I'm sure we'll rush to Fredericksburg and be wed there. I have invited the Wallaces and will tell Mother, if she wants to come down not being disapproving of a civil ceremony. I interviewed a Presbyterian minister—old friend of Mrs. Willis—but how strange I felt discussing Doug and my wedding with a PRESBYTERIAN PREACHER. We may delete him later. We shall see. I'm just marking time until my darling dear comes back to me, or I can get to him.

Now to the visit to Weems, which lifted me above the earth. It was the greatest treat to come home to, excluding Doug. We drove to their rural retreat, past America's most hallowed historic ground: Washington's birthplace, where Jefferson wrote the Declaration of Independence, where Madison had his first law office.

As we drove along, Sonia filled in details. This lovely person born on the border of Yugoslavia and Trieste, telling me with ardor, imagination and pride American Revolutionary history, in her soft European accent. I was captivated beyond words. I also observed how she watched over her George, how she worries when he is restless or moody. She is the farmer of the low rambling domain perched on a riverbank. As I wrote Doug, "I will strive my utmost to be a Sonia Wallace to you, and more as a wife I could not be." I stayed four days, and the conversation was MANNA. I shall try to jot down certain remarks of George's. "Every time you read the word Communism, substitute the word REVOLT, reflecting the conditions that led to this last desperate measure, and you have a truer perspective. Show me the man who is surprised at world events and I will show you a naïve fool—nothing happens without cause and effect. One follows the other. America is in serious trouble right now, very serious. People say blithely, let's go to war with Russia. Assume we do and by a miraculous assumption, let's say we win. Then what have we accomplished? If Italy goes communist on the April 18th elections, we're in for it. One of the greatest organized forces in the world for war today is the Catholic Church."

He advised me not to attempt to discuss the discomforting things I'd seen in China, my impressions of the Russians, etc., because you can put nothing across, you make enemies and stir up resentment. Sonia and I argued this point, both of us feeling what is true should be spoken. His attitude toward the Soviets was very realistic: "They've lived a dog's life under the Tsars. When they rebelled and sent the armies down on them, as well as the rest of Europe, and when Hitler first threatened Czechoslovakia at the outset of World War II only Russia stood up and said it would stand by its treaty pledge. England sold out 'Peace in our Time' and the USA was loathe to get involved."

We took a glorious boat ride in the Wallaces' cruiser. My heart felt a pang of greediness. I was having all this to myself without Doug. The Wallaces were delighted with the prospect of Doug. Spoke of him continually as though he were right there with us. They invited us to come down together, man-and-wife, before we return to China. Both were in sympathy with our defiance of the church and Pope. (Geo. W is outspokenly godless, I'm afraid.)

When I got back to D.C. I had a hasty note from George from which I quote: He speaks of the false premise of the Marshall Plan—the theory being that our millions of aid will "rebuild" Europe's economy. This implies if we can put it back on a pre-war basis all will be well. Nothing would be more untrue—the truth is the good old days of "free enterprise," 1929-33, were the bad old days. He brings out a good point here: the pre-war period in Europe, if restored, will not bring peace nor quiet, nor acceptance, the reason being that the word "communism" holds out a road to travel. After the explosions, Communism at least holds out "HOPE," which they never had before. This is the point Doug has often made. We have no standard method of passing on American democracy or foreign policy. We hardly know what that is ourselves. When the Wallaces drove me back and left me with Mrs. Willis, I felt alone again, with no one to talk over language except—via letters—to my darling Doug.

APRIL 6, 1948—WASHINGTON D.C.—I just talked to Doug a few minutes ago. He called from Las Vegas to tell me the news and that he loved me (and how I love him. Oh, how much I do—more than ever, ever before). We are still not positive if we can be married immediately after his return. Darrell *[Editor's Note: Doug's first wife]* must first return the divorce papers, stating her consent. How we pray she will. Otherwise a 30-day wait. But Doug will be home in about two weeks. And oh, but we count every day. I will be glad to have him home for another reason. I've been continuously ill for the past month and a half, violently upchucking, etc. I must see a doctor, but the expense and being alone has held me off. But if all goes well Doug and I will be married in Fredericksburg on April 26th or as soon afterward as possible. The plan for the civil ceremony at Mrs. Willis' home still goes. Do hope George and Sonia Wallace can make it, too, and that I'm not upchucking sick from the trip down.

Now to my professional life. I went to New York last week to interview Clare Boothe Luce on YOUTH TODAY—an article I do hope the *Ladies' Home Journal* will take. Lady Clare looked exquisite, her hair now champagne-colored with the gray showing through. She was so cordial and responsive to my questions, if in sharp disagreement with most of them. Henry Luce came in as I was finishing up. Very charming when Lady Clare told him I was just back from China, spoke Russian, etc.

Oh yes, I told Mrs. Luce about making up the women in Kuldja and how lipstick and cold cream had a night of triumph over Joe Stalin looking down his nose and mustache at us from the wall. "You write that up for *Reader's Digest*, send it to Paul Palmer. Tell him I told you to," she said. Well, today in the mail comes the assignment direct from Palmer himself, telling me he'd had lunch with Lady Luce and she told him my story. Bless her. So I've got a big chicken in my pot.

Also, while in New York, the pennies are low. I got the basics for my trousseau and my wedding dress—a simple and blessedly inexpensive pink pure silk print with no trim but a soft flounce around the throat. I also came away with loot from the wholesale millinery district—five hats. But they must do me for a goodly stretch. And quickly I might note Vada Ward, my unexpectedly good friend, dropped down from New York and hauled me off to the Women's Press Club's annual banquet—formal affair—long gowns et al. Saw, at close range, President Truman for the first time. Must say that for all his limitations and blunders, when you're in the same room with him, he has a compelling, human appeal. But when he said a few extemporaneous words and let go "Everybody must do THEIR part," my heart sank. His daughter, Margaret, is quite attractive and sweet seen in person, but poor Bess Truman is impossible, poor soul.

Oh yes, might note too that the answer I got from Monsignor Ehardt after telling him I was going to marry Doug with a civil ceremony—was contemptuous—he had overrated my intelligence, quoth he, much less my faith.

MAY 2, 1948—A memorable walk up Massachusetts Avenue this afternoon must be recorded for the love story annals. First, Doug could not return on schedule because his former wife did not sign the papers agreeing to the divorce. So we face the 30-day extended wait in hopes the papers will come back before another month. This way my darling's return is so indefinite it's almost twice as nerve-straining. Also, the delay had to be explained to everyone immediately concerned. Most difficult of all, to Mother. I decided the personal discussion was best. Then, too, Mother knew nothing of the Fredericksburg plan. She came down Friday afternoon, stayed at Scott's. The anticipated discussion did not go as smoothly as I had hoped.

Mother stood more in dread of Daddy's fury at a civil ceremony than in hopes of attending our little ceremony. Tension mounted. I felt she was letting me down in being so preoccupied with Daddy's displeasure that she couldn't see the big issue of my wedding day. She was so upset she went back over her initial objections to my marrying a divorced man, etc. I was drastically hurt, let down—almost on the brink of blaming Doug for causing this added unhappiness. I've been through a lot and have come a long way to marry him and here we are separated and with no wedding date in sight. Mother and I finally came to un-reconciled point.

Into this clouded, delicate atmosphere came a lovely, white-haired angel with a Southern accent—Mrs. Carrie Willis, up from Fredericksburg for a day's visit. The subject of the wedding was scrupulously avoided until after luncheon when we went for a walk on Massachusetts Avenue. When we got back to Scott's, drenched by a sudden shower, I was made to see that it would be harder for Mother to sit in Harrisburg with the secret of the day locked inside than to walk out on Daddy and come down to Fredericksburg. Mother had a strong suggestion that SOMEHOW she must get to her daughter's side on the big day. I felt so relieved—enough to try on my wedding dress for Mother after Mrs. Willis had gone home. Then I rushed her to her bus—and really felt twice as close to her. The visit was a success. Now I just feel I need reassurance from Doug. The battle of obstacles mounts and must be outweighed by HIM alone as he stands before me. Meanwhile my investigation check has finally ended and tomorrow I begin a humble job in the Russian section of the State Department. So glad for the incoming ready, but little, cash. Hoping to hear soon from *Reader's Digest* about the story on Kuldja I sent them a week ago. Ann Cottrell is back from China and called a week ago. Wish I were free to tell her about marrying Doug, but don't want to until our plans are more definite.

Oh, yes, just completed a temporary job for the State Department—an International Tin and Rubber Conference. Memorable because of a reception for the delegates at the Carlton Hotel. As I circulated among delegates from various parts of Asia, I was introduced to the man who "owns half of Malaysia"—Sir John Hay—white-haired rubber plantation king. He was extremely interesting and interested in knowing I had been recently in Malaysia. As we said goodbye he presented me with his business and personal cards, urging me to let him know if I were ever to return to Malaysia or London. He also invited me to dinner, but Mother's visit curtailed that. Also for the record, received a joyous telegram dated April 30, 1948, from John Wilson saying my darling Dassie had given birth to a daughter Anne, "weighing 9 lbs. 4 oz., length 22 inches." So happy for all of them—but for myself I would be so disappointed in not having a son.

MAY 9, 1948—I just distinguished myself for a rash act of uncontrolled emotion. Doug sent me the news that proceedings will now be delayed until May 30. This blow—meaning he won't be home until June, coming on top of last weekend and emotional upsets—was too much. I wept myself to exhaustion. On top of this came an ecstatic letter from D. A. Wilson describing the birth experience of wee Anne's issue into the world. It was a divinely sweet and inspiring letter. I burst into fits of weeping again as I thought of Doug and I having a child and how terribly unlike the Wilson experience it would be. I've given up wedding plans completely and it were not for thoughts of the child, I would give up Doug and RUN like mad away, away. I began to feel there must be some purpose—some hand of providence in this—the unbroken series of obstacles—walls between us and our marriage. WHY? A certain amount could be circumstantial, but all we've had.

As per pre-arranged time, Doug called from Las Vegas at 10 p.m. The call, usually on the dot of the hour, was 15 minutes late. My nerves were taut, drawn to the last possible reserve of strength. When the phone finally rang and Doug sounded very casual and said he had no news, I broke down. I was almost speechless. My reaction probably came as a surprise to Doug. I told him not to call me on the 13th. I wanted to forget what that day meant. "Now, listen—no—you're wrong," he began. Then I gasped out— If I could round up money for the fare one way (to fly, I was thinking), would he muster the return? He readily volunteered to pay both fares, implying as we spoke he'd either come back himself or I could go out there. Again the emotion drained me—I wanted to explain why I was so engulfed, but unable to be coherent, I just hung up. He didn't call back, and now I'm afraid he'll come home without the divorce. I don't want him to do that, but feeling as I do now I almost don't care. The dread ordeal of our future—all the trials we have already been through, still without accomplishing our end, make me wish I had left Doug in Tihwa and gone about my life. I don't believe any solid LIFETIME foundation—a marriage to the death—can be built on this. Life is a profound experience. Unless something happens to alter my mental state, I will be glad our wedding—eventually—will be just a civil one, unsanctified and easily obliterated, or with a minimum of effort. NOTE FOR THE RECORD: As a last ditch reserve I have in the National City Bank of New York, as of April 5, 1948, $793.04 which I want to leave intact and forget about for the time being.

MAY 10, 1948—The tears on the phone last night got action, all right. At 2 a.m. this morning a telegram: DARLING LEAVING HERE FIRST AVAILABLE AIR OR RAIL. DON'T GIVE UP (MY TEARS) LOVE. That was exciting enough, but the phone on my desk rang about 2 p.m. Doug!!! I nearly popped, and not a whit of privacy. Just said he was definitely leaving today and that he loved me very, very much. He didn't get a chance to say that last night. Little tingles surged through me. I loved him with all my heart for saying that.

About an hour ago, another telegram. He's coming in on United Airlines—due at noon tomorrow. I'm just quaking with anticipation after so long—after being without him and just taking the dreary toll day after day—to have him home tomorrow is too much. I will go to the airport looking, I hope, my most scrumptious. I feel in my bones that I can never let him leave me again. If he must go back, I will have to go with him—somehow we must not be separated. Oh, how I long to just hold him in my arms.

JUNE 9, 1948—I have been reading a most penetrating, conducive book, one which has driven me to taking out this fragmentary catch-all of Parker antics and putting down a word, I thought. The book is Somerset Maugham's *On a Chinese Screen,* a Maugham catch-all of people, impressions, feelings which marked his travels in China. He describes fewer rice paddies than PEOPLE—and in the people it is their mental personality and behavior he discusses with such acumen and suave portrait words. I think of a true thing George Wallace told me once—the greatest travels and adventures are exploring human mentality and conduct. This diary of mine seems a trashy waste. How sketchily have I recounted scenes, incidents, people. Henceforth may I mature and use the pen for loftier purposes and have done with starring P. Parker against exotic scene and circumstance.

A very great and rather sad thing has happened to me since last I wrote. I do not feel I can emote the astounding news here and now. Only Doug shares my secret, and I love him almost helplessly, depending on him. He flew back from the West. We had a happy, consoling reunion. I love him deeply and completely. Then he returned to Nevada for what we thought was the final hearing on the divorce. All plans were made. Rings bought, We were sure we were at least free to have each other—NO—the decree was contested at the zero hour. Doug was away a week, then again flew back to Washington. Now we have no plans and no idea WHEN we can be married. I have at least been driven to my knees in the most imploring prayers of my life. For I feel now only God can help me. But the hell—torture—the waiting is almost unendurable.

Might record briefly that Doug and I attended a dinner party last night and met Owen and Eleanor Lattimore, well-known travelers— dull but accurate and intelligent writers on China. They had driven in from Baltimore especially to meet Doug, and everything was very interesting. But Lattimore surprised me—a wisp of a man in a business suit lacking even the traveler's vitality in his speech, which was conspicuously BRITISH for an American. He referred occasionally to the TIB-etans and spoke of SIN KEE ANG when our fateful province is Sin Jong. It is perhaps presumption to judge him on an evening's parlor chatter. But I just felt he was like a schoolmaster of geography and his travels had been physical, mental and professional.

JULY 4, 1948—WASHINGTON, D.C.—It is incredible to look back on one year's entry and contemplate the harried plot of my life and Doug's since then. What I didn't record in this journal last July 5 was that Doug kissed me for the first time. I was so distant and frightened that night after my Russian Consul General interview I went clandestinely to visit Doug at the British Consulate. Doug was friendly, willingly helpful, amused that the incident lightened up the monotony. About midnight we went out to the kitchen for some coffee. The electricity had gone off—Doug took a flashlight; I picked up a can of powdered coffee. As we ventured into the darkened kitchen, Doug grabbed my arm—"Watch it—there's a step here," We passed through the narrow doorway together. The nearness and the darkness touched us. Suddenly Doug seized me passionately in his arms. He did not love me then—he had no intention of doing it and probably never would have again. But in my state of mind I clung to him, seeking shelter, protection, a confidant. I felt only relief that he had broken the aloof reserve between us. This was the first kiss. Womanlike, I remember the incident and the date photographically.

So much has happened since then—and two of the biggest events are yet to happen before the year is out. One in August when we think the divorce will be granted, and one in October. During the worst of our mental trials in trying to clear the way for our marriage, I had a remarkable letter from George Wallace, my sage, my mentor and standby. He wrote to describe what he called the "heat treatment." Until one had undergone that—"some searing, crushing, beating down"—the person is not ready for battle or does not know life. Character, or one's human existence, must be "tempered in heat, white-hot" at some point along the way, and the great test comes in HOW YOU TAKE IT, HOW YOU COME THROUGH. I'm having this now for the first time in my human span, and it has been an ordeal—one not finished yet. Through it all, Doug, my dearest darling, has sustained me—always—not once has he humanly had enough, let me down. He has been dearer to me than ever, and I love him with such dependence, such gratitude, I can only hope that my deliverance in October will bring Doug the reward of happiness from me he so justly deserves.

Wallace's letter continued, "Don't forget—you're playing for the biggest of stakes—real self-expression in the world—and when you play for big stakes you have to put up a big entrance fee. If you want to play penny ante, you'll never win the Calcutta sweepstakes." How well I know, but the heat treatment has had its moments of serenity—of mountaintops. Last weekend Doug and I went to Norfolk on the Potomac riverboat. I could not sleep because it was so hot in the cabin, so I went out on deck. The river was wide and soft and liquid black. Overhead the moon was gold as a lantern, lone and friendly—companionably there overhead. I leaned back in my chair, the wind blew the full skirt of my housecoat about my legs, and my hair slipped back from my face. I felt supremely unafraid of what might come in the next few months. Then this 4th of July weekend,

Mrs. Ann Wheeler, whom I met through Doug and through whom I got my job—turned her house in Bethesda over to me, to my peaceful delight. I cooked all our meals for Doug and me, and we ate by candlelight on a screened porch overlooking a garden of tall trees. It was heavenly. Doug bought me a book I've long wanted (*Rickshaw Boy*, translated by Robert WARD, once Consul at Tihwa and good friend of Doug's). The next day Doug, by odd circumstance, met him on the street near Mrs. Wheeler's home. He's now writing and taking life in stride, having resigned from the foreign service. It was a happy interlude in a real HOME with my darling Doug.

JULY 14, 1948—WASHINGTON, D.C.—ONE YEAR AFTER THE HISTORY ENTRY—A vase of long-stemmed pink rosebuds stands on my dressing table. I have crossed an anniversary line: July 13, 1947-48. I recall that the original date is engraved in two beautiful gold wedding bands we have not yet been able to put on our fingers. In the year's interval two things stand in tribute to that vow and memory, our love, matured not by the brief passage of a year's time but by our shared suffering and disappointment, worries that were unending—prayers—tears—dejection to the dungeon pits marked the Himalayan of OBSTACLES to Doug's legal freedom to marry me—and we still face the last stages due next month. But our love for each other has sustained us and bound us together, man and woman, forever. The second is our son-to-be, our sorrow, our anxiety, our hope, at very great cost.

To spare the strenuous trip to Boston to pack our things, Doug went home on a late train last evening. Before that we celebrated the famous first anniversary of the 13th. It was a human experience. First, the day was like the original—rainy—but without bringing relief from the frightful heat. We went to the Watergate Inn, a fashionable and charming place along the Potomac, but not air-cooled and horribly hot. Doug mopped his face. I fanned myself with the menu. Doug mentioned that I was only too wrong in assuming the inn was air-conditioned. The hostess said we could sit outdoors when a table was vacant. We waited nearly an hour, fanning and mopping and making in-between conversation. I felt little pricks inside that it wasn't a "real 13th." We ordered sparkling burgundy—it bubbled and frothed in chilled glasses, but when Doug raised his glass, all he said was: "Well, here's how." I made a pleading reference to Tihwa and the 13th. Doug smiled but somehow wasn't with me. It wasn't an I-love-you evening. It was a splurge, a treat, and we enjoyed it, but I thought in my heart, maybe next year's 13th, when we'll be married and alone in our own home and in Tihwa, it will be different. But tonight when I came home wilted by the heat and feeling very alone and unsheltered without Doug, and there were his roses waiting, I had to hurry to my room, for my happiness and gratitude broke out in tears. So for the 13th July, 1948, I must again record: How much I LOVE, LOVE, my dearest darling Doug.

AUGUST 8, 1948—WASHINGTON, D.C.—And so we're about to take the first step toward China. I leave tomorrow for San Francisco. Flying, to my intense dread, but by doctor's orders because the train trip would have been too jolty and jarring. I'll be back where I started from two years ago almost to the day. Doug, my dear darling, is going to drive out in our very own brand new jeep-oo-chaw, as the Chinese call them. We went down to the show room last evening and selected the one according to my preference for a green-color model! I was as thrilled as a kid. Tihwa, here we come, AT LAST. Doug will wait in Las Vegas for the final hearing on the divorce and then join me in San Francisco where we will be married briefly and then be on our way, FLYING to Nanking. I dread that long hop over the Pacific, but again it's doctor's orders. There isn't much time until October 20th, which is the big day. Seems so unreal. I've had so much else to think about I look forward to that day as my LIBERATION. My return to slim (I weigh a mere 150) NORMALCY. Meanwhile the world situation looks touchy. Soviet blockade in Berlin—Ambassadors talk with Stalin—nothing happens, publicly anyway—Dewey and Truman are offered to an unenthusiastic U.S.A. for the presidency and popular feeling seems to be that anyone would be better than Truman. So Dewey's chances look good on that basis. China's news is about as unfailingly bad but sustaining as ever.

AUGUST 10, 1948—SAN FRANCISCO—Two years later I return to the scene of my first embarkation to China—and what a harvest of experience marks the passage of that time. I left Washington Sunday on a United Airlines plane and arrived here on Monday. Doug drove me to the airport in our new spanking green "jeep oo chaw" (Chinese for small gas wagon), which we were trying out on our last weekend in D.C. I felt every jar and bump in the road, but ignored the warning— so thrilled and happy to be on the jeep's maiden jaunts through the Maryland and green-treed Virginia countryside. We were as pleased with ourselves and the spunky little jeep as if it were a new Rolls. I dreaded the plane trip out here. I have never been so frightened as I was when I kissed Doug goodbye and started out the gateway. My plane scare in China I guess—plus the other wee passenger tucked away inside, and being alone. But the night crossing of America (oh, what a country we've got) was beautiful. The black oblivion was aglow with a thousand twinkling eyes. The plane simply glided all the way. Except for being unable to sleep or recline with my feet up and consequently that my feet and ankles became badly swollen, I felt no ill effects of the long trip and am all set for the cross-Pacific hop. The doctor was so right—flying is the only kind of traveling at my advanced stage that relieves la petite mère of any jolt or strain.

Maizie Blinn came to see me today, and I was panicky at first about my appearance—wore a loose jacket—as we talked, couldn't bring the "moment" for the news to a head. So I talked of past preliminaries—the church obstacles, legal delays, etc. I was terribly nervous all during her visit, wanting to tell her and get it over with, yet holding off. She's coming again, and I'll make IT the big issue. Despite sophistication, this situation is damnable—and how clumsy and heavy-footed I feel in this ultra-chic, smart town. The stores are opulent, gay, vividly placarded with new fall fashions. It is crisply cool and chill here. In Magnins marten scarves are blended with gold marble murals and gift décor. As I strolled through the new store (I had worked in their former store), I was torn between tingling rapture at the beauty and luxury of the lovely things in cases and draped on heavy glass counters, and the contrasting feeling of personal horror at myself physically—and "fashionably."

Doug just telephoned from Washington. This was his second call—he called the first night I arrived to make sure I had arrived safely, etc. How I loved him for doing it! Tonight's call brings a touch of bad news—He's been delayed four days in Washington, business of course—but delays increase the urgency of MY PREDICAMENT. I can't see us getting away to China now until sometime in September.

AUGUST 13, 1948—Doug called me this morning for our anniversary. "Remember that I love you very specially for today," he said. He doesn't expect to leave Washington for some days. Has had no news on the divorce—and he sent me another $100 just to make sure I wouldn't run short on anything—bless his darling heart—I've got myself resigned now to just waiting out the delays—come what may.

Maizie Blinn—handmaid of God himself, truly—came in for the day. I told her what she had already known. I was truly upset for a moment. She is the only woman to know, and it was such a relief to talk to her. "Don't you cry," she spoke up, "I'd give my right arm for what you've got. I've never been able to have any myself—so you will have to be the daughter I never had." We talked for hours on end. She assured me if worst came to worst I could stay with her in San Anselmo until after the baby is born and join Doug later—the only hitch to my being with her now is Gen living with them. Gen (Ed Nannary's sister) won't be leaving until the first of September. She does know I'm here, of course. One laughing point in the predicament was Maizie and I trying to concoct something for me to wear for our very DELAYED wedding. I am normally Maizie's size. Since I can't get to her house to try things on, Maizie was my stand-in, trying on her clothes with a pillow tied to her tummy, howling at the situation and herself the while. She telephoned this afternoon to say the forces of destiny are at work—a priest came to visit her—she put my case up to him, and he said a Catholic marriage is not impossible and doesn't mean a boon from the Pope. If only Madame X were NOT baptized. I must find out.

AUGUST 29, 1948—SAN FRANCISCO—I sat deep in a book. In the nun-like isolation of this hotel room the only companionable sound was the ticking of my small alarm clock. The phone rang suddenly. Doug from Las Vegas. The divorce hearing which has been DEFINITELY SET for August 31st at 10 a.m. (and now fervently, desperately I cling to that POSITIVE, FIXED DATE OF DELIVERY) was now held pending return of the papers from Madame X, who has now decided NOT to contest the case. We have waited for signed papers to be returned before. When I hung up the receiver I burst into hysterical tears. My God—to have been at his divorce and its delays and postponements and papers for so many heart-aching, worry, dread, and mental-anguish-filled months—after all we've been through or I've been through. For Doug the protraction has been a responsibility and man's affair. For me, the woman, the penalty has been upon my heart, soul and body. The price was greater than the gem that was snatched. Now I see that Doug was my love and I yielded in defiance of church, the social law, everything. The suffering that followed far, far outweighed the ecstasy of love. Now that this experience has taught me that much—and when weeping gave way to cold reason, I began to visualize a future of far different perspective, Operation Parker again. As soon as this child is delivered from me. I've been sitting here thinking and thinking—First, I will NOT marry Doug unless I do, by some 11th hour miracle, go to China with him. I've had all the divorce procedure I want and I guess I want to CUT AWAY CLEAN and won't be sorry if I HURT him in leaving. I can see him doing his work very well without me in Tihwa and actually if I left him, I think he would be relieved of an enormous weight. We've had our wild love—now there are other things to think of. As soon as I am strong enough, I want to go to Alaska. I've even thought of asking my old swain, Art Bremer, to pay my plane fare one way. I'd like to see him—not that there's the faintest spark of any love there. But I'd want to fling myself in the arms of Eva McGown. I'd tell her everything—then I'd come back to San Francisco. What to do with the baby would be one problem. To keep him somehow and try to land a newspaper job in San Francisco.

That's one idea. It's been in the back of my mind these long days. I might make a start here. Until the baby's place is set, I can't go flinging off into space very well. (Turkey still on the map? That or Europe—or from the west coast—South America still lures me strongly.) However events evolve, this thought will be in my mind. There is, after all, a stimulus in doing, planning, figuring out ways and means for myself. I started from this town just two years ago, almost to the very day. Why not try my luck and courage again?

SEPTEMBER 16, 1948—SHANGHAI, CHINA—I've just read the above entry with a wry grimace. Again, I am alone in a hotel room, torn in mental anguish and plotting escape once I am physically able. To flash back, however, Doug and I were married September

2, 1948 in San Francisco. Thanks to the connivance and ingenuity of Maizie Blinn (for whom I thank God), the wedding went perfectly, in keeping with the underlying desperate situation. Maizie loaned me a pink suit which we split at the seams and covered with furs. Doug said not a word about how I looked, so there was no "bride" loveliness whatsoever. There were no flowers. We just went through with it. The judge whom Maizie had gotten for us was white-haired and distinguished and did not read a routine ceremony. He spoke it with dignity and great seriousness. A band concert—American Legion—boomed forth in mid-ceremony and though the judge's assistant closed the window, we still heard its muffled clash–bang. Our wedding bands—ordered last May—were too tight, and we had to cold cream our fingers to get them on. When we were "pronounced man and wife," Doug gave me a tight, hard hug. Then the three of us went to the St. Francis Hotel for sparkling burgundy. After that, Maizie left us. Doug and I went out to a little apartment near Golden Gate Bridge on Lombard Street and ended our day drinking champagne and eating chocolate wedding cake. Doug was gay and very dear, and held me in his arms like any bride. For that I was grateful.

Next day we began household shopping, changing the name on my passport, getting my shots, etc. Before we departed the most memorable events were receiving a telegram from Eva McGown in Alaska, driving to visit a Col. and Mrs. Ellsworth—friends of Doug's, who were darling to us—and spending a day with Maizie at San Anselmo.

Finally at midnight September 10, 1948, we flew out over the ink-black Pacific, via Pan American to Honolulu. We hired a taxi, drove over the island, gazed on the multi-colored Pacific and the flowering paradise of trees and shrubs, then got back on the plane—Midway to Wake Island and an engine went dead. We flew at half speed and got into Wake Island late in the evening. Stayed on the ground overnight while repairs were made. Then at noon the next day we went on to Tokyo. Again it was night when we arrived, so I saw nothing of

Japan. The trip was taking its toll, and I was terribly tired. My feet were swollen and I could wear only bedroom slippers. Deep in my woman's heart I detested my appearance. At 2 a.m. September 13 we arrived in Shanghai, where we were met by a chap from the consulate and taken to the Metropole Hotel. Next day Fern Cavender—an old Consulate friend—popped in, amazed that I was here and wed to Doug and so exceedingly pregnant. I look as though I'd swallowed a basketball. We had a luncheon date at Broadway Mansions with the PAPANIAS, friends of Doug and parents of a year-old daughter. Mrs. P. was very solicitous that I see a doctor at once after the long trip. So to her private physician, one Dr. McClain, we went. He examined me with solemn thoroughness. Then he broke the news—two heartbeats, but to be absolutely certain I must have an X-ray. I went to the hospital today, and it is true—I am to have TWINS.

SEPTEMBER 23, 1948—SHANGHAI—The threesome is doing well. I have "come around" on accepting the rigors and ardors of two cherubs to be raised helplessly on my abysmal ignorance in the wilderness. Everyone at the Consulate has been kind and extremely keen on the DOUBLE event. Doug, too, seems all for the double production so that makes me feel better. I have been checked in at the Broadway Mansions Army Hospital and have been assured it will be a normal delivery. I have sufficient space for the wee ones to slip safely through. (I would dread a Caesarean out here unless I knew my surgeon WELL). The only back-of-mind concern now is—Can I bundle these wee Mackiernans up in an airplane by the end of November and fly them at 13,000 feet into the wild hinterlands of western China? If not, we will be completely cut off from Doug and Tiwha. I want terribly for this BIG EVENT to be over so that I can be flitting around doing things—any delays separate me from my darling, beloved husband, who comes first in my heart always. To my surprise, had a charming and gallant letter from Art Bremer, loyal to his Parker regardless.

OCTOBER 19, 1948—French Town State Department billet. How can I recount the greatest story I've ever written: the birth of my BABIES, my beautiful daughter and son? For a newspaper woman writing for herself, the story is perhaps best recorded in city desk fashion—A son and daughter were born to Mr. and Mrs. Douglas Mackiernan at 2:10 a.m. September 30, 1948, the first pair of twins ever born in the U.S. Army Hospital in the Broadway Mansions Hotel. The attending physician, 1st Lt. Jean L. Bolduc, was assisted and supervised by the hospital Commandant and Surgeon, Lt. Col. JOSEPH CAPLES, and a Seventh Day Adventist missionary surgeon, Dr. WAGNER. The multiple birth presented many physical difficulties and complications, and army physicians were widely praised and highly regarded for their exacting and skilled delivery, which through a prolonged labor of 48 HOURS, spared the mother a major operation.

The first child, Mary Mackiernan, weighing 6 lbs. 8 oz., was removed with forceps by Dr. Bolduc. Great care was exerted in this removal, and the child was born without a single scratch or head injury.

Both parents were exceedingly eager to have a son, and when the girl's birth was made known to the father, waiting outside, he was increasingly anxious for his wife. "She will be disappointed," he told the nurse. Mixed sex in twins is a comparative rarity, and the mother, fully conscious during the entire 3-hour delivery, prepared for the second child's arrival with hopeful cries to the doctor: "Work hard on my little Irishman—let's produce Michael Alowishus and call it a night's work."

The age-old birth ritual began at 2:30 a.m. and the mother was instructed to PUSH—PUSH—PUSH. She strained every muscle in her wracked, perspiring body. "Come on, Michael—come on, Michael Alowishus," she cheered herself and the hustling attendants, including three doctors, one army nurse—1st Lt. RUTH I. LEE—and three Chinese nurses. Looking down at 2:50 a.m. at the feet of the second baby, the mother gasped on hearing it was—oh, miracles COME TRUE—A SON! Sheer ecstasy at seeing a little, HOMELY blond boy with sleepy blue eyes, weighing 6 lbs. 14 oz., soon gave way to frightful physical agony for the exhausted mother. The pain-numbing spinal injection had long since worn off, and all the stitches had yet to be taken. Removal of the afterbirth—each child was born from his own sac, hence their individual formation avoids identical appearance—was a worse ordeal than the twin births. Every stitch in the deep incision was counted in pain. "Oh, hurry, sew quickly—are there many more?" the mother moaned. Her babies' whimpering cries as Lt. Lee bathed them were exquisite sounds, healthy cries.

In a few seconds, the delivery room tension relaxed as the babies were hustled across the hall to a waiting nursery. The doctors, interested surgically in the delivery, gathered in the adjoining wash-up room for shop talk, every word of which carried to the mother's ear. Every worry of disaster or serious malfunction, dread of Caesarean, was expelled as the doctors removed their gowns. "My God, my God, my God. You brought me through safely—and I never asked your help or raised my heart to you. But now, thanks—thanks from my soul."

I lay quivering and spent, limp and sodden with perspiration, on the hard, narrow delivery table when suddenly I looked up into my husband's face. He had come right into the delivery room. He bent down to kiss me. I saw his eyes red-rimmed from sleeplessness and exhaustion—there was rough stubble on his chin. "Oh, darling, we have our son," I told him. I'm afraid we didn't even mention Mary then—the surgeon saw Doug. "Come on, Papa Mac—we're going up to my apartments and break out champagne. We've put in a good three-day workout." They went out, giddy with relief and the first spell of relaxation.

So it was over—we were the parents of a SON and daughter. I was wheeled into a room with two other mothers and lay wide awake in the dark thinking. It was sweetly impossible to grasp. I was a mother of TWO children. I felt gratified and relieved to have a SON, but in my heart of hearts, it was tiny MARY I loved with swift bondage the instant I saw her lovely face. She is a pretty child, but when I first saw her she was beautiful—her skin was petal clear, pink and white—her eyes, large and bluey blue and curious in her small face—I knew she was blind, as all babies are at first, but she seemed to look right down at me, seriously taking stock of her mother. Her dark brown head and general features resembled mine. She was MY VERY OWN—my little girl, who came where a BOY was so ardently on order. I LOVED HER. But Michael, then and even now, gives me no response. He doesn't seem to belong to me. I feel toward him a detached, preening satisfaction so traditionally rigid in this country where SONS are worth more than land or rice. I am more amused at him than tender. He is a serious, intense, little man and ALL MAN. He submits helplessly to being loved and cooed over and his blue eyes look up resistingly. He cries like a worried old man—nervously, almost crankily and irritably. As the days passed and his face filled out a bit, he began to look more and more SCOTCH. His head is covered with blond duck fuzz. His chin is long and pointed—his face is just plain HOMELY and wholly male. When the nurses brought him in for feeding and he was crying in hunger, we used to laugh at him and call him Sandy McGregor who lost his last dollar!

One Chinese night nurse told me one evening in Chinese, "You have something very special: a piece of jade and a piece of porcelain. The son is jade, the daughter porcelain—nice but of little value."

I nursed both at alternate feeding hours. When asking which baby to bring, the Chinese nurses would say, "Piece of jade or porcelain?"

The twins created a furor, of course—and for obvious reasons I was dreading any notoriety or someone putting it in the newspaper. I wondered at Doug's private heart-of-hearts feeling over the twins' arrival. He didn't react like an ordinary father. No cigars. No conspicuous bounce, boast or pride. He sent me two baskets of flowers with loving cards, but he wasn't fatherly in any way. He calls the twins "brats," to my pained horror. I lay awake one night weeping into a towel so the others wouldn't hear. When Doug calls them "brats" I remember the physical cost of bearing them and my heart breaks that he doesn't understand. Even as I write, it is impossible to keep my eyes from misting. Perhaps it was self-consciousness or mental depression after the ordeal, but I felt farther away from Doug and less beloved by him those two weeks in the hospital than ever before. He came frequently to see me, but he was like a friend. He spoke of his doings, getting our shipment together, etc., but he made no effort to see the babies or to ask the nurse to let him see them. He went to Nanking, and days passed with no word. With cringing anguish I again recalled the good telephone service before we were married. I'd then lie by the hour looking at the ceiling thinking my old theme. Somewhere there's music, the tune that woos me far away, away from all that began in Tihwa. Away from Doug. Somewhere ELSE there's music, I promise myself—I promise Pegge Parker. Then I snap back to normal—at home—twins doing well—Doug and I can escape to our heavenly mountains. I'll wait for that. If it doesn't come—woe, woe, woe.

As the hospital days dragged into two weeks, I began turning a story over in my mind. One day a young lieutenant's wife came in for the castor oil treatment. It seems when babies are late they can be brought on with a good jigger of castor oil and an enema. This girl, a fluffy blond of nice, small-town, rather pampered background, brought a raft of silks and satins, a make-up kit. Got herself glamorous every evening after her son was born. Next day after the birth she refused to nurse her baby. "I'm putting him on the bottle," she said.

We other mothers said nothing, but the nurse brought the doctor in. Sizing her up, he began pleading the cause of nursing by appealing to her vanity. If she nursed she'd get her figure back sooner, etc. The other mothers all nursed away and tried hard to produce more and more milk. She was self-conscious in her apologies. Mother's milk was all watery—didn't always agree with babies, etc. We all said nothing. One day the truth came out. She admitted thinking nursing a repulsive, animal procedure.

Another mother was a snapshot impression—Russian girl, slim, tall, quite lovely in a simple, sweet way. Wife of a pudgy, red-faced, middle-aged Major. She was foreign to the other American mother and me. We blabbed away by the hour about everything, back home, etc. She lay isolated, silent, unconfiding. I felt her dread of going to the U.S. some day and having so little in common with Americans like us. The Chinese nurses had a slightly condescending attitude toward her. Yet as my heart went out in pity it was checked. She spoke with brutal callousness about the Chinese one day. They were so many beasts of burden, subhuman to her—and she was unspeakably selfish. Her attitude toward generous, open-handed Americans was—fools to pay the price. While we loaned, swapped and freely donated little things to each other, she wouldn't even loan a flower vase to anyone.

After nearly three weeks, I came home from the hospital and moved into a State Department billet in French town. What sheer panic. I had to rely wholly on Amah, who made the formulas in the kitchen out of sight. We had no pans big enough to sterilize four bottles. Then the nipples clogged. I had no brushes to clean them. Babies howling. Amah burned a needle and pinched the nipple, popped it into mouths. I was again panicky—that black, burned nipple going into the babies' most sterile inner sanctums—their MOUTHS.

Fern Cavender moved us home in her car. Then as a reward she wanted to hold and play with the babies and she had a wracking cough—maybe a cigarette cough, I don't know—but I was desperate to grab my babies and obligated to spare the person that had done us. a generous favor. Then well-meaning friends and neighbors descended, all smoking, all with outsider germs. I was quaking and quivering, just in a panic. The first two days were a nightmare. The third day we relaxed. Today Daddy Doug sent a package from Nanking. Shirts and bottles. Amah and I were beside ourselves, thrilled to death at the bottles. The makeshift "NO HAVE GOT" supplies is hell. And I ranted at my meek submission to Doug's "Don't get this—or that—I resented everything he had brought in our precious air luggage that might have been baby clothes, bottles, etc. But we're coasting on our own now. Amah is the slave of the babies. I do hope she goes to Tihwa with us, at least until I get hold of the technique—and MYSELF.

OCTOBER 21, 1948—What a FRANTIC time we all had last night. I've had four conflicting messages on when Doug will be back. At 6 p.m. feeding time I had a phone call. I turned Mike over to a visitor to start his bottle (since Amah had Mary). The visitor has two children herself, but she didn't give Mike the bottle correctly. A few minutes later more visitors arrived, and when we peeked in Mike's bassinet he vomited the whole feeding. This was the first time either baby had done that. I yelled for Amah. She was off somewhere having chow. Another visiting mother took over as I stood quaking. Michael is our problem and my growing concern. He is difficult to feed, has sometimes violent hiccups despite our slowest bottle giving. He still isn't as quick as Mary; when turned on his tummy he can't lift or turn his head (which makes him FURIOUS). His crying is a wild burst of temper and rage, and he resists all cuddling and adoring affection. Mary is the exact opposite. She is sweet, performs her baby functions easily, can lift and turn her silken soft brunette head and cries only—or usually—from hunger and wet pants (or "poo poo," as Amah calls a bowel movement). Maybe Mike is to be Doug's child— male response to male attendance.

SATURDAY, OCTOBER 24, 1948—I am so FURIOUSLY WILD angry at Doug this minute I must write it out for a safety valve. Master came home from the first shipment to Lanchow of Consulate supplies. I was beside myself with relief and delight to see him. We have been close and busy with plans of what we'll do about going up to Tihwa. Last night we were invited to dinner—my first trip out after having the twins. Felt all excited and so I was disappointed I had no clothes to wear. Since my tummy is perfectly flat in a tight girdle and I'm so slim, could wear my best things—Alack! Memorable reaction: At 10 p.m. I was very conscious of the feeding hour—wondering what poor Amah was doing with the two alone. We got back after 11 p.m. and when we walked in, my heart contracted, there sat Amah, looking tired and worn, holding wee Mary, just finishing her bottle. The big eyes, the moon cheeks and soft down-covered head. My tiny baby I had deserted for what—a dinner party! It was Mary again who moved my heart just now. Doug and I were talking in the mid p.m. Amah brought Mary in from her sun bath, gave her some water to stop her fussing and play. I took water, then she was ready to play. I took her and Oh! SHE IS SO CUTE. She was wearing her pink sweater and I could have hugged her to pieces. After bouncing around I passed her over to Doug. He refused her. "No, no, you hold her; I've got a cold." I had made him a mask to wear and noticed it went unused all day yesterday. I handed it to him playfully. He too turned it back. I could have annihilated him. Refusing my darling Mary. I'll NEVER, NEVER hand the babies to him again. Amah was sitting right beside me, so to preserve face I passed it off. But oh, how I am seething inside. If Amah weren't here I think I'd be telling Doug I'm not coming to Tihwa. He can go and stay forever for all I care at this moment. I've got the twins. He's a mere man. He hasn't even wanted to hold them. He doesn't look at them in their bassinets and I had to tell him not to call them brats. Still a sore point, but a request complied with.

Pictures of Pegge and the twins.

OCTOBER 25, 1948—My, what a tear-splattered page! But now all is well. Doug and I had a little talk and he was very sweet, loving and understanding. I calmed down and felt so gratefully relieved—it was like falling in love with him again. But the next day Fern Cavender came out. She dotes on Mike, and as she was holding him Doug kept making kidding but gruff-sounding remarks. He made no attempt to hold either one. All day he sat in the other room from them. He never goes near the bassinets to even take a curious peek. We were going out to dinner and I'm glad I had the bathroom to escape to—and a thick towel to sob into. I swore to myself if he didn't voluntarily pick up Mike without my prompting before he went to Tihwa, I wouldn't go on that fateful plane. We joined our friends, Captain and Mrs. RALPH PAPANIA, at the Broadway Mansions. Mrs. P took pity on my attire—my one skirt—and loaned me a wool suit of hers. As we dressed in the other room I broke down and told her about Doug. She immediately counter confided she had the same experience with her husband. Plus the 'brat" calling etc. Other young wives have had the same experience. All have been in hysterical tears, ready to leave their husbands, etc. I was agog at this. What a difficult experience and a regrettable, sad one when husband and wife should be close and happy with their new baby! Doug still hasn't picked up the babies, but he talks about them more, asks how they are, what's wrong, when they cry for prolonged WAILING periods. Mike still cries like a SQUEALING, senile invalid—but to my delight he now wants to be cuddled and talked to and held. He looks up shyly and adorably when loved.

I like going out with Doug as his wife—looking my best, and being with his friends, sharing the sensation of being the parents of the TWINS. It has its proud moments. We are so well known everywhere as the twin producers.

I'll interrupt the chronicle of Parker-Mackiernan and the world to attach some memorable documents. Just for the record, this adorable verse by Blake:

My Mother groan'd, My father wept,

Into the dangerous world I leapt,

Helpless, naked, piping loud,

Like a fiend hid in a cloud.

[Editor's Note: Then in her diary are the following:

A telegram from Consul Paxton in Tihwa to Mackiernan in Shanghai: "10859 can you confirm rumored arrival Shanghai two new Americans boy and girl query congratulations and best wishes to all four of you end it."

A cable from Fairbanks, Alaska to Pegge Mackiernan: ALL HAPPINESS CONGRATULATIONS GOD BLESS YOU BOTH DEAREST LOVE EVA (McGown).

Next, the fourth page of a letter from Art Bremer from Alaska with a clipping from the newspaper with headline: Pegge Parker Weds Vice Consul, Returns to China.]

OCTOBER 31, 1948—I can't believe a month has gone by since that exclamation point event Sept. 30, 1948. But here we three are, still going strong. I took the babies to the hospital for their first checkup yesterday. Mary is up to 8 lbs. 14 oz.; she has out-gained Mike, who started at 6 lbs. 14 oz. and yesterday was 8 lbs. 6 oz. To visit the hospital was memorable for another reason. It was the first time Doug HELD Mike. I schemed that he would carry his son down the steps and into the hospital. Mike was all done up in his company best—booties, bonnet, jacket. Papa said he looked HOMELY—as he does. I put him in Doug's arms and leaned over to kiss him. For all Doug protested that he knew how to carry a baby, he held Mike as though he were made of glass.

Well, so much for babies.

Now the fates conspire to trouble us. China's teapot is about to pop from all undercurrent information. The military and economic situation is on the brink of total collapse. I've known bad moments in China before so took these lightly when Doug knit his brows. But now, facing the flight to Tihwa with these two babies, I feel sobering chills down my spine. Doug sometimes over-alarms the situation, but now when he says we will be wholly isolated in Tihwa from any supplies, we may never get our jeep or household effects, sitting for all we know on the strike-bound docks in San Francisco.

Then comes the "crossroads" decision:

If dependents are evacuated, what to do? Go with Doug and take the roughing it? Or take the babies home for their safety's sake?

Love and common sense are in conflict. In the old days of our first romance NOTHING could or would have kept me from Doug. But the feeling between us now is so difficult. Doug is a love at night. The rest of the time his prime concern is the supply caravan to Lanchow. While for me, back to normal, my figure slimming, I want violin playing—ROMANCE—pretty clothes and from Doug a thousand little things. I sit here at night—dinner for one—young MOTHER—with soft radio music—one soft light on—the boy glides in and out serving my dinner. I am lost in imaginings and I am dancing. I am wearing a white dress, discerningly wicked—bare-bosomy, and I have red roses in my hair and a lush red fire feeling inside. I would give anything to be dressed like that sometime for Doug. Not to charm him—to defy him—to stand him off as I imparted the challenge—so you didn't know I was THIS WOMAN underneath. I wonder how other women feel in their heart of hearts toward their husbands when mother bearing is all over?

NOVEMBER 3, 1948—SHANGHAI—Helen Papania just called. She has gotten a passport for her 6-month-old daughter in preparation for being evacuated to the States. Doug is still in Nanking, so I don't know yet what our status is. But I gather that dependents are to be moved out fast. Doug must be beside himself in trying to get us to Lanchow or Tihwa before the commotion begins. The currency here has gone under, and merchants, especially rice dealers, locked up their stocks. A hungry populace has become a threatening menace, doubly so when the military situation is on the verge of collapse. Riots were feared, but now price controls have been lifted, shops are gradually reopening. The currency is rampant and everyone is alert to whatever must come next. I would be in a somewhat embarrassing position going home with TWINS before next May, but in an emergency I could stay in California, I guess. Mike, who is under my eye here on the sun-warmed veranda, is howling furiously. He's been fed, dry-diapered and given water, so I've got to let him yell. He's my problem child, all right. I've had him to the hospital twice this week for a mild obstruction of the nasal passage. Seems better now.

NOVEMBER 5, 1948—SHANGHAI—DAWN PATROL—Vapors of morning are a silvery blur outside. The air is cold. I have just bed both my children AT ONCE all night. I feel new confidence in my "motherhood." Before, without Amah I'd have been fussed, floundering, wild-eyed. Since we have Mike's livelihood to watch more closely than Mary's, he gets first attention. Mary has to feed herself lying down with the bottle propped up in a rolled diaper. Bless her big-eye'd little self. She's so good about everything. Mike is getting better looking. His face is filling out. His coloring is lovely. He will be a blondie and keep his blue eyes, I think. I had a fuss with Amah over Mike. I felt she didn't like him because he was more trouble than Mary and his crying does set nerves and patience on edge. Hence my conciliation (after stern words) in letting Amah sleep all night while I took over the 10 p.m. and dawn feeding, diapering, etc., myself. Amah is in a sunny mood again. I DO PRAY she goes to Tihwa with us.

Now to events. I had a letter from Doug in Nanking which was more reassuring. "Am doing my damnedest to get us all to Tihwa. I'm afraid if we don't make it on this November 21 plane, chances are nil of getting there this year or (worse) next spring." So while the army prepares its evacuation, looks as though I go on to the wilds. I wouldn't mind if we were better equipped. I still have no clothes. Helen is going to sell her suit to me. (It is so warm, thank heaven.) The suitcase with my entire wardrobe in it has never shown up.

Meanwhile, to external events—I had a wonderful luncheon date with the British Consul General yesterday, SIR MICHAEL GILLETT, the famed character of Kashgar. Doug has always wanted to meet him so I took the initiative of going down so that when Doug gets here we could take him to dinner. Red goatee, monocle et al. He was wonderful. His genuine homesickness for Sinkiang (after serving some time in gaudy Shanghai) moved him to hospitality toward me, I'm sure. He expressed confidence Tihwa was as safe a place—or safer—than any in China for going with two infants. He felt Sinkiang would only be a hot spot if an international incident occurred. Even then, he felt, with the British regularity, the Soviets would afford us exit on the Trans-Siberian. Commenting on Truman's ASTOUNDING re-election, Gillet said, "Well, you have a good Secretary of State in George Marshall." He added a kind word for Truman: "He is an honest man. Study a photograph of his face and Dewey's. Nothing in Dewey's face gives you the convincing honesty of Truman." True diplomat. Describing his first trek over the pass to Kashgar, as a hot-house young foreign office lad from London, Gillet said it was "rather fun" because anti-British feeling was keen at the time and wayfarers refused to shelter him or sell him fuel. He's been over the pass twice. Quite a jaunt, especially on the rope bridges.

NOVEMBER 10, 1948—SHANGHAI—The Consulate car sped smoothly through the Shanghai countryside, the fields were green with late fall harvest. Along the shoulder of the road marched Chinese Army troops in padded, clumsy uniforms. American rifles were slung over their shoulders. Their tennis shoes made a dull shuffling sound as they passed. Their cheeks were ruddy and wind-burned. Their faces were set in blank, unthinking expressions as though they marched in automatic response to orders without thinking of their own or China's imminent fate.

I turned from them, snuggled closer to my darling husband. "Remember me on Christmas Eve," I whispered. He is going to Kianguan Airfield and eventually Tihwa. And I am to stay in Shanghai to await shipment to San Francisco for the duration of China's political earthquake. We reached the separation discussion simultaneously after working uphill for many anxious days—the babies' tender age decided us. We feel we couldn't expose them to unnecessary risk. How—where—and WHEN we shall meet again, we don't know.

I was resigned in my heart, however, as far as Doug and I are concerned—our love is our iron bondage—and for the few days he was here he reacted more intimately toward the babies. During the night feedings he willingly took Mike or Mary, fed and burped them. The discharge from Mike's left eye concerned him. He will be a solicitous and devoted parent when he's been around him longer and they are older—I hope. At the airport we stood in a whipping cold wind saying last things, practical details and financial affairs, etc. I got back in the Consulate car. Doug leaned in the doorway.

"Remember I love you extremely much, my darling," he said and kissed me long and hard.

The collapse of China's Chiang Government is expected weekly. Already the money is rampant. Food prices are wildly beyond the means of ordinary people. My Amah, whose salary of $25 U.S. a month is considered very high, asked for food instead. I got her a load of commissary supplies instead.

Oh, to flash back—Doug and I took the British Consul General—Gillet—to dinner at the correspondents' club atop the Broadway Mansions. I was proud of myself for having instigated the affair, which I knew Doug enjoyed.

I went to the hospital today for my six weeks' post-pregnant check-up. All is well. I am up to 130 lbs, but I may have occasional backaches. My uterus is tilted back slightly. One stitch still bothers me a bit. The skin feels puckered and sensitive. When I finished with the doctor, I took Lt. Lee, the army nurse who assisted in my delivery, to lunch at the correspondents' club. I had wanted to know her life story and love mishap. We sat for two hours. Born in Philadelphia and raised in a religious atmosphere, she decided at an early age that she wanted to come to China and contribute her service as a nurse "because Christ died for love of me." She calls herself a Christian and refuses any other formal denomination. She came to China at her own expense because all missions insisted she was too young, etc. For five years she worked at a small mission inland from Tsing Tao, learned fluent Chinese, grew to love the people. She moved on later to other missions, finally given job in Nanking, came the war, evacuated to Manila, joined the army, began associating freely with men, began experimenting in worldly good times, drinking. Later, sent to the States, was told to give a speech on her wartime experiences at a money-raising affair—told to lay it on thick about her grim experience. She was presented with her first orchid and sat on a platform with blind young GI veterans—awful ordeal—especially because she insisted on telling the truth and some of her Jap captors had been fairly decent. She came back to Shanghai in the army's Broadway Mansions hospital. The nursing staff is composed of locally trained nurses of mixed nationality—Chinese and particularly Portuguese. Through one of these she met a young Englishman and fell madly in love. He was married but estranged. The romance came to nothing because he fell in love with another Portuguese girl, a physical affair. So Ruth, who wants not just a home and children but a hospital in the interior, has nothing. Drinking was a way of finding oblivion for a time. Once she was called to deliver a baby after an all-night round of hilarity—the baby boy was perfect, but she was filled with self-loathing afterward. Was embarrassed when the Chinese nurses told her she smoked a cigar in celebration afterward. To add to her feeling of frustration and dread of an eternity of empty days ahead, there is the threat of China's upheaval. As she is head nurse at B'way she was asked by the head surgeon to have coffee and a talk (Colonel Caples—my doctor). He digressed from the emergency measures—the staff plans to feed the Chinese personnel in lieu of salary, etc.—long enough to suggest he would be seeing lots of her after hours during the siege when his wife goes home. The wife, a truly nice person unable to bear children and addicted to indiscretions in alcoholic intake, will depart in the emergency evacuation soon.

"But oh, Pegge," she told me, looking out of her window down the Bund where two American cruisers lay anchored conspicuously, "He's not for me. Grand person, has everything in common with me for wanting to do hospital work among the humble, ordinary people. But I couldn't imagine kissing him."

Wonderful story in Ruth Lee—I hope I pick up the thread later on.

NOVEMBER 14, 1948—MIDWAY TO MIDWAY (ISLE) VIA PAN AMERICAN—Going home. I'm the first State Department "evacuee" to leave China because of the fast-imperiled internal situation. Fern

Cavender literally EJECTED me from Shanghai by plane. I wanted to go by ship, feeling the plane accommodations were too confining. Fern was right, however—this is the only way to travel, and I've got my hands full. Both babies are at my feet in their Chinese bassinets. The stewardesses think they're "cute punkins" and at their age far less trouble than 1-2-3-year-old pranksters tearing up and down the aisle. The plane vibrations and the altitude make the cherubs sleepy, so they are comparatively easy to handle. As we approach San Francisco I begin to grow apprehensive. Will Maizie meet us? What will she tell Lou about the twins? Will I—as I suppose—have to go into hiding until Mike and Mary can be declared in May? My reservation came awfully late. As I was in the midst of packing, Doug called from Nanking. He expects to get to Lanchow soon. He held out hope that I'd be back in the Spring, coming in to Sinkiang via India—astride a mule. I was loathing to end the conversation. "I love you, Darling," I kept saying. He answered in Russian, as we always do: "I mojna" (I also).

It was a thrill to see San Francisco in all her gaudy spangles. I was giving Mike his bottle when we came in over the city. I was so excited I dropped his bottle and held him up to the window for his first glimpse of America. He looked out and didn't even howl for more chow. Maizie and Lou Blinn met us. I was overjoyed to see Maizie, and I could hardly wait to ask her what she had told Lou about Doug and me. Her story was convincing. Doug and I were married at Tihwa thinking his divorce was final. Had to keep it secret because of a "bigamy" angle. At first I was thrilled to be here. Fresh orange juice, sunshine, a clean kitchen to use for the formula making, great stir and clamor in the Blinn household to have the first evacuees, and twins to boot. Now, however, it boils down to Lou and Maizie having words about my being "taken in" and Lou's impossible (poor soul), unlivable, selfish old mother being invited out also. I am doing the work of two Amahs—EVERYTHING from getting my own meals to feeding, fending entirely for the twin Mackiernans. I am completely

EXHAUSTED—the only reward is the response of the cherubs to me and being so CLOSE to them, knowing every move and mood and baby function of both. Keeping a keen eye on Mike, who upchucks his whole bottle often. Both babies caught colds and I had a doctor in to see them. They're okay now, but I am soon to face the CLIMAX of telling Mother and sending for her to help me.

NOVEMBER 29, 1948—SAN ANSELMO, CALIFORNIA—I had a cable this morning from Fern Cavender saying Doug left Lanchow for Tihwa November 27 and I was lucky to be out of Shanghai. I felt very detached from news of Doug. I'm already thinking of going on from here without him. I have no feeling of being married to him at all, and my most recent memories of being with him in Shanghai leave little bondage in my heart. My love affair was out of this world—that was that—and all I had with Doug. Last night I wrote Art Bremer a letter, suggesting he come down next Spring to see me. I felt as free as "Pegge Parker" doing it. My mind is in a constant quandary about Doug and my own future. I can't see going back to China. Doug's indifferences or detachment as far as the twins are concerned—and his omission of little things—the heart's things—for me make the separation more than distance. I have a baby nurse here now. The colds are still with my cherubs, but Mary has the pinkest cheeks and Mike is fine, too. I love and adore them more and more every day.

DECEMBER 4, 1948—SAN ANSELMO—Well, I've come through another week with the cherubs. I had a practical nurse for five days, 9 a.m. to 5 p.m., $40, but she was grand. Gave me a chance to get some luxurious sleep during the day. The babies had their first Pablum and applesauce today. Mary wriggles like a puppy with a bone, and a wad of Pablum landed in her eye. I have trouble keeping her covered, too. She kicks her feet straight up in the air—almost rocks over on her head. Covers fly to all sides when she has a good spell on. Mike just set off, so I'm writing this with him slung over my left shoulder. Oh. He just burped. He's been turning on the charm lately. SMILING whenever he wakes up—waiting for Mary to be fed first and nary a yip out of him. He's still homely, but so cute withal. I wrote both grandmothers a letter this week saying I was to be evacuated— seemed such a shame to deny them the news and pictures of their grand-twins.

I can scarcely sleep these nights trying to connive somewhere to go with the twins. I've a plan to exit to South America in mind. Native help, and possibly the Yankee dollar goes further somewhere there than it does up here. I'm still undecided about Doug and wonder where he is and if we'll ever be reunited. Expenses in this part of the world are terrific. I went to the bank this week and no salary checks have been deposited for Doug yet. I wrote the State Department in Washington about it.

DECEMBER 9, 1948—SAN ANSELMO—I had a letter from Doug, written in the airplane en route to Lanchow, which has set my mind straight on where I go next. Back to him in Tihwa. He suggests I come in over the pass in Northern India—or fly in the usual way across China, depending on the internal situation. The letter made me very happy deep in my heart, where I do love my Doug terribly, but where I have been disappointed and alone.

Mike is really making up for lost time. He's bigger than Mary, eating Pablum like mad and TALKING. He's just discovered he can make noises besides crying. A wee tickle under his chin gets him grinning and goo-gooing adorably. He is the hit of the combination, although Mary is the prettier baby. But as Amah used to say, "he proper boy." Doug sent me a $100 check and set my mind at ease financially, for which I was very grateful, as living at Blinn's has been a strain at times. I am so nervous when the twins howl, especially at night, knowing they can be heard, vibrating the walls. Lou has taken an unexpected shine to Mike, and the other evening Maizie amazed me by saying in baby talk to Mike that Lou had suggested leaving this sumptuous house to my wee son since neither Maizie nor Lou have any close kin. May have only been a remark. No matter how difficult the makeshift arrangements are, I now count the days until I'll be off to China or India. I am reluctant to take the babies while they're still so young. Will all depend on what Doug writes from Tihwa after he gets there. Letter from Mother—seems fantastic she knows nothing about Mike and Mary.

CHRISTMAS EVE, DECEMBER 24, 1948—SAN ANSELMO, CALIFORNIA—How impossibly real this is, sitting here in a glamorous leathery, color-clad reading, lounging den at the Blinn's. Can it be true that this time last year I was in that drafty boarding house in Belfast? To think that 1948 brought my marriage to Doug whom I loved madly—heart over head—a flight to China—TWINS (Ah, my son, my son, my darling son) and another flight back from China. Never was my life so marked for HARVEST at the year's end. And as I approach the moment for analysis and inventory I think—next to my children, the greatest accomplishment of the year was the experience of LIFE—the suffering of 1948 far outweighed any other of my life, and all in all out-balanced the happiness—but Oh, the attainment of spiritual, or is it philosophical, citizenship in the universe was BEGUN. Yet I must rescind all declarations of past anguish when I think of Mikey. He is more precious, more passionately treasured than anything else I have ever known. Mary is pretty, roly, chubby, but Mike is my heart's supreme treasure. And so is Christmas at Blinns—two baby Christmas trees, one for Mike and the other for Mary. Satin damask love seats HEAPED with big bowed boxes for Mike and Mary. I enjoyed opening them far more than my own—hand-knit legging sets, rattle ducks and a PIN POTTY. (I remember Amah, so proud of Mary who took to her first potty like a little wetting puppy. But MIKE—he HOWLED and SCREAMED, scared to death of it.) Maizie and Lou gave me lavish gifts and to my great surprise Doug's two brothers, Stu and Mackie, sent me LeLong's Tailspin perfume—AIR MAIL. And Doug's mother Mary sent two pairs of black nylon stockings.

All my Christmas cards were filled with sympathy that I, the new bride, would be spending my first Christmas miles from my husband. Not at all. This supposed bereavement the twins fill to capacity any "alone" feelings. And Doug's attitude in Shanghai removed any longing or instinct to be in the beloved presence and arms. I am tormented at times with remembrances of his cool, casual air with the babies. His "distance" from Mike. His unfeeling or unresponsive or ungrateful husband acceptance of our son and daughter have separated my heart from his. I must, however, give him a chance. He was under strain in Shanghai. I was far from glamorous looking and he was more worried perhaps about taking the babies to Tihwa than the proud, indulgent father he might have been in the USA. Being separated this way, without even mail communication, leaves me (and, I fear, him) adjusting mentally and emotionally to getting along, quite well in a way, without the other. I had thought I was more sweetheart than mother—not so. I love my two with a deeper passion. (I am feeding Mary with one hand and writing with the other.) I think of Doug before I fall asleep, and I've already checked steamships for getting back to Shanghai, but I am even more concerned with getting a place of my own, being on my own, establishing a household and landing a newspaper job, if possible.

The babies were baptized last Sunday. They wore velvet corduroy— Mary peach with a sash in the back, Mike blue with a pleated back. The full names given them were Mary Rose and Michael Lewis, the latter for Uncle Lou, the first father Mike ever knew. Mikey was an angel. He sat up, taking it all in. When the priest put the salt on his tongue, he smacked his lips and grinned. The priest read the next passage in uncontrollable laughter. Mike threw him up in his lines.

Poor Mary was so hungry she was chewing her fists and making noises LOUDLY (for the record, the church was San Anselm's, in San Anselmo, and the date was December 19, 1948).

1949

JANUARY 1, 1949—This time last year—London and no Doug. This year, a family gathering, mild eggnog, and no Doug. Just for the record, we spent the day taking pictures of the twins. A neighbor's daughter, Betty Grant, who may go back to China with me, took the pictures. One of them was Mike in the tub. We put the tub on Maizie's marble coffee table in front of the fire. Just as I lifted Mike into the water Maizie shrieked—Mike had sprayed over the edge of the tub onto her satin damask settees!

The New Year's Eve observance was a rather strained one for me. I'd received a letter from Doug's mother saying the State Department had notified her Dec. 15 that Doug reached Tihwa safely Dec. 10. I felt I wasn't a wife, just a girl he married en route. The feeling of depression is getting under the skin. I lie awake between baby feedings scheming an escape. I have my twins and they are so completely mine. Doug can never belong to them. But he doesn't care, doesn't realize his loss.

My own feelings about Doug are at a dangerous point. One false move on his part and he will never see me or the cherubs again. I've also made up my mind to buy myself the gift he didn't realize was due when the twins were born. Mama is going to have a fur coat, thank you. I'm learning the hard way—no sweet little wifey—I do furiously resent not being notified of Doug's arrival and not hearing the news from him directly. Anyway, Maizie and Lou had the Grants in for the evening. We looked at Betty's color pix on screen, drank eggnog at midnight. I fed the babies shortly afterward—more chatter—a buffet—goodnight and so to bed. Next year: where?

By the way, for the record: I climaxed a week of intense mental torment about Doug (I am haunted by his lack of fatherly affection for the twins) with a deluge of weeping over a letter from my long-lost friend, Monsignor Ehardt. He wrote that when he was fixing up a manger for Christmas at his home, her remembered me. Picking up one of his lambs, he took it into the house, painted it black, and returned it to his model nativity. "There was no question where to put the black sheep christened Pegge—closest to the crib." I answered at once, telling the whole story of Mike and Mary. His letter, by the way, was addressed to Miss Pegge Lyons! He does not recognize P. Mackiernan.

JANUARY 30, 1949—I have had a letter, $600, and a cable from Doug since my last entry, but I feel in my heart no close bondage to Doug. He writes that he wants me to hurry back to him, but I don't feel the urgency of returning as to a lover and darling I can't live without. Shanghai and its memories cured all that. Meanwhile I have given a little talk at a local ladies club, and they LOVED it. They really did pour out their hearts in ecstasy over it. I thought of George Wallace. He almost had me convinced Americans had no interest or concern for the rest of the world. I hope my success will bring in some money which I badly need and want. I particularly want to get my professional standing back again and financial independence from Doug. I want to snap my fingers at him. Mother knows "a baby" is on the way. I want to get her out here to lend a hand before I tell her the "real story"—that Doug and I were first wed in Tihwa.

FEBRUARY 8, 1949—Just a quick catch-up and a chance to add a few lines about a lecture I heard last night by LOUIS FISCHER, a Russia specialist. Just at random, here are some quotes. Gandhi was the greatest Christian since Christ. In Gandhi's hut in India many years back Fischer sat on the floor to interview the wizened little man. On the walls the only ornament was a head of Christ. Fischer questioned him. He wasn't Christian—why the picture of Christ? Gandhi's answer: "I am a Christian, I am a Hindu, I am a Jew, I am an Indian, I belong to the world." Fischer decried a recent purge of the college faculty of the University of Washington when several "Communists" were ousted. Fischer said, "If I were a college president I'd insist on having a Communist on my faculty. Let the students hear his arguments, and the ANSWERS democracy presents. If Democracy can't surpass anything Communism offers, we've got to do something about it. Moral weapons are our greatest defense." He praised the North American Alliance which has Stalin worried. He disparaged the United Nations, whose charter is a barren, impotent prescription for warless debate among nations.

More personally, I've had a letter from Doug that leads with how much he loves me and seems quite urgent about getting me over there with him. It was appealing enough to get me to write him two letters telling him exactly how I feel that we got off on the wrong foot, but I'd try to get back to him.

FEBRUARY 13, 1949—Uncertainties on top of uncertainties. Now I don't know what's what with housing for my family—Tihwa— Doug—My feeling for him vacillates. I wrote him a long letter about how I feel, then wisely re-read it before sealing the envelope. Now I have to re-write it all.

MARCH 10, 1949—The Mackiernan question still unsettled. I've heard from Doug but he doesn't know my mental dis-union. Meanwhile I go on here with Lou and Maizie, who adore the babies and play with them. Lou has given Mike all the love he'd have given his own son. The babies are more demonstrative now and aware of people. They smile, gurgle and shriek when you talk to them. And Mary has found her toes. She grabs each foot and rocks herself. Mike watches all this with male detachment but hasn't played rocking horse with his footies yet. His big job is on the thumbs, and he is a fiend at that. Neither has much hair yet. Mike is easier to feed than Mary. I sing "if a body meets a body comin' through the rye" to both when I try to slip a little spinach over on them.

The income tax of $700-plus worries me. I hate to check off my New York bank account to pay it in full. I've tried to save on Doug's expense by opening his divorce case to reduce the $100 a month paid to Gail. No word yet on that.

This week had one treat—or fillip. I was a guest on a radio luncheon interview over KSFO (on March 8 to be exact) atop the Mark Hopkins hotel. Bill Robinson, famed Negro dancer, sat beside me.

MARCH 18, 1949—Letter from Doug—lots of practicalities on Tiwha. Then in the last paragraph, lots of "love you, remember that." He ignores answering or explaining my letdowns in Shanghai that cool my interest in returning to China and him. I HATE this quandary of uncertainty. I can visualize only too well the rough going in Tihwa if Doug and I are not in love. I feel so stuck with the babies. I'm not sure how I can strike out on something and let Doug keep his Tihwa. I keep thinking ardently of Chile. I have a fixation for Santiago. I am sending Doug a magazine condensation of John Gunther's *Death Be Not Proud*, the moving story of how he lost his only son. I made a speech this week at the Junior College of Marin, expect a check for $35 for it.

APRIL 2, 1949—Status quo—No further word from Doug, and I feel the same about him, but more vaguely so. He seems like someone who never existed or would be a stranger. I cannot associate him with any intimacy or relationship to me or the twins. They are ADORABLE—wobbly, curious, fatty, toe players. Can't quite sit up or drink from a cup. Their hair is only a token covering. They realize the duo existence but are not "company" for each other yet. If they are in the pre-teeth stage you'd never guess it from howling. They're very sound, healthy babies. Mike is the pride and joy around here. Yesterday in exercising his vocal range he got out "DA-DA."

To my amazement I got a card stating that Doug's third brother, Duncan, and his wife had twin girls on March 22nd: Meredith and Judith. So the twin bug is Mackiernan.

APRIL 10, 1949—This may be of insignificant note, but I have just removed my wedding ring and will not put it back on my finger until I truly feel—again—in love with Doug. I have had two long letters from him ignoring my emotional laments of the Shanghai letdown—his lack of response to the babies, etc. He has been wonderful about money, sending practically every cent he gets. As for everything else, he just writes as though all my letters were FINE and we were an old married couple of 10 years standing. I have been so FURIOUS I am almost afraid to face him. I have penned up such resentment and remembered indifference. I am reading books on CHILE, SOUTH AMERICA, and trying to figure a way to get there. Doug? It's on the fence.

APRIL 27, 1949—Wedding ring's back on the finger—long thought of Doug's loyalty and generosity during the previous ordeal made me feel childish for having thrown my ring in the kitchen sink! The war in China is reaching its culmination—Nanking has fallen, which means I'll be more delayed getting back. But when I do go, I'll be more assured of prevailing conditions remaining unchanged until I get to Tiwha. Bought a winter coat in a sale for $48 and feel very extravagant spending Doug's money. Also bought a crib—one—for about $30. They're so expensive. We're going to send the telegrams on Saturday announcing the TWINS. Mother will have upchucks.

MAY 1, 1949—MAY DAY—Mike made an earnest bid for room service at 5:30 a.m. I fumbled sleepily to the kitchen and got two bottles. Now he's asleep. The babies are in their new crib, Mike at one end, Mary at the other. Maizie and Lou sent the telegrams announcing the birth. Lou was a good sport about it. When he came home he bounced Mike on his knees. "One day old, hey, Smaltzie. You're awful heavy for a 6 lb. 14 oz. boy!" (We nicknamed him Smaltzie because is so Dutch-looking—pink-white-gold, blue-eyed and plump.)

Eva McGown has come to San Francisco, and I went in to see her. "Tra-la-la-la, Tra-la-la" I heard when I stepped off the elevator. "Is that my darling Pegge?" she trilled, rushing toward me in a peach chiffon and lace negligee. She was bounding along telling me all the news, never giving me a chance to tell her about Mike and Mary. She was open-mouthed but speechless when I told her—"Gawd save us. Oh no!" she gasped. I shocked her out of her senses. She spent an afternoon out here. Mary let out a yell first, then Eva took her on her knee. Eva and Maizie clicked, to my great delight. I had one day alone with Eva—told her how estranged I was from Doug.... To my surprise she rushed to his defense. "That boy's got good stuff in him," she declared. "He should make an excellent father for those wee children." She reached into her own store of experience and told me her Albert left her alone at times and she resented it. His explanation was a peremptory "Little girl, I am looking to our ramparts."

As I look back on it now, I can see more clearly what turned me from Doug...

MAY 21, 1949—Fern Cavender in from China. I met her ship, an ordeal and thrill—half Shanghai's Russians were aboard. Fern had no new leads on Doug or Tiwha. She was not very encouraging about an early return: "Wives have to expect separation in the Foreign Service," she stated, as though that would settle me. She expects to be married while here, though she told me she's not in love with the man. It's a companionship arrangement. Fern said there were indications the Chinese Communists would be all diplomatic banter toward Americans because they'd need our dollars, trade and economic support, which means further delay in clearing the way to Doug.

Returning home from my day with Fern, I had a cable from Doug, sent from Shanghai to Washington D.C. It just said all mail and cable communication had been suspended. My return via China impossible—TRYING INDIA LOVE DOUG, it concluded. I was momentarily heartened. He wasn't resting on the obvious barriers with a "NOTHING-I-can-do" attitude. He seems DETERMINED to get me over there. Why, aside from practical convenience, I can't understand. I've read his letters and though they end in dutifully ardent I miss you's, there is no plea to touch or move me to dire action. My feeling for Doug boils down to gratitude for financial responsibility and a feeling of "Well, one trip to India is LURE in itself," but to the man I once loved with all my might and main, I am building up an intense, deep grown, explosive anger and disappointment. I can't imagine that this time last year I was madly in love, or that I ever shall be again. At least with Doug. Have a hunch he will come out over the pass this summer when the Paxtons leave their post.

JUNE 11, 1949—The plot rises... letter from Doug posted in Hong Kong, stressing his utmost desire to have the twins and me join him THROUGH INDIA, over the Kara Korum. I ran all the way up the dusty, tree-lined road, yelling for Maizie. We thought it out for half a second. Then I cabled him OK INDIA WITH TWINS through

Canton, which is still open. I've had butterflies inside ever since. How in the name of God above can the babies be fed, diapered, SAFELY managed—for a month over the pass, then about two weeks by truck to Tihwa. If I go by ship to Bombay (2½ months and terribly expensive), we'll just make the border about the time the pass closes. Doug said if I were willing to undertake such a trek, he'd foot the bill if the State Department won't authorize it. I am quite willing to go to India even if I shouldn't get over the pass. It would be sheer luxury to remain, say, in New Delhi, have an amah for the twins, WRITE, earn money, and be out in the world again. I would travel halfway round the globe just to see Doug and get straightened out on whether we're really still in love and will remain married... or what. I want to LOOK out of this world and put his eyes out. I don't want to rush to him all "dears and darlings." If I am woman-wise at least I shall hold myself quite aloof and apart until the Shanghai score is settled.

JUNE 12, 1949—To wake one morning and find yourself 30!!!— with a son and daughter vocalizing for their bottles. I had some disconnected birthdays. This one passed as any Sunday except for my growing impatience to know if I'm going or not going to China, India or whatever. I have a feeling the whole thing is still on flimsy ground. The trip through India is typical of things Doug and I have undertaken; we rush toward an objective at all costs, and the costs have been terrific, though the end was finally reached... I'm afraid Washington's reaction to my letter on India will be a chilly "considered highly inadvisable," etc.

JUNE 15, 1949—No further word. Maizie's learning to drive her car. Mary is beginning to pull herself up to standing. Old Mike is chewed up with mosquitoes and hasn't progressed an inch, expect to grow fatter and cuter. As for the trip ahead, I keep visualizing myself in

Delhi instead of Tihwa. Getting a late ship start, I don't see how I'll make all the connections in time.

JUNE 25, 1949—Terrific setback… wire from State Department saying no dependents may return to China (or Tihwa) at present. Therefore they would not forward my cable to Doug, sent through their office. I had been getting everything lined up. Found only PAA could take us—at a terrific fare—to Calcutta where Doug would have to meet us. Barred from any communication, I can only turn away from China and Doug and face the reality of pitching for myself and the twins here. I can only see going to a less expensive place to live— Canada or South America, where I can be freed of the babies and get a job. What enforced separation will do to Doug and me and this so-called marriage, I don't know. Carol Pomeroy, my friend from Alaska, came through San Francisco. Through mischance she insisted on coming out to the house to see the twins. We first had lunch in town; however, she got off on to Christian Science. While I could never be drawn to the religion, I was impressed with Carol herself, and one little slogan of hers which so soothed my frantic beginning against four walls of obstacles, insecurity and fear of the future. Said Carol, "Let go. And let God." She was shocked when she saw the twins, supposedly no more than 6 weeks old. So I wrote her a letter telling her the exact truth. Back came a beautiful letter of understanding and loyalty. But she does urge me to consult a practitioner. Maizie has counter-talked that move. Actually, I'm not on the market for any religion, but I was deeply moved by Carol's intercession.

JULY 4, 1949—This day reminds me of the beginning of this Mackiernan episode. Is it possible this is only the second year since I met Doug and here we are indefinitely separated plus being parents of a son and daughter which are really mine, not his or "ours"? It is even more incredible that I no longer love him. I guess I don't mean that with such finality, but it will take a reunion and a lot of understanding to make amends and I don't think Doug is capable of appreciating the disillusionment Shanghai and the birth of the twins was. If he sends no word on the 13th of this month I will know that he really has forgotten our love affair, for I am sure as long as Canton remains open, so does the State Department wire. Meanwhile I am looking for a small house in this vicinity to get myself established until at least next spring. I hope gradually to work myself into a newspaper job of some kind hereabouts. Out of the corner of my eye I am picturing us in Canada or Chile. I want so very much to have a career again—and with my darling chilluns I'll never be alone. Mary, whom I have rechristened Posey, is now STANDING—she pulls herself up in the playpen and hangs on, her little fattie legs are quite bowed, but funniest of all is the slow sag of her didies until finally they slide down to her ankles. While ol' Mike can't even hold his own bottle and doesn't creep yet.

JULY 7, 1949—What mental HELL Maizie and I went through yesterday. I got a letter, relay from Washington, of a cable from Doug. He told me to fly to India and meet him in Kashmir by mid-August. Maizie and I went over and over every angle. The decision was staggering. I would have loved the trip alone, but taking the kids floored me—plus the expense. Two things finally decided me. An instinctive RELIEF whenever I weighed NOT going (here is everything for the babies), and as Maizie said, "It all depends on how much you love Doug, because that is all you'll accomplish by going back, plus being out all your money." So I took stock of my feelings and decided Doug wasn't worth it. That decision was so SLAM-THE-DOOR final I knew I was right. So today I sent a cable: DEPT REFUSES PERMISSION AWAIT SPRING REMEMBER THIRTEENTH PEGGE.

JULY 11, 1949—I have gone through another firebrand over Doug—unexpectedly received a letter from Clare Boothe Luce saying she would use her influence to get Doug transferred to a post so we could be together. The slight reopening of the door to Doug upset me deeply because it all boils down to the question of Doug and me. I feel grimly now that he is not worth all the mental anxiety and exasperation to straighten out our affair. I am having enough difficulty trying to find a place to live and get established on my own without taking Doug on too. I've been going around muttering, "The hell with him, the hell with him and trying to take care of the kids at the same time."

Just for the record, Nat. City Bank $540.09.

JULY 13, 1949—Posey and Mike, feet to feet, in the crib beside me. This has been a terrific day. First, when I awoke I was dimly aware that this was my second anniversary and it would mean nothing. I shoved the thought from my mind and was really not expecting the cable when the phone rang. I remember the girl saying she couldn't pronounce the name of the place. Then I heard DEAREST LOVE ON OUR DAY STILL WORKING ON TRIP DOUG.

I was quite excited that Doug had not forgotten, that he'd planned and timed his cable against every obstacle, and what he said came from his heart. I really felt for the first time that I wanted to get to him, throw my arms around him. I could recall what it was like to be in love with him, and most of all I could forgive him with grace for the letdown in Shanghai. Maizie was touched to tears of relief for me that the cable came, and we spent maddening hours going over possibilities including the flight using the Clare Luce angle. I called the Indian consulate about a visa. Then in the afternoon mail came a long and very "diplomatic" letter from Doug's chief in Washington saying under no circumstances was I to go to Tihwa, and there was the slight hint that American citizens would be evacuated from

Sinkiang... That decided me with finality. I would not make any attempt to go back now. Meanwhile, Maizie and I have found a house on a hilltop for $5,000 that is darling—near the shopping center and post office. I'm sure I can manage the payments. Lou drove me over this p.m. so that he could go over the structure himself. He thought it a good buy also. So tomorrow I'll take steps to acquire it. Maizie and I already have it "designed" in our minds. To top everything Posey, who loses her diapers while standing up in the playpen, got a yellow jacket sting on her little pink bottom today while I was in the midst of my weighty affairs.

JULY 25, 1949—I am about to move to my new, my FIRST home, without Doug, but with Maizie. She is decorating with an elegant hand. How KNOCKOUT the living room will be. And the babies' room... it's a lot of fun... and on the hilltop I can call all my own... the view from the little porch—Posey hanging sleepily but stubbornly to the rail of her crib prompts me to be brief and turn off the light.

AUGUST 19, 1949—Dateline: 67 Rocca Drive, Fairfax, Calif. FIRST HOME.

On August 2nd a boxcar on Burma Road tires rolled up to the Blinns. This s'zit, the young truck driver from BEKINS moving and storage swung down, then stopped short regarding Mike and Mary sitting on the grass waiting to be moved to their first home a half hour later. All I call my own, including kids, rolled into the back yard of a white bungalow perched like a robin's nest on a topmost branch, wobbly maybe, but wonderful for the VIEW. Although a Swede grandpa carpenter I got in for about two weeks told me, "Them underpinnins ain't much good come a bad winter," all my whole heart tells me the MOUNTAINS and TREES all around are enduring personal and close companions. With all the shambles, repairs, bills and babies around me, bearing down on me single-handed, I have but to retreat to my porch and its view for brotherhood and balm. I love my trees and my VERY OWN, OWN HOUSE. My INDEPENDENCE AT LAST. Yes, this little hilltop house was worth twice what I paid—$5,500 plus $100 for oddments of furniture. Pictures will have to be taken. The "Before" horrors. Maizie is doing the decorating as I forecast. We've knocked "bats" (wooden stripes) off walls, shoved things around, painted the living room a sort of jade green—my labor charges for carpenter have been very high, $2 an hour—father and son—but a lot of changes have been made. On top of everything else I got a lot of overripe fruit as a gift and had to stop and make jelly. My cooking has not been anything rave'able— trying to reduce recipes to single servings, or else, like some Spanish rice I made, eating the same dish all through the week… solid. I do want to improve and get some really good dishes down pat before Douglas himself returns.

My first friend in the new neighborhood was the public health nurse, an Armenian war widow and a dear: Esther Baxter. What's more, she sent the babies to the clinic for a checkup and shots at no cost to me. Second friend is the boy next door, George, who works in the butcher shop. He sees my light in the kitchen (my blessed reading time) and comes visiting. Nothing deters him—once I was scrubbing the bathtub, determined to finish. He sat down and talked to me through the wall: The other night, for privacy, I took my book (Kipling's short stories) into the bathroom, leaving the invadable parts of the house in darkness.

AUGUST 26, 1949—Speaking of darkness, today was really the day of black despair. I had an armload of Mike en route to the chow trough for eggs and oatmeal when the phone rang. Mike didn't get his oats for an hour afterward and he raised a vigorous inquiry. Posey wondered about the slack service and made pointed reminders to the management. But the pillar of twins and motherhood had a complete collapse over a telegram from Washington: AM CONSULATE OFFICIALLY CLOSED BUT YOUR HUSBAND REMAINING TEMPORARILY HANDLING DISPOSAL U.S. INTERESTS DATE HIS DEPARTURE NOT YET DETERMINED. This came COLLECT, after a week of fool's paradise. Last Sunday, Doug's father had telegraphed a Boston paper that carried a story saying that the consulate was closed and all hands identified by name were coming out, presumably through India. Mother also sent a Chris Rand, *New York Trib* story about the same thing, so I wired Washington for confirmation and waited in a daze of emotion. What would I wear when I met his plane? Must get my hair done, etc., then this ice water deluge... so added to my disappointment is the increased anxiety. The longer Doug stays, the more danger he is exposed to.

SEPTEMBER 3, 1949—One year later. A set of twins, a house on a hill, and round trip to China. A long and meaningless march of month after month, taking care of twins, that about sums up a year of "marriage." No husband. Not even a spiritual marriage, this, for I have no heart-of-heart love bond with Doug. I think about him, alone in my little private lookout on the mountains, but my thoughts are more calculating and anticipating the reality of his return for an extended stay, than any romantic dreaming of my love. I am getting myself ready for his return by more or less building up my defenses. I have no guarantee that anything as flimsy as "love" will be the main element of reunion and RENEWAL of the bond, which will eventually grow into a feeling of marriage, home and family.

SEPTEMBER 7, 1949—As a belated P.S. to above entry. Maizie telephoned this cable from Doug. ALL MY LOVE ON OUR FIRST STOP IMPORTANT NEWS COMING BY MAIL. So he did remember... the cable was sent on Sept.1 direct from Tihwa. I must honestly admit the cable did not strike a chord in my heart for Doug, just an added anxiety for the letter. A mystery as to how it's coming, WHEN, etc. I've had no word from Washington either, so I know nothing. Maizie came to lunch today and I let go on Doug about this separation of endless months, for I interpret the "mail" part of the cable to be the explanation of why he's not coming home. The constant trickle of cables over the month have (has) increased my feeling of insecurity and unsettledness. Maizie, as always, went on in loyal defense of Doug. Progress on the house is like unto the diligent anthill toil. I get so little done each day and the incoming bills just make me shudder.

Just for the word—My New York bank account lists $540.09 as of August 1949. Looks exquisite and very tantalizing under the name Pegge Parker.

SEPTEMBER 19, 1949—Letter from Chris Rand, *New York Tribune* correspondent in China (Hong Kong now) with some reassuring news about Doug… everyone expects him to leave soon… they have contact with him by radio—some charter flights are due up his way soon. Paxton should be arriving in India with Doug's letter one of these days. Frank Robertson, who was in Tihwa when I was and who caused me so much trouble with the gravediggers (past history) is also in Hong Kong and not yet free to marry Jackie, who dragged around with him in hopes. How I pity her. The effect of the letter was reassuring but I will still WAIT for some POSITIVE words before getting any tingles of anticipation and some dread and uncertainty on our personal standing. As a house "wife" and decorator and twin keeper, I am on an unending 6 a.m. to midnight shift. I stained my living room floor one day, was paralyzed and even so it has to be gone over and smoothed out. I'm so new at everything, the cooking too. I do want to have the chow department in perfect eating order by the time Doug gets back.

SEPTEMBER 30, 1949—TWIN'S FIRST BIRTHDAY—Posey looked at the yellow fluff of cake on the tiny spoon. Her big, inky eyes were doubtful, suspicious, but no, maybe a taste wouldn't be so bad. She opened her baby pearled mouth and took in her first birthday cake. Fairy stuff, it melted away on her tongue! It was gone! Mike grabbed his off the spoon, then sat deliberating solemnly the handful of yellow crumbs, hoisting them to his mouth. Alas, they tumbled and spilled down his front. He stared down at his flaky shirt front. Confounded stuff!

The first birthday was a golden California day. Having no room or place to receive guests, I had to set up a table on the porch. But the sun, uninvited, soon moved us out. The twins received a beautiful set of clothes from the Blinns. Posey in pink organdy was just a big-eyed cloud tottering up and down in her crib. And Mike was very natty in a yellow and lime checked suit. I thought of Doug with pride when I looked at the children—and with a kind of anxious longing. It seems so unlikely he should be on his way home now. I was greatly upset the other day to receive a letter of sharp rebuke from the Mackiernans, accusing me of great indiscretion in Doug's job and whereabouts. I sent the letter to Maizie for judgment. The thought of a split with the in-laws is distasteful. I would dread it. I am afraid, too, Doug might side with them against me. Alas, it seems my hold on him and "marriage" is hair-thin.

OCTOBER 3, 1949—The letter from Doug is here, and it tells me nothing. I look at these pages of hastily misspelled, strikeover typed correspondence in vain. I wanted to know two things: WHEN he is coming home (he has no idea) and IF he loves me. It says so here, blandly, nicely, repeated at times. But the words only antagonize me, for they are not the language of my long-lost lover. The details of his letter are not important, except that I feel the same exasperation. I MUST, MUST write my way out of this existence, somehow.

NOVEMBER 16, 1949—Letter from the embassy in New Delhi this morning, saying my note forwarded to Paxton had been delivered on his arrival from Tihwa—over the pass—the papers and *TIME* carried a picture of dear ol' Pappy Paxton looking very rough and tough, whiskers et al. I do hope to see him and Tai Tai on arrival here, and young Dreeson, Doug's pal in Tihwa. In regard to my "husband"— have been in a mental muddle weighing my imprisoned frustrations on him.

The other night the old deep, deep wound of Shanghai was reopened. Neighbors, the John *Polk*s, came by for a minute to show off newborn (one-month-old) Mike in a brand new jockey hat. We laughed, I cooed, and it was only after they left that I reflected on the beaming happiness and pride the father had showed for that little bundle that was his son. Remembering Doug and Mike— remembering cruelly and too clearly—I wept my eyes out and despised Doug to the point of passion. I feel so maddened to picture myself waiting for him, so anxious, when he himself is no "goal" for us. The mental wretchedness of his Shanghai husband-and-father unlovingness tears my whole being to be UP—OUT OF HERE AND AWAY—FAR–FAR–AWAY, to SOUTH AMERICA IF POSSIBLE. Letter from Eva McGown urging I get Mother out here to help me and that I tell her the truth. I'm of two minds on that. I somehow don't think my poor darling Mother could take it, any more than I could bear such a shock from my adorable, beloved little Posey.

The children are a million rewards for everything. Posey teeters around on her chicken wishbone, bent baby legs. Old butternut Mike is too heavy for his feet. He goes very flash-quick on all fours though. Odd how he curls one leg under him, kind of makes a tractor tread of it. Terrible knock-me-out struggle to get their clothes on, like running down a gridiron to get the pants on a touchdown star. Mike can drink marvelously from a glass and he eats everything in sight. But Posey is a trial in the high chair, very spitty on any lumps or new food. They can't say any words yet.

Spending thanksgiving with Esther, my nurse friend, at her apartment. Going with the kids. I'll really enjoy it more than at the Blinns, where I'd be nervous every minute the babies would touch things. I seldom see them. Lou is so full of football he rarely makes the 10-minute ride over to see "Mikey."

Saw Carol Pomeroy the other week. She's still keen on my becoming a Christian Scientist. but I don't think I could get a prayer out of my heart any more. She also told me my darling Dassie Wilson is to have another baby. I'm so happy for her, just wish she'd write and tell me herself. Carol is to be married, too, in the spring. She really has gone all out for me. Bless her.

NOVEMBER 28, 1949—FAIRFAX, CALIFORNIA—Doug is in Tibet. I just had a letter this morning saying our State Department was notified Doug left Tihwa the first of October for India via Tibet. He is expected to be in India the first of December and HOME FOR CHRISTMAS! I had been at the very last thread of my endurance when I got word Doug was truly and officially and positively on his way home. Paxton got out over the Leh route. Terrible time. Write-up in *TIME* magazine. When he flew into Washington he telephoned me to say he had no news of Doug, but he might be out in the Spring, six more months. Oh no. I could not bear it!

In my anguish and despair I began to pray. I guess it was my first real prayer since before the twins were born. I just said one "Our Father." Now I am just holding my breath that he does come home and actually gets here by Christmas. I'm working like mad on the house so it will look good when Doug gets here.

DECEMBER 1, 1949—No more word from the "intimate stranger" to whom my thoughts fly wildly with visions of our reunion. Will I be arm's-length "cordial" with the pained heartache of Shanghai in my heart—and eyes. Or will I be carried away with sheer relief at his safe physical presence? Will I fly into his arms and hang on for dear life? This, and HOW I will look at that moment are prime concerns. Had a long letter from my dearest D.A. Wilson announcing the oncoming wee one. For my own: I put Mike on his upsy-daisy potty seat for the first time after his lunch. Posey came on the run to see what was going on. Mike sat there chuckling and wiggling his toes, delighted and thrilled at the new experience, then a little pink flush came over this face—he frowned and grunted and a lovely doo-doo was achieved—on his very first sitting. I fed Posey and tried her—not even a tinkle! They are coasting along smoothly now, sleep all night, eat well, play reasonably well unattended. Posey loves to wrap herself in any fallen or low-hanging garment. She got a pink nightie of mine off a hook, got her neck through the armhole, and I found her strutting around with the nightie trailing behind like a court of St. James train. Mike, who has 12 darling teeth, loves to bump his head on the floor. He gets on all fours and kow-tows to the blue linoleum. He does not walk yet; pulls himself up and goes like a shot—but no steps.

DECEMBER 24, 1949—FAIRFAX, CALIFORNIA—Baby narcissus at my table—Christmas Eve—scent is sweetest spring. Christmas Eve. The twins in their cribs, bottoms up, thumbs in mouths—they had a very bewildering and bountiful Santa visit. We went over to the Blinn's. Maizie had a lush Christmas spread and presents—boxes and bows. Posey blinked and withdrew a little, her hands clutching me for security. It took her an hour or so to relax. She sat in her little blue PJ's close beside me and hardly budged. Old Mike was gleeful (the taffy polish on the floors was ripe for zoomie crawling). Their toys were so profuse they couldn't concentrate on them. Posey seemed to enjoy the sparkly ribbon most.

Christmas this year was truly felt, but mostly inwardly. I enjoyed the approaching holiday more by myself. I loved getting out the boxes

I sent east. Listening to the music and plays on the radio. Reading the Other Wise Men—the cards I got—the incoming gift packages. I really felt quite serene and happy... Doug? He seems so far away and now is so unaccustomed to my life and thoughts. I can't say I really mind him. His parents were lavishly generous with gifts for the babies. And to me. In summing up: my isolation is becoming my world, and I am happier and richer for it.

1950

FIVE MINUTES TO MIDNIGHT, NEW YEAR'S EVE—JANUARY 1, 1950—The nicest memories of today are... Mike's first haircut!!! And the surprise of a box of lovely flowers from Doug's brothers, Stu and Malcolm. Mike was a man among men in the barbershop. He sat atop a board laid across the arms of a regular barber chair. Lou Blinn stood by, balancing him. I stood on the other side. Posey clutched at my throat. Mike took the clipping very easily, and what a trim, polished little gent emerged under the scissors and comb. His head is in perfect contour, his ears close fitting. He was so good during the whole process, which lasted about fifteen minutes. Clipping cost $1.25. Esther, my trusty friend, bounced in on me, and we had dinner together—one she brought: New Year's stew.

After she left, the flowers arrived. I was quite surprised, so much so, I told the delivery boy to wait until I had read the card to be sure they were for me! I recalled all the flowers Doug had sent me so long ago as I arranged these. New Year's brings Doug sharply to mind: the delay in news makes me feel he had to dig in along the way and will be indefinitely delayed. I also have a premonition that news from him direct will be a shocker and a terrible letdown, such as a telephone call from Doug in Stoughton—his arrival on the East Coast and his going "home" first. I feel he will never see my little hillside roost—and—I may be predicting overtime—I am afraid his return will present unhappy, upsetting, nerve-straining difficulties. Of one thing I am SURE—and so sure I RESOLVE it from my heart: I will not be writing a New Year's memento for 1950 from Fairfax, California. It will either be Doug or South America ... Chile.

Sum total of 1949, as I observed at Christmas, was a year of inner spiritual and mental activity—emerging hand-in-hand with God is a mark of progress and certainty that RIGHT will make things RIGHT in the end.

[Editor's Note: At this point, there is a break of more than five weeks in Pegge's almost daily entries in her diary.]

FEBRUARY 9, 1950—FAIRFAX, CALIFORNIA—Resuming the private papers of Pegge Parker Mackiernan, like beginning a new book of fate—and beginning with a jolt at that. I was suddenly informed a radio newscast had carried a story from Peking, China, that Doug S. Mackiernan was a spy. That he had "fled" into the Himalayas bound for India, after organizing resistance groups in the now Communist province of Sinkiang. The phone began ringing—the *San Francisco Chronicle* and the *San Rafael INDEPENDENT.*

But the next day things really got underway—even to making a radio broadcast over the Mutual Broadcasting Co. (a telephone recording). A reporter and photographer—then another photographer arrived. Posey ran and crawled onto the blanket shelf in the closet. The reporter followed her, so she met the press revealing two licorice eyes over a foxhole of woolly blankets! Mike—old "butternut" as I call him, slept heavily, soundly through it all—until I had to wake him, dress him, then trot him out before the flash bulbs and a cold world. Naturally, the string of questions about them came up. How old? Where born?

etc., etc. The subsequent stories were happily balled up on that score. Eva McGown in Alaska was in a loyal flutter up there when three stories and two pictures appeared in the *NEWS MINER!*

The day was bedlam—I listened to two or three newscasts at the same time, rolling the dial from one to the other. The next day, January 31, early in the morning (Mike on potty, Posey ready for her oats and drops), Washington D.C. called. A Mr. Friedman—then Brad Connors (of China days—uncomfortable memories—he opposed my going to Tihwa in the first place). Anyway, they had a message from Doug—from somewhere en route: "Am safe and well. Expect to return in the Spring." They said another message was expected in 4 to 5 days. I immediately called AP (old loyalty) and gave them the news, for which they were grateful. Then I called the Mutual Station (KFRC), which had been so helpful before, and another broadcast was made—heard coast to coast on an evening broadcast called "Mutual Newsreel"—the local station called too, and we recorded a 15-minute interview. All the papers called—and in between the news came over the air. Were it not for my dear Armenian nurse friend, Esther Baxter, I don't know what I'd have done with the twins while all this was going on.

Just as I was sitting down to dinner, a phone call from Boston— Doug's mother! I had not wired her on receipt of the news, because of an earlier incident when she sent me a sharp rebuke for "pestering the State Dept. for news—just the first wife, Darrell, etc." It was tactless but not really unkind, though it made me reluctant to wade into any entanglements. Mrs. Mackiernan was simply floored to open a Boston paper and see our picture! She has not written or communicated since. And I am apprehensive about their disapproval of the way I handled the news release. In-law crossfire is a delicate matter—and they have been so very kind on other occasions that I must overlook little things.

Clippings have poured in from Fairbanks, Alaska, to Miami, Florida. One of Doug's former sergeants from Tihwa wrote. Lois

Fegan in Harrisburg retold my life story on page one of the local paper. Mother and Daddy had a field day. For Mother, it was the thrill of a lifetime to open her pet *New York Journal American* one evening and there see Pegge and twins with caption: "Where's Daddy?" She was in raves. I made every big paper in the country. Poor Doug hardly got a mention.

Al Morano sent clips from Connecticut. (I suppose Clare Boothe Luce also knows.) Colonel (Ed) Kearney, my old Shanghai boss, called the Torians (Ed and Lou) in Carlisle, and Ed told him. He was amazed—didn't even know I was wed. Now he will understand why I didn't rush home from Tihwa! J. Hall Paxton sent me a penny postcard from Florida.

And then there is another incident to record. Young neighbors asked if I'd "baby sit" their 4-month-old son, Mike. Mike arrived with his diapers, etc., at about 7 p.m. I was so absorbed in him that I didn't get my dishes done or the floor mopped. Then Esther had brought me her pressure cooker, with which I decided to experiment before cleaning up. I was in the midst of stewing dried apricots when there came a slap-rap on the door. "Is this the Mackiernan residence?" There in the dim rainy night stood BILL MACFAYDEN—a friend of Doug's from Nanking in the days before Doug trucked up to Tihwa and met me! MacFayden entered—the kitchen was fumey with apricots. I looked hideous—goggles, no make-up, knee socks, flat shoes. I waved him into the living room, where Mike began to howl. MacFayden stumbled over the mop and bucket, and the key to my floor furnace. For a smoothie, a sort of young Mr. Sophisticate, all this must have been nonplusing indeed. I was frantic. For a friend of Doug's, I would have wanted to put up a charming front. I finally got the goggles off, some lipstick on, made coffee, and then we talked. And the talk was disquieting. We talked of Doug, and Bill knew and understood this long-lost husband of mine very well. About Darrell and Gail—about his brilliant fits and quirks, and his loneliness. "When I read about you in the papers," Bill said frankly, "I knew the girl Doug would marry must be something. I know physical attraction wouldn't get him—that the girl would have to be quite exceptional." I winced—I wasn't appearing anything but a housewife.

We talked on, the mood confiding. I rashly admitted my estrangement, because I felt Doug did not appreciate or love his twins. To my horror, I began to cry. Bill offered a shoulder and I was self-conscious of his touch. I felt horrible. All the spiritual resources I'd built up that helped me past Christmas etc., seemed dashed. I felt Doug's presence and the accompanying dread that Doug may be not at all in love with me when he gets back, alone. Bill, who is shrewd, dig-down perceptive, said that whatever "marriage" survives will be my making. Every woman, every wife's job is to be the kneader of all disseminating parts into the whole piece. Doug will be twice the job of the twins, twice the "baby" for my solicitude. He warned me to not make an issue of the twins, to let Doug get to know them gradually. But most of all to give Doug SECURITY, the rock foundation of family and home he has never had outside his parents' household.

Every sensitivity, every lone star in my heart, every buried, tender hurt and anguish, the unspeakable thoughtlessness and preoccupation of Doug in Shanghai, every giddy doubt of my own future and security rose to skin surface. To climax this brutal evening, as we stood in the doorway, Bill mentioned something about finances, the finances of a friend with yachts, etc. I shrugged, "How little those people have really," etc. He looked at me, digging an arm into his overcoat, "That's because you live so close to economic realities!" Wham—the squalor of my dear little self-made house on the hill, rose up a monster of defeat! I broke down, wept wildly—failure, failure—I saw this house, and myself, as perhaps we will look to Doug. The nightmare of feelings, thoughts, emotions continued until the wee hours, nearly 3 a.m. when the neighbors came for their son—again yelling, though he is a dear little fellow!

EASTER SUNDAY—APRIL 9, 1950—FAIRFAX, CALIFORNIA—
Another holiday comes goldenly in California, without Doug and
with only a vague expectation of his return—a remote feeling of
never belonging to him at all. Meanwhile, the only spark of news was
a surprise phone call from a Mrs. H. W. BESSAC in Lodi (California).
She said she is sure her son, a wandering language student, is with
Doug and he would be a boon companion on such a rugged trek
out.

The only other event to mark the work-work-wash-baby-baby was
the arrival of Mother from Harrisburg. I sent for her on impulse one
day, feeling she should see the twins and me, and know the truth.
Daddy came forth with her fare, and out she came. I met her in
Oakland, supremely unafraid, sure everything would be fine. She saw
them asleep the first night and was awakened early the next morning
with their bottle cries. She seemed to accept their size, and I did not
get around to saying anything for several days. It came on a sunny
afternoon on the porch after lunch. She said a major I knew in China
had made a blundering remark at the Torians' in Carlisle. All of them
had been stunned in embarrassment and denial—it must have been
a nightmare. Mother didn't know what to believe and finally decided
never to mention it unless I did. As long as my father never found
out, she accepted it in the spirit of one-of-those-things, now done
and past and not to be mentioned again. I have written Doug in New
Delhi that Mother will be here on his return and she will know all.
What Mother doesn't guess is how I feel about Doug. To my surprise,
her only "anti"-reaction to the whole thing seems to be an aloofness
and subconscious resentment of Maizie. She and Lou have not been
here to see us for two weeks, and Mother just refused to go over for
dinner. Too glamorous, too much being "dressed up and talking" and
worrying about the "bugs" as we call the twins, getting into things.
Lou has been having a time with ulcers, so Maizie has had her hands
and mind full these past weeks.

My darling babies are as always my supreme solace and reassurance that all this lone-machine-drive household routine is not meaningless waste. Posey is lovely and lively. Mother adores her. Butternut got in her bad graces by howling at 2 and 3 a.m. every night for her first week here so she got no sleep at all. (One evening at 11:00, the Bill of the preceding episode called and wanted to come visiting at that hour. I had just fallen asleep, was angry and barely coherent to him.) Posey can say "baby" and "duck" but still takes a bottle and is unsatisfactory on the potty. Mike walks now, in a funny, stiff, fanny-wiggling way, eats everything in sight. He is slower than Posey, but to me, adorable and blond. I do, do wonder what comes next—where we go from here.

MAY 7, 1950—Taking the thread of my last words, we "go" nowhere from here via suitcase and haste, but in an anguish of rebelling and impatience, we go very far and very fast. There is no news, and now, no hope, no anticipating. I have gone through wild, sword-in-air battles of refusal to wait longer, even to be still bound to Doug. Mother has listened in patient sympathy, not taking seriously the rage I feel at the destruction of any love, bondage or belonging to Doug. She feels certain when Doug gets back we will pick up on our life together, etc. "The children are his, too. You've got to think of them, you know." Yes, I remember how they "belonged" to Doug in Shanghai very well and bitterly, that soul wound. Well, as the days drag on, meaningless except that they are busy with livelihood, I am resolved that something must be done. I cannot—and will not—go on, pointlessly waiting and waiting for Doug. I pray, however, that I shall not do an impulsive thing, a wrong thing, for well I know the brutal penalty of a mistake. I tell myself on this imprisoning situation I must ride with it, not fight it. What cannot be cast aside or surmounted must be carried along, to some purpose. If my days are meaningless or empty, that will be my own omission.

Today, Mother is off for a visit and I have been alone again. A good thing, for I am an "alone" creature at heart. Anyway, I began the day despondent. I went to Mass and found response and warmth in it, but walking home I felt my rebellion and helplessness strike at Doug in abounding fury, even hate and detestation. Then, after Mother went off—half reluctant, sensing my mood—I resolved to test myself. Could I take this day in my bare hands, as it were, and make a success of it, a triumph? Now it is over, and to my honest satisfaction, I must record that this was a good day. Some change, some plan and pattern will clear this muddled bewilderment of the moment. I am sure I feel no hope or expectation of Doug's return. Almost I can imagine his NEVER returning—and that being a freedom to live my own life again.

My darling wee ones are fine. They just got over colds, which were costly in medicine. Posey's one foot still toes in, but the $50 it would cost, plus the difficulty of transportation for doctor visits, has stopped me from doing anything just now. The Blinns had us all over to dinner, and I put Posey in her best bestest, a pink pique fluff-skirted dress with a matching bonnet. I put two little bunches of white forget-me-nots over each cheek. She was enchanted with herself, conscious of our raves and adoration. Her bright black eyes danced with lights. I could have hugged her to pieces. In a white linen outfit, old Butternut looked as though he were making his first communion. Now that "Banie" (Mother's baby name for herself) devotes herself to Posey, I feel my heart going out to Mike. He takes quite a beating from sissy. She pulls his hair HARD, really sinking her fingers deep in his silken, taffy topping and pulling with all her might. As I was feeding Posey her dinner in the high chair tonight, Butternut, on the loose, came duck waddling by and on tippy toes grabbed her spoon away. In a flash, Posey sank her fingers into the back of her filcher's head and dragged him back. He yielded without a word!

On April 19, received a telegram from D.A. (my Dassie) saying her son, Richard, was born in Boston. I rejoice with her and feel even closer to my dearest friend. For now we share a son-and-daughter bond. The Mackiernans were lavishly generous in their gifts to the twins on their "birthday," April 30.

SUNDAY, JUNE 11, 1950—FAIRFAX, CALIFORNIA—Oh, to write the following is anguish. For while my stricken brain finds the words, my heart and soul cry out to the Great God for a Miracle, for Doug's life, that he be spared, even when we have already been told to anticipate his tragic death in a raw and barren Tibetan outpost.

Wednesday morning, June 7, a Mr. Fulton Freeman, Bureau of Chinese Affairs, Department of State, Washington, D.C., called in person. He had flown here from Washington to tell me the ghastly news that Doug's evacuation party had been ambushed in Northern Tibet. The Tibetans, being very anti-foreign anyway and not realizing Doug was a friendly U.S. official, fired on them. The messages relayed to New Delhi did not mention Doug by name but stated that an American Mongolian language student, Frank Bessac (whose fine family I visited recently in Lodi, California) was the "sole survivor," and he, I believe, was shot in the leg. Another non-American was also killed. Further details should be forthcoming next week. Washington will phone me direct. I was too stunned with shock and disbelief to do more than thank him for coming and to say I would not give up hope—well did I know Doug to be indestructible—until there is the inexorable, unmerciful truth—the full, positive truth. We also discussed financial matters, as the twins' needs and their jeopardized future compels me to concentrate on reality. Mother, who went ashen and expressionless at the news, spoke up sharply that, in answer to Mr. Freeman's offer to "do anything possible," the Department must get me a job to secure my future, on behalf of the twins. Mr. Freeman said that was an excellent idea. He would see about it on his return to Washington. He left.

Every day since, and every hour, I have prayed in desperation, and every time the phone rings, the beat of my heart is a painful bellow. I wait in terror for Mother to answer. A ban of utmost secrecy has been put on us for reasons of international and political security (one special reason we are confident the Department will move quickly to find a berth for me, once the facts are established).

I wrote Mrs. Mackiernan (we were told she was simultaneously informed, in person, as I had been) that I would bring Doug's babies to her in Stoughton as soon as the facts are established. The following day she telephoned me, asking first guardedly, "Pegge, have you had any news?" I burst into tears, and she urged me to continue talking, said Daddy Mac refuses to believe Doug is gone, is holding out to the terrible end, and she begged me to come to her big, now-empty house, with the twins, which I assured her I would, by flying with them to Boston as soon as possible. God love her. How glad I am I have my precious, my beloved, my beautiful son and daughter, Doug's life in them, to take to her.

My own heart of hearts has been deeply grieved that there was this estrangement, now perhaps never to be banished except in my sorrowful forgiveness and forgetting. I truly feel I had stopped loving Doug in Shanghai and only lived through all this long waiting in California to begin all over again, from scratch if possible. Our love and then our marriage—as the days pass since the terrible news, I am overcome with sorrow for Doug, for the waste of his gifts and intellect. The sum total of his life being so meager and oh, his poor lonely soul, like his poor lonely life, have an even lonelier eternity. This morning at Mass, though I prayed and wept and cried out desperately, desperately for his survival, if it must be, my future wifehood must be a service of atonement for the shadowed pattern of my poor, once passionately loved, beloved Doug. I offered first to God the months of waiting, these empty days and weeks, totaling nearly two years, as a service for Doug. My grief for Doug, as a human being, as a man, as a soul of God's—is profound and wholly separate from any semblance of self-sorrow. I know that my life will go on, and my future will perhaps find this tragedy a beginning of life for me and the children. But until that call comes, until we KNOW, I can hold onto the hope that Doug may yet come home to me. No matter what, however, at least in these crucial hours, I am at God's knees. Before, when the children were born, I was bitterly alone. Now, I know that HE has given me many kindnesses before exacting the penalty. God help us.

JUNE 20, 1950—FAIRFAX—It has come—and he is gone to eternity as though he merely hurried in and out of my life, leaving in my soul a bitter sorrow and in my heart and arms, the brief transmission of his being, Mike and Mary. It is too fantastic, too staggering, too cruelly dramatic for any real-life tragedy. On the sunny, normal afternoon of JUNE 14, 1950, the call came through from Mr. Freeman in Washington. He simply said quickly, "Pegge, we have positive word now, and the incident occurred exactly as we feared. Bessac, himself, sent the cable from the capital of the country we discussed. Doug is buried in a village; we can't find it on the map." I cried out in anguish that I will not even have his poor broken remains, his poor ashes. What were the details, why did they leave him there alone? Bessac would give a full report on his return, and I gathered he would be ordered to come to me with the details, in about two weeks. Mr. Freeman had not yet called Doug's family. My heart broke for the blow about to come to them. I cut the line then with a quick goodbye. The vision of that lonely grave on a Tibetan hillside smote my heart in unspeakable sorrow—poor, poor darling boy of mine. Mother was overcome and wept and wailed and squealing! I called Maizie—then quickly had to bring myself together to run to the bank, closing out my joint account in San Francisco and transferring an emergency advance (from the Department) of $900 to a single checking account.

Later that evening, I called Stoughton to talk to Doug's mother. Her voice broke, so humanly grieved, but holding up for the sake of the others. Her grief shook my emotions, and I could barely express my love and sympathy. I spoke to Dad Mackiernan, too. Oh, Doug was his dearest son, his great pride. I said I'd come to them as soon as Bessac returns with the details and whatever effects can be salvaged. I slept that night with a strong straight whiskey numbing my senses. Certain things will bring Doug ALIVE and near. I can remember as much of him. I do feel a positive certainty, though, that Doug had lived his life, and God was kind. We had so little time and with circumstances so against us, God was kindly on our side—that we were together in our love and our children were created in time—softly and in love. Though we seemingly broke every law of society and church, we did not transcend God's loving understanding. I am terribly, desperately impatient to begin my life in the outside world again and to somewhere find someone else. I am beside myself with eagerness to know what kind of job might be ahead and if it will be possible to go out of the country. I am a bit apprehensive over how the Mackiernans will accept the circumstances of the twins' birth, since there is still a note of condemnation in Mother's knowing. I am afraid I will not want to stay long in Stoughton, and I want so much to have my job lined up, my prospects at hand when I get there. The house is for sale and to outward appearances I merely go about as though "there is no news," even to Carol Pomeroy Elwell who was here the other day with her kind and elderly husband. With my heart dead inside, it was torture to listen to their cajolements of do-not-lose-faith, etc.

As for the twins: the other morning while Mother and I were having a late breakfast, Mike crawled out the window of his room onto a flower bed of pansies—from there he fell to the ground, over 20 feet, and screamed in terror and shock. We heard the yells, but they sounded so far away they didn't seem to be "our two." When I opened the nursery door and grasped the disappearance of Mike, I nearly died until I got across the porch and down the steps to him. He was unhurt except for one arm which seems to pain him somewhat. Mother and I were so shaken and upset over this that we groped our way to the bathroom for aspirin tablets. While swallowing them, I turned in time to see Posey flying head-over-heels out of her crib onto the floor. All's well now, however.

JULY 4, 1950—FAIRFAX, CALIFORNIA—July is my month of keenest remembrance of Doug. How fantastic, utterly out of life and like some installment melodrama is my series of July 4th notations from 1947 on. Now the events to record are absurdly disconnected with the theme. Yesterday an application blank arrived from Mr. Freeman—first step into the gray mist of my uncertain future. Mother and I are here, quietly biding our time waiting for the return of FRANK BESSAC. A few firecrackers bang and pop in the neighborhood, but this is no holiday for us. Our job of the babies and housework goes on. Mike's arm, which seemed to "pain him somewhat," was broken— "greenstick" break at the right elbow, which meant X-rays and a bone specialist, and a plaster cast from shoulder to wrist, not that it slows him down one bit. Posey has her dear little feet in a metal splint to hold them in an out-toeing position. She has been very agreeable about this restriction, too. In this interval I've had a message from Bessac saying he wished to express his "deepest regrets" to "Mrs. Mackiernan" and that "Mackiernan's personal effects" are being sent to India (my heart will be torn in unspeakable sorrow at the tangible emptiness of "effects" without their owner). Bessac is writing me a letter giving full details (oh, my heart—what are "details" since my beloved will never return to us?).

Bill MacFayden, that bowtie GI student friend of Doug's, descended on me the other evening. It was good to fill my ears with talk of Doug in the present tense, the LIVING TENSE. Also, he made a point clear to me regarding the reason for my letdown in Shanghai. Could it not have been my poor darling was just overcome instead of overjoyed with twins? Under all personal and political circumstances, did he not need me to share his arduous efforts to get us (the two of us) to Tihwa? His need for me didn't come to me at all. But how can I, the mother of my two adorable, heart's love babies, feel I should not have brought them to being? They cost me dearer than dear. I am deeply pained to realize now how much more I would have given Doug in his so-little-time. Alas, in actual physical acquaintance, nearness, I knew Doug only about a year! I've had wonderfully kind and generous letters from Doug's parents agreeing to keep the twins for as long as need be, even forever! Until I get "adjusted." Even if I leave the country with the State Department.

SEPTEMBER 3, 1950—FAIRFAX—I have had two letters recently that were worth noting. One struck a shattering, bitter, horrible blow. It came from Lhasa—from FRANK BESSAC—and for all the worth of its contents and the great effort to get it out over the mountains to me, it might as well never have been written. "That Mac's dead while I am alive and well appears to me to be a gross injustice," he began. Then he got off onto a business summary of Doug's "effects"—nearly all of which have been SOLD, and at a profit, he hastens to assure me, listing each price and adding this is "about three times the price in India or the United States." Our ring, or Doug's wedding ring, and wallet are "lost"—or at least Bessac seems rather haphazard on this point. I was just outraged over the letter and Bessac, but have since contained myself, holding my faith and personal judgment of him until he gets home. He has arrived at last in Delhi, narrowly escaping a severe earthquake in northeast India. His mother (whom I admire greatly, and feel warmly toward) wrote to say they had no direct word from him yet. She has invited me down there, and I have delayed returning to the East Coast until Bessac does get back. Everything concerned with this nightmare has been such a disappointment. I must expect little or nothing from my visit with Bessac. It is also an odd fact—the less I know about Doug's tragedy, the more unreal and painless it is. The other day, his mother sent me a map of Tibet with the village marked. I was sick and aghast to look at it. In these days, I do not dwell overlong on carrying vivid and loving remembrances of Doug. He seems a phantom, an illusion, even the twins are not tie or proof of Doug's existence in my life, because he was never part of them—a daddy to them.

I still feel God has HIS reasons and own intent in taking Doug, and I feel Doug was never meant for me. So many things were wrong from the very start. Only the twins, and they are such beloved darlings, come of all the entanglements and anguish. I hope desperately I shall marry, and love, again. With security and a home.

The other letter I mentioned was a very kind and personal one from CLARE BOOTHE LUCE. She wrote from her own heart with the understanding of her own sorrow (the loss of her daughter Anne). She said in gist "no one escapes some profound agony soon or later, but no one." And that there must be a REASON—the Hand of God moves with purpose and meaning.

In the interval of not writing, my father made a sudden and brief visit out here. He came to help me in my affairs, but as the house sale is at a standstill, there was nothing he could do. We also thought the State Department was sending a representative to see me with the papers that I, as Doug's beneficiary, would need to go over and sign. We've also been in a muddle over the absence of a will, or any trace of one. Daddy's visit was rather ill-timed in a way. I was so upset over Bessac's letter that I was a very poor hostess. Mother was at her wit's end too.

Paxton wrote he was afraid he'd "stuck his neck out" in his first letter to me, saying he'd lost sleep over Doug's death, worrying over ways he might have been saved. The Mackiernans are firmly holding out for just compensation for the twins and me—and we three will really make a stand if we feel Doug's affairs are not adequately handled. Meanwhile, the hardest part to bear now is the pall of activity, just waiting for Bessac. I am assured my papers are being processed for a job. I stressed my keen desire for New Delhi, but oh, this vacuum. The day after day of routine nothing. I am sorry also to note Maizie's ordeal. Lou is in the last stages of C *[cancer]*, and she is worn to the point of collapse. I feel sorry for Lou, but sorrier for the utter waste and uselessness of his life, in a way.

OCTOBER 4, 1950—STOUGHTON, MASSACHUSETTS—Can't believe that I am here in Doug's home, with all his brothers, his parents, and his TWINS. And that I should have let myself in for the heart tugs of staying here. I flew with Mother to New York. ANN BOTTORFF met us, and kind George Keibel. Ann had not received word from Bessac and thought it very odd. I flew on to Boston alone with the babies, and we were warmly met by the Mackiernans Sr. and Malcolm, the youngest, who looks somewhat like Doug. The first day was difficult for me. I felt since they are such STRANGERS to me, Doug too, as one of them, was a stranger also. Then I got going in the attic looking for some papers. Doug left so few, in fact all I did find were my letters to him. He had saved every one, tied in a bundle. I was oddly touched but after sorting through them, I will burn them. I found also his to me, and they tore my heart open. They did remind me that once we had loved each other with a great desperation and determination to be together. There are other reminders of Doug's absence—the brothers themselves, one newly married—Stuart—and all they have together.

Then I went to visit my dearest friend, DOROTHY ANN WILSON. She is so solidly established with her home, husband and children. I stayed overnight, and watching John with his little girl, who looks a bit like Posey, sent a sharp stab through me, sharper still because Doug cared so little for Mary. It was hard to see all D.A. had for her children—and she herself. Her own car, a summer house at Marblehead that was a mansion compared to my Rocca Drive monstrosity and the dirt yard my beloved little ones had. But one little incident sent a comforting measure of balance and perspective. John's manufacturing company had an obscure paragraph news story in the remote financial pages of the *New York Times*, and he mentioned with pride that he had gotten "extra copies," etc. I thought, when Doug's story was told, even before his death, it was Page One in the nation's press and radio.

We have gotten no satisfaction from Washington on the financial settlement of Doug's affairs, and after seeing so much CONTRAST to my way of life in Fairfax (on $118 a month) I am determined to take action if I must go to Washington in person. I am sorry not to have mentioned more on the twins. They were never happier. The Macks love them. The boys are fine to them, too. I am so very grateful. I am sorry being here is so great an anguish to me. I have not yet told Doug's mother about the twins' birth in China. It will be very hard to do and may change whatever feeling she has for me.

OCTOBER 19, 1950—BETHESDA, MARYLAND—Frank Bessac has just left and my anguish of soul is extreme, for Frank, at my insistence, related the final chapter of Douglas Mackiernan with brutal candor. I'm so shaken in my feeling of sustained love or loyalty, in any faith in my tie bond with him, that I am beyond anything to hold on to, except a vague hope that had Doug returned our tragedy might have been worse. I am confirmed in my belief that Doug's life was spent, and therefore concluded according to plan.

These are the highlights of Bessac's discussion: that Doug labored under some strain. Once he attempted to confide in Frank, and he withdrew. Doug snapped out of it, and nothing more was said. But Frank knew something was bothering Doug, made him irrational at times. Made him want to remain behind in villages, even to the point of risk. There were periods of flare-ups and arguments and strong differences of opinion. But they got over them. In the Black Gobi, Doug did a foolhardy thing: said they'd "manage" without water, at the cost of three days without any. He removed his ring when his fingers began to swell from frostbite. He referred to me as "my wife" not frequently and not often as Pegge. He said often to Frank, "Don't ever get married," although he seemed proud that "my wife" could and would go anywhere with him. He spoke little of the twins, but mentioned Mike and was glad he had his son. This is most painful, but Bessac said Doug had mistresses—Tartar women. It was his weakness that foreign women, and just plain foreigners, appealed to him. (This ugly truth wounded my heart sickeningly.)

"The most I did for Douglas was offer some stabilizing influence and probably held him, as best he could, to the long road out. But Doug sought death," Bessac explained, "and meeting you probably prolonged his life or his effort to live." Once he almost committed suicide. He walked off from camp with a revolver through his belt. Vasili (a Russian in the party) followed him. Doug sat on a rock with the revolver beside him for a long time, and then he came back to camp after the mood passed. Bessac said it may have been thoughts of "my wife" that helped him get over this. Bessac suspected a strain of hero-illusion in Doug. He wanted to appear tough and rugged before the Russians and others. Had Doug survived (pure conjecture) and had Bessac been killed, the experience would have snapped Doug out of his somewhat erratic mental state, or he would have gone to the other extreme. Bessac said of the two of them, Doug's survival would have been of greater value. "I wish I knew what the hell was eating Mac," Bessac said.

Doug was shot on April 30 or May 1, about midday. He was left unburied for about two months, but in Lhasa, orders were given for burial, with crosses to mark the spot. "Mac died in the Cold War," Bessac said. "He did some good in a sense of security to his country.

Don't forget him to spare a hurt to your pride at his unfaithfulness. You were the only woman who meant anything to him. Think of him with compassion for his weaknesses."

Next day—Tony Freeman has been here. His solid, protective assurances and sympathy for my plight were calming after the destructive story told by Bessac. I feel sure the finances will be worked out, but a job and something to occupy my mind are what I need most urgently. I suggested to Bessac that Doug's "company" might find me useful on a trip to Lhasa. He will let me know, he said. I phoned J. Hall Paxton and will try to learn from him whether Doug was such a mental and physical wreck out there. Then I am going to Weems, Virginia, to the good company of the George Wallaces. When I return I hope to get settled and job hunt.

Oh yes, the Medal. Doug was awarded a State Department Foreign Service distinguished service medal. I was invited, expenses paid, to Washington D.C. The Mackiernans came with me. The ceremony was composed of Marine Band music—blah blah speeches—but DEAN ACHESON made a brief talk. I was first to receive the medals and on the platform stood beside Acheson, as the Assistant Secretary read the citation. Then I said to him, "Thank you on behalf of my TWINS." He smiled automatically. Then the word TWINS registered. "Er. Oh—well—well," he blurted. The medal is dull silver on a red ribbon.

OCTOBER 27, 1950—WASHINGTON—I walked into Thebolt Taylor's office this p.m. at the new State Department building and did not at first notice Frank Bessac sitting at a desk. I was asked to wait, and as I turned away, Bessac spoke up. My heart leaped in surprise and remembered pain. I was rather cold and abrupt—inwardly in quivers. He came over to me, bent his six-foot frame to an Asian hunch beside me. "May I see you before I go home?" We stepped out in the hall and I turned up my eyes to study him. We stood quite close and wordless for a time. "You will not distress and upset me further?" I asked. He embarrassedly said he would not. He seemed to want privacy and to have something important to say. I have had inner flip-flops ever since. What use to relate the bewildering state of my affairs. I have seen Tony Freeman twice. I learned my FBI check, due perhaps to Brad Connor's negligence, never left his office from the end of July until yesterday. However, with swift action on Tony's part, my clearance is on a priority list, and I have been assured the job for me in India is waiting the minute I am free. Meanwhile, an effort will be made to get me on some kind of payroll until the clearance comes through. In the background of all this lurks "the company." I am very eager to establish contact, but they appear reluctant to come forth—however, my trump card is their jittery fear that I "know all." I intend to use it for all it's worth. Out of all this my heart goes on feeling and longing. Every time I see a little child the age of my own, it tears at my heart. I am beside myself at moments. I must build a home around them and have some kind of love and marriage. This I want so desperately I am afraid my longing may show and certainly I would fall in love again, very blindly and helplessly.

NOVEMBER 8, 1950—WASHINGTON, D.C.—Of all the incredible experiences and rare vignettes of this Washington Saga, this was the most exquisite. I felt like a heroine moving in my own mystery thriller. First, some background: When Bessac came to see me he strongly urged me to phone the man Doug had named as my emergency SOS contact. Bessac's visit yielded nothing, incidentally, but a friendly feeling. We took a long walk. He told me about the ceremony of visiting Genghis Khan's dubious, but picturesque tomb crypt in the wastes of the desert. He stressed the fact that the "effects" coming back were all his own except for an old sleeping bag and the Kazak belts. He saw me off on the bus to Harrisburg, where I had a nice home visit, saw Ed Torians, etc. The following weekend,

I went to New York and spent a long day and two nights with Bessac's friends, the Bottorffs. I believe they are more MY friends now. Sum total of our compared notes was Bessac is suffering shock and various psychological shock reactions to his experiences, which have warped and twisted his chronicle of how it happened. That he resented, envied, and to a degree, hated Doug is quite clear. Twice in his life, his worth has been considered of secondary importance to another's—first, the favored brother, Arthur, and then Doug. He told the Bottorffs he often sees Doug's face before him in haunting nightmares. Seems Bessac also worked out a nice deal with *LIFE* magazine for which he was handsomely paid. I was so infuriated over this I was speechless. Heaven help him if he attempts to cash in on Doug's experience. I was so bitterly upset over Bessac's profiteering on the side, and so stirred to even the score with him that I wept myself to sleep, murmuring desperately to myself: "Vengeance is mine, vengeance is MINE, sayeth the Lord." John Bottorff was very sympathetic. I think he had some genuine feeling for me, though Bessac is his friend. He gave me one of his Chinese gowns, which I've been wearing as a housecoat.

Visited the PAPANIAS. Helen large with second child. Ralph as warmly cordial as Doug's close friend would be. Oh yes, had a brief chat with LOWELL THOMAS on the phone about Tibet. I had hoped to visit him and sound him out on his desire to return to the Roof of the World. I am now doing a temporary job at State, in a dismal section, however—Lebanon, Syria, and Iraq—but my loyalty check should soon be through, if my experience tonight did not squelch that: I telephoned—shall we call him "John." His voice and manner were true detective story—smooth, deep-toned and calculating. Yes, he would see me, about 5:30 in my office. Instinct told me to be strictly on guard, At just 5:30, while my boss was droning dully through a Lebanon policy statement, a man walked into our office asking for me. I looked up swiftly with a mounting pulsation. We spoke, and for all his trained, experienced composure, as we looked across that office in recognition, an indefinable current of feeling flashed between us. He was tall and slight and dark, mustached, lean-faced, with intense black eyes. But in general appearance, the color of his tie, shirt and jacket marked him for—oh, say an actor or radio commentator between jobs. My heart raced in my throat. At last! At last—one to speak to of Doug. At last someone, the one, who knew the whole inside story! We sat in the corner of a semi-deserted office. I asked him first to identify himself by giving me his Arlington address. He eyed me with swift professional approval and gave me the correct address. Then we spoke. It is not professional to say what we discussed in any but barest detail. But he did admit an admiration and fondness for Doug and a tremendously high regard for his integrity and ability. He spoke not so feelingly of Bessac, assured me Doug knew every minute what he was doing—sent regular reports of his progress and came within hair's breadth of capture, which at the hands of the Chinese Communists would have meant sure and speedy death. Hence, "What was eating Mac" was that he had lots to worry about. Complete rejection of Bessac's story about Doug wanting to die, lagging behind. Somehow my faith in Doug's loyalty to our love is restored. John left no doubt whatsoever in my mind that the full responsibility of a dangerous job involving great security would not permit Doug to have women in his quarters. John's picture of Doug so thoroughly agrees with mine (before Bessac) that I am almost restored in my heart to my poor lost darling. One disturbing note, however, came when John rather rejected the idea of my going to India... Feels I'd be on the spot as the widow of a Communist declared spy. This threat may knife my chances of getting to go to Delhi. He entirely vetoed my secret itch to get to Lhasa. Incidentally, John indicated his agency would have had other plans for Doug on his return than a foreign post for two to three years. "We needed his technical skill, and he would have been kept right here." John drove me to the hotel and left me with the assurance that I would hear from him in about 10 days.

NOVEMBER 13, 1950—WASHINGTON—A rather fateful series of events has taken place. One morning, as I was hustling belatedly to get off to work, the phone rang. A kind friend asked, "Have you seen the *Washington Post?* Brace yourself." Bessac's *LIFE* story—a gory glorified account of Doug's most tragic journey—was too shocking for words. Full-page pictures of the Tibetans who killed Doug, and a long one-sided account of it. I was enraged and bitterly saddened. Thel Taylor was loyally sympathetic (he, like Tony Freeman, is a fine, good man and genuine friend). I went to see Tony at his home. He was appalled at Bessac's caddish, selfish behavior. He pointed out also that the State Deparement went to extremes of secrecy and had me play acting for months, all for Bessac's safety. What was to prevent my going right to AP and selling the first exclusive? Bessac's safety, as long as he was within the borders of the U.S. My case had, Tony felt, been ethical appeal, but nothing legally substantial, the one hope: a personal letter to Mrs. Clare Boothe Luce. I wrote one, putting it this way: Can the magazine bring pressure to bear on Bessac? Certainly, if anyone was to profit by Doug's death saga, his children have first or equal claim. I wrote it all out in longhand, and mailed it with the feeling that part of me went out to that brilliant and lovely lady with the letter—now that I have thought about it, my life, future, and certainly my beloved darling babies. If Mrs. Luce is sympathetic to my appeal and I receive any payment from the magazine, I shall use it as the first contribution to the Plan growing to the point of intensity, where there is no turning back. Maybe this is a moment, a phase of my life, maybe not, maybe this is the Reason, the long way I am to go from here, always God's road, with my children and others.

I want most passionately to buy a big old house and fill it with children from all over the world—little ones of my own—I want, most passionately of all, a Tibetan. My idea basically is this: to fill up the heart and the house with children who need both, to give them a life start and send them back to their own country. I can get the thing started with whatever pension I finally receive from the

Government, and I can keep it going with what I shall write about it. This time, until I hear from Mrs. Luce, will be my period of decision. I'd like to have God's okay and to know He thinks it a good idea and that I have the makings of being the mother of, say, 12 kids of as many nationalities and colors. So we'll use Mrs. Luce as the signal. If she gives me my "starter," I'll go to see her with my idea. Golly, I can see my House of Nations, with Esther Baxter, Mother and me to get it started. Somewhere in New England, I think. Maybe Connecticut. Another encouraging move in this direction came in the news that my house in California sold for $6,000 cash. I felt a tug at my heart, as so much happened in that house.

NOVEMBER 24, 1950—WASHINGTON, D.C.—I have had no sign or encouragement yet on the children's project. No word from Mrs. Luce, and I am beginning to be concerned that she may not answer or at any rate that she can do nothing. The idea is still worth keeping in mind.

Meanwhile I have seen John again. Mother had come down for a nice weekend. We were getting ready for breakfast when John called. Could I see him Monday night? I was in a trance until then. His fascination, his dark-of-night interviews, his voice (this, with his manner, is exactly like a three-act Broadway mystery drama technique). It poured rain. He picked me up at the hotel, not coming into the lobby, or the light, of course. We drove to a side street and parked for four hours. It stopped raining, and a misty midnight moon glowed dully on the still wet shiny streets. And John asked and asked and asked, even with a threat, what did I know, how much did I know. He would MAKE me tell him. I must tell him. Doug would want me to. He was Doug's boss. But not a word. Nothing, nothing did I say. We reached a crossroads dead stop. He adroitly changed the subject, indicating (1) he could offer me a job in Washington editing long reports, boiling them down, etc. (My reply: not interested unless there were a Boston office); (2) There will be no objections to my going to India, but as a cooling-off "period" so that my name would lose its associations; (3) If I am not satisfied with my financial settlement, he will see what can be done. He feels I could be useful in their work with careful training, but he's afraid I am not free to do a real job. "You always go back to your children, your attachment for them is very deep, and close concern for them might limit your activity." John touched on the sides of the Bessac story. "Just what you'd expect from him." He also said he'd turned Bessac down on a job. John knew Bottorff also—did not indicate very high regard for him (I was a bit hit on that, poor Ann.) In discussing Doug, the past came up: "We are not concerned with morals, only security." It cut at my heart to speak of my poor Doug like this—of course John knew everything. Under what circumstances the twins were born, about Madame X—saddest of all, about the Russian episode. John's comment: "It was a hell of a lonely place, Tihwa."

DECEMBER 7, 1950—WASHINGTON, D.C.—I opened the kitchen door and stopped still. The little girl with the plain jane shiny brown hair and round little face stopped still also, hesitated, then ran shyly away, from Mommie. I went home to Boston last weekend and found my beloved "babies" so big and grown up (in a month, the change!). Mary ran away, but was irresistibly drawn back. In her baby mind was some instinct, perhaps, that told her this "lady" in the little feathered hat, brown coat and mink scarf was someone to whom she belonged. I found Mike under his high chair. He crawled out, grinning, and cried, "Scissors—scissors." He is fascinated with the "s's" and says the word over and over and over in great triumph and delight. I held him on my lap, and gradually Mary crept near. "See the kitties, see the kitties," she ventured, crooking a little finger at my furs. Finally, she got near enough to touch them, and I swept her to my heart. Mrs. Mack had cut her hair quite short and straight and dressed her in boys' blue jean pants. It moved my heart oddly to see her—almost homely plain, but her glorious eyes and pretty nose and mouth (on second study) offset the first-glance plainness, She touches the inner heart of me for little things. For instance, her devotion to Malcolm, Doug's youngest and only unwed, as yet, brother, is almost pathetic. "Mackie" she calls him, and he is awfully nice to her. She still sucks her thumb and Mackie tries to wean her away from it. She is so ashamed when he asks to see "the thumb." She hides her hands and if teased further, will burst into tears.

Mrs. Mack has been quick to teach the twins everything possible. When out in the car, they learn colors: blue sky, green trees, red traffic light, green lights, etc. Mary knows them. Mike, who is all mimic, imitates Grammie Mack to a "t." Mary, however, knows what she says, her letters "w" and "r" she pronounces adorably. And she knows her animals in the storybooks too!

My joy and pride and soul-restoring happiness in seeing them is beyond description, so much of anguish and distress in the month or so since I'd seen them all fell away from me when I was alone with them in the room and they were as sound asleep as angels with heads tucked in their wings. I found myself saying as I looked at them, "Dear God in Heaven, I have them and ask nothing more, There can be no more than this." The fact that I had to scold and even smack Mike a few minutes later (for tantrum, howling and head beating) did not detract from the ecstatic bliss of our reunion.

I presented the Macks with Doug's watch. I did not mention my anger over Bessac claiming all the Tibetan presents as his, and I've already gotten notice of the effects—they were shipped from Calcutta Nov. 7, so should be back soon. Also, for the record I received my first paycheck on this temporary job: $148.64—not sure what that means "per week." Also for the record I had a very kind and moral-support bolstering letter from Mrs. C. B. Luce's secretary. She said Mrs. Luce, upon reading my letter, "lost no time in getting in touch with the editors of *LIFE*. We have not had word from them yet, but you may be certain that as soon as anything comes along, Mrs. Luce will be in touch with you. I am sure I need not tell you all that is in Mrs. Luce's heart for you during these trying months."

DECEMBER 14, 1950—Well, if the Answer to the Tibetan Incident was to be my Baby Project, I got the first "sign" from above—Mrs. Luce and the coffers of *Time-Life* magazine. A check for $750 was sent to me—with it came a heart-softening, kneeling, apology-begging letter from one *LIFE* editor, EMMETT J. HUGHES, who said, "My reaction to your letter is one of almost as much shock as you must have had upon seeing the article. For having quite unwittingly added to your troubles, please accept my sincere regret. When Mr. Bessac was in the office at the time the article was being finished, he stated quite explicitly that he was going to see you. It was beyond anyone's imagination here that he would see you without informing you of what he was doing. While we shall try to ascertain more about the use and final disposition of your husband's camera (which may have taken the pictures *LIFE* ran), this fact in itself has little to do with the elementary justice of your feeling. For while authorship has its own claims, the story of Douglas Mackiernan's last performance of service belongs first of all to his family" etc. He was bleeding his penance, and I wrote, dear diary, the discreet line on the bottom, "cc: Mrs. Clare Boothe Luce" explains everything. I immediately wrote Mrs. Luce that receipt of the check gave me a "humble and quite self-conscious feeling of God looking over my shoulder, that there was a little story behind the letter I'd written her. "Should any money come to me through you, I had promised God it would all be given away again," in her name and Doug's. "I've got a special project in mind," I confided, "of which I'm sure you would approve, since it involves (appropriately at Christmas) homeless children. I haven't worked out all the details yet, but," I concluded, "I will let you know later how far your efforts succeeded to an end you did not guess, and with as yet unforeseen results." I go around thinking of my Project, aghast at all the practical details to be worked out—half girding for a campaign to get a baby column going, on a Washington paper, immediately as the initial down payment. On the other hand, torn with impatience to get to India to acquire the celebrities of the Project, my two Tibetan babies. Nothing seems to be moving in that direction, the loyalty papers may be bogged down somewhere. However, in my heart of hearts is the weakening self-knowing misgiving, if I go to India, that I shall stick to any Project. Oh well, it's in the Good God's Hands since HE saw fit to start me off with $750. Can I let Him down or do anything else without His Hand at my heels?

1951

JANUARY 3, 1951—WASHINGTON—Mike and Mary awoke Christmas morning all unaware that a pack of adult elves and Santa Claus Mackiernans had been at work in the living room, which was overpowered with a twinkling tree—presents—gleam-glow tinsel and sparkle! When awake, pottied and dressed, they were led into the room. Mary was all gasping "Oohs" and "O O" eyed. Mike took the situation in at a glance. His bright eyes fastened on a shining new truck. He made a dive for it, down on the floor, cheek on rug, pushing it back and forth, intent and fascinated watching its wheels go round. Mary was handed toys and sparkly bowed packages—dollies, tea sets, a mop and broom set, clowns that wind up—a snowstorm paperweight, books by the score. Mike got himself detached from the trucks and cars long enough to explore other wonders and curious all about. We had a lot of fun over them. Nice gifts went 'round for the "Santa Clauses" themselves. I am genuinely pleased to note that Madame X—Darrell Brown M.—sent the twins nice gifts from "Gail," So she must know she has a half-brother and sister. Frank Bessac

592   *Slow Boat to China*

astounded us by sending Mrs. Mackiernan a postal money order for $25 to "buy the twins something."

The Christmas visit home was a good one. Mary wears a corrective shoe, but her legs should straighten out eventually. Mike has learned two nursery rhymes, "Hey Diddle Diddle" and "Mistress Mary Quite Contrary." He has his howling spells, devours his food, sleeps like a laborer—and is quite the little guy. Mary is quite aware of her dear brother's shortcomings. Howls when he does anything he shouldn't, like putting his fingers in his food or spilling things on the floor. (Whenever she sees any spills on the floor, from kitchen to living room, she runs and points them out, pointing down self-righteously. "Mike—Mike," she assures you.) We had a day at the Wilsons' which went well—picture taking—gifts exchanged. D.A. dashed off, leaving me to fend with four lunches from Rich (baby) to the twins. But she came back with a fabulous emerald-green chiffon dinner-dance dress for New Years's. Our "visit" consisted of conversation on the ride home. She darts and flits at a jarring pace around her house, until the quickened pace is disconcerting by contagion. I return joyously from our visits (I do love her dearly—my closest standby friend), but with butterflies in my tummy and vaguely aware of a panicky pace—over what? I bought a coat at Bonwit's, $98, and a hat to go with it, $25, at a swank shop. Winter navy, trimmed with Persian, princess, dressmaker touch lines, but it's only size 12. Though the Mackiernans approved, I wondered what their private opinion was. The same day I made this major purchase, I lunched with Aunt Ethel Mackiernan. I do enjoy her and admire her. There is good, genuine stock in the Mackiernan family. But our lunch conversation in the Revere Room of the Parker House (alas—an "anniversary" of January 13, 1948 was spent in that very room with Doug) turned to Doug, speculation on Bessac's brutal tale to me—his accusations, which Aunt E. immediately and indignantly swept aside. I found myself telling her (perhaps in a subconscious effort to have someone in the Mack family understand "my story" and my experience with Doug) about the dread and painful Russian episode. She was aghast, relived only that her brother (Dad) and Doug's mother would never know. I was shaken and distressed myself that the episode had come out. It is remote that the Russian girl would ever come forward. But at least Ethel knows, and she can protect the family's interests. I wonder what Ethel thought afterward. She too had regarded Doug as a Boy Scout—from such a high plane and by such conventional (Boston) standards. Poor darling—if I did him an unnecessary disservice I am sorry. The same day or evening, I looked up Sonia Wallace's daughter, Diana Charleson, had dinner in her apt, liked her, felt a warm appeal toward her. Felt also the absolute stone-cold wall of isolation from her stepfather, my mentor and guiding light, George Wallace! Though, since my last visit there, my heart is with Sonia. Diana's "chances," as they say, seem limited in Boston. She, with her very correct and glamorous childhood in Europe and her British citizenship, finds herself just a routine nurse at Mass-General. Not meeting interesting (eligible) interns, doctors or men. Or any to speak of. Wise Mother, seeing this, suggested my visit of course. I left my beloved dear, darling twins (they are so wonderful, are developing so well they "give" so much to me, in my heart of hearts, so much delight and reward for all the cost) and went on to New York in time to see Ahmee and the Papanias. Ahmee I found shrunken and weak and low, but mentally (in conversation diverted from herself) keen. She had warned me before that the end was near (inevitable, what else?), but I shushed her, etc. (what can be done now?). Alas, I left my Ahmee in my fondest recollections long ago. She seems most vitally and belovedly associated with my "green years." I shall always remember her as the beautiful voice—perfume—and long, jangling beads striking me in the face whenever she bent down to kiss and primp over her plain, alas, second-image granddaughter: "Margaret, who looks like me, poor child."

Helen and Ralph, on Long Island, have just had a son, Jerry—and Judine is quite a little miss. My New Year's was spent in Helen's kitchen doing dishes—drinking coffee—folding a mountain of laundry. Ralph was conked out, asleep in bed. His studies at the Army Weather College are overpowering. He's not by aptitude a "scholar." Helen and I had a real gal-gab, all about how Ralph, so engrossed in his studies and anxious about making the grade, has lost "lover" interest, is even vague in rejoicing over his son, precious man child. I listened and much came back to me—Doug and our man child. The baby is as newborns are, but fine, healthy and appealing. I arrived back in Washington with a hollow, almost depressed reluctance. This State Department "routine"—the salary!—I still weigh India against my baby schemes.

JANUARY 16, 1951—WASHINGTON—I was astounded to pick up a routine document in the office today. "Daily report—Foreign Broadcasts China" on page 1. "Former British Consul Exposed as Spy," Peking, in English Morse to North America, Jan. 14, 1951, Tihwa, Jan.—delayed. G. Fox Holmes, former British Consul in Tihwa, who collaborated with the AMERICAN SPY, D.S. MACKIERNAN, and carried out espionage activities and other activities against the People's Government in Sinkiang Province, was deported by the Public Security Office on Dec. 16, 1950. After his arrival in Tihwa in 1948, G. Fox Holmes worked hand in glove with Mackiernan in anti-Soviet and anti-Communist activities. He (Holmes) also gave one thousand five hundred U.S. dollars to Criminal Mackiernan to help him escape. He (Holmes) took over from Mackiernan important intelligence reports and materials, two radio sets, etc. On Dec. 4, Members of the Public Security Office reached Holmes' home and found six reports on the revolution in Ili (Kuldja where I had been in 1947), etc. 10 documents pertaining to collaboration between Mackiernan and Osman, etc. Holmes has made a written confession of his crimes and signed his name to the intelligence reports found in his possession.

Dear God, poor Holmes must have had a rough time, and heaven only know what stuff of Doug's they found. Paxton called Waddell from New York to check if we had any further information on the fate of Fox-Holmes (who owes him $500, incidentally). I was sure "John" had seen this transcript and more!

The battle on my case continues. The first release of funds has bogged down to the point where I made and fully intended to follow through with drastic appeals to highest authority. I am keeping daily worksheets of "Progress" and every conversation. Mr. Waddell and I have our ups and downs. Today I went in person to the Civil Service Commission, armed with birth and marriage certificates. Was assured "within a week" I will know what figure will be set. That may be. Still have alerted Mr. Mack, Sr. that he may have to come down and help expedite.

Mildred Allport (first meeting Bern 1947—press attaché American Legion), who is across the hall from me, has been a gem-treasure out of the blue—confident young mother—interested ear—a darling. She is going to Frankfurt, but leaving much of her great charm and ideals for life behind with me for always.

JANUARY 23, 1951—WASHINGTON, D.C.—There have been many astounding events to mark my stay in The Department. Today was another. But first let me record some vital statistics. CAS is the center of "John's" and Doug's affiliation, "The Company" which paid him an annual salary of $8,344 (this may include the Department's Vice Consul "bit" also). Also a regular "line" was prepaid in advance for the Macks and me—particularly was T.F. (Tony Freeman) to watch for any "hunch" I might have of Doug's true job. This information has been disturbing and unnerving. Certainly, it estranges me from the one man I held my most loyal and faithful friend—how well he played the role assigned him.

Next item: I had lunch with a certain rather high-placed lady today, who almost shocked the ears off me. We were in the Department cafeteria, within earshot of dozens of fellow diners, and the charming lady imported a most outrageous tale to me .... concerning the morals and general deportment of an Ambassador's wife. The stunned effect of the lady's glib calumny hung over me like an evil fascination, since I may someday meet her dazzling victim. (What a story, too—what a story.)

And now to grimmer stuff. Last Friday night when I came home, three checks from the Civil Service Commission fell out of my mail box: one for $88 for each twin, ($176) and one for me for $168. Papers were attached showing something about retroactive payments to May 1, 1950 (retirement pension). I showed it to Mildred—we rejoiced—I phoned the Mackiernans in Boston. They were gratified at such a high monthly pension. Mike was lured to the phone to recite "Mistress Mary Quite Contrary—How Does Garden GROW." I was thrilled. Mildred and I discussed over milkshakes how I should invest my money—bonds, etc. Then, before hopping into bed I read the fine print on the attached paper and learned the cruel truth. These were the retroactive payments, and henceforth the pension would be $11 a month per child. Nothing for me whatsoever! I was too shaken to phone the Mackiernans again. I wrote them a letter, enclosing the checks and all the papers. I slept little, but the next day I was even more determined to make money, that I have got to earn an INCOME, perhaps at the writing again, when Mildred goes and I am isolated here. The pension figure can be appealed, but if that is as long and dragged out a procedure as the $4,000 check, I haven't the heart or endurance. I hope Mr. Mack can take it from there. No word to date on the check letter.

JANUARY 31, 1951—I have just talked to John... will see him in a few days. I do want to pin him down on finances and also tell him about leaving the country if I do. Since last I took up the record, my FBI clearance has come through and I was offered a post in East Bengal, DACCA. My second thought on this was to consult "John." More decisive though than this is the burning DECISION I must make and apparently soon: shall I go to India—or stay here and exploit every possibility in this Baby Column? I keep thinking of baby items—ideas—promotions as I pore over dispatches on Afghan-Pakistan border disputes (Pushtoonistan) and long, heavy-worded tomes on economic particulars of Chittagong! I've got the title of the Baby Column: "Small World." And ideas come flooding. Could be a magazine feature also. I've got a letter out to a former contact on *Ladies' Home Journal* and a note to Wayne Randall, who first hired me for the TIMES HERALD. He is now with the *Washington Post.* "Dad" Mackiernan came down quite unexpectedly Monday to see about our case, which is still dragging. That night (I treated him to cocktails and dinner) we discussed the case, and in conclusion, I mentioned my Baby idea. He agreed with me it had unlimited scope financially and otherwise and seemed to think it a better bet. "You could then have the babies," he remarked. My heart stopped, could there be the slightest inference in that comment that they wanted to take them. No, I decided, it couldn't be. I was, however, tremendously encouraged by his approval. The mental strain of indecision is exhausting. But more and more I see it. I am NOT going to India to do the job assigned, but to Pakistan for the intrigue and association of the country, for the hope of learning more of Doug's fate and for the social advantages and the companionable feeling of Bob Dreeson's being in Kabul across the way. Balance this with "Small World," a career for the rest of my days—great financial scope (baby products on the side perhaps)—remaining with and close to my beloved babies. Travel not barred at all. I can initiate my own trips. But it all boils down mostly to A JOB I LOVE PERFORMED WITH TOOLS BORN IN ME. The pressure on me now is stalling on the India job— at least long enough to make sure of "Small World." It seems to me a daily newspaper, possibly syndicated, would be a better starter than a magazine, but each has possibilities. Washington might be as good a start as Boston. Maybe by the time I reach Boston I'll be syndicated. Oh, sweet delight.

FEBRUARY 2, 1951—WASHINGTON—I am enjoying the tingling, exquisite, wonderful delight of an evening, the very best evening, with "John." Really, truly wonderful. I dressed for him painstakingly, wearing Boston's Best. The navy blue coat and Carnegie-copy hat—a dash of Shalimar. He met me just outside the lobby. He looked debonair, delighted—as though he had (as I) anticipated the meeting. We drove to the same spot where we had talked the last time in the rain. And the atmosphere of our interview was the same, though on a more companionable footing. I mainly wanted to tell him three things. First, my going to India. Next, what about Doug's unpaid salary, then, the insurance. He said he'd checked their accounting department and was assured State was in charge and everything was in the clear. About the insurance, there is no record of any at all. He did say, too, that everyone in his agency wholeheartedly agreed we were entitled to compensation.

Before meeting "John" I had a message to telephone Waddell (handling the case) at home "after 8 p.m." We drove to a Hot Shoppe. I went to a phone booth. John got two coffees and returned to the car. Waddell's message was: The Bureau of Employees Compensation has arrived and the figure for the pension: $161.67 for me, monthly, and for the twins, until they are 18 yrs old, $94.31 a month. Gail *[Editor's Note: Doug's daughter with Darrell]* will receive $47.15 a month. These figures are gauged on 40% of Doug's total base pay. Checks for retroactive payments from April 14 to January 1 will be forthcoming in the amount of $2,448—which includes the twins' and my income. John and I thought $255.98 a month was not bad. He promised to investigate the insurance, which he said, should be $10,000 and the unpaid salary and let me know. (So I shall see him again.)

We chatted and laughed often of many things. Apparently the new boss (Smith) has cracked the whip, weeding out about 150 dreamers and dead wood. He described Smith as a prestige man, former Ambassador to Moscow, confidant of General Marshall. Personally, he's an electric force—whiplash. He said certainly Smith would see me, if I asked for an appointment (to this I said I'd go and cross my legs). John laughed. "Yes, but" he checked the thought, "were I held responsible for the case, and if the general got a look at you and the legs, he might sense some plot." He advised another check on finances before we resort to that. I planted a remark that Doug's father knew about CAS. It was intelligently received. John confided he'd been primed to take the Southeast Asia conference trip to Colombo, but his chief is detaining him, to John's great disappointment. "I'll get to go next time," he confided. It struck me I had imagined seeing him in Delhi. "Oh," I chimed in, "were the boy to bring in a chit with your name on it, I'd put on a gold sari and come flying" (oh, wouldn't I). The evening's conversation was a special satisfaction, because John's manner was easily co-confiding. He assumed I well knew "everything" (I did, too, incidentally mention I know about the planned conversation for Tony Freeman. John evinced no surprise at my learning; he just confirmed it.)

It was a restoring, glorious feeling, this being with John—really the prelude to a deep attachment to love, for certainly, were he free, I would love him. Oh, what a champagne delight was the highlight experience of John—all our meetings, but especially tonight—and a gold thread to run through my thoughts and days. I shall see him again—soon. Odd thing tonight, too: When I came home from the office, a telegram. I shuddered—Ahmee, Lou Blinn, Genevieve Blinn? Filled with anticipation of John, I felt incapable of an obituary. I just peeked inside the wire to see the signature, BLINN. Alas, poor Lou. Not until now did I rip it open—message, "Love to see you."

Alice Blinn. That's *Ladies' Home Journal* and Small World. I shall spend the precious time of this week on making a presentation, then scurry up to New York to sell it. But oh—my gypsy heart is dancing, dancing with the laughing man with the gray-flecked black hair. The mustache that seems to move and accent the quick, gay laugh—the black eyes—the professional, cultured voice—John, who is such a good companion. He did say he thinks about me very often (oh yes, and the $10,000 unaccounted for in Doug's case was State's money, not the Company's). But Doug's plan was always to bury what he couldn't take along. It was John's guess he'd done that, figuring he, or someone, would get back someday to uproot it. I brought up the point of wanting to know who ordered Doug to stay behind—John looked at me sharply—denied it had been the Colonel. "State's orders," he said. "I wonder," I continued, "had it been Butterworth?" John wisely "wasn't sure." He added he had a special loathing for Mr. B, having known him in China. His replacement, Rusk, is a fine gentleman. Oh yes, two more points: There would be no harm in my seeing Vasili Swansdorf in Delhi if he is still there. And the "Major," to whom Doug wrote in formal notes, was John's colleague in the "Company." He is no longer an associate, however.

FEBRUARY 6, 1951—WASHINGTON—This has been a day of twists and turns—sharp needles in my heart. First, a nice chap, MULLIN, whom I'd casually met, invited me to lunch. It was a startling surprise when he hailed a taxi and took me to the very swish Watergate Inn along the Potomac. Also, it was in this very same restaurant that Doug and I had celebrated our only 13th (July 13th) anniversary together—of all places to take me. This young, smiling chap insists I get to Delhi, though some pressure has been put on me to go to Madras in South India. But (thinking of my Baby "Small World), I coolly insisted it must be Delhi. No progress on my case, no word from John.

Now to the tense little drama in my room tonight. The "effects" of—Frank Bessac? Or Douglas Mackiernan?—are here. I was totally alone tonight, and the news that "two wooden boxes" awaited my claim, smote me with dull dread. One box was very small, the other just a bit larger than a footlocker. A handyman ripped off a lid. I had them delivered to my room, and then I went through them, bit by bit. Fascination and wonder and pleasure came to me as I lifted silver bowls and heavy musk-odored garments from the boxes. There are two Buddhas—and most prized of all, a long heavy gold and silver prayer wheel. Really, this exquisite, meaningful object is my favorite piece. There were little weather-beaten volumes of Leo Tolstoy's *War and Peace*, with Robert Ward's name written in the front and a Chinese dictionary. There was a large picture of the Dalai Lama with his name (autograph) written in red ink—rugs—some wild ones I never recall seeing in Tihwa—lengths of brocade, the Z-Kazak belts, which definitely were Doug's, Bessac said—and two worn, reeking fur-lined hats—really horrid things. A number of winter garments, gowns cut on the China pattern. A long pair of worn, heavy leather boots. Three Tibetan scrolls, one with very lovely colors, two quite hideous. Except for the prayer wheel and one or two other things, I wanted to get rid of them. I was tempted to call John. I do want him to see some of the things, and I'd like to give him some memento.

FEBRUARY 11, 1951—WASHINGTON—Letter from Frank Bessac out of the blue: "Enclosed are the color negatives which were in the camera from Tibet." (I notice he avoids mentioning Doug's camera.) "I hadn't told you about their existence, because I thought they were all classified. However, some of them were. It seems that the camera, as with mine, must have been clogged with dust as soon as we left Urumchi. All the negatives are in this envelope." The pictures were not very startling. Doug was in none of them. I shall show them all to John next time we meet. My future seems confused from here.

I have been too bogged down mentally and emotionally with the Mackiernan case to give much energy to "Small World," though I have done research, interviewed pediatricians on my lunch hour, etc. If I don't go to India or to Delhi, I'm not sure what's ahead there. I miss the twins so terribly.

FEBRUARY 13, 1951—WASHINGTON—What a distressing postscript to the Mackiernan saga. Last night, Ann Wheeler came home with me to see the Tibetan oddments. We had just gotten settled in the room, when a long-distance call came in: Mr. Mack, Sr. He told me he'd gotten, at last, the check from GAO for $4,000 plus. Then I asked how the insurance is coming out. Mr. Mack seemed a bit touchy on this point, resentful and quite emphatic that he wanted no meddling or interference. I tried to explain (though it was an embarrassing strain with Anne right in the room) that the only possible hope of insurance lies with the Company (John's outfit) and I am not meddling. It is just that I alone have the personal contact with them. There was an immediate blind spot on understanding. At this point, Mrs. Mack took over the phone, making a great effort—as though exerting every ounce of patience to reason with an irascible child. I became very upset, more so because Anne was right here, and I had no privacy. Finally, Mrs. Mack lashed out in exasperation: "You have nothing whatsoever to do with this. You don't know the policy numbers or anything about it. Furthermore, you are completely out of this. The policy will either be made out to Darrell or to me!" The conversation became more strained. The crowning blow-up was a blast from Mr. Mack. He took the phone from Mrs. Mack and burst out: "Either I handle this or I resign right now as administrator. You can do what you like about it." I was speechless. The conversation ended abruptly.

The day had not been a successful or smooth one. I had a raging, splitting headache. I was very, very tired. The affront and the tone of the entire conversation sickened me. I was overcome—could it be the eagerness for the insurance was based on the possibility that Mrs. Mack would come into the ten thousand? I rejected that conclusion as too abominable. Then I wondered about the bonds made out to her and the stress on the twins' pension payments being made out to her! Anne, who has had some experience in mixing families and finances, urged me to get an attorney at once. And by ALL MEANS to take the children, and as soon as possible. My heart quailed. I could not bear a family break. For part of it would destroy the flickering, faint bondage with Doug. For if I take the babies from the Mackiernans, it will be an act of disassociation, disaffection, dis-relationship. I have never been so utterly, utterly distant—so angry and so saddened. It is a good thing my life to date has equipped me to stand alone. "Tough," that's what Bessac called me. Thank God I am. My day—this wretched one—began with a rather pointless, though interesting interview with an attorney from CAS. John had phoned and said he was sending over one Chuck Price to see me. He will have all the facts at his fingertips, be able to answer all my questions. Although he impressed me as possessing that certain keen watching, concentrated manner—and the VOICE quality—that sets these men apart in their own rare and exclusive genus, Mr. Price (ex-Navy man, and clad in his ex-Navy windbreaker) had only one thing to say to me: "I assure you, Mrs. Mackiernan, that steps are being taken to conclude this case and to track down this confusion over unpaid salary." About insurance (though I was very guarded in this), he said what John had: No record—not a single document in writing, but he would check further.

Incidentally, while this nerve-straining pursuit on my case continues, I am thinking about the two possible jobs in the future. The Department's USIE people first had me slated for Delhi, then today mentioned Lahore, in north Pakistan. But I do truly feel "Small World" is my true career. Little progress on it, however, with the concerns over the case.

On top of everything, last night I had a telegram from Eddie: "Ahmee very ill. Can you come on immediately. Ans at once." I really felt my shoulders giving way under the load. I felt, however, very shoddy and unfilial to send a reply that I could not come now—that for one thing, finances were low.

FEBRUARY 20, 1951—WASHINGTON, D.C.—Just talked to John. There has been no follow-up of my conversation with Mr. Price, so I enquired, what was up? John had no answer either. Yes, he admitted, there was still money outstanding—unpaid—no, nothing on insurance that he knew. Also nothing from the Mackiernans all this time. I suppose they were quite annoyed and out of sympathy with me. But I have been to see a lawyer, Samuel Horne, who is Mildred Allport's attorney also. I felt the stress of a "drastic step" when I first approached his office, but the ease, assurance and sense of security our conversation gave me, has made me more adult. And henceforth I shall have legal advice for my affairs. The best thing he told me was the Mackiernans have no custody claim on my beloved babies. The guardianship papers only protect them financially, as Mrs. Mack must keep books for the court's approval. It is a protection for the babies and me. I shall see Mr. Horne for further advice soon.

Meanwhile I'm still slated for Lahore—or hadn't I mentioned that? After shuffle from Dacca to Madras, then Delhi, now it's Lahore, Pakistan. Been working on my "Small World" presentation—going to New York next week to give it a whirl.

MARCH 7, 1951—WASHINGTON—So much has happened— my whole world—heart—has changed—DRASTICALLY, since my last notation. First, I am in love, whole heart, whole mind, whole terrible, terrible longing to be loved in return. Gone, gone, forever from me now, is any emotional tie to Doug. I was working on "Small World" one night at the office (the Pakistan political desk is a most unlikely spot for Baby-Diaper-Dan inspiration—but the typewriter is available). In came a Mr. MALCOLM JONES. He is a tall, 40-ish, Midwestern engineer, bachelor—period. He recently did a special job for the Department, assisting in settling a dispute over the Helmand River between Iran and Afghanistan. Mr. Jones sat on a desk opposite me and began to read a letter from an Afghan cabinet minister to me. One word led to more. I was sensitively aware of him, his homey warmth for people and something in his plain simple face—his kind eyes. But he left. I continued typing, but my mind was following our conversation. I left shortly afterward and went to see Lowell Thomas Jr.'s film-lecture on his trip to Lhasa. But the connection with Doug was lightened—detached.

The next day, wearing the pink suit in which I had married Doug, oddly enough, I saw my Mr. Jones in the hall. I had something for him, a poem about the courage of one's convictions—I was thinking of "Small World"—if I had enough faith in that and myself, I would leave the Department and go forth into the baby world. Mr. Jones, flattered that I would consult him, instantly suggested dinner that very night. It was, oh dear, exquisite—highest peak of sheer delight I have known for a long—long—LONG time.

And so I fell madly in love with Mr. Jones. It was—for the record—the velvet, star-sparkling night of February 27, 1951. We had dinner at the Watergate, that fateful restaurant on the Potomac where Doug and I had our only (July 13, 1948) anniversary. His dinner conversation revealed a man of discernment, humor, good self-expression and always that warm kindness was in him. We came out and looked at the lights on the river. "To think this time last week I didn't even know you," I said to him. We got in the car and drove, just rambled along, driving and talking. Oh, such delightful companionship—his words and mine hand in hand. We were unaware how far we had gone, or where, until the headlights picked up a small sign: MOUNT VERNON, the beautiful reverent Washington home. "Oh, let's get out a moment and take a look," I suggested on irresistible impulse—the night was starry enchantment. Malcolm took my arm and I walked close beside him, my hair falling on his shoulder as I gazed upward. It was inevitable that my face should escape. It too, came to rest on his shoulder and he held me lightly, gently against him. He did not kiss me, for there is in him a restraint, almost primness. He did not dare kiss me, despite his instincts. He scarcely knew me. But driving back to Washington, I sat with my head against him, in the curve of his arm. The night had been above the earth, a shared vault above ourselves together. I was so shaken and disturbed over the sensations and rush of feelings—tenderness and longing for him—I could not sleep.

The next day I was told to report for training for my overseas post. I put it off until Monday, March 5, and left the next day for New York—with "Small World." Alice Blinn at *Ladies' Home Journal* liked it—the title, what I had written, etc. I left the presentation with her, went on to Boston. The babies were a thrilling rediscovery. Mary is advanced beyond Mike, who is still baby—puppy. Mary knows colors and words—by herself. The Macks were cordial—"business" was not immediately discussed. When we got down to it, all was in complete harmony and understanding. I was relieved. Though really my love for Malcolm releases me from them, and any association with Doug. Also, poor Doug. All the way home on the train my thoughts raced to Malcolm. What would it be like to see him again? He must, MUST kiss me. I would not bear it not to be close to him—in his arms! Love me he must! I saw him next at the office. We did have dinner that night and drove to the foot of the Washington Monument where he did kiss me. But—alas—the kiss was without meaning, or flame, or heart even! Nor did he yield to me. His line seemed to be "How could anyone as gifted, beautiful and creative as you, care for just an ordinary guy like me?" I told him he was all I ever wanted and never had—that Doug had not made me happy. I hopelessly overplayed my hand. I practically begged him to adore me and he resisted, backed away and brought me home at 10:00. I was so terribly disappointed in him, that kiss, that poor little 16-year-old farm boy wisp of ardor. God help me!

New tactics are in order: indifference—though it makes me more wretched than him. I saw him twice and all but ignored him completely, which he must have been aware of. Then today, most blessed stroke of all, a new man walked into my life, invited me to lunch and dinner all in the same breath. I held him off—my mood is still all Malcolm, but the new man sends my woman's conquest powers racing. I will be the Belle Parker of old—and if I cannot make Malcolm love me, I shall wound him to unforgetfulness. But nonetheless he has freed me of Doug. My heart is new and eager and outrushing as the new Spring all around us. (But, oh dear blessed God—How I do love him, my darling Malcolm.)

Meanwhile, I have been made a Vice Consul—given a rating of FSS-7 and a salary of $5370 plus allowances and a 25% post differential. I am attending class lectures at the Foreign Service Institute. At first my mind wandered out the window and across the void to other things and Malcolm—but now I've almost decided I will go to Lahore after all. If Malcolm is not true love, then I will find another (if only, only I can have Easter with Malcolm). Oh yes, "John" (my charming Mr. X) called tonight. He'd been away. He'd called before, couldn't get me—How were things? Nothing has happened, I said, so I wrote a letter to Lt. Gen. Walter B. Smith, head of the CIA, asking for an appointment. I told this to "John," who was at once alarmed. He warned me the general is away fishing for three weeks and requested I keep him informed. He wants to brief me before I see him. I was amused at the irony of this, that in a sense John's interests hang by the thread of my regard and fascination in him.

MARCH 16, 1951—WASHINGTON—I'm sitting here in a little pink hat (from Garfinkles, with a rose over one eye, dusted with sparkly sequins), waiting to go to dinner with Malcolm Jones. Also the mad skylark is already on the wane, most devastating blow: an enchanting evening last night with my fascinating Mr. X—"John." I saw him to discuss an interview with General Smith. The letter had been intercepted, so that I am sure the General never saw it. I am so weary, heart and soul weary, of this battle for Doug's salary. The crowning touch was a letter from the "Office of the Director," written in a manner to wash his hands—his agency's hands—of any association with Doug. I was so terribly, desperately hurt. I called Mr. X, who was kind, but his explanations did little. I burst into furious tears. So when he came to see me last night I wore my new Pink Hat and a gleam in each eye. All of which he noticed. He admitted he "doesn't mind" having to see me on his own time. He also, suavely, remarked I was a dangerous woman who knew too much, more than most wives. Also, he expected me to weep on his shoulder. (I gave him a liquid look on that.) We finished our interview with coffee, in the car. I dashed in to get it. I also told him I wanted to give him one of the Tibetan relics—a bowl—as a "memoire" of me. He was charmingly appreciative. When I left him, I had the minx-taunting sensation of attraction—of more passing between us than was said or admitted. Oh yes, he made one slashing remark… I was lamenting my financial status—and said there was the twins' future—all my responsibility. He said, "Now, Pegge, you aren't seriously worried about that—not for long." The inference was sharp—almost ridiculing me. John has no illusions about my "widowhood." I am glad I shall see him again, the contrast in his virility and flashing charm and wit—his "knowing-ness"—with Malcolm's reserve and Scot deliberation—was striking. Although we had dinner and sat talking afterward, head on shoulder, arms about each other, the longing for him was almost casual. He is leaving me for Easter, and for two weeks to have a visit in his staid life—fiddlesticks! And farewell, Malcolm!

Meanwhile, *Ladies' Home Journal* telephoned from New York. Mary Bass—would I meet her (Senior Editor) for lunch in Philadelphia next Thursday? My thoughts raced. "Have you seen 'Small World'?"

I asked. "Yes," was the answer, "but it is not necessarily about that I want to see you." I am really betwixt—for I am 75% in the mood to be a Vice Consul in Pakistan. However, if the job offer they make is good and the salary equal to the Vice Consul, I will take it.

Not sure what my Easter plans will be.

APRIL 21, 1951—BAKER MEMORIAL HOSPITAL, BOSTON—A year ago, who would have guessed I'd be here, recuperating from an operation on my foot. A bone was cut from the side of my left foot by Dr. Carter Rowe, and he did a highly skilled, beautiful, clean cut job. I came in April 16 and April 17 I was shot three times in the arm and hauled away to "OP." I was O-U-T from 10:30 a.m. 'til 5:30 p.m. when they had to waken me. My first sensation was as though a truck had run over my foot and crushed all my toes. But my own pain has been a mere sneeze compared with the three other women in my ward. One young girl with an abdominal operation tore my heart out, distressed me so my temperature went up, and I couldn't sleep. This has been a redeeming experience in many ways, a suspended conning tower indeed, for as I lay here a week, gazing long and musing out my life as my eye glided down the sparkling ledge of the Charles River dancing with copper fire in the April sunset, I saw many things clearly—leaving my beloved babies behind me when I go will cost me dear. There is a "wrong" element in my planned future. These two years of diplomatting—a mother to so remove herself from her mother's bond. Although I think any way I turn, my widowhood removes me from their lives to a good extent.

The *Ladies' Home Journal* offered something: a high-paying fiction reader-editor's job. But not "Small World." I went to Philadelphia— lunched with Mary Bass and another feather-in-hat, intent lady editor. Just boy-meets-girl la-de-da fiction, somebody else's output— is not my bowl of noodles. I didn't say so on the spot, and later they sent me a wire and long-distance calls, bidding we meet the Goulds (publishers). I wired back I felt committed to the Department—Oh—the Department. I do not consider the case closed—no indemnity from the Tibetans—then a bill could be put through Congress. I saw harassed Mr. James Webb, who implied plainly that I'd been "taken care of"—have been given a job at the highest possible salary. (I shall not forget his "gift.") I didn't know where next to turn, but out of the blue Al Morano, dear, kind, old acquaintance Al Morano—now a Congressman. Our re-meeting was fantastic—as though all the years and all the surge of events had never come between us, nor the eight years (My God!) we have known each other. The conversation naturally turned to my affairs—how the Department handled it—and Al was swiftly on the defensive. Certainly there would be a bill for Congress. All he wanted was a definite statement of the Department's position. I went to Mr. Hummeline's office, was referred to a Mr. Victor Purre. I was impressed with him as a very fine person—at least he was sympathetic to my stand that Doug's pitiful estate leaves no funds for our secure future. Mr. Purre showed me a top-secret letter from the CIA, giving a complete financial statement of my earnings. The estate, etc. It showed me earning $8500 a year—and volunteered the comment "This is considerably more than her husband earned. We do not feel there is any cause for a sympathetic claim to Congress for additional funds." Mr. Purre and I pursued the conversation along the lines that the staggering income they listed for me—$8500—had to be earned; it was no reserve put aside for the twins in the event of my own death. And it still did not release the obligation of the indemnity from the Tibetan government. We are to have a further conference on this before my ship sails.

Before going into all this I must record briefly my farewell with "John." I had two engagements for cocktails the evening I was to see him. In fact, I wasn't even home when he called. But he waited—though a bit "floating" (with no dinner) I was quite aware of him—the mood—and the magnet. He was dark-eyed and expectant—extravagant—he had set the stage and knew what the night held for us. As he helped me into the car, his arm encircled me, and as we drove away he burst out with "Don't sit way over there, Pegge, come over here beside me where I can see you." How I had cherished this last interview, how I had posed every dart of intrigue, every turn of phrase—and then the dazzling last, last goodbye that would be one rare, perfect friend less. But John was all man, helping himself to the desirable. He stopped the car and seized me, lion tight: "I'm going to kiss you until you're black and blue" and so he did, my throat, my legs, my knees. He was beside himself. He brought back Doug in a sharp flash—I had forgotten—man.

It did neither of us any good. I had not expected this, nor wanted it. There was constraint and abandonment of all we'd had together in our silence driving home. I gave him a Tibetan silver wok, which he accepted with some reluctance knowing its value. But what distressed me most was the finality of his goodbye. Nothing further between us is possible or wise—under any circumstances—the loss to me was painful, for such a phantom companion had he been during such dark anguish—and then later—so gay—so satisfying to discuss the finances—the case—with him. I had been so proud of him. Now I am not so sure he was my "friend" except so far—as a man. He found me—pleasurable.

For future reference, I met a girl I liked very much while in the last stages of overseas training—Barbara Ward. She is going to Delhi— USIE—I believe I shall see her.

MAY 7, 1951—NEW YORK, FOR THE RECORD—Claims board, Office of Budget and Finance Dept of State. From Edward B. WILBER—Claims approved to amount of $2530.75 (my figure $3,044.15).

The last week in New York was hectic. The sailing time was so uncertain. I finally got the last word for going aboard at 4:30 the day before and one day before the regular sailing date. Mother stood nobly by—trotting earnestly, exhaustingly around town with shopping lists. She had come over to spend the last week with me. LOIS FEGAN came too, and though she left me at the last minute to see someone else, a man (at the cost to me of seeing Al Morano and having Mother over a day earlier), she was generous and sincere in making amends for not coming to my "aid" when Doug was killed.

My days in New York were exceedingly complex because I was given "a job." It was one to content me, however—a background story on Sinkiang, angled to show Soviet persecution of the Moslems in Turkestan. I read reams of background material I had not seen before—stories in the *New York Times* on OSMAN BATOR (whom Doug must have known well). I called young Walter Sullivan and went to the new, unfinished UN building on 42nd Street to have lunch. I was amused at one or two things he said. In regard to my trip to Kuldja: "God, I'd have split a gut to go there!" About all the odd ducks and women who came to Tihwa: "Never saw anything like it—nothing but raving beauties came there except Tai Tai Paxton, of course." Pat English was good-looking. I wondered about her and if Doug had found her attractive. Sullivan said he had some pictures of Doug at Osman's camp.

I took J. Hall Paxton and Vincoe (to think she introduced me to Doug) to lunch. For the occasion, Vincoe was attired in a Turki coat from Kashmir and a Tihwa Moslem cap. No make-up. Rimless glasses and the perpetual smile of the clean of heart and mind. Hall was cordial and human at least. When Vincoe left the table, I asked him about Doug's suicide episode as related by Bessac. "Utter nonsense," said Paxton. Doug had no thought but to get the twins and me to Tihwa or himself out to us. The wife of the British Consul General had boy-girl twins, too, and she and Doug were frequently comparing notes on how well Mike and Mary would take Tihwa. I was glad to hear this. I believe I'll get the truest (kind or cruel— hurting cruel) version of Doug in Tihwa from Dreeson when he gets down from Nepal.

My foot was slow to heal. I wore bedroom slippers around New York to save my foot. When I went back to Boston the last weekend before I sailed, I was confronted by a bill from Dr. Rowe for $45. I was billed for every office visit, including the first one when he told me what operation he would perform. I was indignant—usually all charges are included in the operation fee.

I had an elegant lunch date with D.A. Wilson. We talked at such length I did not get to the doctors. In time, I suppose I'll feel the benefit of the bone removal. D.A. met me at the Ritz. She looked perfectly lovely in a new custom-made gray hat with yellow flowers— gay—on one side. I told her about the babies in China. She told me about one of her brothers whose child was born five months after his wedding. She seemed more astounded at how I bore the ordeal of the experience than the revelation of my relationship to Doug. The twins' birthday, September 30, is her husband's also. As she told me about her brother, I got a swift insight to the reaction of the Mackiernans to ME. The woman is always the one to bear the condemnation, the moral taboo. D.A.'s mother was so distressed for her son; never mind the girl at all. Her mother's heart rushed to her son, how she had "failed" him in his upbringing. Perhaps this, and other things, explain the Mackiernans' utter lack of regard for me. My sailing day, Mother's Day, went by with this comment from Mrs. Mack: "I don't want to load you down with something you wouldn't want anyway" (a gift). I had intended sending her flowers for Mother's Day, but thought I wouldn't go to so much trouble. I had sent them $10 to go to the circus with the babies. Comment: must thank you, but "you needn't have done that." I am more an outsider—less than a friend, neighbor, or fourth cousin twice removed—than ever. This feeling increases my intense longing to have the babies in my own care.

My departure, which aside from the memorable, really wonderful visit with D.A. (a good, good friend is a treasure beyond price. She is my most supreme friend. Esther Baxter next), including a lengthy confession visit to a little French church, a communion the next morning.

Ladies Home Journal has come again to the fore. I was invited to lunch to meet the publishers, the really charming, warmly human, interested and interesting Bruce Goulds. I'm glad Mother was on hand for this, seeing I was dressed at my best, cheering me on with "remember they sent for You."

Mr. Gould, I must say, insisted I have an air conditioner. I demurred, the cost being far beyond me. To press his point, Mr. Gould bent his eye upon me: "You install an air conditioner in your bedroom," he declared, "and everyone'll be fighting to get it."

Mrs. Gould was envious of the trip—the stops I'd make—asked that I do a running letter on what I find along the way. Also to keep in touch from Lahore, let them know what I find in magazine material—what ideas I have, etc. I reminded them that I need serve only ONE YEAR, and at their bidding I would come home (Mike and Mary and me under one roof, away from Stoughton).

Al Morano came to dinner one night—alas, when Helen Papania also came. So the three of us had dinner. He called the day I was to sail. He was coming through New York on his way to Connecticut, but I missed him. I had had a letter from WEBB—under secretary— saying what I anticipated. No petition to Congress—I have been "taken care of." Foreign Service implies certain risks. I must "expect them." I haven't had Al's reaction to Webb's letter yet. Or the Macks. But any case I make to put a claim in will have to be strictly my doings with Al. I will no longer involve the Macks in anything. When Doug's estate is settled, I wonder about two points: Whether the $1,000 I borrowed (and repaid) from Daddy for the Fairfax house will be deducted, and whether Mrs. Mack will keep the bonds, some of which are made out to her—although I had told her they were "hers." She made no reply to this.

The departure from the babies was tearful and saddening. We had taken a long drive, ending at the station. As Mr. Mack removed my things, Mary caught the meaning of our stop. She began to cry, really in earnest, her face smudged wet with great tears. Mrs. Mack swooped her into the front seat so I could get out. Mike, usually worse in upsets than Mary, fell on the floor of the car screaming and yelling. I reached for Mary. "Mommie, Mommie!" she cried in panic. Her little hands closed tightly on my coat. She clung to me in desperation. I put her down and took up Mike. He cried and wiggled and was upset. But I don't believe he comprehended as did Mary that a genuine separation was upon us.

Perhaps not for longer than a year.

FRIDAY, MAY 18, 1951—NEW YORK CITY—Tomorrow I sail for what I hope is a new life in Pakistan...

Index

TRAVEL THE WORLD
WITH TITLES FROM HLUCKY BOOKS

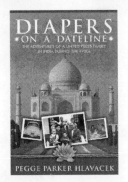

Hlucky Books

www.HluckyBooks.com